TAKING SIDES

Clashing Views in

Gender

SIXTH EDITION

Selected, Edited, and with Introductions by

Jacquelyn W. White
University of North Carolina at Greensboro

3, 4, 5, 8

Connect
Learn
Succeed™

Connect
Learn
Succeed™

TAKING SIDES: CLASHING VIEWS IN GENDER, SIXTH EDITION

Published by McGraw-Hill, a business unit of The McGraw-Hill Companies, Inc., 1221 Avenue of the Americas, New York, NY 10020. Copyright © 2013 by The McGraw-Hill Companies, Inc. All rights reserved. Printed in the United States of America. Previous editions © 2009, 2007, and 2005. No part of this publication may be reproduced or distributed in any form or by any means, or stored in a database or retrieval system, without the prior written consent of The McGraw-Hill Companies, Inc., including, but not limited to, in any network or other electronic storage or transmission, or broadcast for distance learning.

Some ancillaries, including electronic and print components, may not be available to customers outside the United States.

This book is printed on acid-free paper.

Taking Sides® is a registered trademark of the McGraw-Hill Companies, Inc.
Taking Sides is published by the **Contemporary Learning Series** group within the McGraw-Hill Higher Education division.

1 2 3 4 5 6 7 8 9 0 DOC/DOC 1 0 9 8 7 6 5 4 3 2

MHID: 0-07-805030-8
ISBN: 978-0-07-805030-5
ISSN: 1526-4548

Managing Editor: *Larry Loeppke*
Senior Developmental Editor: *Jade Benedict*
Senior Permissions Coordinator: *Lenny J. Behnke*
Senior Marketing Communications Specialist: *Mary Klein*
Project Manager: *Erin Melloy*
Design Coordinator: *Brenda A. Rolwes*
Cover Graphics: *Rick D. Noel*
Buyer: *Nicole Baumgartner*
Media Project Manager: *Sridevi Palani*

Compositor: MPS Limited
Cover Image: © Purestock/SuperStock RF

www.mhhe.com

Editors/Academic Advisory Board

Members of the Academic Advisory Board are instrumental in the final selection of articles for each edition of TAKING SIDES. Their review of articles for content, level, and appropriateness provides critical direction to the editors and staff. We think that you will find their careful consideration well reflected in this volume.

TAKING SIDES: Clashing Views in Gender

Sixth Edition

EDITOR

Jacquelyn W. White
University of North Carolina at Greensboro

ACADEMIC ADVISORY BOARD MEMBERS

Editors/Academic Advisory Board continued

Preface

Issues having to do with females and males, "femaleness" and "maleness," are omnipresent in Western culture and around the world. Our lives revolve around presumed distinctions between females' and males' attitudes, characteristics, emotions, behaviors, preferences, abilities, and responsibilities. We have clear definitions of what females and males can and should do differently from one another. In some cultures, there are third and fourth gender categories, complete with their own expectations and proscriptions. What has triggered such a deep gender divide? Is it rooted in our biology? Is it a cultural creation that gets reproduced through socialization practices and interpersonal interaction? What is the future of gender? Controversy abounds. *Taking Sides: Clashing Views in Gender* is a tool for stimulating critical thought about females and males, femaleness and maleness, and beyond. Consideration of the complexity of sex and gender necessitates a multidisciplinary perspective. Thus, you will learn about definitions and views of sex and gender from such fields as sociology, ethnic studies, women's studies, men's studies, gay and lesbian studies, queer studies, gender studies, transgender studies, education, language, political science, global studies, religion, history, medicine, law, psychology, and biology. The multidisciplinarity of inquiry on sex and gender has created a rich, exciting, and emotionally and politically charged body of theory, research, and practice. The study of sex and gender is so dynamic that it is one of the most fast-paced areas of inquiry, characterized by great fervor and rapid growth. It is also one of the most contentious areas of thought, distinguished by deep theoretical and philosophical differences. Such division also marks public discourse on sex and gender. This book contains 21 issues, organized into 6 units, each focusing on a hotly debated question in contemporary scholarly and public discourse on sex and gender. They are phrased as yes/no questions so that two distinct perspectives are delineated and contrasted. Each issue is prefaced by an *Issue Introduction* containing background material contextualizing the dual positions. Additional perspectives are presented in an *Is There Common Ground?* section following each issue to enrich and enliven debate and discussion. No issue is truly binary, adequately represented by only two points of view. Considering other perspectives will broaden your understanding of the complexity of each issue, enabling you to develop an informed ideology. The *Additional Resources* that appear at the end of the *Is There Common Ground?* section should help you find resources to continue your study of the subject. Additionally, on the *Internet References* page that accompanies each unit opener, you will find Web sites that are relevant to the issues in that unit. They should prove useful as starting points for further research. At the back of the book is a listing of all the *Contributors to This Volume*, which will give you information on the various writers whose views are debated here.

You begin this quest with an existing personal gender ideology of which you may not even be aware. It serves as a filter through which you process information about females and males, femaleness and maleness. It draws your attention to some information and points of view and allows you to disregard other more dissonant perspectives. Your challenge is to probe your personal gender ideology (and intersecting ideologies such as ethnicity, sexual orientation, social class, gender identity) so that you can open your mind to other perspectives and information and develop a more informed ideology. To do so takes courage and active thought. As you work through this book, note your reactions to different points and perspectives. Exchange reactions and relevant experiences with your peers. "Try on" different perspectives by trying to represent a view with which you initially disagree. Explore the *Additional Resources* provided for issue. Challenge yourself to explore all angles so that your own theories or views become more reasoned and representative. No matter what field of study, career path, and/or other personal choices you pursue, issues of sex and gender will be pervasive. Great sociohistorical change in sex and gender marked the twentieth century, catalyzing even greater momentum in the twenty-first century. The goal of this book is to help you develop an ideological tool chest that will enable you to intelligently and responsibly navigate the changing gender landscape. Collectively, you will chart the course of the future of gender.

Changes to this edition   This edition contains 21 issues organized into six units. The book outline has changed substantially, with the addition of a new section, several rephrased issues, 2 new issues, and 22 new, more current selections that reflect the YES and NO perspectives. Unit openers and issue introductions have been revised accordingly, along with a new *Is There Common Ground?* section added to the end of each issue. Each issue opener calls attention to the consideration of cross-cutting issues that enrich and complicate in meaningful ways the clashing views presented in each unit. Students and instructors are encouraged to discuss each of these questions:

1. *The role of biology:* What does emerging research on brain differences tell us about gender-related patterns of behavior? How can one separate cause, consequence, and correlates in this growing body of knowledge?
2. *Intersecting identities:* How do race, ethnicity, class, and other status-defining attributes relate to gendered patterns of behavior? Does the consideration of how multiple identities intersect contribute to new understandings of gender?
3. *Media representations:* How do media portrayals of gender-related issues affect our understanding of the phenomenon? How and when do media portrayals, including images and language, reinforce or defy gender stereotypes?
4. *Cross-cultural and intra-cultural generalities:* To what extent is understanding of gender-related concepts shaped by culture? Can results of studies conducted in one country generalize to other countries? Do results of a study conducted in a particular country actually reflect the values of that entire country? That is, are there intra-cultural differences within a given country? For example, are students at a

university in a given country more similar to students at universities in other countries than they are to other social groups within their own country?

A word to the instructor An *Instructor's Resource Guide with Test Questions* (multiple-choice and essay) is available through the publisher for the instructor using *Taking Sides* in the classroom. A general guidebook, *Using Taking Sides in the Classroom*, which discusses methods and techniques for integrating the pro–con approach into any classroom setting, is also available. An online version of *Using Taking Sides in the Classroom* and a correspondence service for *Taking Sides* adopters can be found at http://www.mhhe.com/cls. *Taking Sides: Clashing Views in Gender* is only one title in the Taking Sides series. If you are interested in seeing the table of contents for any of the other titles, please visit the Taking Sides Web site at http://www.mhhe.com/cls.

Acknowledgments First and foremost, the contributions of Elizabeth Paul, editor of the first two editions, are acknowledged. The insights and knowledge she brought to this project provided a solid platform from which to move forward into the following editions. Her understanding of the issues facing the study of gender and her ability to cogently frame the issues set a high standard. I also want to express great appreciation to my many undergraduates who helped me understand which issues resonate most with them. Many colleagues in the Women's and Gender Studies program at UNCG provided an articulate sounding board as I debated which issues to include and how to frame them. I must also acknowledge Jade Benedict at McGraw-Hill/Contemporary Learning Series, who provided me with expertise, support, and encouragement at each step of the process. Lastly, my husband and children Ian and Elaine were enormously supportive and patient, filling in for all those household tasks I simply ignored. I have learned much from them about what it means to have an equal partner and to attempt to raise children free of gender constraints in a society that really does not want that to happen.

Jacquelyn W. White
University of North Carolina at Greensboro

Contents In Brief

Contents

Cornelieke van de Beek and colleagues demonstrated that testosterone, estradiol, and progesterone levels measured during pregnancy are related to gender-related play in 13-month-old girls and boys and found clear sex differences in preferences for masculine and feminine toys. Vasanti Jadva, Melissa Hines, and Susan Golombok, using a preferential looking task, found sex similarities in infants' preferences for shapes and colors and suggest that later gender-related patterns of toy preferences may be related to socialization or cognitive development factors rather than inborn differences.

Janet Shibley Hyde makes the case that gender similarities are just as interesting and important to understand as are gender differences. By adopting a social structuralist perspective and considering gender as a social stimulus rather than a person variable, she uses meta-analyses to support the argument that women and men are more alike than different. Marco Del Giudice follows the assumptions of evolutionary theory to accept the premise that women and men are different. He argues that effect sizes derived from meta-analyses underestimate the true magnitude of gender-related differences.

Clinical psychologist Heino F. L. Meyer-Bahlburg and his colleagues report that sexual orientation is related to specific molecular genotypes in women with classical congenital adrenal hyperplasia (CAH), supporting a sexual-differentiation perspective involving the effects of prenatal androgens on the development of sexual orientation. Psychologist Lisa M. Diamond and her student Molly Butterworth use a feminist theoretical framework of intersectionality to analyze data from the experiences of individuals who claim neither an unambiguously female nor a male identity to demonstrate that sexual orientation, sexual identify, and gender identity are fluid and change over time.

UNIT 2   FROM OZZIE AND HARRIET TO MY TWO DADS: GENDER IN CHILDHOOD   75

The Human Rights Campaign (HRC), America's largest gay and lesbian organization, explains why same-sex couples should be afforded the same legal right to marry as heterosexual couples. John Cornyn, U.S. senator from Texas, says a constitutional amendment is needed to define marriage as permissible only between a man and a woman. Senator Cornyn contends that the traditional institution of marriage needs to be protected from activist courts that would seek to redefine it.

Walter R. Schumm examined data from several sources and concluded that there is evidence for the intergenerational transfer of sexual orientation, especially for female parents or female children, but the pathways for such an effect are not well understood. Paige Averett, Blace Nalavany, and Scott Ryan found evidence that the sexual orientation of adoptive parents had no relation to the likelihood that their children would have behavioral problems. They studied internalizing and externalizing problems, and did not consider the sexual orientation of the child a problem.

Professor of human development Natasha J. Cabrera reports that father engagement has positive effects on children's cognition and language, as well as their social and emotional development. Jane Waldfogel, Terry-Ann Craigie, and Jeanne Brooks-Gunn, in a detailed analysis of various family structures, find that family instability has a negative effect on children's cognitive and health outcomes, regardless of structure, meaning that children with single or cohabiting parents are not necessarily at risk.

Physicians Z. O. Merhi and L. Pal discuss the conditions under which selection of the sex of a child does not breach any ethical considerations in family planning among infertile couples. The American College of Obstetricians and Gynecologists' Committee on Ethics supports the practice of offering patients procedures for the purpose of preventing serious sex-linked genetic diseases, but opposes sex selection for personal and family reasons.

Nancy Henley and Cheris Kramarae, adopting a social contextual approach, suggest that patterns of communication are due to inequalities and are multi-determined. Daniel Maltz and Ruth Borker adopt a cultural differences approach and suggest that men and women, by virtue of their sex, live in different cultures.

Issue 9.   Do Nice Guys Finish Last?   191

Psychologist Peter Jonason, taking an evolutionary perspective, demonstrates that the "dark triad" of attributes (narcissism, psychopathy, and Machiavellianism) promotes a reproductively adaptive strategy, especially for short-term mating behaviors. Psychologist Adrian Furnham found consistent sex differences that revealed women's preference for "nice guys," that is, those who were intelligent, stable, conscientious, better educated, with good social skills and political and religious compatibility.

Issue 10.   Gender Symmetry: Do Women and Men Commit Equal Levels of Violence Against Intimate Partners?   212

Murray A. Straus and his colleague Ignacio L. Ramirez argue that women are just as likely to commit physical aggression against dating partners as are men, suggesting that gender symmetry exists in different cultural contexts. On the other hand, social psychologists Christopher T. Allen, Suzanne C. Swan, and Chitra Raghaven argue that women's use of aggression does not equate to gender symmetry. Rather, cultural context, motives, and history of trauma must be considered.

Issue 11.   Does Pornography Reduce the Incidence of Rape?   236

Professor of law Anthony D'Amato highlights statistics from the most recent National Crime Victimization Survey that demonstrate a correlation between the increased consumption of pornography over the years with the decreased incidence of rape. Some people, he argues, watch pornography in order to push any desire to rape out of their minds, and thus have no further desire to go out and actually do it. Judith Reisman, president of the Institute for Media Education, asserts that sex criminals imitate what they see depicted in the media, providing examples of serial rapists and killers who had large stores of pornography in their possession, and research in which approximately 33 percent of rapists said that they had viewed pornography immediately prior to at least one of their rapes.

UNIT 4   IS IT A MAN'S WORLD? MATH, SCIENCE, AND THE CYBER-WORLD   249

Paula Olszewski-Kubilius and Seon-Young Lee analyzed data from over 250,000 gifted students who took a variety of different tests and concluded that the ratio of talented math and science students remains at about 3 males:1 female. Sara Lindberg and colleagues use meta-analysis to analyze 242 studies of mathematics performance and concluded that there are no gender differences.

Tim Olds and his colleagues examined how much time adolescents spent in different activities during the school day and found that boys had higher levels of screen time, which included television, video games, and computer use, which peaked in the peripubertal years. Susan McKenney and Joke Voogt studied children's use of technology both within and outside school settings and found no gender differences in young children's perceptions of their own use of computers or in ability level.

The Government Equalities Office presents data suggesting that women are experiencing more challenges than men due to the economic recession. Teri Fritsma, in an analysis of data based on employment patterns in Minnesota, suggests that men are being more negatively affected by the recession than are women.

In contrast, Hilda Kahne, professor emerita at Wheaton College in Massachusetts, and Zachary Mabel, research analyst with the Center for Education Policy Research at Harvard University, make the argument that incomplete education and few training programs, rather than gender discrimination, make it more difficult for low-age single mothers to raise their earnings. They advocate for policies that foster economic advancement. Hadas Mandel of the Department of Sociology and Anthropology at Tel Aviv University reviews extensive data from 14 countries and concludes that social policies have the counterintuitive impact of decreasing women's opportunities for access to more desirable and powerful positions. His analyses show distinct profiles of gender inequality and their relations to ideology and public policy.

Alice Eagly and Linda Carli contend that barriers exist for women at every stage of their career trajectories, resulting in, not a glass ceiling, but a labyrinth. Mark van Vugt and Anjana Ahuja assert that the division of labor by sex is rooted in biologically based differences between women and men. Evolutionarily based natural selection has led to inclinations that make women and men better suited for different types of jobs.

Correlation Guide

The *Taking Sides* series presents current issues in a debate-style format designed to stimulate student interest and develop critical thinking skills. Each issue is thoughtfully framed with an issue summary, an issue introduction, and challenge questions. The pro and con essays—selected for their liveliness and substance—represent the arguments of leading scholars and commentators in their fields.

Taking Sides: Clashing Views in Gender, 6/e, is an easy-to-use reader that presents issues on important topics such as *cyberbullying, pornography*, and the *gender wage gap*. For more information on *Taking Sides* and other *McGraw-Hill Contemporary Learning Series* titles, visit www.mhhe.com/cls.

This convenient guide matches the issues in **Taking Sides: Clashing Views in Gender, 6/e,** with the corresponding chapters in three of our best-selling McGraw-Hill Human Development textbooks by Kelly, Yarber et al., and Miller.

Taking Sides: Gender, 6/e	Sexuality Today, 10/e by Kelly	Human Sexuality: Diversity in Contemporary America, 8/e by Yarber et al.	Intimate Relationships, 6/e by Miller
Issue 1: Is Anatomy Destiny?	**Chapter 2:** Female Sexual Anatomy and Physiology **Chapter 3:** Male Sexual Anatomy and Physiology	**Chapter 3:** Female Sexual Anatomy, Physiology, and Response **Chapter 4:** Male Sexual Anatomy, Physiology, and Response	**Chapter 3:** Attraction
Issue 2: Are Women and Men More Similar Than Different?	**Chapter 5:** Developmental and Social Perspectives on Gender	**Chapter 5:** Gender and Gender Roles	**Chapter 6:** Interdependency
Issue 3: Is Sexual Orientation Innate?	**Chapter 7:** Adult Sexuality and Relationships	**Chapter 5:** Gender and Gender Roles	**Chapter 9:** Sexuality
Issue 4: Should Same-Sex Marriage Be Legal?	**Chapter 13:** Same-Gender Orientation and Behavior		
Issue 5: Does Parents' Sexual Orientation Affect Their Children's Psychological Outcomes?	**Chapter 5:** Developmental and Social Perspectives on Gender	**Chapter 1:** Perspectives on Human Sexuality **Chapter 2:** Studying Human Sexuality	**Chapter 10:** Stresses and Strains
Issue 6: Are Fathers Necessary for Children's Well-being?	**Chapter 5:** Developmental and Social Perspectives on Gender	**Chapter 5:** Gender and Gender Roles	**Chapter 1:** The Building Blocks of Relationships

(Continued)

Taking Sides: Gender, 6/e	Sexuality Today, 10/e by Kelly	Human Sexuality: Diversity in Contemporary America, 8/e by Yarber et al.	Intimate Relationships, 6/e by Miller
Issue 7: Should Parents Be Allowed to Choose the Sex of Their Children?	**Chapter 10:** Reproduction, Reproductive Technology, and Birthing	**Chapter 12:** Conception, Pregnancy, and Childbirth	
Issue 8: Are Gendered Patterns of Communication Related to Power Differentials?	**Chapter 5:** Developmental and Social Perspectives on Gender	**Chapter 5:** Gender and Gender Roles	**Chapter 12:** Power and Violence
Issue 9: Do Nice Guys Finish Last?	**Chapter 9:** Sexuality, Communication, and Relationships	**Chapter 8:** Love and Communication in Intimate Relationships	**Chapter 12:** Power and Violence
Issue 10: Gender Symmetry: Do Women and Men Commit Equal Levels of Violence Against Intimate Partners?	**Chapter 16:** Sexual Consent, Coercion, Rape, and Abuse	**Chapter 17:** Sexual Coercion: Harassment, Aggression, and Abuse	**Chapter 12:** Power and Violence
Issue 11: Does Pornography Reduce the Incidence of Rape?	**Chapter 15:** Sex, Art, the Media, and the Law **Chapter 16:** Sexual Consent, Coercion, Rape, and Abuse	**Chapter 18:** Sexually Explicit Materials, Prostitution, and Sex Laws	**Chapter 12:** Power and Violence
Issue 12: Do Men Outperform Women in Mathematics?	**Chapter 5:** Developmental and Social Perspectives on Gender	**Chapter 5:** Gender and Gender Roles	**Chapter 10:** Stresses and Strains
Issue 13: Is Gender Related to the Use of Computers?	**Chapter 5:** Developmental and Social Perspectives on Gender	**Chapter 5:** Gender and Gender Roles	**Chapter 5:** Communication
Issue 14: Is Cyberbullying Related to Gender?	**Chapter 5:** Developmental and Social Perspectives on Gender **Chapter 16:** Sexual Consent, Coercion, Rape, and Abuse	**Chapter 5:** Gender and Gender Roles **Chapter 17:** Sexual Coercion: Harassment, Aggression, and Abuse	**Chapter 5:** Communication
Issue 15: Is the Gender Wage Gap Justified?		**Chapter 5:** Gender and Gender Roles	**Chapter 10:** Stresses and Strains **Chapter 11:** Conflict **Chapter 12:** Power and Violence
Issue 16: Has the Economic Recession Been Harder on Women's Employment than Men's Employment?			**Chapter 10:** Stresses and Strains

Taking Sides: Gender, 6/e	Sexuality Today, 10/e by Kelly	Human Sexuality: Diversity in Contemporary America, 8/e by Yarber et al.	Intimate Relationships, 6/e by Miller
Issue 17: Do Social Policies Improve Gender Inequalities in the Workplace?	**Chapter 5:** Developmental and Social Perspectives on Gender	**Chapter 5:** Gender and Gender Roles	**Chapter 10:** Stresses and Strains
Issue 18: Are Barriers to Women's Success as Leaders Due to Societal Obstacles?	**Chapter 5:** Developmental and Social Perspectives on Gender		**Chapter 10:** Stresses and Strains
Issue 19: Is There Something Wrong with the Content of Comprehensive Sex Education Curricula?	**Chapter 8:** Sexual Individuality and Sexual Values **Chapter 9:** Sexuality, Communication, and Relationships	**Chapter 6:** Sexuality in Childhood and Adolescence **Chapter 7:** Sexuality in Adulthood	**Chapter 9:** Sexuality
Issue 20: Is "Gender Identity Disorder" an Appropriate Psychiatric Diagnosis?	**Chapter 5:** Developmental and Social Perspectives on Gender **Chapter 13:** Same-Gender Orientation and Behavior **Chapter 14:** The Spectrum of Human Sexual Behavior	**Chapter 9:** Sexual Expression **Chapter 10:** Variations in Sexual Behavior **Chapter 14:** Sexual Function Difficulties, Dissatisfaction, Enhancement, and Therapy	**Chapter 4:** Social Cognition
Issue 21: Should Transgendered Women be Considered "Real" Women?	**Chapter 14:** The Spectrum of Human Sexual Behavior	**Chapter 9:** Sexual Expression **Chapter 10:** Variations in Sexual Behavior	**Chapter 9:** Sexuality **Chapter 10:** Stresses and Strains

Topic Guide

This topic guide suggests how the selections in this book relate to the subjects covered in your course. You may want to use the topics listed on these pages to search the Web more easily. On the following pages a number of websites have been gathered specifically for this book. They are arranged to reflect the units of this *Taking Sides* reader. You can link to these sites by going to http://www.mhhe.com/cls. **All the articles that relate to each topic are listed below the bold-faced term.**

Introduction

Sex and Gender: Knowing Is Believing, but Is Believing Knowing?

As people go through their day-to-day lives, when is their sex or gender relevant, that is, in the foreground, and when is it in the background? Think about this question regarding your own life. Are you always aware of being a female or a male? Probably not. Does your femaleness or maleness cause you to behave the way you do all the time? Probably not. Thus, we arrive at the perplexing and complicated question: When do sex and gender matter? To begin to answer this question we need to consider what we mean by the terms *sex* and *gender*. We also need to identify and make explicit the fundamental assumptions that lead us to put so much importance on questions regarding sex and gender. Within any species of living organisms, there is variation. In Western thought, a primary individual difference is sex. What do we "know" about the ways in which individuals differ by sex? Of course, an obvious response is that individuals are either female or male. We treat it as fact. What else do you *know* about human variation by sex? Are there other *facts* about human females and males? Perhaps you will state such facts as males' greater physical strength than females, males' taller stature than females, and females' unique capacity for childbearing. Make a list of what else you *know* about human variation by sex. Most of us have a vast network of knowledge about human variation by sex. Many of the claims stem from knowledge of the differential biology of females and males and extend to variation in human emotion, thought, and behavior. In fact, some individuals maintain that females and males are so different that they are from different planets! For most of us, this is an interconnected network of "givens" about the far-reaching effects of femaleness and maleness. Given that we consider human sex variation to be an undeniable fact, we rarely question these claims. Instead we see them as essential truths or facts—unquestionable, unchangeable, and inevitable. The goal of this book is to guide your critical evaluation of this network of knowledge. What you may discover as you critically consider the controversial issues in this book is that many of the things we believe to be factually true and objectively provable about human sex variation are instead unsupported beliefs.

Knowledge and Beliefs in the Study of Sex and Gender

Cross-Cutting Issue: The Role of Biology

For decades, in public discourse and in numerous academic disciplines, there has been widespread debate and discussion of the extent of human variation by sex. In addition, there is extensive consideration of the cultural meaning and significance attached to femaleness and maleness. The terms *sex* and *gender* are used to refer to these various phenomena. Although sex and gender are commonly thought to be synonyms, many scholars attempted to assign different meanings to these terms. Sex was often used to refer to the biological distinction between females and males. Gender referred to the social and cultural meaning attached to notions of femaleness and maleness. Depending on one's theory of how sex and gender were related, there were varying degrees of overlap or interconnection between these two terms. Many scholars now question the usefulness of the distinction, suggesting that the notion of biological sex itself is socially constructed. This more contemporary view rests on two arguments. First, biological organisms cannot exist or be studied devoid of a social context, making the sex and gender dichotomy arbitrary. Second, as Myra Hird has suggested, there is a persistent yet unchallenged belief that biological sex is the "original sign through which gender is read." That is, what we know about a person's anatomy provides the basis for prescriptions and proscriptions regarding appropriate behaviors. However, some recent feminist theorists, reflecting on transgenderism, suggest that gender identity, not anatomy, is core to a person's true self. Thus, if biological anatomy does not match identity, it is the anatomy that is "wrong," a medical condition worthy of fixing. Biological features of sex have been assumed to include genetic factors of female and male chromosomes, hormones and the endocrine system, internal and external sexual and reproductive organs (appearance and functionality), and central nervous system sex differentiation. The assumption or the defined norm was that there is consistency among these different biological factors, differentiating individuals into females and males. However, research with transgender people and intersexed individuals challenges the assumption that various biological features of organisms "naturally" co-occur. Research suggests that variations among these features occur naturally. Defining these variations as "normal" or "deviant" is a social construction. Gender has been employed in theory and research in various ways and toward various goals. The study of gender has been used to assess the validity of claims of human sex differences. It has also been used to challenge assertions of biological roots of gendered behavior by testing alternate causal theories (e.g., environmental, learning, cognitive theories). Some studies of gender aim to analyze the social organization of female/male relations, elucidating gendered power dynamics and patterns of dominance and subordination. Gender studies have also been used to show how burdens and benefits are inequitably distributed among females and males in society. Other scholars have used conceptions of gender to explain the structure of the human psyche, individuals' sense of self, identity, and aspiration. How are elements of gender produced? Biological essentialists believe that biological sex differences directly lead to behavioral, cognitive, and emotional differences between females and males. In other words, there are *essential* differences between females and males that stem from biology and pervade human psychology and sociality. Evolutionary theorists believe that ancestral responses to environmental challenges created physiological differences between females and males that underlie contemporary behavioral differences. In contrast, social constructionists believe gender to be a social or cultural creation. Infants and children are socialized and disciplined so as to develop sex-appropriate gender attributes and skills. As individuals mature, they develop a gender identity or a sense of self as female or male. They internalize the dominant cultural gender ideology, develop expectations for self and others, and assume sex-congruent gender roles, behaving in gender-appropriate ways. Symbolic interactionists point to the power of pervasive cultural gender symbolism in the production and reproduction of gender in cultures. They show how gender metaphors are assigned to cultural artifacts and how language structures gender meanings and dynamics, creating a dominant cultural meaning system. Standpoint theorists show us how our position in the social hierarchy impacts our perspective on and involvement in cultural gender dynamics. Throughout all the issues in this book, you will see these various perspectives being contrasted. Recent technological advances are permitting greater opportunities to examine genetic constitution and expression, as well as neurological and hormonal functioning in humans. Sophisticated methods provide for careful evaluation of cardiovascular and immune functions as well. All of these have been applied to the study of sex differences. The big debate is whether this work is clarifying or confusing the study of sex and gender.

Cross-Cutting Issue: Intersecting Identities

Adding to the complexity is a growing appreciation that what it means to be female or male in a given culture is affected by one's race, ethnicity, social class, and sexual orientation, with some scholars arguing that these too are social constructs. Contemporary analyses suggest that the fundamental construct is *oppression*—that is, those in power have the authority to declare who is and is not "acceptable," with access to resources (such as education or political influence) based on criteria defined by the powerful. Thus, gender is seen as one system of power intersecting with other systems of power (such as race, ethnicity, heterosexuality, and social class). The concept of intersecting identities suggests that some people may experience status incongruence as they forge a sense of identity. Identity is a dynamic ongoing process involving the negotiation of social relationships across time and contexts. The view that people's identities are dynamic and negotiated indicates that one's senses of self (e.g., psychological characteristics or traits, physical features, roles, abilities) are contextually dependent. The negotiation of power relationships can be informed by the dynamic process of identity development and maintenance and vice versa. Theories of identity bring social structural variables (e.g., ethnicity, gender, class) associated with varying degrees of status, to the individual and interpersonal levels. In any given situation, a person's perception of how social structural variables are incorporated into her/his identity may inform the perception of relative power. Different levels of social power may produce different behavioral, cognitive, and affective consequences, making the presentation of self, even at the biological level, fluid across time and context. It is likely that as we more consciously consider the notion of intersecting identities into discussions of sex and gender, much of what we think we know will need to be reevaluated. Such analyses provide opportunities to challenge the essentialist notion of the universal male and female.

Cross-Cutting Issue: Media Representations

Consider what constitutes "proof" for you. What are your standards of "truth"? How do we know that a piece of information is a fact rather than a belief? Do we base our classification on evidence? What kind of evidence do we require? What constitutes enough evidence to classify a claim as a fact rather than a belief? Starting with what we *know* to be the most basic fact about human variation by sex, that humans are either female or male, how do you know that? Did someone tell you (e.g., a parent, a teacher)? Did you read it somewhere, in a magazine or a scientific journal? Did you observe differences between yourself and others or among others? How did this information or observation get generalized from a few individuals to all humans? How have your observations played out in movies or television programs? Is this kind of generalization warrantable, based on human variation? Are there any exceptions (i.e., individuals that do not fit neatly into the categories of female or male)? Would such exceptions lead you to question the *fact* of sex as female or male? For something to be fact, must it be universally true of all individuals within a given species? Have you ever thought critically about this before? How have media portrayals challenged gender constructions? Think of *M. Butterfly* or *Brokeback Mountain*. Consider the public reaction to Chaz Bono, especially his decision to appear on *Dancing with the Stars*. If gender is a culturally specific construct, then many time-honored assumptions about sex and gender are challenged. Most people do not read scientific journals to get their facts. They rely on various media—magazines, television, and increasingly, the Internet. Consider how current media reports of scientific findings may privilege an essentialist, causal role of biological forces in gender differences over social constructionist views. For example, the *Science Daily* (February 29, 2008) recently proclaimed, "Sex Differences Extend into the Brain." "The New Sex Scorecard" in *Psychology Today* (July/August 2003) proclaimed that "men and women's minds really do work differently." What is the impact of such headlines from supposedly reputable sources on everyday people's understanding of the women and men? A fundamental question is whether the media reflect reality or contribute to the creation of reality. Consider the marketers of Halloween costumes for children. Adie Nelson did a content analysis of 469 children's costumes and sewing patterns. She found that less that 10 percent were gender neutral. Costumes for both girls and boys were predominantly hero costumes. Costumes for girls tended to depict beauty queens, princesses, and other traditionally feminine images (including animals and foodstuffs). Costumes for boys often followed a warrior theme, featuring villains (agents or symbols of death). She concluded that "children's fantasy dress reproduces and reiterates more conventional messages about gender" (see her chapter "The Pink Dragon Is Female" in Spade and Valentine's *The Kaleidoscope of Gender: Prisms, Patterns, and Possibilities*, 2010). The same conclusion can be said about many media messages. Exposure to sexist media has been shown to lead to less achievement in girls and more sexist attitudes in boys. It is important to also consider what media messages say to members of various racial, ethnic, and cultural groups. How do these messages frame and reinforce the marginalized status of many groups? For example, to be beautiful is to be thin, blond, and heterosexual. One study found that the more mainstream TV young white women watch, the more negative their body image, but that the more black-oriented TV that young black women watch, the more positive their body image. Finally, there is growing interest in how Internet use might change "doing gender." In the game world, gamers are known to take on many different personae, experimenting with different ways of interacting. We know that switching genders is common. In chat rooms, people may present themselves differently and express themselves in ways they might not in the real world. What implications does this have for gamers' and chat room participants' real-world sense of themselves as females and males? Does experimenting in virtual reality matter? Research has only begun to scratch the surface of the myriad ways that Internet use can alter one's gender-related attitudes, cognitions, and behaviors.

Cross-Cutting Issue: Cross-Cultural and Intra-Cultural Generalizations

Scholars have asked that we pay close attention to differences between cross-cultural comparisons, studies of cultural processes, and intra-cultural differences. For example, some cultures, mainly Eastern cultures, are considered to be more collectivist in comparison to the more individualist orientation of Western cultures. Although this is an oversimplification of the rich diversity within any given culture, this general difference reveals that people from individualistic cultures have a tendency to self-enhance and brag in ways absent in Eastern cultures. North Americans tend to view individuals as free agents and ascribe autonomous and agentic dispositions to individuals, whereas East Asians view individuals as more constrained by the situation, less agentic, and more subject to collective level influence. Does this not sound quite similar to the ways in which masculinity and femininity are contrasted in Western culture? Thus, what does it mean when we observe that Asian men are more deferential and modest than American women? Similarly, cultural differences in values relate to aggression. We find that in more collectivist cultures people generally are less aggressive than people in more individualistic cultures, revealing that Westernized women may be more aggressive than Asian men. Similarly, there are cultural differences in the expectation that romantic love is a prerequisite for marriage, with more collectivistic cultures placing less emphasis on romantic love and more on the wishes of family and other group members. There are even cultural differences in views of gender identity and attitudes toward sex change surgeries. Consider, for example, that there are more of these surgeries in the Muslim countries of Thailand and Iran than in more Westernized countries. What are the teachings of the Quran that might make sex reassignment more acceptable than teachings of the Roman Catholic Church? As intriguing as such cross-cultural comparisons are, critics of cross-cultural comparison research, similar to critics of sex differences research, warn of the dangers of looking at surface differences. These types of comparisons give no insight into the whys of the differences. Here, a deeper exploration of specific cultural practices is necessary. That is, causal processes may have less to do with being female or male or a member of one cultural group or another and more to do with some underlying dynamic, such as power, social systems, or socioeconomic level. Furthermore, there are striking intra-cultural differences that are often ignored. Take, for example, research on the culture of honor among southern white males, which reveals that this particular group of men tends to be more aggressive than men in other regions of the United States. How does this observation challenge our assumptions about aggression as a universal, biologically based male attribute? As another example, consider a study of attitudes toward breast self-examinations in immigrant women from Mexico, Puerto Rico, Cuba, El Salvador, and South America now residing in the United States. The researchers identified various barriers, as well as facilitative factors, that affected the likelihood of breast self-exam. For this discussion, the findings revealed vast differences in various attitudes among these groups of Latina women. For women of Mexican and Puerto Rican descent, embarrassment about touching their breasts was a major barrier, whereas this was not the case for women from South America. So, can we make a sweeping generalization about Latina women's attitudes toward breast self-exam? No—intra-cultural diversity must be considered. As you consider the various issues presented in this book, you are challenged to remain cognizant of whether results observed are generalizable across cultures as well as to various sub-cultures within any given culture.

Tools for Argument Analysis

The concept of gender has been construed in many ways, spawning a highly complex field of inquiry. Some scholars perceive gender as an attribute of individuals or something we "have." Others see gender as something we "do" or perform; gender is seen as a product of interpersonal interaction. Gender has also been construed as a mode of social organization, structuring status and power dynamics in cultural institutions. Some see gender as universal; others believe gender to be historically—and culturally—specific. The latter perspective has yielded a proliferation of investigations into how, why, when, where, and for whom gender "works." Recently similar logic has been applied to biological sex. That is, the concept of biological sex itself is a social construction. Some individuals champion gender as stimulating complementarity and interdependence among humans; others see gender as a powerful source of segregation and exclusion. Some scholars emphasize differences between females and males; others allow for greater individual variation that crosses sex and gender boundaries or they even emphasize similarity between females and males. Some people think of gender as invariant and fixed; others think of gender as malleable and flexible. Some scholars see gender as politically irrelevant; others see gender as the root of all social and political inequities. Some view "gender-inappropriate" behavior with disdain and fear, labeling it problematic and pathological and in need of correction; others see gender variance as natural and cause for celebration. Some individuals believe "traditional" differentiated sex roles should be preserved; others believe that these conventional notions of gender should be redefined or even transcended. Some individuals view gender processes and dynamics as personally relevant; others have little conception of the role of gender in their lived experience. As you can see from this brief review of many of the ways in which gender has been construed and studied, there are differences and even contradictions among the various perspectives and approaches. How do we deal with this controversy? How can we evaluate and weigh different assertions and arguments? What is the difference (if any) between facts and beliefs? Do we treat knowledge differently if we classify it as fact versus belief or opinion? Are facts more important to us than beliefs? Do we question the veracity of facts as much as that of beliefs? Why not? What are the ramifications of not submitting facts to critical questioning? In the opening of this introduction you were asked to make a list of facts. Rethink the facts you listed about human variation by sex. How do you know these are facts? What is your evidence? Does your evidence indisputably support the claim as fact? Do you detect defensiveness about or resistance to critically questioning facts? Why? Each pair of selections in this volume presents opposing arguments about sex and gender. How do you decide which argument is "right" or, at least, which argument is better? Argument analysis is a field with many approaches and standards. Here a few major components and criteria are briefly presented to help you in making judgments about the quality of the arguments advanced in the book. To assess an argument's quality it is helpful to break it down into seven components, including its *claim, definitions, statements of fact, statements of value, language and reasoning, use of authority,* and *audience.* However, first we must touch on the issue of *explicit versus implicit elements* within an argument. Real-world arguments contain many implicit (unstated) elements. For example, they may use unstated definitions of key terms or rely on value judgments that are not made clear within the body of the argument itself. Occasionally, these elements are left out because the author wants to hide the weaknesses of her or his argument by omitting them. However, it is probably more often the case that they are omitted because the author assumes the audience for their work knows about the missing elements and already accepts them as true. The job of the argument analyst begins with identifying implicit elements in an argument and making them explicit. Since we usually do not have direct access to the argument's author, making implicit elements explicit requires a good deal of interpretation on our part. However, few arguments would stand up to analysis for long if we did not try our best to fill in the implicit content. Specific examples of making implicit elements explicit are provided in what follows.

Claim

The first component one should look for in an argument is its claim. What, specifically, are the authors trying to convince us of? The notion of a claim in an argument is essentially the same as that of a thesis in a term paper. In almost all cases it is possible to identify a single overarching claim that the authors are trying to get their audience to accept. For example, in Issue 3 Diamond and Butterworth claim that fluidity in one's sexual orientation across time is evidence that it is not innate. Once the claim of an argument is identified, the analyst can begin to look for and evaluate supporting components. If no claim can be identified, then we do not have an argument that is well formed enough to evaluate fairly.

Definitions

At first thought, an argument's definitions might not seem a very interesting target for analysis. However, definitions are often highly controversial, implicit, and suspect in terms of their quality. This is especially the case in the study of sex and gender. How are the key terms in an argument's claim and supporting reasons defined, if at all? Does the author rely on dictionary definitions, stipulative definitions (offering an original definition of the term), definition by negation (saying what the term does not mean), or definition by example? Dictionary definitions are relatively uncontroversial but rare and of limited application. Stipulative definitions are conveniently explicit but often the subject of controversy. Other types of definitions can be both implicit and not widely accepted. Once you have identified definitions of the key terms in an argument's claim and supporting reasons, ask yourself if you find these definitions to be acceptable. Then ask if the argument's opponent is using these same definitions or is advocating a different set. Opposing arguments cannot be resolved on their merits until the two sides agree on key definitions. Indeed, many long-term debates in public policy never seem to get resolved because the two sides define the underlying problem in very different ways. For example, in Issue 9, Furnham defines male advantage in terms of number of sex partners, but Jonason sees advantage in more long-term relational terms.

Statements of Fact

Claims have two fundamentally different types of supporting reasons. The first type is statements of fact. A fact is a description of something that we can presumably verify to be true. Thus the first question to be answered about an argument's factual statements is how do we know they are true? For example, in Issue 15, we are given the fact that on average women earn 75 cents to each dollar earned by men. Authors may report original empirical research of their own. With an argument that is reporting on original research, the best means of checking the truth of their facts would be to repeat, or replicate, their research. This is almost never realistically possible, so we then must rely on an assessment of the methods they used, either our own assessment or that of an authority we trust. Authors may be relying on facts that they did not discover on their own, but instead obtained from some authoritative source. Aside from the question of the truth of facts is the question of their sufficiency. Authors may offer a few facts to support their claim, or many. They may offer individual cases or very broad factual generalizations. How many facts are enough? Since most arguments are evaluated in the context of their opponents, it is tempting to tally up the factual statements of both arguments and declare the one with the most facts the winner. This is seldom adequate, although an argument with a wealth of well-substantiated factual statements in support of its claim is certainly preferable to one with few statements of fact that are of questionable quality. In persuasive arguments it is very common to see many anecdotes and examples of individual cases. These are used to encourage the audience to identify with the subject of the cases. However, in analyzing these arguments we must always ask if an individual case really represents a systematic trend. In other words, do the facts offered generalize to the whole or are they just persuasive but isolated exceptions? On the other hand, it is also common to see the use of statistics to identify general characteristics of a population.

The analyst should always ask if these statistics were collected in a scientific manner and without bias, if they really show significant distinct characteristics, and how much variation there is around the central characteristics identified. Debates about the gender pay gap are highly influenced by how the pay gap is measured (see Issues 15 and 16). A final question about statements of fact concerns their relevancy. We sometimes discover factual statements in an argument that may be true, and even interesting reading, but that just don't have anything to do with the claim being advanced. Be sure that the forest is not missed for the trees in evaluating statements of fact—in other words, that verifying and tallying of factual statements does not preempt the question of how well an author supports the primary claim.

Statements of Value

The philosopher David Hume is famous for his observation that a series of factual statements (that something "is" the case) will never lead to the conclusion that something "ought" to be done. The missing component necessary to move from "is" to "ought," to move from statements of fact to accepting an argument's claim, are statements of value. Statements of value declare something to be right or wrong, good or bad, desirable or undesirable, beautiful or ugly. For example, "It is wrong for boys to play with dolls." Although many people behave as if debates can be resolved by proving one side or the other's factual statements to be true, statements of value are just as critical to the quality of an argument as are statements of fact. Moreover, because value statements have their roots in moral and religious beliefs, we tend to shy away from analyzing them too deeply in public discourse. Instead, people tend to be *absolutist,* rejecting outright values that they do not share, or *relativist,* declaring that all values are equally valid. As a result, statements of value are not as widely studied in argument analysis and standards of evaluation are not as well developed for them as for factual statements. At the very least, the argument analyst can expect the value statements of an argument to be part of what has been referred to as a "rational ideology." A rational ideology is one in which value statements are *cogent* and *coherent* parts of a *justifiable* system of beliefs. A cogent value statement is one that is relevant and clear. Coherent value statements fit together; they are consistent with one another and help support an argument's claim. A system of beliefs is justifiable if its advocate can provide supporting reasons (both facts and values) for holding beliefs. A morality that makes value judgments but refuses to offer reasons for these judgments would strike us as neither very rational nor very persuasive. Although we rarely have the opportunity to engage in a debate with authors to test their ability to justify their value statements, we can expect an argument's value statements to be explicit, cogent, coherent, and supported by additional statements of fact and value as justification. As in the case of definitions, it is also fruitful to compare the value statements of one argument with those of the opposing view to see how much the authors agree or disagree in the (usually) implicit ideology that lies behind their value statements. Throughout the issues in this book you will see an implicit clash of values: The sexes *should* be different versus opportunity for variations should be encouraged.

Language and Reasoning

There are a vast number of specific issues in the use of language and reasoning within arguments. Any introductory book on rhetoric or argumentative logic will provide a discussion of these issues. Here just a sample of the most common ones will be touched on. The analyst gives less weight to arguments that use language that is overly emotional. Emotional language relies on connotation (word meanings aside from formal definition), bias or slanting in word choice, exaggeration, slogan, and cliché. Emotional language is sometimes appropriate when describing personal experience but it is not persuasive when used to support a general claim about what should be believed or done in society. The analysis of reasoning has to do with the logical structure of an argument's components and usually focuses on the search for logical fallacies (errors in logic). A common fallacy has already been discussed under statements of fact: hasty generalization. In hasty generalizations claims are made without a sufficient amount of factual evidence to support them. When authors argue that one event followed another and this proves the first event caused the second, they are committing the *post hoc* fallacy (it may just be a coincidence that the events happened in that order). Two fallacies often spotted in arguments directed at opponents are *ad hominem* and straw man. The first involves attacking the person advocating the opposing view, which is generally irrelevant to the quality of their statements. The second is unfairly describing an opponent's argument in an overly simplified way that is easy to defeat. Fallacies directed at the argument's audience include false dilemma, slippery slope, and *ad populum*. Authors commit the fallacy of false dilemma when they argue that only two alternatives exist when, in fact, there are more than two. Slippery slope is an unsupportable prediction that if a small first step is taken it will inevitably lead to more change. An appeal to public opinion to support a claim is an *ad populum* argument if there is reason to believe that the public is prejudiced or plain wrong in its views, or if what the public believes is simply not relevant to the issue. In general, the argument analyst must not only look at the individual statements of an argument but must also ask how well they are put together in an argument that is logical and not overly emotional.

Use of Authority

The issue of authority is relevant in argument analysis concerning what is the authority of the argument's author. Analysts should use whatever information they can gather to assess the expertise and possible biases of authors. Are authors reporting on an issue that they have only recently begun to study, or have they studied the issue area in considerable depth? Do they occupy a professional position that indicates recognition by others as authorities in the field? Do you have reason to believe that their work is objective and not subject to systematic biases because of who pays for or publishes their work? Be careful not to commit *ad hominem* on this one yourself. The brief biographies of contributors to this volume give you a bit of information about the authors of the arguments that follow.

Audience

The final component of argument analysis is consideration of an argument's intended audience. Clues to the intended audience can be found in the type of publication or forum where the argument is presented, in the professional standing of its author, and in the type of language that the author uses in the argument itself. Knowledge of audience is critical in evaluating an argument fairly. Authors writing an argument for an audience that shares their core values and general knowledge of the subject tend to leave definitions and statements implicit and use language that is highly technical, dense, and symbolic. This applies equally well to scientists writing for a journal in their field and politicians addressing their supporters. Authors writing for an audience that is very different from them tend to make the various components of their arguments much more explicit. However, if authors believe the audience disagrees with them on, for example, an important value statement, they tend to make statements that are both explicit and yet still very general or ambiguous (this is a skill that is highly developed in politicians). It is difficult to make a fair judgment across these two basic types of author–audience relationships, since the former requires much more interpretation by the evaluator than the latter.

Summary

Analyzing arguments by evaluating their quality in terms of the seven components listed above is by no means guaranteed to give you a clear answer as to which argument is better, for several reasons. The relevant criteria applicable to each component are neither completely articulated nor without controversy themselves. In the process of making implicit elements explicit, analysts introduce their own subjectivity into the process. It should also be clear by this point that argument analysis is a very open-ended process— checking the truth of statements of fact, the justifiability of statements of values, the qualifications of authorities—could go on indefinitely. Thus the logic of argument analysis is underdetermined—following each step exactly is still no guarantee of a correct conclusion. However, if you apply the analytical techniques outlined above to the essays in this volume you will quickly spot implicit definitions, hasty generalizations, unsupported value statements, and questionable authorities as well as examples of well-crafted, logical, and persuasive argumentation. You will be in a much stronger position to defend *your* views about the arguments you find in this book.

Issues in This Volume

The critical examination of sex and gender in this text is segmented into six units. In Unit 1, fundamental assumptions about sex and gender are considered, revealing that "simple" definitions of sex as female or male and gender as direct derivative from biology are shortsighted. Moreover, debate over these fundamental assumptions has yielded some of the most contentious controversy in this field. This unit also addresses the "difference model," the primary paradigm for conceptualizing and studying sex and gender. Sex and gender are usually construed as binary oppositions: female versus male, feminine versus masculine. Thus, a primary way in which sex and gender are studied is the comparison of groups of females and males (i.e., sex comparison or sex difference). In this section, you will grapple with underlying theoretical rationales for excavating such differences (including biological, evolutionary, and learning theories), and you will critically evaluate the difference model in terms of methodology, social meaning and significance, and political impact. Is the search for differences between females and males a useful approach to elucidating gender or is it meaningless and even politically dangerous? Unit 2 examines gender in a critical social domain—family. Gender is influential before conception, in making decisions to carry a fetus to term, and in the life expectancy of female and male children. Sex selection is a common practice in many cultures, including Western cultures. Why is higher value placed on male versus female offspring? From some theoretical perspectives, gender begins with early socialization and is affected by family composition. One of the most gendered social institutions is the family. Traditional Western family ideology is heterosexist (regarding the heterosexual union as the only acceptable family context) and sexist (prescribing different roles for husbands and wives). In Unit 2, these fundamental values and assumptions are examined. Gender ideology riddles the construction of parenthood. Does gender influence women's and men's capacities for and approaches to parenting? How are traditional family gender ideologies challenged by same-sex parents? Unit 3 focuses on the dark side of relationships, including whether women and men want different things in relationships and whether they communicate differently. Also, violence in the daily lives of women and men is examined. One of the most pervasive stereotypes is that of sex differences in aggression. It is often assumed that males have an inborn predisposition toward aggression and females do not. As a result, girls and women should give up authority to men in exchange for their protection. This section addresses the issue of the extent to which aggression is gender-based, whether girls and boys, women and men do or do not express aggression equally and in similar or dissimilar ways. In what ways does patriarchy (masculine/male) ways lead to dominance and control? Two issues related to gender and violence are gender symmetry and pornography. Gender symmetry, as used in the domestic violence domain, reflects the assertion that women and men are both aggressive toward intimate partners; hence, domestic violence is not about gender. Various perspectives on this issue influence research agendas, intervention programs, arrest policy (i.e., dual arrest), and services (should there be shelters for battered men?). Similarly affecting research agendas, intervention programs, public policy, and services is the debate over the causal role of pornography in rape. Does viewing pornography increase men's proclivity to rape or do men with a propensity to rape prefer to view pornographic material? Unit 4 examines gender in the STEM areas, science, technology, engineering, and mathematics. Stereotypes of science and math geeks—always male—come to mind easily. Unfortunately, such common stereotypes may deter women for pursuing careers in math and science. The goal of this section is to explore what we know about gender-related patterns of performance in the sciences, especially mathematics. Sound training and skills in the sciences are considered critical twenty-first century tools for success. In particular, competence in the use of technologies, including computers and other Web 2.0 skills, is of growing importance. One question is whether women and men are destined to differential success in the STEM areas, and is this difference related to biological or social factors. A dark side of these technological skills is explored in the issue of gender and cyberbullying. In Unit 5, the world of work is explored. It is a well-established fact that women on average earn 75 cents for each man's dollar. We want to know why. Is it career choice, and if so, what factors determine individuals' career choices? It is highly likely that advanced training in mathematics and the sciences opens more doors of opportunity and increases the likelihood of a larger paycheck. How do gendered factors, be they biological or societal, affect girls' and boys' career choices and opportunities for advancement? Do these factors justify the gender wage gap? It is well understood now that most families cannot achieve a comfortable lifestyle without two paychecks. What are the implications of this for single parents, especially poor women? This section also explores how the recent economic down turn has or has not differentially affect women's and men's ability to work and earn a decent wage. In Unit 6, issues of gender and sexuality are explored. In particular, this section is interested in exploring the double standard and double bind that women and men often find themselves in. When considering the circumstances of a transgender person, the question of a triple standard arises. What does it mean to be a sexual person and how can society go about teaching young people about responsible sexual behavior? Throughout history there has been greater acceptance of male than female sexuality. Societies traditionally have endorsed various explicit and implicit means of controlling sexual expression. For example, sex education programs in the schools are explicitly aimed to control adolescent sexuality.

Conclusion

Equipped with your new tools for analyzing arguments, begin your exploration of knowledge and belief in the study of sex and gender. Remain open to considering and reconsidering beliefs and knowledge in ways that you never imagined. Your "gender quest" begins now; where you will end up, no one knows!

Internet References . . .

Alice Dreger Talks About Anatomy as Destiny

View a video that features Alice Dreger, a professor of clinical medical humanities and bioethics at Northwestern University, talking about anatomy as destiny.

http://www.ted.com/talks/alice_dreger_is_anatomy_destiny.html

Gender and Medicine

The Web site of the Monash University Medicine, Nursing and Health Sciences faculty talks about when it is sex difference and when is it gender difference.

http://www.med.monash.edu.au/gendermed/difference.html

Hyperemesis Education & Research Foundation

This foundation is dedicated to providing education and support for mothers suffering from hyperemesis gravidarum and those who care for them. This link provides information on human chorionic gonadotropin (hCG) and estrogen hormones.

http://www.hyperemesis.org/hyperemesis-gravidarum/theories-research/hormones.php

Men, Women, and Sex Differences: The Attitudes of Three Feminists—Gloria Steinem, Gloria Allred, and Bella Abzug

A paper by Russell Eisenman entitled "Men, Women, and Sex Differences: The Attitudes of Three Feminists—Gloria Steinmen, Gloria Allred, and Bella Abzug" is presented on this Web site. This paper is a case study of perspectives on sex differences of three prominent feminists.

http://www.theabsolute.net/misogyny/eisenman.html

PFLAG

PFLAG is an international organization with 490 chapters. Founded in 1981, its goal is to help families understand and accept gay, lesbian, bisexual, and transgendered family members. It offers help in strengthening families, support groups for families and friends, educational outreach, a newsletter, chapter development guidelines, grassroots advocacy, information, and referrals. It also has a Transgender Network (PFLAG TNET).

http://www.pflag.org

The National Gay and Lesbian Task Force

The National Gay and Lesbian Task Force was founded in 1973 to advocate and organize for the rights of gay, lesbian, bisexual, and transgendered people. Technical assistance for state and local organizers is provided, along with publications, materials, and a newsletter.

http://www.thetaskforce.org

Definitions and Cultural Boundaries: A Moving Target

*W*hat is sex? What is gender? What is gender identity? What is sexual orientation? Must there be congruence between biological aspects of sex (chromosomes, hormones, internal organs, and genitals) and social aspects of gender (assigned sex, gender identity, sexual orientations, and career aspirations)? These are controversial questions with a diversity of answers. In fact, the vast array of contradictory "answers" loosens the boundaries of these concepts to the point of losing any sense of certain definition. Definitions often reveal important theoretical standpoints underlying much of the controversy in the study of sex and gender. Moreover, they raise the question of cultural relativity of definitions. Can these concepts be objectively defined, or is the most objective and scientific definition still a product of culture? This section explores the limits and limitlessness of definitions and boundaries of sex and gender within biology, psyche, and culture. As you read these selections, consider the role of biology. Is the newest scientific evidence convincing regarding the causal role of biological factors? Does correlation mean causation? Do issues of gender identity, sexual orientation, and career choice based on biological factors play out the same way across race, ethnicity, class, culture, and other status-defining categories? How do the media shape the public's understanding of these issues?

- Is Anatomy Destiny?

- Are Women and Men More Similar Than Different?

- Is Sexual Orientation Innate?

ISSUE 1

Is Anatomy Destiny?

YES: Cornelieke van de Beek, Stephanie H. M. van Goozen, Jan K. Buitelaar, and Peggy T. Cohen-Kettenis, from "Prenatal Sex Hormones (Maternal and Amniotic Fluid) and Gender-Related Play Behavior in 13-Month-Old Infant," *Archives of Sexual Behavior* (2009)

NO: Vasanti Jadva, Melissa Hines, and Susan Golombok, from "Infants' Preferences for Toys, Colors and Shapes: Sex Differences and Similarities," *Archives of Sexual Behavior* (2009)

Learning Outcomes

As you read the issue, focus on the following points:

- Correlations between hormonal levels and behavior do not always mean that biological factors drive the behavior. You should be able to distinguish correlation from causation.
- Consider how various factors, such as environmental ones, might explain various hormonal—behavioral relations, especially at very young ages. You should be able to think about other factors that might account for a correlation between two variables.
- Consider why it is important to use experimental research designs to answer research questions related to hormonal–behavioral relations.

ISSUE SUMMARY

YES: Cornelieke van de Beek and colleagues demonstrated that testosterone, estradiol, and progesterone levels measured during pregnancy are related to gender-related play in 13-month-old girls and boys and found clear sex differences in preferences for masculine and feminine toys.

NO: Vasanti Jadva, Melissa Hines, and Susan Golombok, using a preferential looking task, found sex similarities in infants' preferences for shapes and colors and suggest that later gender-related patterns of toy preferences may be related to socialization or cognitive development factors rather than inborn differences.

Do we really know what constitutes one's "sex" and "gender"? Why do girls and boys, women and men behave the way they do? Typically, people assume that being male or female is a clear and absolute distinction. Biologically based theories of sex differentiation support the argument that genetic make-up and resultant hormonal influences determine fundamental differences between women and men. Given the ethical constraints associated with doing research on humans, researchers have had to rely on animal experimentation to demonstrate, for example, that hormones contribute to sexual dimorphism (i.e., sexual differentiation) on neural systems, brains, temperament, and behavior. The assumption is that sex is an unquestionably natural dichotomy rooted in an organism's genetics. Various research traditions have attempted to validate the biological basis of sex differences. These include animal studies, anthropological and cultural studies, and studies of newborns. Examples of each are provided below.

A review of animal studies has found "every imaginable mode of relationship between the sexes exists in different species." Some animal studies offer evidence of the effects of environment on something as fundamental as biological sex. For example, it is known that the depth at which sea turtle eggs are buried and the resultant temperature determine whether the turtle will be female or male (known as temperature-dependent sex determination). Even with scientific experiments (i.e., with manipulation of variables and random assignment of animals to experimental conditions), no sweeping conclusions can be drawn because, depending on the species studied, diametrically opposed results have been found.

In contrast to animal studies, anthropologists have studied various cultures in the search of universal patterns of sex differences, premised on the assumption that such patterns would be evidence for some biological basis. However, they have found that humans are incredibly malleable. Cultural analyses question the immunity of biological constructs and suggest that we must recognize that the practice of science occurs within a sociopolitical context. Therefore, notions about the biological basis of sex differences result from a dynamic interplay of cultural, social, religious, and political thought and practice. Scholars have uncovered compelling evidence that even when a binary view of sex is embraced, there are still cultural underpinnings. For example, within both Judeo-Christian and Islamic traditions, sex is seen as binary; a person is either male or female. These dominant views of sex delineate two "normal" categories: male and female. Notions of gender follow suit, typically contrasting masculine and feminine behavior patterns. However, religious traditions also deal with the reality of gender/sexual diversity in different ways. The medical procedure of a sexual reassignment surgery is understood very differently by religious leaders: for instance, while the Vatican does not think individuals can "change" sex through hormone replacement or plastic surgery, there are some Shii clerics who believe this transformation may be required in cases where the gender identity does not match external genital.

However, is this dichotomy universal? Some scholars argue that when looking for binaries, we observe only a dichotomous reality. But what remains unseen—gender diversity—is also an important reality. Dichotomous definitions of sex are not universal. Instead many cultures acknowledge multiple genders. For example, the *Turnim man* (meaning "expected to become a man") has been recognized in Sambian society (New Guinea). As a result of a genetic variation known as delta-4-steroid-5-alpha-reductase deficiency, individuals are born with a pseudo-female appearance and may be raised as a boy or girl; however, at puberty, as a result of an increase in testosterone, the individual becomes male-like. However, they typically experience a life of ridicule and rejection. This is unlike the treatment that individuals with the same genetic variation receive in the Dominican Republic. Here, the transformation of these individuals, called *guevedoces,* is celebrated. Contrast these two examples with that of the *berdache* (now considered an outdated term by some anthropologists) in Navajo society, where not only are three sexes recognized, but the berdache ("two spirits") are valued. Among various indigenous peoples more than two sexes are recognized, with remarkable variation in how they are treated by their own cultures. However, whether reviled or celebrated, for the purpose of this discussion, the point is that many cultures acknowledge more than the two traditional sexes, male and female.

Another research tradition relies on studies of newborns, on the assumption that the environment has not yet had a chance to shape gender-related patterns. However, there is the question of whether any of these can be truly unbiased. The YES and NO selections you will read for this issue were based on studies of newborn infants. These studies attempt to establish explanations for often-observed sex differences in color, shape, and toy preferences among children.

What we do know is that females and males differ in amount of various sex-related hormones in their system, sex hormones enter the brain and affect its activity, but research is inconclusive regarding causality and behavioral ramifications. Indeed, a large body of research with numerous species of animals, as well as with humans, suggests that environmental factors provide the major determinants of gender-related patterns of behavior. That is, gender is a socially constructed constellation of feelings, attitudes, and behaviors, thus strongly influenced by cultural forces.

Some revisionists have begun to "reinvent sex" by replacing dichotomous conceptions of sex with arrays reflecting the complexities of sexual variability in natural characteristics of humans. For example, terms such as "gender-crossing" have been coined. The problem with such concepts is that they still rely on the fixed binary of male/female, and they problematize deviations. As an alternative, sexologists have grappled with the idea of fluidity, such as in the "lovemap," a term first coined in 1981 by sexologist John Money. It is a "a developmental representation or template in the mind and in the brain depicting the idealized lover and the idealized program of sexual and erotic activity projected in imagery or actually engaged in with that lover." He claims that each person's map is as unique as a fingerprint. He describes the lovemap as an "entity," the facets of which include one's reproductive structure, one's sexual identity, mechanisms of reproduction, sexual orientation, and patterns and roles that are related to gender.

Whether or not you find the idea of a lovemap compelling, such a conceptualization challenges us to stretch our understanding of sex and gender in more complicated, nuanced, and multidimensional ways than most of us typically think. We may be able to more easily conceive of the possibility of multiple genders, transcend binary notions, and reconsider the notion of deviance typically associated with nonmale and nonfemale genders.

Prenatal Sex Hormones (Maternal and Amniotic Fluid) and Gender-Related Play Behavior in 13-Month-Old Infants

Introduction

Toy preference is one of the earliest manifestations of gender-related behavior. Girls have been found to prefer playing with toys such as dolls and household supplies, whereas boys prefer playing with toys such as vehicles and weapons. Several studies have demonstrated that sex differences in play behavior are present in the second year of life. One study showed that girls and boys chose different toys as early as the age of 12 months.

The fact that parents engage in some form of sex typing of their infant's play behavior in the first year of life suggests that socializing influences already may play a role. However, there are also indications that the child himself or herself may have certain innate preferences, i.e., the tendency to be focused on specific aspects of objects, like movement, color or form, which may prime them to prefer specific toy categories. The findings of sex differences in toy preferences in non-human primates, in which the influence of social learning and cognitive concepts or beliefs on toy preference can be considered nil, give additional reason to assume that there is a biological basis for the development of sex-typed toy preferences.

Among the biological determinants of play behavior, sex hormones are likely candidates. Prenatal sex hormones can permanently influence postnatal human sex-typed behaviors by altering fetal brain development. Moreover, since there is also much within-sex variation in gender-typical behaviors, such as tomboy behavior, sex hormones are probably not only responsible for behavioral sex differences, but also for within-sex variations in gender-related behavior.

Animal studies have shown that there are a few critical periods in development in which the brain regions that are responsible for the regulation of the sex-typed behavior are highly sensitive to the effects of sex hormones. In humans, the period between weeks 8 and 24 of gestation may be particularly important for sexual differentiation because this is the period when the male fetus shows a peak in serum testosterone (at its highest at about week 16).

It has been clearly shown that prenatal androgens can have masculinizing and defeminizing effects on postnatal human behaviors. Very little is known about the function of "female-typical" hormones in sexual differentiation and their effects on human behavioral differentiation. Although rodent studies indicate that estradiol is very important in behavioral masculinization and defeminization, its role in humans is less obvious. Findings in both girls and boys, exposed to diethystilbestrol (DES) (a synthetic estrogen), suggest a general lack of influences on childhood gender typical play.

Studies that have investigated the behavioral effects of prenatal progestagens mostly focused on exogenously administered synthetic progestins. The interpretations of the findings are complicated by the fact that different types of progestins were used. Prenatal exposure of girls to androgen-based synthetic progestins seemed to result in more male-typical behavior, such as more tomboyism and a stronger preference for male-typical toys, whereas exposure of girls to progesterone-based synthetic progestins produced fewer and opposite effects. Similar but less pronounced effects of these two types of exogenous progestins were found in boys. Less is known about the effects of normal circulating progesterone levels during pregnancy, although an antiandrogenic effect on the fetus has been proposed.

Currently, most evidence of a prenatal effect of androgens on human play behavior comes from studies in girls with congenital adrenal hyperplasia (CAH). CAH is a genetic condition that results in the production of high adrenal androgens beginning very early in gestation. Girls with CAH show both masculinization and defeminization of behavior: they have a stronger preference for traditionally masculine toys and activities than unaffected control girls (relatives or matched comparisons). Indications for a dose–response relationship have also been found: more severely affected girls with CAH were more interested in masculine careers and toys than less affected girls. Furthermore, the timing of exposure on behavior has been demonstrated: prenatal androgen exposure, but not early or later postnatal exposure, was related to more male-typical play behavior. In boys with CAH, elevated prenatal adrenal androgen exposure does not seem to result in more masculine play behavior.

There is also evidence that normal variations in androgen levels are systematically related to early sex differences and within-sex variations in gender-typical play behavior of children without clinical conditions. This evidence comes from studies using maternal blood to infer hormonal effects on the fetus. . . . Recently, a positive correlation was found between maternal and fetal blood testosterone. This suggests that testosterone may cross the placenta, but it may also reflect a genetic relationship. However, maternal androgens do not appear to come from the fetus, as several studies have failed to find a difference in serum second trimester testosterone levels between women carrying a male and those carrying a female fetus.

Another approach to investigate the organizational effects of prenatal sex hormones is used by amniotic fluid studies. Amniotic fluid can only be obtained from amniocentesis conducted for purposes of diagnosing fetal anomalies. Coincidentally, this medical intervention usually takes place around week 16 of gestation, a time that appears to correspond well to the male testosterone peak. Amniotic fluid seems to provide information about the sex steroid production by the fetus since several studies have found large sex differences in amniotic androgens. However, currently there is no hard evidence of a direct relationship between amniotic testosterone and fetal serum testosterone. The mostly low and/or non-significant correlations between androgens measured in amniotic fluid and in maternal serum suggest that these measures reflect something different. In addition, there is also another methodological difference between these two measures: amniotic fluid measures are only available for a specific population, which contains generally older mothers, while maternal blood measures can be relatively easily measured in a representative sample of the general population. Therefore, both measures have their advantages and disadvantages, and might provide convergent evidence of the relationship between prenatal hormones and postnatal behavior.

Until now, there are two groups of investigators that have examined the relationship between early androgen exposure by investigating prenatal amniotic hormones and postnatal behavior. One research group mainly looked at measures of cognition and cerebral lateralization. The other group of investigators primarily focused on aspects of early social development, but also included one aspect of gender role behavior in their design, namely game participation. They did not find amniotic testosterone to be related to individual differences on the Masculinity and Femininity scales of the Children's Play Questionnaire at age 5/6 years, despite the fact that this measure showed large sex differences in the same sample. However, this parent report instrument might not have been sufficiently sensitive to within sex variability in behavior, as opposed to between-sex differences. Also, the very small sample size may have increased the chance of negative results.

In the current study, we focused on toy preference observed in a laboratory situation. Rather than using parental reports, play behavior was scored by trained observers. Our first goal was to replicate previously reported sex differences in masculine and feminine toy preference in normally developing 13-month-old infants. Furthermore, we investigated whether prenatal testosterone, estradiol, and progesterone levels, as assessed in amniotic fluid and maternal serum, were related to sex differences and within-sex variations in gender-related play behavior.

Since the literature suggests most clearly an effect of prenatal androgens on play behavior, we hypothesized that higher levels of testosterone would be related to more masculine and less feminine play behavior. Previous studies on children with CAH indicate that these effects are clearly observed in girls, but are absent in boys. [T]he maternal blood study reported the same pattern in a normative population. Therefore, we predicted that this relationship would be sex-specific, i.e., more clearly present in girls than boys. We did not have clear predictions with respect to the behavioral effects of variations in estradiol and progesterone.

Method

Participants

All participants were enrolled in a prospective longitudinal project on the effects of prenatal sex hormones on gender development. Participants were recruited from a consecutive series of referrals, between January 1999 and August 2000, to the Department of Obstetrics at the University Medical Centre in Utrecht (UMCU) to undergo an amniocentesis because of prenatal diagnostic screening. All participants lived in relative close vicinity (30 km) of the UMCU. Amniotic fluid samples were provided by 153 participants with a normal healthy singleton pregnancy. Each participant gave informed consent to the procedure and the UMCU Medical Ethical Committee approved the study.

For the majority of the women (96%), the reason for amniocentesis was a higher risk of age-related (36 years or older) genetic changes and their implications. The others had an amniocentesis because of their medical history (e.g., a previous child with Down syndrome or radiation cancer treatment) (3.3%) and one participant had a high result on the triple test (indicating an increased risk for Down syndrome) (0.7%). Seven participants reported that they did not become pregnant spontaneously; $n = 4$ had ovulation induction of which one also had donor insemination, $n = 1$ had artificial insemination, and $n = 2$ had in vitro fertilization (IVF).

For 18 participants, data could not be collected at follow-up. Three children could not be tested because of illness or pregnancy of their mothers. Two children were excluded when their mother's command of the Dutch language appeared to be insufficient to complete questionnaires. One child was excluded because of extreme prematurity (gestational period less than 35 weeks) at birth. Furthermore, we lost participants ($n = 12$) because they moved abroad ($n = 1$) or were no longer interested to participate in the study ($n = 11$).

In total, 135 children were seen at the age of 13 months. Two girls were so timid that behavioral observations were not possible. The observations of three other children were not reliable because of illness or fatigue and the play behavior of four children could not be scored because of technical problems. In the end, the data of 126 children (63 boys and 63 girls) were used for further analyses. The mean age of the children was 56.4 weeks ($SD = 1.2$, range, 53.6–60.6). The mean age of the mothers at amniocentesis was 37.5 years ($SD = 2.1$, range, 28–45). The mean parental education score was 9.8 ($SD = 3.1$, range, 2–14). With respect to the presence of older siblings, there were: no older brother ($n = 69$), one older brother ($n = 43$), two or more older brothers ($n = 10$), no older sister ($n = 86$), one older sister ($n = 31$), and two or more older sisters ($n = 5$). None of these variables differed significantly between boys and girls.

Measures

Sex Hormones in Amniotic Fluid

The amniotic fluid samples were collected between week 15.3 and 18.0 of pregnancy ($M = 16.3$, $SD = .46$). The length of gestation was determined by the last menstrual period and/or ultrasonic measurement of crown-rump length (CRL). Because we had to adjust to the time schedule of the clinic, it was not possible to standardize the hormone sampling time completely; however, all samples were taken between 8:00 am and 13:00 pm. The material was stored at –30°C until assayed. The lab employees who analyzed the samples were masked to the behavioral data. Testosterone was determined by radioimmunoassay (RIA) after extraction with diethyl ether. . . .

Sex Hormones in Maternal Serum

We were able to collect serum in 115 mothers-to-be (57 boys, 58 girls). The maternal serum samples were collected immediately following the amniocentesis. The hormonal analyses were conducted as described above except for testosterone. In maternal serum, free testosterone, the biologically active part of this sex hormone, was calculated using existing procedures. . . .

One girl with an extremely high (because of skewed distributions, a criterion of >4 SD was used) amnion testosterone level (2.50 nmol/l) and whose mother had an extremely high progesterone level (2,860.0 nmol/l) and one girl whose mother had an extremely high plasma testosterone level (42.40 nmol/l) were not included in the data analyses.

Play Observations

In a structured toy play session, nine different toys that previously had been classified by parents and non-parents as masculine, feminine, or neutral were used. Each toy category was equally presented. Neutral toys were a plastic friction dog, a wooden puzzle, and a stacking pole with rings. Masculine toys were a trailer with four cars, a garbage truck, and a set of three plastic pieces of equipment. Feminine toys were a teapot with a cup, a soft doll in a cradle with a blanket, and a doll with beauty set (brush, comb, and mirror).

The toys were arranged in a standard order in a semicircle (from left to right: tea set, dog, trailer, doll in cradle, rings, truck, doll with beauty set, puzzle, and equipment). The mother was asked to place the child in the center of the semicircle, at the same distance from all toys, and then take a seat in the chair just outside the semicircle (1.5 m). She was instructed to let the child play on his or her own, but was allowed to give neutral verbal reactions if the child specifically asked her attention. When giving verbal reactions, she was asked to avoid naming the objects and guiding the child in its actions. The child was videotaped for 7 min, starting by the first touch of a toy. If play behavior was not present for longer than 30 s (e.g., if the child started to cry and sought comfort with his/her mother), this time was added to the original 7 min. In this way, every child had 7 min real playing time. The play session took place at the beginning of a more extensive testing session, after a short (5–10 min) talk with the mother. The entire visit took approximately 1 h.

For each toy, we recorded the number of seconds the child played with that particular toy. Each "play action" was scored from the moment that physical contact started until the physical contact stopped, unless there was still obvious "involvement" (e.g., pushing a car and crawling behind it). "Involvement" was defined as looking at, pointing at, and moving behind the object. If the child played with several toys simultaneously, physical contact time was scored for each toy separately. Thus, the total playing time of a child (all time spent with the different objects in sum) sometimes was longer than the 7 min of play observation. For each toy category, the total amount of time was counted and the percentage of the total playing time was calculated, resulting in the variables "% masculine play," "% feminine play," and "% neutral play." Two participants with a deviant total playing time (>3 SD) were excluded; one boy showed an extremely high (730 s) and another boy an extremely low (36 s) total playing time.

The videotapes were scored by trained observers who were masked to the hormonal values. The inter-rater reliability was high. Kendall's tau correlations ranged from .95 to 1.00 for masculine play, from .94 to .99 for feminine play, and from .99 to 1.00 for neutral play.

Developmental Assessment

A home visit took place within a week after the play session. During this visit, the Bayley Scales of Infant Development II (BSID II) was administered to assess motor and mental development.

Background Variables

Information was collected on several social and demographic variables by means of a short questionnaire. The following variables were used in the analyses: age of the mother at the time of amniocentesis, parental educational level, and number of older brothers and sisters. For each parent, the educational level was scored on a 7-point scale, with a score of 1 indicating "no formal qualifications" to 7 representing "a university degree." The scores of both parents were combined. . . .

Results

Prenatal Sex Hormones

There were no significant sex differences in maternal serum. In amniotic fluid, male fetuses had significantly higher testosterone levels, and female fetuses had significantly higher estradiol levels. No significant sex difference was found with respect to amniotic progesterone levels.

No significant relationship was found between maternal age and the hormone levels, and the same applied for gestational age at sampling and maternal hormones. In male fetuses, but not in female fetuses, there was a gestational age effect with respect to the amniotic data. With the progression of pregnancy, a significant decrease was found in testosterone, progesterone, and estradiol. To control for these effects, we used in further analyses the standardized residual of the calculated regression lines instead of the actual hormone levels.

Play Behavior

The total sample had a mean total playing time of 415 s (SD = 87; range, 181–692). There was no significant sex difference in the total time that the toys were handled.

. . . Boys (M = 40.96, SEM = 3.59) spent a significantly higher percentage of time playing with the masculine toys than girls (M = 27.10, SEM = 2.87). . . . The percentage of time with feminine toys was significantly higher for girls (M = 45.74, SEM = 3.43) than for boys (M = 36.62, SEM = 3.56). . . . Boys and girls did not differ significantly with respect to neutral play.

Gender-Related Play and Non-Hormonal Variables

In boys, no clear relationships were found between the age of mother, parental education, the number of older sisters, and mental and motor development, on the one hand, and masculine and feminine play behavior, on the other, except for a marginally significant positive relationship between parental educational level and masculine play behavior. For feminine play, a marginally significant relationship was found for boys, but in the opposite direction. In addition, the percentage of masculine play behavior tended to be lower, and feminine play higher, with an increase in the number of older brothers.

In girls, no significant relationships were found between any of the background variables and gender-related play, except for a significant negative relation between percentage of feminine play and number of older sisters.

Prenatal Hormones and Gender-Related Play

No significant relations were found between maternal sex hormones levels and masculine or feminine play behavior in either boys or girls. With regard to the sex hormones measured in amniotic fluid, a positive correlation between progesterone and time spent with masculine toys . . . was observed in boys. No other significant relationships with masculine or feminine play were found in either boys or girls.

Regression Analysis Within the Sexes

Because there were no significant relationships between prenatal hormones and feminine play in boys or girls, and because there was no relationship between prenatal hormone levels and masculine play behavior in girls, we further explored the relationship between hormones and masculine behavior in boys only. First, the variables that were related to masculine play (at a p < .10 level) were entered in the model simultaneously. These variables were progesterone in amniotic fluid, parental educational level, and the number of older brothers. Although amniotic testosterone was not significantly correlated with masculine play, we included it in the regression, because amniotic testosterone and progesterone were positively related. . . . In the final model, only progesterone in amniotic fluid significantly and positively predicted masculine play. With respect to the non-hormonal variables, masculine play was predicted by the number of older brothers (less masculine play with more older brothers) and parental educational level (less masculine play with lower educational level).

Regression Analysis Including Both Sexes

Using a similar procedure, we also entered sex, and the interactions between sex and amniotic progesterone and testosterone, respectively, in the model. Again, progesterone positively predicted masculine play, but now at a trend level. Sex of child strongly predicted masculine play, as did parental educational level. Finally, at a trend level, an inverse relation was found between the number of older brothers and masculine play.

Discussion

In the present study, we observed significantly higher amniotic testosterone levels in male pregnancies, significantly higher amniotic estradiol levels in female pregnancies, and no sex difference in maternal plasma sex hormone levels. This is in line with previous findings. Furthermore, sex differences in toy preference were clearly present at the age of 13 months. Boys spent significantly more time playing with masculine toys than girls and girls played significantly more with feminine toys than boys.

For both sexes, no significant relations were found between amniotic testosterone or other hormones and masculine or feminine play behavior, except for an unexpected positive relationship between amniotic progesterone and masculine play. This effect was clearly present in boys and was present at a trend level in the total sample (girls and boys together).

We can think of several reasons for the absence of a significant relationship between amniotic testosterone and play behavior. In our study, there are several methodological gaps that may have led to insufficient experimental power. First, it may be that one single sample of hormones does not represent actual individual differences in fetal hormone exposure. Little is known about circadian rhythms of sex hormones during pregnancy, but it has been reported that several hormones show fluctuations within a day and across days, even in fetuses. Furthermore, the relationship between testosterone measured in amniotic fluid and fetal blood is not established, so it is still uncertain what the amniotic level really represents.

Second, it may be that, at the age of 13 months, sex differences in play behavior were too small to study hormone–play relationships in the currently used sample size. At 13 months of age, we found clear sex differences in masculine and feminine toy preference, but the effect sizes were small (feminine play: $d = .35$) to moderate (masculine play: $d = .53$). This is much smaller than what is usually reported in studies in somewhat older pre-school children (e.g., $d = 1.92$ for masculine toys and $d = 1.23$ for feminine toys in 3-year-olds. However, other hormone studies did find a relationship between amniotic testosterone and behaviors that show sex differences of moderate effect size, i.e., eye-contact ($d = .53$) and vocabulary size ($d = .67$). Therefore, we expected to find at least significant results for masculine play.

Third, in a study on hormone–behavior relationships, an instrument is needed that captures behavioral differences between boys and girls, but that is also sensitive to within sex differences. Despite the fact that we did find sex differences, it may be that our method was not sensitive enough to measure within sex variability. Although the mothers in our study were instructed not to interfere, it may be that their presence has caused some error.

The positive and unexpected relationship between amniotic progesterone and masculine play behavior in boys may have reflected a Type I error, considering the multiple comparisons. Yet, in the Stanford Longitudinal Study, which used umbilical cord blood assessments, some significant relationships were found between progesterone and traits that can be labeled masculine. However, it is questionable whether umbilical cord blood levels are a good index of organizational effects of sex hormones and little is known about the relationship between progesterone levels from cord blood at birth and progesterone levels in second trimester amniotic fluid.

Finally, some attention should be paid to the few potentially relevant non-hormonal variables we incorporated in our study to control for their possible effects. Although the design of the study does not allow for definite conclusions, the results indicate that, already at 13 months of age, variables such as parental education and the number of older brothers are related to gender-related play behavior. In boys, there were indications for a tendency of masculine play to be less frequent, and feminine play to be more frequent, when the child had more older brothers. Although having one older brother is associated with more masculine gender role behavior, studies that included families with more than one sibling suggest that having two or more brothers is related to a decrease in masculine behavior. Rather than considering sibship as a social factor some researchers consider it as a biological factor, propos[ing] that each succeeding male fetus leads to the production of antibodies that can pass through the placental barrier, enter the fetal brain, and impede the sexual differentiation of the brain in the male-typical direction.

Although both biological and social factors play a role in gender role development, there is no real consensus as to if and how the different factors interact and whether there is a specific point in time at which social or cultural factors might, in fact, overrule potential biological influences. Parental behavior may strengthen biologically based differences, augmenting small differences present at 13 months. However, parents may also modify individual preferences, and overrule biological predispositions, for example in the case of very feminine boys. It is important to follow up the participants of this study and establish whether the studied relationships between prenatal hormones and gender-related play behavior increase or change over time or only appear later in development.

Vasanti Jadva, Melissa Hines,
and Susan Golombok

Infants' Preferences for Toys, Colors, and Shapes: Sex Differences and Similarities

Introduction

Children show clear sex-typed toy preferences, with girls showing more interest than boys do in dolls and boys showing more interest than girls do in vehicles. In addition to these differences between the sexes, within sex analyses show that boys play more with masculine toys, like vehicles and weapons, than with feminine toys, like dolls and tea sets. In contrast, although girls play more with feminine toys than with masculine toys when the feminine toys are sufficiently interesting, they sometimes show no significant preference for feminine over masculine toys. The strong male preference for same-sex toys has sometimes been described as boys avoiding girls' toys.

Sex-typed toy preferences have been seen in infants grow larger as childhood progresses and have been reported into young adulthood. These sex differences have been documented using an array of research methodologies, including inventories of children's toys at home, observation of children's toy contact in a playroom, parental interviews and questionnaires, and visual preferences and eye-tracking.

Perspectives on the acquisition of sex-typed play, including toy preferences, can be categorized broadly into social learning theories, cognitive theories, and hormonal theories. Social learning theories posit that children are socialized into different gender role behaviors, including toy play. Boys are reinforced for engaging with male-typical toys and girls for engaging with female-typical toys. Opposite sex-typed behavior is punished or not rewarded, which leads to extinction. Children can also learn which behaviors to adopt by modeling individuals of the same sex as themselves or by complying with labels identifying behaviors as appropriate for children of one sex or the other.

From a social learning perspective, infants' preferences for sex-typed toys would suggest that the differential treatment of boys and girls begins at an early age. In support of this view, studies have found that fathers of 12-month-old infants were less likely to give dolls to their sons than to their daughters. In one study, parents of boys called their sons' attention to the clown more than

From *Archives of Sexual Behavior*, vol. 39, 2010, pp. 1261–1273. Copyright © 2010 by the International Academy of Sex Research. Reprinted with kind permission of Springer Science + Business Media via Rightslink.

the doll and parents of girls called their daughters' attention to the doll more than the clown. Similarly, parents of infants aged 5–25 months may create different home environments for boys and girls. Boys have more sports equipment, tools and vehicles, and girls have more dolls and fictional characters. Thus, socialization of very young infants may be occurring not only through parents' interactions with their sons and daughters, but also in the way in which they design their infants' home environments.

Cognitive theories include cognitive developmental theories and gender schema theories. According to cognitive developmental theories, gender role acquisition involves three stages: gender labeling, gender stability, and gender constancy. It is at this last stage, where the child understands that gender remains the same across different situations, that sex-typed preferences were originally thought to emerge. More recently, researchers have suggested that gender constancy is not a prerequisite for gender-typed behavior and, indeed, young children show sex-typed preferences before gender constancy is attained. Gender schema theorists posit that children develop gender schemas to organize and structure gender-related information from their environment. The process of gender typing is thought to begin once the child is able to categorize him/herself as belonging to a particular gender. For cognitive theorists, sex-typed behavior follows from a child knowing his or her own gender and becoming aware of the stereotypes that exist in the social environment.

From the hormonal perspective, sex differences arise, in part, from early hormonal differences between boys and girls. In particular, sex differences in the prenatal hormonal environment are thought to produce differences in neural organization, such that high concentrations of androgens, hormonal typically produced in large amounts by the male fetus, lead to brain masculinization and increased male-typical behavior. One approach to understanding the effects of sex hormones has been to study children with congenital adrenal hyperplasia (CAH), a genetic condition where the female fetus is exposed to abnormally high concentrations of androgens. These studies have shown that girls with CAH spend more time playing with masculine toys and less time playing with feminine toys compared to control group girls. The suggestion that this may result from parents encouraging male-typical toy play in girls with CAH has not been supported by research finding that parents encourage feminine toy play, not masculine toy play, more in their daughters with CAH than in their unaffected daughters. Normal variability in androgen exposure prenatally also relates to male-typical childhood behavior, suggesting that the findings for girls with CAH relate to their androgen exposure, not to other aspects of the disorder. Sex-typed toy preferences similar to those seen in children have also been reported in two species of non-human primates, vervet monkeys and rhesus monkeys, providing additional evidence of some innate contribution.

Given the evidence that sex differences in toy preferences emerge early in life and appear to relate, in part, to hormonal or other inborn influences, some researchers have begun to ask what properties of sex-typed toys differentially attract boys and girls. For example, are boys attracted to wheels and motion, and girls to faces and imaginary role-play? Perhaps toy preferences result from what the toy can do, rather than from children knowing that a toy is appropriate for their own gender. Similarly . . . sex-typed toy preferences may result from a preference for different object features, including color, movement, or form.

Sex-Typed Toys and Color

Toys for boys and girls tend to differ in many ways. One of the most obvious is color. [G]irls' toys tended to be colored in pastel shades, especially pink and lavender, and boys' toys tended to be colored in intense colors, such as red, blue, and black. These colors are also differentially preferred by girls and boys. One study asked 3- to 7-year-old children to choose their favorite felt pig from a choice of pigs colored in either stereotypically masculine colors (navy blue, brown, maroon) or stereotypically feminine colors (light pink, bright pink, lavender), and found that they were likely to choose a pig in a color stereotyped as for their own sex. . . . Girls use more "warm" colors, including pink, than boys, whereas boys use more "cold" colors, such as gray and blue, compared to girls. Sex-typed color preferences appear to persist into adulthood; . . . females prefer reddish purple and males . . . prefer blue-green.

Few studies have examined the color preferences of children below the age of 3 years, and none have looked at sex differences in infants' preferences. However, babies as young as 3 months can see color and both male and female infants between the ages of 3 and 5 months appear to like red most and green least. It is not known, however, if infants display sex-typed color preferences similar to those of older children and adults or, if so, when these sex differences emerge.

Sex-Typed Toys and Shape

In addition to color, sex-typed toys differ in their shape. For instance, cars and other vehicles tend to be angular, whereas dolls tend to be rounded. Although research has not examined preferences for different shaped toys per se, some studies have examined the content of drawings, finding sex differences in images produced by adults, as well as children. [M]en tend to "close off" stimuli, to enlarge images (mainly by extending the image upwards), and to emphasize sharp or angular lines, while women tend to leave the stimulus areas "open", to elaborate the drawing within the confines of the presented lines and to blunt or round off any angular lines. Among children, girls are more likely than boys to draw flowers, butterflies, the sun, and human motifs, whereas boys are more likely than girls to draw mobile objects, such as vehicles, trains, aircraft, and rockets.

The present study examined toy preferences, as well as color and shape preferences, in infants ages 12, 18, and 24 months. We evaluated the hypotheses that these young children show preferences for sex-typical toys and colors, for sex-typed toys in sex-typed colors, and for angular versus rounded shapes. Infants across a range of ages were studied in anticipation of determining not only infants' sex-typed preferences, but also the age at which any such preferences emerge.

Method

Participants

Parents of infants were contacted through nurseries and mother and baby groups in London, UK. Infants were recruited into three age categories: 12 months . . . , 18 months, and 24 months. Each age category consisted of 20 boys and 20 girls. Most infants (N = 116) participated with their mothers; four infants participated with their fathers. Each parent–infant pair was paid £10 sterling (about $20) for taking part in the study.

The majority of mothers (72, 60%) and fathers (81, 67.5%) had a professional occupation, . . . and 94 (78.3%) mothers and 96 (80%) fathers held a university degree. Sixty-six (55%) of the mothers were not working at the time of study, 13 (10.8%) worked full-time, and 41 (34.2%) worked part-time. Ninety-eight (81.7%) infants were Caucasian. . . .

Measures

We used a preferential looking task, whereby two images were shown simultaneously to the infant in a darkened room. Each image in each stimulus pair was mounted in a square, colored in gray. . . . The infant's face was recorded by videotape and later coded for the length of time that the infant looked at each image. The stimuli used for the preferential looking task were chosen to test specific hypotheses, and these stimuli, and the hypotheses they were chosen to assess, are described below.

Color Stimuli

Four pairs of stimuli were used to evaluate infants' preferences for colors on their own. These stimulus pairs examined the hypotheses that boys prefer blue and girls prefer pink, as well as that infants show these sex-typed color preferences when brightness is controlled. Two pairs of stimuli compared pink . . . and blue. . . . To ensure that the color of the stimuli matched the shades of pink and blue of existing toys, two toys (a doll's dress and a building block) were scanned directly into the computer and their shades of pink and blue were recorded. Because pink and blue are made up of different brightness (luminance) levels, with pink being brighter than blue, and because differences in the brightness levels of colors have been shown to modify infants' color preferences two additional stimulus pairs were used to control for brightness. The pink was matched for brightness with the blue to produce red, and the blue was matched for brightness with the pink to produce pale blue. Thus, there were four pairings: pink/blue; red/pale blue; pink/pale blue; and red/blue.

Toy Stimuli

Two sex-typed toys (a doll and a car) provided the toy stimulus pairings. Simple line drawings of a doll and a car were scanned into a computer to create the stimuli. To allow assessment of relationships between toy and color, as well as toy preferences on their own, the car and the doll were colored in the same four colors used for the color stimuli (pink, blue, red, pale blue).

The stimuli were paired to examine specific hypotheses. To test the hypothesis that boys and girls prefer sex-typed toys in sex-typed colors, we compared the doll to the car when colored in sex congruent colors, i.e., pink doll/blue car. To test the hypothesis that the preference for sex-typed toys would be weaker when they are colored in cross sex-typed colors, we compared the doll to the car when colored in sex incongruent colors, i.e., blue doll/pink car. To examine the same hypotheses with brightness controlled, we paired the doll to the car when colored in sex congruent colors and sex incongruent colors controlling for the difference in brightness levels of pink and blue. As all possible color combinations were included, this resulted in four pairings: two pairings of toys colored in sex congruent colors (i.e., red doll/blue car and pink doll/pale blue car) and two parings of toys colored in sex incongruent colors (i.e., red car/blue doll and pale blue doll/pink car).

We also tested the hypothesis that boys and girls differ in their preference for the car and doll when both toys were of the same color or no color, by pairing the doll with the car of the same color, i.e., pink car/pink doll, blue doll/blue car, and by pairing a colorless car with a colorless doll. Finally, to test the hypothesis that boys and girls differ in preferences for the colors pink and blue, we paired pink to blue with the toy held constant: blue doll/pink doll and pink car/blue car.

Shape Stimuli

Three pairs of stimuli tested the hypothesis that boys and girls differ in their preferences for angular shapes versus rounded shapes: an angular triangle paired with a triangle with rounded edges (rounded triangle), an angular star paired with a star with rounded edges (rounded star), and an overlapping square and rectangle (rectangles) paired with an overlapping circle and oval (circles). The shapes were colored in white.

Procedure

. . . On arrival, parents and infants were taken into a reception room where they were informed about the procedure for the study and parental consent was obtained. They were then taken into the laboratory where parents were asked to seat their infants in their laps. In front of them, at a distance of 2 m, was a large white screen onto which the prepared images were projected. Hidden behind the screen was a stand holding a video camera and speakers. Only the lens of the video camera, which protruded from a hole cut out of the screen, was visible from the front of the screen. Parents were advised not to direct their child to a particular stimulus, either verbally or physically. They were also told that they could stop the testing procedure at any time by getting up from their seat. The experimenter sat in the observation room, separated from the laboratory by a one-way mirror.

As in other preferential looking studies, two stimuli were presented simultaneously, one on either side of the child's central gaze. The stimuli measured 45×45 cm and were located approximately 45 cm apart when projected onto the screen. The experimenter waited for the child to have a central gaze before showing each pair of stimuli. The infant could also be encouraged to look centrally at the screen by projecting a red spot onto the central point of the screen (used when the infant was looking in the direction of the screen) or by playing a sound (used when the infant was looking away from the screen area or was being especially fidgety). Generally, these devices were only required before the first pair of stimuli were presented.

The first sets of stimuli shown were the four pairs of color stimuli combined with the 11 pairs of toy stimuli. To ensure counterbalancing, each pairing was shown twice, with each stimulus within a pair appearing once on the left and once on the right side of the child's gaze. Thus, 30 pairs of stimuli were shown for 5 s each. The shape stimuli were shown after the color and toy stimuli. The three pairs of shape stimuli were counterbalanced producing six pairs shown for 5 s each. Order of presentation was randomized within each of the two groups of stimuli.

Data Analysis

Coding of the videotapes from the toy, color, and shape presentations was carried out by playing the tape on a VHS video-recorder and freezing the initial image. The frame advance function was then used to move the picture frame by frame. Data were coded directly onto a spreadsheet where it was noted whether the infant was looking at the left hand image, the right hand image or neither image during each frame. There were a total of 25 frames per second. . . . To assess inter-rater reliability, a randomly selected sample of the videotapes was coded by two scorers. Pearson correlation coefficients for the pairings, calculated using the combined raw scores for each pair of stimuli, ranged from .80 to .99 with an average correlation of .95. . . .

Some infants looked longer at the pairings than others. To adjust for these differences, scores were converted into the proportion of time spent looking at one stimulus over the total looking time for both stimuli. Proportions were transformed into percentage values; thus, an infant looking at a particular stimulus for 50% of the time meant that no preference was shown. All subsequent analyses were conducted using these percentage values.

Results

Mean proportions of time that infants looked at each of the color, toy, and shape stimulus pairings [were] broken down by sex and age. . . . Sex and age differences and their interaction were evaluated using analysis of variance for each of the pairings.

Color Stimuli

No main effects of sex were found for any of the four color pairings. A significant main effect of age was found only for the red/pale blue pairing, . . . with 12-month-olds looking significantly longer at red compared to 24-month-olds. . . . There were no significant interaction effects. A composite score was computed to examine sex and age influences on preferences for pink/red versus blue/pale blue collapsed across all four pairings. There were no significant main effects of sex or age and no interaction between sex and age.

Toy Stimuli

Five of the 11 pairings designed to test specific hypotheses were significant, and, contrary to the expectation that sex-typed toys would be of most interest when of sex-typed colors, findings suggested that infants preferred looking at sex-typed toys whether or not they were of sex-typed colors, but only when the brightness of colors was matched. In addition, means, even when not significant, were in the direction consistent with a preference for sex-typed toys, regardless of their color.

Shape Stimuli

No main effects of sex or age and no interactions were found for any of the three shape pairings comparing rounded shapes to angular shapes. An overall score, collapsed across all three pairings, also showed no main effects of sex or age and no interaction between sex and age.

Composite Stimuli

We next combined stimulus pairs to provide more reliable, composite estimates of children's preferences for sex-typed toys and sex-typed colors. Preferences for sex-typed toys were assessed by computing infants' average scores for looking at the doll versus the car, irrespective of color, across all pairings. Preferences for sex-typed colors were assessed by computing infants' average scores for looking at pink/red versus blue/pale blue, across all color pairings and, irrespective of the toy, across all toy pairings. . . .

The combined analysis of toy type revealed a main effect of sex. Girls looked longer at the doll than boys did, and boys looked longer at the car than girls did. . . . There also was a main effect of age. . . . Infants looked significantly longer at the doll at 12 months of age than at either 18 months . . . or 24 months . . . , but 18- and 24-month-olds did not differ. There was no significant interaction between sex and age. The combined analysis of color preferences across all toys and color pairings showed no significant main effects of sex or age and no significant interaction.

Using the composite scores, we also looked at within sex preferences for same sex-typed toys over other sex-typed toys (i.e., boys' preferences for cars over dolls and girls' preferences for dolls over cars) in each age group. Girls showed a significant preference for the doll over the car at ages 12 months . . . and 18 months . . . , but this difference, though in the same direction, was not statistically significant at 24 months. Boys also showed a significant preference for the doll over the car at 12 months. . . . At ages 18 and 24 months, boys no longer showed a preference for the doll, and, although they looked longer at the car than the doll at these later ages, their preference for the car was not statistically significant.

Finally, at the suggestion of a reviewer, we analyzed difference scores, obtained by subtracting percentage looking time at the colorless doll and car from percentage looking time at the same stimuli when colored. These analyses also suggested that infants did not show sex typed color preferences. There were no significant main or interaction effects for the composite color difference scores, and only one main effect and no interactions for any of the individual pairings.

Infant Preferences Regardless of Sex and Age

Because no sex or age differences emerged for the color or shape stimuli, we examined color and shape preferences, irrespective of sex and age. For the color stimuli, infants looked longer at red than blue and longer at red than pale blue. For the shape stimuli, infants looked longer at circles than squares and longer at rounded triangles than triangles. For the four color stimuli combined, infants looked longer at pink/red than blue/pale blue. . . . For the three shape stimuli combined, infants looked longer at rounded images than angular images. . . .

Discussion

Our results found both sex differences and sex similarities in infants' toy, color, and shape preferences. We saw the expected sex differences in toy preferences, with girls showing more interest than boys in dolls, and boys showing more interest than girls in cars. These results did not interact with age. The differences were most apparent in stimulus pairings when colors were controlled for brightness. Contrary to prediction, however, sex-typed toy preferences were not stronger when toys were of sex-typed colors. In addition, infants did not show the predicted sex differences in color or shape preferences. Instead, we saw sex similarities in these areas. Both boys and girls preferred reddish colors to blue colors, and rounded shapes to angular shapes. There was also an age effect for interest in the doll. Both boys and girls looked longer at the doll at age 12 months, than at 18 or 24 months.

Controlling the brightness of colors was a novel aspect of the current study and, given that sex differences in toy preferences were most obvious when brightness was controlled, this could be a useful design feature for future studies. Controlling brightness may be particularly important in studies such as ours, which present images in a darkened room, allowing the brightness of a color, as well as its hue or other characteristics to influence its attractiveness.

Our observations that 12- to 24-month-old boys show more interest than girls do in cars, and that girls of this age show more interest than boys do in dolls, resemble observations of sex differences in toy preferences in older children, and add to evidence that these sex differences emerge at a very young age. Such early sex differences could reflect inborn tendencies for girls and boys to prefer different toys. This interpretation is consistent with findings linking prenatal androgen exposure to toy preferences in children and with findings of similar sex differences in toy preferences in non-human primates. Additionally, early socialization could contribute to sex differences in infants, since they have already been provided with sex-typed toys. Thus, their looking preferences may reflect the type of toys that they have been exposed to in their environment. This interpretation would suggest that children learn sex-typed behaviors at a very young age.

Cognitive developmental processes related to gender are not likely to explain sex-typed toy preferences in 12- to 24-month-old infants. At this age, many infants would not have reached even the first stage of gender acquisition (gender labeling). In addition, although there is evidence that female infants may display some understanding of gender by the age of 18 months, this is apparently not the case for boys. The role of gender identity in the acquisition of gender role learning needs to be re-evaluated, because toy preferences are found in male infants, even though they do not appear to be aware of their gender identity. Our findings also argue for reconsidering the role of cognitive understanding of gender, at least in the initial phase of children's acquisition of sex-typed toy preferences. Cognitive factors may play a role in later years, however, as sex-typed toy preferences become increasingly evident.

We did not see sex differences in preferences for pink or reddish colors over blue, nor did we see sex differences in preferences for angular versus rounded shapes. Therefore, our findings did not support [the] suggestion that differences in color or shape preferences explain sex differences in toy preferences, at least at this early stage of development. Indeed, the causal relationships may be the opposite. Sex differences in toy preferences may contribute to sex differences in preferences for colors or shapes. For example, girls may learn to like pink because many of the toys they play with are pink. Alternatively, or additionally, they may learn this color preference through social or cognitive mechanisms. For example, girls may learn to prefer pink through modeling older girls who like pink, or through cultural labeling of pink as for girls. Similar mechanisms could explain sex differences in shape preferences. In addition to suggesting that the different colors of sex-typed toys could drive boys and girls differential interest in them, [it] has [been] suggested that females and males may have evolved to prefer pink and blue, respectively, a suggestion that has been reiterated by others. Our findings argue against these suggestions as well.

Our observation that boys at 12 months of age, like girls, prefer the doll to the car . . . argue against suggestions that boys' strong preference for masculine toys or avoidance of feminine toys, such as dolls, is inborn, and argue instead for the importance of social learning or cognitive developmental processes in the development of this particular aspect of sex-typed toy preferences. Consistent with this argument, boys' avoidance of feminine toys has been found to increase with age, and to be stronger when an observer is present. Boys also receive stronger reinforcement than girls do to avoid cross sex toy play, and they are more likely than girls are to imitate the behavior of same sex models. Thus, reinforcement and modeling could play an important role in boys' eventual strong preference for masculine toys or avoidance of feminine toys.

Instead of providing evidence of sex differences in infants' visual preference for pink and blue, our findings suggest that infants prefer red, irrespective of their sex. Other studies also have reported that infants from as young as 2 months of age look longer at red than at other colors. . . . The absence of sex differences in infants' and young children's color preferences, coupled with findings that older children display sex-typed color choices, suggests that children learn these preferences. The timing of the emergence of sex-typed color preference (after age two, or maybe even five, years) is also consistent with cognitive developmental perspectives, which suggest that sex differences in children's behavior emerge as children develop a cognitive understanding of their gender and its stability and constancy, a process that continues after the age of two until as late as age seven years or older.

Our results also suggest sex similarity rather than difference in infants' shape preferences; irrespective of sex, infants looked longer at rounded shapes (circles, rounded triangles) than at angular shapes (squares, triangles). The preference for rounded over angular shapes could relate to the emotional responses that different shapes elicit. A study asking college students to rate their emotional response to stimuli consisting of either an ellipse or a straight line found that roundedness conveyed warmth and acute angles conveyed threat. . . . Sharp angles may convey a sense of threat which results in a negative bias. It also has been suggested that the visual properties of angularity could reflect the facial attributes of an angry face and roundedness could reflect the facial attributes of a happy face. . . .

In addition to seeing unexpected sex similarities in the color and shape preferences of infants, we saw an unpredicted effect of age. Regardless of sex, infants looked longer at the doll at age 12 months than at later ages. The interest of 12-month-old infants of both sexes in dolls might relate to infants' interest in faces. If so, our results suggest that this interest is more pronounced in younger infants than in older infants. . . .

The current study adds to growing evidence that infants younger than 2 years of age display sex-typed toy preferences, with boys showing more interest than girls do in cars, and girls showing more interest than boys do in dolls. Within sex analyses found that the female preference for dolls over cars begins as early as 12 months of age, whereas boys of this age also prefer dolls to cars. The male preference for cars over dolls, or avoidance of dolls, emerges later, suggesting that socialization or cognitive development, rather than inborn factors, causes the male avoidance of feminine toys. Similarly the lack of sex differences in color or shape preferences in infants suggests that sex differences in these areas emerge later, perhaps also under the influence of socialization or cognitive developmental processes. In addition to seeing sex differences in infants, we also observed sex similarities. Infants of both sexes preferred reddish colors to blue and rounded shapes to angular shapes. One implication of our findings is that sex differences in toy preferences in infancy are not driven by sex-linked preferences for different colors or shapes, since sex differences in these areas are not yet present. Instead, the direction of influence could be the opposite. Girls may learn to prefer pink, for instance, because the toys that they enjoy playing with are often colored pink. Finally, our results suggest that different types of factors influence different aspects of children's sex-typed preferences. Inborn factors, such as the prenatal testosterone surge in male fetuses, may be particularly important for boys' greater interest than girls in vehicles and girls' greater interest than boys in dolls. In contrast, sex-typed color and shape preferences, and the male avoidance of girls' toys, which appear to emerge later in life, may depend more extensively on sex-related differences in socialization or cognitive developmental processes.

EXPLORING THE ISSUE

Is Anatomy Destiny?

Challenge Questions

1. Jadva and colleagues describe a number of different theories that might account for sex differences in toy preferences. What are these theories?
2. Given that toy preferences, especially the nature of sex differences, appear to change with age, how might these age-related changes be explained? Do some theoretical accounts do a better job of explaining such changes than others?
3. Explain the concepts of sex-similarities and sex-differences.
4. What findings might argue against explanations that focus on inborn causes of the differences? Make a list of what these might be, including such things as parents' educational level or number and sex of older siblings in the home.
5. What findings might argue against explanations that focus on environmental causes of the differences? Make a list of what these might be, including such things as prenatal hormonal levels.
6. Do studies such as these shed light on the question of whether anatomy is destiny? Why or why not?
7. How might the issue of gender-related patterns in toy preferences be studied cross-culturally?

Is There Common Ground?

Both YES and NO selections suggest that clear gender-related preferences for toys exist, but the question of why remains to be answered. Van de Beek and colleagues note that although their focus was on the relation between prenatal hormones and toy preferences, there is clearly room for various environmental factors to affect toy preferences. Conversely, Javda and her colleagues do admit that although socialization and cognitive development factors probably account for sex similarities and differences, inborn biological factors including hormones may also make a contribution. Thus, although different authors may emphasize one set of factors over another, they do leave room for the possibility that there is a dynamic interaction between the biological and the environmental factors.

Nature versus nurture? Biology versus social determinism? Just as some scholars argue that we need to move beyond gender binaries to better understand human complexity, we must also move beyond neat either/or propositions about the causes of sex and gender. Traditional thought dictates that biology affects or determines behavior and that anatomy is destiny. But behavior can also alter physiology. Recent advances explore the complex interaction between biology (genes, hormones, brain structure) and environment. We have learned that it is impossible to determine how much of our behavior is biologically based and how much is environmental. Moreover, definitions of gendered behavior are temporally and culturally relative. Yet, why do researchers continue to try to isolate biological factors from environmental factors? Advancements in the study of biological bases of sex and critiques of applications of biological theory to human behavior challenge many long-held assertions. Many traditional biologists recognize species diversity in hormone–brain–behavior relationships, which makes the general application of theories based on animal physiology and behavior to humans problematic. Moreover, species diversity challenges male/female binaries. The validity of the presence/absence model of sex dimorphism has been challenged. In embryonic development, do females "just happen" by default in the absence of testosterone? No, all individuals actively develop through various genetic processes that are integrally linked to environmental factors that either activate or alter these processes. Moreover, the sexes are similar in the presence of, and need for, both androgens and estrogens; in fact, the chemical structures and derivation of estrogen and testosterone are interconnected and imbalances of either in females and males cause serious anomalies in the development and lifetime functioning.

Additional Resources

Jill B. Becker, *Sex Differences in the Brain: From Genes to Behavior* (New York: Oxford University Press, 2008).

Anne Fausto-Sterling, *Sexing the Body: Gender Politics and the Construction of Sexuality* (New York: Basic Books, 2000).

Colin Hamilton, *Cognition and Sex Differences* (New York: Palgrave Macmillan, 2008).

http://www.hyperemesis.org/hyperemesis-gravidarum/theories-research/hormones.php

http://www.ted.com/talks/alice_dreger_is_anatomy_destiny.html

ISSUE 2

Are Women and Men More Similar Than Different?

YES: **Janet Shibley Hyde**, from "New Directions in the Study of Gender Similarities and Differences," *Current Directions in Psychological Science* (vol. 16, pp. 259–263, 2007)

NO: **Marco Del Giudice**, from "On the Real Magnitude of Psychological Sex Differences," *Evolutionary Psychology* (vol. 7, pp. 264–279, 2009)

Learning Outcomes

As you read the issue, focus on the following points:

- Pay attention to the basic assumptions each author makes and how the assumptions lead to a different interpretation of the results of meta-analyses.
- You should be able to explain the differences between evolutionary theory and social structural theory.
- Understand what an effect size is and how it can be used to interpret the strength of relations between variables.
- Understand what it means to say a psychological construct is multidimensional.

ISSUE SUMMARY

YES: Janet Shibley Hyde makes the case that gender similarities are just as interesting and important to understand as are gender differences. By adopting a social structuralist perspective and considering gender as a social stimulus rather than a person variable, she uses meta-analyses to support the argument that women and men are more alike than different.

NO: Marco Del Giudice follows the assumptions of evolutionary theory to accept the premise that women and men are different. He argues that effect sizes derived from meta-analyses underestimate the true magnitude of gender-related differences.

What is the most fruitful approach for better understanding sex and gender? For decades, the dominant approach in social scientific research on sex and gender has been the study of sex differences, termed a difference model. The goal is to examine whether or not sex differences exist and to describe the differing group tendencies. In this research, sex differences are identified from a comparison of the average tendency of a group of males to the average tendency of a group of females. The result is typically expressed in the form of generalizations about the ways in which males and females differ, presuming within-sex homogeneity (i.e., all females are alike). The contrasting view is the similarities model, one that is less popular in general. Some feminist scholars warn of the overrepresentation of findings of sex differences in published scholarship. Many scholars argue that the comparison of males and females is as much a political as a scientific enterprise. The finding of similarities between groups is thought to be a "null" finding and thus not publishable in its own right. The popular press is eager to disseminate evidence of sex differences; indeed, findings of sex similarity are viewed as not newsworthy. Often, the description of a sex difference is accompanied by a presumption that the difference is innate and thus immutable. An ongoing debate surrounds whether women and men are more similar than different and whether it is worthwhile to continue to study differences, especially if they are small. There appears to be a trade-off in the costs and benefits of each perspective. Noted feminist psychologist Rhoda Unger once said, "Consider a rainbow. Given the full spectrum of color, we perceive red and magenta as being similar. If, however, we eliminate all other hues, red and magenta are now perceived as being different. But the price of emphasizing this difference is the loss of the rest of the spectrum. Similarly, relationships relevant to both sexes have been obscured by the limitation of research to the difference between them." Where do you think it is most fruitful to be on the similarity–difference spectrum? Will we learn more by focusing on one end or the other? Is it possible to embrace both approaches?

Maccoby and Jacklin's 1974 classic *The Psychology of Sex Differences* triggered other in-depth analyses of the existence or lack thereof of sex differences in numerous areas. In general, conclusions reflected skepticism about the presence of sex differences. In the 1980s, this area of research took another step forward by moving from an impressionistic normative reviewing process to a more formal, quantitative technique for synthesizing research: meta-analysis. Meta-analysis provides a common metric with which studies can be compared directly and the magnitude of sex differences can be represented numerically. Moreover, meta-analysis looks at the consistency of findings across studies and tries to identify variables (such as measurement strategies, the historical moment when the study was conducted, and sample characteristics) that explain inconsistencies and even contradictions across studies.

Researcher and psychologist Jacquelyn James in "What Are the Social Issues Involved in Focusing on *Difference* in the Study of Gender?" *Journal of Social Issues* (Summer 1997), outlines five critical issues to consider when reviewing the status of the difference model, which remain important today as we examine the similarities–differences debate:

1. *Very small differences can be statistically significant*: Because of the social weight of scientific evidence, even misrepresented and statistically weak differences get exaggerated by public accounts and therefore misused, typically to the detriment of women.
2. *False universalism*: Interpretations of group differences often presume within-group similarity. In fact, other individual differences (e.g., social power) may explain differences better than similarities.
3. *The "tyranny of averages"*: Sex differences are usually based on group averages, interpreted as if they represent absolutes. Within-group variability or the overlap between distributions of males and females are not examined.
4. *The revelations of within-group differences*: Careful examination of within-group variation can be very effective in challenging gender stereotypes and examining the conditions under which differences do and do not occur. Furthermore, methodological practices may skew the meaning of sex differences (e.g., measurement bias). It is often the case that the differences within each sex are far greater than the difference between the average for women and the average for men.
5. *Some differences are diminishing over time*: Weakening differences over time suggest the sociohistorical change. As opportunities for women and men expand, each is able to acquire skills previously associated with the other sex, such as combat skills for women in the military and care-taking skills for men in the nursing profession.

Has the difference model outlived its purpose? In the YES selection, Janet Hyde, using results of several meta-analyses, documents that women and men are quite similar in a number of psychological domains. Only for the domains of motor performance and physical aggression, behaviors that depend largely on muscle mass and bone size, and for sexuality (at least masturbation and attitudes accepting of casual sex) have moderate-to-large sex differences been found. She highlights the importance of considering social context when examining gender-related behaviors and concludes that the overinflation of sex differences is costly for girls and boys. In contrast, in the NO selection, Del Giudice takes an evolutionary approach and accepts the premise that women and men are different, arguing that the very same meta-analyses Hyde relies on to document similarities actually document differences. He does so by doing additional analyses of these numbers to show that meta-analyses can underestimate the true magnitude of gender-related differences. Del Giudice would disagree with the point made by Jacquelyn James above that small differences are misrepresented. Rather, he argues that many small differences can accumulate to be meaningful.

Although most of the research on sex differences has been descriptive, assumptions and theories of what causes these sex differences abound. As you read YES and NO selections, consider the role of biology. Are new developments in neuron imaging that show which areas of the brain are most active during various tasks clarifying or confusing our understanding of the role of biology in explanations of sex differences and similarities? How do issues of sex differences/similarities play out across race, ethnicity, class, culture, and other status-defining categories? Are women and men alike or different across these various categories? Do media representations of women and men "fan the fires" of difference?

YES

Janet Shibley Hyde

New Directions in the Study of Gender Similarities and Differences

For at least the last century, psychological scientists, as well as members of the general public, have been convinced that human males and females differ psychologically in important and substantial ways. Psychological scientists, basing their ideas on key reviews, have thought and taught that there are reliable gender differences in verbal ability (females scoring higher), mathematical and spatial abilities (males scoring higher on both), aggressiveness (males higher), and activity level (males higher). Members of the general public, influenced by bestsellers such as John Gray's *Men Are from Mars, Women Are from Venus* and Deborah Tannen's *You Just Don't Understand: Men and Women in Conversation,* believe that men and women are fundamentally different. Here I review current scientific evidence on psychological gender differences and similarities, as well as current and future directions to advance this area of research.

Gender Similarities and Differences

Gender-differences research is an extremely active area; often 50 or more studies can be found on a single aspect of gender differences. *Meta-analysis* has emerged as an excellent method for assessing these large research literatures to determine which findings are reliable. Meta-analysis is a statistical method that allows the researcher to synthesize the statistical findings from numerous studies of the same question—for example, "Are there gender differences in aggression?" An important statistic in meta-analysis is the *effect size,* which measures the magnitude of the gender difference:

$$d = \frac{M_M - M_F}{s_w}$$

where d is the effect size, M_M is the mean score for males, M_F is the mean score for females, and s_w is the pooled within-gender standard deviation. Positive values indicate that males scored higher and negative values indicate that females scored higher; d measures how far apart the average male and female scores are, in standard-deviation units.

From *Current Directions in Psychological Science,* vol. 16, 2007, pp. 259–263. Copyright © 2007 by the Association for Psychological Science. Reprinted by permission of Sage Publications via Rightslink.

Table 1

A Sample of Effect Sizes Extracted from 46 Meta-Analyses of Research on Psychological Gender Differences

Variable	No. of reports	Effect size (d)
Cognitive variables		
Mathematics problem solving	48	+0.08
Mathematics	6*	+0.16
Reading comprehension	5*	−0.09
Mental rotation	78	+0.56
Communication		
Self-disclosure	205	−0.18
Smiling	418	−0.40
Social and personality variables		
Physical aggression	111	+0.33 to +0.84
Verbal aggression	68	+0.09 to +0.55
Helping behavior	99	+0.13
Leadership effectiveness	76	−0.02
Self-esteem	216	+0.21
Depression symptoms	49	−0.16
Attitudes about casual sex	10	+0.81
Miscellaneous		
Throwing velocity	12	+2.18
Moral reasoning: Justice orientation	95	+0.19

Asterisks indicate that data were from major, national samples.

In a recent review, I was able to identify 46 different meta-analyses that assessed psychological gender differences. They spanned a wide range of domains, including cognitive abilities, communication, social behavior and personality, psychological well-being, and other miscellaneous areas. A sample of these meta-analyses and the associated effect sizes is shown in Table 1.

I extracted the effect sizes from the meta-analyses and analyzed them for patterns. Which are the large gender differences? Which are the small ones? Cohen provided guidelines for interpreting the magnitude of effect sizes based on the d statistic: .20 is a small effect, .50 is a moderate effect, and .80 is large. I therefore grouped effect sizes into those that fell in the small range ($0.11 \leq d \leq 0.35$), the moderate range ($0.36 \leq d \leq 0.65$), and the large range ($d = 0.66$ to 1.00). I added two categories: differences that are near zero or trivial ($0 \leq d \leq .10$) and differences that are very large ($d > 1.0$).

The surprising result was that 48% of the effect sizes were in the small range and an additional 30% were near zero. That is, fully 78% of the effect sizes for gender differences were small or close to zero. Stated another way, within-gender variability is typically much larger than between-gender variability.

These findings led me to propose the Gender Similarities Hypothesis, which states that males and females are similar on most, but not all, psychological variables. This view is strikingly different from the prevailing assumptions of difference found among the general public and even among researchers.

Exceptions to the pattern of gender similarities do exist, but they are few in number. The largest gender differences were in the domain of motor performance, for behaviors such as throwing velocity ($d = 2.18$). Large gender differences were found in some—but not all—aspects of sexuality, including incidence of masturbation and attitudes about sex in a casual, uncommitted relationship. Across several meta-analyses, aggression showed a moderate gender difference ($d = 0.50$), with males being more aggressive.

Meta-analyses also provide abundant evidence that effect sizes in a given domain are heterogeneous and that not only the magnitude but even the direction of gender differences depends on the context in which behavior is measured. A classic example comes from Eagly and Crowley's meta-analysis of research on gender differences in helping behavior. Averaged over all studies, $d = 0.34$, indicating that men helped more. However, for studies in which onlookers were present and participants were aware of it, $d = 0.74$, and when no onlookers were present, $d = -0.02$. These findings were consistent with Eagly and Crowley's predictions based on social-role theory; chivalrous and heroic helping is part of the male role and is facilitated when onlookers are present, resulting in a large gender difference.

I argue that gender similarities are, scientifically, as interesting as gender differences. Future researchers, whether they are gender researchers or researchers who have conducted casual tests for gender differences in research focused on another question, should report both differences and similarities so that we have a balanced view of the two.

Gender as a Stimulus

In the preponderance of psychological research, gender is considered to be an individual-difference or person variable. An alternative approach recognizes that gender is a social-stimulus variable as well. Here I review two lines of research that support this view: research on gender bias in evaluations of leaders, and the Baby X studies.

In experimental research on gender and the evaluation of leaders, evaluators receive information about a leader, typically as a written vignette but sometimes as a videotape or live scenario by a person trained to engage in a standard set of behaviors. The gender of the leader is manipulated while all other factors are held constant. Thus any differences in ratings of male and female leaders must be due to gender and not to other confounding factors.

Eagly and colleagues meta-analyzed this research literature, locating 61 relevant studies. Overall, there was little evidence of gender bias in the evaluation of leaders ($d = 0.06$). In certain circumstances, however, gender bias was larger. For example, female leaders portrayed as using an autocratic style were evaluated less favorably than comparable male leaders ($d = 0.30$).

A second example comes from a classic experiment by Condry and Condry. Participants viewed a videotape of a baby's emotional responses to a jack-in-the-box popping open. The baby stared and then cried. Half the adult viewers were told that the baby was a boy and half were told it was a girl. Those who thought the baby was a boy labeled the emotions "anger"; the other half called the "girl's" emotions "fear." In short, the adults read the emotions differently depending on the baby's gender. Numerous studies using this Baby X paradigm have replicated the finding that adults respond differently to an infant depending on whether they think the child is a boy or a girl.

The broader implication here is that, both in laboratory experiments and in real life, an individual's gender acts as a stimulus that influences people's responses to the person. This principle deserves more theoretical, empirical, and methodological attention. Methodologically, for example, participants' behavior may be substantially influenced by the gender of the experimenter, but researchers rarely test this effect.

Sociocultural Influences on Gender Differences

Some of the most exciting research and theory on sociocultural influences on psychological gender differences is coming from cross-national research and research on gender and ethnicity in the United States.

Cross-National Research

The availability of major databases such as the United Nations data on gender equality (or lack thereof) in nations around the world (http://hdr.undp.org/hdr2006/statistics/indicators/229.html) has contributed to important developments in the ability of psychological scientists to test hypotheses about links between sociocultural factors and gender differences and similarities in behavior. These advances in research capabilities have been accompanied by advances in theory.

Eagly and Wood proposed social-structural theory as an explanation for the origins of gender differences in human behavior. According to social-structural theory, a society's division of labor by gender drives all other gender differences in behavior. That is, gender differences in behavior are created by social structures, and particularly by the different roles that women and men occupy. Psychological gender differences result from individuals' adaptations to the particular restrictions on or opportunities for their gender in their society. Eagly and Wood acknowledged biological differences between women and men, such as differences in size and strength and women's capacity to bear and nurse children, but they argued that these physical differences are important mainly because they are amplified by cultural beliefs and roles. Men's greater size and strength have led them to pursue activities such as warfare that in turn gave them greater status and power than women. Once men were in these roles, their behavior became more dominant and women's behavior accommodated and became more subordinate. The division of labor by gender, in which women were responsible for home and family, led women to acquire role-related skills such as cooking and caring for children. In this way, women acquired nurturing behaviors and a facility for relationships.

Eagly and Wood reanalyzed Buss's 37-cultures data, which are widely believed to support evolutionary-psychology theories, to examine variations in patterns of mate preferences across cultures, making use of the U.N. database on gender equality across nations. Their hypothesis was that the greater the gender gap in status in a culture, the greater would be the psychological gender differences. Societies characterized by gender equality should show far less psychological gender differentiation. Consistent with predictions, correlations were high between societies' gender inequality and the magnitude of the difference between women and men in that society on psychological measures of mate preferences. Studies such as this represent an important future direction for gender research.

Gender and Ethnicity in the United States

Scholars in women's studies have long urged the study of the intersection of gender and ethnicity. Translated to the language of psychological science, this is equivalent to a hypothesis of an interaction of gender by ethnicity. That is, gender differences—or gender phenomena more generally—are expected to differ across ethnic groups. Because so much research is based on samples of college students and because the great majority of them are White, most of what we know about gender differences and similarities is actually about gender differences and similarities among Whites. Clearly, investigations of gender phenomena in different U.S. ethnic groups are an important new direction for research.

One example comes from a meta-analysis of studies of gender differences in self-esteem, based on 216 effect sizes. It is widely believed that girls and women have lower self-esteem than men and boys do, particularly beginning in adolescence. The meta-analysis found, in contrast, that the effect size was small ($d = 0.21$). The important point here, though, is that the effect size for White samples was $d = 0.20$, whereas the effect size for Black samples was $d = -0.04$ (insufficient numbers of studies of other ethnic groups were available to permit computation of average effect sizes). That is, the much-touted gender gap in self-esteem is small in Whites and nonexistent in Blacks. This illustrates the extent to which psychology has been a psychology of Whites and, in particular, gender psychology has been a psychology of White women and men. An important new direction in research will be to examine whether "well established" gender phenomena are similar or different across ethnic groups.

Neuroscience and Gender Differences

Although members of the general public tend to believe that any pattern of behavior that is rooted in the brain is "hard wired," immutable, or something one is "born with," contemporary neuroscientists are in fact immersed in the study of brain *plasticity*: the capacity of the nervous system to change its organization and function over time. As the brain develops, certain synapses form and stabilize, whereas others are pruned and removed. Brain plasticity can be affected by many factors including experience, drugs, hormones, maturation, and stress. For example, a repeated experience that results in the activation of a particular set of synapses can lead to long-term potentiation (or alternately, depression) of the activity of those synapses.

In the era of functional magnetic resonance imaging research, it is common to see reports of studies finding that different brain regions are activated in males compared with females during activities such as solving difficult mathematics problems. It is easy to assume that these differences are "hard wired" and that they explain gender differences in performance, but an equally viable interpretation is that males and females have different experiences related to mathematics as they grow up, and that these different experiences have, on average, enhanced synaptic connections in some regions for males and in other regions for females. Moreover, gender similarities in performance can be associated with activation of different brain regions in males and females, and gender differences in performance can be found when similar brain regions are activated in males and females. Certainly the study of gender-related brain plasticity will be an important direction for new research.

Conclusions

I have identified four current and future directions for gender research: the gender similarities hypothesis, analysis of gender as a stimulus variable, studies of sociocultural variations in gender differences, and the recognition of brain plasticity. These ideas lead to four suggestions for future research. First, researchers should strive for balanced reporting of both gender differences and gender similarities. Second, although the tradition in psychological research has been to view gender as an individual-difference or person variable, gender can also be a potent stimulus variable. Research and theory analyzing ways and situations in which gender acts as a stimulus are important directions for the future. This approach could effect a major change in the way in which we conceptualize gender in psychology. Third, cultural psychology is a rapidly expanding area, providing researchers with new tools to measure and understand sociocultural influences on women's and men's behavior. I envision far more ambitious studies of gender roles cross-nationally, as well as more dedicated attention to patterns of gender differences and similarities across ethnic groups in the United States. Fourth, the nervous system is characterized by great plasticity. Future neuroscience research can profitably seek to discover linkages between gender-differentiated experiences on the one hand and gender differences in brain structure and function on the other.

Marco Del Giudice  **NO**

On the Real Magnitude of Psychological Sex Differences

Introduction

Psychology has a long tradition in the study of sex differences in personality, cognition and behavior. For more than a century, psychologists have tried to measure them and to evaluate their impact on social and interpersonal processes. More recently, a large number of meta-analyses have become available to researchers, thus offering a valuable yardstick against which to assess the magnitude of psychological sex differences. The results have been widely variable, but a pattern clearly stands out: Most of the studies find rather high levels of statistical overlap between the male and female distributions, with conventionally "large" effects being the exception rather than the rule. This applies to studies of spatial abilities (overall Cohen's $d = .37$), self-disclosure ($d = .18$), self-esteem ($d = .21$), personality ($d = .10$ to $.50$), aggression (overall $d = .24$), and the list could go on. Hyde conducted a second order meta-analysis of sex differences on 128 published meta-analyses, and found that 78% of all the effect sizes fell below a standardized mean difference of $d = .35$, which is conventionally regarded as "small to moderate." In terms of statistical overlap, $d = .35$ means that—assuming normality—the male and female distributions share about 75% of their joint area. Hyde used this result in support of the "gender similarities hypothesis," i.e., that males and females are similar rather than different on most psychological variables. While Hyde's analysis has been criticized for omitting some large-effect studies and for not organizing variables in biologically relevant categories, it is true that the effects reported in the empirical research often seem to imply little statistical separation between male and female distributions.

Is this a valid assessment of the data? And most importantly, should we care? I surmise that, if we want to build a comprehensive evolutionary theory of sex differences, we need to proceed in two directions at once: On one hand, we should aim to build more detailed models, develop finer distinctions between functionally distinct subtypes of traits and behaviors, and identify the specific contexts in which sex differences are magnified or reduced. On the other hand, we should try to measure the global patterns of sex differences in different areas of human psychology, and use the quantitative information carried by effect sizes to better understand the selective processes that have shaped our male and female minds. In addition, comparing the magnitude of effect sizes across different psychological domains may provide useful support in the evaluation of competing explanatory hypotheses on the origin and function of mental and behavioral traits.

In the present article I will argue that mainstream research has severely underestimated the magnitude of human sex differences by failing to fully appreciate the multidimensional nature of many psychological constructs. I will then show how to address this shortcoming by calculating multivariate indices of effect size (ES). In particular, I will introduce the multivariate generalization of Cohen's d: the Mahalanobis distance D, a standardized mean difference calculated simultaneously on k correlated variables. Finally, I will illustrate the practical import of multivariate ESs with two reanalyses of published datasets on sex differences in personality and aggression.

The Interpretation of Effect Sizes

With few exceptions, psychological researchers adhere to the convention of interpreting the magnitude of group differences after a set of guidelines supposedly recommended by Cohen. As the convention goes, $d = .20$ represents a "small" effect, $d = .50$ is a "moderate" effect, and group differences of $d = .80$ or more are "large." Many would be surprised to learn that Cohen did, in fact, advise *against* the use of conventional ES measures; he reluctantly proposed his famous guidelines as a last-resort approximation to employ when researchers need to perform power analysis, but have no previous information on the investigated variables. Indeed, there is no justification in statistical theory or methodology for using such conventional labels in the *interpretation* of research findings; it is impossible to evaluate the practical magnitude of an effect size without considering the theoretical relationship between variables, their measurement error, and the context in which they are measured and analyzed. In some contexts, a statistically small deviation from a set value may have important consequences (think of the rigidly controlled mechanisms that regulate body temperature), while in others even "large" differences may be inconsequential or comparatively small (e.g., a drug reducing depressive symptoms by $d = .80$, when all other drugs on the market reduce them by $d = 2$ or more).

The practical significance of a difference between means also depends on where one is looking: differences that have almost undetectable effects in the central region of a distribution can be amplified by orders of magnitude as one moves toward the distribution extremes. For example, even if males (on average) were only slightly superior to females in their visuo-spatial abilities, the male:female ratio would increase dramatically when considering people with *extremely* high levels of the same abilities. Whereas such a small difference might have virtually no consequence in most aspects of everyday life, it could still determine large sex biases in specialized contexts where high visuo-spatial abilities are required (e.g., skilled hunting in traditional societies). This distribution-tail effect is often compounded by the larger variance exhibited by males in many psychological traits, perhaps especially in those with a history of strong sexual selection. Finally, division-of-labor social and interpersonal processes may amplify initially small psychological sex differences, ending up in large differences in the actual behavior of the two sexes.

Effect Sizes and the Evolutionary Psychology of Sex Differences

Evolutionary theory provides reasons to expect reliable sex differences in personality, cognition, and behavior and evolutionary psychological research has often focused on the adaptive value of male-female differences. Although current models are still too coarse to make quantitative predictions about the *absolute* magnitude of sex differences, it is already possible to generate several predictions on their *relative* magnitude in different traits or constructs. First of all, the strongest psychological sex differences are expected—and found—in reproduction-related traits and in those subject to divergent sexual selection pressures; for example, in the literature on mate preferences ESs are often in the $d = .80$–1.50 range, higher that those found in most other psychological domains. Careful application of sexual selection theory suggests additional, subtler predictions: Sex differences in a sexually selected trait are likely to be small (or even nonexistent) if (1) the trait is subject to reciprocal mate choice, or (2) both sexes need to possess the same psychological machinery, in order for members of one sex to evaluate the quality of the trait when it is expressed by members of the other sex.

Importantly, several psychological constructs that on the surface may appear unrelated to reproduction turn out to be involved in mating as well. For example, Big Five personality traits show remarkable evidence of reciprocal sexual selection and assortative mating. At the same time, some of the same traits are linked to sex-typical mating strategies: Both openness to experience and extraversion predict increased numbers of sexual partners, and males might be expected to show higher average levels of these traits in many (but not all) ecological contexts. Similarly, sex differences in visuo-spatial abilities may have been indirectly shaped by sexual selection because of the involvement of these abilities in sex-typical activities that contributed to mating success, such as hunting. Effect sizes can be used to compare the magnitude of sex differences among different psychological constructs and, potentially, to adjudicate between alternative explanations of their evolution (e.g., a model involving reciprocal mate choice versus one positing divergent sexual selection pressures). Depending on the level of analysis, effect size comparisons can involve narrow traits such as extraversion or physical aggression, as well as complex multidimensional constructs such as mate preferences or personality.

Multidimensional effect sizes can also be useful when evaluating the magnitude of sex differences across different social and ecological contexts. For example, there is evidence that sex differences in personality traits vary among cultures; however, this may or may not translate in a change in the overall statistical overlap between male and female personality profiles, since different combinations of univariate sex differences may result in the same overall ES. The study of ecological variation in the overall patterns of sex similarity/difference has fascinating evolutionary implications; in this context, multivariate indices can be a valuable addition to standard univariate measures, and can be employed in cross-cultural studies to explore variation at a level higher than that of individual variables.

Another potential application of multivariate effect sizes is in the study of the folk psychology of sex differences. Are people's perceptions of sex differences basically accurate, or are they prone to distortion by socially transmitted stereotypes? To begin answering this question, one has to know how large sex differences *are* in the first place; and the case can be made that overall, multidimensional sex differences (for example in personality or aggression) may be a more natural and intuitive metric than differences in the narrowly specified, individual traits measured by psychologists. It is then possible that what appear as inflated stereotypes might actually turn out to be realistic and accurate representations of the overall statistical distance between male and female profiles. Such findings would be highly relevant to the evolutionary study of social cognition, folk psychology, and social learning.

Finally, the rhetorical impact of effect sizes should not be underestimated. The argument that males and females possess evolved, sexually differentiated psychologies has been met with especially strong skepticism; findings of "small" effect sizes tend to reinforce the skepticism by suggesting that sex differences are trivial, unimportant, or too small to be of "real" biological significance. While this kind of interpretation is often unwarranted and based on inadequate criteria (see above), the present reality is that most researchers are likely to be intrigued by a "large" ES much more than by a "small" one. Showing that the overall sex differences in constructs such as aggression or personality are substantially larger than previously assumed can alert many researchers to the fact that sex differences are not an ignorable nuisance of human psychology, but a robust phenomenon deserving satisfactory theoretical explanation.

The Logic of Multivariate Differences

As stated in the introduction, the standard approach to the evaluation of sex differences dramatically underestimates their overall magnitude when dealing with multidimensional psychological constructs. The common procedure employed in meta-analyses of sex differences goes as follows: (1) sex differences are measured on a set of variables making up an integrated, multidimensional construct (e.g., the Big Five personality factors, multiple measures of aggression, or a battery of visuo-spatial tasks); (2) sex differences on these variables are not combined into a multivariate effect size, but considered only one at a time; and (3) an average measure of the univariate effect sizes is taken, and is then treated as an estimate of the overall sex difference in the investigated construct.

Why is this procedure inadequate? When measuring a multidimensional construct, the overall difference between two groups is *not* the average of the effects measured on each dimension, but a combination of those effects in the multidimensional space: Many small differences, each of them on a different dimension, can create an impressive effect when all the dimensions are considered simultaneously. Crucially, such overall differences are likely to matter more than their individual components, both in shaping people's perceptions and in affecting social interaction. . . . Failing to combine univariate sex differences into a proper multivariate measure [may] lead to underestimate [an] overall male-female difference. . . .

A Multivariate Effect Size: The Mahalanobis Distance

The Mahalanobis distance D is a generalized distance metric calculated on two or more correlated variables. Like the popular Cohen's d, it is a standardized distance, i.e., distances are expressed in terms of the standard deviation of the measured variables. . . . The interpretation of D is straightforward, as it represents the difference between two groups in terms of the standard deviation of the multivariate distribution. Thus, the interpretation of its magnitude is the same as that of Cohen's d. . . . The main difference between d and D is that the latter is an unsigned coefficient (always positive), and as such cannot be used to test directional predictions. To understand the pattern of directional differences between groups, one has to refer to univariate d values; thus, univariate and multivariate ESs should be seen as complementary rather than alternative tools.

As with Cohen's d, Mahalanobis D can be translated into approximate measures of statistical overlap by assuming multivariate normality. . . .

In summary, computing multivariate effect sizes will give researchers a more accurate estimate of the overall difference between males and females on any truly multidimensional construct. First, the standard procedure almost invariably leads to underestimate the magnitude of sex differences construct-wise, and such underestimation bias becomes more severe as the number of measured variables increases. Second, there simply is no way of properly taking into account the effect of correlations between variables without calculating a multivariate effect size such as D.

Example 1: Sex Differences in Personality

I will now turn to a real-world example that strikingly demonstrates the importance of calculating multivariate effect sizes in addition to univariate ones. In a large Internet-based survey, a Big Five personality inventory (the BFI) was administered to 5,417 female and 2,901 male students. Standardized sex differences on the five personality scales ranged from $d = .10$ to $d = .53$ in module, with an average unsigned effect size $\bar{d} = .27$. Correcting for attenuation due to scale unreliability brings the average effect size to $\bar{d}_c = .30$.

These results are entirely typical of sex differences research and would fit neatly in Hyde's meta-analysis; by looking at the average ES, one might conclude that the male and female distributions of Big Five personality traits in this sample show about 80% overlap. In fact, multivariate effect sizes tell a rather different story. I reanalyzed the same data by calculating the Mahalanobis distance from Cohen's d values and the correlation matrix of the five BFI scales. The overall male-female difference on the construct defined by the five personality scales was $D = .84$ (with a 95% upper bound of .87). Correcting for scale unreliability raised the estimated ES to $D_c = .98$, i.e., a sex difference of about one standard deviation. The corresponding overlap between the male and female distributions is about 45%; the statistical separation between the sexes in the Big Five personality space is clearly much larger than could be inferred by looking at individual scales one at a time. Given that both d values and inter-scale correlations . . . are typical of personality research, this result is most likely to generalize to the entire field of sex differences in personality traits.

Example 2: Sex Differences in Aggression

In a recent article, Archer discussed the hypothesis that sexual selection is responsible for the consistent pattern of sex differences observed in same-sex human aggression. He presented a summary of the meta-analytic findings in aggression research clearly showing that males are higher than females in physical and verbal aggression, and lower in indirect (or "relational") aggression. . . . The largest sex differences are found in physical aggression (average $d = .58$), the smallest in relational aggression (average $d = -.16$). While it is important to discriminate between different aspects of aggression and to interpret the univariate effect sizes one at a time, it can also be useful to ask how much males and females differ in their overall aggression profiles. The average univariate effect size module is $\bar{d} = .34$; correcting for attenuation by assuming measurement reliability equal to .80 (a realistic estimate for psychological measures) produces a slightly higher average of $\bar{d}_c = .38$.

In order to compute D, an estimate of the correlations between different types of aggression is needed. For the purposes of this illustrative example, rough estimates of typical correlation magnitude can be obtained by surveying the relevant literature. Correlations between physical and verbal aggression are typically around .40, ranging from about .35 to .55. Very similar correlations are found between physical and indirect aggression. A correlation coefficient of .40 was chosen as a reasonable approximation of both correlations. There are fewer published data on the correlation between verbal and indirect aggression; however, the overall correlation between direct (physical plus verbal) and indirect aggression was estimated at .60 in the meta-analysis by Card and colleagues. I computed D twice, using two different estimates of the verbal-indirect correlation: the .60 coefficient and a more conservative .40 (i.e., the same correlation as that between physical and indirect aggression).

[T]he estimated overall sex difference in aggression is $D = .75 - .80$. Assuming .80 reliability, the disattenuated estimate is $D_c = .89 - 1.01$; in other words, males and females differ about one standard deviation in their overall aggression profiles. This corresponds to a statistical overlap of about 44–49%. Despite the error margin due to the rough estimates of correlations and reliabilities, this illustrative re-analysis indicates that the overall size of sex differences in human aggression may be more than twice as large as the average of the univariate ESs.

Limitations

The above examples show that proper aggregation of effect sizes can reveal substantial sex differences in multivariate psychological constructs. Of course, this does not mean that aggregation will always be useful or meaningful.

I want to underline once again that I'm not proposing to automatically substitute univariate ESs with their multivariate counterparts; rather, the latter offer a *complementary* source of information, one that can be more or less interesting depending on the research question at hand. Most evolutionary hypotheses are highly domain-specific, and may be best answered by comparisons on single variables. In some instances, differences between males and females may be qualitative rather than quantitative, with distinct processes at work in the two sexes; clearly, in such cases any simple calculation of effect sizes (univariate or multivariate) would be uninformative or even misleading.

Methodological Remarks

Before concluding, I will briefly discuss some additional methodological aspects of using D as a summary effect size. First of all, the reader may be wondering about the relationship between the number of measured variables and the magnitude of D. If D tends to increase with the number of variables making up the construct of interest, won't aggregating large number of variables produce inflated estimates of sex differences? To answer this question, one has to remember that D depends on the pattern of correlations between variables in addition to their number. Imagine that researcher A measures personality using only 5 scales, whereas researcher B employs 30 different scales. The 30 scales of researcher B are likely to show more content overlap with one another, and larger between-scale correlations; if the many scales he/she uses are psychometrically redundant, this will lead to relatively smaller estimates of D. In other words, adding variables contributes to D only as long as they provide new information about sex differences. Conversely, if the "true" dimensionality of that personality space is closer to 30 than to 5, and/or if some of the 30 scales reveal interesting sex effects that are masked in the 5 scales of researcher A, then researcher B may *correctly* get a higher estimate of the overall sex difference. The issue of how many variables to aggregate is, at bottom, a theoretical one: Careful definition of the traits under investigation is essential to ensure that the chosen variables provide a satisfactory coverage of the intended construct.

That said, it is true that sampling error will tend to inflate estimates of D when large numbers of variables are aggregated together. Even if all the univariate sex differences in the population were equal to zero, it would be virtually impossible that all the sample d's turned out exactly zero as well. The same phenomenon leads to inflated R^2 estimates when adding large numbers of independent variables to a multiple regression model. For this reason, when computing multivariate effect sizes researchers should (1) avoid including unnecessary or clearly redundant variables, and/or reduce the dimensionality of the construct via factor analysis; (2) in particular, keep the number of variables small when sample size is not large; and (3) when possible, compute confidence intervals on D to check the reliability of the estimate.

Finally, a note on correlation matrices: sometimes sex differences in two or more variables create spurious correlations between those variables that can muddle up the interpretation of D. For example, imagine that females were both more nurturing and less dominant than males, but that nurturance and dominance were otherwise completely unrelated *within* each sex. When computing whole-sample statistics, dominance and nurturance would be negatively correlated, but that would be solely due to sex differences in the two variables. Using the overall correlation coefficient to compute D would count the effect of sex differences twice, thus biasing the result in potentially misleading ways. For this reason, it seems advisable *not* to use whole-sample correlation matrices when computing Mahalanobis D to measure sex differences; whenever possible, a better estimate of correlations (unbiased by between-group differences) can be obtained by computing separate correlation matrices for males and females, then pooling them with one of the available methods. Of course, computing a pooled estimate is only meaningful if the within-sex correlation matrices are reasonably similar to one another.

Conclusion

Current research practices lead to inadequate assessment of the overall psychological differences between males and females; relatively small univariate differences are taken at face value, without properly aggregating them into multivariate ES indices. When differences are measured on multidimensional constructs, multivariate indices will almost invariably produce larger estimates of the statistical distance between the sexes. Luckily, the appropriate multivariate ES indices are readily available, although seldom presented in data analysis textbooks; the Mahalanobis distance D is a highly intuitive measure of multivariate differences between groups, and has the same basic interpretation of Cohen's d.

In this article I argued that accurate assessment of the magnitude of sex differences can foster progress in evolutionary research; indeed, I believe that evolutionary psychologists are especially likely to benefit from better measurement in this area. While the available models are still rudimentary in some respects, they already make it possible to predict the relative weight of sex differences between different psychological domains; and as theory will grow more sophisticated, empirical tests will increasingly depend on accurate quantification of between-sex variation, thus making effect size computation ever more important. I hope the present article will contribute to bring this important topic to the attention of researchers interested in human sex differences; I also hope it will prompt psychologists (regardless of their theoretical background) to challenge the received wisdom and consider the possibility that, taken as groups, human males and females are more different from one another than we currently believe.

EXPLORING THE ISSUE

Are Women and Men More Similar Than Different?

Challenge Questions

1. How is it that the results from similar meta-analyses can be interpreted in such a way as to lead to differing conclusions regarding the magnitude of sex differences?
2. Is the magnitude of sex differences identified for various attributes and behaviors the same?
3. Why might some differences be greater than others?
4. What is the difference between thinking about gender as a person variable and thinking about gender as a social stimulus?
5. Where do you think it is most fruitful to be on the similarity–difference spectrum? Will we learn more by focusing on one end or the other? Is it possible to embrace both approaches?

Is There Common Ground?

Both YES and NO selections use meta-analysis and the resultant statistic, the effect size, as the basis of their arguments. However, each comes to a different conclusion. Hyde places emphasis on similarity and Del Giudice on difference. Both rely on the same numbers but each uses a different perspective. Hyde's reliance on social constructivist theory considers gender a stimulus; thus, when sex differences are observed, they can be explained by the nature of social expectations and interactions. On the other hand, Del Giudice uses the tenants of evolutionary theory to explain the nature of sex differences. Given the variability in the magnitude of effect sizes across various domains of attributes and behaviors, the door remains open for a balanced view that allows for the possibility that there is a dynamic interaction between the biological and the environmental factors. Where do you think it is most fruitful to be on the similarity–difference spectrum? Will we learn more by focusing on one end or the other? Is it possible to embrace both approaches?

The issue of similarity and difference is one of degree and perspective. Although many meta-analyses inform us that most differences between women and men are statistically quite small, there are differences. What do we make of small differences, especially when the differences within women and within men typically exceed the average difference between the groups?

Should we move beyond the difference model for studying sex and gender? Debate has focused on social costs and benefits incurred as a consequence of sex difference findings, the statistical and social meaning of sex difference findings, the overemphasis on difference and underrepresentation of findings of similarity, and the questionable efficacy of sex difference findings in elucidating the phenomena of sex and gender. Whether or not scholars believe that the continuation of sex difference research would be beneficial or at least benign, there is widespread agreement that this research alone is insufficient to explore the complexities of sex and gender as social categories and processes. Difference research has been primarily descriptive in nature, although assumptions abound about the "natural" causes of sex differences. But knowing what differences exist between males and females does not help us to understand why, how, when, and for whom they exist. Furthermore, descriptive research alone does not help us understand the social meaning or significance of such differences. Some assert that sex comparisons obscure an understanding of gender as social relations and do little to help us understand the processes that expand or delimit the significance of the difference.

Others argue that focusing on categorical differences helps us to avoid the hard work we have to do to improve our society. At the very least, scholars urge that we move beyond the individual as the focus of difference research to examine the way gender is produced in interpersonal and institutional contexts. In moving beyond the difference model, what other approaches can be used to better understand sex and gender? One suggestion calls for an approach to studying gender that transcends the difference model. The focus is on the *process* of gender. Research should explore and document "gender coding," or how society is gendered (e.g., unequal expectations, opportunities, power), and how individuals (particularly those who are disenfranchised) cope with or negotiate such inequality (ranging from acceptance to resistance). It is important to view individuals not only as having some agency to affect their environment but also as being constrained or shaped by social situations and structures. Another suggested innovation reflects an effort to move beyond essentialist overgeneralizations about "generic" men and women as distinct groups. What does a categorical variable like sex actually mean? Many argue that such variables are too simplistic and therefore meaningless for representing the complexity among individuals, identities, and experiences that make up the group. Some state that assertions about sex differences are usually based on comparisons of white middle-class men and women and therefore have limited generalizability. Thus, some scholars advocate exploring within-sex diversity and attending to a host of contextual and structural variables that are inseparable from sex. This kind of approach has led some to ask, Can we move to a point where difference no longer makes so much of a difference? How do we get there? One view differentiates between approaches that "turn the volume up" and that "turn the volume down" on categories of difference. Should we eliminate sex and gender dichotomies from the definition of normal and natural (turn the volume down) or proliferate categories of sex and gender into as many categories as needed to capture human complexity? Or is the focus on categories obscuring more specific and critical concepts such as privilege, conflict of interest, oppression, subordination, and even cooperation?

Additional Resources

R. Barnett and C. Rivers, *Same Difference: How Gender Myths Are Hurting Our Relationships, Our Children, and Our Jobs* (New York: Basic Books, 2004).

M. M. Kimball, "Gender Similarities and Differences as Feminist Constructions," in R. K. Unger, ed., *Handbook of the Psychology of Women and Gender* (New York: John Wiley & Sons, 2000).

http://www.theabsolute.net/misogyny/eisenman.html

http://www.med.monash.edu.au/gendermed/difference.html

ISSUE 3

Is Sexual Orientation Innate?

YES: Heino F. L. Meyer-Bahlburg, Curtis Dolezal, Susan W. Baker, and Maria I, from "Sexual Orientation in Women with Classical or Non-Classical Congenital Adrenal Hyperplasia as a Function of Degree of Prenatal Androgen Excess," *Archives of Sexual Behavior* (vol. 37, no. 1, 2008)

NO: Lisa M. Diamond and Molly Butterworth, from "Questioning Gender and Sexual Identity: Dynamic Links over Time," *Sex Roles: A Journal of Research* (vol. 59, 2008)

Learning Outcomes

As you read the issue, focus on the following points:

- Are there specific genotypes that might serve as a basis for sexual orientation?
- What hormones might affect sexual orientation?
- Does evidence of changing experiences of sexual orientation suggest that it is not immutable?
- Both YES and NO selections report on studies of women in the United States. What might results look like for men? Are the results generalizable?

ISSUE SUMMARY

YES: Clinical psychologist Heino F. L. Meyer-Bahlburg and his colleagues report that sexual orientation is related to specific molecular genotypes in women with classical congenital adrenal hyperplasia (CAH), supporting a sexual-differentiation perspective involving the effects of prenatal androgens on the development of sexual orientation.

NO: Psychologist Lisa M. Diamond and her student Molly Butterworth use a feminist theoretical framework of intersectionality to analyze data from the experiences of individuals who claim neither an unambiguously female nor a male identity to demonstrate that sexual orientation, sexual identify, and gender identity are fluid and change over time.

Psychosexuality, or psychological behaviors and phenomena presumably associated with biological sex, has typically been defined as having three components: gender role, gender identity, and sexual orientation. A fundamental assumption is that these are congruent.

The term *gender role* refers to attitudes, behaviors, and personality characteristics that are designated by society (in particular sociohistorical contexts) as appropriately masculine or feminine (i.e., typical of the male or female role, respectively). Thus, assessments of gender role behavior in children have included toy preferences, interest in physical activities, fantasy role and dress-up play, and affiliative preference for same-sex peers versus opposite-sex peers. It is also assumed that although the specific features of gender roles are learned from societal customs, they also flow from biologically based gender identity and sexual orientation.

Gender identity is one's sense of self as belonging to one sex: male or female. Most people reply, if asked, how do you know? "I just know" and if pressed to answer why, they would make some reference to their genitalia. Cognitive developmentalists such as Lawrence Kohlberg add the criterion of gender constancy to an understanding of gender identity. Gender constancy starts with the ability of a child to discriminate accurately between females and males and to identify accurately her or his own status correctly (based on genitalia). The child also comes to know that gender is invariant. That is, if you were to put girl's clothing on an anatomically correct boy doll, the child would know the doll is still male. If a child were to put on clothes typically associated with the other sex, she or he would know that his or her own sex had not changed. However, in some cases, the acquisition of gender identity is affectively loaded and sometimes marked by negative emotion, otherwise known as gender dysphoria. Those who experience gender dysphoria will report that something feels wrong. This is often the case for transgender people. They often report that they feel like one sex is trapped in the other sex's body.

Gender identity disorder (GID) is defined as a strong psychological identification with the opposite sex and is signaled by the display of opposite sex-typed behaviors and avoidance or rejection of sex-typed behaviors characteristic of one's own sex. It is not related to sexual orientation. Distress or discomfort about one's status as a boy or a girl frequently accompanies these behaviors. The age of onset is 2–4 years. Some children self-label as the opposite sex, and some self-label correctly but wish to become a member of the opposite sex. Other children do not express cross-sex desires but exhibit cross-sex-typed behavior. Some children cross-dress, sometimes insistently. Less characteristic are cross-sex-typed mannerisms (e.g., body movements, voice, pitch). Cross-sex peer affiliation preferences, poor peer relations, and alienation are typical. It has been reported that women with classical congenital adrenal hyperplasia (CAH), which is related to a deficiency of the enzyme 21-hydroxylase, show variable degrees of masculinization of the body, interests, and behavior due to excess adrenal androgen production. One result may be related to increased bisexuality and homosexuality.

Sexual orientation refers to the match between one's own sex and the sex of the person to whom the person is erotically attracted. Typically, sexual orientation has been considered categorically as heterosexual, homosexual, or bisexual, although some research suggests that sexual orientation is actually a continuum rather than a category. It has been suggested that understanding bisexuality in particular may be crucial to understanding the complexity of sexual orientation.

It is important to consider the definitions and associated distinctions among gender roles, gender identity, and sexual orientation. A consideration of GID is relevant here (also see issues 1 and 21 for further information and reflection). As we think about gender identity, what questions does it raise about sexual orientation? In 2003, there was a movie entitled *Normal* about a man, married with an adult son and teenaged daughter, who announces to his family that he plans to have a change of sex operation. In one scene the son asks the mother, upon her announcement that she may stay in the marriage after the surgery, if that would make her a lesbian. She replies in the negative; she says that this is about the dad finding his true self, not about her, and that she would still love the person he is. What does this say about distinctions between one's sense of self, their genitalia, and the person to whom they are erotically attracted? If the father after becoming a woman continues to love his wife, is the new "she" a lesbian? What does would it mean for a woman identified as heterosexual to stay in an intimate relationship with her husband after he becomes a woman? What does such a scenario say about one's sexual orientation? Does it change? Is this the evidence for the fluidity rather than constancy of sexual orientation?

There is considerable controversy concerning whether gender identity and sexual orientations are socially constructed or innate. Researchers studying the effects of prenatal hormones on brain structure, gender identity, and gendered behavior, including sexual orientation, have challenged the claim that gender identity is socially constructed. A pivotal case was that of John/Joan, a boy (with a twin brother) who at 8 months of age was injured in a botched circumcision and subsequently reared as a girl. This created the opportunity to study "naturalistically" whether or not gender identity could be socially constructed. But at the age of 14, upon learning the facts of his birth and sex reassignment, the child rejected his reassigned sex and began living as a man. In May 2004, he committed suicide.

The YES and NO selections presented here argue from very different perspectives and rely on different research traditions. In the YES selection, Meyer-Bahlburg and colleagues compared responses on self-report questionnaires, psychometric tests, and interviews of women with CAH for whom their molecular genetics had been determined with a group of non-CAH women (sisters and female cousins). In contrast to a "snapshot in time," in the NO selection, Diamond and Butterworth considered interview data collected over a 10-year period from four young women who were identified as nonheterosexual. The results are arguments that on the one hand consider sexual orientation as a result of prenatal androgens and on the other hand consider sexual orientation and gender identify as fluid and changing over time as a result of multiple factors.

YES  Heino F. L. Meyer-Bahlburg et al.

Sexual Orientation in Women with Classical or Non-Classical Congenital Adrenal Hyperplasia as a Function of Degree of Prenatal Androgen Excess

Introduction

Sexual orientation is a trait with very large differences between men and women . . . one of the largest for any gender-related behavior or trait. . . . The demonstration of familiality and heritability of homosexuality has led to numerous attempts to provide genetic explanations. Given the focus of evolutionary theory on reproduction and survival of the offspring, a sexual orientation of women to men and of men to women is eminently plausible. It is much more difficult to come up with a compelling evolutionary raison d'être for homosexuality and bisexuality. A number of non-endocrine explanatory hypotheses have been formulated. In the framework of evolutionary theory, overdominance kin altruism, and sexually antagonistic selection have been suggested as potential mechanisms explaining the gene polymorphism that is presumed to underlie homosexuality, and mathematical models have recently been formulated that should facilitate their empirical testing. However, the variability of homosexual behavior across vertebrate species has not led to a consensus on an explanation in terms of evolutionary theory, and the demonstration of learning mechanisms in the acquisition of sexual preferences in animal models has further complicated the issue. Identification of specific genes has not yet led to consistent success, but new findings on extreme skewing of X-inactivation by DNA-methylation in mothers of gay men have added additional genetic possibilities.

. . . New data from the AddHealth project . . . (indirectly) supports a social-influence hypothesis explaining same-sex attractions in adolescents. Other non-genetic explanations include the progressive immunization hypothesis, which is derived from the well-replicated association of homosexuality in males with the number of older brothers in the sibship and assumes that successive pregnancies with male fetuses leads in some mothers to the development of male-specific antigens. The developmental instability theory explains homosexuality as a perturbance of the complex processes of prenatal brain development by exogenous influences and was originally stimulated by findings of increased non-right handedness among homosexuals of both sexes, but attempts at finding an association of homosexuality with fluctuating asymmetry as a broader index of developmental instability have been unsuccessful.

The most commonly offered theory places sexual orientation in the context of the sexual differentiation of brain and behavior in general, with a focus on the role of pre- and perinatal sex hormones in this process. This approach was presumably prompted by the association of human homosexuality with gender-atypical (non-sexual) behavior and goes back to the mid-19th century, when scientific embryology began focusing on the development of the sex-dimorphic reproductive tract and its disorders. Such research yielded medical explanations of somatic hermaphroditism, and analogous medical concepts were applied to the explanation of homosexuality. In this context, homosexuality was often categorized as an inversion (of gender roles). With the rapidly advancing techniques of measurement and synthesis of sex hormones in the second half of the 20th century, behavioral-endocrinology research in non-primate mammals demonstrated the profound "organizational" influence of sex hormones during early developmental periods on later mating behavior and sexual orientation, with perinatal androgens and estrogens (derived by aromatization of androgens within brain cells) supporting the development of masculine behavior, and estrogens supporting the defeminization of behavior, followed by "activating" effects of sex-specific hormones from puberty on. The analogous processes in primates may be limited to androgen effects, but the determinants of sexual orientation in primates are not yet clear. Early attempts to identify sex hormone abnormalities in human homosexuality were unsuccessful in men and only partially successful in women. In the absence of systemic hormone abnormalities and of any signs of somatic intersexuality in human homosexuality, some investigators have suggested that causal endocrine abnormalities might be limited to the central nervous system (CNS-limited pseudohermaphroditism), which is compatible with the recently growing evidence of tissue specificity of hormone production and/or metabolism and of hormone receptors. During the last two decades, advances in genetics have broadened the focus of research on sexual differentiation to include the many genes involved in the sexual differentiation of the gonads and, possibly, of the brain. Although research on the specific genetic mechanisms involved in the brain is still in its early stages, the recent use of cellular-biology techniques to unravel the chain of mechanisms involved in the hormone-based sexual differentiation of specific sex-dimorphic nuclei of the limbic system and the amygdala in the neonatal and pubertal periods of development is likely to contribute in a major way to the identification of genes with specific functions in these processes.

Recent quite large-scale behavioral data on humans continue to support the "inversion" perspective regarding homosexuality, and the attempts to find a hormonal cause continue. Considerable efforts have been made to identify somatic markers of prenatal sex hormone effects, such as shifts in the second to fourth finger length ratio (2D:4D) in homosexuals of both sexes; the findings are suggestive, but far from uniform. Another such marker may be the reduction of spontaneous otoacoustic emissions in lesbians, which is awaiting replication by independent teams. Clearly, more direct evidence of prenatal sex hormone effects would be desirable.

However, experimental variations of the prenatal sex-hormone milieu solely for behavioral research purposes cannot be ethically justified. [A] team at Johns Hopkins introduced as an alternative the behavioral study of syndromes of intersexuality, which represent naturally occurring extreme variations of the sex-hormone milieu. Classical (prenatal-onset) congenital adrenal hyperplasia (CAH) in 46,XX individuals is the most prevalent of the classical intersex syndromes and by far the most thoroughly investigated in terms of endocrinology and psychology. About 90% of CAH patients suffer from the deficiency of the enzyme, 21-hydroxylase. As one of several endocrine consequences, 46,XX fetuses with CAH are exposed to unusually high levels of androgens during fetal development, which variably masculinize the genitalia and presumably also the brain and later behavior.

If sexual orientation is sexually differentiated in a similar fashion, 46,XX women with classical CAH should show an increase in bisexuality and homosexuality. . . .

Even if the majority of . . . findings . . . support an association of classical CAH with bisexual or homosexual orientation in women, a causative interpretation of these findings in terms of androgen effects on sexual orientation is not as compelling as would be findings from randomized control trials of androgen treatment. Human studies of this kind only use "quasi-experimental designs" with, in the best case, "patched-up controls." One could strengthen the case for the role of androgens by demonstrating a dose–response relationship between the degree of prenatal androgen exposure and the degree of later sexual orientation. Ideally, we would measure prenatal hormone levels repeatedly over the course of fetal development and derive from such measurements an index of the degree of prenatal androgen exposure. However, the health risks of even one-time cross-sectional determinations of androgen levels in the amniotic fluid, for instance, can be justified only if there are compelling medical indications for the procedures involved. A relatively crude alternative is the demonstration of dose–response relations on the group level using the clinical-endocrine or molecular-genetics classification of CAH subtypes that differ in severity, i.e., degree of 21-hydroxylase deficiency and, thereby, degree of androgen excess. Within classical CAH, commonly two major subtypes are distinguished, the more severe salt-wasting (SW) variant and the simple virilizing (SV) variant, and several studies have shown that bisexuality and homosexuality are increased more in the SW than the SV variant or in CAH women with higher Prader stages of genital masculinization at birth, which are also (moderately) correlated with CAH severity. . . .

Our current study had several goals: (1) To replicate the published findings on sexual orientation in a relatively large sample of adult women with classical CAH using a systematic assessment of multiple aspects of sexual orientation, and to establish at which age the women reach the respective romantic/erotic milestones; (2) to extend the dose–response approach to the mildest form of CAH, the non-classical (NC) variant, which becomes clinically symptomatic (in somatic terms) only after birth, in childhood or adolescence; (3) to examine to what extent sexual orientation and global measures of gender behavior other than sexual orientation are correlated; (4) to test whether the prediction of the behavioral phenotype from the endocrine phenotype can be enhanced by the molecular-genetics classification; (5) to answer the question how commonly CAH women see themselves as men in their romantic/erotic imagery; and (6) to perform a methodological study of the interrelationship of the sexual orientation variables.

Method

Participants

The current study is part of a comprehensive long-term follow-up project of women with CAH. . . . During an initial pilot phase of this project, a small number of women with CAH was recruited from two pediatric endo-crine clinics in New York City. . . . Eligible were all adult women with CAH due to 21-hydroxylase deficiency for whom the molecular genetics of the 21-hydroxylase gene had been determined and who spoke English. Geographically, the participating women were spread over the entire United States and other continents. Transportation reimbursement was provided for women within the continental US.

The total analysis sample for CAH women in this report included 40 SW women, 21 SV women, and 82 NC women. Almost all CAH women were on glu-cocorticoid replacement treatment at the time of the study. A total of 24 non-CAH control women (labeled COS) consisted of sisters and female cousins of participating CAH women. Ages ranged from 18–61 years (subgroup means, 28.8–34.7 years). . . .

In addition to the control group of sisters and female cousins, we included for selected comparisons and illustrations two control groups (labeled COD) from our preceding project on the long-term behavioral after effects of prena-tal diethylstilbestrol (DES) exposure. . . .

Study procedures were approved by the appropriate institutional review boards, and all participants gave written informed consent.

Measures and Procedure

All women underwent an 8–10 h protocol (often spread out over several days) of standard self-report questionnaires, psychometric tests, physical examina-tions, and systematic interviews. Sexual orientation was assessed as part of the Sexual Behavior Assessment Schedule, a comprehensive sexual-history inter-view schedule that covers psychosexual milestones, sexual orientation, sexual activity level, and sexual dysfunctions. Its administration takes approximately 1 h. The SEBAS-A was placed late in the overall protocol in order to facilitate rapport development between interviewer and interviewee and, thereby, increase disclosure of sensitive information, and the SEBAS-A instructions to the interviewee emphasized the importance of accuracy to enhance the participants' motivation. All SEBAS-A interviews (as well as most other study interviews) with women were conducted by female interviewers in order to facilitate self-disclosure. Interviewers were clinical psychologists who were specifically trained for sexual research interviewing. Procedures were introduced to keep the interviewers from identifying the group membership of the study participants along with instructions for the women against the disclosure of their medical histories to the interviewers. All interviews were audiotaped to permit monitoring of interviewer performance. Excellent interrater reliability of the SEBAS-A has been demonstrated.

SEBAS-A variables pertinent to sexual orientation covered masturbation fantasies, masturbation erotica, romantic/erotic fantasies during sexual relations with a partner, romantic/sexual daydreams, romantic/sexual nightdreams, sexual attractions, "Total Imagery," actual sex partners ("Actual Partners"), and overall sexual responsiveness ("Overall Kinsey"). The first six variables addressed "current" sexual orientation, with "current" defined as the 12 months prior to interview, and each was preceded by a question concerning its frequency (e.g., "How often did you have romantic or sexual nightdreams during the past 12 months?"). The remaining three aspects were rated separately for the past 12 months and for lifelong ("Lifetime") patterns (thus, yielding six variables), with lifelong defined as "since puberty" (for "Total Imagery" and overall sexual responsiveness), or as "since becoming sexually active, excluding prepubertal sexual activities" (for sexual relations); both definitions of lifelong included the past 12 months.

For each sexual-orientation variable, interviewers' ratings used the Kinsey Rating Scale with the following formulations: 0 = entirely heterosexual; 1 = largely heterosexual but incidentally homosexual; 2 = largely heterosexual but also distinctly homosexual; 3 = equally heterosexual and homosexual; 4 = largely homosexual but also distinctly heterosexual; 5 = largely homosexual but incidentally heterosexual; and 6 = entirely homosexual. Since the Kinsey team had not defined "distinct," "a distinct" homosexual history (Kinsey score 2 or "K2") was rated when the woman had experiences such as homosexual dreams or fantasies over a period of at least 1-year recurring with some regularity (not less than "about once a month"). Whenever a subscale was rated "K2," the corresponding global score could not be rated less than "K2."

The variables on actual sex partners were based on detailed structured interview sections concerning diverse romantic and sexual activities, separately for male and female partners. The definition of sexual relations as used here for actual sex partners required genital contact including but not limited to penile–vaginal intercourse; it did not require orgasm. Total Imagery was a global rating encompassing the preceding six variables on imagery and attractions and taking into consideration the frequencies of the respective experiences as reported by the interviewee. Overall sexual responsiveness was a global rating based on Total Imagery and Actual Partners. . . .

Results

Psychosexual Milestones

. . . Substantial minorities of women in all groups experienced same-sex crushes, while fewer women experienced same-sex love and same-sex genital sex. CAH women were increased above control women in all three categories, and SW women were highest. . . . The NC group was higher than the COS group on all 3 variables (significantly so for genital sex and marginally significantly for love). The ages at first occurrence of these states or events appeared to be relatively late. However, this does not indicate a general delay of psychosexual milestones (heterosexual and homosexual combined) in CAH. Rather, among those women with a history of both heterosexual and homosexual experiences, the first experience tended to be heterosexual. . . .

Sexual Orientation: Lifetime

. . . The data show a rather consistent progression of Kinsey score means . . . , except for the SV group on Actual Partners and Overall Kinsey, and of K2-6% for all three variables with increasing degree of androgenization. . . .

The K2-6% for women with classical CAH (SV and SW combined) was 42% for Total Imagery, 15% for Actual Partners, and 37% for the Overall Kinsey rating. The NC group was significantly higher than the COS group on all three Kinsey scores. . . . The Kinsey scores for lifetime Total Imagery were higher than for lifetime Actual Partners. The number of women with any actual same-sex partner experience was relatively small, and the number of those with considerable experience in terms of same-sex partner numbers or same-sex occasions was even smaller. In interpreting these data, one has to take into consideration that women with classical CAH, and especially those with the SW variant, had significantly lower lifetime actual-partner numbers and lower total lifetime sex occasions (heterosexual and homosexual combined in both variables) than the other groups. . . .

Sexual Orientation: Current (Past 12 Months)

The current data on sexual orientation also show Kinsey scores for all three CAH subgroups in an apparent dose–response fashion. The gradual increase in Kinsey scores from non-CAH controls to the most severe SW variant applied to all variables, and was highly significant for all categories except for fantasies during partner sex. Again, the NC group had higher Kinsey scores than the COS group on all 9 variables . . . , the SW group was significantly higher than the two other CAH variants . . . , but the difference between SV and NC women reached conventional and marginal significance on only 1 variable each.

Sexual Orientation and Non-Sexual Gender-Related Behavior

The global lifetime and 12 months Kinsey scores were correlated with selected global variables of gender-related behavior (not including sexual orientation). The expected correlations were significant and in the predicted direction, but of modest size, and stronger for childhood measures than adulthood measures. . . .

Cross-Gender Imagery

At the end of the imagery section, the participant was asked about the frequency with which they saw themselves as "a person of the opposite sex" in their erotic imagery, separately for the past 12 months and lifetime (since puberty, excluding the past 12 months). All groups except SV included some women with such experience. The percent of women with such experience and the frequency of having that experience, especially for lifetime, was significantly increased in the SW subgroup above all other groups.

Predicting Sexual Orientation from Prenatal Androgenization and Gender Variables

. . . We tried to predict the Overall Kinsey Score for the past 12 months successively from the degree of prenatal androgenization in terms of the four CAH-severity groups, childhood gender-related behavior (the Gender scale of the RCGQ-R), adult gender-related behavior (the sum score of the Hobby Preferences Scale), and Seeing Self as Man during Romantic/Erotic Imagery, Frequency: Lifetime (Excluding the Past 12 Months). Prenatal androgenization and RCGQ-R Gender contributed significantly to the prediction . . . , but Hobby Preferences and Seeing Self as Man was not.

Role of the Molecular Genotype

Finally, we wanted to test whether the CAH subtypes as defined by endocrine criteria or their classification by molecular genotype is more closely associated with sexual orientation. . . . The two classifications did not differ in their association with the Kinsey score. In this particular sub-sample, the endocrine and genetic classifications correlated Pearson $r = .90$ with each other, i.e., there was little room for divergence between molecular genotype and endocrine phenotype. . . .

Discussion

Our data clearly showed increased sexual orientation towards females (i.e., bisexuality and homosexuality) in women with classical CAH (SV and SW combined) compared to non-CAH controls. . . . Thus, our study corroborates earlier findings on sexual orientation in CAH. We also clearly replicate earlier demonstrations of increased bisexual/homosexual orientation in SW women compared to SV women, and earlier reports indicating that these shifts are more strongly accentuated in romantic/erotic imagery than actual sex-partner experiences.

More surprising is the finding of increased bisexual/homosexual orientation in NC women above controls in the diverse variables evaluated here. This finding is in line with our earlier report on mild, but significant shifts of the same

NC women towards masculinized gender-related behavior other than sexual orientation. In the endocrine literature, NC is usually described as a syndrome characterized by onset of clinical (somatic, physiological) symptoms of androgen excess after birth, in childhood or later. Since there is consensus that the masculinization of gender-related behavior in classical CAH is due to the effect of prenatal androgens on the developing brain, these behavioral shifts in NC women were not expected. The finding raises the question whether the mild androgen excess that is likely to be present in NC fetuses from the first trimester on, but is insufficient to noticeably affect the sexual differentiation of the genitalia, is nevertheless sufficient to slightly affect the sexual differentiation of the brain. Alternatively, the data suggest an unexpected postnatal effect of mild but persistent androgen excess on brain and gender-related behaviors. Our study does not provide data that would help us to argue in favor of one or the other explanation.

In conjunction with the other CAH subgroups and the control women, our NC data further strengthen the notion of a dose–response relationships of androgens with sexual orientation, at least on the subgroup level, given that the other hormone abnormalities seen in the CAH syndrome (e.g., deficiency of cortisol and aldosterone, excess of ACTH and 17-hydroxyprogesterone) are not known to be associated with masculinization of gender-related behavior in animals or humans (although specific studies of this kind are yet to be conducted). As we had found analogous relationships with CAH severity for non-sexual gender-related behavior, we also could confirm significant, but modest-sized correlations of sexual orientation scores with non-sexual gender-related behaviors, which had been shown by others. Such findings are also in line with an understanding of sexual orientation in the context of sexual differentiation. Given the many differences in sexual orientation and associated variables between men and women, the question arises, whether the increased sexual orientation towards females associated with CAH severity in 46,XX individuals is a model of the role of androgens in sexual-orientation development in males rather than lesbian women. Early developmental research on non-sexual sex-dimorphic behavior in animals sought to explain sex differences in behavior, and experimental manipulations of pre- and perinatal androgen levels served to show to what extent one could create male-typical behavior in females so treated. Later, such findings were also used to explain interindividual variations of gender-related behavior among females, and there is some supportive evidence for this approach in humans. That this may apply also to sexual orientation in at least a subgroup of women is suggested by the fact that earlier research has repeatedly shown that about one third of homosexual women have (modestly) increased levels of androgens.

One of the major limitations of the interpretation of findings in classical CAH in relation to animal studies is the hormone treatment that females with classical CAH typically receive throughout postnatal life. The classical animal study of sexual differentiation of brain and behavior exposes the female fetus to androgen treatment during the known early hormone-sensitive period of sexual differentiation of the brain and then again around the time of puberty/young adulthood. That combination tends to maximize the development of cross-gender sexual behaviors, especially when ovariectomy after puberty preceded the treatment with testosterone propionate. By contrast, human 46,XX individuals with CAH are initially exposed to excess, endogenous androgens from their adrenals during the presumed hormone-sensitive prenatal period of sexual differentiation of the brain, and in the severe variants at even higher levels than normal males and more chronically so; however, from birth on, the excess androgen levels are suppressed by glucocorticoid replacement therapy (sometimes to levels even lower than is normal for healthy females), the ovaries are left in place, and female puberty is induced by an endogenous, largely normal female hormonal milieu. Unfortunately, there are no behavioral studies of non-human primates that mimic the androgen history of 46,XX humans with CAH, so that we cannot be sure if we should expect to see much more bisexuality and homosexuality in 46,XX individuals without postnatal androgen suppression. . . .

Another potentially confounding factor is the fact that insufficient glucocorticoid replacement or treatment interruptions lead to virilization, i.e., somatic symptoms of androgen excess, and, if occurring early enough during childhood development, also to stunting of growth, while overtreatment brings about variable degrees of obesity, all of which may reduce attractivity to men and romantic approaches by men, and to related body-image concerns of the CAH women. This raises the question whether associated inhibition of romantic practice in adolescence, perhaps also supported by less-stereotypic feminine leisure time activities and, at least for some CAH women, relative isolation in the peer group, might increase the chance of bisexual/homosexual development rather than exclusively a direct effect of androgens on brain circuits that regulate sexual behavior. If so, this might be an example of the interaction of social and biological factors in the development of bisexuality/homosexuality, for which Bearman and Brückner (2002) argued.

In our data set, the clinical-endocrine classification of CAH was highly correlated with the classification based on molecular genetics, and knowledge of one did not add to the predictive power of the other in terms of gender outcome. Thus, there is no suggestion that the molecular-genetic defect influences sexual-orientation outcome through any other physiological route than the hormonal abnormalities caused by the degree of enzyme deficiency.

It is noteworthy that our data suggest an influence of CAH severity on cross-gender identity in sexual situations. . . . Perhaps, gender-atypicality in non-sexual behavior along with later emerging atypical sexual orientation facilitate in some CAH women an identification with selected aspects of the male role, which may subsequently broaden and thereby lead to late overall gender identity change, as it has been documented to occur in some 46,XX individuals with CAH.

Our data show that current sexual orientation is not only predicted from the degree of prenatal androgen exposure as indicated by the CAH-severity classification, but in addition also from the degree of masculinization of gender-related behavior during childhood. The latter variable could reflect variable brain responsiveness to prenatal androgens as well as postnatal psychosocial influences, provided retrospective reporting bias can be ruled out. This study does not provide an opportunity to decide between these options. . . .

The current data set on sexual orientation suffers from the same overall limitations as the previous one on gender development, namely, small sample size, questionable representativeness, and cross-sectional design. However, our findings on a dose–response relationship of androgens and sexual orientation appear even stronger than for non-sexual gender-related behavior and make a persuasive case for the extension of this association to women with NC CAH. Overall, our findings support a sexual-differentiation perspective involving prenatal androgens on the development of sexual orientation.

Lisa M. Diamond and
Molly Butterworth

 **NO**

Questioning Gender and Sexual Identity: Dynamic Links over Time

Introduction

Historically, research on both sexual identity development (generally understood as the process by which individuals come to acknowledge same-sex
attractions and to gradually conceive of themselves as nonheterosexual)
and gender identity development (understood as the process by which children come to think of themselves as unequivocally and permanently male
or female) have adopted dichotomous and essentialist models of gender and
sexuality, in which individuals possess and seek to publicly embrace one and
only one true identity (male or female, heterosexual or gay-lesbian). Individuals whose experiences of gender and sexuality involve multiplicity and fluidity
have been ill-described by such models. For example, sexual identity researchers have long critiqued traditional sexual identity models for failing to account
for the experiences of men and women who experience attractions for both
men and women, and who do not consider one form of desire to be a "truer"
representation of their sexuality than another. Historically, such individuals'
resistance to dichotomous models of sexual identity and orientation has been
attributed to denial, internalized homophobia, or false consciousness.

These views are now changing. Research increasingly demonstrates
that categories such as "gay," "lesbian," and "heterosexual" are not, in fact
unproblematic natural "types." Furthermore, patterns of same-sex and other-
sex desire show far more fluidity and complexity than previously thought. A
similar adherence to fixed, categorical notions of identity has also historically characterized interpretations of transgender experience. Transgender is a
broad category typically used to represent any individual whose gender-related
identification or an external presentation either violates conventional conceptualizations of "male" or "female" or mixes different aspects of male and
female role and identity. The word and concept "transgender" came into use
specifically because many individuals with fluid experiences of gender felt that
this phenomenon was not well-described by clinical discussions of transsexualism. The term "transsexual" is typically used to refer to individuals who feel
that their true psychological gender is the opposite of their biological sex, and

From *Sex Roles: A Journal of Research*, vol. 59, 2008. Copyright © 2008 by Springer Science and
Business Media. Reprinted by permission via Rightslink.

who seek surgical or hormonal modifications in order to bring these two into alignment.

There has been increasing social scientific acknowledgment and investigation of transgender individuals, but much of this work presumes that the primary "dilemma" of all transgender experience is a conflict between one's psychological gender and one's biological sex that inhibits expression of the individual's "true" gender identity. Hence, just as the healthy endpoint of sexual identity development was once presumed to be a stable, integrated, unambiguous lesbian, gay, or heterosexual identity, the normative and healthy endpoint of transgender development is often thought to be adoption of a stable, integrated, unambiguous identification as 100% male or 100% female, often achieved via some form of physical transformation (for example, some combination of clothes, makeup, demeanor, hormones, or surgery) aimed at bringing one's psychological gender and one's physical gender presentation into direct alignment.

Yet just as research increasingly demonstrates the inadequacy of historical, dichotomous models of sexuality, there is increasing evidence that dichotomous models of gender fail to capture the complexity, diversity, and fluidity of transgender experience. . . . Theorists have argued against a "master narrative" of transgender experience in which all experiences of gender fluidity and multiplicity must be resolved in favor of a singular, unified gender identification/presentation. In resisting this universalized narrative, they challenge the presumed essential basis of sexual differentiation and the corresponding, sociopolitical (and fundamentally patriarchal) sex/gender hegemony. . . .

The Relevance of Intersectionality

In this article we maintain that the feminist theoretical framework of intersectionality provides a generative starting point for theorizing women's experiences of multiple, partial, and fluid gender identifications. Historically, intersectionality has been articulated as a framework for analyzing the way in which multiple social locations and identities mutually inform and constitute one another. A key tenet of theories of intersectionality is that the process of identifying with more than one social group produces altogether new forms of subjective experience that are unique, nonadditive, and not reducible to the original identities that went into them.

Although intersectionality is perhaps most widely used as a theoretical approach for analyzing relations among different forms of oppression, our focus is more intrapsychic in nature, and emphasizes intersectionality's challenge to the notion of primary sites of identity and selfhood. Contrary to interpretations of transgender experience, which emphasize conflicts between an individual's (true) psychological gender and (discordant) biological sex, the framework of intersectionality calls attention to experiences of multiplicity in gender identification, and how these experiences—embedded within specific social, cultural, and interpersonal contexts—create altogether new, emergent forms of experience and identity.

We also find intersectionality relevant to understanding how gender identity and sexual identity interact and co-create one another. Historically, gender and sexual identity have been viewed as orthogonal dimensions, and social scientists have taken pains to emphasize that variability in one dimension does not neatly map onto the other: Being gay/lesbian/bisexual obviously does not mean that one is transgendered (and being heterosexual does not mean that one is *not* transgendered), just as being transgendered does not mean that one is necessarily gay/lesbian/bisexual. Rather, the linkage between sexual identity and gender identity takes a wide array of forms. But in emphasizing distinctions between gender and sexual identity, social scientists may have given short shrift to the complex processes through which individuals' experiences of gender and erotic desire mutually influence one another over time. We believe that such intersections and reciprocal influences deserve closer analysis if we are to create developmentally accurate models of gender and sexual identification over the life course. In other words, when examining women with "non-mainstream" gender and sexual identities, we must account for the fact that their attractions and identities are in dynamic interaction with one another, yielding diverse constellations of identity and erotic phenomenology over time. Theories of intersectionality call direct attention to these processes via their emphasis on the ways in which intersections between different identities and social locations give rise to altogether novel forms of subjective experience.

To elucidate how the framework of intersectionality helps to interpret complex, multiple, partial experiences of gender, in this article we discuss experiences of gender/sexual intersectionality as experienced by four women, each of which has been interviewed intensively over the past 10 years in the course of an ongoing longitudinal study of sexual identity development. These four women's journeys through nonheterosexual sexual identities eventually—and unexpectedly—prompted each of them to explore transgendered identifications. None of these women described feeling "trapped" in the "wrong" gender, and none sought to irrevocably replace her female body and identity with a male one. Rather, they all articulated experiences of multiplicity regarding their gender identities, and resisted selecting one form of identity as inherently "primary." These women's reflections about their own gender-sexual phenomenology resonate with the challenge that theorists of intersectionality have historically posed to dichotomous, essentialist models of identity and selfhood. . . .

Four Women's Unexpected Journeys

Cynthia/Mark was an avid tomboy growing up, and greatly enjoyed boys' company and games. She first began questioning her sexuality at the age of 12, when she developed a strong crush on a female friend and sent her a love poem. This unfortunately triggered a barrage of social stigma and school harassment. Yet Cynthia persevered, becoming an active and proud bisexual at the age of 14, and identifying as lesbian by the age of 15. By her mid-20s she had met the woman of her dreams and the two of them were planning a lesbian wedding. Several years later, however, she was working at a male-dominated profession and found that she was increasingly adopting a masculine "stance" when interacting with colleagues. She gradually began reflecting on her own subjective sense of gender, and increasingly felt that she would be more comfortable adopting a more masculine gender identity. Her lesbian partner urged her not to do so, and once Cynthia finally made the decision to change her name to Mark and began dressing and appearing as a man (although not consistently identifying as "male," as we will see below), her partner left her. Mark now identifies as queer; he continues to present himself as male on a day-to-day basis, but has no plans to pursue sex-reassignment surgery. At the time of the 10-year follow-up, Mark was 30 years old, and happily married to a bisexually-identified woman.

Lori was a proudly-identified bisexual woman when she first enrolled in the study at the age of 23. She had longstanding memories of experiencing attractions to both women and men, and enjoying satisfying friendships with both female and male peers, although her most substantive emotional ties were formed with women. As Lori's college years progressed, she started reading about transgender issues and meeting transsexual people, and began thinking more and more about her own sense of gender. By the time of our third interview, when she was 27 years old, she had started identifying as transgendered, and an important part of this identification was a rejection of the notion of "two and only two" genders. Although she has never adopted a male identity, she began taking testosterone, and by the time of the ten-year follow-up interview, at age 33, she described her physical appearance as decidedly masculine. Over the years she continued to experience attractions and relationships with both women and men, but had become seriously involved with a woman.

Ellen first remembers feeling attracted to women at the age of 12 or 13, and by age 14 she had admitted to herself that she was a lesbian. She regularly attended gay-lesbian support groups, and felt both certain and proud of her sexual identity when she first enrolled in the study at age 19. Questions of gender identity had always been lurking in the back of her mind, from a very early age. Sometimes she thought that it would just be easier to be a man, given that she knew she was attracted to women. Yet toward the end of adolescence, she realized that she actually enjoyed being a woman. As she progressed through her 20s, her lesbian identity remained rock-solid, while her gender identity continued to fluctuate. She eventually began an intensive process of spiritual questioning that led her to affirm her own complex, multidimensional experience of gender and sexuality. She still identifies as a lesbian, but remains deeply ambivalent about identifying as a "woman." By the 10-year point, at age 29, she was unsure whether she might someday pursue full-blown gender reassignment.

Karen identified as bisexual when she first participated in the study at age 17. She had long been aware of experiencing attractions to both women and men, and pursued relationships with both sexes. By the age of 18, she had also started to question her gender identity. She began taking testosterone and started describing herself as a female-to-male transsexual. Yet through this process, she became aware that "male" was not necessarily a more comfortable identity for her than "female," and that she was more comfortable living and identifying "somewhere in the middle." Around this time she also became increasingly aware that her attractions to other people, too, were not strongly oriented around gender, but instead revolved around personal attributes. She continued to pursue relationships with both women and men, but by the time of the 10-year follow-up, at age 27, she was happily involved with a man.

Multiplicity of Female and Male Identifications

A longstanding assumption about transgender individuals is that they uniformly and unequivocally desire permanent re-identification as the other gender. This can be seen in many first-person accounts collected from transsexuals, in which they recount having dressed or acted as the other gender from an early age. For individuals who seek complete re-identification as the other gender, this goal involves changes in self-concept and corresponding changes in the outward presentation of one's gender, including changes in name, in gender role behavior, and in physical gender presentation. The latter can be achieved through a variety of routes, pursued separately or concurrently, including alterations in hairstyle and clothing, hormonal modification of secondary sex characteristics, and most drastically, surgical modification of the genitals.

This developmental trajectory presumes that female and male identities are irreconcilable, and that one of these identities must occupy a psychologically primary status. Hence, the process of becoming more and more masculine— in one's appearance, demeanor, and physicality—gradually supplants one's previous femininity, and is desirable for this specific reason.

Yet none of the women profiled here were following such a trajectory. Rather, despite adopting observably masculine gender presentations, they expressed ambivalence about taking on a male identity. . . .

Two aspect's of Lori's experience stand out from the perspective of intersectionality. First, Lori is acutely aware—and wary—of the sociopolitical ramifications of taking on a conventional "male" identity in light of the other identity statuses that she would simultaneously occupy. Given her ethnicity and her sexual interest in women, she perceives that identifying as male would entail identifying as a heterosexual white male, suddenly placing her in a position of power and privilege that runs counter to her previous experience with, and political activism regarding, social marginality. Her ambivalence about "being a guy" reflects an implicit awareness—consistent with the framework of intersectionality—that she cannot simply subtract out the aspects of a male identity she finds troubling.

Second, and perhaps most notably, Lori's overall resistance to "picking a box" and designating either a female or male identity as her true identity resonates with intersectionality's challenge to the notion that any one particular identity status (i.e., ethnicity, social class, gender) must be personally and socially "primary," such that other identity statuses are analyzable chiefly with respect to how they add or subtract from forms of social marginality associated with the primary one.

This particular aspect of Lori's experience was echoed by other respondents. Mark, for example, also resisted adopting a wholly male identity, despite changing his name and presenting himself as male on a day-to-day basis. He had specifically elected not to pursue sex reassignment surgery or to pursue a formal legal change to his gender status, instead crafting his own, hybrid combination of maleness and femaleness. . . . Thus, for Mark a feeling of "otherness"—which, from the perspective of intersectionality, can be interpreted as the emergent product of Mark's social marginalization on the basis of both his gender and sexual identity—was not necessarily undesirable, and was not something to be obliterated and replaced with a more fixed, categorical sense of self. Rather, Mark had come to embrace dynamic, partial, and intersecting experiences of gender and sexuality.

The notion of dynamism and continued change and transformation is important, because although all of these individuals embraced gender-ambiguity to some degree, they did not turn it into its own fixed category (i.e., "androgynous"). Rather, their experience of gender identity involved continued movement between, around, and within gender polarities. Hence, for these women the experience of "transition" was not a unilateral movement from female to male, but an ongoing oscillation between more feminine and more masculine aspects of internal gender identity and outward physical presentation. This is perhaps the clearest challenge to conventional notions of transgender, because it posits change and transition as a potential outcome rather than just a temporary process. This, importantly, is consistent with feminist perspectives on intersectionality which emphasize the simultaneous occupation of multiple social and psychological identities, and how dynamic interactions among these identities, embedded within specific contextual, interpersonal, and developmental circumstances, create altogether new senses of selfhood. . . .

Written on the Body: Physical Transformation and Intersectionality

Many conventional understandings of transgender experience, particularly those drawn from the narratives and experiences of self-identified transsexuals, suggest that transgender women and men typically feel they were born with the "wrong body," and hence experience a persistent hatred of their bodies which can only be remedied through bodily transformation. Such transformations are supposedly aimed at replacing all signs and manifestations of one's given gender with one's desired (and ostensibly, psychologically primary) gender. Yet among the women profiled here, the aforementioned phenomenon of multiplicity in gender identification extended to the way in which they perceived and experienced their physical bodies, and their corresponding motives for different types of body modification. Although all of them pursued some form of physical transformation, these "body projects" did not involve the straightforward erasure of femininity and the taking on of an unambiguous male role. Rather, women pursued complex, contradictory forms of gender presentation that seemed to inscribe, in physical terms, the multiplicity and partiality that characterized their psychological sense of gender.

Lori, for example, was an avid bodybuilder with a long history of body modification, including tattoos, body piercing, and experimenting with different modes of dress and posture. When she eventually sought a breast reduction, it was not because of any sort of "female body hatred"—in fact she stated straight out that she loved her breasts—but was linked to a certain muscular aesthetic. . . .

Lori did, in fact, eventually have her breasts removed. Yet as with the breast reduction, her account reveals no persistent body hatred. . . . Lori also expressed no desire to change her genitals. Despite the fact that she had been taking testosterone and was passing as male on a day-to-day basis. . . . In fact, by the 10-year interview, she was considering going off of testosterone in order to get pregnant, and was clearly comfortable with the prospect of combining her masculine-appearing body with perhaps the ultimate symbol of femininity: A pregnant belly.

Karen, in fact, actually lived out this experience, having served as a surrogate mother for one of her relatives despite having transformed her body through years of testosterone. . . .

The framework of intersectionality is relevant to Karen's and Lori's approaches to their bodies because intersectionality directly counters essentialist assumptions about the primacy of biologically-based forms of identification over others. . . .

Of all the respondents, Ellen was the only one who gave voice to a distinct dissatisfaction with the gendered nature of her body. . . .

Ellen enacted her own questioning process by pursuing other forms of body modification, and at the time of the 10-year interview was engaged in a long-term tattoo project which would eventually cover 75% of her body. . . .

Ellen's tattoo had everything to do with her own personal experience of identity transformation and emergence, and replacing old scars (both psychological and physical, in her case) with powerful, healing images whose symbolic meaning was contextualized within her own personal history. . . .

Links Between Gender and Desire

Perhaps the most fascinating aspect of these women's experiences of multiplicity regarding gender identity is the effect that it has had on their erotic attractions. Of course, the notion that gender identity and sexual desire are fundamentally linked has a long history: In the 19th and early 20th century, it was widely believed that same-sex sexuality was caused by gender "inversion," as if the only way to be attracted to a woman was to be male, and the only way to be attracted to a man was to be female. In this formulation, all desire is fundamentally heterosexual desire. Accordingly, if you possess same-sex desires it is not because you are homosexual, but because your natural, heterosexual desires are trapped in the wrong gender identity.

Now, of course, the pendulum has shifted, and gender and sexual identity are considered to be orthogonal constructs. Yet the experiences of the women profiled here indicate that for many women who have undergone substantive processes of sexual questioning, it is impossible to completely disentangle one's own sense of femaleness and maleness from one's own understanding, experience, and interpretation of sexual desire for female and male partners.

Theories of intersectionality provide useful conceptual tools with which to make sense of this phenomenon. Whereas conventional understandings of gender identity and sexual identity presume that each has its own independent, essential basis, making it possible to analyze each separately from the other, intersectionality challenges this notion. According to the theoretical framework of intersectionality, no identity status is experienced—or can be meaningfully understood—in isolation. Hence, a sexual-minority woman's experiences of same-sex and other-sex desires are always embedded within the social and interpersonal context of her gender presentation and gendered experience, and changes in one domain necessarily shape the other. The relationship between gender and desire is dynamic and reciprocal, relating not only to a woman's own sense of gender, but her appraisal of how social others appraise and understand her.

It is not surprising, then, that women who began to explore multiplicity and fluidity with respect to their gender identity became progressively more aware of multiplicity and fluidity in their erotic attractions as well. This is perhaps most evident in the case of Mark, whose attractions were predominantly directed toward women prior to the point at which he began to question his gender identity. But as Mark delved deeper into the masculine sides of his personality, and took on an increasingly masculine role in self-presentation and interpersonal interaction, he found himself unexpectedly attracted to men. . . . Mark's own experience of desire for men was, to some degree, constituted by his appraisal of men's social location with respect to his own. Previously, men's position of power and privilege rendered their erotic reactions to Cynthia troublesome. Yet now that Cynthia identified as Mark, a man's desire was no longer experienced as threatening, and in fact represented a willingness to threaten conventional gender locations (because male desire for Mark was now same-sex desire). It is also notable that Cynthia/Mark experienced changes in the types of men she/he found attractive after taking on a masculine gender presentation, and these changes were directly related to issues of power and social location. Previously, Cynthia had found only "feminine" men attractive, but after identifying as Mark, he found a broader range of men—and masculinities—to be desirable. This suggests that the critical "trigger" for Cynthia/Mark's desire was never, in fact, some sort of stable, trait-like "degree" of femininity or masculinity, but instead a particular interpersonal dialectic regarding gender and—necessarily—social power. Mark noted that it was the traditional male-female heterosexual dynamic that he had always found distasteful, and which he had subverted—as Cynthia—by seeking "feminine" men. Now that he identified as Mark, all desires for men now fell outside the purview of the conventional male-female heterosexual dynamic, thereby opening up new erotic possibilities. . . .

Similar intersections among gender, desire, and power were voiced by the other three respondents, making it clear that our culture's complex interbraiding of gender and power fundamentally shapes individuals' experiences of erotic attractions. Thus, some of the new desires for men that women began experiencing as a function of their increasingly masculine gender presentations had to do with the distinct changes they began to experience in their relative power vis-à-vis men. . . . Although it is common to think about desire as located "within" individuals, and expressed outwardly through behaviors and expression, these women's experiences demonstrate that desire itself takes shape (and is reshaped) through direct engagement with different social partners across different social contexts. Just as no form of identity is inherently "primary," neither is any specific form of "desire." Changes in one domain necessarily change the terrain on which the other is experienced. Intersectionality provides a valuable framework for interpreting this phenomenon because of its emphasis on the nonadditive relations among different social categories, and the potential for intersections between these categories to create novel forms of experience. . . .

Giving Voice to Multiplicity

Each of the women profiled has made a certain amount of peace with her own experience of multiplicity in gender identity and sexual desire. Yet according to conventional norms regarding sexuality and gender, no such peace is truly possible. Rather, it is presumed that the most desirable, psychologically healthful state is to have a unitary, primary identity which provides not only a solid foundation for ego development, but a permanent social location that is understandable to the rest of the culture. The women profiled here have already experienced society's relentless pressure toward categorization in the domain of sexual orientation and identity. All of these women experienced attractions to both men and women (even if they did not all identify as bisexual), and all of them were well-aware of the cultural unintelligibility of such attractions. In order to avoid being misunderstood, some of them actively censored themselves with friends or family members to present a more categorical portrait of their desire/behavior than was actually the case. . . .

Our culture's difficulty in making sense of individuals with multiple identities, multiple subjectivities, and multiple social locations is manifested in the lack of language to describe such experiences. As noted earlier, the word "transgender" came into use because many individuals with fluid experiences of gender felt that this phenomenon was not well-described by discussions of transsexuality, which instead emphasize experiences of conflict between psychological gender and biological sex.

Similarly, each of the women profiled here expressed dissatisfaction with the term "bisexual," feeling that it failed to adequately convey the open, expansive way in which she experienced her sexual desires. Some found it ironic that although the phenomenon of bisexual attraction posed a challenge to categorical models of sexual orientation, slapping the "bisexual" label on this phenomenon seemed to be an attempt to revise and reinvigorate such categorical models. Why is it so difficult, some wondered, to get beyond these categories?

Some noted that their main problem with the word bisexual was that it placed so much emphasis on gender as a category of desire. . . .

This ambivalence about labeling was also reflected in the way that these women dealt with "the pronoun thing." In other words, did they think of themselves—and prefer to be called—"he," or "she?" None of the four respondents expressed a preference for a single pronoun usage across all contexts. Rather, each reported using both "he" and "she" in different contexts. . . .

The difficulty that society continues to experience in giving voice to complex, multiple, fluid experiences of gender is exemplified by the difficulty that we encountered in choosing and using pronouns for Mark. In deference to his own unwillingness to consistently use "she" or "he," we initially experimented with randomly alternating among "he," "she," "her," and "him." Yet it soon became apparent that to readers (and writers!) accustomed to consistency in linguistic gender-markers, this proved both confusing and distracting. We therefore settled on consistently male pronouns for Mark, despite our own ambivalence about the erasure of multiplicity that this necessarily entails.

Conclusion

The struggles recounted by the women profiled here in reaching awareness and acceptance of the multiplicity in their gender status demonstrate the importance of fostering an increased appreciation for intersectional gender and sexual identities. Continued longitudinal observation is obviously critical for understanding how the experiences of multiplicity that we have emphasized play out over time, and the degree to which theories of intersectionality can, in fact, make substantive contributions to their interpretation. It is also critical to examine how the dynamics described in this article manifest themselves with younger cohorts of transgendered individuals, who have greater awareness and appreciation for social constructionist perspectives on gender than do older generations. . . .

Clearly, much has changed, and continues to change. The last 20 years have witnessed incredible strides with respect to conceptualizations of sexual identity and orientation. Multiplicity and fluidity in patterns of sexual attraction—which were long considered "impossible," "invalid" or "transitional"—are now widely acknowledged and even celebrated by both activists and social scientists, and have become one of the most exciting and productive areas of social scientific inquiry into sexuality.

Multiplicity in gender identification deserves similar theoretical attention, and the framework of intersectionality provides a valuable starting point for such analyses via its dismantling of the historical emphasis on "primary," "core" loci of identity. This does not necessarily suggest that we are—or should be—headed toward a future in which there are *no* terms or concepts to represent gender and/or sexual identities. As Mark pointed out, identity labels play a potentially important role in helping individuals to "find others like yourself," to build alliances around salient or personally significant aspects of one's experience and identification. A greater appreciation of intersectionality, however, helps to guard against the fallacy that these identities—once claimed and named—function as stable and essential "types" of selfhood. From the perspective of intersectionality, adopting and proudly embracing an identity is fully compatible with a critical appreciation for the fact that these identities are always moving targets, reforming and reshaping themselves across diverse social and interpersonal contexts.

Along these lines, perhaps the greatest potential contribution of intersectionality to our understanding of transgender experience is the way in which it recasts and reconstitutes the phenomenon of *change*. Traditional perspectives on transgender experience examine change from the perspective of *transition:* men transitioning to a new (and purportedly permanent) female identity, or women transitioning to a new (and purportedly permanent) male identity. . . . Change, for these women, was an ever-present possibility rather than a temporary phase. Theories of intersectionality help to make sense of this experience by emphasizing how *all* subjective experiences of selfhood are continually transformed, reenacted, and renegotiated as a function of shifting landscapes of social context. From an intersectionality perspective, instead of representing a woman's journey to transgender identification as having a distinct beginning, middle, and end, we should treat each successive stage of her life course, each of her (fluid) social locations, and each of her intimate relationships as continually interacting with her experiences of gender and desire to produce multiple, dynamic senses of self over time. . . .

EXPLORING THE ISSUE

Is Sexual Orientation Innate?

Challenge Questions

1. What are the relations between biological sex, sexual orientation, gender identity, and gender roles?
2. What does it mean to say biological sex, sexual orientation, gender identity, and gender roles are congruent? Is incongruence, or should incongruence be, the basis for determining one has a disorder?
3. Is it necessary to include data on genotypes or hormonal levels in a discussion of whether sexual orientation is innate?
4. If sexual orientation is fluid, what are the implications of this for our understanding of the biological basis of sexual orientation?
5. What are some of the social and political implications of knowing whether sexual orientation is innate or not? Would this knowledge have any medical or ethical implications?

Is There Common Ground?

The etiology (cause) of sexual orientation is still more unknown than known. The biological perspective explores the effects of prenatal androgens and maternal prenatal distress on gender atypicality. This research is primarily conducted on lower animals, intersexual humans, or persons with atypical hormonal exposure, such as CAH women (even though GID is not typical in intersexuals). Social scientists examine sex-related socialization practices, including parental attitudes, social reinforcement processes (consistently and without ambiguity rearing a child as a boy or a girl, including encouragement of same-gender behavior and discouragement of cross-gender behavior), and self-socialization. An interactionist perspective suggests that sexual biology makes some individuals more vulnerable to certain psychosocial rearing conditions.

Different ideologies about whether or not sexual orientation is a disorder seem to rest on this question: do we view sex, gender, and sexual orientation as distinct domains or as inextricably linked? Phyllis Burke notes in *Gender Shock: Exploding the Myths of Male and Female* (Anchor Books, 1996) that "when you look at what society pathologizes, you can get the clearest glimpse of what society demands of those who wish to be considered normal." It appears, then, that our society expects congruence among sex, gender, and sexual orientation and believes that to be the norm. But some critics caution that the biodiversity of nature is greater than our norms allow us to observe. Moreover, we have little understanding, beyond stereotype and presumption, of the association between this biodiversity and gender identity and sexual behavior. For example, how many of us have biological evidence (beyond visible external genitalia) that we are the sex that we believe ourselves to be? There have been cases where female athletes were surprised to find that they have a Y chromosome, yet by other biological measures they are clearly female. What, then, is this individual's "appropriate" gender identity? (See Issue 21.) Currently, cross-cultural studies, such as Herdt's work in Papua New Guinea, studies of transgenderism, and analyses of historical changes in lesbian/gay identities in the late nineteenth century have begun to challenge the biological, bipolar notion of sexual orientation. Furthermore, the definition of sexual orientation is becoming more "complicated" as scholars pay more attention to diversity in sexual, affectional, and erotic attraction; that is, they do not all fit together. Erotic and affectional feelings may or may not match fantasies and behaviors. Sexual identity, sexual behavior, and sexual desire appear to be fluid and changeable over time, context, and cultures. Thus, there are likely multiple pathways to sexual orientations.

Additional Resources

J. Colapinto, *As Nature Made Him: The Boy Who Was Raised as a Girl* (New York: HarperCollins, 2000).

National Gay and Lesbian Taskforce. http://www.thetaskforce.org/

Parents, Families and Friends of Lesbians and Gays. http://www.pflag.org

Cheryl L. Weill, *Nature's Choice: What Science Reveals About the Biological Origins of Sexual Orientation* (Routledge/Taylor & Francis Group, New York, 2009).

Internet References . . .

The Future of Children

This Web site is sponsored by the Woodrow Wilson School of Public and International Affairs at Princeton University and the Brookings Institution. Its goal is to promote effective policies and programs for children by providing policymakers, service providers, and the media with timely, objective information based on the best available research.

http://www.futureofchildren.org/

The Children's Defense Fund

This nonprofit organization, begun in 1973, advocates for preventive programs to help children stay healthy and out of trouble.

http://www.childrensdefense.org

Institute for Ethics and Emerging Technologies

Read an essay by James Hughes, Ph.D., the Executive Director of the Institute for Ethics and Emerging Technologies, a bioethicist and sociologist at Trinity College in Hartford, Connecticut, on sex selection and women's reproductive rights.

http://ieet.org/index.php/ieet/more/hughes20070510/

National Fatherhood Initiative

Founded in 1994, the National Fatherhood Initiative advances the view that "Fathers make unique and irreplaceable contributions to the lives of children; Father absence produces negative outcomes for children; Societies which fail to reinforce a cultural ideal of responsible fatherhood get increasing amounts of father absence; Widespread fatherlessness is the most socially consequential problem of our time."

http://www.fatherhood.org/

Resolution of the American Psychological Association

Read the APA resolution on sexual orientation, parents, and children that reviews research that supports same-sex parenting.

http://www.apa.org/about/governance/council/policy/parenting.aspx

Tufts University's Child and Family Web Guide

This Web site provides links to the best sites on same-sex parents.

http://www.cfw.tufts.edu/topic/2/189.htm

From Ozzie and Harriet to My Two Dads: Gender in Childhood

In contemporary America, the "ideal" family continues to be defined as one in which mother and father are married, father is the breadwinner, and mother maintains the home and cares for the children. This ideal is no longer matched by actual family structure, with more and more alternative family structures, including families with same-sex parents and single-parent families being developed to meet personal desires and needs and to cope with societal pressures and changes. Nonetheless, traditional family ideology remains dominant in America. Traditional family ideology institutionalizes conventional gender roles, so much so that many gender scholars view the family as a "gender factory." The institutionalization of gender roles also extends to parental desires regarding the sex of one's children. In this unit, we examine issues surrounding what constitutes a "normal" family, from the perspective of couples themselves. In evaluating the selections in this unit, consider what role biology plays in the construction of parenthood. One argument supporting traditional families rests on the assumption that women and men have biologically based attributes that render each uniquely suited for particular parenting roles, and that having sons and daughters creates a more balanced family. Do data support such an assumption? Is there a maternal instinct? How do race, ethnicity, class, culture, and other status-defining attributes contribute to definitions of family? How might variations in family arrangements across these dimensions challenge essentialist notions of mother and father? Traditional media representations of the family supported a 1950's Ozzie and Harriet view of a stay-at-home-mother and a working father. What views are presented in contemporary media? Consider movies such as Three Men and a Baby *and* Transamerica. *How do media portrayals of parenting affect our understanding of healthy relationships? How and when do media portrayals, including images and language, reinforce or defy gender stereotypes?*

- Should Same-Sex Marriage Be Legal?
- Does Parents' Sexual Orientation Affect Their Children's Psychological Outcomes?
- Are Fathers Necessary for Children's Well-Being?
- Should Parents Be Allowed to Choose the Sex of Their Children?

ISSUE 4

Should Same-Sex Marriage Be Legal?

YES: **Human Rights Campaign,** from *Answers to Questions about Marriage Equality* (Human Rights Campaign, 2009)

NO: **John Cornyn,** from "In Defense of Marriage: The Amendment That Will Protect a Fundamental Institution," *National Review* (July 2009)

Learning Outcomes

As you read the issue, focus on the following points:

- Consider the assertions pertaining to the effects of same-sex couples or their unions on different-sex couples.
- What effect do you think the relationship status, choices, and behaviors of heterosexual couples have on lesbian and gay individuals and couples?
- Does allowing same-sex couples to marry have an effect on different-sex couples? Does the institution of marriage as traditionally understood need to be protected?
- What would be the advantages of marriage for a same-sex couple?

ISSUE SUMMARY

YES: The Human Rights Campaign (HRC), America's largest gay and lesbian organization, explains why same-sex couples should be afforded the same legal right to marry as heterosexual couples.

NO: John Cornyn, U.S. senator from Texas, says a constitutional amendment is needed to define marriage as permissible only between a man and a woman. Senator Cornyn contends that the traditional institution of marriage needs to be protected from activist courts that would seek to redefine it.

Many people believe that a person should have the same rights as anyone else, regardless of their race, age, gender—or sexual orientation. When this discussion moves into the arena of same-sex marriage, however, those beliefs start to waver a bit. The past few years have seen the topic of same-sex marriage rush into the forefront of the news and other media. Vermont became the first state to make civil unions legal between two people of the same sex. Although a same-sex couple cannot have a marriage license or refer to their union as a marriage, the benefits are the same as they would be for a heterosexual marriage. These unions are not, however, recognized in many states. This is due in great part to the Defense of Marriage Act, which was signed into law in 1996 by the then President Bill Clinton. This Act says that no state is required to recognize a same-sex union and defines marriage as being only between a man and a woman. Therefore, same-sex unions that are legal in one state do not have to be recognized as legal in another. In anticipation of efforts to have state recognition of civil unions, more than 30 states have passed legislation saying they would not recognize a same-sex union that has taken place in another state. In the 2004 national election, few issues were more hotly debated than same-sex marriage. In that election, 11 states passed constitutional amendments that effectively banned same-sex marriage. The then President Bush was quoted as saying "The union of a man and a woman is the most enduring human institution, honored and encouraged in all cultures and by every religious faith." Political conservatives claimed that the election results indicated that the country generally rejects same-sex marriage. However, in spite of President Obama's stated opposition to same-sex marriage, in February 2011 he decided that the 1996 Defense of Marriage Act was unconstitutional and ordered the Justice Department to stop defending the law. However, a May 2011 Gallup poll found that the majority of Americans (53 percent) now support gay marriage, especially Democrats, independents, and those who label themselves liberal. Contrast this to the 77 percent who favor interracial marriages.

However, beneath the political rhetoric are questions about what is really wrong with gays and lesbians being granted the same legal rights as of heterosexual couples. Those who oppose same-sex marriage believe that marriage is, and always has been, between a man and a woman. They believe that a key part of marriage for many heterosexual couples is reproduction or another type of parenting arrangement, such as adoption. In those cases, they believe that any child should have two parents: one male and one female. Many do not oppose granting domestic partner benefits to same-sex partners, or even, in some cases, civil unions. They do, however, believe that if lesbian and gay couples were allowed to marry and to receive the legal and social benefits thereof, it would serve only to further erode the institution of marriage as it is currently defined, which, in the United States, boasts one divorce for every two marriages. Furthermore, as Michele Bachmann, a tea party member running for the Republican nomination for president, has said, "the 501(c)(3) tax-exempt status given to thousands of churches, nursing homes, schools, ministries, universities and radio stations may be at risk if an organization 'discriminates' against a legally protected status, such as same-sex marriage. What does this mean? If gay marriage is legalized, then any church or religious organization that doesn't agree with same-sex marriage will likely come under intense pressure to either change their views or go silent. Tax-exempt status for faith-based organizations that fail to agree with same-sex marriage will be at risk" (*WorldNetDaily*, April 24, 2004).

Supporters of same-sex marriage believe that if lesbian and gay couples wish to make a lifetime commitment, they should be afforded the same rights, privileges, and vocabulary as heterosexual couples. Although some would be as happy with the term "civil union," accompanied by equal rights, others believe that making marriage available to all is the only way to go. An argument that is raised in this debate is that granting same-sex couples the right to marry would open the door for adult pedophiles to petition to marry the children with whom they engage in sexual relationships. Most lesbian and gay individuals and their supporters find this offensive, as well as an invalid comparison. What do you think? As you read, consider what is at the basis of each argument. Consider the assertions pertaining to the effects of same-sex couples or their unions on different-sex couples. Do you agree? What effect do you think the relationship status, choices, and behaviors of heterosexual couples have on lesbian and gay individuals and couples? In the YES and NO selections, information from the Human Rights Campaign provides facts about same-sex marriages and addresses commonly raised concerns opponents, such as Senator John Cornyn, raise, such as why do we need a federal constitutional amendment, when we already have the Defense of Marriage Act? He argues that the traditional institution of marriage is the "gold standard" for raising children.

Answers to Questions about Marriage Equality

10 Facts

1. Same-sex couples live in 99.3 percent of all counties nationwide.
2. There are an estimated 3.1 million people living together in same-sex relationships in the United States.
3. Fifteen percent of these same-sex couples live in rural settings.
4. One out of three lesbian couples is raising children. One out of five gay male couples is raising children.
5. Between 1 million and 9 million children are being raised by gay, lesbian and bisexual parents in the United States today.
6. At least one same-sex couple is raising children in 96 percent of all counties nationwide.
7. The highest percentages of same-sex couples raising children live in the South.
8. Nearly one in four same-sex couples includes a partner 55 years old or older, and nearly one in five same-sex couples is composed of two people 55 or older.
9. More than one in 10 same-sex couples include a partner 65 years old or older, and nearly one in 10 same-sex couples is composed of two people 65 or older.
10. The states with the highest numbers of same-sex senior couples are also the most popular for heterosexual senior couples: California, New York, and Florida.

Why Same-Sex Couples Want to Marry

Many same-sex couples want the right to legally marry because they are in love—either they just met the love of their lives, or more likely, they have spent the last 10, 20, or 50 years with that person—and they want to honor their relationship in the greatest way our society has to offer, by making a

---

These facts are based on analyses of the 2000 Census conducted by the Urban Institute and the Human Rights Campaign. The estimated number of people in same-sex relationships has been adjusted by 62 percent to compensate for the widely-reported undercount in the Census. . . .

public commitment to stand together in good times and bad, through all the joys and challenges family life brings.

Many parents want the right to marry because they know it offers children a vital safety net and guarantees protections that unmarried parents cannot provide.

And still other people—both gay and straight—are fighting for the right of same-sex couples to marry because they recognize that it is simply not fair to deny some families the protections all other families are eligible to enjoy.

Currently in the United States, same-sex couples in long-term, committed relationships pay higher taxes and are denied basic protections and rights granted to married heterosexual couples. Among them:

- **Hospital visitation.**   Married couples have the automatic right to visit each other in the hospital and make medical decisions. Same-sex couples can be denied the right to visit a sick or injured loved one in the hospital.
- **Social Security benefits.**   Married people receive Social Security payments upon the death of a spouse. Despite paying payroll taxes, gay and lesbian partners receive no Social Security survivor benefits—resulting in an average annual income loss of $5,528 upon the death of a partner.
- **Immigration.**   Americans in binational relationships are not permitted to petition for their same-sex partners to immigrate. As a result, they are often forced to separate or move to another country.
- **Health insurance.**   Many public and private employers provide medical coverage to the spouses of their employees, but most employers do not provide coverage to the life partners of gay and lesbian employees. Gay employees who do receive health coverage for their partners must pay federal income taxes on the value of the insurance.
- **Estate taxes.**   A married person automatically inherits all the property of his or her deceased spouse without paying estate taxes. A gay or lesbian taxpayer is forced to pay estate taxes on property inherited from a deceased partner.
- **Retirement savings.**   While a married person can roll a deceased spouse's 401(k) funds into an IRA without paying taxes, a gay or lesbian American who inherits a 401(k) can end up paying up to 70 percent of it in taxes and penalties.
- **Family leave.**   Married workers are legally entitled to unpaid leave from their jobs to care for an ill spouse. Gay and lesbian workers are not entitled to family leave to care for their partners.
- **Nursing homes.**   Married couples have a legal right to live together in nursing homes. Because they are not legal spouses, elderly gay or lesbian couples do not have the right to spend their last days living together in nursing homes.
- **Home protection.**   Laws protect married seniors from being forced to sell their homes to pay high nursing home bills; gay and lesbian seniors have no such protection.
- **Pensions.**   After the death of a worker, most pension plans pay survivor benefits only to a legal spouse of the participant. Gay and lesbian partners are excluded from such pension benefits.

Why Civil Unions Aren't Enough

Comparing marriage to civil unions is a bit like comparing diamonds to rhinestones. One is, quite simply, the real deal; the other is not. Consider:

- Couples eligible to marry may have their marriage performed in any state and have it recognized in every other state in the nation and every country in the world.
- Couples who are joined in a civil union in Vermont (the only state that offers civil unions) have no guarantee that its protections will even travel with them to neighboring New York or New Hampshire— let alone California or any other state.

Moreover, even couples who have a civil union and remain in Vermont receive only second-class protections in comparison to their married friends and neighbors. While they receive state-level protections, they do not receive any of the *more than 1,100 federal benefits and protections of marriage.*

In short, civil unions are not separate but equal—they are separate and unequal. And our society has tried separate before. It just doesn't work.

Marriage:	Civil unions:
• State grants marriage licenses to couples.	• State would grant civil union licenses to couples.
• Couples receive legal protections and rights under state and federal law.	• Couples receive legal protections and rights under state law only.
• Couples are recognized as being married by the federal government and all state governments.	• Civil unions are not recognized by other states or the federal government.
• Religious institutions are not required to perform marriage ceremonies.	• Religious institutions are not required to perform civil union ceremonies.

"I Believe God Meant Marriage for Men and Women. How Can I Support Marriage for Same-Sex Couples?"

Many people who believe in God—and fairness and justice for all—ask this question. They feel a tension between religious beliefs and democratic values that has been experienced in many different ways throughout our nation's history. That is why the framers of our Constitution established the principle of separation of church and state. That principle applies no less to the marriage issue than it does to any other.

Indeed, the answer to the apparent dilemma between religious beliefs and support for equal protections for all families lies in recognizing that marriage has a significant religious meaning for many people, but that it is also a legal contract. And it is strictly the legal—not the religious—dimension of marriage that is being debated now.

Granting marriage rights to same-sex couples would *not* require Christianity, Judaism, Islam, or any other religion to perform these marriages. It would not require religious institutions to permit these ceremonies to be held on their grounds. It would not even require that religious communities discuss the issue. People of faith would remain free to make their own judgments about what makes a marriage in the eyes of God—just as they are today.

Consider, for example, the difference in how the Catholic Church and the U.S. government view couples who have divorced and remarried. Because church tenets do not sanction divorce, the second marriage is not valid in the church's view. The government, however, recognizes the marriage by extending to the remarried couple the same rights and protections as those granted to every other married couple in America. In this situation—as would be the case in marriage for same-sex couples—the church remains free to establish its own teachings on the religious dimension of marriage while the government upholds equality under law.

It should also be noted that there are a growing number of religious communities that have decided to bless same-sex unions. Among them are Reform Judaism, the Unitarian Universalist Association, and the Metropolitan Community Church. The Presbyterian Church (USA) also allows ceremonies to be performed, although they are not considered the same as marriage. The Episcopal Church and United Church of Christ allow individual churches to set their own policies on same-sex unions.

"This Is Different from Interracial Marriage. Sexual Orientation Is a Choice."

"We cannot keep turning our backs on gay and lesbian Americans. I have fought too hard and too long against discrimination based on race and color not to stand up against discrimination based on sexual orientation. I've heard the reasons for opposing civil marriage for same-sex couples. Cut through the distractions, and they stink of the same fear, hatred, and intolerance I have known in racism and in bigotry."

— Rep. John Lewis, D-Ga., a leader of the black civil rights movement, writing in *The Boston Globe,* Nov. 25, 2003

Decades of research all point to the fact that sexual orientation is not a choice, and that a person's sexual orientation cannot be changed. Who one is drawn to is a fundamental aspect of who we are.

In this way, the struggle for marriage equality for same-sex couples is just as basic as the fight for interracial marriage was. It recognizes that Americans should not be coerced into false and unhappy marriages but should be free to marry the person they love—thereby building marriage on a true and stable foundation.

"Won't This Create a Free-for-All and Make the Whole Idea of Marriage Meaningless?"

Many people share this concern because opponents of gay and lesbian people have used this argument as a scare tactic. But it is not true. Granting same-sex couples the right to marry would in no way change the number of people who could enter into a marriage (or eliminate restrictions on the age or familial relationships of those who may marry). Marriage would continue to recognize the highest possible commitment that can be made between two adults, plain and simple.

Organizations That Support Same-Sex Parenting

American Academy of Pediatrics

American Academy of Family Physicians

Child Welfare League of America

National Association of Social Workers

North American Council on Adoptable Children

American Bar Association

American Psychological Association

American Psychiatric Association

American Psychoanalytic Association

"I Strongly Believe Children Need a Mother and a Father."

Many of us grew up believing that everyone needs a mother and father, regardless of whether we ourselves happened to have two parents, or two *good* parents.

But as families have grown more diverse in recent decades, and researchers have studied how these different family relationships affect children, it has become clear that the *quality* of a family's relationship is more important than the particular *structure* of families that exist today. In other words, the qualities that help children grow into good and responsible adults—learning how to learn, to have compassion for others, to contribute to society and be respectful of others and their differences—do not depend on the sexual orientation of their parents but on their parents' ability to provide a loving, stable and happy home, something no class of Americans has an exclusive hold on.

That is why research studies have consistently shown that children raised by gay and lesbian parents do just as well on all conventional measures of child development, such as academic achievement, psychological well-being, and social abilities, as children raised by heterosexual parents.

That is also why the nation's leading child welfare organizations, including the American Academy of Pediatrics, the American Academy of Family Physicians and others, have issued statements that dismiss assertions that only heterosexual couples can be good parents—and declare that the focus should now be on providing greater protections for the 1 million to 9 million children being raised by gay and lesbian parents in the United States today.

"What Would Be Wrong with a Constitutional Amendment to Define Marriage as a Union of a Man and Woman?"

In more than 200 years of American history, the U.S. Constitution has been amended only 17 times since the Bill of Rights—and in each instance (except for Prohibition, which was repealed), it was to extend rights and liberties to the American people, not restrict them. For example, our Constitution was amended to end our nation's tragic history of slavery. It was also amended to guarantee people of color, young people, and women the right to vote.

The amendment currently under consideration (called the Federal Marriage Amendment) would be the only one that would single out one class of Americans for discrimination by ensuring that same-sex couples would not be granted the equal protections that marriage brings to American families.

Moreover, the amendment could go even further by stripping same-sex couples of some of the more limited protections they now have, such as access to health insurance for domestic partners and their children.

Neither enshrining discrimination in our Constitution nor stripping millions of families of basic protections would serve our nation's best interest. The Constitution is supposed to protect and ensure equal treatment for *all* people. It should not be used to single out a group of people for different treatment.

TEXT OF PROPOSED FEDERAL MARRIAGE AMENDMENT

"Marriage in the United States shall consist only of the union of a man and a woman.

Neither this [C]onstitution [n]or the constitution of any state, nor state or federal law, shall be construed to require that marital status or the legal incidents thereof be conferred upon unmarried couples or groups."

— H.J. Resolution 56, introduced by Rep. Marilyn Musgrave, R-Colo., in May 2003. It has more than 100 co-sponsors. A similar bill was introduced in the U.S. Senate in November 2003. In February 2004, President Bush said that he would support a constitutional amendment to define marriage as between only a man and a woman.

"How Could Marriage for Same-Sex Couples Possibly Be Good for the American Family—or Our Country?"

"We shouldn't just allow gay marriage. We should insist on gay marriage. We should regard it as scandalous that two people could claim to love each other and not want to sanctify their love with marriage and fidelity."

— Conservative Columnist David Brooks, writing in
The New York Times, Nov. 22, 2003.

The prospect of a significant change in our laws and customs has often caused people to worry more about dire consequences that could result than about the potential positive outcomes. In fact, precisely the same anxiety arose when some people fought to overturn the laws prohibiting marriage between people of different races in the 1950s and 1960s. (One Virginia judge even declared that "God intended to separate the races.")

But in reality, opening marriage to couples who are so willing to fight for it could only strengthen the institution for all. It would open the doors to more supporters, not opponents. And it would help keep the age-old institution alive.

As history has repeatedly proven, institutions that fail to take account of the changing needs of the population are those that grow weak; those that recognize and accommodate changing needs grow strong. For example, the U.S. military, like American colleges and universities, grew stronger after permitting African Americans and women to join its ranks.

Similarly, granting same-sex couples the right to marry would strengthen the institution of marriage by allowing it to better meet the needs of the true diversity of family structures in America today.

"Can't Same-Sex Couples Go to a Lawyer to Secure All the Rights They Need?"

Not by a long shot. When a gay or lesbian person gets seriously ill, there is no legal document that can make their partner eligible to take leave from work under the federal Family and Medical Leave Act to provide care—because that law applies only to married couples.

When gay or lesbian people grow old and in need of nursing home care, there is no legal document that can give them the right to Medicaid coverage without potentially causing their partner to be forced from their home—because the federal Medicaid law only permits married spouses to keep their home without becoming ineligible for benefits.

And when a gay or lesbian person dies, there is no legal document that can extend Social Security survivor benefits or the right to inherit a retirement plan without severe tax burdens that stem from being "unmarried" in the eyes of the law.

These are only a few examples of the critical protections that are granted through more than 1,100 federal laws that protect only married couples. In the absence of the right to marry, same-sex couples can only put in place a handful of the most basic arrangements, such as naming each other in a will or a power of attorney. And even these documents remain vulnerable to challenges in court by disgruntled family members.

"Won't This Cost Taxpayers Too Much Money?"

No, it wouldn't necessarily cost much at all. In fact, treating same-sex couples as families under law could even save taxpayers money because marriage would require them to assume legal responsibility for their joint living expenses and reduce their dependence on public assistance programs, such as Medicaid, Temporary Assistance to Needy Families, Supplemental Security Income disability payments, and food stamps.

Put another way, the money it would cost to extend benefits to same-sex couples could be outweighed by the money that would be saved as these families rely more fully on each other instead of state or federal government assistance.

For example, two studies conducted in 2003 by professors at the University of Massachusetts, Amherst, and the University of California, Los Angeles, found that extending domestic partner benefits to same-sex couples in California and New Jersey would save taxpayers millions of dollars a year.

Specifically, the studies projected that the California state budget would save an estimated $8.1 million to $10.6 million each year by enacting the most comprehensive domestic partner law in the nation. In New Jersey, which passed a new domestic partner law in 2004, the savings were projected to be even higher—more than $61 million each year.

(Sources: "Equal Rights, Fiscal Responsibility: The Impact of A.B. 205 on California's Budget," by M. V. Lee Badgett, Ph.D., IGLSS, Department of Economics, University of Massachusetts, and R. Bradley Sears, J.D., Williams Project, UCLA School of Law, University of California, Los Angeles, May 2003, and "Supporting Families, Saving Funds: A Fiscal Analysis of New Jersey's Domestic Partnership Act," by Badgett and Sears with Suzanne Goldberg, J.D., Rutgers School of Law–Newark, December 2003.)

"Where Can Same-Sex Couples Marry Today?"

In 2001, the Netherlands became the first country to extend marriage rights to same-sex couples. Belgium passed a similar law two years later. The laws in both of these countries, however, have strict citizenship or residency requirements that do not permit American couples to take advantage of the protections provided.

In June 2003, Ontario became the first Canadian province to grant marriage to same-sex couples, and in July 2003, British Columbia followed suit—becoming the first places that American same-sex couples could go to get married.

In November 2003, the Massachusetts Supreme Judicial Court recognized the right of same-sex couples to marry—giving the state six months to begin issuing marriage licenses to same-sex couples. It began issuing licenses May 17, 2004.

In February 2004, the city of San Francisco began issuing marriage licenses to same-sex couples after the mayor declared that the state constitution forbade him to discriminate. The issue is being addressed by California courts, and a number of other cities have either taken or are considering taking steps in the same direction.

Follow the latest developments in California, Oregon, New Jersey, New Mexico, New York and in other communities across the country on the HRC Marriage Center. . . .

Other nations have also taken steps toward extending equal protections to all couples, though the protections they provide are more limited than marriage. Canada, Denmark, Finland, France, Germany, Iceland, Norway, Portugal, and Sweden all have nationwide laws that grant same-sex partners a range of important rights, protections, and obligations.

For example, in France, registered same-sex (and opposite-sex) couples can be joined in a civil "solidarity pact" that grants them the right to file joint tax returns, extend social security coverage to each other and receive the same health, employment and welfare benefits as legal spouses. It also commits the couple to assume responsibility for household debts.

Other countries, including Switzerland, Scotland, and the Czech Republic, also have considered legislation that would legally recognize same-sex unions.

"What Protections Other Than Marriage Are Available to Same-Sex Couples?"

At the federal level, there are no protections at all available to same-sex couples. In fact, a federal law called the "Defense of Marriage Act" says that the federal government will discriminate against same-sex couples who marry by refusing to recognize their marriages or providing them with the federal protections of marriage. Some members of Congress are trying to go even further by attempting to pass a Federal Marriage Amendment that would write discrimination against same-sex couples into the U.S. Constitution.

At the state level, only Vermont offers civil unions, which provide important state benefits but no federal protections, such as Social Security survivor benefits. There is also no guarantee that civil unions will be recognized outside Vermont. Thirty-nine states also have "defense of marriage" laws explicitly prohibiting the recognition of marriages between same-sex partners.

Domestic partner laws have been enacted in California, Connecticut, New Jersey, Hawaii, and the District of Columbia. The benefits conferred by these laws vary; some offer access to family health insurance, others confer co-parenting rights. These benefits are limited to residents of the state. A family that moves out of these states immediately loses the protections.

10 Things You Can Do

Every Family Deserves Equal Protections. How Can I Help?

1. Urge your members of Congress to oppose the Federal Marriage Amendment, or any constitutional amendment to ban marriage for same-sex couples. Make a personal visit if you can. HRC's field team can help you. Or fax a message through HRC's Action Network. . . .
2. Sign the Million for Marriage petition . . . and ask 10 friends and family to do the same.

3. Talk to your friends and family members about the importance of marriage for same-sex couples and their children. Recent polls of the GLBT community show that many people have not yet talked to parents, siblings, or other family members about the discrimination they face. Nothing moves the hearts and minds of potential straight allies more than hearing the stories of someone they know who is gay, lesbian, bisexual, or transgender. For more information, download "Talking about Marriage Equality" from HRC's Online Action Center.

4. Write a letter to the editor of your local newspaper saying why you support marriage for same-sex couples and why a constitutional amendment against it is a bad idea.

5. Next time you hear someone say marriage is only meant for heterosexual couples, speak up. If you hear this on a radio program, call in. If you hear it on television, call or send an e-mail. If it comes up in conversation, set the record straight.

6. Host a house party to educate your friends and family about marriage equality. Invite a diverse group and inspire them to write letters to Congress and your state government at your house party. . . .

7. Meet with clergy and other opinion leaders in your community and ask them to join you in speaking out in support of marriage equality and against the Federal Marriage Amendment. Let HRC know the results. . . .

8. Share your story about why marriage equality matters to you and send it to HRC's family project. . . . Personal stories are what move hearts and minds.

9. Become a member of HRC and support our work on behalf of marriage equality. . . .

10. Register to vote and support fair-minded candidates. . . .

Additional National Resources

Human Rights Campaign . . .

HRC is the nation's largest national organization working to advance equality based on sexual orientation and gender expression and identity to ensure that gay, lesbian, bisexual, and transgender Americans can be open, honest, and safe at home, at work, and in their communities. Of particular interest to people following the marriage issue:

The Human Rights Campaign Foundation's FamilyNet

The FamilyNet Project . . . offers the most comprehensive resources about GLBT families, covering marriage, parenting, aging, and more. HRC's Action Center . . . offers important updates about what's happening in legislatures nationwide and the latest online grassroots advocacy tools.

Other important resources include:

American Civil Liberties Union . . .

ACLU works in courts, legislatures, and communities throughout the country to defend and preserve the individual rights and liberties guaranteed by the Constitution and laws of the United States.

Freedom to Marry Collaborative . . .

A gay and non-gay partnership working to win marriage equality.

Children of Lesbians and Gays Everywhere (COLAGE) . . .

Fosters the growth of daughters and sons of GLBT parents by providing education, support, and community, advocating for their rights and rights of their families.

Dignity USA . . .

Works for respect and justice for all GLBT persons in the Catholic Church and the world through education, advocacy, and support.

Family Pride Coalition . . .

A national education and civil rights organization that advances the well-being of GLBT parents and their families through mutual support, community collaboration, and public understanding.

Federation of Statewide LGBT Advocacy Organizations . . .

The GLBT advocacy network of state/territory organizations committed to working with each other and with national and local groups to strengthen statewide advocacy organizing and secure full civil rights in every U.S. state and territory.

Gay & Lesbian Advocates & Defenders . . .

The GLBT legal organization that successfully brought the case that led to the civil union law in Vermont and the recognition of marriage equality in Massachusetts.

Gay & Lesbian Victory Fund . . .

Committed to increasing the number of openly gay and lesbian public officials at federal, state, and local levels of government.

Lambda Legal . . .

A national legal group committed to achieving full recognition of the civil rights of, and combating the discrimination against, the GLBT community and people with HIV/AIDS through impact litigation, education, and public policy work.

Log Cabin Republicans . . .

Operates within the Republican Party for the equal rights of all Americans, including gay men and women, according to the principles of limited government, individual liberty, individual responsibility, free markets, and a strong national defense.

Marriage Equality USA . . .

Works to secure the freedom and the right of same-sex couples to engage in civil marriage through a program of education, media campaigns, and community partnerships.

National Center for Lesbian Rights . . .

A national legal resource center devoted to advancing the rights and safety of lesbians and their families through a program of litigation, public policy advocacy, free legal advice and counseling and public education.

National Black Justice Coalition . . .

An ad hoc coalition of black GLBT leaders who have come together to fight against discrimination in our communities, to build black support for marriage equality, and to educate the community on the dangers of the proposal to amend the U.S. Constitution to discriminate against GLBT people.

National Gay & Lesbian Task Force . . .

Dedicated to building a national civil rights movement of GLBT people through the empowerment and training of state and local leaders, and research and development of national policy.

National Latina/o Lesbian, Gay, Bisexual & Transgender Organization (LLEGÓ) . . .

Develops solutions to social, health, and political disparities that exist due to discrimination based on ethnicity, sexual orientation, and gender identity affecting the lives and well-being of Latina/o GLBT people and their families.

Parents, Families & Friends of Lesbians & Gays (PFLAG) . . .

Promotes the health and well-being of GLBT people, their families and friends, through support, education, and advocacy with the intention of ending discrimination and securing equal civil rights.

Soulforce . . .

An interfaith movement committed to ending spiritual violence perpetuated by religious policies and teachings against GLBT people through the application of the principles of non-violence.

Universal Fellowship of Metropolitan Community Churches . . .

A worldwide fellowship of Christian churches with a special outreach to the world's GLBT communities.

John Cornyn  **NO**

In Defense of Marriage:
The Amendment That Will
Protect a Fundamental Institution

In 1996, three fourths of the House and Senate joined President Bill Clinton in a strong bipartisan effort to defend the traditional institution of marriage, by enacting the federal Defense of Marriage Act (DOMA). That act defined, as a matter of federal law, the institution of marriage as the union of one man and one woman—reflecting the views of the vast majority of Americans across the country. Today, as it debates a constitutional amendment to defend marriage, the Senate will revisit precisely the same question: Should the institution of marriage continue to be defined as the union of one man and one woman—as it has been defined for thousands of years?

Since the 1996 vote, two things have changed. First, activist courts have so dramatically altered the meaning of the Constitution, that traditional marriage laws are now under serious threat of being invalidated by judicial fiat nationwide—indeed, the process has already begun in numerous states across the country. Second, the broad bipartisan consensus behind marriage that was exhibited in 1996 has begun to fracture. Some who supported DOMA just a few years ago are, for partisan reasons, unwilling to defend marriage today. Although the defense of marriage should continue to be a bipartisan endeavor—and kept out of the hands of activist lawyers and judges—there is no question that both the legal and the political landscapes have changed dramatically in recent years.

Commitment to Marriage

One thing has never changed, however: Throughout our nation's history, across diverse cultures, communities, and political affiliations, Americans of all stripes have remained committed to the traditional institution of marriage. Most Americans strongly and instinctively support the following two fundamental propositions: Every human being is worthy of respect, and the traditional institution of marriage is worthy of protection. In communities across America, adults form caring relationships of all kinds, while children are raised through the heroic efforts of parents of all kinds—including single parents, foster parents, and adoptive parents. We admire, honor, and respect those relationships and those efforts.

At the same time, most Americans believe that children are best raised by their mother and father. Mankind has known no stronger human bond than that between a child and the two adults who have brought that child into the world together. For that reason, family and marriage experts have referred to the traditional institution of marriage as the "gold standard" for raising children. Social science simply confirms common sense. Social science also confirms that, when society stops privileging the traditional institution of marriage (as we have witnessed in a few European nations in recent years), the gold standard is diluted, and the ideal for raising children is threatened.

There are a number of important issues facing our nation—and the raising and nurturing of our next generation is one of them. Nearly 120 years ago, in the case of *Murphy v. Ramsey,* the U.S. Supreme Court unanimously concluded that "no legislation can be supposed more wholesome and necessary in the founding of a free, self-governing commonwealth" than "the idea of the family, as consisting in and springing from *the union for life of one man and one woman in the holy estate of matrimony*" (emphasis added). That union is "the sure foundation of all that is stable and noble in our civilization; the best guaranty of that reverent morality which is the source of all beneficent progress in social and political improvement." Moreover, that same Court unanimously praised efforts to shield the traditional institution of marriage from the winds of political change, by upholding a law "which endeavors to withdraw all political influence from those who are practically hostile to its attainment."

False Arguments

Today, however, the consensus behind marriage appears to be unraveling. Of course, those who no longer support traditional marriage laws do not say so outright. Instead, they resort to legalistic and procedural arguments for opposing a marriage amendment. They hope to confuse the issue in the minds of well-meaning Americans and to distract them from the importance of defending marriage, by unleashing a barrage of false arguments.

For example:

- *Why do we need a federal constitutional amendment, when we already have DOMA?*

The need for a federal constitutional amendment is simple: The traditional institution of marriage is under constitutional attack. It is now a national problem that requires a national solution. Legal experts and constitutional scholars across the political spectrum recognize and predict that the *only way* to preserve the status quo—the *only way* to preserve the traditional institution of marriage—is a constitutional amendment.

Immediately after the U.S. Supreme Court announced its decision in *Lawrence* v. *Texas* in June 2003, legal experts and commentators predicted that, under *Lawrence*, courts would begin to strike down traditional marriage laws around the country.

In *Lawrence*, the Court explicitly and unequivocally listed "marriage" as one of the "constitutional" rights that, absent a constitutional amendment, must be granted to same-sex couples and opposite-sex couples alike. Specifically, the Court stated that "our laws and tradition afford constitutional protection to personal decisions relating to *marriage*, procreation, contraception, family relationships, child rearing, and education. . . . Persons in a homosexual relationship may seek autonomy for these purposes, just as heterosexual persons do" (emphasis added). The *Lawrence* majority thus adopted the view endorsed decades ago by one of its members—Justice Ruth Bader Ginsburg. While serving as general counsel of the American Civil Liberties Union, she wrote that traditional marriage laws, such as anti-bigamy laws, are unconstitutional and must be struck down by courts.

It does not take a Supreme Court expert to understand the meaning of these words. And Supreme Court experts agree in any event. Legal scholars are a notoriously argumentative bunch. So it is particularly remarkable that the nation's most recognized constitutional experts—including several liberal legal scholars, like Laurence Tribe, Cass Sunstein, Erwin Chemerinsky, and William Eskridge—are in remarkable harmony on this issue. They predict that, like it or not, DOMA or other traditional marriage laws across the country will be struck down as unconstitutional by courts across the country.

Indeed, the process of invalidating and eradicating traditional marriage laws nationwide has already begun. Most notably, four justices of the Massachusetts Supreme Judicial Court invalidated that state's marriage law in its *Goodridge* decision issued last November, which it reaffirmed in February.

Those decisions were breathtaking, not just in their ultimate conclusion, but in their rhetoric as well. The court concluded that the "deep-seated religious, moral, and ethical convictions" that underlie traditional marriage are "no rational reason" for the institution's continued existence. It argued that traditional marriage is a "stain" on our laws that must be "eradicated." It contended that traditional marriage is "rooted in persistent prejudices" and "invidious discrimination," rather than in the best interest of children. Amazingly, it even suggested abolishing the institution of marriage outright, stating that "if the Legislature were to jettison the term 'marriage' altogether, it might well be rational and permissible." And for good measure, the court went out of its way to characterize DOMA itself as unconstitutionally discriminatory.

Without a federal constitutional amendment, activist courts, and judges will only continue striking down traditional marriage laws across the country—including DOMA itself. Lawsuits challenging traditional marriage laws are now pending in courtrooms across America—including four lawsuits in federal court.

In 2000, Nebraska voters ratified a state constitutional amendment protecting marriage in that state. Yet that state constitutional amendment has been challenged in federal district court as violating federal constitutional law. As Nebraska's attorney general, Jon Bruning, testified last March, the state expects the federal district judge to strike down its constitutional amendment. A federal lawsuit has also been filed in Florida to strike down DOMA as unconstitutional under *Lawrence*. Lawyers are similarly claiming that DOMA is unconstitutional in a pending federal bankruptcy case in Washington state. And in Utah, lawyers have filed suit arguing that traditional marriage laws, such as that state's anti-polygamy law, must be struck down under *Lawrence*. And that just covers lawsuits in federal court—in addition, dozens of suits have been filed in state courts around the country.

A representative of the Lambda Legal organization—a champion of the ongoing nationwide litigation campaign to abolish traditional marriage laws across the country—recently stated: "We won't stop until we have [same-sex] marriage nationwide." This nationwide litigation campaign also enjoys the tacit, if not explicit, support of leading Democrats—including Sens. John Kerry and Ted Kennedy, Rep. Jerrold Nadler, and former presidential candidates Howard Dean and Carol Moseley Braun. All of them have attacked DOMA as unconstitutional, and thus presumably *want* DOMA to be invalidated by the courts—and without a constitutional amendment, their wishes may very well come true. The only way to stop the lawsuits, and to ensure the protection of marriage, is a constitutional amendment.

- *Why do we need an amendment now?*

Last September, the Senate subcommittee on the Constitution, Civil Rights and Property Rights examined the threat posed to the traditional institution of marriage by the *Lawrence* decision.

Detractors of the hearing scoffed that the threat was a pure fabrication, motivated by partisan politics. But then, just two months later, the Massachusetts *Goodridge* decision, relying specifically on *Lawrence,* struck down that state's traditional marriage law—precisely as predicted at the hearing.

Detractors then scoffed that the *Goodridge* decision would not stick. They argued that the state's own constitutional amendment process would be sufficient to control their courts. But then, the Massachusetts court reaffirmed its decision in February. The court even refused to bend after the Massachusetts legislature formally approved a state constitutional amendment—an amendment that can only take effect, if ever, no earlier than 2006.

Detractors then scoffed that DOMA had not been challenged, so there was no reason to take constitutional action at the federal level. But then, lawyers began to challenge DOMA. Cases are now pending in federal courts in Florida and Washington. Additional challenges are, of course, inevitable.

The truth is that, for these detractors, there will never be a good time to protect the traditional institution of marriage—because they don't want to protect the traditional institution of marriage. The constitutional amendment to protect marriage is not a "preemptive strike" on the Constitution, as detractors allege—it's a precautionary solution. Parents take responsible precautions to protect their children. Spouses take responsible precautions to protect their marriage. Likewise, government has the responsibility to take precautions to protect the institution of marriage.

- *Why can't the states handle this? After all, isn't marriage traditionally a state issue?*

This argument borders on the fraudulent. There is nothing that a state can do to fully protect itself against federal courts hostile to its laws except a federal constitutional amendment. Nebraska has already done everything it can, on its own, to defend marriage—up to and including a state constitutional amendment. Yet its amendment has already been challenged in federal court, where it is expected to be struck down. As state and local officials across the country have repeatedly urged, when it comes to defending marriage, the real threat to states' rights is judicial activism—not Congress, and certainly not the democratic process.

Moreover, the Constitution cannot be amended without the consent of three-fourths of the state legislatures. States can protect marriage against judicial activism—but only if Congress provides them the opportunity to consider a federal constitutional amendment protecting marriage.

- *Isn't our Constitution too sacred for such a political issue as defending marriage?*

No one is suggesting that the Constitution should be amended lightly. But the defense of marriage should not be ridiculed as a political issue. Nor should we disparage the most democratic process established under our Constitution by our Founding Fathers.

Our Founding Fathers specifically insisted on including an amendment process in the Constitution because they humbly believed that no man-made document could ever be perfect. The constitutional amendment process was deliberatively considered and wisely crafted, and we have no reason to fear it.

We have amended the Constitution no fewer than 27 times—most recently in 1992 to regulate Congressional pay increases. The sky will not fall if Americans exercise their democratic rights to amend it again. Surely, the protection of marriage is at least as important to our nation as the regulation of Congressional pay, the specific manner in which we coin our money, or the countless other matters that can be found in our nation's charter.

Moreover, there is a robust tradition of constitutional amendments to reverse constitutional decisions by the courts with which the American people disagree—including the 11th, 14th, 16th, 19th, 24th, and 26th Amendments.

Opponents of the marriage amendment apparently have no objection to the courts amending the Constitution. Yet the power to amend the Constitution belongs to the American people, through the democratic process—not the courts. The courts alter the Constitution—under the guise of interpretation— far more often than the people have. Because of *Lawrence,* it is inevitable that the Constitution will be amended on the issue of marriage—the only question is how, and by whom. Legal scholars across the political spectrum agree that a constitutional amendment by the people is the only way to fully protect marriage against the courts.

- *Why would we ever want to write discrimination into the Constitution? Why would we ever want to roll back the Bill of Rights?*

This argument is offensive, pernicious—and revealing.

Marriage is not about discrimination—it is about children. It is offensive to characterize the vast majorities of Americans who support traditional marriage—individuals like Reverend Ray Hammond of the Bethel African Methodist Episcopal Church in Boston, Reverend Richard Richardson of the St. Paul African Methodist Episcopal Church in Boston, and Pastor Daniel de Leon, Sr., of Alianza de Ministerios Evangélicos Nacionales (AMEN) and Templo Calvario in Santa Ana, California—as bigots. It is offensive to characterize the laws, precedents, and customs of all fifty states as discriminatory. And it is offensive to slander the 85 senators who voted for DOMA as hateful.

Moreover, it is *precisely because* some activists believe that traditional marriage is about discrimination, and not about children, that they believe that all traditional marriage laws are unconstitutional and therefore must be abolished by the courts. These activists leave the American people with no middle ground. They accuse others of writing discrimination into the Constitution—yet they are the ones writing the American people out of our constitutional democracy.

Just last week, representatives of Sens. John Kerry and John Edwards said that the marriage amendment would "roll back rights." If you believe that traditional marriage is only about discrimination and about violating the rights of adults—as Sens. Kerry and Edwards apparently believe—then you have no choice but to oppose all traditional marriage laws. Any other position is incoherent at best—and deceptive at worst.

Marriage Protection

So the issue has been joined—precisely as it was in 1996. Despite typical Washington Beltway tricks to overcomplicate and confuse matters, the question remains a simple one: Should marriage, defined as the union of one man and one woman, be protected against judicial activism and the will of legal and political elites? If you believe that the answer is yes—as vast majorities of Americans do—then you have no legal option but to support a federal constitutional amendment protecting marriage.

The American people believe that every human being deserves respect, and the traditional institution of marriage deserves protection. As members of Congress continue to debate this issue, we should also remember what else the American people deserve: honesty. . . .

EXPLORING THE ISSUE

Should Same-Sex Marriage Be Legal?

Challenge Questions

1. What is the difference between a civil right, a legal right, and a human right?
2. In society, beyond the same-sex couple, who would benefit from making same-sex marriage legal?
3. How do status variables such as race, class, and ability status affect the debate regarding same-sex marriage? Do you think the issues are the same across these status variables?
4. There is great concern about the impact of parents' sexual orientation on their children (see Issue 5). Would the marital status of same-sex couples, legal or not, affect children?
5. How does the debate over same-sex marriage tie in with the fact that an increasing large number of people think the institution of marriage is obsolete? What is the possibility that same-sex marriage could "save" the institution of marriage?

Is There Common Ground?

Part of this discussion is whether marriage is a civil right, an inherent right, or a moral right. Those supporting marriage rights for lesbian and gay couples cite the struggles of the civil rights movement of the 1960s in their current quest for equality for all couples. Among the points they make is that up until 1967, it was still illegal in some states for people of different races to marry. Many opponents find the idea of comparing same-sex marriage to the civil rights struggles of the 1960s and earlier offensive; they say it is like comparing apples and oranges. Many of these individuals believe that sexual orientation is chosen, rather than an inherent part of whom one is—unlike race, which is predetermined. Most sexuality experts, however, agree that although we do not know for sure what "causes" a person to be heterosexual, bisexual, or homosexual, it is clear that it is determined very early in life, perhaps even before we are born. Regardless, is marriage a civil right? A legal right? An inherent right? It has also been argued that if sexual orientation is not "normal," then same-sex couples would not have "healthy" relationships. However, there is no evidence that would support such a claim. In fact, some studies would suggest that some aspects of same-sex relationships are in fact healthier than heterosexual relationships. At least two factors may contribute to this. First, neither person in a same-sex couple is constrained by gender role expectations; that is, each person has more latitude to be himself or herself rather than the "bread-winner" or "homemaker." Second, because there are few role models for same-sex couples, they may actually spend more time negotiating aspects of their relationships in ways that heterosexual couples do not. Currently, no heterosexual has to pass a "mental health test" in order to marry. Additionally, heterosexual couples do not have to demonstrate a "healthy" relationship in order to either marry or remain married. Is it possible that heterosexual couples could learn something from same-sex couples?

Additional Resources

George Chauncey, *Why Marriage? The History Shaping Today's Debate over Gay Equality* (New York: Basic Books, 2004).

How Same-Sex Marriage Threatens Liberty. http://www.wnd.com/news/article.asp?ARTICLE_ID=38195#ixzz1XCGCeRFv

Jonathan Rauch, *Gay Marriage: Why It Is Good for Gays, Good for Straights, and Good for America* (Toronto: Owl Books, 2004).

http://law-library.rutgers.edu/SSM.html

http://www.gallup.com/poll/147662/First-Time-Majority-Americans-Favor-Legal-Gay-Marriage.aspx

ISSUE 5

Does Parents' Sexual Orientation Affect Their Children's Psychological Outcomes?

YES: **Walter R. Schumm**, from "Children of Homosexuals More Apt to Be Homosexuals? A Reply to Morrison and to Cameron Based on an Examination of Multiple Sources of Data," *Journal of Biosocial Sciences* (vol. 42, pp. 721–742, 2010)

NO: **Paige Averett, Blace Nalavany, and Scott Ryan**, from "An Evaluation of Gay/Lesbian and Heterosexual Adoption," *Adoption Quarterly* (vol. 12, pp. 129–151, 2009)

Learning Outcomes

As you read the issue, focus on the following points:

- What constitutes "good" parenting?
- What are the best indicators of one being an effective parent? Does a child's sexual orientation constitute a problem that should be studied?
- Why do some children seem to thrive in the presence of "bad" parenting, whereas those with "good" parents still have problems?
- How should the effects of parents' sexual orientation be studied? Should only same-sex and heterosexual parents who adopt be studied? If so, how might what we know about parenting of one's biological children in couples who do or do not marry affect the discussion of quality of parenting?

ISSUE SUMMARY

YES: Walter R. Schumm examined data from several sources and concluded that there is evidence for the intergenerational transfer of sexual orientation, especially for female parents or female children, but the pathways for such an effect are not well understood.

NO: Paige Averett, Blace Nalavany, and Scott Ryan found evidence that the sexual orientation of adoptive parents had no relation to the likelihood that their children would have behavioral problems. They studied internalizing and externalizing problems, and did not consider the sexual orientation of the child a problem.

Currently, there are thousands of children awaiting adoption. In many cases, there are strict requirements as to who can and cannot adopt. In one country, for example, a heterosexual couple must be married for at least 4 years—and if they already have one child, they can adopt a child only of a different sex. Most countries do not allow same-sex couples or openly lesbian or gay individuals to adopt children. In the United States, same-sex couples can adopt in a number of ways. Some state laws support same-sex couples' right to adopt children, and some do not. In New Jersey, California, Connecticut, and Massachusetts, for example, joint or second parent adoption is currently available. In Utah, married heterosexual couples are given priority for foster or adoptive children, and in Mississippi, there is a law that outright bans a same-sex couple from being able to adopt children.

When gays and lesbians do adopt, some will adopt as single parents, even though they are in a long-term, committed relationship with another person, because the state or agency does not permit same-sex couples to adopt together. Others will do what is called "second parent" adoption—where one partner is the biological parent of the child, and the other can become the other legal parent by going through the court system. In other cases, the biological parent must terminate her or his own rights so that there can be a "joint adoption." Both parents jointly adopt the child and become equal, legal parents. This applies to unmarried different-sex couples, too.

There is a range of feelings about who should or should not parent children. The American Psychological Association's 2004 Policy Statement on Sexual Orientation, Parents, and Children concludes that there is no empirical evidence to support the claim that children raised by same-sex parents are harmed psychologically and that all children benefit from legal ties to both parents. Others assert that gay men are sexually promiscuous, and are therefore poor role models and parents for children. Likewise, these same people claim that lesbians are ineffective parents because they are raising a child without the presence and influence of a father figure, which some theorists argue is vital to the psychosocial development of children, male and female. Some individuals feel that children should be raised by a man and a woman, who are married, not by a gay or lesbian, individual or couple. They begin with the premise that homosexuality is wrong; thus, they feel that such a relationship is an inappropriate context in which to raise children. For some of these opponents of lesbian and gay parenting, homosexuality is defined by sexual behaviors. Opponents believe that children would be harmed if they grew up in gay or lesbian families, in part because they would grow up without a mother figure if raised by gay men or without a father figure if raised by lesbians. Additionally, because they fear that sexual orientation and behaviors can be learned, they also fear that children raised by a lesbian or gay couple will be more likely to come out as lesbian or gay. Other people do not believe that a person's sexual orientation determines the ability to parent. Whether a person is raised by one parent, two men, two women, or a man and a woman is less important than any individual's or couple's ability to love, support, and care for a child. They oppose the concept that a heterosexual couple in which there is abuse or where there are inappropriate sexual boundaries would be considered preferable to a lesbian or gay couple in a long-term, committed relationship who care for each other and their children. They point to the fact that most lesbian, gay, and bisexual adults were raised by heterosexual parents. Therefore, they believe, being raised by a lesbian or gay couple will not create lesbian, gay, or bisexual children, any more than being raised by a heterosexual, married couple would guarantee heterosexuality.

As you think about the issue of sexual orientation and parenting, consider the challenges of doing research. It is highly likely that there can be confounds due to shared genetic make-up when the child has a biological parent, and this fact may affect attitudes and beliefs about the child ("she's just like her mother"). Most heterosexual couples raise their own biological children. This can affect the parents' attitudes toward their children in ways that might not happen with adoptive parents, which most same couples are more likely to be. Some lesbian couples conceive by artificial insemination so that the child is the biological offspring of one of the partners. Or consider the case of Sir Elton John and his partner David Furnish. They both contributed sperm to a surrogate mother, so their child is the biological offspring of one of them but, at least for the time being, they do not know which one. Due to all the possible complications and confounds associated with comparing same-sex and heterosexual parents when at least one of the parents is genetically related to the child, many researchers turn to the study of only adoptive parents. How do you think limiting the scope of study to just this group of parents affects what we hope to learn about the parenting of same-sex couples?

As you read this issue, think about what you think the characteristics of a good parent are. Can these characteristics be found only in heterosexual relationships, or can they be fulfilled by a same-sex relationship? Does the gender of a same-sex relationship affect your feelings on the subject? For example, do you find two women raising a child more or less threatening than two men?

YES

Walter R. Schumm

Children of Homosexuals More Apt to Be Homosexuals? A Reply to Morrison and to Cameron Based on an Examination of Multiple Sources of Data

Introduction

Cameron presented data from three sources of popular literature concerning the important question of the extent to which children of gay or lesbian parents would tend to adopt a homosexual orientation or preference themselves. In spite of Cameron's evidence, . . . the question remains controversial. . . .

Cameron [has been] criticized for not including other books that concerned the children of gay or lesbian parents. . . . While analysis of . . . other popular sources may not improve generalizeability, it may allow a more thorough test of the hypothesis of intergenerational transfer of sexual orientation. . . . I . . . argue that we can do better than merely reviewing 'books on gay parents' and finding 'that some of the adult children interviewed were non-heterosexual'; it is possible to evaluate the matter statistically. The authors of these . . . books have done important data collection for the entire scientific community. While their samples may not be random, they may be no worse than the convenience and snowball samples used in much of previous research with gay and lesbian parents; certainly, their combined dataset is far larger than many of the early studies on gay and lesbian parenting. . . .

Clearly, the question of the impact of a parent's sexual orientation is important. Just as clearly, at least some of the authors of [ten] popular narratives on the lives of the children of gay and lesbian parents have dismissed any notion that the null hypothesis had ever been, or ever would be, rejected scientifically. [S]ocialization is assumed to have nothing at all to do with one's sexual orientation. . . . Thus, it is of particular interest what these authors'own narratives might tell us, if examined systematically and evaluated statistically, because many of the authors and their participants reject any notion that parental sexual orientation could have any influence on a child's sexual orientation.

From *Journal of Biosocial Sciences*, vol. 42, 2010, pp. 721–742. Copyright © 2010 by Cambridge University Press. Reprinted by permission.

Social Science Claims: A Few Examples

. . . An idea commonly reported by social scientists is that intergenerational transfer of sexual orientation does not occur. Gottman concluded from her own research that there was 'no evidence to suggest that daughters of lesbian mothers became homosexual themselves' and from her review of literature that parental sexual orientation did not influence children's sexual orientation directly or indirectly. As part of his discussion of the myth that being exposed to a homosexual parent might have adverse effects on a child, Herek indicated that, 'Researchers similarly have not observed differences between children from gay and heterosexual households in development of sexual orientation,' and that 'nor does [having a gay male or lesbian role model] influence the sexual orientation eventually adopted by a child.' Likewise, Falk stated that, 'The second assumption with respect to gender or sexual development, and perhaps the most uniformly cited assumption, is that the child will be more likely to become homosexual than a child raised by heterosexual parents.' She noted a court decision in which it was argued that 'there is substantial consensus among experts that being raised by a homosexual parent does not increase the likelihood that a child will become homosexual.' Patterson (1995, p. 265) stated that, 'Research to date gives no evidence to support the view that having non-heterosexual parents predisposes a child to become lesbian or gay'; later she echoed the same claim, 'There is no reason to believe that the offspring of lesbian or gay parents are any more likely than those of heterosexual parents to become lesbian or gay themselves.' . . . It is clear that the standard 'scientific' answer for the past twenty years is little or no intergenerational transfer of sexual orientation.

Legal Implications

[It has been] observed that courts often denied parents custody of children because of a belief that, 'Their children are more likely to become gay or lesbian themselves' . . . [and] that all restrictions on gays and lesbians in the courts were based entirely on prejudice because social science research was 'remarkable' in, among other things, showing no indication that the 'children of lesbian and gay parents . . . were likely to become gay or lesbian themselves.' In other words, the public, the courts, and the legislatures were wrong, biased and prejudiced, refusing to recognize what social science had allegedly proven.

Recent Questioning of Social Science Claims

In spite of the apparent consensus among the authors of [the ten] books and among many scholars, some scholars, as early as 1995, began to question the null hypothesis regarding intergenerational transfer of sexual orientation. . . .

[Some have] argued that sociological and psychological theory would predict at least some influence of parental sexual orientation on the sexual orientation of children. . . .

[Although] empirical data on the association between parental and child sexual orientation [are] 'limited,' [a recent review] found evidence across several studies that children (particularly girls) raised by lesbigay parents were 'somewhat more likely to experience homoerotic attraction and homosexual relationship.' . . .

Thus, it appears that the scientific consensus against intergenerational transfer of sexual orientation may have begun to evolve, at least slightly, from 'myth' with no evidence (1991–1996) to theoretically plausible but little evidence (1995–2001) to some, ambiguous evidence (2004) to limited but irrelevant evidence (2006–2008).

Hypotheses

Hypothesis One

While Cameron argued in favour of the intergenerational transfer of sexual orientation, he offered no statistical evidence to support his argument. Morrison was right to question Cameron's argument, especially since that argument was not supported with statistical evaluations. If it is assumed, rather generously, that 10% of the children of heterosexual parents might become gay or lesbian in their sexual orientation, the results found in the ten books can be compared statistically with an equivalent size artificial sample of heterosexuals, using a chi-squared test and odds ratios for comparison purposes.

Hypothesis Two

A reviewer of an earlier draft of this report suggested that the data be analysed at the family level in addition to the individual level. Here the hypothesis was keyed to gender of child and of parent: within families, would female children or mothers be more likely to have higher rates of intergenerational transfer of sexual orientation for at least one child? If gay or lesbian parents had a male and a female child, would daughters be more likely to model their sexual orientation after their lesbian mother and sons after their gay father?

Methods

Sample

Ten books that concerned the children of gay, lesbian or transsexual parents were reviewed, including the three books previously analysed by Cameron and the two recommended by Morrison. Each of the 277 children discussed in the ten books was assessed by name, gender, age and sexual orientation of parent(s). However, on a reviewer's recommendation, no transgender parents or children ($N = 15$) were included in the following analyses, leaving $N = 262$. Evidence for each child's sexual orientation was identified by quotations in most cases; in a few cases by the narrative, as indicated by specific pages in each book. When no mention was made regarding a child's sexual orientation, it was coded as heterosexual ($N = 122$ cases), in order to minimize the risk of overestimating the percentage of gay or lesbian children. . . . Sexual orientation was coded as heterosexual, homosexual, bisexual and unsure with the latter three categories being collapsed to form a heterosexual versus non-heterosexual contrast. . . . Likewise, all children of unstated sexual orientation were coded as heterosexual regardless of age, even though none of the children under seven years of age ($N = 34$) reported anything other than a heterosexual (or unstated) sexual orientation. . . .

In addition, for comparison purposes, a simulated database of 280 heterosexual parents, divided evenly between mothers and fathers with male and female children, was created with 10% homosexual children. . . . Assuming that 10% of the children of heterosexuals would develop non-heterosexual identity, attraction or behaviour is generous in the direction suitable for disproving the hypothesis; it could easily be argued that assuming 5% non-heterosexual preference or less would have been quite adequate for testing the hypothesis.

To evaluate the second hypothesis, a second database was created using family-level data from the same ten books. In addition to the sexual orientation of the parents, families were coded in terms of the reported number of sons and daughters in each family and whether the family included gay sons or lesbian daughters. Data were also coded in terms of whether or not all children were over 15 years of age, based on research that indicates that many children only become aware of a GLBT sexual orientation at puberty, if not later in life. . . .

Results

Descriptive Results

Data were coded for 262 children of gay fathers or lesbian mothers. Of those 262 children, 63 were coded as non-heterosexual (homosexual, 22; bisexual, 26; unsure of sexual orientation, 15). Of the 262 children, 140 (53.4%) included relatively clear evidence of their sexual orientation; all of the unclear assignments were coded as heterosexual, though it is quite likely that some of them were not heterosexuals. One hundred and five daughters and 63 sons had lesbian mothers; 38 daughters and 39 sons had gay fathers; and 8 daughters and 9 sons had both a gay father and a lesbian mother.

The average age of the children of the gay and lesbian parents was 18.8 years (SD = 10.5 years) with a median age of 19 years (eight cases had missing data on age). Male children were slightly older (mean = 19.7 years, SD = 12.0 years) than female children (mean = 18.1 years, SD = 9.3 years) but the difference was not statistically significant by an independent samples t-test. . . . The difference in age by child's sexual orientation was significant . . . : heterosexuals (mean = 17.3, SD = 10.5), homosexuals (mean = 27.3, SD = 8.8), bisexuals (mean = 23.9, SD = 6.2) and unsure (mean = 15.9, SD = 11.1). The differences in ages for heterosexuals versus homosexuals and bisexuals were significant . . . , as was the difference between homosexuals and those unsure. The unsure were significantly different . . . from bisexuals. . . .

Hypothesis One

When comparing all children, those children who had both a gay father and a lesbian mother were included. There were eighteen children who had mutually homosexual parents, of whom four (22.2%) were not heterosexual. The difference in percentages of non-heterosexual children was not significant across homosexual parent gender (lesbian mother, 26.9%, 46/171; gay father, 19.3%, 16/83). When comparing children on the basis of each parental gender, the children of mutually homosexual parents were omitted from the analyses. . . .

As a check on the robustness of the data, an error rate of $N = 20$ was assumed in classifying children incorrectly, but the resulting odds ratio of 1.77 (16.4%, 43/262) remained significant statistically ($p < 0.03$) (compared to 10%, 28/280; with parental sexual orientation predicting child's sexual orientation. Using only the best data, a higher odds ratio of 3.99 ($p < 0.001$) (30.7%, 43/140) was obtained.

Hypothesis Two

The objective of the second hypothesis was to examine, at the family level rather than the individual level of the child, indications of non-heterosexuality as a function of parental gender, child gender and the interaction of parental and child gender. Controls were used for age of child (age 16 or older) and clarity (specified/not specified) of evidence regarding children's sexual orientation. . . .

Gender of Parent

When data were collapsed into 218 families, 31.9% (43/135) of the families of lesbian mothers, 19.4% (12/62) of the families of gay fathers, and 25.0% (3/12) of the families of both a gay father and a lesbian mother indicated a non-heterosexual child. When the evidence was clear for children's sexual orientation, 57.3% (43/75) of the families of lesbian mothers and 34.3% (12/35) of the families of gay fathers included a non-heterosexual child. When the analyses were restricted to children older than 15 years of age, 46.7% (35/75) of the families of lesbian mothers and 22.4% (11/49) of the families of gay fathers included a non-heterosexual child. When the analyses were restricted to both older age and clear evidence, 58.3% (35/60) of the families of lesbian mothers and 33.3% (11/33) of the families of gay fathers included a non-heterosexual child. In all of the previous analyses, families of lesbian mothers were more likely to include a non-heterosexual child than were families of gay fathers.

Gender of Child

When families with only all male or all female children were examined, 29.0% (27/93) of the only female children families and 11.3% (8/71) of the only male children families included a non-heterosexual child. Corresponding percentages for families restricted to children over age 15 were 38.3% (23/60) and 15.9% (7/44); for families restricted to children with unequivocal evidence of sexual orientation, 55.1% (27/49) and 21.6% (8/37); with both restrictions applied, 57.5% (23/40) and 21.2% (7/33). In all cases, families with only female children were significantly more likely to include a non-heterosexual child than were families with only male children.

Gender of Parent and of Child

Limiting the analyses to families with only female or only male children reduced the sample size and statistical power considerably; therefore, significance levels obtained from one-sided Fisher's Exact tests are reported hereafter and results for $p < 0.10$ are also reported. Twenty-eight per cent (7/25) of the daughters from families of gay fathers were non-heterosexual compared with none (0/22) of the sons from families of gay fathers ($p < 0.01$). For families of lesbian mothers, the corresponding percentages were 30.5% (18/59) and 17.1% (7/41) ($p < 0.10$). When only clear evidence was used, 53.8% (7/13) of the daughters of gay fathers compared with none (0/11) of the sons of gay fathers were non-heterosexual ($p < 0.01$); the corresponding percentages for lesbian families were 60.0% (18/30) and 36.8% (7/19) ($p < 0.10$). When only data from children over age 15 were used, the corresponding percentages were 31.8% (7/22), 45.2% (14/3l) and 30.0% (6/20) ($p < 0.02$, for gay father families only). Applying both restrictions yielded percentages of 58.3% (7/12), 60.9% (14/23) and 40.0% (6/15) ($p < 0.005$, gay father families only). Although families with daughters were consistently more likely to have a non-heterosexual child, the gender differences were only significant statistically for families with a gay father.

Gender-Mixed Families

When there was exactly one male and one female child in a family and no more than one child was non-heterosexual ($n = 30$, 9 gay fathers, 21 lesbian mothers), 33.3% of both types of families (gay father, lesbian mother) had one non-heterosexual child; notably, all of the non-heterosexual children were of the same gender as their non-heterosexual parent, an unlikely outcome. The percentage rate of non-heterosexuality in those 30 families was significantly higher than expected had they been compared with 30 heterosexual families with a 10% rate of non-heterosexual children. Two other lesbian-led families with one son and one daughter featured both children being non-heterosexual. Aside from the gender-mixed families with two children, there was one family that included two boys and two girls of a lesbian mother, with one son being gay. Therefore, of the 24 lesbian mother families with equal numbers of children, 41.7% (10/24) included at least one non-heterosexual child and 8.3% (2/24) included two non-heterosexual children.

A reviewer suggested analysing the data for only those children age 25 years or older, assuming that sexual orientation would be more certain by then, and only for children based on their 'final' orientation (i.e. if they had been LGB but were now heterosexual). . . . The strongest influence occurred for daughters of lesbians (15/31, 48.4%, $p < 0.002$). Eliminating the heterosexual cases that had merely been assumed to be heterosexual yielded stronger results, 44.9% non-heterosexual ($p < 0.001$) for all 69 children, 55.6% for daughters of both gay fathers (5/9, $p < 0.01$) and lesbians (15/27, $p < 0.001$)

[handwritten marginalia: "° Are all these children adopted?"]

and 33.3% (11/33, $p < 0.01$) for sons of gay fathers and lesbian mothers combined.

Examining the children from gay father families in more detail, there were 22 families with one daughter (seven were non-heterosexual), 3 with two daughters, 16 with one son, 3 with one son and two daughters (one lesbian daughter), 9 with one son and one daughter (3 gay sons), 5 with two sons, 3 with two sons and one daughter (one gay son), and one family with three sons. The only gay father families with gay sons were families that included both sons and daughters.

Discussion

The consensus among the authors of the ten books and among most scholars was remarkable as to the lack of any expected relationship between parental and offspring sexual orientation. . . . Results here differed from that previous scholarly consensus.

A total of eighteen statistical tests were performed in the analysis of hypothesis one. Only five of those tests were not significant. All of the results for the 'clear evidence' subgroup, despite its smaller sample size and lower statistical power, were significant. All of the odds ratios exceeded 1.66, regardless of their statistical significance. Odds ratios were greatest for daughters, lesbian mothers and the daughters of lesbian mothers. . . .

When the data from the ten books were re-analysed at the family level, percentages of families with non-heterosexual children remained higher for families with daughters and for families led by lesbian mothers, generally confirming the results obtained from the individual-level analyses. . . .

There appeared to be a tendency for children of the same gender rather than for children of the opposite gender as their gay or lesbian parent to adopt that parent's sexual orientation. Female gender, of either parent or child, appeared to be associated with higher rates of non-heterosexual sexual orientation. Rates of intergenerational transfer appeared to be lower for gay fathers or sons of gay parents than for combinations of families with a female parent or female child.

If there is nothing morally deficient with homosexual behaviour, then the reproduction of homosexual attraction, behaviour or identity should not be a problem. . . .

Other Research Perspectives

Since it has been argued recently that science has proven that sexual orientation is not subject to the influence of *any* social factors, other research perspectives might be useful in corroborating a hypothesis that societal or family social factors might influence sexual orientation. After all, many types of bias could be involved in the selection and analysis of ten popular books on gay and lesbian parenting. It could be argued that between the bias of the books' authors and bias in the interpretation and analysis of the books, little of merit might remain. Is there any other evidence to support the outcomes of the analysis of these ten books? In other words, how would the results presented here fit within the *larger context* of other types of research, including ethnographic research or meta-analysis of research on lesbigay parenting?

Ethnographic Evidence

If sexual orientation is entirely genetic in origin, then there should be little effect of societal factors on sexual orientation. Likewise, if one assumes that the family is a microcosm of society, it would be logical to argue that if society can influence the expression of homosexual orientation, it should be possible for parents/families to do so. [E]thnographic data [have been reported] in which cultures [were classified] in terms of whether homosexuality was rare or not rare and in terms of whether it was culturally accepted or not accepted. . . . [I]t appears that a majority of cultures listed did not approve of homosexuality (28/37, 76%). Furthermore, of those cultures that accepted homosexuality, 89% (8/9) featured higher rates of homosexual behaviour compared to 44% (11/25) of cultures that did not approve of homosexuality. . . . Therefore, it appears reasonable to conclude that sociological factors, such as general societal acceptance, could be associated with rates of expression of homosexual behaviour and that therefore it is plausible that such effects might also operate at the family level. Such findings do not rule out genetic effects—rather they merely contradict the null hypothesis that social variables have *nothing* to do with expression of sexual orientation. . . .

Research on Pathways

. . . [W]hile further research on the pathways involved in the intergenerational transfer of sexual orientation is much needed, at least five pathways seem possible: parental modelling of sexual orientation, parental preference for child's sexual orientation, child's greater questioning of their sexual orientation, parental desire for grandchildren, and non-parental adult modelling of sexual orientation.

Conclusion

In the foreword to Bigner (2006), Doherty observed that researchers must not be afraid to publish research that could be used or misused by political opponents, noting that, 'If those of us who value GLBT families are not willing to ask difficult questions and follow the evidence where it leads us, you can be sure that others will do so . . .' (p. xxii). He warns against GLBT family researchers censoring credible research, even if it might not fit preconceived notions.

Here, the evidence appears to support Cameron's (hypothesis regarding the intergenerational transfer of sexual orientation, from a number of different directions, using narrative data, ethnographic data, and data from over two dozen previous studies on gay and lesbian parenting. Not only were these results statistically significant but the percentages and odds ratios indicated substantive or clinical significance. It was surprising that Cameron's estimate of 35–47% of children of a homosexual parent becoming homosexual themselves was not as outrageous as some might have thought, given the percentages presented here, which ranged as high as 61% when data were restricted to lesbian mothers' older daughters whose sexual orientations had been clearly discussed or reported. Results from the 26 previous studies on gay and lesbian parenting confirmed higher rates for gay and lesbian parents but at lower percentages (14–31%) than observed in the ten narrative sources. The higher rates of transfer observed for daughters of mothers may corroborate research in which daughters of lesbian mothers were more likely than their sons to adopt more of a same-sex sexual orientation even before the age of 13.

Further research is needed to assess the mechanisms by which parental sexual orientation may be influencing child sexual orientation. Parental preference and modelling may play an important role, among many other possible factors. Another area of research is whether the apparent gender-linkage of transfer of sexual orientation is related to genetic or to social influences. Are women more responsive to social factors? Are genetic influences tied to (female) gender? Either possibility might account for the apparently larger intergenerational transfer observed for mothers and for daughters than was observed for fathers and for sons. This study cannot determine the relative likelihood of either possibility. . . .

Clearly, the intergenerational transfer of sexual orientation is an idea that, in the past, has been vigorously opposed, even ridiculed. However, it appears that as our scientific theory and research have improved and continue to evolve, research in this area may be moving into Schopenhauer's third phase.

*It can be passed down.
⌐Nature & nurture   but doesn't mean it will always happen

Paige Averett, Blace Nalavany,
and Scott Ryan

 **NO**

An Evaluation of Gay/Lesbian
and Heterosexual Adoption

Introduction

As of 2007, there were approximately 130,000 children in the child welfare system waiting to be adopted. Yet congress noted in 2007 that there were "serious shortages" of qualified adoptive parents. The American Civil Liberties Union stated that many gay and lesbian families are interested in adopting and willing to adopt children and are often open to accepting the harder to place children such as those who are older. . . . Yet policies of adoption agencies, social stigma, and state laws have created barriers for gay and lesbian couples in the adoption process.

Last year, the Florida law that for over 3 decades banned adoptions by gays and lesbians was ruled unconstitutional. Florida has been the only state with an outright ban on adoption by gays and lesbians, although in both Arkansas and Utah there are bans any unmarried persons adopting or fostering children. Mississippi bans homosexual couples, but not single lesbian, gay, bisexual, and transgender (LGBT) persons, from adopting. In 2007, New Hampshire repealed a 15-year ban on gay and lesbian adoption, after hearing extensive testimony from children's advocates.

Many experts in the fields of child psychology and social work have agreed that there is no scientific evidence to support a gay and lesbian adoption ban. . . . [T]here is no reliable scientific evidence that proves that lesbian or gay parents arrange their homes differently or are inept parents or that their children develop differently from those in heterosexual homes. Organizations such as the American Academy of Pediatrics, the American Medical Association, the American Psychiatric Association, and the National Association of Social Workers all support permitting same-sex couples to adopt.

Yet there continues to be persistent mythology pertaining to outcomes for children adopted by gay and lesbian parents. For example, in the Florida case experts called by the state claimed there was a higher incidence of drug and alcohol abuse among gay couples, that they were more unstable than heterosexual unions, and that the children of gay couples suffer from social stigma. Many of the persistent and pervasive myths are grounded in homophobia and a heterosexual bias that views heterosexual couples as the gold standard of parenting practices. . . .

(handwritten margin note: not the intergenerational transfer of s. orient.)

From *Adoption Quarterly*, vol. 12, 2009, pp. 129–151. Copyright © 2009 by Taylor & Francis Journals. Reprinted by permission via Rightslink.

[T]his study will present findings from a sample of gay and lesbian adoptive parents and heterosexual adoptive parents. This study compared the extent of emotional and behavioral problems of adopted children given the sexual orientation of their adoptive parents. Specifically, controlling for various confounding variables, we hypothesized that parent sexual orientation would not have a significant impact upon the emotional and behavioral functioning of their children.

Literature Review

Research on gay and lesbian adoptive families has generally been scarce. However, the literature is growing. There are a few studies that have looked particularly at the functioning level of gay and lesbian adoptive families. . . . [They] conclude that the children were "growing up in healthy families with strong, capable parents which has resulted in the children themselves showing many areas of strengths." . . .

Thus, the current literature on gay and lesbian adoption and comparison of gay and lesbian adoption to heterosexual adoption supports New Hampshire's and Florida's recent decisions to repeal bans on gay and lesbian adoption. The current, albeit limited, literature continues to demonstrate that gay and lesbian parents are viable, strong, and an untapped source for children in need of adoption. Building on the need for continued research on gay and lesbian family functioning and specifically in comparison to heterosexual functioning, the current study was completed.

Methodology

Design and Data Collection Process

This study utilized a cross-sectional survey design and consisted of two data sets. The first data set consisted of families participating in the Florida Adoption Project (FAP). The goal of the FAP is to examine key indicators of success among the population of parents who had adopted a child through Florida's public child welfare system and were receiving a special needs subsidy payment. Adoptive parents in Florida receiving an adoption subsidy for at least one adopted child in their care were eligible for the study. . . . Parents were sent a coded packet that included a cover letter, informed consent form, and survey instrument; . . . 1,694 families returned surveys for 2,382 children.

The second data set consisted of gay and lesbian individuals and couples throughout the United States. The sample gay and lesbian adoptive parents were obtained through a variety of media in order to ensure an adequate sample size for this comparative study. Newspaper ads were placed in several metropolitan gay and lesbian weekly newspapers, adoption magazines, and gay parenting magazines as well as a designated Web site. Once contact was initiated by the participants via e-mail or phone, a research team member would contact parents and describe the purpose of the study and the procedures, and if they wished to participate, the researcher obtained their address. A cover letter, consent form, and survey were sent to all participants who were interested in participating in the survey. Of the 281 surveys distributed, 183 surveys were returned.

Sample

To ensure comparability between the two data sets, three sampling criteria measures were followed. First, only gay and lesbian adoptive couples and heterosexual adoptive couples met inclusion criteria for this study. Regardless of sexual orientation, single adoptive parents were excluded. Second, although some FAP adoptive parents completed surveys on siblings whom they adopted, only the oldest adopted sibling was included in this study. This is consistent with the gay and lesbian data set where the child of focus was the oldest adopted child when they had adopted siblings. Thus, the data set included adoptive parents who had adopted one child or the oldest child in sibling adoptions. Finally, the subsample for the present analysis included parents who adopted children aged 1.5 through 18 years.

The subsample of children were classified as having a gay and lesbian adoptive parent ($n = 155$) or heterosexual adoptive parent ($n = 1,229$). For the analyses that follows, we divided the sample into two age groups of children, 1.5 to 5 years ($n = 380$) and 6 to 18 years ($n = 1,004$). Of the 1.5- to 5-year-old children, 86 (22.6%) were children of gay or lesbian parents and 294 (77.4%) were children of heterosexual parents. In terms of the 6- to 18-year-old children, 69 (6.9%) were children of gay or lesbian parents and 935 (93.1%) were children of heterosexual parents.

Measures

Although the gay and lesbian survey contained information specific to gay and lesbian parents, both surveys contained common domains that are reported on in this study, including information about parent and child characteristics, family composition and dynamics, the child's pre-adoptive history (maltreatment history), and current emotional and behavioral functioning. Measures were treated as independent, dependent, and control variables. The main independent variable in this study was parent's sexual orientation (1 = heterosexual; 0 = gay and lesbian). The main dependent variable was child internalizing and externalizing behavior. In order to rule out alternative explanations for child behavior, we include several covariates in the models. . . .

Control Variables

Based on their empirical associations with adoption outcomes, control factors were included in the multivariate models. These include sex (1 = female, 0 = male), child age, pre-adoptive history of maltreatment (1 = yes, 0 = no), co-sibling adoption, adoption preparation, family income, and family functioning. . . .

Results

. . .

Sample Characteristics: 1.5 to 5 Years

The ethnic makeup of the parents was not diverse, in that 100% of the gay and lesbian and 78.8% of the heterosexual parents were Caucasian. A significant majority of gay and lesbian parents (58.1%) had obtained master's or doctoral degrees, whereas 71.2% of the heterosexual parents had completed high school, GED, or associate's degrees. As such, the annual income of gay and lesbian parents (M = \$118,619) was significantly more than that of heterosexual parents (M = \$62,798). Significantly more heterosexual parents (38.7%) had adopted a child of different ethnicity than did gay and lesbian parents (11.6%). The average age of gay and lesbian parents (M = 43.69 years) and heterosexual parents (M = 42.37 years) was approximately equal. Gay and lesbian parents were partnered for significantly less years (M = 10.45 years) than heterosexual parents were married (M = 14.19 years). The majority of gay and lesbian parents resided in the West (34.5%), followed by the Northeast (25.9%), Midwest (20.1%), Southeast (9.8%), Southwest (8.6%), and Canada (1.1%).

The ethnic makeup of the children of gay and lesbian adoptive parents was predominately biracial (44.2%), whereas the majority of children of heterosexual parents were Caucasian (46.7%). The age of placement in the adoptive home was approximately equal for children of gay and lesbian parents (M = 1.06 years) and heterosexual parents (M = 1.01 years). In terms of current age, children of heterosexual parents were significantly older (M = 4.28 years) than children of gay and lesbian parents (M = 3.69 years). Sex was approximately equally distributed, with 62.5% and 54.4% of children of gay and lesbian parents and heterosexual parents, respectively, being male. A significant majority of children of heterosexual parents were adopted with their sibling(s) (16.7%) as compared to children of gay and lesbian parents (7.0%). A higher percentage of children of heterosexual parents had pre-adoptive histories of neglect (49.3%) and physical abuse (17.7%) as compared to children of gay and lesbian parents (31.4% and 4.7%, respectively).

Sample Characteristics: 6 to 18 Years

The ethnic makeup of the parents was not diverse, in that 94.2% of the gay and lesbian and 76.4% of the heterosexual parents were Caucasian. A significant majority of gay and lesbian parents (49.3%) had obtained master's or doctoral degrees, whereas 72.7% of the heterosexual parents had completed high school, GED, or associate's degrees. Accordingly, the annual income of gay and lesbian parents (M = \$111,207) was significantly more than that of heterosexual parents (M = \$58,222). There were no differences in transracial adoptions between heterosexual parents (26.1%) and gay and lesbian parents (18.8%). The average age of gay and lesbian parents (M = 46.06 years) and heterosexual parents (M = 48.02 years) was approximately equal. Gay and lesbian parents were partnered for significantly less years (M = 12.79) than heterosexual parents were married (M = 19.62).

The ethnic makeup of the children of gay and lesbian adoptive parents was predominately Caucasian (39.1%) and biracial (44.2%), whereas the majority of children of heterosexual parents were Caucasian (56.9%). The age of placement in the adoptive home was approximately equal for children of gay and lesbian parents ($M = 3.72$ years) and heterosexual parents ($M = 4.07$ years). In terms of current age, children of heterosexual parents were significantly older ($M = 12.1$ years) than children of gay and lesbian parents ($M = 10.47$ years). Sex was approximately equally distributed, with 58.0% and 51.6% of children of gay and lesbian parents and heterosexual parents, respectively, being male. A significant majority of children of heterosexual parents were adopted with their sibling(s) (38.8%) as compared to children of gay and lesbian parents (18.8%). Over half of the children of gay and lesbian parents (53.6%) and heterosexual parents (67%) had pre-adoptive histories of neglect, whereas approximately equal proportions had pre-adoptive histories of physical abuse (33.3% and 34.4%) and sexual abuse (23.2% and 17.6%), respectively.

Bivariate Analyses

. . . In the 1.5- to 5-year-old group, the results indicated that gay and lesbian parents reported significantly more satisfaction with the adoption preparation process and significantly less externalizing problems of their adopted children than heterosexual parents reported. However, no statistically significant associations were found between family functioning and internalizing problems.

The results for the 6- to 18-year-old group indicated that heterosexual parents reported significantly higher levels of family functioning and more externalizing problems among their children than reported by gay and lesbian parents. However, no statistically significant associations were found between adoption preparation services and internalizing problems. . . .

Internalizing and Externalizing Problems: 1.5 to 5 Years

[O]nly one variable emerged as a predictor of internalizing problems. An adopted child who was adopted as part of a sibling group would have significantly higher levels of internalizing problems compared to children not adopted as part of a sibling group, holding all other variables constant. The variables included in the model accounted for only 4.2% of the variance in internalizing behavior.

Two variables emerged as predictors of externalizing problems. [A]n adopted child who was adopted as part of a sibling group would have significantly higher levels of internalizing problems as compared to children not adopted as part of a sibling group, holding all other variables constant. Adopted children's externalizing problems significantly decreased as their adoptive parents reported more satisfaction with the adoption preparation process. The variables included in the model accounted for only 3.5% of the variance in internalizing behavior. As hypothesized, the sexual orientation of adoptive parents was not a significant predictor of internalizing problems or externalizing problems.

Internalizing and Externalizing Problems: 6 to 18 Years

A 1-year increase in child age at survey and pre-adoptive sexual abuse was predictive of more internalizing problems. On the other hand, an increase in annual income, family functioning, and parental satisfaction with adoption preparation services was predictive of significantly fewer internalizing problems. The variables included in the model accounted for 10.1% of the variance in internalizing behavior.

. . . [A] 1-year increase in child age at survey, pre-adoptive history of physical abuse, and pre-adoptive history of sexual abuse accounted for more externalizing problems. Overall, girls were significantly less at risk for externalizing problems as compared with boys. The control variables of annual income, family functioning, and parental satisfaction with adoption preparation services were predictive of fewer externalizing problems. The variables included in the model accounted for 16.0% of the variance in externalizing behavior. As hypothesized, the sexual orientation of adoptive parents was not a significant predictor of internalizing problems or externalizing problems.

Discussion

Limitations and Strengths

As with many adoption studies, the present study possesses some limitations that need to be considered in order to understand the influence on the findings and their implications. First, as this study utilized a nonrandom sample and cross-sectional design, the findings cannot be generalized to the broader population of adoptive parents and children nor can causal inferences be made. . . . Second, secondary confirmation of variables was absent. . . . Third and perhaps most significantly, the comparability of the gay and lesbian and heterosexual parents may be suspect since both samples were collected for different study purposes. There were also considerably more heterosexual parents than gay and lesbian parents in both analyses. . . .

Notwithstanding these limitations, the study contained several strengths. The study adds to our understanding of the factors that may contribute to adopted child internalizing problems and externalizing problems in gay and lesbian families and heterosexual families. In doing so, this study used measures with sound psychometric properties and variables that were measured similarly between the two samples, and to the best of our knowledge, it is the largest comparative study on gay and lesbian and heterosexual adoptive parents. . . .

Parent Sexual Orientation

In terms of sexual orientation, there were no significant differences between the heterosexual and homosexual parents. This finding is consistent with prior research that compares these two specific groups of adoptive parents. . . .

The sexual orientation of the adoptive parents in this sample had no significant impact on the internalizing or externalizing behaviors of the

<u>children</u>. The results support the ACLU's demand that gays and lesbians be given an equal and fair opportunity to pursue adoption. Access to a just and open adoption process requires changes in both practice and policy. First, the findings support the need for specialized training of adoption workers in order to prepare them to make nondiscriminatory assessments and to engage in sensitive practice with gays and lesbians. Logically, this training would begin during the education experience. [H]aving a class that explicitly explores homophobia [will] cultivate a greater acceptance of gays and lesbians for social work students. . . .

The results also have timely policy implications. It is important to note that while the Florida ban on gay adoption was ruled unconstitutional, it was appealed by the state and is likely to go to the Florida Supreme Court for a final decision. . . . The results of this study support the growing body of knowledge that could aid in overturning the unconstitutional laws currently in effect.

Many of the adoptive parents in this sample faced stressors; however, their sexual orientation was not a predictor of those stressors. The following sections discuss the findings in regard to these stressors, specifically the emotional and behavioral issues of the adoptive children and the factors that might buffer such behavior.

Sex

The adoption analyses in 6- to 18-year-olds revealed that boys were more at risk for poor behavioral outcomes. . . . This may be partially a result of adopted boys' inclination for externalizing disorders. In contrast to internalizing behavior, adoption outcome research suggests that externalizing behavior, such as breaking rules, running away, fighting, and threatening behavior, is most disconcerting to adoptive parents and is associated with placement instability and adoption disruptions.

Pre-Adoptive History of Sexual Abuse

None of the pre-adoptive abuse variables emerged as significant predictors of internalizing and externalizing problems in the younger child analyses. There are a host of possible explanations for this counterintuitive finding. . . . One possible explanation is that younger children may lack to vocabulary to disclose sexual abuse or may keep it a secret due feelings of betrayal, powerlessness, and shame. It is only when they feel safe with their adoptive parents that they may disclose sexual abuse.

It is possible that the effects of sexual abuse may lay dormant until a later developmental stage, such as in adolescence when symptoms may be triggered by certain stressors related with that developmental stage. Lending support to this developmental theory is that pre-adoptive sexual abuse was a significant predictor of more severe internalizing and externalizing behavior among the older children. . . .

Interestingly, pre-adoptive history of physical abuse emerged as a significant predictor of externalizing problems only for the older child analyses, albeit the magnitude of the effect was less pronounced as compared to children with pre-adoptive sexual abuse. On the other hand, pre-adoptive neglect was not significant in any of the analyses. It is unclear whether a similar developmental trajectory exists for physical abuse and neglect. . . .

Sibling Adoption

Although much of the previous research findings on sibling adoptions in adoptive families and child behavior is mixed, sibling adoption was the only significant predictor of both more problematic internalizing and externalizing problems for children 1.5 to 5 years old. . . . In comparison to children not adopted in sibling groups, adopted siblings may be at more risk for behavioral problems because they have at least one common parent and experience similar emotional, behavioral, and social experiences overtime. . . .

Adoption Preparation

Parents' perceived satisfaction with adoption preparation services was a significant factor positively influencing the emotional and behavioral outcomes of the youth in all analyses except internalizing behavior of the younger children. The consistency across the analyses suggests that early in the adoption life cycle, the degree to which adoption workers exemplify concern for the child and family, demonstrate knowledge of adoption-related issues, and respond to adoptive parent problems and questions appears to be of importance to adoptive parents. This suggests that perceived satisfaction with adoption services at adoption may be salient in indirectly helping the child and family adjust to adoption. As potential parents are prepared for their adoptive child's entrance into the family, it is essential that they have a realistic understanding of the emotional and behavioral challenges that they may experience and the understanding of the deleterious impact of a pre-adoptive risk history (e.g., sibling adoption, pre-adoptive child abuse, intellectual disabilities) and its effect on adoption adjustment. . . . Thus, adoption agencies should ensure that information about these resources is provided to parents prior to placement.

Child Age

The findings suggest that older children (as a proxy for placement age) were at risk for more severe internalizing and externalizing problems, but only for the analyses in older children. . . . [O]ne possible reason for adoption adjustment problems among children adopted at older ages is that there may be profound emotions associated with the loss of their biological families and fears of rejection by their adoptive families. . . . Once the children are adopted, these problems may stress the ability of families to successfully incorporate the children in their families.

Family Functioning and Family Income

Family functioning was a nonsignificant predictor in the younger child analyses but emerged as significant for both emotional and behavioral problems in the older child analyses. As predicted, better family functioning was associated with less severe emotional and behavioral problems among the older children. . . .

As a proxy for resource availability, our findings demonstrate that higher family income predicted less severe internalizing and externalizing symptoms. An increase in financial supports may buffer some of the barriers and stresses adoptive parents experience in securing medical and behavioral services for their adopted children and enhance family functioning.

Conclusion

. . . Deciding to adopt is an important step and should be meaningfully considered and weighed by potential parents. However, the sexual orientation of the person should not affect that choice or keep that person from pursuing the option if so desired. Gay and lesbian couples should be considered and assessed via an adoption process that is respectful, culturally sensitive, and strengths-based. Gay and lesbian adoptive parents, as well as heterosexual adoptive parents, face challenges and issues in their families. Although the emotional and behavioral issues of their children can provide challenges for adoptive parents, their parents' sexual orientation does not impact their ability to face those challenges.

Social work educators, adoption professionals, and policy makers have a responsibility to face the growing body of knowledge that proves that gay and lesbian parents are as fit as heterosexual parents to adopt. As a result, we must not only educate and practice and create laws that respect the 2 million gay and lesbian potential adoptive parents but we must also serve the 130,000 children in the child welfare system waiting to be adopted.

EXPLORING THE ISSUE

Does Parents' Sexual Orientation Affect Their Children's Psychological Outcomes?

Challenge Questions

1. Do you think that homosexuality is "contagious"?
2. Why might there be an increased likelihood of children raised by same-sex couples to themselves have a nonheterosexual sexual orientation?
3. Does sexual orientation affect the characteristics of a good parent? What are these characteristics?
4. Does the sex of the same-sex couple make a difference in parenting style?

Parenting is an area that has so many unknown factors, influences, and outcomes. Two-parent, high-income families sometimes have children who grow up with emotional and/or behavioral problems. Single parents can raise healthy, well-adjusted children. Some heterosexual couples raise children effectively, and some do not; some lesbian or gay couples raise children effectively, and some do not. Some parents abuse their children; most do not. Although there is much research exploring correlations between economic health, number of parents, and other factors, literature reviewing the connections between a parent's sexual orientation and the ability to parent increasingly supports the conclusion that same-sex couples are just as likely to be good parents as are heterosexual couples. There are studies maintaining that children need to be raised by a married, heterosexual couple, and there are studies asserting that a same-sex couple can do just as effective a job. There is also insufficient information about sexual orientation itself and the effects that having a lesbian, gay, or bisexual parent may or may not have on a child. The lack of information and plethora of misinformation breed fear. When people are afraid, they want to protect—in this case, people who do not understand the basis of sexual orientation feel they need to protect children. In doing so, they sometimes make decisions that are not always in the best interest of the child. For example, in 1996, a divorced heterosexual couple living in Florida was battling over custody of their 11-year-old daughter. The male partner had recently completed an 8-year prison sentence for the murder of his first wife, and had married his third. His ex-wife, however, had since met and partnered with a woman. A judge determined that the man and his new wife would provide a more appropriate home for the child than the child's mother because she was in a relationship with another woman. In the end, the judge believed that the child would do best in a home with a mother and a father, even though the father was convicted of second-degree murder and accused of sexually molesting his daughter from his first marriage. How do you feel about this? If you feel that heterosexual couples are more appropriate parents than same-sex couples, how would the fact that one of the heterosexual partners had committed a serious (capital crimes are by definition those punishable by death, which would not include 2nd-degree murder) crime affect your opinion? Sometimes, we argue for what we think "should be" in a given situation. A challenge arises when comparing the "should be" to the "is"—what we think is best as opposed to the reality. If you feel that heterosexual married couples make the best parents, what should be done with those same-sex couples who are providing a loving, stable home for their children? Would it be best to leave the child where she or he is, or do you think the child would be better off removed from the existing family structure and placed with a heterosexual couple? Clearly, this is a discussion and debate that will continue as more and more same-sex couples not only adopt, but also have biological children of their own.

Additional Resources

Jane Drucker, *Lesbian and Gay Families Speak Out: Understanding the Joys and Challenges of Diverse Family Life* (New York: HarperCollins, 2001).

Patricia Morgan, *Children as Trophies? Examining the Evidence on Same-Sex Parenting* (Newcastle: The Christian Institute upon Tyne, 2002).

R. U. Paige, Sexual Orientation, Parents, and Children, Minutes of the meeting of the Council of Representatives, July 28 and 30, 2004, Honolulu, HI. Retrieved November 18, 2004, from http://www.apa.org/about/governance/council/policy/parenting.aspx

http://www.cfw.tufts.edu/?/category/family-parenting/2/topic/same-sex-parents/189/

ISSUE 6

Are Fathers Necessary for Children's Well-Being?

YES: Natasha J. Cabrera, Jacqueline D. Shannon, and Catherine Tamis-LeMonda, from "Fathers' Influence on Their Children's Cognitive and Emotional Development: From Toddlers to Pre-K," *Applied Developmental Science* (2007)

NO: Jane Waldfogel, Terry-Ann Craigie, and Jeanne Brooks-Gunn, from "Fragile Families and Child Well-Being," *The Future of Children* (vol. 20, pp. 87–112, 2010)

Learning Outcomes

As you read the issue, focus on the following points:

- What is the difference between family structure and family stability?
- Can certain family structures affect some child outcomes but not others?
- Is one sex naturally better at parenting than the other? Are there essential characteristics of fathering versus mothering?
- Is having a parent of each sex necessary for the well-being of children?

ISSUE SUMMARY

YES: Professor of human development Natasha J. Cabrera reports that father engagement has positive effects on children's cognition and language, as well as their social and emotional development.

NO: Jane Waldfogel, Terry-Ann Craigie, and Jeanne Brooks-Gunn, in a detailed analysis of various family structures, find that family instability has a negative effect on children's cognitive and health outcomes, regardless of structure, meaning that children with single or cohabiting parents are not necessarily at risk.

On Father's Day, June 21, 2009, President Obama gave a speech in which he said, "We need fathers to step up." He used his own experiences as a child growing up without a father, as well as his observations as a community organizer and legislator as a basis for his plea. His concerns reflect long-standing assumptions that fathers are necessary for children's well-being. But are they? For decades there has been active debate about parenting roles and responsibilities. Traditionalists assume that there is a maternal instinct and that children will just naturally fare better if there is a mother in the home and a father who fulfills the role of breadwinner. Myths abound about single mothers. These include: Today's family problems are due to the increase in single parenthood; the increase in unwed motherhood was due to the sexual revolution; children of unwed or divorced mothers are doomed to fail; and the male-breadwinner family is the best model. Another myth is reflected in the claim that so many young, poor urban males are involved with gangs, drugs, and guns because they lack a father figure.

The twentieth century saw significant changes in the American family. Well over half of mothers are currently in the paid workforce. More than half of all new marriages end in divorce. One-third of all births are to single women. The traditional family ideal in which fathers work and mothers care for children and the household characterizes less than 10 percent of American families with children under the age of 18. Mothers' increased labor force participation has been a central catalyst of change in the culture of fatherhood. Mothers began to spend less time with children, and fathers began to spend more time. Thus, the cultural interest in fatherhood increased, and it was assumed that fathers were becoming more nurturing and more essential. The history of the ideals of fatherhood reveals that fathers have progressed from distant breadwinner to masculine sex-role model to equal co-parent. Despite changes in the *ideals* of fatherhood, some family scholars observe that fathers' behavior has not changed. Rather, it appears that mothers' behavioral change may be responsible for the change in the culture of fatherhood. A recent review of comparisons of fathers' and mothers' involvement with their children (in "intact" two-parent families) reveals a gap: fathers' engagement with their children is about 40 percent that of mothers'; fathers' accessibility is about two-thirds that of mothers. Fathers' lesser involvement is even more characteristic of divorced and never-married families. Nearly 90 percent of all children of divorced families live with their mothers. Most single-parent fathers are "occasional" fathers. More than one-third of children in divorced families will not see their fathers at all after the first year of separation. Only 10 percent of children will have contact with fathers 10 years after divorce. Yet, at the same time, research has documented the important ways in which fathers influence their children. But does this mean that fathers are essential? Some contend that fathers are not mothers; fathers are essential and unique. Many reject a gender-neutral model of parenting, arguing that mothers and fathers have specific roles that are complementary; both parents are essential to meet children's needs. Proponents of this model assert that fatherhood is an essential role for men and pivotal to society. They maintain that fathers offer unique contributions to their children as male role models, thereby privileging their children. Moreover, fathers' unique abilities are necessary for children's successful development. However, some scholars have shown that boys raised without fathers, even when their mothers are of low income, can turn out remarkably well. Such findings challenge traditional views of fathering, that is, boys can thrive without fathers. Responsible parenting can occur in a variety of family structures, including single parents and same-sex parents.

At least four contextual forces challenge a redefinition of fathering: (1) Legal notions of fatherhood disregard nurturing. Adequate fathering is primarily equated with financial responsibility. (2) Concepts of masculinity conflict with nurturant parenting. Nurturant fathers risk condemnation as being "unmanly." How can nurturant fatherhood fit into notions of maleness and masculinity? (3) Homophobic attitudes further obstruct nurturant fatherhood. Ironically, active legal debate about sexual orientation and parenting might be influential in reconstructing fatherhood. Is there a model of shared parenting within the gay community? (4) Whether with a two-parent marriage or with parents living in separate households, one parent usually does most, if not all, of the nurturing. Interestingly, it is the case that nurturance is a better predictor of effective parenting than is sex.

Gender neutrality and equality in parenting is undefined. How would you conceptualize a model of shared parenting (taking care not to discriminate against single-parent families)? What would parental equality look like in practice? Is it essential that children be exposed to both female and male role models? If so, why? If women and men were not expected to conform to a specific set of expectations associated with their sex, would the sex of the people raising children matter? Which benefits the child more, a heterosexual set of parents who are bound by strict gender-related conventions, which results in an overbearing, abusive father, or a loving single father or loving, nurturing gay parents?

The following selections advance two models. In the YES selection, Natasha Cabrera and her colleagues' paper suggest that a father's presence has positive effects on children's cognition and language, as well as their social and emotional development, and that the timing of these effects is important. They believe programs that increase fathers' education in particular can contribute to fathers developing positive parenting skills. In contrast, in the NO selection, Jane Waldfogel and her colleagues show that it is the stability within a family structure that is more important than the structure itself.

YES ↵

Natasha J. Cabrera,
Jacqueline D. Shannon, and
Catherine Tamis-LeMonda

Fathers' Influence on Their Children's Cognitive and Emotional Development: From Toddlers to Pre-K

In recent years, scholarship on *resident low-income fathers* has made important contributions to our understanding of how fathers affect children's development. It has shown that men are involved with their young children in multiple ways through their accessibility, responsibility, and engagement; the quality of father engagement, or father–child interactions, can be positive and supportive; positive father–child interactions matter for children's development, with different effects emerging at different points in development; and, that father–child interactions are embedded in a larger ecology that includes mother–father relationship and the family human and financial resources. This article presents an integration of findings across several of our recent studies that have contributed to each of these areas.

First, we present findings that address the question of how resident fathers are engaged with their young children at 2 years, 3 years, and pre-kindergarten (pre-K). These findings are important because they are based on observed rather than survey data and show that the quality of father–child interactions is consistent across time and that fathers, like mothers, can be sensitive and supportive to their children.

Second, we highlight central fathers' personal and contextual characteristics that affect fathers' engagement. In particular, we focus on fathers' human and financial resources and mother–child interactions. These findings shed light onto particular personal and contextual factors that are central to positive parenting over time, which programs and policies can target for effective interventions.

Third, we focus on how fathers' engagements affect their young children's cognitive, language and social, and emotional outcomes over and above mothers' contribution. The extant literature on low-income fathers has focused on the effects of absent fathers and men's lack of resources on children's development. In contrast, our findings show that fathers who engage with their children in positive ways have significant effects on their cognition and language at 2 and 3 years and their social and emotional development at 2 and 3 years

From *Applied Developmental Science*, vol. 11, no. 4, 2007, pp. 208–213. Copyright © 2007 by Taylor & Francis Journals. Reprinted by permission.

and at pre-kindergarten. These findings are important because they show that fathers uniquely contribute to children's cognitive and social and emotional development above the effects on mothers' engagement on children.

These studies are guided by the Dynamics of Paternal Influences on Children over the Life Course Model that stipulates the important contribution of parent characteristics, child, and context to parenting and children's outcomes. These findings add to the literature in several ways: First, they focus on an ethnically/racially diverse, low-income sample of fathers who reside with their young children. Second, they show that low-income fathers can make significant contributions to their children's development. Third, these findings are based on observations of fathers and their children and hence move us beyond methodologies that rely on mothers as proxy respondents for fathers.

Methods

Participants

Participants were drawn from research sites that participated in both the National Early Head Start Research and Evaluation Project (EHS study) and the EHS Father Study's Project. Ten of 17 EHS sites participated in the father component of the main study at 2 and 3 years, and 12 participated at pre-K time point. Families ($N = 1,685$ at 2/3 years, $N = 2,115$ at pre-K) were enrolled into the study when they initially applied to have their children receive childcare and parenting services at the local Early Head Start program that is partners in the EHS study. Written consent to participate in the EHS study and family baseline data (e.g., maternal age, race/ethnicity) were obtained from mothers at the start of the research and from fathers at their initial visit.

Because the majority of fathers who participated in the video portion of the study were biological and resident (i.e., 85% at 2 and 3 years, 75% at pre-K), we only include families with a resident biological father at each age point. For the 2 and 3 year time points, we report on a sample of 290, and at pre-K we report on a sample of 313. These samples include families for whom we had father video data on at least one assessment.

Given the design of the study (mothers identified fathers, but not all identified fathers agreed to participate in the study), the fathers who ultimately participated in study 1 (2 and 3 year time point) and study 2 (pre-K time point) of the EHS father study are a select group of men. Compared with those who did not participate in the father study, participating fathers and their children's mothers were more likely to be married and/or cohabiting, White or Latino, completed more years of education, and were more likely to be employed. Additionally, their children had higher scores on cognitive and social and emotional tests than children from nonparticipating families.

The majority of fathers in these reported studies were White (60%, 60%, and 51%, respectively); the remaining fathers were largely African American followed by Latino. Across the three ages, approximately 1/3 to 1/2 of fathers had less than high school degree; remaining fathers had high school degrees or more. Almost all fathers reported working full-time or part-time at the various ages, ranging from 84% to 96%. However, the annual income for families at pre-K was larger ($59,459) than it was at 2 and 3 years ($18,820 and $25,440, respectively). Children averaged 25 months at the time of the 2-year visit, 37 months at the 3-year visit, and 64 months at the time of the pre-kindergarten visit; about half at all three ages were boys.

Procedures

Once fathers had been identified by the child's mother, they were contacted to participate in the study. Participating fathers were administered a father questionnaire and mother–child and father–child dyads were videotaped in separate home visits when children were 2 and 3 years, and about to enter kindergarten. Children's cognitive, language, and social and emotional development were assessed by a trained tester at the mother visit. Fathers were given $20 at the 2- and 3-year visits and $30 at the pre-K visit, and children were given a gift.

Father–child interactions were videotaped during three activities, including 10 or 15 min of semi-structured free play, which was the focus of the investigation. During free play, toys were presented to fathers in three separate bags. Toys were selected to be age appropriate and to offer dyads the opportunity to engage in both concrete and symbolic forms of play (e.g., at 2 years, the father toys included: bag #1—a book, bag #2—a pizza set and telephone, and bag #3—a farm with farm animals). Fathers were asked to sit on a mat with his child, try to ignore the camera, and to do whatever felt most natural. They were instructed to only play with the toys from the three bags and to start with bag #1, move on to bag #2, and finish with bag #3. They were told that they could divide up the 10 min or 15 min as they liked.

Measures

Parent Characteristics

The majority of demographic characteristics were collected from the father interview. Family income was gathered from standards measure of employment. Measures to assess children's development included mental and behavior ratings scales (i.e., emotional regulation and orientation/engagement factors) . . . and children's sociability and emotional regulation.

Parent–Child Interactions

The quality of father–child interactions as well as mother–child interactions were assessed. . . . We assessed three dimensions of positive parenting (i.e., sensitivity, positive regard, and cognitive stimulation) as indicators of fathers' and mothers' *Supportiveness*, which represents parenting that is characterized by emotional support and enthusiasm for the child's autonomous work, responsiveness, and active attempts to expand the child's knowledge and abilities. We included one negative aspect of parenting: *Intrusiveness*, which indicates that the parent is over-controlling and over-involved. All coders were unaware of children's scores on child assessments and father interviews.

Results

Findings from these studies are organized around the three research questions: (1) How do resident fathers engage with their young children? (2) How do human and financial resources and mothers' engagements predict the quality of fathers' engagements with their young children? (3) How do resources and father engagements affect their young children's development, over and above mother engagement?

Fathers' Engagements with Their Young Children

Building on past research that fathers and mothers engage with their children in distinct but also similar ways, our work offers further evidence of the similarities between some parents. Fathers were as sensitive as mothers, and both parents showed low levels of intrusiveness, countering common stereotypes of fathers as aloof. At all child ages studied, fathers and mothers received comparably high scores on their supportiveness . . . and equivalently low scores on their intrusiveness. . . . As observed in the videotaped father–child interaction episodes, children experienced supportive and positive parenting from both their parents.

Financial Resources and Mother–Child Interactions to Father Engagement

Although the samples in our studies represented all resident fathers who were generally higher functioning than nonparticipating fathers, for example, the majority were employed and obtained at least a high school degree, there was variation in the sample that accounted for differences in father engagements.

In terms of human and financial resources, fathers were more supportive at all three ages and less intrusive at 2 years when they had at least a high school education. . . . Income was positively related to fathers' supportiveness at 2 years and pre-K, but not at 3 years . . . , whereas income negatively related to fathers' intrusiveness at these same two ages. . . . At all three ages, mother supportiveness to her child related to father supportiveness. . . . Mother intrusiveness with her child related to father intrusiveness at 2 and 3 years . . . , but not at pre-K. . . .

In summary, fathers' resources and mother supportiveness are significantly related to supportive father engagement at most ages. Also, the finding of covariation between father and mother engagement quality underscores the need to covary mothers' engagement when considering the unique influence of fathering on children's outcomes.

Human and Financial Resources and Parent Engagement in Relation to Children's Development

Children's scores on the mental scale . . . , language scores . . . and word-recognition and applied problems . . . averaged .5 to 1.0 SD below the national norms. However, children were highly regulated and interactive during the administration of child assessments as indicated by their high scores on the orientation/engagement and emotional regulation factors . . . and on the cognitive-social and emotional regulation composite scales. . . .

Predictors to Children's Cognition and Language

Fathers' education (*more* than high school) was significantly related to children's scores. . . . Family income was significantly related to all child outcomes at pre-K. . . .

After accounting for financial and human resources (and mother engagement), the association between father engagement and child outcomes varied slightly over time depending on type of father engagement. In general, mothers' supportiveness related to children's cognitive outcomes at 2 and 3 years, and at pre-K. . . . Fathers' supportiveness related to children's outcomes at 2 and 3 years, but not at pre-K. . . . Intrusiveness varied in its relation to child outcomes by child age. Neither mother nor father intrusiveness were related to child outcomes at 2 and 3 years. . . .

Predictors to Children's Social and Emotional Behaviors

. . . As with cognitive outcomes, fathers' education (more than high school) consistently predicted children's emotional regulation at 2 and 3 years. . . . Family income, on the other hand, mattered only for children's orientation-engagement at 3 years and emotional regulation at pre-K . . . and approached significance to their cognitive-social behaviors at pre-K. . . .

In terms of parent engagement, surprisingly, maternal supportiveness was unrelated to children's outcomes at all ages . . . , however, father supportiveness was positively associated with children's emotional regulation at 2 years . . . and marginally related to their orientation-engagement at both 2 and 3 years. . . . Expectedly, maternal intrusiveness was negatively related to children's emotional regulation at 2 years and pre-K as well as their cognitive-social scores at pre-K. At 2 years, father intrusiveness was positively related to orientation-engagement but inversely related to emotional regulation. . . . Father intrusiveness was unrelated to children's social and emotional outcomes at 3 years and pre-K. . . .

Discussion

To date, studies of how fathers matter to their children have produced inconsistent findings. Some studies have reported that father engagement has no direct effect on children's outcomes. First, it is less likely to find an association between father *report* of engagement and child outcomes than when the quality of father engagement is observed. Second, it is possible that fathers have different effects on children's development across time. Findings from this study support both explanations. We also find that fathers' education and income are key predictors of positive father engagement.

It is noteworthy that the quality of fathers' and mothers' parenting is very similar to each other. Insofar as the brief videotape of parent–child interaction provides a window to how children are parented, we find that both parents are more sensitive than intrusive. In line with prior research, we also find that the most consistent predictors of supportive fathering across children's ages are fathers' education and income. It might be that fathers who have more than high school education are more motivated to parent and are more aware of the developmental needs of children than those with less education.

The next question we were interested in was whether parenting has an effect on children's outcomes. Although children in our study scored .5 to 1.0 SD below national norms of cognitive tests, they were highly regulated across ages. As with predictors to father engagement, in general, fathers who have more than high school education have children performing better in all developmental domains—cognition, language, and social and emotional development. Family income, however, matters more at later ages than earlier; presumably as children get older they need more stimulating materials and opportunities to promote learning. This is consistent with resource theories that posit that parents who have more resources are more likely to invest on their children by providing a stimulating environment that promotes growth and learning than fathers with fewer resources.

Once we accounted for the effect of resources on children's development, we examined the unique contribution that parenting had on children's outcomes. For cognitive development, mothers' and fathers' supportiveness were positively related to children's language and cognitive outcomes across ages, although fathers' supportiveness did not matter at pre-K. For social and emotional development, fathers' supportiveness mattered only at earlier ages, while mother supportiveness was not related at any age. It might be that supportive mothering alone might not be enough to teach children to regulate and pay attention. Perhaps supportive parenting coupled with other dimensions of parenting, not measured here, such as discipline, might be more effective, especially with older children. It is also possible parents in our study were not intrusive enough to have a negative effect on children. Our findings are consistent with past research that supportive parenting is important for children's cognitive development across time and it adds to the literature by showing that *supportive fathering* has similar effects on children's cognitive functioning and emotional development especially with younger children, whereas *supportive mothering* only affects cognitive development across ages.

Our results also shed light on the effects of one dimension of negative parenting. We found parent intrusiveness less consistently related to children's development across domains and ages. In contrast to our findings for supportive parenting, intrusive parenting has an expected negative effect on children's cognition and language, but only for older children. Perhaps over controlling parents tend to inhibit older children's autonomy to verbalize and ask questions hence diminishing opportunities for learning. However, parent intrusiveness related to children's emotional regulation differently depending on child's age and gender of parent. At 2 years, both parents' intrusiveness mattered. Parents who are over controlling and over-involved have young children who are less regulated (i.e., less attentive, less able to stay on task) than non-intrusive mothers and fathers. At 3 and pre-K, maternal intrusiveness was almost consistently related to less emotional regulation whereas paternal intrusiveness was not related at all. It is possible that children, especially older children, interpret paternal intrusiveness in a more positive way than they do maternal intrusiveness.

In summary, fathers who have at least a high school education were more supportive and less intrusive than parents with fewer resources. Over and above mother engagements, fathers' supportiveness matters for children's cognitive and language development across ages as well as children's social and emotional behaviors, but less consistently. In contrast, father intrusiveness is not related to older children's social and emotional behaviors; it matters only at 2 years. These findings have important implications for policy and programs. Programs that aim at increasing fathers' education and that promote and encourage father's positive parenting will yield large benefits for children.

Jane Waldfogel, Terry-Ann Craigie, and Jeanne Brooks-Gunn

 **NO**

Fragile Families and Child Well-Being

For much of the nation's history, the vast majority of American children were born into and spent their childhood in intact married-couple families. Almost the only exceptions were children whose families suffered a parental death. Over the course of the twentieth century, however, as divorce became more common, an increasing share of children experienced a breakup in their families of origin and went on to spend at least some portion of their childhood or adolescence living with just one parent or with a parent and stepparent. A large research literature developed examining the effects of such living situations on child outcomes.

More recently, as unwed births have risen as a share of all births, family structure in the United States has increasingly featured "fragile families" in which the mother is unmarried at the time of the birth. Children born into fragile families spend at least the first portion of their lives living with a single mother or with a mother who is residing with a partner to whom she is not married. For simplicity, we will refer to the first of these types of fragile family as single-mother families and the second as cohabiting-couple families.

An astonishing 40 percent of all children born in the United States in 2007 were born to unwed parents and thus began life in fragile families. That share was more than twice the rate in 1980 (18 percent) and an eightfold increase from the rate in 1960 (5 percent). Half of the children born to unwed mothers live, at least initially, with a single mother who is not residing with the child's biological father (although about 60 percent of this group say they are romantically involved with the father), while half live with an unwed mother who is cohabiting with the child's father. These estimates imply that today one-fifth of all children are born into single-mother families, while another fifth are born into cohabiting-couple families. Therefore, in examining the effects of unwed parenthood on child outcomes, it is important to consider both children living with single mothers and those living in cohabiting-couple families.

Single parenthood and cohabitation have lost much of their stigma as their prevalence has increased. But there are still many reasons to be concerned about the well-being of children in fragile families, and, indeed, research overwhelmingly concludes that they fare worse than children born into married-couple

From *The Future of Children*, vol. 20, 2010, pp. 87–112, a collaboration of the Woodrow Wilson School of Public and International Affairs at Princeton University and the Brookings Institution. Copyright © 2010 Princeton University, all rights reserved.

households. What remains unclear is how large the effects of single parenthood and cohabitation are in early childhood and what specific aspects of life in fragile families explain those effects.

In this article, we review what researchers know about the effects of fragile families on early child development and health outcomes, as well as what they know about the reasons for those effects. Many underlying pathways or mechanisms might help explain the links between fragile families and children's cognitive, behavioral, and health outcomes. Identifying these mechanisms is important to efforts by social scientists to understand how family structure affects child outcomes and to develop policies to remedy negative effects. A challenge that must be addressed is the role of "selection." The characteristics of young women and men who enter into single parenthood or cohabiting relationships differ from those of men and women in married-couple families, and those pre-existing characteristics might lead to poorer outcomes for children regardless of family structure. Parents in fragile families, for example, tend to be younger and less educated than those in married-couple families, and they may also differ in ways that cannot readily be observed even using detailed survey data. A final question is the degree to which the stability of the family setting affects how well children fare. In fact, recent research holds that it is in large part the stability of the traditional family structure that gives it its advantage.

We highlight new answers to these questions from studies using data from the Fragile Families and Child Wellbeing Study (FFCWS)—a data set designed specifically to shed new light on the outcomes of children born into single-mother and cohabiting families and how they compare with those of children in married-couple families. The study follows children from birth and collects data on a rich array of child health and developmental outcomes, thus providing evidence on how children's outcomes differ depending on whether they grow up in single and cohabiting versus married-couple families and on the factors that might underlie those differences.

We review the evidence on the effects of fragile families on child well-being by comparing outcomes for three types of families. The first type is families where children live with two married parents (for simplicity, we refer to these as traditional families). In this category are children living with their married biological parents as well as children living with married stepparents. (Research has documented differences in outcomes between these two subgroups of children, but those differences are not our focus here.) Rather, we are interested in two other types of families—both fragile families—that have become increasingly prevalent in recent years. One is single-mother families in which the mother was not married at the time of the birth and in which she is not currently living with a boyfriend or partner. The other is cohabiting-couple families in which the mother was not married at the time of the birth but is currently cohabiting with a boyfriend or partner, who might be either the child's biological parent or a social parent (someone who is not biologically related to the child but who functions at least partially in a parental role). We do not distinguish between families that share and do not share households with extended family members or with other families or friends. We also do not distinguish between single mothers who are in a dating or visiting relationship and those who are not. Such distinctions likely matter, but our focus is on the three more general family types: traditional married-couple family, single-mother family, and cohabiting-couple family.

Explaining the Links between Fragile Families and Poorer Child Well-Being

Many studies, reviewed below, concur that traditional families with two married parents tend to yield the best outcomes for children. But the specific pathways by which growing up in traditional families lead to this advantage are still being debated. The key pathways, or mechanisms, that likely underlie the links between family structure and child well-being include: parental resources, parental mental health, parental relationship quality, parenting quality, and father involvement. As noted, the selection of different types of men and women into the three different family types also likely plays a role, as does family stability and instability. We discuss each of these mechanisms in turn. . . .

Past Research on the Links between Family Structure and Child Outcomes

An extensive body of work has examined the effects of parental divorce on child outcomes. As noted, however, most of this work was published before the massive increase in unwed parenthood that now characterizes American families. Thus, informative as it was about the effects of divorce, this early wave of research lacked data to explain how unwed parenthood might affect child outcomes.

The classic study by Sara McLanahan and Gary Sandefur, published in 1994, bridged the gap by bringing together an array of evidence on how growing up in various types of nontraditional families—including both divorced families and unwed-mother families—affected child well-being. Even after controlling for the selection of different types of individuals into different types of family structure, the authors concluded that children who spent time in divorced- or unwed-mother households fared considerably worse than those remaining in intact two-parent families throughout their childhood and adolescence. While they were still in high school, they had lower test scores, college expectations, grade-point averages, and school attendance, and as they made the transition to young adulthood, they were less likely to graduate from high school and college, more likely to become teen mothers, and somewhat more likely to be "idle" (a term that refers to those who are disengaged from both school and work). . . .

With regard to mechanisms, McLanahan and Sandefur found that income was an important explanatory factor for the poorer outcomes of children in single-parent families (but not for children in stepparent families). On average, single-parent families had only half the income of two-parent families, and this difference accounted for about half the gap between the two sets of children in high school dropout and nonmarital teen birth rates (in regression models that also controlled for race, sex, mother's and father's education, number of siblings, and residence). The other important mechanism was parenting. When McLanahan and Sandefur entered parenting into the regressions (instead of income), they found that the poorer parenting skills and behaviors in single-parent families explained about half the gap in high school dropout rates, but only a fifth of the gap in teen birth rates (again controlling for race, sex, mother's and father's education, number of siblings, and residence). Because the authors did not control for income and parenting in the same models, the question of how much overlap there was in their effects remains.

Although child health was not a focus in the McLanahan and Sandefur analysis, other analysts have consistently found effects of family structure on children's health outcomes. Janet Currie and Joseph Hotz found that children of single mothers are at higher risk of accidents than children of married mothers, even after controlling for a host of other demographic characteristics. Anne Case and Christina Paxson showed that children living with stepmothers receive less optimal care and have worse health outcomes than otherwise similar children living with their biological mothers (whether married or single). An extensive body of research also links single-parent and cohabiting-family structures with higher risk of child abuse and neglect.

As McLanahan and Sandefur noted at the time, their findings were worrisome given the burgeoning growth in unwed parenthood in the United States at the time. Although an earlier generation of researchers had debated whether or not divorce affected children's well-being, McLanahan and Sandefur's findings left little doubt that children of unwed parents were worse off than other groups. Concern about how children would fare in unwed families ultimately led to the Fragile Families and Child Wellbeing Study.

The Fragile Families and Child Wellbeing Study

The Fragile Families and Child Wellbeing Study is a new data set that follows a cohort of approximately 5,000 children born between 1998 and 2000 in medium to large U.S. cities.

Approximately 3,700 of the children were born to unmarried mothers and 1,200 to married mothers. The study initiated interviews with parents at a time when both were in the hospital for the birth of their child and therefore available for interviews. As a consequence, FFCWS is able to comprehensively detail the characteristics of both parents and the nature of their relationship at the time of the child's birth.

The study also contains extensive information on early child developmental and health outcomes. . . .

Interviewers gather data on children's behavior problems by asking mothers questions from the Child Behavior Checklist about both externalizing and internalizing behaviors—that is, both outward displays of emotion, including violence and aggression, and introverted behavioral tendencies, including anxiety, withdrawal, and depression. The study assesses prosocial behavior (which includes the child's ability to get along in social situations with adults and peers). . . .

Finally, FFCWS includes several measures of child health. The initial survey records whether a child had a low birth weight. In addition, at the age-three and age-five in-home assessment, the interviewer records physical measurements of the child's height and weight to make it possible to calculate the child's BMI and to determine whether the child is overweight or obese. At the same interviews, the mother is asked about four other health outcomes: whether the child has ever been diagnosed with asthma; the child's overall health, from the mother's perspective; whether the child was hospitalized in the past year; and whether the child had any accidents or injuries in the past year. The study also includes fairly extensive information on child abuse and neglect, which captures another aspect of child health and well-being. The primary caregiver's use of discipline strategies is measured by the Conflicts Tactics Scale (including the child neglect supplement). Parents are also asked whether their family has ever been reported to child protective services for child abuse or neglect.

Studies using data from FFCWS have found that in general, children in traditional married-couple families fare better than children living in single-mother or cohabiting families. We summarize separately below the evidence on cognitive development, child behavior, and child health.

Fragile Families and Child Cognitive Development

. . . [A]mong couples unmarried at the time of the child's birth, marriage improved cognitive scores for children whose parents later married. . . . [However, there is] no difference in children's vocabulary scores at age three between stable two-parent families (whether cohabiting or married) and stable single-mother families, but . . . scores are lower in unstable families (whether cohabiting or married) than in stable families. . . .

Fragile Families and Child Behavior Problems

. . . [C]hildren living with cohabiting parents have more externalizing and internalizing behavioral problems than children living with married parents, even at age three. One explanation may be the pre-existing risks that accompany nontraditional families. . . . [W]hen single mothers have more material and instrumental support, children have fewer behavior problems and more prosocial behavior. . . . [R]elationship conflict exacerbates externalized behavioral problems in children regardless of past family structure transitions.

. . . [B]ehavioral problems are intensified with each additional change in family structure the child experiences (changing from single to cohabiting parent, or cohabiting to single, for example), with this association mediated at least in part by differences in maternal stress and parenting quality. . . . [B]oth cohabiting and dating mothers confirm that mothers experiencing instability in their relationships go on to report more stress and to engage in harsher parenting.

It appears, however, that there is an important interaction between family structure and stability. . . . [S]tability seems to matter in cohabiting families, but not in single-mother families, where the risk of behavior problems is elevated even if that family structure is stable. . . . [H]aving a social father involved in a child's life can lower behavioral problems just as having an involved biological father can. . . .

Fragile Families and Child Health

. . . [C]hildren born to unwed mothers have worse health across a range of outcomes, even after controlling for other differences in characteristics such as maternal age, race and ethnicity, and education. Children living with single mothers have worse outcomes on all five health measures than children living with married parents, while children in cohabiting-couple families tend to have worse outcomes on some but not all measures. . . . [I]nstability for the most part does not affect children's health outcomes (the exception is hospitalizations, where they find, unexpectedly, that children who experienced more instability are less likely to have been hospitalized). These findings suggest that what negatively affects health among children in fragile families has to do with living with single or cohabiting parents (rather than experiencing changes in family structure). . . .

[S]ome of the mechanisms that link unwed parenthood with greater risk of low birth weight [include smoking cigarettes and using] illicit drugs during pregnancy, and less [receipt of] prenatal care in the first trimester of their pregnancy. . . . [However,] unwed mothers who received support from the baby's father are less likely to have a low-birth-weight baby, as are those who cohabited with the father.

Studies based on FFCWS also confirm earlier research finding that children living with single mothers are at higher risk of asthma. . . .

A few studies have taken advantage of the data in FFCWS to examine the effects of family structure on child abuse and neglect. . . . [A]lthough marriage appears to be protective in the raw data, that effect disappears in models that control for parental and family characteristics. . . . [B]oth single-mother families and cohabiting families where the mother is living with a man who is not the biological father of all her children are at higher risk of having been reported than are families where the mother is living with the biological father of all her children. . . . [The] presence of a social father in the home is associated with increased risk of abuse or neglect.

Our Own Analyses of FFCWS

The many studies in this area, including the recent ones using FFCWS data, do not always define family structure or stability in a consistent way. Studies also vary in the extensiveness of other controls that are included in the analyses. These differences across studies can make it difficult to generalize across studies and to summarize their results.

Accordingly, we carried out our own analyses of FFCWS data, estimating the effect of a consistently defined set of family structure and stability categories on a set of child cognitive, behavioral, and health outcomes at age five. The family categories we defined account for both family structure at birth and stability since birth. We divide families into the following six categories: stable cohabitation, stable single, cohabitation to marriage, married at birth (unstable), cohabiting at birth (unstable), and single at birth (unstable). We then contrast them with the traditional family reference group (that is, families in which parents were married at the child's birth and have remained so). . . .

Cognitive Outcomes

[A]ll types of nontraditional or unstable families are associated with lower scores, with the exception of the cohabitation to marriage category, which is [not] significantly different from the stable married category. The possible mediators explain some, but not all, of these negative effects.

Aggressive Behavior Outcomes

[A]ll types of nontraditional or unstable families are associated with worse scores. . . . However, in contrast to the results for cognitive outcomes, it appears that for aggressive behavioral problems, growing up with a single mother (stable or unstable) is worse than growing up with a cohabiting mother. The effects of growing up with a single mother . . . remain significant after controlling for demographic differences . . . plus possible mediators.

Health Outcomes

Results for the health outcomes reveal a different pattern. [F]or obesity, the worst outcomes are associated with growing up with a single parent (whether stable or unstable) or an unstable cohabiting parent. This pattern is true as well for asthma, although after controlling for demographic differences (or demographic differences plus the possible mediators), instability appears to be most important (with the worst outcomes found for children of unstable single or unstable cohabiting mothers).

These results suggest that the relative importance of family structure versus family instability matters differently for behavior problems than it does for cognitive or health outcomes. That is, instability seems to matter more than family structure for cognitive and health outcomes, whereas growing up with a single mother (whether that family structure is stable or unstable over time) seems to matter more than instability for behavior problems.

Summary and Conclusions

In this article we summarize the findings from prior research, as well as our own new analyses, that address the question of how well children in fragile families fare compared with those living in traditional married-parent families, as well as what mechanisms might explain any differences. . . .

Until recently, most . . . research focused on divorced parents. The sharp rise over the past few decades in births to unwed mothers, however, has shifted the focus to unmarried single and cohabiting parents. These demographic changes make it difficult to compare research done even ten or fifteen years ago with research on cohorts from the beginning of this century. Rapid changes in the characteristics of parents over time also could result in different selection biases in terms of which parents (both mothers and fathers) have children when married or when unmarried (for example, as the pool of parents having unwed births grows, the characteristics of unwed parents may become more similar to those of married parents, which would result in smaller estimated associations between fragile families and child outcomes). And given that recent cohorts of children born to single and cohabiting parents are relatively young, an additional complication involves comparing outcomes across studies (that is, analysts cannot yet estimate effects of family structure on adolescent and adult outcomes for cohorts such as FFCWS). Therefore, although growing up with single or cohabiting parents rather than with married parents is linked with less desirable outcomes for children and youth, comparisons of the size of such effects, across outcomes, ages, and cohorts, is not possible. In addition, analysts have used vastly different controls to estimate family structure effects, again complicating the quest for integration across studies. We addressed this latter problem by carrying out our own analyses using a consistent set of controls across outcomes. . . .

As noted, past research focused mainly on children whose parents were married when they were born but then separated or divorced (and subsequently lived on their own or remarried). Today, an increasing share of American children is being born to unwed mothers and thus the children are spending the early years of their lives in fragile families, with either a single mother or a cohabiting mother.

That worrisome change informed the launch of the Fragile Families and Child Wellbeing Study a decade ago. Today FFCWS provides a wealth of policy-relevant data on the characteristics and nature of relationships among unwed parents. . . .

Studies using the FFCWS data have shed new light on how family structure affects child well-being in early childhood. The findings to date confirm some of the findings in earlier research, but also provide some new insights. In terms of child cognitive development, the FFCWS studies are consistent with past research in suggesting that children in fragile families are likely at risk of poorer school achievement. Of particular interest are analyses suggesting that some of these effects may be due to family instability as much as, or more than, family structure. That is, some studies find that being raised by stable single or cohabiting parents seems to entail less risk than being raised by single or cohabiting parents when these family types are unstable. Because findings are just emerging, the relative risks of unmarried status and turnover in couple relationships cannot be specified yet. . . .

With regard to child behavior problems, evidence is consistent that children in fragile families are at risk for poorer social and emotional development starting in early childhood. In contrast to the results for cognitive outcomes, it appears that behavioral development is compromised in stable single-mother families, but, in common with the results for cognitive outcomes, such problems are aggravated by family instability for children in cohabiting families.

The research also sheds a good deal of light on mechanisms, such as maternal stress and mental health as well as parenting, that might help explain why behavior problems are more prevalent in fragile families.

FFCWS is also providing some new insights on the effects of family structure on child health. Across a range of outcomes, findings suggest that children of single mothers are at elevated risk of poor health; evidence of health risks associated with living with cohabiting parents is less consistent. Findings for child abuse and neglect are also intriguing and suggest that children of single mothers and cohabiting mothers are at elevated risk of maltreatment, although marital status per se may be less consequential than whether a man who is not the child's biological father is present in the home. . . .

To the extent that children in fragile families do have poorer outcomes than children born into and growing up in more stable two-parent married-couple families, what are the policy implications? In principle, the findings summarized here point to three routes by which outcomes for children might be improved. The first is to reduce the share of children growing up in fragile families (for example, through policies that reduce the rate of unwed births or that promote family stability among unwed parents). The second is to address the mediating factors that place such children at risk (for example, through policies that boost resources in single-parent homes or that foster father involvement in fragile families). The third is to address directly the risks these children face (for example, through high-quality early childhood education policies or home-visiting policies).

EXPLORING THE ISSUE

Are Fathers Necessary for Children's Well-Being?

Challenge Questions

1. Do you think there is such a thing as a maternal instinct?
2. Are fathers essential? Are male role models essential? If so, for whom—boys or girls or both?
3. Even if the two-parent family often has an easier time at effective parenting, does it mean that it is the only acceptable model?
4. Should fathers move beyond the provider or breadwinner role and become more involved in the physical and emotional care of their children? Should fathers emulate mothers' traditional nurturing activities?
5. Can parenting partnerships be truly egalitarian? What might they look like?

Is There Common Ground?

In the NO selection, Jane Waldfogel, Terry-Ann Craigie, and Jeanne Brooks-Gunn suggested that there are five pathways related to family structure that affect child outcomes: parental resources, parental mental health, parental relationship quality, parenting quality, and father involvement. Their analyses suggest that the presence of a father can often be a plus, at least in the context of a stable family structure. However, given these multiple pathways, one could conclude that fathers are good for children but not essential. Likewise, one could argue to opposite. Mothers are good for families but not necessary. Unfortunately, much less research has been conducted on father-only families.

Researchers have explored under what conditions optimal father involvement is possible. Some state that the three necessary conditions are (1) when a father is highly motivated to parent, (2) when a father has adequate parenting skills and receives social support for parenting, and (3) when a father is not undermined by work and other institutional settings. The reconstruction of fathering, whatever the redefinition, has proven to be very difficult and contested by many cultural forces. At issue is the assumption that there is something natural and thus rooted in the basic nature of women and men that makes a two-parent family, with a mother and father, essential and ideal for children's well-being. The fundamental assumption of different parenting styles and roles of men and women has led to debates about whether "fathers can mother." That is, can men, and should they, begin to fill the role of nurturer? The result is that men's "job description" as fathers is less clear than expectations of women as mothers. Therefore, fathering is very sensitive to context (including the marital or co-parental relationship, children, extended family, and cultural institutions). The role of mother is especially delimiting. Mothers often serve as gatekeepers in the father–child relationship. Father involvement is often contingent on mothers' attitudes toward, expectations of, and support for the father. Many mothers are ambivalent about active father involvement with their children. The mothering role has been a central feature of adult women's identity, so it is no wonder that some women feel threatened by paternal involvement in their domain, which affects their identity and sense of control. In the absence of social consensus on fathering and counterarguments about the deficits of many fathers, many mothers are restrictive of father involvement. However, some maintain that responsible mothering will have to evolve to include support of the father–child bond. In addition, with increasing latitude for commitment to and identification with their parental role, men are increasingly confused about how to exercise their roles as fathers. This also makes them sensitive to contextual factors such as others' attitudes and expectations. Worse yet, they frequently encounter disagreement among different individuals and institutions in their surrounding context, further complicating their role choices and enactment.

Additional Resources

Esther Dermott, *Intimate Fatherhood: A Sociological Analysis* (Routledge, New York, 2008).

Armin A. Brott and Jennifer Ash, *The Expectant Father: Facts, Tips, and Advice for Dads-to-Be* (New Father Series, Abbeyville Press, New York, 2001).

Single Mother Assistance. http://www.singlemoms.org/

National Fatherhood Initiative. http://www.fatherhood.org/

ISSUE 7

Should Parents Be Allowed to Choose the Sex of Their Children?

YES: **Z.O. Merhi and L. Pal,** from "Gender 'Tailored' Conceptions: Should the Option of Embryo Gender Selection Be Available to Infertile Couples Undergoing Assisted Reproductive Technology?" *Journal of Medical Ethics* (2008)

NO: **American College of Obstetricians and Gynecologists Committee on Ethics,** from "Sex Selection," Opinion No. 360, *Obstetrics and Gynecology* (2007)

Learning Outcomes

As you read the issue, focus on the following points:

- What is the relation between sex of a child and gender of a child?
- Is the question of parental selection of their child's sex a social or an ethical issue?
- Is the question of parental selection of their child's sex a question of parental rights or children's rights?
- What is the position taken by the American College of Obstetricians and Gynecologists' Committee on Ethics?

ISSUE SUMMARY

YES: Physicians Z.O. Merhi and L. Pal discuss the conditions under which selection of the sex of a child does not breach any ethical considerations in family planning among infertile couples.

NO: The American College of Obstetricians and Gynecologists' Committee on Ethics supports the practice of offering patients procedures for the purpose of preventing serious sex-linked genetic diseases, but opposes sex selection for personal and family reasons.

The potency of sex and gender as explanations for differences between males and females escalates early in life. By early childhood, a host of differences are observed between boys and girls as children internalize a sense of themselves and others as gendered. Concern has been raised about inequities and deficits resulting from the effects of sex and gender. All of these concerns are compounded by issues of preference for, and ability to select prenatally, a particular sex. Even before conception many people think about the sex of their child—which sex they want. For some, the decision even to carry a fetus to term can be influenced by gender. Research has consistently documented the preference and desire for sons in America and in other cultures. In many cultures, such as India and China, maleness means social, political, and economic entitlement. Men are expected to support their parents in their old age. Moreover, men remain with their family throughout life; women, upon marriage, become part of the husband's family. Thus, women are traditionally seen as a continuing economic burden on the family—particularly in the custom of large dowry payments at weddings. In some cultures, if a bride's family cannot pay the demanded dowry, the brides are often killed (usually by burning). Although dowries and dowry deaths are illegal, the laws are rarely enforced. In such cultures, there is an expressed desire for male children and an urgency to select fetal sex. In contrast to this pattern, a recent 2010 study based on data from several health and demographic surveys, by Kana Fuse, published in *Demographic Research*, suggests that in some developing countries there has been a shift in attitudes toward a preference for balance (i.e., sons and daughters), with some countries showing a preference for daughters. In general, Fuse found that the preference for daughters is strongest in Latin America and the Caribbean (with the exception of Bolivia) and in some Southeast Asian countries. Southern Asia, Western Asia, and Northern Africa show a preference for sons, which was also the pattern in 16 of the 28 countries sub-Saharan Africa studied with the remaining countries showing a daughter preference. Thus, it appears that there may be much more heterogeneity currently in preferences for sex of children than in the past.

Recently, sex-determination technology is most commonly used to assay the sex of fetuses, although in many cultures the use of such technology has been banned. When the fetus is determined to be female, abortion often follows because of cultural pressures to have sons. Such sex-determination practices have led to many more male than female infants being born. The gap grows even wider because of a high childhood death rate of girls, often from neglect or killing by strangulation, suffocation, or poisoning. Furthermore, women are blamed for the birth of a female child and are often punished for it (even though, biologically, it is the male's sperm, carrying either X or Y chromosomes, that determines sex). Research shows that in contemporary America, 78 percent of adults prefer their firstborn to be a boy. Moreover, parents are more likely to continue having children if they have all girls versus if they have all boys. Faced with having only one child, many Americans prefer a boy.

The issue of prenatal sex selection can be considered within the larger context of the "sexual revolution" and the burgeoning expansion in reproductive technologies. As a child, my peers and I would taunt each other with the saying, "First comes love, then comes marriage, then comes [name] with a baby carriage." Such childhood teasing reflected the cultural understanding that the order of things was love, marriage, and then children (with hetero-sexuality assumed). This is no longer the case. Sexual activity, without a repro-ductive goal, at earlier ages, parenthood without marriage, and the increase in the number of same-sex parents challenge much of what we understand about relationships and parenting. Additionally, discussions of the desired sex of one's child, along with the possibility of prenatal fetal sex selection, become even more real given all the reproductive technologies that are readily available. These include the use of sperm donors, *in vitro* fertilization, artificial insemination, and surrogate mothers, to the more controversial techniques of artificial wombs and cloning.

The availability of sex-selection technology in the last quarter of the twentieth century has been met with growing interest and widespread willing-ness to make use of the technology. Available technologies for sex selection include preconception, preimplantation, and postconception techniques. Pre-conception selection techniques include folkloric approaches like intercourse timing, administering an acid or alkaline douche, and enriching maternal diets with potassium or calcium/magnesium, all thought to create a uterine environment conducive to producing male or female fetuses. There are also sperm-separating technologies whereby X- and Y-bearing sperm are separated, and the desired sperm are artificially inseminated into the woman, increasing the chance of having a child of the chosen sex. Preimplantation technolo-gies identify the sex of embryos as early as 3 days after fertilization. For sex-selection purposes, the choice of an embryo for implantation is based on sex. Postconception approaches use prenatal diagnostic technologies to determine the sex of the fetus. The three most common technologies are amniocentesis (available after the 20th week of pregnancy), chorionic villus sampling (avail-able earlier but riskier), and ultrasound (which can determine sex as early as 12 weeks but is not 100 percent accurate). The American demand for social acceptance of sex-selection technologies has increased in the past decade. Pre-conception selection techniques are becoming quite popular in the United States, and preimplantation technologies (though more expensive) are also more frequently used. It has become more and more socially accepted to use prenatal diagnostic technologies to determine fetal sex. But incidence rates for sex-selective abortions are difficult to obtain. There is mixed opinion about the frequency of sex-selective abortions, tinged by political controversy.

In the following selections, Physicians Merhi and Pal argue that a desire for gender balance in the family is ethical. In contrast, The American College of Obstetricians and Gynecologists' Committee on Ethics asserts that fetal sex selection is always unethical, except in the case of preventing sex-linked genetic diseases. They suggest that parents are really not interested in the gen-italia that their infants are born with. What they are really choosing is an "ideal," defined by gender role expectations: a boy dad can play ball with or a girl who can wear mom's wedding gown when she marries.

YES

Z. O. Merhi and L. Pal

Gender "Tailored" Conceptions: Should the Option of Embryo Gender Selection Be Available to Infertile Couples Undergoing Assisted Reproductive Technology?

Preimplantation genetic diagnosis (PGD) was introduced at the beginning of the 1990s as an adjunct to the prenatal diagnostic armamentarium, allowing for genetic diagnoses earlier in the gestational period. This diagnostic option allows couples the opportunity of reaching decisions regarding terminating a genetically compromised fetus earlier in the course of the pregnancy, thus minimising the psychological stress as well as medical risks associated with terminations performed at more advanced gestations. Since its inception, PGD testing has been utilised for evaluation of a spectrum of inherited diseases (e.g., cystic fibrosis, sickle cell disease, hemophilia A and B, Lesch-Nyhan syndrome, thalassemia, Duchenne muscular dystrophy, and recently, Marfan's syndrome) allowing parents to avoid the lengthy, fearful wait for results of traditional testing (e.g., amniocentesis, chorionic villous sampling) while their pregnancy continues to progress. However, the application of PGD has raised multiple ethical issues, many of which were addressed by the President's Council on Bioethics in a recent paper in which the council sought to improve the application of PGD. One of the thorniest issues currently being confronted is the use of PGD for gender selection.

The methods used for preconception gender selection have evolved over time. An influence of coital timing on the gender of the conceptus was proposed by Shettles, who described an exaggerated motility by the smaller Y-bearing sperm in the mid cycle cervical mucus, and hypothesised that there would be male offspring dominance if the timing of coitus was proximate to ovulation. The length of the follicular phase of the menstrual cycle (i.e., period of maturation of the ovarian follicle and the contained egg therein), risk modifications by changing vaginal PH, possible effects of ionic concentrations in the woman's body, susceptible to dietary modifications and pre-fertilisation separation of X-bearing from Y-bearing spermatozoa, have all been stated to

From *Journal of Medical Ethics*, vol. 34, 2008, pp. 590–593. Copyright © 2008 by Institute of Medical Ethics. Reprinted by permission of BMJ Publishing Group via Rightslink.

demonstrate varying degrees of success in gender determination. However, while some of these methodologies offer successes greater than predicted by the "toss of a coin," the results remain far from "guaranteed."

Among the prominent motivations driving a demand for preconception gender selection is the desire for children of the culturally preferred gender, and to achieve gender balance within a given family. Recently, an interest in PGD testing for the purpose of "gender selection" for social reasons seems to be escalating, although no concrete data are available. This use of PGD for "family tailoring" has engendered debate and controversy. While the acceptability of PGD for traditional medical indications is generally condoned, utilisation of this modality for non-medical purpose has generated ethical concerns. The American College of Obstetricians and Gynecologists has taken a clear stance on this issue as reflected in the following committee opinion, "The committee rejects the position that gender selection should be performed on demand. . . ." Additionally, the American Society of Reproductive Medicine states that "in patients undergoing IVF, PGD used for gender selection for non medical reasons holds some risk of gender bias, harm to individuals and society, and inappropriateness in the use and allocation of limited medical resources." An introspective assessment of the published literature on clinical practices suggests that, while the stance of the principal governing bodies on the issue of PGD for gender selection is unambiguous, the actual practice of the technology of "gender tailoring on demand" is not uncommon. In fact, a recent survey of IVF clinics in the United States, an access to and provision of PDG services for sex selection was acknowledged by as many as 42% of the providers of assisted reproductive technique (ART) services; furthermore, beyond these geographical boundaries, the literature is replete with documentation of couples undergoing ART specifically wishing for family completion and/or balancing requesting that embryo(s) of a preferred gender be utilised for transfer.

Acknowledging the contrasting stance of the licensing and governing bodies on ethical concerns related to a wider availability and access to gender selection option versus the prevalent practices (as mentioned above), the authors herein attempt to explore whether the explicit utilisation of PGD for the purpose of gender selection by the infertile couple already undergoing a medically indicated ART procedure encroaches on breach of basic dictates of medical ethics.

It is currently not the "standard of care" (an individualised paradigm of diagnostic and treatment plan that an appropriately trained clinician is expected to pursue in the care of an individual patient) to perform PGD in the absence of a medical indication. However, "standards of care" should remain receptive to evolving scientific data, both that which supports and that which stands in opposition to changes in the standard. Accordingly, the opportunity to explore ethical arguments for and against the utilisation of PGD for gender selection by infertile couples undergoing ART is undertaken in this paper. This process might enable the patient and the provider to make informed and rational decisions when considering PGD utilisation for such a non-medical indication.

Beneficence and Non-Maleficence

Within the context of beneficence-based clinical judgment, a physician's inherent obligation towards his/her patient (i.e., the potential benefits of PGD) *must* be balanced against the risks of the proposed technique. For the infertile patients undergoing ART, and therefore already anticipating a procedure with some treatment related inherent risks, that is, minimal and yet real risks of anaesthesia, infection, bleeding, and ovarian hyperstimulation syndrome (a potentially lethal complication of attempts at inducing multiple ovulation), PGD for targeted genetic anomalies has been shown to improve ART outcomes (i.e., successful pregnancy following treatment), and to significantly reduce the risk of aneuploidy and miscarriage rates in a high-risk population. We believe, that in this patient population, use of additional gene probes per request, that is, for sex chromosomes, would not in any way jeopardise the principle of beneficence.

The limiting factor within this prototype of allowing PGD for gender selection "on request" will be the availability of an adequate number of cleaving embryos. A small yet real possibility does exist for a failure to achieve an embryo transfer either because of evidence of aneuploidy in the entire cohort of the tested embryos, a scenario that can be easily conjured for an older woman, or because of a procedure-related embryo loss due to the mechanisms used to create an opening in the zona pellucida (a membrane surrounding the egg) for the explicit purpose of removing a cell from the dividing embryo for PGD. The proposed benefits of PGD for the sole intention of gender selection in a patient undergoing ART must be thus balanced against the small yet real risks of embryo loss, and even failure to achieve an embryo transfer, as well as the incremental costs incurred (approximately $2500 per cycle above the costs of approximately $7500–$10 000 for the IVF cycle and related procedures). To date, there are no reports of increased identifiable problems (fetal malformations or others) attributable to the embryo biopsy itself. On the contrary, data suggest that PGD for aneuploidy screening may significantly reduce the risk of spontaneous abortions and of aneuploidies in the offspring of women undergoing IVF, particularly so in the reproductively aging patient population.

The principle of beneficence is maintained in offering PGD to couples undergoing ART (the analysis of risks and benefits being based on the physician's assessment, and the risks being primarily confined to the embryo, and not to the patient). However, the same may not hold for otherwise fertile couples. In that case, the female partner would be subjected to medically unindicated risks as well as substantial financial costs ($10 000–$15 000), driven solely by a desire for a child of the preferred gender. Such couples may represent a "vulnerable population" whose vulnerability lies within a potential, enticed by a promise of a child of the preferred gender, for making impetuous decisions regarding an expensive and medically non-indicated intervention that has an uncommon, yet real potential for health hazard. For the fertile population, this desire may lead them to "medicalise" the spontaneous procreative process, transforming it into a controlled and expensive process.

While the authors believe that the principles of beneficence and non-maleficence are upheld within the context of allowing couples anticipating undergoing ART for the management of infertility, we believe that the medical community needs to pause and ponder on any potential for generation of *unwanted surplus embryos* of the undesired sex prior to declaring this as an "acceptable practice." Aspects for further "beneficence" may be appreciated within the folds of this latter concern as couples may consider donation of discard embryos of the non-desired gender to the less fortunate infertile patients. These plausible scenarios must be discussed at length with any couple wishing to discuss the possibility of embryo gender selection while undergoing a medically indicated IVF.

In contrast to an infertile patient anticipating undergoing medically indicated IVF and requesting embryo gender selection, a similar request from an otherwise fertile couple merits additional consideration. A decision to discard embryos of an undesired gender may be less onerous to a reproductively competent individual, although data in support of such a conjecture are lacking. Whether or not this concern regarding abandonment of the "unwanted" embryos is legitimate depends on the perception of the status accorded to the embryos. Although debatable, some would agree that since embryos are too rudimentary in the developmental paradigm to have "interests," there is simply no basis upon which to grant the embryos "rights." Additionally, the ethical principle of non-maleficence is not violated since this principle is directed to "people" rather than "tissues." Future debates on this particular concern might be needed to settle this issue.

To summarise, the performance of PGD per request specifically for gender selection in an infertile couple already planning to undergo ART for medical indications may not breach the principle of beneficence nor hold undue harm for the patient. However, the principles of justice and autonomy must also be considered.

Justice

The principle of justice requires an equitable distribution of the benefits as well as the burdens associated with an intervention. While at one end of the spectrum, this concept addresses the concern of societal gender imbalance resulting from utilisation of PGD for gender selection, at the other extreme, there may be concerns of gender imbalance in relation to socioeconomic strata, as an economic differential in the utilisation of ART services is well recognised.

Concerns are voiced regarding a potential of PGD, if deemed acceptable for the explicit purpose of sex selection, for disrupting the societal gender balance. Indeed, examples of gender preferences abound in existing communities and societies. For example, in certain regions of China, termination of pregnancies, infanticide, and inferior medical care for baby girls have created a shift in the population to a ratio of approximately 1.5 to 1 favouring males. Gender preference for the firstborn can thus overwhelmingly favour male gender, particularly if "one child per family" population policies continue to be implemented. Similarly, a preference for male offspring is recognised in other regions across the globe including India and the Middle East. In contrast, in Nigeria, anecdotal tradition suggests that although a son is beneficial for propagating the family's name, a female infant is preferentially hoped for, as a daughter holds promise for eventual financial gains at the time of marriage. Similarly, in Haiti, a female firstborn is welcomed as a potential caregiver to the future siblings (personal communication).

It is important to appreciate that concerns voiced by the community regarding a potential for creating a gender differential across global regions if PGD for sex selection while undergoing a medically indicated IVF indeed achieves wider acceptability, while not unreasonable, appear based on "snap shot" views of cultural preferences. One is reassured by results of a recent cross-sectional web-based survey of 1197 men and women aged 18–45 years in the United States which revealed that the majority of those surveyed were unlikely to utilise "sperm sorting," an already existing, cheaper and less invasive technology, as a means for preferential preconception gender selection (sperm sorting employs flow cytometric separation of the 2.8% heavier "X chromosome" from the relatively lighter "Y chromosome" bearing sperm, thus providing an "X" [destined to contribute to a female fetus] or "Y" [destined to create a male fetus] enriched sperm sample for subsequent utilisation for artificial insemination or ART). Given the lack of enthusiasm for this simpler modality for preconception gender selection (an intervention that involves no risks to the patient or the embryos), at the population level, individuals are even less likely to opt for a more aggressive approach, that is, proceeding with ART and PGD, just for gender selection reasons. Similarly, a study from England on 809 couples revealed that gender selection is unlikely to lead to a serious distortion of the sex ratio in Britain and other Western societies. Yet another survey performed on a sample of German population (1094 men and women aged 18–45 years were asked about their gender preferences and about selecting the sex of their children through flow cytometric separation of X- and Y-bearing sperm followed by intrauterine insemination), revealed that the majority did not seem to care about the sex of their offspring and only a minority expressed a desire for gender selection. These authors concluded that preconception gender selection is unlikely to cause a severe gender imbalance in Germany. Similar conclusions, that is, the lack of an overwhelming interest in preconception gender selection were deduced in a survey of infertile Hungarian couples with regard to utilisation of sperm sorting for gender selection. These data are thus reassuring and suggest that, at least in the developed world, even if given access to technology facilitating preferential gender selection, and subsequently while undergoing a medically indicated IVF, use of such methods is not likely to significantly impact on the natural sex ratio within the communities. It needs to be appreciated however, that surveys generated within the industrialised nations are not representative of global perceptions regarding access to and utilisation of similar technology for ensuring conception of progeny of a preferred gender.

Another concern regarding the possibility of breaching the principle of justice is the ART-related cost as well as the additional expenditure related to the use of PGD. The financial burden is likely to preclude a section of the infertile population from using this service, hence holding the potential for a breach in the principle of justice. However, given that utilisation of PGD for gender selection may be limited secondary to financial constraints, such a differential would render significant shifts in population gender distribution very unlikely (like in ART, the issue of social and economic differences pose a distributive bias here that is beyond the scope of our paper).

Given the lack of information regarding the magnitude of utilisation of technologies for gender selection (PGD or sperm sorting) within societies, it may not be unreasonable to suppose that PGD would not be accessible to large enough numbers of people to make a real difference in the population gender balance. A potential donation of the undesired embryos by couples who opt to utilise PGD for gender selection is likely to negate any concerns regarding eventual disturbance of the sex ratio, enhance the balance towards "benefi-cence" by offering a possibility of parenthood to those who would otherwise not be able to afford the cost associated with ART and thus address some con-cerns regarding the principle of "justice" voiced earlier.

To summarise, although the existing literature touches upon aspects of preferential and differential biases in terms of gender preferences in the various communities around the world, data specifically addressing this aspect in infer-tile couples undergoing medically indicated ART are nonexistent, and voice a need to more formally assess the use of preconception gender selection technol-ogies globally, so as to fully evaluate the impact of these practices on the prin-ciple of justice. It follows that performing PGD for gender selection might be consistent with substantive justice–based considerations until more thorough analysis for societal disruptive imbalance of the sexes has been performed.

Patient Autonomy

The freedom to make reproductive decisions is recognised as a fundamen-tal moral and legal right that should not be denied to any couple, unless an exercise of that right would cause harm to them or to others. Access to and use of contraceptive choices, recognition of a woman's right to request for a termination of an unplanned and/or undesired pregnancy, and an emerg-ing acceptance of an individual's right to determine his or her sexual orienta-tion reflect evolving social and societal perceptions as relates to "reproductive autonomy, the authors believe that utilisation of PGD for the purpose of gen-der selection by infertile couples already undergoing ART may be incorporated within this paradigm of "reproductive autonomy." Across the societies, while parental autonomy in shaping the social identity of their progeny (behaviour, education, attire, . . . etc.) is an acceptable norm, this debate proposes that, in defined clinical situations, allowing parents to shape the genetic identity of a much-desired child will be within the purview of patient autonomy.

It is of interest that most of the ethical debates around use of PGD for gender selection stem from concerns regarding termination of pregnancies. Opponents to use of PGD for gender selection project that acceptability of such a practice will add yet another indication to justifying pregnancy termi-nation, namely termination of a conceptus of an undesired gender. This latter concern however pales against the escalating requests for "selective reduction" of fetuses (a procedure in which one or more fetuses in a multiple pregnancy is/are destroyed in an attempt to allow the remaining embryo/s a better chance to achieve viability as well as minimise health risks to the mother) resulting from ART, driven by patients' "demands" for transfer of surplus embryos so as to ensure "success," albeit at escalating health risks for the mother and the fetus(es). If indeed a request for "selective reduction" of fetuses by an infertile couple is an acceptable exercise of parental autonomy, the authors put forth that compliance with a request for "gender selection" by an infertile couple undergoing ART be viewed in a similar vein.

By the same token of parental autonomy, the couple has to assume all responsibility of consequences resulting from such a decision, including a possibility of not achieving an embryo transfer secondary to failure of embryos to demonstrate ongoing development following the biopsy, a possibility of all embryos being of the less desired gender, as well as of the child of the desired gender failing to conform to their expectations! Extensive counselling of the couple must therefore be an integral part of the consenting process, if couples and practitioners are considering utilisation of such procedure.

Conclusion

While concerns regarding a potential for breach of ethical principals related to a generalised acceptance of such a practice are real, this paper attempts to evaluate the integrity of principles of ethics within the context of acceptability and use of PGD for the purpose of gender selection, exclusively in patients undergoing ART for the management of infertility. The authors believe that given the current prevalence of such practices despite a stance to the contrary taken by the licensing bodies, the needs and desires of an individual seeking care within the context of the overall society's perspective be considered; this extrapolation seems not to breach the basic four principles of ethics, nor does it hold harm for the patient/embryos. Accessibility of PGD for gender selection to couples undergoing ART for management of infertility is unlikely to influence the gender balance within this society and is very distant from being in the "bright-line" areas described by the President's Council on Bioethics.

American College of Obstetricians and Gynecologists

 **NO**

Sex Selection

Sex selection is the practice of using medical techniques to choose the sex of offspring. Patients may request sex selection for a number of reasons. Medical indications include the prevention of sex-linked genetic disorders. In addition, there are a variety of social, economic, cultural, and personal reasons for selecting the sex of children. In cultures in which males are more highly valued than females, sex selection has been practiced to ensure that offspring will be male. A couple who has one or more children of one sex may request sex selection for "family balancing," that is, to have a child of the other sex.

Currently, reliable techniques for selecting sex are limited to postfertilization methods. Postfertilization methods include techniques used during pregnancy as well as techniques used in assisted reproduction before the transfer of embryos created in vitro. Attention also has focused on preconception techniques, particularly flow cytometry separation of X-bearing and Y-bearing spermatozoa before intrauterine insemination or in vitro fertilization (IVF).

In this Committee Opinion, the American College of Obstetricians and Gynecologists' Committee on Ethics presents various ethical considerations and arguments relevant to both prefertilization and postfertilization techniques for sex selection. It also provides recommendations for health care professionals who may be asked to participate in sex selection.

Indications

The principal medical indication for sex selection is known or suspected risk of sex-linked genetic disorders. For example, 50% of males born to women who carry the gene for hemophilia will have this condition. By identifying the sex of the preimplantation embryo or fetus, a woman can learn whether or not the 50% risk of hemophilia applies, and she can receive appropriate prenatal counseling. To ensure that surviving offspring will not have this condition, some women at risk for transmitting hemophilia choose to abort male fetuses or choose not to transfer male embryos. Where the marker or gene for a sex-linked genetic disorder is known, selection on the basis of direct identification of affected embryos or fetuses, rather than on the basis of sex, is possible. Direct identification has the advantage of avoiding the possibility of aborting an unaffected fetus or deciding not to transfer unaffected embryos. Despite

From *ACOG Committee Opinion*, vol. 109, 2007, pp. 475–478. Copyright © 2007 by American College of Obstetricians and Gynecologists. Reprinted by permission.

the increased ability to identify genes and markers, in certain situations, sex determination is the only current method of identifying embryos or fetuses potentially affected with sex-linked disorders.

Inevitably, identification of sex occurs whenever karyotyping is performed. When medical indications for genetic karyotyping do not require information about sex chromosomes, the prospective parent(s) may elect not to be told the sex of the fetus.

Other reasons sex selection is requested are personal, social, or cultural in nature. For example, the prospective parent(s) may prefer that an only or first-born child be of a certain sex or may desire a balance of sexes in the completed family.

Methods

A variety of techniques are available for sex identification and selection. These include techniques used before fertilization, after fertilization but before embryo transfer, and, most frequently, after implantation.

Prefertilization

Techniques for sex selection before fertilization include timing sexual intercourse and using various methods for separating X-bearing and Y-bearing sperm. No current technique for prefertilization sex selection has been shown to be reliable. Recent attention, however, has focused on flow cytometry separation of X-bearing and Y-bearing spermatozoa as a method of enriching sperm populations for insemination. This technique allows heavier X-bearing sperm to be separated; therefore, selection of females alone may be achieved with increased probability. More research is needed to determine whether any of these techniques can be endorsed in terms of reliability or safety.

Postfertilization and Pretransfer

Assisted reproductive technologies, such as IVF, make possible biopsy of one or more cells from a developing embryo at the cleavage or blastocyst stage. Fluorescence in situ hybridization can be used for analysis of chromosomes and sex selection. Embryos of the undesired sex can be discarded or frozen.

Postimplantation

After implantation of a fertilized egg, karyotyping of fetal cells will provide information about fetal sex. This presents patients with the option of terminating pregnancies for the purpose of sex selection.

Ethical Positions of Other Organizations

Many organizations have issued statements concerning the ethics of health care provider participation in sex selection. The ethics committee of the American Society for Reproductive Medicine maintains that the use of preconception sex selection by preimplantation genetic diagnosis for nonmedical reasons is ethically problematic and "should be discouraged." However, it issued a statement in 2001 that if prefertilization techniques, particularly flow cytometry for sperm sorting, were demonstrated to be safe and efficacious, these techniques would be ethically permissible for family balancing. Because a preimplantation genetic diagnosis is physically more burdensome and necessarily involves the destruction and discarding of embryos, it was not considered similarly permissible for family balancing.

The Programme of Action adopted by the United Nations International Conference on Population and Development opposed the use of sex selection techniques for any nonmedical reason. The United Nations urges governments of all nations "to take necessary measures to prevent . . . prenatal sex selection."

The International Federation of Gynecology and Obstetrics rejects sex selection when it is used as a tool for sex discrimination. It supports preconception sex selection when it is used to avoid sex-linked genetic disorders.

The United Kingdom's Human Fertilisation and Embryology Authority Code of Practice on preimplantation genetic diagnosis states that "centres may not use any information derived from tests on an embryo, or any material removed from it or from the gametes that produced it, to select embryos of a particular sex for non-medical reasons."

Discussion

Medical Testing Not Expressly for the Purpose of Sex Selection

Health care providers may participate unknowingly in sex selection when information about the sex of a fetus results from a medical procedure performed for some other purpose. For example, when a procedure is done to rule out medical disorders in the fetus, the sex of a fetus may become known and may be used for sex selection without the health care provider's knowledge.

The American College of Obstetricians and Gynecologists' Committee on Ethics maintains that when a medical procedure is done for a purpose other than obtaining information about the sex of a fetus but will reveal the fetus's sex, this information should not be withheld from the pregnant woman who requests it. This is because this information legally and ethically belongs to the patient. As a consequence, it might be difficult for health care providers to avoid the possibility of unwittingly participating in sex selection. To minimize the possibility that they will unknowingly participate in sex selection, physicians should foster open communication with patients aimed at clarifying patients' goals. Although health care providers may not ethically withhold medical information from patients who request it, they are not obligated to perform an abortion, or other medical procedure, to select fetal sex.

Medical Testing Expressly for the Purpose of Sex Selection

With regard to medical procedures performed for the express purpose of selecting the sex of a fetus, the following four potential ethical positions are outlined to facilitate discussion:

Position 1: Never participate in sex selection. Health care providers may never choose to perform medical procedures with the intended purpose of sex selection.

Position 2: Participate in sex selection when medically indicated. Health care providers may choose to perform medical procedures with the intended purpose of preventing sex-linked genetic disorders.

Position 3: Participate in sex selection for medical indications and for the purpose of family balancing. Health care providers may choose to perform medical procedures for sex selection when the patient has at least one child and desires a child of the other sex.

Position 4: Participate in sex selection whenever requested. Health care providers may choose to perform medical procedures for the purpose of sex selection whenever the patient requests such procedures.

The committee shares the concern expressed by the United Nations and the International Federation of Gynecology and Obstetrics that sex selection can be motivated by and reinforce the devaluation of women. The committee supports the ethical principle of equality between the sexes.

The committee rejects, as too restrictive, the position that sex selection techniques are always unethical (position 1). The committee supports, as ethically permissible, the practice of sex selection to prevent serious sex-linked genetic disorders (position 2). However, the increasing availability of testing for specific gene mutations is likely to make selection based on sex alone unnecessary in many of these cases. For example, it supports offering patients using assisted reproductive techniques the option of preimplantation genetic diagnosis for identification of male sex chromosomes if patients are at risk for transmitting Duchenne's muscular dystrophy. This position is consistent with the stance of equality between the sexes because it does not imply that the sex of a child itself makes that child more or less valuable.

Some argue that sex selection techniques can be ethically justified when used to achieve a "balance" in a family in which all current children are the same sex and a child of the opposite sex is desired (position 3). To achieve this goal, couples may request 1) sperm sorting by flow cytometry to enhance the probability of achieving a pregnancy of a particular sex, although these techniques are considered experimental; 2) transferring only embryos of one sex in assisted reproduction after embryo biopsy and preimplantation genetic diagnosis; 3) reducing, on the basis of sex, the number of fetuses in a multifetal pregnancy; or 4) aborting fetuses that are not of the desired sex. In these situations, individual parents may consistently judge sex selection to be an important personal or family goal and, at the same time, reject the idea that children of one sex are inherently more valuable than children of another sex.

Although this stance is, in principle, consistent with the principle of equality between the sexes, it nonetheless raises ethical concerns. First, it often is impossible to ascertain patients' true motives for requesting sex selection procedures. For example, patients who want to abort female fetuses because they value male offspring more than female offspring would be unlikely to espouse such beliefs openly if they thought this would lead physicians to deny their requests. Second, even when sex selection is requested for nonsexist reasons, the very idea of preferring a child of a particular sex may be interpreted as condoning sexist values and, hence, create a climate in which sex discrimination can more easily flourish. Even preconception techniques of sex selection may encourage such a climate. The use of flow cytometry is experimental, and preliminary reports indicate that achievement of a female fetus is not guaranteed. Misconception about the accuracy of this evolving technology coupled with a strong preference for a child of a particular sex may lead couples to terminate a pregnancy of the "undesired" sex.

The committee concludes that use of sex selection techniques for family balancing violates the norm of equality between the sexes; moreover, this ethical objection arises regardless of the timing of selection (i.e., preconception or postconception) or the stage of development of the embryo or fetus.

The committee rejects the position that sex selection should be performed on demand (position 4) because this position may reflect and encourage sex discrimination. In most societies where sex selection is widely practiced, families prefer male offspring. Although this preference sometimes has an economic rationale, such as the financial support or physical labor male offspring traditionally provide or the financial liability associated with female offspring, it also reflects the belief that males are inherently more valuable than females. Where systematic preferences for a particular sex dominate, there is a need to address underlying inequalities between the sexes.

Summary

The committee has sought to assist physicians and other health care providers facing requests from patients for sex selection by calling attention to relevant ethical considerations, affirming the value of equality between the sexes, and emphasizing that individual health care providers are never ethically required to participate in sex selection. The committee accepts, as ethically permissible, the practice of sex selection to prevent sex-linked genetic disorders. The committee opposes meeting other requests for sex selection, such as the belief that offspring of a certain sex are inherently more valuable. The committee opposes meeting requests for sex selection for personal and family reasons, including family balancing, because of the concern that such requests may ultimately support sexist practices.

Medical techniques intended for other purposes have the potential for being used by patients for sex selection without the health care provider's knowledge or consent. Because a patient is entitled to obtain personal medical information, including information about the sex of her fetus, it will sometimes be impossible for health care professionals to avoid unwitting participation in sex selection.

EXPLORING THE ISSUE

Should Parents Be Allowed to Choose the Sex of Their Children?

Challenge Questions

1. What assumptions about sex and gender underlie the desire to have boy or girl children?
2. Is fetal sex selection ever ethical? Does the method used to make the selection affect your answer to this question?
3. Is using sex-selection as a "small family planning tool" an acceptable use of sex-selection technologies?
4. Are sex differences located in biology and/or culture?
5. Can children's gender roles be redefined?

Is There Common Ground?

A primary focus of critics' concern about sex-selection technologies (and cultural biases toward males) is their impact on population sex ratios. A skewed sex ratio, they fear, will cause dire consequences for a society, particularly for heterosexual mating (although it is ironic that the same class of reproductive technological advances not only facilitates sex selection but also makes reproduction less reliant on conventional heterosexual mating). But what about social concerns about sex-selection? How will the increasing frequency of the use of sex-selection technologies impact families? How will it affect gender assumptions and sex discrimination? Is the acceptability of sex selection conditional? If Americans were not as biased toward having just boys or just girls, and therefore the population sex ratio would not be threatened, would sex selection be acceptable to control the birth order of the sexes, to ensure a mixture of boys and girls, or to have an only child of a certain desired sex? Sex selection technology might reduce overpopulation by helping families who already have a child of one sex "balance" their family with a second child of the other sex, rather than continue to have children "naturally" until they get the sex they want. Is using sex-selection as a "small family planning tool" an acceptable use of sex-selection technologies? Many feel that using sex selection to balance a family is not sexist. But others argue that it is sexist because it promotes gender stereotyping, which undermines equality between the sexes. Some feminists argue that sex selection for any reason, even family balancing, perpetuates gender roles and thus the devaluation of women. Some people in the disabilities rights movement have joined with this perspective, suggesting that if it is permissible to select against female embryos (is sex per se a genetic "abnormality"?), then so it is permissible to select against embryos with genetic abnormalities of all types; and who is to define what is "abnormal"—height, IQ? Then the door is open to increasing discrimination against people with disabilities. Should abortions solely for the purpose of sex selection be allowed? This is a profound dilemma for many pro-choice feminists for whom a woman's right to choose an abortion for any reason is opposed to gross sex discrimination in the form of sex-selective abortions (usually of female fetuses). It is interesting to note that when parents choose to abort based on fetal sex in an effort to "balance" their family, sex selection is regarded as more acceptable than when only female fetuses are aborted because of a preference for males.

Additional Resources

K. M. Boyd, Medical Ethics: Principles, Persons, and Perspectives: From Controversy to Conversation, *Journal of Medical Ethics, 31* (2005).

Susan M. Wolf, *Feminism and Bioethics: Beyond Reproduction* (New York: Oxford University Press, 1996).

The Future of Children. http://www.futureofchildren.org/

J. Hughes, "Sex Selection and Women's Reproductive Rights," Institute for Ethics and Emerging Technologie. Retrieved May 10, 2007, from http://ieet.org/index.php/ieet/more/hughes20070510/

Internet References . . .

Gender and Communication Section of the International Association for Media and Communication Research

The IAMCR is the worldwide professional organization in the field of media and communication research. Its members promote global inclusiveness and excellence within the best traditions of critical research in the field.

http://iamcr.org/s-wg/cctmc/gco

Educational Communications Board

This Web site is a state agency focused on public radio and television programs throughout Wisconsin that reflect Guide to Healthy Dating, including a series of videos on intimacy, sex, breaking up, communication, the role of the media, dating violence, and date rape.

http://www.ecb.org/guides/dating.htm

Center for Young Women's Health

This Web site from the Children's Hospital of Boston provides information on different kinds of relationships, what makes them special, and how to communicate in a positive way. Stories and fun ways to work on many kinds of relationships are offered.

http://www.youngwomenshealth.org/healthy_relat.html

National Online Resource Center on Violence Against Women

This Web site is the online resource for advocates working to end domestic violence, sexual assault, and other violence in the lives of women and their children. It provides resources and research.

http://www.vawnet.org/

Men Against Violence

This group is a nonprofit corporation dedicated to reducing domestic violence. It is a group of committed men and women who actively provide early intervention to reduce domestic violence through the education and support of individuals who have been or may be at risk of offending.

http://www.menagainstviolence.org/

Same-Sex Dating Violence

This Web site is maintained by Student Services at Brown University to provide a wide range of information and resources regarding same-sex dating violence.

http://brown.edu/Student_Services/Health_Services/Health_Education/sexual_ assault_&_dating_violence/dating_violence_in_LGBTQ_communities.php

Enough Is Enough

Enough.org is dedicated to protecting children and families from the Internet dangers of pornography and sexual predators.

http://www.protectkids.com/effects/

UNIT 3

Does Gender Disrupt Relationships? The Dark Side of Getting Along

*G*iven myriad stereotypes about women and men and their suppos-edly different styles of interaction, the issue of how these differences may affect the way women and men navigate relationships arises. All relation-ships have a life cycle that begins with initial attraction. One important question is what attracts individuals to each other. More importantly, once the attraction phase is over, what happens? Those features of a per-son which contributed to the initial attraction may or may not facilitate the next phase in a relationship, the build-up phase. During this phase aspects of relationships, such as learning about each other's interests and values, as well as building trust, become important. Communica-tion patterns contribute such learning. As relationships grow, conflicts will occur—they are an inevitable aspect of all relationships. How con-flicts are resolved depends on patterns of communication as well as con-flict resolution styles. Furthermore, conflict resolution style may have an impact on the whether relationships endure and their long-term quality. One unfortunate mode of conflict resolution is violence. A major question regards the extent to which patterns of violence are gendered, for vic-tims and for perpetrators. One of the most enduring stereotypes is that of aggressive men and passive women. But just how accurate is that stereo-type? Research would suggest that the answer depends on how aggression is defined and whether one is looking at discrete behaviors or other forms of psychological control and abuse. Additionally, the meaning, motive, and outcome can alter how the gendered nature of violence is construed. What insights does the study of race, ethnicity, and social class lend to our understanding of violence? How do media portrayals of aggressive women and men, as well as portrayals of male and female victims, fuel or challenge stereotypes?

- Are Gendered Patterns of Communication Related to Power Differentials?

- Do Nice Guys Finish Last?

- Gender Symmetry: Do Women and Men Commit Equal Levels of Vio-lence Against Intimate Partners?

- Does Pornography Reduce the Incidence of Rape?

163

ISSUE 8

Are Gendered Patterns of Communication Related to Power Differentials?

YES: Nancy Henley and Cheris Kramarae, from "Gender, Power, and Miscommunication." In Susan Erlich (ed.), *Language and Gender* (New York: Routledge, pp. 133–154, 2008)

NO: Daniel N. Maltz and Ruth A. Borker, from "A Cultural Approach to Male–Female Miscommunication." In Susan Erlich (ed.), *Language and Gender* (New York: Routledge, pp. 75–93, 2008)

Learning Outcomes

As you read the issue, focus on the following points:

- What are the key differences between a social contextual approach and a cultural differences approach to explaining communication patterns?
- Does culture shape language or does language shape culture?
- Does one's gender define the culture to which one belongs?
- If cultural differences explain conflict in male–female communication, how does one account for smooth, non-problematic interactions?

ISSUE SUMMARY

YES: Nancy Henley and Cheris Kramarae, adopting a social contextual approach, suggest that patterns of communication are due to inequalities and are multi-determined.

NO: Daniel Maltz and Ruth Borker adopt a cultural differences approach and suggest that men and women, by virtue of their sex, live in different cultures.

T heories of communication generally focus on three aspects of the communication process: the speaker, the recipient, and the message. These theories argue that the meaning of the message is not constant; rather, it changes depending on who the two communicators are. Many scholars would add the social or cultural context to this model. That is, there is a larger backdrop against which any communication takes place. Furthermore, the communication process is influenced by many nonverbal aspects of communication—posture, tone of voice, and facial expressions, including tilt of head, gaze of eyes, and presence of a smile. Feminists view the study of communication and gender as very important because language is a powerful agent in the creation and maintenance of the gender system. Because the gender system is marked by inequality, language maintains that inequality. Consider, for example, what men do if asked to imitate a woman or a woman is asked to imitate a man. To see the power of verbal and nonverbal cues, extend this example by considering what people do if asked to imitate a gay man or lesbian. The stereotypes come to mind all too readily and their mere existence perpetuates and reifies them.

In 1978, a major review of the scientific literature on gender and language by Cheris Kramer, Barrie Thorne, and Nancy Henley entitled "Perspectives on Language and Communication" (*Signs: Journal of Women in Culture and Society,* vol. 3, 1978) was published. This review summarized the three central research questions of the time: (1) Do men and women use language in different ways? (2) In what ways does language—in structure, content, and daily usage—reflect and help constitute sexual inequality? (3) How can sexist language be changed? Over thirty years later, these same three questions continue to dominate the field, but they have been reframed in more contemporary work because of an interest in *specificity* and *complexity*. Rather than studying "generic" groups of males and females, we must study particular men and women in particular settings and examine the interactions of gender and other identity categories and power relations, including race, ethnicity, class, sexual orientation, and other markers of identity. In an issue of *Ladies Home Journal* (June 2005), an article on "Why Communication Counts" declared "Over and over again, communication problems are targeted as the number-one cause of marital strife. In many cases, couples think they're communicating, but the messages aren't getting through. Communication problems stem from differences in conversational styles between men and women." The article then proceeded to give readers (presumably mostly women) tips on how to communicate more effectively with their partner. The popular press is quick to agree with assertions such as these. In fact, most of these claims are based on the widely cited work on gender and language by author Deborah Tannen. Following up on her classic *You Just Don't Understand: Women and Men in Conversation* (1991), she has examined women and men's "conversational rituals" in the workplace in *Talking from 9 to 5: Women and Men at Work* (2001). In her writings she argues that "men and women live in different worlds . . . made of different words," and that how women and men converse determines who gets heard and who gets ahead in the workplace, via a verbal power game. Tannen parallels male–female differences to cultural differences. She regards males and females as different but equal. She explores how this cultural difference manifests itself in male–female (mis)communication. Her aim in her popular publications is to reassure women and men that they are not alone in experiencing miscommunication and communication problems because of sex-differentiated communication styles. Moreover, she says that she does not value one style over the other. If anything, she praises women's communication styles. Tannen urges that males and females need to respect each other's differences so that they understand why they misunderstand each other. Interestingly, although Tannen's most recent books reflect the current focus on greater specificity in analyses of who says what to whom, and how, in her books *You're Wearing THAT?: Understanding Mothers and Daughters in Conversation* (2009) and *You Were Always Mom's Favorite!: Sisters in Conversation Throughout Their Lives* (2011), her analyses focus on women. Is this because she doesn't think that fathers and sons or brothers talk to each other, or that their patterns of conversation are not interesting or worthy of analysis?

Taking a different perspective, Louann Brizendine in a book on the female brain suggested that gendered communication is a result of biological differences in the brain. She agrees with Tannen that women and men live in different worlds. She goes further by claiming that these worlds differ beginning at conception. She even suggested, for example, that men use only 7,000 words a day compared to women's use of about 20,000. It should be noted that empirical studies of how many words woman do men speak in daily language do not support this claim. Critics claim that analyses such as Tannen's and Brizendine's universalize and generalize, thereby creating generic individuals. Questions of difference are misguided and counterproductive not only because they are invariably marked by a political agenda but also because sex comparisons locate gender in the individual rather than in social relations and processes. Responses to claims of sex difference in communication styles frequently involve blaming women for deficiencies or minimizing conflicts between men and women by reframing them as miscommunication for which we must develop tolerance. Sociocultural inequalities are not addressed. In many analyses two different questions get confounded: What do we *know* about differences between males' and females' communication styles? And, how do we explain gender-patterns of communication when they are found? Some scholars argue that gendered communication patterns are related to power and status differences. In these selections you will find two different ways of accounting for gendered patterns of communication discussed. Henley and Kramarae suggest that patterns of communication are due to inequalities and are multi-determined, whereas Maltz and Borker argue that men and women, by virtue of their sex, live in different cultures, thus miscommunication between them is no different than miscommunication between any two members of different cultures.

YES

**Nancy M. Henley
and Cheris Kramarae**

Gender, Power, and Miscommunication

Females and males seem to have frequent problems of miscommunication, most notably in adult heterosexual interaction. Many magazines and books, in fact, offer to teach one sex, usually women, how to interpret the other. Women's reactions to men's "street talk" is another example that what is ostensibly meant by one sex may not be what is understood by the other. An extreme form of miscommunication is sometimes said to occur in cases of date, acquaintance, and marital rape, when a frequently offered explanation is that a male has interpreted a female's "no" as part of sexual play. Problematic heterosexual communication takes place not only in verbal, but in nonverbal interaction also, as facial expressions, gestures, and other bodily expressions may be intended as one kind of signal but received as another.

Nonsexual interaction also provides the circumstances of miscommunication. Patterns of sex difference in speech interaction may lead to difficulties in communication, as evidenced in such behaviors as interruption, overlap, and "back-channeling," or in hedging and apologizing. There are also sex-related differences in lexical usage which may lead to miscommunication: for example, the different meanings in the terms used by women and men to evaluate, or the different understandings they may have of masculine forms used generically (e.g., *mankind*). . . . All miscommunication does not necessarily lead to immediate disruption and repair of the conversation: It may be unnoted or unacknowledged at the time by the interactants, only to come up, or be discovered, later when the different understandings lead to unexpected different outcomes, such as one voicing support and the other nonsupport for a proposal, or dressing up versus dressing down for a social event.

Female–male miscommunication has been interpreted in a number of ways, most notably as an innocent by-product of different socialization patterns and different gender cultures, occurring in interaction between speakers who are ostensibly social equals. We wish to examine cross-sex miscommunication and the explanations surrounding it with special attention to the context of sexual inequality. This context creates the gender-polarized conditions that give different interpretations and different evaluations of women's and men's language usage; suggest that men and women have distinctive languages which demand interpretation to one another, and tend to create denial and reinterpretation of women's negations in the sexual realm. It is our belief that, viewed in the context of male power and female subordination, the explanation that miscommunication is the unfortunate but innocent by-product of cultural difference collapses.

This pattern of polarization, differential evaluation, denial, and reinter-pretation is the same as that between different ethnic, recial, religious, age, and class groups (for example), when there is social inequality based on these differences: although cultural differences between groups are undeniable and may lead undeniably to miscommunication, that is not the end of the story. Hierarchies determine whose version of the communication situation will pre-vail; whose speech style will be seen as normal; who will be required to learn the communication style, and interpret the meaning, of the other; whose lan-guage style will be seen as deviant, irrational, and inferior; and who will be required to imitate the other's style in order to fit into the society. Yet the situa-tion of sex difference is not totally parallel: sex status intercuts and sometimes contrasts with other statuses; and no other two social groups are so closely interwoven as men and women.

Theories of Female/Male Miscommunication

Explanatory theories of cross-sex miscommunication are based on expositions of gender differences in language usage, so it is to these we must first turn. The most influential theories have been *female deficit* theory and *two cultures* theory. We begin with them. . . . Then we look . . . at other explanations that stress social power, psychological difference, language system-based problems, and cross-sex "pseudocommunication." We have found all of these explana-tions for miscommunication helpful and all of them limited. We next discuss some broad issues that must be addressed in an adequate theory of cross-sex miscommunication, and in the last section of the chapter propose an alterna-tive theory, which we call a multi-determined social context approach.

Female Deficit

Despite women's supposed bilingualism in knowing both men's and women's language forms and often-cited superior female language abilities, women's communication is often evaluated as handicapped, maladaptive, and need-ing remediation. To a notion of deviancy from a masculine norm are added assumptions and statements of the inferiority of "women's language." . . .

Earlier female deficit theories . . . seem to have been based in an unques-tioned biological causation, women having naturally inferior reasoning capac-ity to that of men, for example, or having essential difference from men in interests, assertiveness, and so on. The more recent socio-biological theory would attribute sex difference in speech to behaviors that display and exagger-ate sex difference in order to help select superior mates, as a means to ensure survival of offspring.

Other recent deficit theories, . . . stress environmental rather than bio-logical causation, either through women's socialization to speak "women's lan-guage" or through women's isolation from the cultural mainstream, leading to different life experiences from men's, and therefore deviant perceptions and values.

Consequences and Implications of Female Deficit Theory

Theories of female deficit, along with those of cultural difference (see below), have probably had the most consequence in our daily lives. A primary consequence of female deficit theory is the expansion of notions of male normativeness. By this we mean a view that sees female/male difference as female deviation from what is often called "the" norm, but is actually the male cultural form. The male normativeness is manifested in several ways.

1. *There is a focus on female forms and female "difference."* . . . Although most writing about language and speech is tacitly based on men's actions, very little is written on men's language and speech forms per se, which should merit as much attention as female ones, as distinctive cultural forms. . . . The focus on female difference of course emphasizes the underlying assumption that the female is a deviant while the male is "normal" and speaks "the language." . . .

2. *There is pressure on women to use "men's" language.* . . . In the late 1970s and early 1980s, the general problem with communication between women and men was presented as women's hesitancy in stating their interests and wishes. The basic solution presented by many "experts" was (especially in the U.S.) assertiveness training, which was to help women change their behavior and be more assertive. That is, both the blame and the potential solution were located within the woman experiencing trouble in making others understand her.

3. *There is an expectation that females should (re-) interpret male expressions.* [G]irls and women have to be bilingual, to speak both women's and men's languages. But there is no suggestion that boys or men have to be bilingual, even though . . . young boys learn women's language as their first language, and have to unlearn it by around the age of 10. Why are not men already bilingual, or why are they not too required to become bilingual?

Evaluation of Female Deficit Theory

This requirement of bilingualism, or bidialectalism, if it is true (we know of no empirical research directly on the question), would be more invidious than it might at first appear. We believe there is an implicit deficit theory underlying dominant U.S. culture, which requires (and teaches, through popular magazines) females, not males, to learn to read the silence, lack of emotional expression, or brutality of the other sex as not only other than, but more benign than, it appears. From a young girl's re-framing of a boy's insults and hits as signs that he likes her, to a woman's re-framing of her husband's battering as a perverse demonstration of caring, females are encouraged to use their greater knowledge of males' communication to interpret men's assaultive behavior, to make it in an almost magical way "not so."

Women, on the other hand, are not reinterpreted by men. They are in fact often characterized as uninterpretable and unfathomable by men. Yet many theorists and researchers have written about the ways that dominant groups of a social hierarchy (e.g., men) largely determine the dominant communication system of the society, and about the ways subordinate groups (e.g., women) are silenced and made inarticulate in the language. This *muted group* theory argues that women's voices are less heard than men's in part because they are trying to express women's experiences that are rarely given attention and they are trying to express them in a language system not designed for their interests and concerns; hence their language may at times seem unfathomable to men. . . .

We reject much in the theories of female deficit because of their biased evaluation of female and male speech styles, and we reject biologically based theories as ignoring the large and complex contributions of culture and psychology to speech differences. However, the point . . . that society differentially evaluates women's and men's speech is largely true and must be taken into account in any theory of difference and miscommunication.

Two Cultures

. . . Rejecting social power-based and psychological explanations of female/male difference (explained below), [one two cultures theory prefers] to think of both cross-sex and cross-ethnic communication problems as examples of the larger phenomenon of cultural difference and miscommunication. They put forward what they consider a preferable alternative explanation, that American men and women come from different sociolinguistic subcultures which have different conceptions of friendly conversation, different rules for engaging in it, and different rules for interpreting it. Even when women and men are attempting to interact as equals, the cultural differences lead to miscommunication. . . .

[This theory] compare[s] the situation in cross-sex communication with that in interethnic communication, in which communication problems are understood as personality clashes or interpreted through ethnic stereotypes. . . .

[It] see[s] the sources of the different cultures to lie in the peer groups of middle childhood: The rules for friendly interaction and conversation are being learned at a time when peer groups are primarily of a single sex, and the two styles are quite different. The world of girls, they assert (based on their own experience and on published studies of child play), is one of cooperation and equality of power; but because of heavy emotional investment in pair friendships, girls must learn to read relationships and situations sensitively. The world of boys, on the other hand, is said to be hierarchical; dominance is primary, and words are used to attain and maintain it, also to gain and keep an audience and to assert identity. The adult extension of these group differences in speech situations is that women's speech is interactional: It engages the other and explicitly builds on the other's contributions, and there is a progressive development to the overall conversation;

while men's speech is characterized by storytelling, arguing, and verbal posturing (verbal aggressiveness). [There are] six areas "in which men and women probably possess different conversational rules, so that miscommunication is likely to occur."

1. *Minimal response.* . . . A minimal response is something like "uh-huh" or "mm-hmm," given in response to another's talk. Women's meaning by the positive minimal response (PMR) is said to be something like "continue, I'm listening," while men's is said to be something like "I agree, I follow you." These two different meanings of the expression and interpretation of PMRs can explain . . . several of the sex-related differences and miscommunication findings: (a) women's more frequent use of PMRs than men's; (b) men's confusion when women give PMRs to their (men's) speech, then later are found not to agree; and (c) women's complaint that men are not listening enough when they (women) talk. . . .

2. *The meaning of questions.* Women use questions for conversational maintenance; men tend to use them as requests for information.

3. *The linking of one's utterance to the previous utterance.* Women tend to make this link explicitly, but for men no such rule seems to exist, or they explicitly ignore it.

4. *The interpretation of verbal aggressiveness.* Women see verbal aggressiveness as personally directed and as negative. For men, it helps to organize conversational flow.

5. *Topic flow and shift.* In women's conversations, topics are developed and expanded, and topic shifts are gradual. But men tend to stay on a topic as narrowly defined, and then to make an abrupt topic shift.

6. *Problem sharing and advice giving.* Women tend to discuss and share their problems, to reassure one another and listen mutually. Men, however, interpret the introduction of a problem as a request for a solution, and they tend to act as experts and offer advice rather than sympathize or share their own problems. . . .

Consequences and Implications of Two Cultures Theory

Although earlier "women's" problem with language was seen as non-assertiveness, more recently the basic problem has been named *miscommunication*, and the general solution advocated by many lay and professional researchers is to help everyone recognize that women and men have different cultures, different needs and experiences, which lead to different ways of understanding and relating to one another. . . .

One consequence of the cultural difference approach is this explanation of date and marital rape and other such forms of sexual aggression as extreme examples of miscommunication, in which males and females had different interpretations of their own and each others' behavior, and communication breakdown resulted. Sexual communication is an often difficult matter in western societies, complex in its layers of subtlety, indecision, game-playing, sex-specific prescription, and choices to understand or not understand. . . . To the extent that women communicate imprecisely the distinction between determined and token resistance, and/or men fail to understand the distinction, sexual miscommunication may result. Accuracy in encoding and decoding may be quite consequential here . . . , men's understanding is part of the legal definition of rape. A man must both understand a woman does not want intercourse and force her to engage in it anyway, to be convicted of rape.

But is rape in such a circumstance truly a matter only of "missed" communication? No; in actuality, power tracks its dirty feet across this stage. Greater social power gives men the right to pay less attention to, or discount, women's protests, the right to be less adept at interpreting their communications than women are of men's, the right to believe women are inscrutable. Greater social power gives men the privilege of defining the situation—at the time, telling women that they "really wanted it," or later, in a court.

And greater social power gives men the ability to turn definitions of the situation into physical violation. If the problem really were cultural difference alone, would we have such scenarios? In purely cultural difference, the male's and the female's understanding of the situation would each prevail about equally. The outcome might be arguments in which either party's definition would prevail and the "losing" party would go home angry; or the couple might have sullen evenings of unexpressed expectations and disappointments; or when a man's definition of the situation won out, the woman would only be forced to agree that her interpretation of their interaction was wrong—but she would not be raped as a consequence.

Evaluation of Two Cultures Theory

. . . The first point to be made about the claim of cultural difference is that there is truth in it: Clearly there are differences in communication style between men and women, exacerbated by sex segregation in different situations, which surely are implicated in misunderstandings. As we have been among those cataloguing these differences, we would be among the last to deny them and their potential effect. Our point here is that cultural difference alone cannot adequately explain the full pattern of language difference and miscommunication; and that in fact such an explanation badly misrepresents these phenomena.

Reinterpreting Differences—Culture or Power?

We begin with the six female–male differences that Maltz and Borker cite as innocently underlying miscommunication, and argue that those differences may be interpreted in another light when the context of cultural *dominance* as well as that of cultural *difference* is taken into account.

1. *Positive minimal response.* . . . [M]en respond to women's—and to other men's—PMRs as reinforcement—that is, they keep talking. PMRs are the basis of what is called *verbal reinforcement*; there is an extensive psychological literature showing that people tend to speak more, and more of any particular speech form, when reinforced with PMRs. . . .

   But beyond this, [is] the political use of minimal responses. [M]en . . . use *delayed* minimal response (leaving a silence before giving a minimal response) with women more than vice versa. . . . Such behavior can discourage interaction and lead to the failure of topics initiated by women to become joint topics of the conversation, or even extinguish a speaker's conversation. This seemingly innocent cultural difference, then, has the effect of supporting male dominance of conversation.

2. *The meaning of questions.* Males' understanding of questions as requests for information rather than as conversational maintenance devices may alternatively be heard as taking to themselves the voice of authority.

3. *The linking of one's utterance to the previous utterance.* Men's not having, or ignoring, a rule that demands that their utterance link to and thus recognize another's contribution may be seen as exercising a common prerogative of power. Those with lesser power do not have the option to ignore the other's rules, or common rules.

4. *The interpretation of verbal aggressiveness.* Men's overt use of aggressiveness against an interlocutor in organizing conversational flow may also be seen as a prerogative of power. In situations of inequality, the one of lesser power dare not show aggressiveness to the other, especially unilaterally.

5. *Topic flow and shift.* Men's tendency to make abrupt topic shifts, that is, to ignore basic conversational rules, like their tendency not to link to the previous utterance (even when on the same topic) may likewise be seen as a prerogative of power, the power to define and control a situation.

6. *Problem sharing and advice giving.* Men's tendency to take the mention of a problem as an opportunity to act as experts and offer advice rather than sympathize or share their own problems is, like the tendency to treat questions solely as requests for information, again the prerogative of authority.

In sum, the characteristics [associated with] females' speech are the ones appropriate to "friendly conversation," while the ones cited for males' speech are not neutral but indicate very uncooperative, disruptive sorts of conversational interaction. In addition, they tend to be self-centered, also consistent with the stance of the powerful.

If gender speech differences were *simply* cultural differences, there would be no pattern to them implicating dominance and power. . . . Indeed, two indications point to the *predominance* of power/dominance factors in female–male miscommunication:

a. First, as illustrated above, there is a clear pattern for language style associated with men to be that of power and dominance, and that associated with women to be that of powerlessness and submissiveness.

b. [I]n systematic study of couples, "certain types of communications were *particularly given to misinterpretation*—requests, excuses, explanation; in short, *verbalizations associated with getting one's way.*" "Getting one's way" is a denatured term for "exercising power."

Thus the overall pattern of miscommunication is not random, but rather founded in, and we would add, expressive of, the inequality of women and men. If power differentials simply provided an overlay . . . , they would not be the *predominant* context factor in miscommunication, but a minor one among many. Clearly, the place of power must be recognized in miscommunication problems between women and men, as it must between any two cultural groups differing in power. . . .

Some Considerations for a Better Theory of Female–Male Miscommunication

In working toward a more comprehensive theory of cross-sex miscommunication, we suggest the following broad considerations:

- Theories of female–male miscommunication have been put forward primarily by white theorists (which we are too) and are based largely on explanations of the actions of whites; to this extent their generalizability within the English-speaking, or any broader, community may be limited.
- As with all interactions, we need to recognize talk as an active process in a context that often involves speakers who may have different and changing concerns and who do not always have the conveying of information, politeness, rapport, clarity, agreement, understanding, and accommodation as primary goals. Discussions of miscommunication seldom, for example, talk about *anger* and *frustration* as emotions and expressions present *during* the conversation, not only as results of miscommunication. Women's anger in particular has frequently been denied or interpreted in terms of misunderstanding, inarticulation, and confusion.
- We might usefully consider the contemporary focus on miscommunication between women and men as a device that has encouraged thinking about oppositional spheres, as if women and men have innately quite separate interests and concerns. Attention to miscommunication is often a way to stress *difference* while ignoring *hierarchy*. Usually these discussions of miscommunication ignore the links between problems heard in female–male conversations and the inequities women experience through family policies, property laws, salary scales, and other repressive/discriminatory practices.
- We can recognize that boys and girls, women and men, belong, or are assigned by others, to particular age, sexual orientation, class, and race groups. Media attention to miscommunication pays little attention to this fact, assuming that only *gender variants* are involved. This is probably due in part to the fact that talk about "the battle of the sexes" is still often done flippantly, and casually. . . . One way to trivialize the topic of female–male interaction is to simplify it, ignoring the interaction of race, class, age, sexual orientation, and sex group.
- Women and men need to be asked about what they experience as communication problems. The popular media have found it easy to talk about "miscommunication" which seems to mean primarily women and men talking past each other by unwittingly using terms or concepts not understood by the other. Blame is often equally assigned

to women and men in this (popular for the mass media) battle of the sexes.

- We need to consider further the definition of *miscommunication*. Is it an interpretive error experienced by at least one of the interactants? A mismatch between the speaker's intention and the hearer's interpretation? A response by one that indicates that she or he hasn't understood? How do we know when "misunderstandings" are intentional?
- We can recognize that all confusing talk does not involve "confusion" on the part of one or both interactants. For example, a speaker might deliberately obfuscate. Further, a speaker who says something unintelligible to another may be little interested in hearing a clarifying question; repair of misunderstandings or confusions usually requires work on the part of both speakers. *Not* acknowledging communication problems is a common strategy for speakers who try to avoid confrontation in order to avoid another's anger and laws.

The Interaction of Race/Ethnicity, Gender, and Class in Miscommunication

The types of problematic talk experienced might be quite different for white/ Anglo women and women of color; and for women of different classes. In the case of race/ethnicity, for example, many black women in English-speaking countries have not grown up in patriarchal, nuclear families but in matrifocal or extended families; the same is true for many Native American women. They may experience less sexist female/male interaction. They may also experience a lot of interracial "miscommunication" in talks with both white women and white men. . . .

A basic question we need to pursue here is: Do studies of interracial/ interethnic miscommunication apply equally to women and men? Is there an interaction of race/ethnicity and gender such that different races/ethnic groups have different gender differences and different gender power relations, and consequently different loci of misunderstanding? Future studies need to account for the interrelated influences of culture, class, age, and gender—and of racism, classism, ageism, sexism, and so on. . . .

Same-Sex and Gay-Straight Issues in Miscommunication

Left untouched in this discussion, built as it is on a literature focused on cross-sex communication, is the question of how *same-sex* communication might be detrimentally affected by issues of male dominance. . . .

Same-sex miscommunication may also originate from gay-straight differences and stereotypes. Many gay males and lesbians, for example, report the experience of a straight same-sex friend or acquaintance reacting oversensitively to a touch or other expression of warmth, obviously misunderstanding it as a sexual advance. . . . Here, too is the potential for miscommunication based on cultural difference and dominance—that between homosexual and heterosexual cultures. This topic certainly deserves further exploration.

Polarizing and Reifying Gender Notions

A prominent danger in examining sex differences is that of exaggerating them and ignoring sex similarity. A more insidious danger is that of accepting sex as an unproblematic category. Similarities between the sexes are downplayed and differences exaggerated, as a general rule in Western societies, as is well evidenced by the elaboration of his-and-hers products, from pink and blue baby outfits and gender-typed children's toys to sex-customized razors, deodorants, and household tools for adults. Added to the cultural tendency to exaggerate difference is that contributed by the scholarly literature on sex difference, which has often focused uncritically on difference rather than on its underpinnings.

The exaggeration of sex difference gets much impetus from school settings, where the assumption of essential differences seems virtually institutionalized. Here children are treated as separate social categories by their teachers. . . . Despite the cultural emphasis on group difference, similarities of behavior between females and males, in language as in other areas, are far greater than differences, as many feminist scholars have pointed out. . . . A subtler, and therefore worse, problem is the simplistic and unthinking conception of sex and gender to be found in most writing, scholarly and popular. . . .

A Multi-Determined Social Context Approach to Female–Male Miscommunication

We envision a comprehensive approach that does not have to choose *between* the different explanations offered, but rather that recognizes the important factors of each of these as forces. The difference in feminine and masculine cultures is real, but it is not the only fact of existence for men and women in our society; differences due to race, ethnicity, class, age, sexual preference, and so on may compound and interact with gender differences; and cultural commonality exists too. Most importantly, cultural difference does not exist within a political vacuum; rather, the strength of difference, the types of difference, the values applied to different forms, the dominance of certain forms— all are shaped by the context of male supremacy and female subordination.

Furthermore, cultural segregation and hierarchy may combine to produce psychological effects in both women and men that independently engender and consolidate language forms which express superior and subordinate status. Both macrolevel power (a), based on structural male dominance, and microlevel power (b), based on individual socialization, exist and influence language use and therefore miscommunication. Structural male dominance favors the growth of faulty linguistic systems, including dominant metaphors, which express primarily male experience and further add to making women a muted group—leading to further problems in communication. At the same time, the general assumption that men's and women's words and behaviors mean the same leads to the problem of pseudocommunication, the false belief that we have understood each other, and misunderstandings may compound.

The differences and misunderstandings created by these factors are not equally engaged in all contexts: gender (like dominance) varies in meaning and prominence in different contexts. And this may be so for the different explanatory factors as well. For example, it may be that different speech cultures, to the extent that they exist, come primarily into play with marital/partner communication, as when wives/women say they want husbands/partners to engage in more emotionally sharing communication. Cross-sex pseudocommunication may occur especially in (hetero)sexual or potentially sexual situations. Social power may be said to enter broadly with all these factors, but may most specifically structure conversational interaction patterns. Rather than debating the merits of one factor over another, we would do well to turn our attention to ascertaining the contexts in which different factors enter to make cross-sex communication problematic.

In addition, this social context model assumes that men's as well as women's communicative behaviors are to be explained, to be studied as "caused"; that neither's speech is understood as either norm [or] deviant; that not only women's, but also men's psychology is seen as developing from their situation in the social structure, and as affecting their language style; that patterns of cross-sex misunderstanding may differ between racial, ethnic, age, and sexual preference groups, and the pattern in the dominant white/Anglo and straight culture cannot be taken as indicative of all. The model sees communication within the context of gender hierarchy as well as of gender segregation and socialization and assumes that not only the more noticeable (and often superficial) gender differences in speech are seen as underlying cross-sex miscommunication, but that also to be considered are deeper concerns of women's exclusion from the linguistic structuring of experience.

Conclusion

The patterns of miscommunication we have discussed occur within the cultural context of male power and female subordination: The accepted interpretation of an interaction (e.g., refusal versus teasing, seduction versus rape, difference versus inequality) is generally that of the more powerful person, therefore that of the male tends to prevail. The *metastructure* of interpretation—not what the interpretation is, but *whose interpretation is accepted*—is one of inequality. Females are required to develop special sensitivity to interpret males' silence, lack of emotional expression, or brutality, and to help men express themselves, while men often seem to be trained deliberately to misinterpret much of women's meaning. Yet it is women's communication style that is often labeled as inadequate and maladaptive, requiring remediation in which white-collar masculine norms are generally imposed.

As we have seen, miscommunication may be used to stigmatize: less powerful individuals (because of their ethnicity, class, sex, etc.) may be defined as deviant communicators, incapable of expressing themselves adequately. "Problems of communication" are often diagnosed in difficult interaction to obscure problems that arise from unequal power rather than from communication. The explanation of "separate but equal cultures" has been a means of avoiding reference to power and to racial and ethnic domination, and should be recognized for its implicit denial of sex domination as well. The complex patterns described above fit into the larger structure of female–male myths and power relations. One may in fact ask how well male dominance could be maintained if we had open and equally-valued communication between women and men. The construction of miscommunication between the sexes emerges as a powerful tool, maybe even a necessity, to maintain the structure of male supremacy.

Daniel N. Maltz and
Ruth A. Borker

 **NO**

A Cultural Approach to Male–Female Miscommunication

Introduction

This chapter presents what we believe to be a useful new framework for examining differences in the speaking patterns of American men and women. It is based not on new data, but on a reexamination of a wide variety of material already available in the scholarly literature. Our starting problem is the nature of the different roles of male and female speakers in informal cross-sex conversations in American English. Our attempts to think about this problem have taken us to preliminary examination of a wide variety of fields often on or beyond the margins of our present competencies: children's speech, children's play, styles and patterns of friendship, conversational turn-taking, discourse analysis, and interethnic communication. . . .

Our major argument is that the general approach recently developed for the study of difficulties in cross-ethnic communication can be applied to cross-sex communication as well. We prefer to think of the difficulties in both cross-sex and cross-ethnic communication as two examples of the same larger phenomenon: cultural difference and miscommunication.

The Problem of Cross-Sex Conversation

Study after study has shown that when men and women attempt to interact as equals in friendly cross-sex conversations they do not play the same role in interaction, even when there is no apparent element of flirting. We hope to explore some of these differences, examine the explanations that have been offered, and provide an alternative explanation for them. . . .

Women's Features

Several striking differences in male and female contributions to cross-sex conversation have been noticed in these studies.

First, women display a greater tendency to ask questions. . . .

[T]his question-asking tendency [is] an example of a second, more general characteristic of women's speech, doing more of the routine "shitwork" involved in maintaining routine social interaction, doing more to facilitate the flow of conversation. Women are more likely than men to make utterances that demand or encourage response from their fellow speakers . . . In the earlier social psychology studies, these features nave been coded under the general category of "positive reactions" including solidarity, tension release, and agreeing.

Third, women show a greater tendency to make use of positive minimal responses, especially "mm hmm," and are more likely to insert "such comments throughout streams of talk rather than [simply] at the end."

Fourth, women are more likely to adopt a strategy of "silent protest" after they have been interrupted or have received a delayed minimal response.

Fifth, women show a greater tendency to use the pronouns "you" and "we," which explicitly acknowledge the existence or the other speaker.

Men's Features

Contrasting contributions to cross-sex conversations have been observed and described for men.

First, men are more likely to interrupt the speech of their conversational partners, that is, to interrupt the speech of women.

Second, they are more likely to challenge or dispute their partners' utterances.

Third, they are more likely to ignore the comments of the other speaker, that is, to offer no response or acknowledgment at all to respond slowly in what has been described as a "delayed minimal response" or to respond unenthusiastically.

Fourth, men use more mechanisms for controlling the topic of conversation, including both topic development and the introduction of new topics, than do women.

Finally, men make more direct declarations of fact or opinion than do women, including suggestions, opinions, and "statements of orientation" . . . or "statements of focus and directives." . . .

Explanations Offered

Most explanations for these features have focused on differences in the social power or in the personalities of men and women. One variant of the social power argument is that men's dominance in conversation parallels their dominance in society. Men enjoy power in society and also in conversation. The two levels are seen as part of a single social-political system. . . . A second variant of this argument is that while the differential power of men and women is crucial, the specific mechanism through which it enters conversation is sex-role definition. Sex roles serve to obscure the issue of power for participants, but the fact is . . . that norms of appropriate behavior for women and men serve to give power and interactional control to men while keeping it from women. To be socially acceptable as women, women cannot exert control and must actually support men in their control. In this casting of the social power argument, men are not necessarily seen to be consciously flaunting power, but simply reaping the rewards given them by the social system. In both variants, the link between macro and micro levels of social life is seen as direct and unproblematic, and the focus of explanation is the general social order.

Sex roles have also been central in psychological explanations. . . . Basically . . . having been taught to speak and act like "ladies," women become as unassertive and insecure as they have been made to sound. The impossible task of trying to be both women and adults, . . . saps women of confidence and strength. As a result, they come to produce the speech they do, not just because it is how women are supposed to speak, but because it fits with the personalities they develop as a consequence of sex-role requirements.

The problem with these explanations is that they do not provide a means of explaining why these specific features appear as opposed to any number of others, nor do they allow us to differentiate between various types of male–female interaction. They do not really tell us why and how these specific interactional phenomena are linked to the general fact that men dominate within our social system.

An Alternative Explanation: Sociolinguistic Subcultures

Our approach to cross-sex communication patterns is somewhat different from those that have been previously proposed. We place the stress not on psychological differences or power differentials, although these may make some contribution, but rather on a notion of cultural differences between men and women in their conceptions of friendly conversation, their rules for engaging in it, and, probably most important, their rules for interpreting it. We argue that American men and women come from different sociolinguistic subcultures, having learned to do different things with words in a conversation, so that when they attempt to carry on conversations with one another, even if both parties are attempting to treat one another as equals, cultural miscommunication results.

The idea of distinct male and female subcultures is not a new one for anthropology. It has been persuasively argued again and again for those parts of the world such as the Middle East and southern Europe in which men and women spend most of their lives spatially and interactionally segregated. . . .

When men and women have different experiences and operate in different social contexts, they tend to develop different genres of speech and different skills for doing things with words. . . .

[I]f men and women possess different subcultural rules for speaking, what happens if and when they try to interact with each other? It is here that we turn to the research on interethnic miscommunication.

Interethnic Communication

Recent research has shown that systematic problems develop in communication when speakers of different speech cultures interact and that these problems are the result of differences in systems of conversational inference and the cues for signalling speech acts and speaker's intent. Conversation is a negotiated activity. It progresses in large part because of shared assumptions about what is going on.

[Differences in cues can result] in systematic miscommunication over whether a question was being asked, whether an argument was being made, whether a person was being rude or polite, whether a speaker was relinquishing the floor or interrupting, whether and what a speaker was emphasizing, whether interactants were angry, concerned, or indifferent. Rather than being seen as problems in communication, the frustrating encounters that result [are often] chalked up as personality clashes or interpreted in the light of racial stereotypes which tended to exacerbate already bad relations. . . .

The Interpretation of Minimal Responses

How might [this] approach to the study of conflicting rules for interpreting conversation be applied to the communication between men and women? A simple example will illustrate our basic approach: the case of positive minimal responses. Minimal responses such as nods and comments like "yes" and "mm hmm" are common features of conversational interaction. Our claim, based on our attempts to understand personal experience, is that these minimal responses have significantly different meanings for men and women, leading to occasionally serious miscommunication.

We hypothesize that for women a minimal response of this type means simply something like "I'm listening to you; please continue," and that for men it has a somewhat stronger meaning such as "I agree with you" or at least "I follow your argument so far." The fact that women use these responses more often than men is in part simply that women are listening more often than men are agreeing.

But our hypothesis explains more than simple differential frequency of usage. Different rules can lead to repeated misunderstandings. Imagine a male speaker who is receiving repeated nods or "mm hmm"s from the woman he is speaking to. She is merely indicating that she is listening, but he thinks she is agreeing with everything he says. Now imagine a female speaker who is receiving only occasional nods and "mm hmm"s from the man she is speaking to. He is indicating that he doesn't always agree; she thinks he isn't always listening.

What is appealing about this short example is that it seems to explain two of the most common complaints in male–female interaction: (1) men who think that women are always agreeing with them and then conclude that it's impossible to tell what a woman really thinks, and (2) women who get upset with men who never seem to be listening. What we think we have here are two separate rules for conversational maintenance which come into conflict and cause massive miscommunication.

Sources of Different Cultures

A probable objection that many people will have to our discussion so far is that American men and women interact with one another far too often to possess different subcultures. What we need to explain is how it is that men and women can come to possess different cultural assumptions about friendly conversation.

Our explanation is really quite simple. It is based on the idea that by the time we have become adults we possess a wide variety of rules for interacting in different situations. Different sets of these rules were learned at different times and in different contexts. We have rules for dealing with people in dominant or subordinate social positions, rules which we first learned as young children interacting with our parents and teachers. We have rules for flirting and other sexual encounters which we probably started learning at or near adolescence. We have rules for dealing with service personnel and bureaucrats, rules we began learning when we first ventured into the public domain. Finally, we have rules for friendly interaction, for carrying on friendly conversation. What is striking about these last rules is that they were learned not from adults but from peers, and that they were learned during precisely that time period, approximately age 5 to 15, when boys and girls interact socially primarily with members of their own sex. . . .

But the process of acquiring gender-specific speech and behavior patterns by school-age children is more complex than the simple copying of adult "genderlects" by preschoolers. . . .

Among school-age children, patterns of friendly social interaction are learned not so much from adults as from members of one's peer group, and a major feature of most middle-childhood peer groups is homogeneity; "they are either all-boy or all-girl." Members of each sex are learning self-consciously to differentiate their behavior from that of the other sex and to exaggerate these differences. The process can be profitably compared to accent divergence in which members of two groups that wish to become clearly distinguished from one another socially acquire increasingly divergent ways of speaking.

Because they learn these gender-specific cultures from their age-mates, children tend to develop stereotypes and extreme versions of adult behavior patterns. . . .

What we hope to argue is that boys and girls learn to use language in different ways because of the very different social contexts in which they learn how to carry on friendly conversation. Almost anyone who remembers being a child, has worked with school-age children, or has had an opportunity to observe school-age children can vouch for the fact that groups of girls and groups of boys interact and play in different ways. Systematic observations of children's play have tended to confirm these well-known differences in the ways girls and boys learn to interact with their friends. . . .

The World of Girls

Our own experience and studies . . . suggest a complex of features of girls' play and the speech within it. Girls play in small groups, most often in pairs and their play groups tend to be remarkably homogeneous in terms of age. Their play is often in private or semi-private settings that require participants be invited in. Play is cooperative and activities are usually organized in noncompetitive ways. Differentiation between girls is not made in terms of power, but relative closeness. Friendship is seen by girls as involving intimacy, equality, mutual commitment, and loyalty. The idea of "best friend" is central for girls. Relationships between girls are to some extent in opposition to one another, and new relationships are often formed at the expense of old ones. . . .

There is a basic contradiction in the structure of girls' social relationships. Friends are supposed to be equal and everyone is supposed to get along, but in fact they don't always. Conflict must be resolved, but a girl cannot assert social power or superiority as an individual to resolve it. . . .

Basically girls learn to do three things with words: (1) to create and maintain relationships of closeness and equality, (2) to criticize others in acceptable ways, and (3) to interpret accurately the speech of other girls.

To a large extent friendships among girls are formed through talk. Girls need to learn to give support, to recognize the speech rights of others, to let others speak, and to acknowledge what they say in order to establish and maintain relationships of equality and closeness. In activities they need to learn to create cooperation through speech. . . .

Friendships are not only formed through particular types of talk, but are ended through talk as well. . . .

Second, girls learn to criticize and argue with other girls without seeming overly aggressive, without being perceived as either "bossy" or "mean," terms girls use to evaluate one another's speech and actions. Bossiness, ordering others around, is not legitimate because it denies equality. . . .

Finally, girls must learn to decipher the degree of closeness being offered by other girls, to recognize what is being withheld, and to recognize criticism. Girls who don't actually read these cues run the risk of public censure or ridicule. Since the currency of closeness is the exchange of secrets which can be used against a girl, she must learn to read the intent and loyalty of others and to do so continuously, given the system of shifting alliances and indirect expressions of conflict. Girls must become increasingly sophisticated in reading the motives of others, in determining when closeness is real, when conventional, and when false, and to respond appropriately. They must learn who to confide in, what to confide, and who not to approach. Given the indirect expression of conflict, girls must learn to read relationships and situations sensitively. Learning to get things right is a fundamental skill for social success, if not just social survival.

The World of Boys

Boys play in larger, more hierarchically organized groups than do girls. Relative status in this ever-fluctuating hierarchy is the main thing that boys learn to manipulate in their interactions with their peers. Nondominant boys are rarely excluded from play but are made to feel the inferiority of their status positions in no uncertain terms. And since hierarchies fluctuate over time and over situation, every boy gets his chance to be victimized and must learn to take it. The social world of boys is one of posturing and counter-posturing. In this world, speech is used in three major ways: (1) to assert one's position of dominance, (2) to attract and maintain an audience, and (3) to assert oneself when other speakers have the floor.

The use of speech for the expression of dominance is the most straight-forward and probably the best-documented sociolinguistic pattern in boys' peer groups. Even ethological studies of human dominance patterns have made extensive use of various speech behaviors as indices of dominance. . . .

A second sociolinguistic aspect of friendly interaction between boys is using words to gain and maintain an audience. Storytelling, joke telling, and other narrative performance events are common features of the social inter-action of boys, [b]ut . . . audience behavior is not overtly supportive. The sto-ryteller is frequently faced with mockery, challenges and side comments on his story. A major sociolinguistic skill which a boy must apparently learn in interacting with his peers is to ride out this series of challenges, maintain his audience, and successfully get to the end of his story. . . .

A final sociolinguistic skill which boys must learn from interacting with other boys is how to act as audience members in the types of storytelling situ-ations just discussed. As audience member as well as storyteller, a boy must learn to assert himself and his opinions. Boys seem to respond to the storytell-ing of other boys not so much with questions on deeper implications or with minimal-response encouragement as with side comments and challenges. These are not meant primarily to interrupt, to change topic, or to change the direction of the narrative itself, but to assert the identity of the individual audience member.

Women's Speech

The structures and strategies in women's conversation show a marked conti-nuity with the talk of girls. . . . In friendly talk, women are negotiating and expressing a relationship, one that should be in the form of support and closeness, but which may also involve criticism and distance. Women orient themselves to the person they are talking to and expect such orientation in return. As interaction, conversation requires participation from those involved and back-and-forth movement between participants. Getting the floor is not seen as particularly problematic; that should come about automatically. What is problematic is getting people engaged and keeping them engaged—maintaining the conversation and the interaction.

This conception of conversation leads to a number of characteristic speech strategies and gives a particular dynamic to women's talk. First, women tend to use personal and inclusive pronouns, such as "you" and "we." Second, women give off and look for signs of engagement such as nods and minimal response. Third, women give more extended signs of interest and attention, such as interjecting comments or questions during a speaker's discourse. These sometimes take the form of interruptions. . . . [W]omen often [ask] permis-sion to speak but [are] concerned that each speaker be allowed to finish and that all present [get] a chance to speak. These interruptions [are] not seen as attempts to grab the floor but as calls for elaboration and development, and

[are] taken as signs of support and interest. Fourth, women at the beginning of their utterances explicitly acknowledge and respond to what has been said by others. Fifth, women attempt to link their utterance to the one preceding it by building on the previous utterance or talking about something parallel or related to it. . . .

While the idiom of much of women's friendly talk is that of support, the elements of criticism, competition, and conflict do occur in it. But as with girls, these tend to take forms that fit the friendship idiom. [W]hile "talking smart" is clearly one way women talk to women as well as to men, between women it tends to take a more playful form, to be more indirect and metaphoric in its phrasing and less prolonged than similar talk between men. . . . The target of criticism, whether present or not, is made out to be the one violating group norms and values. Overt competitiveness is also disguised. . . .

These strategies and the interactional orientation of women's talk give their conversation a particular dynamic. While there is often an unfinished quality to particular utterances, there is a progressive development to the overall conversation. The conversation grows out of the interaction of its participants, rather than being directed by a single individual or series of individuals. . . . Not only is the dynamic of women's conversation one of elaboration and continuity, but the idiom of support can give it a distinctive tone as well. . . .

Men's Speech

The speaking patterns of men, and of women for that matter, vary greatly from one North American subculture to another. . . . There are striking cultural variations between subcultures in whether men consider certain modes of speech appropriate for dealing with women, children, authority figures, or strangers; there are differences in performance rules for storytelling and joke telling; there are differences in the context of men's speech; and there are differences in the rules for distinguishing aggressive joking from true aggression.

But more surprising than these differences are the apparent similarities across subcultures in the patterns of friendly interaction between men and the resemblances between these patterns and those observed for boys . . . storytelling, arguing and verbal posturing.

Narratives such as jokes and stories are highly valued, especially when they are well performed for a audience. . . . Loud and aggressive argument is a second common feature of male–male speech. Such arguments . . . may include shouting, wagering, name-calling, and verbal threats. . . . Practical jokes, challenges, put-downs, insults, and other forms of verbal aggression are a third feature of men's speech, accepted as normal among friends. . . .

What Is Happening in Cross-Sex Conversation

What we are suggesting is that women and men have different cultural rules for friendly conversation and that these rules come into conflict when women and men attempt to talk to each other as friends and equals in casual conversation. We can think of at least five areas, in addition to that of minimal responses already discussed, in which men and women probably possess different conversational rules, so that miscommunication is likely to occur in cross-sex interaction.

1. There are two interpretations of the meaning of questions. Women seem to see questions as a part of conversational maintenance, while men seem to view them primarily as requests for information.
2. There are two conventions for beginning an utterance and linking it to the preceding utterance. Women's rules seem to call for an explicit acknowledgment of what has been said and making a connection to it. Men seem to have no such rule and in fact some male strategies call for ignoring the preceding comments.
3. There are different interpretations of displays of verbal aggressiveness. Women seem to interpret overt aggressiveness as personally directed, negative, and disruptive. Men seem to view it as one conventional organizing structure for conversational flow.
4. There are two understandings of topic flow and topic shift. The literature on storytelling in particular seems to indicate that men operate with a system in which topic is fairly narrowly defined and adhered to until finished and in which shifts between topics are abrupt, while women have a system in which topic is developed progressively and shifts gradually. These two systems imply very different rules for and interpretations of side comments, with major potential for miscommunication.
5. There appear to be two different attitudes towards problem sharing and advice giving. Women tend to discuss problems with one another, sharing experiences and offering reassurances. Men, in contrast, tend to hear women, and other men, who present them with problems as making explicit requests for solutions. They respond by giving advice, by acting as experts, lecturing to their audiences.

Conclusions

Our purpose in this paper has been to present a framework for thinking about and tying together a number of strands in the analysis of differences between male and female conversational styles. We hope to prove the intellectual value of this framework by demonstrating its ability to do two things: to serve as a model both of and for sociolinguistic research.

As a model *of* past research findings, the power of our approach lies in its ability to suggest new explanations of previous findings on cross-sex communication while linking these findings to a wide range of other fields, including the study of language acquisition, of play, of friendship, of storytelling, of cross-cultural miscommunication, and of discourse analysis. Differences in the social interaction patterns of boys and girls appear to be widely known but rarely utilized in examinations of sociolinguistic acquisition or in explanations of observed gender differences in patterns of adult speech. Our proposed framework should serve to link together these and other known facts in new ways.

As a model *for* future research, we hope our framework will be even more promising. It suggests to us a number of potential research problems which remain to be investigated. Sociolinguistic studies of school-age children, especially studies of the use of speech in informal peer interaction, appear to be much rarer than studies of young children, although such studies may be of greater relevance for the understanding of adult patterns, particularly those related to gender. Our framework also suggests the need for many more studies of single-sex conversations among adults, trying to make more explicit some of the differences in conversational rules suggested by present research. . . .

We conclude this paper by reemphasizing three of the major ways in which we feel that an anthropological perspective on culture and social organization can prove useful for further research on differences between men's and women's speech.

First, an anthropological approach to culture and cultural rules forces us to reexamine the way we interpret what is going on in conversations. The rules for interpreting conversation are, after all, culturally determined. There may be more than one way of understanding what is happening in a particular conversation and we must be careful about the rules we use for interpreting cross-sex conversations, in which the two participants may not fully share their rules of conversational inference.

Second, a concern with the relation between cultural rules and their social contexts leads us to think seriously about differences in different kinds of talk, ways of categorizing interactional situations, and ways in which conversational patterns may function as strategies for dealing with specific aspects of one's social world. Different types of interaction lead to different ways of speaking. The rules for friendly conversation between equals are different from those for service encounters, for flirting, for teaching, or for polite formal interaction. And even within the apparently uniform domain of friendly interaction, we argue that there are systematic differences between man and women in the way friendship is defined and thus in the conversational strategies that result.

Third and finally, our analysis suggests a different way of thinking about the connection between the gender-related behavior of children and that of adults. Most discussions of sex-role socialization have been based on the premise that gender differences are greatest for adults and that these adult differences are learned gradually throughout childhood. Our analysis, on the other hand, would suggest that at least some aspects of behavior are most strongly gender-differentiated during childhood and that adult patterns of friendly interaction, for example, involve learning to overcome at least partially some of the gender-specific cultural patterns typical of childhood.

EXPLORING THE ISSUE

Are Gendered Patterns of Communication Related to Power Differentials?

Challenge Questions

1. Why does it seem that women are expected to be the gatekeepers of communication in relationships?
2. How might one's status, or position of power, in a group affect style of communication?
3. What features of a situation, besides status, might affect how and what one chooses to communicate?
4. Consider humor as a rhetoric style: How might a gender analysis be used to understand gendered patterns of humor? Why do people seem so tolerant of sexist jokes?

Is There Common Ground?

Research consistently shows that there are gendered patterns of communication. So the question is not whether women and men communicate differently. Rather, we want to know under what circumstances differences emerge and why. It is important to situate discourse about sex differences in communication (indeed in any domain) in a sociopolitical context. Beliefs that the sexes differ, whether supported by empirical evidence or not, are deeply entrenched in our society. Indeed, while academic critics signal the lack of a scientific basis to Tannen's sweeping claims, her popular works have shot to the top of the bestseller list. We, the consumers, have to be very careful about scrutinizing how knowledge has been constructed and used. There is no such thing as a "simple" yes or no answer to a question of sex difference. Scholarly and popular writing on sex differences is impacted greatly by what can be called the "hall of mirrors" effect. As described by Deborah Cameron in "Gender and Language: Gender, Language, and Discourse: A Review Essay" (*Signs: Journal of Women in Culture and Society*, 1998), "in the course of being cited, discussed, and popularized over time, originally modest claims have been progressively represented as more and more absolute, while hypotheses have been given the status of facts." Thus, for example, the originally modest claim made by researchers Don Zimmerman and Candace West in "Sex Roles, Interruptions and Silences in Conversation" (in Barrie Thorne and Nancy Henley, eds., *In Language and Sex: Differences and Dominance*, Newbury House, 1975) that men interrupt women more than the reverse may have been exaggerated by constant repetition and then critiqued for being overstated (much like the "telephone" game played by children). As another example, it turns out that no study had actually counted the number of words used by women and men in natural conversations, that is, not until July, 2007. In contradiction of Brizendine's claim that women utter 20,000 words to men's 7,000 per day, Matthias Mehl and his colleagues found over of period of 17 working hours women average 16,214 words and men averaged 15,669, a highly statistically nonsignificant finding (*Science*, vol. 31). Currently there is less interest in examining sex differences in language and more emphasis on how people use language in everyday life to create and maintain social realities. Mary Crawford points out that feminists have worked to create a more gender-balanced language through the coining of new words and putting old words to new uses. She notes that language is power.

Additional Resources

Daniel J. Canary and Kathryn Dindia, eds., *Sex Differences and Similarities in Communication: Critical Essays and Empirical Investigations of Sex and Gender in Interaction*, 2nd edition (New York: Lawrence Erlbaum, 2006).

Mary Crawford, "Gender and Language," in R. K. Unger, ed., *Psychology of Women and Gender* (New York: John Wiley & Sons, pp. 228–244, 2001).

K. M. Galvin and P. J. Cooper, *Making Connections: Readings in Relational Communication*, 4th edition (Los Angeles: Roxbury Publishing Co., 2006).

International Association for Media and Communication Research http://iamcr .org/s-wg/cctmc/gco

Diana Ivy and Phil Backlund, *Gender Speak: Personal Effectiveness in Gender Communication* (New York: McGraw-Hill, 2003).

Charlotte Krolokke and Anne Scott Sorenson, *Gender Communication Theories and Analyses: From Silence to Performance* (Thousand Oaks, CA: Sage, 2005).

Simma Lieberman, "Gender Communication Differences and Strategies," http://superperformance.com/gendercommunication.html

Deborah Tannen, *Talking from 9 to 5: Women and Men at Work* (San Francisco: HarperCollins, 2001).

J. Wood, *Gendered Lives: Communication, Gender, and Culture*, 4th edition (Belmont, CA: Wadsworth Publishing, 2001).

ISSUE 9

Do Nice Guys Finish Last?

YES: Peter Jonason, Norman P. Li, Gregory D. Webster, and David P. Schmitt, from "The Dark Triad: Facilitating a Short-Term Mating Strategy in Men," *European Journal of Personality* (2009)

NO: Adrian Furnham, from "Sex Differences in Mate Selection Preferences," *Personality and Individual Differences* (2009)

Learning Outcomes

As you read the issue, focus on the following points:

- What is the definition of a "nice" guy?
- What is the "dark triad"?
- What do you find attractive in a future partner?
- Does the notion of what is attractive change depending on whether one is looking for a friend, a one-night stand, or a long-term relationship?
- What factors might motivate women and men to have similar or different concepts of attractiveness?

ISSUE SUMMARY

YES: Psychologist Peter Jonason, taking an evolutionary perspective, demonstrates that the "dark triad" of attributes (narcissism, psychopathy, and Machiavellianism) promotes a reproductively adaptive strategy, especially for short-term mating behaviors.

NO: Psychologist Adrian Furnham found consistent sex differences that revealed women's preference for "nice guys," that is, those who were intelligent, stable, conscientious, better educated, with good social skills and political and religious compatibility.

Google the phrase "What do women want?" and you will get over a 450 million hits. Similarly, if you Google "Do nice guys finish last?" you will get over 250 million hits. These are obviously questions that fascinate, provoke, and frustrate, and there is no shortage of Web sites claiming to have the answer. There are also numerous YouTube posts offering dating advice. The stereotype is that the "bad boy" gets the girl, but not everyone agrees. Why might that be the case? In this issue, we want to examine what it is about men that women seem to want in a partner. Such an examination leads to questions regarding what men look for in a woman, and how does what, if anything, we know about heterosexual attractions tell us about same sex attractions.

All relationships begin with attraction. Research by relationship experts in psychology and sociology attempt to answer these questions using various scientific strategies such as surveys and experimental studies, and by posing theories to explain attraction and relationship development. Some research attempts to identify whether there are physical characteristics that make some people more appealing as a partner than others. In this research, women and men are presented with photos and asked to provide attractiveness ratings. Features of the individuals in the photos are then measured (size of chin, size of eyes, shape of eyes, type of cheekbone, distance between the eyes, etc.), and these measurements are then correlated with the attractiveness ratings. In a "draw an ugly man study," both black and white college students gave "ugly" men larger and broader features. Other studies have looked at bodily features, such as a woman's waist to hip ratio. These studies find remarkable similarity across cultures. In general, large eyes, prominent cheekbones, and a big smile are found attractive in both women and men. Other research focuses on status factors (education, income) or personality attributes, shared values, interests, and character. Some of this research has shown that these attributes may offset physical unattractiveness, especially in men. In these studies, researchers may ask people to rate the attributes they want in a partner and then present them with opportunities to interact with another person, giving them information about several people and letting them select whom they would prefer to meet. Interestingly, these studies suggest that in spite of the fact that women say they value personality, values, and character over looks, physical attractiveness wins out over similarity, just as it does for men. One theory suggests that the physical-attractiveness stereotype is at work. Beautiful people are perceived to be more sociable, extraverted, and socially competent when compared to less attractive people. They are also seen as more sexual, happier, more fun loving, and successful. Thus, first impressions are likely to be based on looks because of the inferences we make about personality and status. However, in spite of this stereotype, we all know that all beautiful people do not have wonderful relationships and that many unattractive people do. So what is going on? The answer lies in what we mean by terms such as "attractive," "relationship," and "partner." When researchers are looking at what men and women want, are they looking at whom they want to hang out with, hook up with, go on a first date, or are they looking at with whom they want a fifty-year marriage? Relationships have a life cycle. The first stage is the attraction phase, when emotions run high, and physical attractiveness plays a prominent role. The vast majority of attraction research has focused on the initial stage of a relationship. However, it turns out that excitement and good looks cannot sustain a relationship. As a relationship develops, its success becomes more dependent on factors such as trust and shared values and interests, with physical attractiveness becoming less important. Violations of trust, as well as the lack of shared values and interests, are often at the core of relationship dissolution. Research on long-term relationships finds that women and men in both heterosexual and same-sex relationships want remarkably similar things in their relationships, such as companionship and the ability to communicate.

Two sets of explanations are advanced to explain patterns of attraction and mating, one resting on evolutionary theory and one on sociocultural theories. Evolutionary theorists tell us that a combination of short-term and long-term mating strategies has the greatest reproductive advantage, especially for men. This approach is used to explain the greater tendency for infidelity among men than women and men's greater intolerance for sexual than emotional infidelity in their female partners. Sociocultural explanations, on the other hand, look at the historically lower status of women and dependence on men for care of themselves and their children. These explanations suggest that women have learned to be more pragmatic in their mate selection. Character traits, values, and status are better indicators of a man's willingness and ability to care for a family than his physical attractiveness. However, with greater opportunities for education and economic security, women may now have more choices than in earlier times for a variety of types of relationships. Yet there are still questions about whether women can express their relationship desires free of societal constraints.

In these selections, think about what stage of a relationship the authors are discussing. Peter Jonason and colleagues suggest that the dark triad of attributes contribute to a successful short-term mating strategy for men. This triad includes narcissism, psychopathy, and Machiavellianism. Typically, psychologists would consider these attributes to be abnormal and maladaptive. So why would women initially be attracted to men who are so clearly self-centered and manipulative? Jonason suggests that these attributes include a drive for power and extraversion that might have at least a short-term advantage in the dating game. Adrian Furnham's research seems clearly opposite in what he finds women desire in a mate. Women reported valuing intelligence, stability, conscientiousness, height, education, social skills, and political/religious compatibility as highly desirous in their ideal mates. Are they lying, or do they really not know what they want? Consider his research methods. Are his findings more reflective of attributes that would contribute to a successful long-term mating strategy?

YES
Peter Jonason, et al.

The Dark Triad: Facilitating a Short-Term Mating Strategy in Men

Introduction

Machiavellianism, narcissism and psychopathy—collectively known as 'The Dark Triad'—are traits that are linked to negative personal and societal outcomes and are traditionally considered maladaptive. However, the persistence of these traits over time and across various societies, as well as linkages to positive traits, suggests that the Dark Triad can be advantageous in some ways. For instance, subclinical psychopathy is associated with a lack of neuroticism and anxiety, which may facilitate the pursuit of one's goals through adverse conditions. Similarly, narcissism is associated with self-aggrandisement, and Machiavellianism is associated with being socially manipulative, both of which may aid in reaping benefits for oneself at the expense of others, especially in initial periods of acquaintance. In the current study, we examine the links between the Dark Triad traits and a short-term mating orientation, and suggest that the Dark Triad traits represent one end of a continuum of individual differences that may facilitate a particular mating strategy.

The Dark Triad Traits: An Exploitative Social Strategy

The Dark Triad is composed of Machiavellianism, subclinical narcissism, and subclinical psychopathy. Machiavellian individuals tend to be manipulative, while demonstrating a "cool" or "cold" approach to others. Subclinical narcissists, sometimes called "normal narcissists," tend to have a sense of entitlement and seek admiration, attention, prestige, and status. Subclinical psychopaths are characterised by high impulsivity and thrill-seeking and tend to have low empathy. Associations among the three traits have been studied in both clinical and nonclinical settings. The three traits are moderately intercorrelated, and each contains a degree of self-aggrandisement, aggression and duplicity. We contend that the three traits may be best viewed as one particular social orientation towards conspecifics.

Specifically, various lines of research suggest that the Dark Triad may facilitate a social style geared towards exploiting others in short-term social contexts. For instance, narcissists tend to be more agentic, with a desire for power and dominance, are less communally oriented, and have a lower tendency to feel guilt or shame. Those with high levels of Machiavellianism are described as charmers and as exploitative demonstrate less empathy, and are less willing to help others in need. Psychopaths have an exploitative nature, with high levels of egocentrism, impulsivity, and irresponsibility, and have low levels of empathy, shame, and guilt.

Clearly the three traits are associated with both high levels of self-interest and low levels of empathic qualities. As such, individuals who score high on the Dark Triad traits are not well suited for or interested in maintaining long-term relationships, where continued reciprocity is integral. Likewise, once their qualities are evident to others, excessively self-serving individuals should be viewed as undesirable, and thus, to be avoided by potential long-term partners. To the extent that this occurs, a self-serving, exploitative nature should be better suited to transacting with others in shorter-term durations (i.e., a "hit and run" strategy).

An Exploitative Short-Term Mating Strategy

In a mating context, those high on the Dark Triad traits may be especially well suited for an exploitative, short-term approach. For example, all three traits are correlated with low agreeableness, which is associated with conflict in long-term relationships and marital dissatisfaction. Machiavellianism is associated with promiscuous, as well as sexually coercive behaviour. Narcissists tend to have an unrestricted sociosexuality and higher levels of infidelity. Narcissists find it easy to start new relationships, but are less committed to and interested in staying in existing relationships, hence, they may pursue exploitative short-term matings to improve their own reproductive interests at the expense of their partners. We predicted that the three individual measures associated with the Dark Triad—narcissism, psychopathy, and Machiavellianism—would be positively associated with behavioural and attitudinal measures of short-term mating.

Pursuing an exploitative short-term mating strategy may be more advantageous for men than women. First, short-term mating may, on average, provide more reproductive benefits to men. That is, women—but not men—are physiologically required to undertake pregnancy and nursing. Because pregnancy was always a possible outcome of sexual intercourse in the ancestral past, casual sex resulted in higher potential costs for ancestral women than men. As such, women may have evolved to be less open than men towards casual sexual opportunities. Indeed, men tend to favour short-term sexual relationships much more than women do, and narcissistic men—but not women—have more illegitimate children. Second, men tend to score higher on the Dark Triad personality traits than women. Therefore, we would expect the facilitation of a short-term mating strategy from having high level of the Dark Triad traits to be more applicable to men than women. Thus, we predicted that the sex of the participant will moderate the positive correlations between scores on the Dark Triad, such that the correlation will be stronger in men than women.

This moderation prediction is informed by the pervasive fact that sex differences persist in mating behaviour. Men's greater interest in short-term sexual relationships compared to women is one of the most consistent and strongest sex differences in the field. However, personality traits like the Dark Triad may facilitate the pursuit of short-term mating in men. Thus, we conducted mediation analyses on the relationship between the sex of the participant and rates of short-term mating. Therefore, we predicted that when the Dark Triad is treated as a unit, it will partially mediate the relationship between the sex of the participant and rates of short-term mating behaviour.

However, only partial mediation is expected because numerous other individual differences, including extraversion, are likely to facilitate short-term mating. Extraversion may be related to extrapair mating in men and lower relationship commitment in women. Extraverts are generally more interested in short-term mating than introverts. Extraversion and the Dark Triad traits are positively correlated. In addition, variables such as age and sex of the participant are also associated with higher self-reports of sexual behaviour. Therefore, we also investigated the correlation between the Dark Triad and short-term mating when we control for the potential confounds of extraversion, age, and sex.

Method

Participants

Two hundred and twenty-four psychology undergraduate students at New Mexico State University (88 men, 136 women) aged 17–43 years (mean = 23.50, median = 21, SD = 6.40) received extra credit for participation. The majority of the sample (88%) was heterosexual, 5% was homosexual, and 6% was bisexual (1% nonresponsive).

Procedures

Participants received a packet that (a) informed them of the nature of the study, (b) asked demographic questions, and (c) asked them to respond to the self-report items described below. Participants completed the survey alone in a room with a closed door and a two-way mirror that allowed an experimenter to monitor the participant's progress. Upon completion, the participants were debriefed and thanked for their participation.

Measures of the Dark Triad

Narcissism was assessed with the 40-item Narcissistic Personality Inventory, a validated and widely used measure. For each item, participants chose one of two statements that they felt applied to them more. One of the two statements reflected a narcissistic attitude (e.g., "I have a natural talent for influencing people"), whereas the other statement did not (e.g., "I am not good at influencing people"). We summed the total number of narcissistic statements the participants endorsed to measure overall narcissism. . . .

The 31-item Self-Report Psychopathy Scale-III was used to assess subclinical psychopathy. This measure has good psychometric properties. Participants rated how much they agreed (1 = strongly disagree, 5 = strongly agree) with statements such as: "I enjoy driving at high speeds" and "I think I could beat a lie detector." The items were averaged to create an index of psychopathy. . . .

Machiavellianism was measured with the 20-item MACH-IV. This measure has good psychometric properties. Participants were asked how much they agreed (1 = strongly disagree, 5 = strongly agree) with statements such as: "It is hard to get ahead without cutting corners here and there" and "People suffering from incurable diseases should have the choice of being put painlessly to death." The items were averaged to create a Machiavellianism index. . . .

We also treated the three Dark Triad measures as a composite measure of an exploitive sexual strategy. We first standardised (z-scored) overall scores on each measure and then averaged all three together to create a composite Dark Triad score. Overall scores were used as opposed to using the complete set of items from all the scales because dichotomous data, like that in the NPI, is problematic in factor reduction procedures. We then conducted analyses on an overall Dark Triad score . . . in addition to the constituent parts. Such an estimate of internal consistency is reasonable for a three-item scale in basic research.

Measures of Short-Term Mating

Sociosexual orientation (SOI) was assessed, measuring both sociosexual attitudes (e.g., "I can imagine myself being comfortable and enjoying casual sex with different partners") and behaviours (e.g., "With how many different partners have you had sexual intercourse within the past year"). As in prior work, individual SOI items were standardised (z-scored) prior to computing an index of sociosexuality. . . .

Participants reported the degree to which they were seeking a short-term mate (1 = not strongly currently seeking, 7 = strongly currently seeking) using a single-item, face-valid question. Such a measure may provide a rough estimate of participants' sociosexual desires. Additionally, we assessed the degree to which participants were seeking a long-term mate as a means of briefly assessing a contrasting mating strategy. It was assessed just as the corresponding item for seeking a short-term partner.

Participants also reported their number of lifetime vaginal-sex partners. Because these numbers were positively skewed, we performed a log-transformation before analyses.

All the short-term mating measures were standardised (z-scored) and then averaged to create an index of attitudes, behaviours, and desires towards short-term mating. . . . The measures of short-term mating were moderately correlated with each other. . . . We did not include the item for degree of seeking a long-term partner in this composite.

Extraversion as a Covariate

Extraversion was measured with seven self-descriptive statements from the NEO-PI-R that are cross-culturally reliable and valid. Participants were asked how much a series of statements fit with their self-concept of how extraverted they were (1 = not at all; 5 = very much). Specifically they were asked: "I see myself as someone who. . ." (e.g., "Is talkative," "Generates a lot of enthusiasm"). The responses to these statements were averaged to create an index of extraversion (α = .75).

Results

Compared with women, men scored higher on Dark Triad traits, as well as short-term mating behaviours and attitudes. Men did not show a significantly . . . higher preference for seeking long-term mates . . . than women. . . .

To examine the possibility that the Dark Triad may reflect a single, underlying social strategy, we conducted three separate tests. First, we tested the intercorrelations among the three measures to determine how strongly correlated they were with one another. Narcissism was significantly correlated with Machiavellianism . . . and psychopathy . . . , and psychopathy was significantly correlated with Machiavellianism. . . . Next an exploratory factor analysis yielded a one factor solution when we considered all three measures of the Dark Triad. . . . Last, we conducted a confirmatory factor analysis to examine the possibility that the three measures reflected a single latent factor that we will call "an exploitive social style." . . . These . . . tests provide convergent evidence that the three measures of the Dark Triad can be treated as a composite. With this support in hand, subsequent analyses were conducted on the Dark Triad composite and its components.

To examine whether the Dark Triad was related to short-term mating, we assessed the intercorrelations between the Dark Triad measures and the short-term mating measures. People's standings on each of the three components of the Dark Triad were related to their history of, orientation towards, and interest in short-term mating, but not long-term mating.

To address the possibility that the Dark Triad is a suite of traits that facilitate short-term mating in men, we tested whether the sex of the participant moderated the relationship between a Dark Triad composite and a short-term mating composite. . . . The Dark Triad composite and short-term mating composite were correlated in men . . . and in women. . . . Second, . . . the Dark Triad was correlated with short-term mating in men . . . and women. . . . [Results] confirmed our prediction that the sex of the participant would moderate the relationship between the Dark Triad and short-term mating.

We hypothesised that the Dark Triad would partially mediate the sex difference in short-term mating. Mediation is present when the relationship between two variables is carried by a third variable that is related significantly to the first two variables. . . . We found significant partial mediation. . . .

To confirm that variables such as age, participant's sex, and extraversion were not driving the correlation between the Dark Triad and short-term mating, we built a hierarchical regression model. . . . The Dark Triad composite remained a significant predictor of short-term mating whereas extraversion did not. This analysis also demonstrated that the mediation was robust after controlling for other sources of variability that have been associated with short-term mating.

Discussion

Although most studies have focused on the negative aspects of the Dark Triad, our evidence suggests that there might be some up-sides to these anti-social personality traits. We found that the scores on the Dark Triad traits were positively related to having more sex partners, an unrestricted sociosexuality and a greater preference for short-term mates. We demonstrated that the association between the Dark Triad composite was correlated with short-term mating above and beyond effects of participant's age, sex and extraversion. We also provide evidence that the three measures of the Dark Triad can be compressed into a composite measure, most notably evidenced in the exploratory and the confirmatory factor analyses.

We confirmed sex differences in all three Dark Triad measures when using a college-student sample. We found a rather high sex difference in psychopathy which may reflect greater rates of secondary psychopathy in some college-aged American men than women. Because we had a smaller amount of men than women in our sample, a few men may have had an undue influence on this sex difference. We confirmed sex differences in short-term mating and a convergence in interest in long-term mating.

Results are consistent with the possibility that the Dark Triad traits may facilitate an exploitative, short-term mating style in men and with work on Machiavellianism, narcissism, and the complete Dark Triad. Our mediation tests showed that personality traits such as the Dark Triad partially mediate the relationships between the sex of the participant and short-term mating. However, this was merely a partial mediation, which we suspect is caused by (a) the reliance on a student sample which may mask some of the extremes of these traits in the population, (b) response biases endemic to self-reports of socially undesirable traits, and (c) the large array of possible individual differences that could also partially mediate the sex difference in short-term mating.

Adaptive Individual Differences?

Whereas personality psychology has been primarily concerned with documenting trait-level individual differences among people, evolutionary psychology has typically been concerned with identifying adaptive, species-typical traits and commonalities among peoples. In recent years, these two approaches have been integrated to yield powerful explanations of individual differences. It is via this adaptive individual difference perspective that we will interpret our results.

An evolutionary view of personality considers traits to have been naturally selected, allowing individuals to compete against conspecifics and deal with the environment. Although directional selection tends to decrease trait variation, localising it in species-typical traits, trait continuums can be maintained in a population if different levels of traits are reproductively useful. For instance, a trait may consist of a dimension whereby both poles of the trait can yield adaptive benefits or bear adaptive costs under certain conditions. That is, one end on a trait (e.g., dominance) might have associated costs and benefits (greater risk and rewards), and the other end of a trait (e.g., submissiveness) might have its own costs and benefits (e.g., lower risks and rewards). However, as long as net fitness gains are achieved by individuals at both ends, then individual differences on this trait may be maintained in the population via balancing selection.

Our study indicates a connection between the Dark Triad and more positive attitudes towards casual sex and more casual sex behaviours. To the extent that lifetime number of sexual partners is a modern-day marker of reproductive success, and given that the Dark Triad traits are heritable and exist in different cultures, we speculate that these traits may represent one end of a set of individual differences that reflects an evolutionarily stable solution to the adaptive problem of reproduction.

Limitations

Personality traits, such as those associated with the Dark Triad, are often considered to be global, continuous measures. We agree that global measures, such as SOI, may obscure the sophisticated or multidimensional nature of personality traits. Independently, the three Dark Triad measures may have distinct implications for psychological and interpersonal functioning. However, in the case of mating, it appears that all three may be measuring the same or a similar social strategy. Specifically, those who score high on the Dark Triad traits may be equipped to engage in exploitative (e.g., deceptive promises of commitment, behaviourally aggressive) short-term mating, which may be a viable reproductive strategy when the relative frequency of exploitable cooperators in a population is sufficiently high. Whereas such a strategy capitalises on quantity at the cost of receiving long-term benefits, individuals who are not high on the Dark Triad traits—the majority of populations—may be better equipped to form cooperative long-term relationships and, to a lesser degree, short-term relationships without deception. This long-term, nonexploitive strategy may represent a slower but more stable approach to reproduction. These two mating strategies have been described as the *Cad* and *Dad* strategies or in literature analyses, the "dark hero" and the "proper hero." Furthermore, because of the asymmetries in reproductive constraints between the sexes, a short-term mating strategy, and by extension, the Dark Triad traits, are more likely to benefit men's reproductive fitness than women's.

This study was based on self-report data offered by psychology undergraduate students from the southwestern United States, and thus, our results are limited in their generalisability. Future work should attempt to replicate our findings with a more diverse, cross-cultural sample. Additionally, we cannot exclude the possibility that the present results were partially caused by some individuals (i.e., high scorers on the Dark Triad measures) positively biasing their sexual success in the form of reported lifetime sex partners. We feel our utilisation of multiple measures of short-term mating should alleviate such concerns. Future research should examine whether scores on the Dark Triad traits mediate the sex difference in sexual success.

In our analyses, we used overall measures of narcissism, psychopathy, Machiavellianism, and sociosexuality. However, work suggests that these measures can be broken down into sub-dimensions. For instance, SOI can be divided into sociosexual attitudes and behaviours or into past behavioural experiences, attitudes towards uncommitted sex, and sociosexual desire; the NPI can be divided into four or seven components; psychopathy can be divided into primary and secondary psychopathy; and at least two different factor structures have been used with Machiavellianism. While we reported only the overall results, we did assess different scale dimensions during our analyses and did not find differences among them. For instance, both socio-sexual behaviours and attitudes were moderately correlated with all three of the Dark Triad measures and with the composite variable of the Dark Triad.

All three Dark Triad traits are associated with an exploitative social style. However, actual exploitative behaviours in mating, and in general, are rarely addressed. Future work should examine the Dark Triad traits along with mating-related deception, mate-poaching, coercive mating, and other more general measures of this exploitative approach to conspecifics.

Conclusion

The personality traits that compose the Dark Triad have typically been considered abnormal, pathological, and inherently maladaptive. Although individuals with these traits inflict costs to others and themselves, the Dark Triad traits are also associated with some qualities, including a drive for power, low neuroticism, and extraversion, that may be beneficial. Together with low amounts of empathy and agreeableness, such traits may facilitate—especially for men—the pursuit of an exploitative short-term mating strategy. Although our study is limited, it suggests a potentially interesting new avenue of research to explore. More generally, the application of evolutionary reasoning to the study of personality traits may yield fruitful insights into the wide array of individual differences that exist on various dimensions.

Adrian Furnham  **NO**

Sex Differences in Mate Selection Preferences

Introduction

There is an extensive literature on mate selection and preferences in evolutionary and social psychology. Studies in the area have been particularly concerned with two areas, namely sex differences and similarity preferences in mate attraction. The fact that women are particularly interested in "resources" and males in "attractiveness" has lead to various theoretical explanations.

The *sex-role socialisation* hypothesis suggests that females' "comparative structural powerlessness" leads them to hypergamy or marrying-upward in socio-economic status while men are more likely to accept the concept of "exchange object." Therefore physical attractiveness becomes the central mechanism or criterion for measuring relative value in exchange commodity. Traditional sex-role socialisation is assumed to be designed to support those structural differences. On the other hand, the evolutionary theory explanation is concerned with reproductive success: females focus on the social and material provisioning for offspring while males seek out fecundity. Whilst there appear to be different explanations for mate choice based on different theories, there is little evidence that they yield dramatically different hypotheses in terms of what they would predict. The aim of this study is primarily to look at sex, personality, and ideological predictors of mate choice.

There is also a *"birds of a feather"* and assortative mating literature which shows that people seek out those similar to themselves. It has been found that newlyweds showed substantial similarity on attitudes but not traits, yet a positive relationship between spouse similarity and marital quality for traits but not attitudes.

There is a literature on the influence of personality factors on their similarity, complementary and assortative mating concepts. My colleagues and I have proposed a "mating market model," which assumes that individuals examine competitors in the mate market and both negotiate and adjust their criteria based on their self and competitor ratings.

Various studies have specifically examined real, media-based personal or lonely-hearts advertisements.

From *Personality and Individual Differences*, vol. 47, 2009. Copyright © 2009 by Elsevier Health Sciences. Reprinted by permission.

There have been a number of studies using "lonely hearts," mate attraction published advertisements which have been surprisingly consistent. One analysed 800 lonely-heart advertisements of American men and women aged 20–59. They found women were more likely than men to offer attractiveness, seek financial security, express concerns about the potential partner's motives, and seek someone who was older. Men were more likely than women to seek attractiveness, offer financial security, profess an interest in marriage, and seek someone who was younger. Offers of, and demands for, financial security varied systematically with age, but concerns about appearance and character did not.

In an analysis of 98 advertisements it was found that males seek attractivity (health, sexiness) and offer resources, while females seek resources and offer attractivity. This is simple evidence of sexually dimorphic mating strategies. Yet another analysis of 1000 advertisements showed, as hypothesised, men sought women of reproductive value (young, attractive) while women looked for ability to acquire resources and provide resources (time, emotions, money, status) in the relationship. Men were more promiscuously indirect while women sought long-term monogamous relationships. . . .

Heterosexual women place emphasis on wealth and status as well as the man's willingness to invest time and effort in the relationship. Females also consistently specify physical attractiveness and social skills; males tend to emphasise physical attractiveness above all other features. The advertisements also indicate that males tend to advertise for females younger than themselves whereas females do the opposite. Further, both sexes know what the other wants. Women offer attractiveness and charm and seek commitment and resources. Men offer attractiveness, charm and resources but seek predominantly the first two.

Some studies have examined the desirability of traits in mate selection. For both males and females the top five most desirable traits are: sincerity, faithfulness, tenderness, reliability, and communicative. This suggests Conscientiousness and Agreeableness of the Big Five are the most desirable traits. In a study using experimentally designed advertisements matched to photographs, it was found that females prefer men of medium rather than high socio-economic status. The idea was that females would be worried that (very) high socio-economic status would be very desirable to all women some of whom might encourage the male to cheat or desert the partner.

In this study participants were asked to freely express what they would say about themselves and the people they are looking for. They were also asked to rate the importance of various characteristics. However, they were also asked to complete a Big Five personality measure and specific details like their height and weight, religious and political beliefs. Hence it was able to look at individual difference predictors of preferences. Whilst studies appear to support the socio-biological theories on mate choice, there appear to have been no individual difference correlates of these factors.

Based on the previous literature, it was hypothesised first, that females would place higher emphasis on education, social skills, emotional intelligence, and conscientiousness while males would place greater emphasis on attractiveness. Second, it was hypothesised that there would be a "birds of a feather"/assortative mating effect in that people would seek out those with personalities similar to themselves, specifically Extraverts would seek out Extraverts, Agreeable participants Agreeable partners, and Open participants, Imaginative partners. Third, it was hypothesised that there would be a strong ideological compatibility effect in that for those of stronger beliefs and commitments to religious and political causes this would be an overwhelmingly important factor in their preference. Specifically that those with strong ideological beliefs would emphasise the role of partner value compatibility.

Method

Participants

There were 250 participants of which 110 were all single male and 140 female. They ranged in age from 18 to 41 with a mean of 22.25 (SD = 5.03 yrs). They rated themselves 5.03 (SD = 1.16) on a 7-point attractiveness scale; 4.48 (SD = 2.03) on a 7-point religious scale (1 Very, 7 Not at All), and 3.98 (SD = 1.12) on a political scale (1 = right wing, 7 = left wing). Their mean weight was 62.38 kg (SD = 13.07) and height 169.80 cm (SD = 9.38). Around a third were Asian from Hong Kong, China, and Singapore, half European, mainly British, and the remainder from North America and Australasia. Around three quarters were students at a variety of higher education institutions, mainly universities.

Questionnaire

They completed either on-line (80%) or on paper (20%) a two page questionnaire. The first part required participants to write down five characteristics that they believed best describes themselves, then write down—in rank order—the five characteristics that they most want in a long-term romantic partner. They then rated the characteristics. These were rated on an 11-point scale where 0 = Not Desirable to 11 = Extremely Desirable.

Personality was assessed by a frequently used brief (15 item) measure of the Big Five questionnaire. It has adequate evidence of internal reliability as well as construct and predictive validity. They were also asked to indicate personal details like age, sex, height, weight, strength of religious beliefs, political leaning, marital status, etc.

Procedure

Ten research assistants contacted around 25 friends mainly by emailing, asking if they or their friends would complete a short and interesting questionnaire. This may mean this is a very unrepresentative sample. They were asked to ensure that they were roughly half male and half female, between the age of 18 and 35 yrs old, unmarried, and heterosexual. They reported on average a 96% response rate. Ethical approval was sought and obtained for the study.

Results

A content analysis of the free responses based on a frequency count of the qualities/traits mentioned by each participant was done. Some categories showed relatively big differences between the descriptions given by the male and female respondents. Females were more likely to describe themselves as outgoing/sociable/extraverted, cheerful/optimistic, and caring/loving compared to males who were more likely to describe themselves as intelligent/competent/capable and good looking/attractive.

The top three categories of adjective/descriptions listed by the males for what characteristics they wanted in a partner were looks/attractiveness, caring/loving, and intelligence. For females it was caring/loving, then funny/humorous, and third loyal/honest.

Rated Preference

. . . Females showed a significant higher preference compared to males for cognitive ability, emotional intelligence, conscientiousness, height, education, social skills, and political compatibility. It was only good looks where male ratings were significantly higher than females. This confirms the first hypothesis. Effect sizes were greatest for height, Conscientiousness, and social skills. . . .

The results showed Agreeableness, Emotional Intelligence and Emotional stability were rated highest (i.e., most desirable) while political and religious compatibility as well as height rated lowest (i.e., least desirable). Abilities and personality tended to be more highly rated than physical factors and looks.

Preferences were correlated with various individual difference factors, two demographic, one self-rating of attractiveness, and the final two of the "ideological" or belief variable. Age of participant showed few correlations. The importance of the physical attractiveness of the partner was confirmed by the ratings. The more religious the person the greater importance they attached to personality (stability, agreeableness, conscientiousness) and values, especially religious compatibility. Religious compatibility was more important to females than males, but the relationship was consistent for both sexes. Political beliefs of the participants had few significant relationships.

The participants' height, weight, and BMI were also correlated with the ratings. Heavier participants rated Conscientiousness . . . , height . . . , and education lower than lighter participants. Taller participants rated good looks more highly . . . but Conscientiousness lower . . . than shorter people. Participants' BMI was correlated negatively with the rated importance of partner conscientiousness . . . , height . . . education . . . and social skills. . . . Height of participant was correlated . . . with ratings of height in a partner. For males the correlation was .63, but for females it was $r = .23$.

Thereafter a set of regressions were performed to examine which, and to what extent, the participant individual difference variables predicted their separate ratings. . . .

A. *Ability:* the only significant regression was for intelligence as criterion factor. Conscientious females rated this more highly. . . .

B. *Personality:* all except one regression was significant. The pattern showed that the participants' personality was the best predictor of personality trait preferences and that there was clear evidence of "like attracts like." Conscientious participants rated Conscientiousness in potential mates highly, as was the case with Openness which predicted ratings of Imaginativeness. Stable, Conscientious females rated Stability in a partner highly while open extraverts rated extraversion highly. However, Neurotic participants preferred stable partners and the participants' Agreeableness scores were unrelated to all ratings. This confirms the second hypothesis.

C. *Physical:* all four regressions were significant. Surprisingly neither sex, nor age, nor BMI were related to the overall ratings of physical characteristics. Agreeableness and Conscientiousness were the only predictors. Disagreeable Conscientious participants rated physical attractiveness highly. Age was related to looks; older, Disagreeable people rated looks less important than younger people. Sex was the only predictor of ratings of height (not BMI) and thus accounted for over 10% of the variance. Open, Disagreeable, Conscientious people rated health most highly.

D. *Social Factors:* again, all regressions were significant and results showed three participant characteristics were consistently significant predictors. Conscientious, low BMI, females rated the overall factor most highly. Slimmer, conscientious people rated education highly, while Conscientious females rated social skills highly. However, it is possible that slimness is a correlate of, and index of, higher socioeconomic status and education. This study did not measure socioeconomic status which would be desirable in future studies.

E. *Values:* all three regressions were significant. . . . Females with a conservative ideology (highly religious and right wing) placed high value on political compatibility. Low Openness participants with a conservative ideology placed considerable emphasis on religious compatibility. This confirms the third hypothesis.

Discussion

The results of this study provide broad support for the hypotheses, which are similar to other studies. Females did rate cognitive ability, social skills, height and conscientiousness more highly than males who in turn rated "good looks" more highly. This confirms nearly all the content analysis studies reviewed in the introduction. However, . . . differences in sex partner preferences are restricted to very specific areas. This study did not include wealth or profession but it could be argued that intelligent (cognitive ability), highly educated, Conscientious, and socially skilled males are most likely to have stable, well-paid, professional jobs. It is interesting to notice that height seemed of particular importance to females though overall it was the third lowest rated factor. Recent studies on height preferences showed that both men and women preferred relationships in which the woman was shorter than the man.

This study showed that there were individual differences, as well as simply sex differences in mate selection. For some factors there was general agreement that the rated factor cognitive ability, emotional intelligence, physical health, social skills—was desirable. However, personality factors did clearly play a part in preferences for personality traits, particularly extraversion and conscientiousness.

There was clear evidence of the "birds of a feather" personality-likeness factor. For each of the regressions, with the exception of Agreeableness, the trait score of the participants on each of the five factors was predictive of the desired trait in a mate. This was strongest for Extraversion and Conscientiousness and throws in dispute Jungian ideas of "opposites" attracting one another, which have not seen much empirical support.

Perhaps one of the most unique aspects of this study was to include political and religious beliefs as both a criterion and predictor variable. Overall religious and political compatibility was not rated as particularly important for these participants but religious compatibility more highly than political compatibility. Further the religious beliefs of participants were a more powerful predictor in their mate choice criteria than political beliefs. Other studies have documented the importance of religion in mate preferences. However, participant ideology did have predictively a very powerful impact on participants' preference for political and religious compatibility. Indeed, together with openness, participant ideology predicted 30% of the variance in the ratings of religious compatibility.

How would evolutionary psychologists explain this? Religion is a strong predictor of values and life style. Religions pre- and proscribe behaviour with respect to money, alcohol, child-rearing. People of similar beliefs are less likely to argue about important social issues and to have similar aims and goals. Most religions still seem conservative with respect to sex-roles and encourage both in-group marriages and having many children to support the youth. People who stay within the faith are likely to be protected and assisted by others while the opposite is true for those who marry out. In this sense there are probably evolutionary advantages to select out people of similar religious beliefs.

Like all others this study has its limitations. The participants were all young and it would have been better to have had a wider age range from a more representative population group. Further it would be most desirable to know about the nature and status of their current relationship and whether they had indeed ever used lonely hearts columns. There is also a problem with respect to questionnaire methodology. Various evolutionary psychology studies have shown that females respond to testosterone-related markers of male physical traits as well as cues to facial and body bilateral symmetry. This means that there may be a mismatch between what females say they may want in a partner and what they actually seek or respond to. This is an important theoretical and methodological issue.

Research using photographs and "live models" suggest that small visual cues have a powerful effect below consciousness on the ratings of attractiveness, . . . such as the symmetry, length and size of fingers, hands, feet and legs, skin-tone, facial hair as well as face structure and shape. These have predictable and consistent relationships with ratings of attractiveness, health, preferences and therefore mate selection. Yet few if any person-descriptions used in questionnaires contain such data preferring to mention more sociological markers like education or ability factors like intelligence or vocabulary. Thus, it may be that results in this area are very methodologically dependent because people actually respond more powerfully to physical cues they rarely mention and maybe are even unaware of. It may be possible to test the relative power of different factors experimentally by varying body-cues and verbal descriptions to see whether mate selection is based more on subtle physical markers of health, than sociological markers of status or wealth. It may also mean that ultimately the self-report methodology of questionnaires may lead to findings that are misleading in the sense that they do not represent how people behave when faced with visual cues.

EXPLORING THE ISSUE

Do Nice Guys Finish Last?

Challenge Questions

1. Is it possible to not have first impressions of someone based on appearance?
2. Have you ever watched a reality dating TV show? What can the lessons learned by relationship researchers tell us about these shows?
3. How do discussions of attraction and mate selection relate to issues of sexuality and sexual expression?
4. Are sex education programs an appropriate site to teach young people about healthy relationships?
5. How would you define a healthy relationship?

Is There Common Ground?

A recent search for dating and relationship reality TV shows revealed 54 hits, including titles such as *the Bachelor*, *elimiDATE*, *The Millionaire Matchmaker*, and *Who Wants to Marry My Dad*. Interestingly, in this search *Cheaters* came up as the first hit. Have you watched any of these shows? What is the basic premise? What do these reality dating shows, from *The Bachelorette* to *Average Joe* to *Hell Date*, have in common? What assumptions do they reflect about what people are looking for in a relationship? What assumptions are they making about how relationships begin? What are the odds that the relationships formed on these shows will last? Do you think it is possible to find true love under the glaring eyes of the camera and millions of TV viewers? Why?

Over the past three decades, women's sexuality has changed—by some accounts dramatically—in ways more commensurate with men's sexuality. In general, women are gaining greater sexual experience. They engage in intercourse at a younger age, they have more sex partners, they engage in sexual intercourse more frequently, and they are increasingly likely to engage in casual sex. Yet, despite this trend toward sex equality in behaviors, traditional gender socialization and the sexual double standard continue to act as an interpretive filter for sexual experience.

Competitiveness, assertiveness, and coercion often characterize males' sexual experiences. Males' self- and peer-esteem are linked to sexual experience and performance. Many future-oriented sexologists caution that in striving for sexual equality, we must not limit ourselves to a preset "male" definition of sexual freedom. Psychologist and sex researcher Leonore Tiefer argues that we need to encourage women's sexual experimentation and explore sexual possibilities. Furthermore, new ideas need to be developed about desire and pleasure. There needs to be freely available information, ideas, images, and open sexual talk. Tiefer asserts that if women develop sexual knowledge and self-knowledge, they can take more responsibility for their own pleasure. Traditional sex education programming has overlooked the possibility of female desire and sexual pleasure, and they do not focus on relationship issues. Some argue that sex education programs can be used to help females protect themselves from being treated as objects but to think of themselves as sexual subjects. Women as sexual subjects would feel free to seek out sexual pleasure and know that they have a right to this pleasure. This argument supports the assertion that we also need to raise boys to avoid treating females as sexual objects. The challenge for sex education programming is to inform women about the possible risks of sexual relationships without supporting the double standard that limits, inhibits, and controls their sexuality. Ideally, sex education programming would include education specifically about gender ideology, as it influences sexual perceptions, decisions, and experiences. Conformity to gender-based norms and ideals for sexual activity and relationships is the most important source of peer sexual pressure and risky sex among youth; youth "perform" gendered roles in sexual relations to secure gender affirmation. Advocates of sex education reform also call for incorporating definitions of "good sex"—sex that is not coercive, exploitative, or harmful. Thus, greater attention to the meaning of healthy relationships is also necessary; young people could learn how to think about attributes to look for in an ideal partner and perhaps, in males in particular, can avoid the "dark triad" in potential mates. They caution not to impose rigid definitions of "sexual normality"; rather, identify some dimensions of healthy sexuality as examples upon which individuals can explore and develop their own unique sexual identity and style. It has been observed that a central practice in the social construction of gender inequality is *compulsory heterosexuality* or societal pressure to be heterosexual. Many sexual revolutionaries argue that an important condition of sexual freedom is freedom from pressures to be a particular "type" of sexual being or to be in a particular type of relationship. Return to the questions asked at the beginning of this commentary about reality dating programs and the impact of watching them in the context of this discussion about sex education programs. Unfortunately, watching these programs may have effects that run counter to good sex education programs. Research has shown that there is a correlation between the amount of reality dating program viewing and sexual attitudes and behaviors, such that greater consumption is associated with stronger endorsement of the sexual double standard, that dating is a game, the belief that appearance is important in dating, strong adversarial sexual beliefs, and that men are sex-driven. This finding is true for women and men, but men report watching these shows for learning more than women do. In discussing this research, Eileen Zurbriggen has said, "Thus, ironically, reality dating programs that purport to show 'real' people in dating situations may actually be an impediment to viewers who hope to create healthy intimacy in their own relationships and to make intelligent decisions about sexuality."

Additional Resources

Joel D. Block, *Broken Promises, Mended Hearts: Maintaining Trust in Love Relationships* (New York: McGraw-Hill, 2001).

Benjamin R. Karney et al., *Adolescent Romantic Relationships as Precursors of Healthy Adult Marriages: A Review of Theory, Research, and Programs* (RAND, 2007).

Julia Ransohoff et al., "ABCs of a Healthy Relationship," http://www.pamf.org/teen/abc/

Leonore Tiefer, "Arriving at a 'New View' of Women's Sexual Problems: Background, Theory, and Activism," *Women and Therapy*, 24, 63–98.

Deborah Tolman, *Dilemmas of Desire: Teenage Girls Talk about Sexuality* (Cambridge, MA: Harvard University Press, 2005).

George Weinberg, *Why Men Won't Commit: Getting What You Both Want Without Playing Games* (New York: Simon & Schuster, 2004).

Naomi Wolf, *The Beauty Myth: How Images of Beauty Are Used Against Women* (New York: HarperCollins, 2002).

Wellsphere, http://www.wellsphere.com/wellpage/healthy-relationships-activities

ISSUE 10

Gender Symmetry: Do Women and Men Commit Equal Levels of Violence Against Intimate Partners?

YES: **Murray A. Straus and Ignacio L. Ramirez**, from "Gender Symmetry in Prevalence, Severity, and Chronicity of Physical Aggression Against Dating Partners by University Students in Mexico and USA," *Aggressive Behavior* (vol. 33, 2007)

NO: **Christopher T. Allen, Suzanne C. Swan, and Chitra Raghaven**, from "Gender Symmetry, Sexism, and Intimate Partner Violence," *Journal of Interpersonal Violence* (vol. 24, 2008)

Learning Outcomes

As you read the issue, focus on the following points:

- What is the definition of intimate partner violence typically used in research? How is it typically measured?
- What does gender symmetry mean?
- Why is it important to distinguish the percentage of women and men who state they have used physical aggression against a partner from the frequency with which they do so from the level of severity of the acts they commit?

ISSUE SUMMARY

YES: Murray A. Straus and his colleague Ignacio L. Ramirez argue that women are just as likely to commit physical aggression against dating partners as are men, suggesting that gender symmetry exists in different cultural contexts.

NO: On the other hand, social psychologists Christopher T. Allen, Suzanne C. Swan, and Chitra Raghaven argue that women's use of aggression does not equate to gender symmetry. Rather, cultural context, motives, and history of trauma must be considered.

One of the most contentious and emotional issues in the intimate partner violence (IPV) literature surrounds the issue of "gender symmetry" in the use of aggression in relationships. Gender symmetry refers to the equivalence in women's and men's use of violence. For many years, the stereotype was of the male batterer and the female victim. Mental health, medical emergency room, and criminal justice data support this assumption. Many more women than men show up at shelters and emergency rooms suffering from the psychological and physical effects of abuse; many more women than men are likely to be murdered by an intimate partner. In contrast, most survey research that asks high school aged youth, college students, and community samples about their use of verbal and physical aggression in intimate relationships finds a very different pattern of results. In these studies, as many women as men, and sometimes more, report aggression against their partners, at least when the Conflict Tactics Scale (CTS) is the research instrument of choice. These data have led some researchers to conclude that such "gender symmetry" indicates that gender is not a central issue in IPV and that the study of IPV should move from the study of gender to other issues such as dominance. However, the same studies that use the CTS still find that women are more likely to be injured than men, suggesting to a different group of researchers that gender is still a central construct of interest. This perspective suggests that it is important to acknowledge and study women's aggression toward male partners, but to maintain a focus on gender. In fact, feminists have suggested that maintenance of the myth of the nonaggressive female contributes to continued discrimination against women. That is, if women are not aggressive, they must turn to men for protection (giving up their independence in exchange for the protection); they are not capable of leadership positions (based on the assumption that aggression is correlated with power, authority, and assertiveness); and if they are aggressive, they must be mentally ill (i.e., deviation from expected gender roles is an indicator of mental illness). Feminist research is challenging this myth in numerous ways, as reflected in several special issues of journals (*Violence Against Women, Psychology of Women Quarterly, Sex Roles*). Scholars such as Kristen Anderson argue that it is essential that we begin to theorize the concepts of gender and violence rather than to assume that everyone understands these concepts.

Family conflict theory and feminist theory are the two primary theories used to describe IPV and they are often pitted against each. According to family conflict theorists, the finding of no sex differences in percentages of women and men who report engaging in partner violence is evidence for gender symmetry. For them, such findings make gender roles and norms theoretically unimportant. Feminist theorists, on the other hand, suggest that researchers need only look at data from emergency rooms and shelters to know that women are the usual targets of far more serious partner violence than are men. For them, it is crucial to focus on the role of patriarchy and societal gender inequality in prescribing how men and women are supposed to both express aggression and to react to it once it happens. They invoke the principles of social learning theory to explain how sociocultural values are transmitted and learned at the individual level. Furthermore, Kristen Anderson notes that family conflict theorists treat gender and violence as individual-level factors, whereas feminists consider them at the interactionist and structuralist levels. That is, for family conflict theorists, sex is an independent variable and therefore, if equal percentages of women and men commit partner violence, partner violence must not be "caused" by sex but by some other individual-level variable(s), such as dominance (as suggested by Murray Straus) or physical size (as suggested by Richard Felson). Anderson notes that these assumptions foster stereotypic and essentialist views of women and men and reduce gender to the behavior of individuals. On the other hand, the interactionist and structuralist approaches suggest that aggression produces gender. That is, people "do gender"; gender is a characteristic of social interactions and societal norms. Thus, behavior defines gender. For example, in order to construct and maintain one's identify, a male may engage in aggressive behavior to demonstrate his maleness, to himself as well as to others. Several lines of research suggest that the meaning of violence depends on the context as well as the sex of perpetrator and victim. Ann Campbell, for example, has shown that male violence is used for instrumental goals, including maintaining control, whereas women's violence is seen as emotional and an indication of a loss of control. Men feel justified in using violence as a right to maintain or regain control over a situation; on the other hand, women are more likely to feel that an aggressive behavior was the result of losing control and they often feel badly about their actions.

In addition to different theoretical perspectives, driving the work of family conflict and feminist researchers is the issue of definition and measurement of IPV. Many empirical studies have used only the CTS that limits the conceptualization of IPV to physical aggression. Although the revised CTS-2 does now include questions about sexual aggression, too few studies that have used it have examined how the inclusion of sexual aggression changes the landscape of IPV. The traditional exclusion of sexual aggression from studies of IPV systematically biases the database on gendered patterns of aggression. According to the FBI, 99% of rape perpetrators are men. Sexual aggression committed by women is more often confined to verbal rather than physical coercion. Also, unwanted sexual acts may co-occur in intimate relationships on the same or on different occasions. The original CTS also excludes many modes of expressing aggression, such as use of indirect methods of aggression, for example, sabotaging another's performance. Cross-cultural research has identified an extraordinary range of harm-doing including verbal, nonverbal, and physical aggression, passive-aggressive behaviors (i.e., nonperformance of duties), property damage, and locking someone out of the house. Other acts of aggression excluded from the CTS include threatening to hurt one's partner economically or socially, humiliation, isolation, controlling what one does and whom one sees, threatening to take the children away, preventing one from getting or keeping a job, and/or not letting her have access to family resources. As one looks at this list of possible ways to harm one's partner, it is easy to see that many of these tactics may be gender-related. Thus, to rely on one instrument, the CTS (or the CTS-2), for a conclusion that there is gender symmetry in IPV, is premature.

In the selections that follow, Straus, the developer of the CTS, and his colleague demonstrate the typical pattern of gender symmetry found in survey research. In contrast, the selection by Allen and his colleagues examines the use of women's aggression toward intimate partners and presents a model for understanding female partner violence from a social contextual perspective that emphasizes one's own history of abuse along with the intersection of race, ethnicity, and class factors.

YES

**Murray A. Straus and
Ignacio L. Ramirez**

Gender Symmetry in Prevalence, Severity, and Chronicity of Physical Aggression Against Dating Partners by University Students in Mexico and USA

Introduction

A controversial issue in research on intimate partner violence (PV from here on) is whether this type of assault is primarily a crime perpetrated by men. A previous paper on this issue shows that when the statistics are based on data from the police or from surveys on crime victimization from 70 to 95% of PV perpetrators are men. On the other hand, the results of almost 200 studies using data from surveys of family problems and conflicts show that ". . . women are as physically aggressive, or more aggressive, than men in their relationships. . . . The aggregate sample size in the reviewed studies exceeds 58,000." The reason why police and crime survey data show PV to be a crime by males, whereas surveys of conflicts between partners in a couple relationship show that it is usually symmetrical or mutual were analyzed in a previous paper and will not be repeated here. Rather, this study is intended to move beyond tabulating the percent of men and women who had assaulted a partner during the time period covered by the study (typically the past year), by providing information on important additional aspects of PV such as the severity, chronicity of the assaults, and gender symmetry of assaults. Specifically, the purposes are:

- To determine the degree to which gender symmetry in PV is found in the diverse socio-cultural contexts in Mexico and the United States.
- To provide more detailed data on gender symmetry by
  - Providing data on the severity and chronicity of attacks by males and females.
  - Classifying couples into three groups: mutually violent, male partner only, and female partner only.
- To compare results based on data provided by male and female respondents.

Methods

Samples

The data [are] from the first four samples of the International Dating Violence Study for which data became available. . . . The data were obtained by administering questionnaires to students in introductory sociology and psychology classes at the Universidad Autonoma de Ciudad Juarez, Mexico, University of Texas at El Paso, Texas Technological University, and the University of New Hampshire.

The data were gathered using procedures reviewed and approved by the boards for protection of human subjects at each of these universities. The purpose of the study and the students' right to not participate were explained orally as well as in printed form at the beginning of each session. Participants were told that the questionnaire asked about their attitudes, beliefs, and experiences they may have had, and that the questionnaire included questions on sensitive issues, including sexual relationships. They were assured of anonymity and confidentiality. A debriefing form was given to each participant as they left. The form explained the study in more detail and provided names and telephone numbers of area mental health services and community resources such as services for battered women. Although 1,554 students completed the questionnaire, as in other surveys, not everyone answered every question. Indeed, to respect the privacy and the voluntary nature of participation the instructions emphasized that respondents were free to omit any question they did not wish to answer. One hundred and eight students (6.9%) did not answer all the questions on violence against a partner. The number of cases analyzed was 1,446 for most of the analyses. However, some analyses are based on as few as 159 cases because they were restricted to the relatively small proportion of respondents who severely assaulted a partner. . . .

Measures

Physical Assault

The revised Conflict Tactics Scales or CTS2 was used to measure physical assault by the respondent. . . . The CTS has been used in many studies of both married and dating partners in the past 25 years and there is extensive evidence of reliability and validity. Respondents are asked to indicate how often they did each of the acts in the CTS and how often their partner did. This allows for analysis of symmetry, as well as patterns of the respondent's behavior. The CTS2 has scales to measure Physical Assault, Injury, Sexual Coercion, Psychological Aggression, and Negotiation. The analyses in this paper used data from the Physical Assault scale.

The CTS2 includes subscales for two levels of severity. The Minor Assault scale includes acts such as slapping or throwing something at the partner. The Severe Assault scale includes acts such as punching and choking. The difference between the minor and severe subscales is analogous to the US legal categories of simple assault and aggravated assault. The following scores were computed:

Prevalence.   Prevalence refers to whether respondents carried out one or more of the 12 acts of physical assault in the CTS in the previous 12 months. The analysis used two measures of prevalence, one for any versus no assault (referred to as "assault"), and one for severe assault versus both no assaults and minor assaults (referred to as "severe assault").

Severity level.   A problem with the Minor Assault scale is that some of the respondents who reported minor assaults probably also carried out more severe attacks on a partner. To have a variable in which the two are mutually exclusive, respondents were classified into one of three categories: 1 = none, 2 = minor only (i.e., one or more acts of minor violence but no instance of severe violence), and 3 = severe.

Chronicity.   The CTS asks respondents to indicate how many times in the previous year they have either perpetrated or been victim of each of the acts in the scale. Chronicity was calculated only for respondents who reported at least one instance of physical assault. Chronicity therefore indicates the number of times that subjects who were physically aggressive to a partner carried out acts of physical aggression. For a discussion of the rationale of the chronicity measure of the CTS2.

Symmetry types.   Three types were identified: *male-only* refers to couples in which violence in the relationship was perpetrated only by the male partner. *Female-only* violence refers to couples where the only violence in the relation-ship was perpetrated by the female partner. *Both* refers to couples in which both the male and female partner committed at least one of the acts of physical assault in the previous 12 months. Symmetry types were computed only if the respondent reported that they, and/or their partner had perpetrated an assault.

Social Desirability Response Bias

Criminological research that uses self-report data need to take into account defensiveness or minimization of socially undesirable behavior. The Limited Disclosure scale of the PRP [Straus and Mouradian, 1999; Straus et al., 1999] was used to control for the variation in individual respondents' tendencies to minimize socially undesirable behavior. This scale is a 13-item version of the widely used Crown–Marlow social desirability scale developed by Reynolds [1982]. The scale measures the degree to which respondents tend to avoid dis-closing socially undesirable behavior.

Socioeconomic Status

Socioeconomic status was measured as a composite of the respondent's moth-er's and father's education, and family income. To control for differences in educational systems and for differences in incomes and purchasing power across countries and geographic regions, parent's education and family income were standardized (z-scored) separately for each sample, before being summed. For interpretability, the sum was then transformed to a z-score. Thus, in each sample, the score of a respondent indicates the number of standard deviations above or below the mean of respondents in that sample.

Results

Prevalence of Assaults on Dating Partners

Combined samples.   When all four samples are analyzed together, a third of the students (33.7%) reported they had physically assaulted a dating partner in the previous 12 months. This is consistent with many other studies of dating violence by university students.

Sample differences.   The percent of students reporting violence was high in all four samples, but also differed significantly between samples. . . . The lowest rate was in New Hampshire (29.7%), followed by Texas, Non-Mexican Whites (30.9%), Texas Mexican American (34.2%), and the highest rate of assault was in Juarez (46.1%).

Gender differences.   Although there were significant differences between samples, . . . the rates for males and females were similar. Thus, the four samples analyzed in this paper had similar rates of partner-assault by men and women. This finding is consistent with previous research on couple conflict discussed in the introduction.

Severe Assaults on Dating Partners

The similar rates of assaulting a partner by men and women could be misleading because the overall rate combines minor acts such as slapping and throwing things with more severe assaults involving punching, kicking, choking, etc. It is possible that the overall rate of assaults could be equal, but a larger proportion of the assaults by men could be in the form of attacks that are more likely to result in an injury. This possibility was investigated by examining the severity level of assaults.

Combined samples.   Overall, more than one out of ten students (11.4%) reported severely attacking a partner (acts such as punching, kicking, or choking).

Sample differences.   The samples differed significantly in the rate of severe violence. The differences were similar to the difference for the overall violence rate, i.e., the lowest rate was in New Hampshire (9.3%), followed by Mexican-Americans in Texas (12.4%), Non-Mexicans in Texas (14.2%) and highest in Juarez (15%).

Gender differences.   [T]he rates of severe assault are almost identical for men and women. Thus, the similarity between men and women in the overall rate of violence against a partner also applies to severe attacks.

When severity level scores were examined, controlling for age, SES, and score on the Social Desirability Response scale no significant differences in the scores of male and female students were found. The interaction of gender and sample was also non-significant indicating that the absence of a gender difference applied to all four samples.

Chronicity of Assaults

Combined samples. The results from these four samples show that, among the couples where there was violence, it was not usually a one-time occurrence. Students who were physically aggressive to a partner carried out a mean of 14.7 acts of physical aggression in the previous 12 months. However, the mean overstates the typical pattern because of a relatively few cases in which violence occurred once a week or more, including a few where it was almost daily. Therefore, the median of four times in the previous year gives a better picture of the typical pattern of violence between dating couples.

A surprising finding was that average number of *severe* assaults (15.6) and the median number of severe assaults (4) was just about the same as mean and medians for the total assault scale. This indicates that when violence is severe, it also tends to be as chronic as minor assaults.

Sample differences. The chronicity of overall assaults was similar across samples. The chronicity of severe assaults was also similar across samples. Thus, the mean chronicity of both overall and severe assaults is similar across the four samples.

Gender differences. There was no significant difference between males and females in the chronicity of physical aggression overall. However, when severe assaults were considered separately, men hit their partner more than twice as frequently as women (mean of 21.9 times versus 9.3 times). The median for severe violence by men was four times in the previous year and for women three times. The large difference between the mean and the median indicates that for both men and women, but especially for men, the high mean score reflects a large influence of a relatively few extremely violent individuals. . . . [R]egardless of whether the mean or median is used, men who severely attacked their partner during the 12 month period covered by this study tended to do so more often than the women who engaged in severe assaults. Tests for a sample by gender interaction were non-significant for both overall and severe assaults. Thus, the analysis indicates that in all four samples, among individuals who assaulted their partners, men and women did so with similar frequency; in contrast, among individuals who were severely violent, men severely assaulted their partners more frequently than women.

Gender Symmetry in Assaults

Combined samples. Among the 553 couples where one or both of the partners were violent, in almost three quarters of the cases (71.2%) gender symmetry was found, that is, both partners perpetrated one or more assault. When only one partner was violent, this was more than twice as likely to be the female partner (19.0%) as the male partner (9.8%). Among the 205 couples where there was an act of severe aggression, symmetry was less prevalent (56.6%), but when only one partner was violent, it was again twice as likely to be the female partner (29.8% female only versus 13.7% male partner only).

The finding that women are more likely to be the only violent partner differs from the results of studies of married and cohabiting couples in the general population. General population studies tend to show that, when there is violence by only one partner, it is as likely to be the male partner as the female partner. . . . [F]or [a] nationally representative sample of couples almost identical rates of partner assault by males and females, except for the youngest couples [has been found.] At ages 18–19, the rate for women is 47% greater than the rate for men. At ages 20–24 women exceed men by 18%, however, among respondents 25 and over, rates of partner assault are almost identical for men and women. A meta-analysis of 37 studies of college students and 27 studies of community samples found that in the community samples the rate of PV by women exceeded the male rate only very slightly. However, among the student samples, the female rate was greater than the rate of PV by males. Thus, the younger the individual, the more the female rate of assaulting a partner exceeds the rate for males. If that generalization is correct, the tendency in this sample of students for women to more often be the only violent partner probably reflects the youthfulness of the sample.

Sample differences. [G]ender symmetry in the overall assault rate across samples [was evident]. [T]he pattern of predominantly mutual violence described above was consistent when the four samples are examined individually. However, [there were] significant differences between samples for severe assaults. The most important difference is that students in the New Hampshire sample had by far the lowest percentage in both categories, and the highest percentage in the Female Only category.

The measure of gender symmetry was based on the questionnaire completed by one partner reporting on both their own behavior and the behavior of the partner. This procedure is open to the possibility that what seems to be symmetry could really be the result of men underreporting their violent behavior. To examine this possibility the Gender Symmetry measure was cross-tabulated by the sex of the respondent, [but] no significant difference in gender symmetry based on reports by male and female partners [emerged].

Discussion

The results of this study provide strong evidence of gender symmetry in respect to violence against a dating partner. First, the results were similar in four different samples with large differences in the socio-cultural setting. Second, the results showing gender symmetry and differences between samples remained after controlling for the age of the respondent, the severity and chronicity of violence, and controlling for socioeconomic status and for social desirability response bias. The results indicate that women and men have similar prevalence rates for both any and severe assaults, and for chronicity of minor assaults. Further, in the majority of couples where one partner is violent, both partners have committed one or more assaults. An important exception to the pattern of gender symmetry was that, among the subgroup of respondents who committed one or more acts of severe violence, men in all four samples did it more often than women. Finally, there is agreement between results based on data provided by males and females.

Methodological Implications

These results have important implications for the methodology of research on PV, and for primary prevention of PV. With respect to methodology, the results show that male or female respondents provide equivalent results. Thus, either partner can be the source of the data in research on PV in non-clinical populations. However, although it is not necessary to obtain data from both partners in a relationship, given that individuals of both sexes appear to underreport their own perpetration, and over-report assaults by partners, in any study of gender differences it is desirable to obtain data from both male and female respondents. Additionally, the parallel results in each of the four cultural settings suggests that the Conflict Tactics Scales is appropriate for use in cross-cultural research.

The robustness of the results cited, and the consistency of the results with many previous studies showing gender symmetry in PV, adds urgency to the need for steps to extend efforts at primary and secondary prevention of PV to women offenders. Also relevant are the studies showing that women initiate PV as often as men and the studies showing that women are injured more often and more seriously than men. Consequently, programs and policies aimed at primary prevention of PV *by women* are crucial for reducing the victimization of not only men but also women.

The High Proportion of Female Violence in New Hampshire

The high percentage in the Female Only and Both Violent category in New Hampshire could reflect the operation of two principles. One is the "convergence theory" of crime by women. This theory holds that as women become equal in other spheres of life, they will also tend to become more equal in respect to committing crime. The data for New Hampshire fit the convergence theory. First, New Hampshire had the highest degree of equality between women and men of the four samples. Second, although New Hampshire had the lowest overall rate of PV, among the couples where violence occurred, it had the largest proportion committed by women.

A second possibility is the cost-benefit theory formulated by Archer. He found that ". . . sex differences in partner aggression follow the perceived costs and benefits of physically aggressing in that social setting." In patriarchal social settings, violation of the male dominance principle in any form, and specifically by hitting a male partner, is likely to elicit severe physical retaliation. However, the social context in New Hampshire is almost the opposite. Women at the University of New Hampshire tend to come from high education and high-income families. Because of the small size of the state, many students live at home and even those living on campus are usually less than an hour from their home. They are thus in relatively protected positions. However, that also tends to be true of students in Ciudad Juarez and El Paso. Perhaps most important, women in New Hampshire have a relatively high degree of equality with men and physical violence against female partners is relatively low compared to other states of the USA. These characteristics may lower the costs women perceive of hitting a partner, and thus alter the cost-benefit ratio enough to produce a higher rate of violence by women than in the other samples.

These comments suggest some issues for future research. For example, why do women, who are on average weaker than men, engage in and initiate violence at least as often as men, whereas outside of family and dating relationships, women engage in a fraction of the violence perpetrated by men? Although Straus has outlined a theoretical model which might explain the discrepancy, it has yet to be tested. Another important avenue of research is twin studies which could provide information on genetic and environmental factors that predict PV. . . . Another needed type of research on gender symmetry in PV concerns the social context. One aspect of social context that has been investigated is the degree to which the society and the family system is male-dominant. However, the many other possible social context effects is illustrated by the Culture of Honor theory which states that violence in defense of honor will be more prevalent in ancestrally herding than in traditionally farming communities. The differences between samples in this study are consistent with that theory. . . .

Prevention Implications

Almost all primary and secondary prevention efforts are based on the assumption that PV is perpetrated primarily by men. There are several reasons for this false assumption. First, programs to end PV were initiated by and continue to be a major effort of the women's movement. Another reason is that women are much more likely to be physically, psychologically, and economically injured than men. Finally, about 90% of assaults and murders outside the family are perpetrated by men and it is easy to assume that this must also apply to PV.

PV by men, but not by women has been decreasing since the mid 1970s but PV by women on male partners have stayed about the same. The failure of prevention and treatment programs to address PV by women may partly explain why PV by men has decreased, but PV by women has remained constant. An ironic aspect is that although the number of male victims has remained high, there is no funding for services for male victims, and almost no research on male victims of PV.

Rather than ignoring assaults by female partners, primary prevention of PV requires strong efforts to end assaults by women. A fundamental reason is the intrinsic moral wrong of assaulting a spouse, as expressed in the fact that such assaults are criminal acts, even when no injury occurs. Second, males are the victims of about a third of injuries inflicted on partners, including about a third of homicides of partners. Third is the unintended validation by women of the traditional cultural norms tolerating a certain level of violence between spouses. A fourth reason for a strong effort to reduce PV by women is the danger of escalation when women engage in "harmless" minor violence. [I]f both partners were violent, it increases the probability that assaults are likely to persist or escalate in severity over [a] 2 year period; whereas if only one partner engages in physical attacks, the probability of a subsequent violence decreases. Finally, when a woman assaults her partner, it "models" violence for the children and therefore contributes to PV in the next generation. This modeling effect is as strong for assaults by women as is assaults by men.

Although it is essential that primary and secondary prevention of PV include a major focus on violence by women as well as men, the needed change must be made with extreme care for a number of reasons. First, it must be done in ways that simultaneously refute the idea that violence by women justifies or excuses violence by their partners. Second, although women may assault partners at approximately the same rate as men, assaults by men usually inflict greater physical, financial, and emotional injury. This means that male violence against women, on average, results in more severe victimization. Thus, a focus on protecting and assisting female victims must remain a priority, despite the fact that services for male victims (now essentially absent) need to be made available. Finally, in many societies women lack full economic, social, political, and human rights. In such cultural contexts, equality for women needs to be given priority as an even more fundamental aspect of primary prevention of PV. Otherwise focusing on PV by women can further exacerbate the oppression of women in those societies.

Christopher T. Allen, Suzanne
C. Swan, and Chitra Raghavan

 **NO**

Gender Symmetry, Sexism, and Intimate Partner Violence

Considerable debate continues regarding the prevalence, direction, and meaning of violence between men and women in intimate relationships. Studies examining men's and women's use of physical violence have indicated that the number of women using physical aggression is either comparable to that of men or higher. Evidence from a different body of studies, in which data are drawn from crime statistics, indicates that all forms of intimate partner violence (IPV) are overwhelmingly perpetrated by men against women.

These findings and subsequent interpretations have led to debates regarding the direction of violence between men and women in intimate relationships. Many of the studies reporting comparable rates of violence perpetration by men and women do not examine contextual factors, such as who initiated the violence, who was injured, whether the violence was in self-defense, and the psychological impact of victimization. For example, a meta-analysis demonstrated that studies using the Conflict Tactics Scale-2 and similar act-based measures found women to be slightly more likely than men to use violence against an intimate partner. However, when contextual factors are examined, a complex picture of gender dynamics in IPV begins to emerge. The data on injury provide a case in point. Although studies indicate that the prevalence of women and men who use violence against intimate partners is about equal, studies consistently indicate greater rates of injury among women. Furthermore, studies that have examined mutually violent couples have found that women tend to suffer more ill effects than men in such relationships.

The Present Study

Contextual Factors

The preponderance of adverse consequences of victimization for women despite debatably equal perpetration rates across genders indicates that further study of the contextual factors that may differ in men's and women's experiences of IPV is necessary. One such contextual factor is raised by the following question: Is women's violence against male intimate partners primarily in response to their partners' violence against them? If so, this would explain why, despite the equivalent prevalence of men's and women's violence perpetration, women experiencing violence tend to experience more physical

From *Journal of Interpersonal Violence*, vol. 24, 2008, pp. 1816–1834. Copyright © 2008 by Sage Publications. Reprinted by permission via Rightslink.

Figure 1

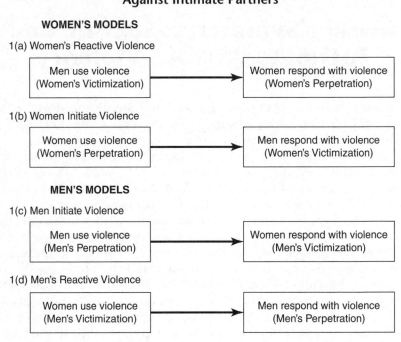

Theoretical Explanations for Women's and Men's Use of Violence Against Intimate Partners

injuries and more detrimental psychological outcomes than men experiencing violence. If women are not typically initiating the violence but are using it reactively, they are not in control of the situation. Rather, they may be using violence to protect themselves from their partners. Indeed, studies have found that male violence against women is a strong predictor of women's violence. A model, 1(a), depicting women's violence and victimization in this direction is shown in Figure 1.

These studies of female violence indicate that women's victimization is a strong predictor of women's perpetration. However, they were not intended to directly compare model 1(a), in which women use violence reactively, with a competing model, 1(b), in which women's perpetration predicts women's victimization (see Figure 1). The competing model 1(b) suggests that women tend to initiate violence first and then their male partners respond with violence, resulting in women's victimization. The comparison of these two models will allow an examination of directionality (with the caveat that the data [are] cross-sectional): Does women's violence tend to be primarily reactive, or do women tend to be the initiators of violence?

This study makes a further contribution toward addressing the "gender symmetry" issue by comparing models between male and female samples with a diverse sample of college students. . . . Although being a recipient of violence predicts women's perpetration of violence, it predicts men's perpetration of violence as well. The present study examines the hypothesis that women's violence is primarily reactive, whereas men's violence is primarily proactive. Model 1(c), shown in Figure 1, suggests that men tend to initiate violence first and then their female partners respond with violence, resulting in men's victimization.

The competing model, 1(d), shown in Figure 1, portrays men's perpetration of violence as occurring in response to women's violence against them. Thus, according to this model, men are victimized by women and then they perpetrate violence reactively.

Sexism and IPV

The second contribution of this study is to consider the utility of sexism in understanding the contexts in which men and women use violence against their partners. Although older writings define sexism as a negative attitude based on the presumed inferiority of women as a group [others] note that currently there are strong social pressures against blatant sexism. Ambivalent sexism theory posits that sexist attitudes have benevolent as well as hostile components. . . .

The research to date regarding how sexism is related to IPV is mixed. Although feminist theory points to patriarchy and sexism as important determinants of violence, not all research has been supportive of this view. Some studies have found that men's traditional sex role attitudes were related to more violent behavior, with abusive men having more traditional attitudes toward women than nonviolent males. However, [the] study of IPV among college students found that men who scored higher on a "Macho" scale were *less* likely to use violence against their female partners, suggesting that sexist attitudes may contain some protective elements that mitigate violence toward women. Ambivalent sexism theory provides an explanation for these inconsistencies by positing that attitudes toward women often have benevolent as well as hostile components. Some of the studies that have found men's more sexist attitudes were predictive of greater violence used the Attitudes Toward Women to assess sexism. This measure contains some items that could be classified as hostile sexism and others that could be classified as benevolent sexism. Perhaps the positive relationship between sexism and IPV in these studies is driven by the hostile sexism-like items.

Studies using [the] Ambivalent Sexism Inventory, which contains different subscales for benevolent and hostile sexism, support this idea. Studies have found that greater endorsement of hostile sexism predicted more positive attitudes toward violence against a female partner. Other studies of IPV among college samples have found that men with more hostile sexist attitudes were more likely to have committed verbal aggression and sexual coercion.

The findings from studies regarding the relationship between benevolent sexism and IPV provide some evidence (albeit mixed) that benevolent sexism may have a protective effect against men's IPV. . . .

There has been almost no discussion of how women's sexism may impact their experiences of IPV. Examining women's sexist notions about their own gender provides a more comprehensive contextual framework by which to understand IPV. A growing body of evidence indicates that women's benevolent sexism, a subjectively favorable view of women, nevertheless can have negative consequences for women if they fail to live up. . . . Hostile sexism, and perhaps IPV as well, may be reserved primarily for women who challenge men's power.

Very little is known concerning women's sexism toward women and their commission of IPV. One study with a college sample did indicate a small but significant impact of women's sexist attitudes on their violent behavior, such that greater sexism predicted more violence. However, other studies of female college students found no relationship between either hostile or benevolent sexism and verbal aggression or sexual coercion.

Hypotheses

The current study examines the following hypotheses regarding gender symmetry and IPV.

> *Hypothesis 1a:* Victimization from male partners will be a strong predictor of women's violence against their male partners (as shown in Figure 1a). . . . If supported, this model suggests that women's violence typically is preceded by violence against them and is reactive in nature.

> *Hypothesis 1b:* A model in which women's perpetration of violence is shown as predicting women's victimization suggests that women initiate aggression first and then their male partners respond with reactive violence (see Figure 1b). We predict such a model will provide a poor fit with the data.

> *Hypothesis 1c:* Men's perpetration of violence will be a strong predictor of men's victimization by their female partners (see Figure 1c). . . . If supported, this model suggests that men typically initiate violence first and then their female partners respond with reactive violence.

> *Hypothesis 1d:* A model in which men's victimization from female partners predicts men's violence suggests that women initiate violence first and then men hit back (see Figure 1d). We predict such a model will provide a poor fit with the data.

The next hypotheses concern the inconsistent findings in studies examining the relationship between men's sexist attitudes and IPV. Although one previous study examined the relationship between ambivalent sexism and sexual and verbal aggression, to our knowledge no studies have explicitly explored the relationship between benevolent sexism, hostile sexism, and physical aggression.

> *Hypothesis 2a:* Men with more benevolently sexist beliefs will be less likely to perpetrate violence against women.

> *Hypothesis 2b:* Men with more hostile sexist beliefs will be more likely to perpetrate violence against women.

Finally, we expand on previous debates by examining women's hostile and benevolent sexism toward their own sex and how these may relate to violence perpetration and victimization.

Hypothesis 3: Women with more benevolently sexist beliefs will be less likely to experience violence from their male partners.

Because so little is known about women's sexism as it relates to IPV and because women's hostile sexism scores are typically lower than both their benevolent sexism scores and men's hostile sexism scores, we make no prediction about the relationship of women's hostile sexism beliefs and IPV.

Method

Participants and Procedure

Data for this study were obtained in a larger study examining risk factors for dating violence in low income immigrant/ethnic minority undergraduates from a large public urban college. The sample was recruited from all entering undergraduates in the first semester of enrollment who were not in either honors-equivalent or remedial programs. The majority of respondents were between 18 and 19 years of age. Fewer than 5% of the potential participants did not participate in the survey . . . resulting in 232 completed questionnaires, of which 92 were male (39.6%) and 140 were female (60.4%). Ethnic/racial composition of this sample was considerably more diverse than most other published college samples: 52% of respondents self-identified as Latino/Latina, 19% as Black, 10% as White, 5% as Asian, 6% as Biracial, 7% as Other, and 1% did not respond. Thirty-four percent of the sample reported having been born outside the United States. . . . Fifteen percent of the sample reported greater reading and speaking proficiency in a language other than English, although 23% reported primarily speaking a language other than English at home. However, all students had to demonstrate proficiency in English to be admitted to the college.

Measures

Ambivalent Sexism Inventory (ASI). The ASI is a 22-item measure that was developed to assess individual levels of hostile and benevolent sexism. . . . An example of a hostile item is: "Women are too easily offended." An example of a benevolent item is: "Women should be cherished and protected by men." . . .

The Conflict Tactics Scale-2 (CTS2). A total of six items from the "minor" violence scales of the CTS2 were administered. (The use of the term "minor" here reflects the CTS2 classification of item severity.) . . . In particular, we selected items for inclusion based on their high item-total correlations and high factor loading on either the "minor" physical, psychological, or sexual aggression subscales, respectively. The CTS2 instructs participants to indicate how many times they committed a given act of aggression against their partners in the past year, and how many times their partners committed that act toward them. . . . The minor aggression items were "I twisted my partner's arm or hair," "I pushed or shoved my partner," "I grabbed my partner," and "I slapped my partner." The psychological aggression item was "I shouted or yelled at my partner." The sexual coercion item was "I insisted my partner have oral or anal sex (but did not use physical force)." . . .

Results

Descriptive Statistics

Fifty-five percent of the female sample reported using violence against their male partners ($M = 1.38$, $SD = 2.36$), and 47% reported being victimized by their male partners ($M = 1.12$, $SD = 2.04$). Women's average level of benevolent sexism was found to be 2.89 ($SD = .69$). Women's average level of hostile sexism was found to be 2.30 ($SD = .76$). . . .

Forty-one percent of the male sample reported using violence against their female partners ($M = .73$, $SD = 1.51$), and 37% reported being victimized by their female partners ($M = 1.00$, $SD = 2.04$). Men's average level of benevolent sexism was found to be 2.89 ($SD = .59$). Men's average level of hostile sexism was found to be 2.79 ($SD = .65$). . . .

In the present study, benevolent and hostile sexism are correlated .40, $p < .00$, in the women's sample, and .24, $p < .05$, in the men's sample. . . .

Comparing Women's and Men's Experience of IPV and Sexism

An ANOVA was conducted to test for differences in levels of perpetration, victimization, benevolent sexism, and hostile sexism between women and men. Women were found to have a significantly higher level of perpetration than men. . . . Victimization did not differ by gender. Benevolent sexism did not differ by gender. Men were found to have a significantly higher level of hostile sexism than women. . . .

Path Analyses

We used four models to test our hypotheses. Hypothesis 1a—victimization from male partners will be a strong predictor of women's violence against their male partners—and Hypothesis 3—women with more benevolently sexist beliefs will be less likely to experience violence from their male partners— were supported by a model in which victimization from male partners strongly predicted women's perpetration. A significant and negative path from benevolent sexism to victimization indicates that women who endorsed benevolently sexist attitudes were less likely to report victimization. . . .

Hypothesis 1b—a model in which women's perpetration of violence predicts their victimization from male partners—provided a poor fit with the data.

Hypothesis 1c—men's perpetration of violence will be a strong predictor of men's victimization by their female partners—and Hypothesis 2a—men with more benevolently sexist beliefs will be less likely to perpetrate "minor" violence against women—were supported by a model in which perpetration by male partners strongly predicted men's victimization. A significant and negative path from benevolent sexism to perpetration indicates that men who endorsed benevolently sexist attitudes were less likely to report perpetration. . . .

Hypothesis 1d—men's victimization predicts men's violence against female partners—was supported by a poor-fitting model portraying men's violence as in response to violence received from their female partners. . . .

Hypothesis 2b—men with more hostile sexist beliefs will be more likely to perpetrate violence against women—was not supported. There was no significant correlation between hostile sexism and perpetration. . . .

Discussion

Women in this sample, on average, perpetrated more "minor" violent acts than their male partners. This result is comparable to findings from other samples of young adult/college populations. The mean number of times women and men victimized by their partners did not differ. However, . . . results indicate women's use of violence occurs in a context that differs from men's violence. As hypothesized, the current study found: Women's victimization from male partners was a strong predictor of women's perpetration, as demonstrated by a path model that fit the data well, and women's perpetration was not shown to predict women's victimization by male partners, as demonstrated by a model that fit the data poorly. Thus, [these] data suggest that women's violence in this sample appears to be primarily a reaction to male violence against them. Furthermore, men's perpetration was found to be a strong predictor of their victimization by their female partners, as demonstrated by a path model that fit the data well; and men's victimization by their female partners was not shown to predict men's perpetration, as demonstrated by a poor-fitting model. These results support the argument that women's violence is often reactive. That is, the data presented here suggest the typical pattern of IPV in this sample is that men hit women first and then women hit back. As women are often at a physical disadvantage in confrontations with males, the doubled rate of perpetration seen in women may indicate that more violence is needed to repel an attack. Of course, because the models presented here are cross-sectional, causality is unknown. Longitudinal models are required to provide a true test of whether men's violence tends to precede women's or vice versa.

This study's findings concerning the relationship between benevolent sexism and IPV are consistent with ambivalent sexism theory. In this sample, benevolent sexism was higher than in normative samples, for both men and women; for men, hostile sexism was also higher than in the normative samples. One possible explanation may be that hostile sexism is higher, on average, in Latinos compared to European Americans; in this study, the large proportion of Latino participants, some of whom were immigrants, may have increased the sample mean. . . . The current study found that men's benevolent sexism protected against their self-reported use of violence against their female partners. That is, men with more benevolently sexist attitudes perpetrated less violence against their partners than men with less benevolently sexist attitudes. Ambivalent sexism theory posits that women who conform to benevolently sexist expectations are "rewarded" with revered status, whereas those who challenge patriarchy are demeaned and punished by men's hostility. The study also found a complementary effect for women: Women's benevolent sexism reduced their risk of victimization from their male partners. This finding suggests that benevolent sexism in women placates male partners. In conjunction with the finding that women's violence is in reaction to men's violence against them, this suggests that the risk of women's victimization may be reduced to the extent to which they accept a subordinate status relative to their male partners. This interpretation is consistent with [the suggestion] that "women's endorsement of benevolent sexism only serves to reinforce gender inequality while offering a highly contingent (and ultimately hollow) promise of protection that is enacted only when women behave in line with sexist expectations and prescriptions." The complementary role of benevolent sexism in women's and men's experience of IPV further supports the notion that IPV must be understood within a contextual framework.

It must be noted that although findings of this study suggest a protective effect of benevolent sexism against male perpetration, we *DO NOT* promote women's acceptance of traditional gender roles as a means for reducing violence against them and we do not believe that women who challenge such roles should be blamed for their partner's violence. In contrast, this finding suggests that it is often unsafe for women to transcend traditional gender roles. These results also suggest that men's attitudes toward, adherence to, and enforcement of rigid gender roles must be targeted for change to eliminate violence against women.

An alternative interpretation of the finding that benevolent sexism predicts less IPV is that participants who report greater benevolent sexist beliefs are also more likely to underreport IPV. This may especially be an issue for Latina participants. [W]omen with more benevolent sexism attitudes may be less likely to define a situation as abuse. . . . Although Latina and Anglo women did not differ in the severity and frequency of victimization, Latinas were less likely to label the behavior as abuse. Though a low number of non-Latino/Latina racial groups in the present study prohibited testing for significant differences in sexism across racial groups, we encourage future studies to examine this alternative explanation.

Results regarding the role of benevolent sexism are particularly intriguing because in other recent studies, no relationship was found between benevolent sexism and verbal aggression or sexual coercion. Perhaps the difference between our findings and the letter studies is that [other] samples were composed exclusively of White Midwestern students. In contrast, in our urban sample, only 10% of the sample are White; 52% are Latino/Latina; and 19% are Black. There may be cultural effects, particularly among the Latinos/Latinas in the sample, that could account for the effect of benevolent sexism on violence found in the study. Latin American societies are characterized by traditional gender roles, strong familism, and patriarchy. Such cultural values may reduce the likelihood of violence by supporting women's acceptance of patriarchy and discouraging their adoption of less traditional gender roles.

According to ambivalent sexism theory, men's violence against women is condoned as a way of reinforcing male social dominance. Thus, the finding that men's hostile sexism was not related to perpetration of violence is curious, given that the levels of hostility reported were higher than in other samples. Again, this finding differs from [others], who found that for men, hostile sexism was positively correlated with self-reports of verbal aggression and sexual coercion perpetration. (Both studies found no relationship for women.) Perhaps hostile sexism operates differently in Latino/Latina and other cultures than it does for European Americans. Another speculation is that the present study assessed "minor" physical violence, whereas the [other] studies examined verbal and sexual aggression. Perhaps hostile sexism operates differently with different forms of aggression. Clearly this is an area in need of further study.

Results of the current study are limited in the following regards. Debate in the extant literature has focused on understanding comparable rates of men's and women's use of physical violence against intimate partners. Although the current article has offered empirical support for the broader contextualization of women's use of violence, more work lies ahead. Specifically, future studies should examine the role of other forms of psychological and sexual abuse in women's use of violence against partners, such as more severe forms of aggression. The findings presented here regarding the context of women's and men's use of physical violence are based on less severe forms of aggression and may not generalize to other forms. Second, the experience of violence was assessed through self-report of both violence perpetration and victimization; data was not collected from couples. Although most survey studies of IPV utilize self-report data, we think it particularly important to note this limitation given the use of complementary models of women's and men's violence. Third, because causality cannot be known from a cross-sectional design, the models suggesting that women's violence occurs in reaction to male violence against them, whereas men tend to initiate violence, need to be examined longitudinally. In addition, the perpetration and victimization scales had low scale reliability in the women's sample. Low reliability of the hostile and benevolent sexism scales could be related to language issues; 15% of the sample reported reading and speaking more proficiently in a language other than English. Finally, though the use of college samples is common in IPV research, the current findings may not generalize to community samples.

This article highlights the importance of studying IPV within a broader sociocultural context. By examining how social factors such as patriarchy and sexism affect the experience of IPV for individuals, we are better able to target our efforts at prevention.

EXPLORING THE ISSUE

Gender Symmetry: Do Women and Men Commit Equal Levels of Violence Against Intimate Partners?

Challenge Questions

1. What are the consequences for the gender symmetry debate of not including psychological and sexual aggression in the usual discussion?
2. How important is it to understand the motive for an act of aggression? Does the motive change the justification for aggression?
3. How expansive should the definition of intimate partner violence be? Should it include all forms of harm-doing, including psychological?
4. Consider various levels of analysis: individual, interactional, and structural. How does each inform our understanding of gender and intimate partner violence?

Is There Common Ground?

The debate about gender symmetry is fueled in part by a continued focus on the question of sex differences rather than on the factors and processes that contribute to intimate partner violence, regardless of the sex of the partners and whether one is considering a heterosexual or same-sex couple. A shift in focus would lead to questions of why some women and some men abuse their partners, whereas others do not. Gender can be reintroduced into the discussion by focusing on how traditional constructions of masculinity and the power associated with it contribute to both women's and men's involvement in partner aggression as victim and/or perpetrator. For example, when women are aggressive, are they trying to gain power in a situation in which they feel powerless? Some studies have suggested that women are more likely to be aggressive out of self-defense, fear, or defense of their children, whereas both women and men are motivated by retribution, but men are more likely to be motivated by need for control. Do men engage in aggression because they are attempting to counter threats to their masculinity? A shift in focus may also encourage researchers to more broadly define intimate partner violence so that it includes not only physical aggression but also verbal and psychological aggression, as well as sexual assault. In doing so, gender again enters the discussion in a way that asks whether there are different patterns of intimate partner violence. For example, men are much more likely to sexually coerce female partners than vice versa. Women may be more likely to persist in use of violence when they have partners who do not engage in aggression; this is known as the "rational choice" strategy. Maureen McHugh has suggested that a postmodern approach to conceptualizing women's use of aggression should include rejecting polarized stances in the debate on gender symmetry; that is, a sex difference approach is not useful. It ignores too much of the context and dynamic nature of intimate partner violence. Rather, there should be a focus on human interactions, examining the meaning and consequences of the experience for all involved. There should be a recognition that patterns of intimate partner violence are multiple and varied, and that perpetrators can be victims and victims can be perpetrators. This latter point raises the possibility that intimate partner violence may be mutual, although it is not necessarily symmetric. Women and men may both commit acts of aggression but in the context of gendered constructions of power and status motives, meanings and consequences are highly unlikely to be symmetric.

ISSUE 11

Does Pornography Reduce the Incidence of Rape?

YES: Anthony D'Amato, from "Porn Up, Rape Down," Northwestern University School of Law, Public Law and Legal Theory Research Paper Series (June 23, 2006)

NO: Judith Reisman, from "Pornography's Link to Rape," WorldnetDaily.com (July 29, 2006)

Learning Outcomes

As you read the issue, focus on the following points:

- What is the definition of pornography? How does it differ from erotica?
- Does viewing porn encourage young people to become sexually active at earlier ages? Does viewing porn psychologically damage kids?
- If pornography is related to increases in violence against women, what mechanisms might explain this effect? If it is related to reduction in the incidence of rape, what mechanisms might explain this effect?

ISSUE SUMMARY

YES: Professor of law Anthony D'Amato highlights statistics from the most recent National Crime Victimization Survey that demonstrate a correlation between the increased consumption of pornography over the years with the decreased incidence of rape. Some people, he argues, watch pornography in order to push any desire to rape out of their minds, and thus have no further desire to go out and actually do it.

NO: Judith Reisman, president of the Institute for Media Education, asserts that sex criminals imitate what they see depicted in the media, providing examples of serial rapists and killers who had large stores of pornography in their possession, and research in which approximately 33 percent of rapists said that they had viewed pornography immediately prior to at least one of their rapes.

According to the Family Safe Media Web site, every second, $3,075.64 is being spent on pornography, 28,258 Internet users are viewing pornography, and 372 Internet users are typing adult search terms into search engines. The site also claims that every 39 minutes a new pornographic video is being created in the United States. The total worldwide revenue of the pornography industry is estimated to be over $96 billion dollars annually, with the United States contributing approximately $13 billion to this total. The site states, "The pornography industry is larger than the revenues of the top technology companies combined: Microsoft, Google, Amazon, eBay, Yahoo!, Apple, Netflix and EarthLink." With these staggering numbers and the huge economic impact, it is little surprise that there is so much interest in the impact of pornography on people's lives. Furthermore while researchers, practitioners, and activists are arguing for the dangers of pornography, the industry itself argues that pornography is not harmful and is a matter of free speech.

Since the creation of the Internet, the world has seen a huge increase in the amount and manner in which information is exchanged with others. This includes the adult entertainment industry, which has become an enormous, multi-billion dollar industry thanks in part to the anonymity and privacy that online pornography provides adults. One challenge, many argue, is that adults are far from the only ones who are able to access porn sites online. Children as young as middle school age are accessing images online, some of which they search for and some of which is targeted to them through spam e-mails or pornographic Web sites that purchase the domain of a similarly sounding Web site; they count on minors to arrive at these sites by accident. The debates about the effects of porn on its users are nearly endless.

There has been a recent interest in the effect of media images on girls, especially as they result in the objectification of the female body with effects on body image and self-esteem. Consequences can range from eating disorders to increased risk for sexual violence victimization. In 2005, the Violence in Video Games and Interactive Media policy was adopted by the American Psychological Association (APA). The review of the literature that led to this resolution summarized results of studies documenting the negative impact of exposure to violent interactive media on children and youth. However, in recognition that this policy did not address issues of sexualization that result from media images, the APA convened the Task Force on the Sexualization of Girls. The task force defined sexualization as occurring when

- a person's value comes only from his or her sexual appeal or behavior, to the exclusion of other characteristics;
- a person is held to a standard that equates physical attractiveness (narrowly defined) with being sexy;
- a person is sexually objectified—that is, made into a thing for others' sexual use, rather than seen as a person with the capacity for independent action and decision making; and/or
- sexuality is inappropriately imposed upon a person.

Guided by this definition, the task force documented the negative impact of media images on girls' cognitive functioning, such as impaired performance on mental activities like math tests. Emotional functioning, in the form of shame and self-disgust, can result from exposure to unrealistic pictures of female bodies. Health, both mental and physical, can be compromised. For example, sexualization of the female body can lead to low self-esteem and depression, as well as eating disorders. Unrealistic expectations about the ideal female body and what sexual relations should be like can impair healthy sexuality. Sexualization can also affect various attitudes and beliefs, such as the acceptance of sexual stereotypes. Furthermore, it is not just girls and young women who are affected by sexualized images of females; others and society are also affected. Men's expectations regarding "ideal" women can undermine healthy relationships and sexism in general can increase. Of particular concern for the present discussion, was the task force's finding that the sexualization of girls through media images was associated with increased rates of sexual harassment and sexual violence and an increased demand for child pornography. Scholars who have been studying human trafficking, such as Norma Ramos with the Coalition Against Trafficking of Women, have argued that pornography is "erotized bigotry." For many, trafficking begins in childhood and takes the form of prostitution, and pornographic images both arouse the appetite for child victims and suggest ways to rape. Ramos has suggested that prostitution is nothing more that pre-paid rape and the world's oldest oppression.

This issue looks at the effects of visual pornography on the incidence of rape in the United States. Since pornography became available, there are many proponents who maintain that by depicting certain sexual acts, sexually explicit media encourages people to try these acts out. In particular, they say, porn that shows rape makes this type of behavior real and, in the rapists' mind, acceptable, thereby encouraging rape. Others maintain that there is no causality between viewing Internet porn and the incidence of rape, that people are exposed to a wide range of information, images, and behaviors every day and do not engage in all of the behaviors they see. These include, they say, sexual behaviors. It has been difficult to demonstrate the causal role of pornography in increasing the likelihood of violence against women. Many studies, such as described in the Anthony D'Amato selection to follow, rely on correlational analyses. With these analyses it is impossible to know whether the presence of pornography causes certain behaviors to increase or decrease, whether people prone to those behaviors or more or less likely to seek out pornography, or whether there is some third factor, such as women's status in a society affects both the amount of pornography consumed and the level of violence against women.

In the following selections, D'Amato provides analyses that suggest a negative correlation: a decrease in rapes in the United States is associated with the increase of pornography availability. He maintains that having pornography available actually *decreases* the incidence of rape. Depicting rape, which is a socially unacceptable (and criminal) behavior, this author argues, actually provides a potential rapist with an outlet for his unacceptable fantasies, thereby keeping him from acting upon them. Judith Reisman counters with stories from actual rapists who discuss viewing porn immediately before raping a victim.

YES

Anthony D'Amato

Porn Up, Rape Down

Today's headlines are shouting RAPE IN DECLINE![1] Official figures just released show a plunge in the number of rapes per capita in the United States since the 1970s. Even when measured in different ways, including police reports and survey interviews, the results are in agreement; there has been an 85% reduction in sexual violence in the past 25 years. The decline, steeper than the stock market crash that led to the Great Depression, is depicted in this chart prepared by the United States Department of Justice:

Rape rates
Adjusted victimization rate
per 1,000 persons age 12 and over

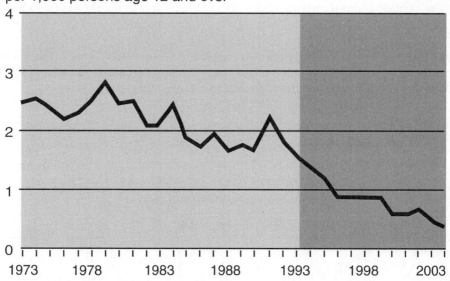

Source: *The National Crime Victimization Survey.* Includes both attempted and completed rapes.

As the chart shows, there were 2.7 rapes for every 1,000 people in 1980; by 2004, the same survey found the rate had decreased to 0.4 per 1,000 people, a decline of 85%.

D'Amato, Anthony, "Porn Up, Rape Down" (June 23, 2006). *Northwestern Public Law Research Paper* No. 913013. Available at SSRN: http://ssrn.com/abstract=913013. Reprinted by permission.

Official explanations for the unexpected decline include (1) less lawlessness associated with crack cocaine; (b) women have been taught to avoid unsafe situations; (c) more would-be rapists already in prison for other crimes; (d) sex education classes telling boys that "no means no." But these minor factors cannot begin to explain such a sharp decline in the incidence of rape.

There is, however, one social factor that correlates almost exactly with the rape statistics. The American public is probably not ready to believe it. My theory is that the sharp rise in access to pornography accounts for the decline in rape. The correlation is inverse: the more pornography, the less rape. It is like the inverse correlation: the more police officers on the street, the less crime.

The pornographic movie "Deep Throat" which started the flood of X-rated VHS and later DVD films, was released in 1972. Movie rental shops at first catered primarily to the adult film trade. Pornographic magazines also sharply increased in numbers in the 1970s and 1980s. Then came a seismic change: pornography became available on the new Internet. Today, purveyors of Internet porn earn a combined annual income exceeding the total of the major networks ABC, CBS, and NBC.

"Deep Throat" has moved from the adult theatre to a laptop near you.

National trends are one thing; what do the figures for the states show? From data compiled by the National Telecommunications and Information Administration in 2001, the four states with the *lowest* per capita access to the Internet were Arkansas, Kentucky, Minnesota, and West Virginia. The four states with the *highest* Internet access were Alaska, Colorado, New Jersey, and Washington. (I would not have guessed this.)

Next I took the figures for forcible rape compiled by police reports by the Disaster Center for the years 1980 and 2000. The following two charts display the results:

Table 1

States with Lowest Internet Access[2]

State	Internet 2001	Rape 1980	Rape 2000
Arkansas	36.9	26.7	31.7
Kentucky	40.2	19.2	27.4
Minnesota	36.1	23.2	45.5
W. Virginia	40.7	15.8	18.3

All figures are per capita.

While the nationwide incidence of rape was showing a drastic decline, the incidence of rape in the four states having the *least* access to the Internet showed an actual *increase* in rape over the same time period. This result was almost too clear and convincing, so to check it I compiled figures for the four

Table 2

States with Highest Internet Access[3]

Alaska	64.1	56.8	70.3
Colorado	58.5	52.5	41.2
New Jersey	61.6	30.7	16.1
Washington	60.4	52.7	46.4

All figures are per capita.

states having the *most* access to the Internet. Three out of four of these states showed declines (in New Jersey, an almost 50% decline). Alaska was an anomaly: it increased both in Internet access and incidence of rape. However, the population of Alaska is less than one-tenth that of the other three states in its category. To adjust for the disparity in population, I took the combined population of the four states in each table and calculated the percentage change in the rape statistics:

Table 3

Combined Per Capita Percentage Change in Incidence of Rape

	Aggregate per capita increase or decline in rape
Four states with lowest Internet access	Increase in rape of 53%
Four states with highest Internet access	Decrease in rape of 27%

I find these results to be statistically significant beyond the 95 confidence interval.

Yet proof of correlation is not the same thing as causation. If autumn regularly precedes winter, that doesn't mean that autumn causes winter. When six years ago my former Northwestern colleague John Donohue, together with Steven Levitt,[4] found that legalized abortion correlated with a reduction in crime, theirs would have only been an academically curious thesis if they had not identified a causal factor. But they did identify one: that prior to legalization there were many unwanted babies born due to the lack of a legal abortion alternative. Those unwanted children became the most likely group to turn to crime.

My own interest in the rape-pornography question began in 1970 when I served as a consultant to President Nixon's Commission on Obscenity and Pornography. The Commission concluded that there was no causal relationship between exposure to sexually explicit materials and delinquent or criminal behavior. The President was furious when he learned of the conclusion.

Later President Reagan tried the same thing, except unlike his predecessor he packed the Commission with persons who passed his ideological litmus test (small wonder that I was not asked to participate). This time, Reagan's

Commission on Pornography reached the approved result: that there does exist a causal relationship between pornography and violent sex crimes.

The drafter of the Commission's report was Frederich Schauer, a prominent law professor. In a separate statement, he assured readers that neither he nor the other Commissioners were at all influenced by their personal moral values.[5] . . .

Although the Reagan Commission had at its disposal all the evidence gathered by psychology and social-science departments throughout the world on the question whether a student's exposure to pornography increased his tendency to commit antisocial acts, I found that the Commission was unable to adduce a shred of evidence to support its affirmative conclusion. No scientist had ever found that pornography raised the probability of rape. However, the Commission was not seeking truth; rather, as I said in the title to my article, it sought political truth.

If pornography does not *produce* rape, I thought, then maybe it *reduces* rape. But no one apparently had any incentive to investigate the latter proposition. But the just-released rape statistics provide the necessary evidence.

Although neither Professor Schauer nor the other Commissioners ever responded to my William & Mary article, now they can forget it. For if they had been right that exposure to pornography leads to an increase in social violence, then the vast exposure to pornography furnished by the Internet would by now have resulted in scores of rapes per day on university campuses, hundreds of rapes daily in every town, and thousands of rapes per day in every city. Instead, the Commissioners were so incredibly wrong that the incidence of rape has actually declined by the astounding rate of 85%.

Correlations aside, could access to pornography actually reduce the incidence of rape as a matter of causation? In my article I mentioned one possibility: that some people watching pornography may "get it out of their system" and thus have no further desire to go out and actually try it. Another possibility might be labeled "Victorian effect": the more that people covered up their bodies with clothes in those days, the greater the mystery of what they looked like in the nude. The sight of a woman's ankle was considered shocking and erotic. But today, Internet porn has thoroughly de-mystified sex. . . .

I am sure there will be other explanations forthcoming as to why access to pornography is the most important causal factor in the decline of rape. Once one accepts the observation that there is a precise negative correlation between the two, the rest can safely be left to the imagination.

Notes

1. E.g., *Washington Post,* June 19, 2006; *Chicago Tribune,* June 21, 2006.
2. Statistics on Internet Access compiled from National Telecommunications and Information Administration. . . .
3. Statistics on forcible rape compiled from. . . .
4. Author of *Freakonimics* (2005).
5. U.S. Dept. of Justice, Final Report: Attorney General's Commission on Pornography 176–79 (1986) (personal statement of Commissioner Schauer).

Judith Reisman  **NO**

Pornography's Link to Rape

Would you try to put out a fire with gasoline?

No? Then you might disagree with an MSNBC online article, "Porn: Good for America!" by Glenn Reynolds, a University of Tennessee law professor. Reynolds suggests that pornography *reduces* rape!

As proof, Reynolds quotes a U.S. Department of Justice claim that in 2004 rape of "people" *over age 12* radically decreased with an "85 percent decline in the per-capita rape rate since 1979" (DOJ's National Crime Victimization Survey of "thousands of respondents 12 and older").

But the FBI also estimates that "34 percent of female sex assault victims" are "under age 12" (National Incident-Based Reporting System, July 2000).

Since the DOJ data *excludes rape of children under age 12,* child rape may be *up 85 percent,* for all we know.

Although the FBI and local police departments are now swamped with teachers, police, professors, doctors, legislators, clergy, federal and state bureaucrats, dentists, judges, etc., arrested for child pornography and for abusing children *under age 12,* the Department of Justice excludes those small victims from its "rape" rates. Why?

Do DOJ, FBI Harbor Pedophiles?

You have to wonder: Are there pedophiles and other sexual predators in the governmental woodpiles?

When I worked for DOJ's Juvenile Justice and Delinquency Prevention in the 1980s, someone high up killed the order to collect crime-scene pornography as evidence in prosecutions. No Democrat or Republican administration has yet mandated such on-site pornography collections. Whom is DOJ protecting?

Reynolds writes less like an objective scholar than a pornography defender:

> Since 1970 porn has exploded. But rape has gone down 85 percent. So much for the notion that pornography causes rape. [I]t would be hard to explain how rape rates could have declined so dramatically while porn expanded so explosively.

He opines that pornography possibly prevents rape (the old discredited "safe-outlet" theory).

The DOJ's preposterous "85 percent" decrease in rape ignores the obvious. The U.S. FBI Index of Crime reported a *418 percent increase* in "forcible rape" from 1960 to 1999. That fear means we now keep our doors, windows, and cars locked. Women seldom walk alone at night. Parents rarely let children go anywhere unaccompanied. Many states let people carry guns for self-defense. Rape Crisis Centers do not report rapes to police. More women perform as sexually required. A conflicting DOJ 2002 report says "almost 25 percent of college women have been victims of rape or attempted rape since the age of 14."

Why Don't the Feds Call Child-Rape "Rape"?

In 1950, 18 states authorized the death penalty for rape; most others could impose a life sentence. Following Alfred Kinsey's "scientific" advice in 1948, many states redefined "rape" so the crime could be plea-bargained down to a misdemeanor like "sexual misconduct."

Missouri redefined rape to mean 11 different crimes for 11 different sentences, magically lowering "rape" rates. Like all states that have trivialized rape, Missouri relied on the Kinsey-based 1955 American Law Institute Model Penal Code.

"Rape" was eliminated from New Jersey's laws and replaced with a variety of terms during a 1978 penal law revision.

For example, Dr. Linda Jeffrey notes that the charge to which child-molesting teacher Pamela Diehl-Moore pleaded guilty was reduced to a second-tier crime, "sexual assault"—i.e., sexual contact with a victim under 13, or penetration where the "actor" uses physical force or coercion, but the victim doesn't suffer severe personal injury, or the victim is 16 or 17, with aggravating circumstances, or the victim is 13 to 15 and the "actor" is at least four years older. (Whew!)

Sex Criminals Copy What Porn Depicts

DOJ experts should read reports such as "Sex-Related Homicide and Death Investigation" (2003). Former Lt. Comdr. Vernon Geberth says today's "sex-related cases are more frequent, vicious and despicable" than anything he experienced in decades as a homicide cop.

In "Journey into Darkness" (1997), the FBI's premier serial-rape profiler, John Douglas wrote, "[Serial-rape murders are commonly found] with a large pornography collection, either store-bought or homemade. Our [FBI] research does show that certain types of sadomasochistic and bondage-oriented material can fuel the fantasies of those already leaning in that direction."

In "The Evil That Men Do" (1998), FBI serial-rape-murderer-mutilator profiler Roy Hazelwood quotes one sex killer who tied his victims in "a variety of positions" based on pictures he saw in sex magazines.

"Thrill Killers, a Study of America's Most Vicious Murders," by Charles Linedecker, reports that 81 percent of these killers rated pornography as their primary sexual interest. Dr. W.L. Marshall, in "Criminal Neglect, Why Sex

Offenders Go Free" (1990), says based on the evidence, pornography "feeds and legitimizes their deviant sexual tendencies."

In one study of rapists, Gene Abel of the New York Psychiatric Institute cited, "One-third reported that they had used pornography immediately prior to at least one of their crimes." In 1984, the U.S. Attorney General's Task Force on Family Violence reported, "Testimony indicates that an alarming number of rape and sexual assault offenders report that they were acting out behavior they had viewed in pornographic materials."

More pornography equals more rape of children and women. We need to ask whether Big Government is now selling out to Big Pornography as it did to Big Tobacco for half a century.

EXPLORING THE ISSUE

Does Pornography Reduce the Incidence of Rape?

Challenge Questions

1. Should pornography be protected as a first amendment free speech right?
2. Is pornography ever okay? What if it is only consumed only by adults?
3. Does the content of the explicit images make a difference? Does it depend on what it depicts?
4. Do adults who view porn develop unrealistic expectations of beauty and sexual expression in their own relationships?
5. If some kind of causality could be shown, that pornography *does* indeed increase behavior, what role do you think the government should or should not play in regulating the industry?

Is There Common Ground?

Throughout history, people have looked for answers to why people perpetrate violent crimes on others. Mental health professionals, law enforcement officials, politicians, parents, and others have pointed fingers at many different potential causes without coming up with a clear answer. Is a person biologically determined to be a rapist? Is a rapist "created," and if so, by what or by whom? One of the first sources people go to for these reasons is the media. One type of indictment against the media focuses on their role as the pulse of the culture. The claim is that media depictions of behavior cause viewers to take actions that they would not otherwise take. Some argue, for example, that depictions of violence in the media lead to greater violence in real life. These arguments have even been brought to the legal system and used during trials. In a well-known court case at the time (*Huceg v. Hustler Magazine*, 1983), a family brought suit against *Hustler*, an adult pornographic magazine, in which a description appeared of autoerotic asphyxiation, a sexual practice in which a person restricts her or his breathing through partial hanging or other method, masturbates, and releases the air restriction at the moment of orgasm. The family's underage son tried this, did it incorrectly, and ended up hanging himself. The family sued *Hustler* magazine, arguing that if this had not been printed, their son would not have done it and died. The Court ruled for the magazine, saying that just reading a description of something does not necessarily encourage someone to do it—especially a young person for whom the material was not created. To say, however, that the media have *no* effect on people's attitudes or behaviors would be inaccurate. Advertisers spend billions of dollars every year on television, print, Internet, and other ads to sell a wide variety of products. The ads are designed to influence people's behaviors—that if we see a particular commercial or hear a particular song, we will be more likely to purchase one product over another. If advertisers are successful at this—at actually influencing people enough to purchase something they may not have necessarily known they wanted—is it possible that the creators and producers of adult sexually explicit media could be doing the same? For right now, the data are inconclusive—and there seem to be as many reports supporting each side of the debate. Be sure to consider a range of reasoning as you establish your own opinion on this topic.

Additional Resource

Family Safe Media's Pornography Statistics: http://www.familysafemedia.com/pornography_statistics.html

Internet References . . .

National Network for Childcare

Read an article from the network's newsletter on math, science, and girls: Can we close the gender gap?

http://www.nncc.org/Curriculum/sac52_math.science.girls.html

Wired Science

Read an article that shows that the gender gap vanishes in female-empowered cultures.

http://www.wired.com/wiredscience/2011/08/women-math-science-culture/

Women's History

Read about the role of Esther Dyson in the history of computer on the women's history section of the about.com Web site.

http://womenshistory.about.com/od/computers/p/esther_dyson.htm

InfoWorld

InfoWorld is the leading source of information on emerging enterprise technologies, and the only brand that explains to senior technology decision makers how these technologies work, and how they can use them to drive their business. This link provides a call to action to right the gender imbalance in the IT world.

http://www.infoworld.com/d/developer-world/women-in-technology-call-action-919

The *New York Times*

Read an article in the *New York Times* by Cornelia Dean that discusses the problems girls who are good at math encounter.

http://www.nytimes.com/2005/02/01/science/01math.html

WiredKids, Inc.

This organization is dedicated to protecting children from Internet-related child sexual exploitation, and creating a safer Internet for all. Stop cyberbullying is one of the Web sites it sponsors.

http://stopcyberbullying.org/

Cyberbullying Research Center

This Web site is dedicated to providing up-to-date information about the nature, extent, causes, and consequences of cyberbullying among adolescents. It is a clearinghouse of information concerning the ways adolescents use and misuse technology.

It is a resource for parents, educators, law enforcement officers, counselors, and others who work with youth. The site provides facts, figures, and detailed stories. It includes ways to help people prevent and respond to cyberbullying incidents.

http://www.cyberbullying.us/

Is It a Man's World? Math, Science, and the Cyber-World

*M*athematics, science, computers—when people think about who occupies these domains, boys and men come to mind readily. Stereotypes of science and math geeks—always male—come to mind easily. Unfortunately, such common stereotypes may deter women for pursuing careers in math and science. There is a well-established need for an increased number of students with career aspirations in information systems and computer sciences. Furthermore, there are far more job openings in computer information specialties, education, and community service than there are interested students, and across all fields of interest students are least prepared in the sciences. There is also a need for students with interests in the social behavioral sciences to be fully facile with cutting-edge technologies and able to develop applications to enhance their work, whether it is basic research or applications. Unfortunately, too few students have adequately developed scientific literacy and too few, especially women and ethnic minorities, are interested in careers in the sciences. Women and ethnic minorities, especially black women, are interested in traditional careers, the social sciences and helping professions in particular. However, focusing on developing self-efficacy and fostering interests in nontraditional fields can ameliorate these patterns. In general, men are more confident in the use of hardware than women, but women are just as likely to see various technologies as intelligent and socially acceptable. What insights does the study of race, ethnicity, and social class lend to our understanding of aptitude for and interest in the sciences and technology? How do media portrayals of women and men as users and consumers affect our beliefs about girls' and boys', women's and men's aptitude for and interest in the sciences and technology? Do these portrayals fuel or challenge stereotypes?

- Do Men Outperform Women in Mathematics?

- Is Gender Related to the Use of Computers?

- Is Cyberbullying Related to Gender?

ISSUE 12

Do Men Outperform Women in Mathematics?

YES: Paula Olszewski-Kubilius and Seon-Young Lee, from "Gender and Other Group Differences in Performance on Off-Level Tests: Changes in the 21st Century," *Gifted Child Quarterly* (vol. 55, pp. 54–73, 2011)

NO: Sara M. Lindberg, Janet Shibley Hyde, Jennifer L. Petersen, and Marcia C. Linn, from "New Trends in Gender and Mathematics Performance: A Meta-Analysis," *Psychological Bulletin* (vol. 136, pp. 1123–1135, 2010)

Learning Outcomes

As you read the issue, focus on the following points:

- Is there a biological basis for gender-related patterns of math performance?
- Do all tests measure the same basic mathematical skills? What are the different skill sets?
- How can you explain gender differences on some tests but not others?
- How might differences in analytic approaches such as meta-analysis and means comparisons lead to different conclusions?

ISSUE SUMMARY

YES: Paula Olszewski-Kubilius and Seon-Young Lee analyzed data from over 250,000 gifted students who took a variety of different tests and concluded that the ratio of talented math and science students remains at about 3 males:1 female.

NO: Sara Lindberg and colleagues used meta-analysis to analyze 242 studies of mathematics performance and concluded that there are no gender differences.

$\mathbf{C}$ognition represents a complex system of skills that enable the processing of different types of information. Cognitive processes underlie our intellectual activities and many other daily tasks. For three decades, researchers have actively explored whether or not males and females differ in their cognitive abilities. The most common taxonomy of cognitive processes used in cognitive sex differences research is based on the type of information used in a cognitive task: verbal (words), quantitative (numbers), and visual–spatial (figural representations). The study of cognitive sex differences became especially active after the publication of Eleanor Emmons Maccoby and Carol Nagy Jacklin's now famous book entitled *The Psychology of Sex Differences* (Stanford University Press, 1974). While concluding with a generally skeptical perspective on the existence of sex differences, the authors maintained that one area in which the sexes did appear to differ was intellectual ability and functioning. Specifically, the sexes appeared to differ in verbal, quantitative, and spatial abilities. This compilation and synthesis of sex comparison findings spawned extensive research on sex differences in numerous areas of functioning but especially in the domain of cognitive abilities. Researchers began to use the quantitative technique of meta-analysis, which has been used to explore whether or not any sex differences change in magnitude over the life cycle or over time, whether or not there is cross-cultural consistency in any sex differences, and whether or not cognitive sex differences are found across various ethnic groups. At an academic conference in January 2005, Harvard's then president Lawrence Summers gave a talk in which he suggested that innate differences in the math ability of women and men help explain why so few women are found at the highest levels in careers in mathematics and sciences. His speech generated a huge outcry from feminists and numerous scholars who dispute such claims. Summers's comments have refueled the ongoing debate regarding the biological basis of math and science abilities. We know that in careers in mathematics and the sciences, women tend to earn 25 percent less than men. They are twice as likely to be out of a job. Consider as well that only 2.5 percent of Nobel Prize winners and only 3 percent of the members of the U.S. National Academy of Sciences are women. There has been contradiction among findings. Some researchers document what they describe as important sex differences; others report negligible sex differences that have become smaller over time. When sex differences are described, males show better visual–spatial ability, especially the ability to mentally rotate three-dimensional figures. Males are also found to have greater mathematical ability. Females show better verbal fluency. This is a politically charged area of research because the stakes are high for the more and less cognitively able. Cognitive abilities relate to valued and "marketable" occupational and societal skills, often putting males at an advantage for higher social status and advancement. This "cognitive ability hierarchy" is determined not so much by findings of sex differences but may reflect differential societal valuation of different cognitive abilities. A criticism of explanatory research (including both biological and sociocultural studies) is the lack of direct testing of causal links. For example, sex differences in brain structure may exist, as might sex differences in spatial test performance. But do sex differences in brain structure *cause* sex-differentiated performance on spatial tests? Evidence is lacking for such causal claims. Observers caution that we must discriminate between causal theory and scientific evidence when evaluating causal claims. The debate falls into the classic concern that correlation does not mean causation. Consider a study that was done examining visual–spatial skills in children. Boys on average outperformed girls. However, the sex disparity was eliminated after girls had been given training in the requisite skills.

From the 1940s to the 1960s, boys tended to surpass girls in math and science, but those discrepancies have lessened more recently. Today girls and boys tend to be equal, especially in basic math skills, although in advanced math, high school girls tend to outperform boys in the classroom. Even at the college level, although males receive higher scores on standardized tests such as the SAT, females tend to earn higher grades in college math courses. It has been suggested that numerous factors affect females' math performance, such as differential treatment of girls and boys in the classroom and girls' lower expectations and lower confidence because of cultural messages that math is a male domain and that girls are not supposed to do well. There was briefly a Barbie doll on the market that said "math is tough." As recently as September 2011, JC Penney had on the market a T-shirt that said "I'm too pretty to do homework so my brother has to do it for me." It was pulled off the shelves quite quickly because of public objection. Even highly competent girls may suffer from stereotype threat in standardized testing situations. That is, although they may know they are good at math, the testing context arouses anxiety because of the stereotype; ironically, this can impair their performance. Research has suggested that girls who resist the pressure to conform to gender-role expectations are more likely to take math and science courses, compete in sports, and be more creative and achievement oriented. Interestingly, it helps to not have a brother, especially an older brother. Birth order, as well as the sex composition of the siblings, makes a difference. Girls without brothers tend to have higher self-esteem and find it easier to resist the pressure to conform to gendered expectations. Jacquelynne Eccles has proposed the Expectancy by Values Theory that helps explain girls' and boys' differential interest in math. She maintains that one's expectations for success interact with the subjective value of various options. Women, as well as men, must believe they can do it and must enjoy doing it. Her research demonstrates that parental attributions are very important. Parents very strongly influence their children's beliefs about their skills, which in turn shapes their academic and, ultimately, career choices. Very frequently, men are socialized to value career over family and vice versa for women. This emphasis on the development of attitudes toward math and science and their impact on career choices is important because it gives us insight into why there is a gender wage gap and why so many single mothers find themselves on welfare. Recently, organizations have launched campaigns to narrow the computer technology gap, which may contribute to the math and science gap for girls and boys. For example, in 2002 the American Association of University Women began the Nebraska Girls and Technology Project in cooperation with the Girl Scouts. The project includes *Girls Click*, which is a computer-based hands-on learning experience.

In the YES and NO selections, you will be reading about the work of two different sets of scholars who used different analytic approaches to address the question of gender differences in mathematical performance.

**Paula Olszewski-Kubilius
and Seon-Young Lee**

Gender and Other Group Differences in Performance on Off-Level Tests: Changes in the 21st Century

Background

It is currently the case in our society that males predominate the faculties of American universities in the fields of mathematics, engineering, and science. An important question is—what accounts for the underrepresentation of females in these occupations and fields? Is it due to gender differences in abilities or aptitudes related to those areas, interest in these fields or careers, socialization practices that differentially encourage or support males and females to enter these fields, cultural factors, or likely, some combination of all these factors? While this situation is very complex, a major source of controversy is the extent to which gender differences in abilities and aptitudes contribute to gender differences in occupational choices and career success.

Differences in the performances of males and females on cognitive tasks and tests have long interested psychologists because of the possible link to gender differences in occupational choices and achievement, particularly within the STEM (science, technology, engineering, and mathematics) fields. Based on several meta-analyses, Hyde [and colleagues] concluded that when samples of children who are heterogeneous with respect to ability and achievement are studied, gender differences on cognitive tests appear to have decreased over time and are currently minimal. However, [others] report that some verbal tasks show large gender differences favoring females such as synonym generation or verbal fluency with effect sizes in the moderate to large range . . . [and] that males tend to perform higher than females on those tests taken mostly by men (math and science tests) and there were small or no gender differences on tests taken mainly by females (literature, foreign language). . . . Males' test scores were relatively higher on political science, physics, European history, computer science, and chemistry. . . . [T]he differences on some of these tests [may be] large enough to affect the admissions decisions of selective institutions. . . .

When gifted students are studied, a consistent and reliable gender difference is that among participants in talent search programs, middle-school-aged males outscore middle-school-aged females on the SAT-Math. . . .

Research suggests that differences in test scores during middle school may have importance in the future. The Study of Mathematically Precocious Youth (SMPY) followed students with varying patterns of SAT scores longitudinally and found that gender differences in middle school favoring males on the SAT-Math had implications for career choices and professional and creative achievements in adulthood. . . .

Gender differences in performances on the SAT, ACT, and EXPLORE are not the only differences that warrant the attention of educators and researchers. Another concern among educators and policy makers is performance discrepancies between ethnic groups and by socioeconomic status. Previous research amply documents that African Americans and Hispanics are severely underrepresented among students who score in the top 1%, 5%, and 10% on standardized tests and who are underrepresented in the top 25% of students at all levels of education, a situation that has changed little over the past 30 years. Comparably, the overrepresentation of Caucasian and Asian students has been steady over decades and across all grade levels and even among high achieving students. . . .

Major causes of this achievement gap are the larger percentage of African American and Hispanic students who came from low-income circumstances compared with Caucasians and Asians—what [is referred] to as the "between-class" dimension of the high achievement gap. At all socioeconomic status levels, African American and Hispanic children achieve at significantly lower levels compared with Caucasian and Asian American students.

In summary, although gender differences on cognitive tests may be small and disappearing when heterogeneous samples of students are studied, they appear to remain robust for gifted samples. These gender differences for gifted students have implications for the representation of the most able females in STEM professions. Therefore, gender and other group differences among the gifted warrant further investigation.

About This Study

The purpose of the study was to explore gender and other group differences in performances on the verbal and math subtests of the SAT, ACT, and EXPLORE tests for academically gifted students who participated in Northwestern University's Midwest Academic Talent Search (NUMATS) since 2000. Students qualify to participate in talent search testing in multiple ways. They must (a) qualify for gifted programs at their school, (b) be nominated by a teacher or parent as achieving several years above grade level, or (c) have achievement test scores (≥ 95th percentile) on a nationally normed achievement test or a norm-referenced state test. Students in Grades 3 through 6 can take the EXPLORE test, and students in Grades 6 through 9 can take the SAT and/or ACT tests. . . .

In this study, we wanted to see if previously reported gender differences and ratios of males to females for specific scoring levels, particularly at the high-end of the score distribution, hold for the Midwest sample of talent search participants; if those ratios have changed over a 9-year period from 2000 to 2008; and whether gender differences among gifted adolescents have declined as they have in heterogeneous populations. Also, we were interested in understanding the demographic characteristics (e.g., grade, ethnicity, household income) of students scoring at different levels on the SAT, ACT, and EXPLORE tests. . . .

Method

Data Collection and Participants

Off-level test scores of 257,829 students were obtained from Northwestern University's Center for Talent Development (CTD) database. The students all met the eligibility criteria for talent search testing through CTD and took the SAT (n = 111,796), ACT (n = 94,054), or EXPLORE (n = 51,979) tests during the years 2000 to 2008 when they were in Grades 4 to 9. The students were almost evenly distributed by gender: 52.2% male and 47.8% female. . . . Overwhelmingly, the students were Caucasian (79.2%), followed by 8.3% Asian, 6.9% African American, and 1.8% Hispanic. . . . Of those who reported family income (59.6% of test takers), more than half (57.3%) came from families with $80,000 or higher annual income. . . .

Generally, slightly more than half of the students scored at the lowest end (SAT 200–399 or 400–499, ACT 1–14 or 15–19 and EXPLORE 1–13 or 14–16) of the score distribution on the SAT, ACT, or EXPLORE subtests. About 1% to 8% of the students scored at the top end (SAT 700–800, ACT 30–36, and EXPLORE 23–25) of the score range on each subtest. Consistently for male and female students on the SAT and the ACT, a greater percentage of students scored at the lowest end of the score range on the verbal (reading and English) subtests than on the math or science subtests. On the EXPLORE, more males and females scored at the lowest end of the score range on both the verbal (reading and English) and math subtests than the science subtest. So, overall, these gifted students who were taking these tests off level found the math and science subtests to be "easier" than the verbal (reading or English) subtests. . . .

Results

Analysis of Mean Score Differences on the SAT

From 2000 to 2008, higher mean scores were found for male students compared with female students on the SAT-Math, . . . with small effect sizes ($.3 < d. < .4$) for the mean differences for each of the 9 years. On the SAT-Reading, females had significantly higher means than males over the 9-year period, . . . though effect sizes for these differences were negligible ($d < .1$). No significant differences were detected between genders in 2000, 2001, 2005, and 2008.

Both on the math and reading subtests, higher mean scores were found for older students and students from families with higher family income.

Differences by ethnicity were also statistically significant on both subtests. Asian students overall obtained the highest mean scores on the math and reading subtests; specifically, Asian males had the highest mean score on the math subtest, followed by Asian females, Caucasian males, and Caucasian females. Asian females obtained the highest mean score on the SAT-Reading, followed by Asian males, Caucasian females, and Caucasian males. African American female students had the lowest mean scores on both the math and reading subtests of the SAT. All these mean differences were very consistent across the years from 2000 to 2008 for male and female students, and all resulted in small effect sizes ($d < .3$). . . .

Analysis of Proportional Differences on the SAT

SAT-Math

Data for the 9-year period revealed that male and female students were different in their proportions in each of the score ranges on the math subtest. . . . Particularly, males outnumbered females at the higher end of the score distribution; more males than females earned scores ranging from 500 to 800 with a gradual increase in the male-to-female ratio across the range of scores. . . . Among the top-scoring students (700–800, top 2% of the testers), about three times the number of males was found compared with females for all 9 years. . . .

[A]t the top end of the score distribution (700–800), overwhelmingly, students were older . . . in that the eighth-grade students performed better than the seventh-grade students although the SAT test takers were split evenly by grade. The majority of the top scorers had families with $80,000 or higher annual household incomes, and thus, students from families with higher incomes were overrepresented among the top-scoring students compared with their representation in the SAT testing pool.

Most of these top-scoring students were Asian or Caucasian. Asian students comprised about two thirds of the top-scoring students, although they represented only 10.5% of the SAT test takers during the 9-year period, whereas Caucasian students were underrepresented (about 2.5 times) in that they comprised only one third of the top-scoring students overall. The overrepresentation of Asian students in the top range increased over the years. . . . Generally, the proportion of top scorers who were Asian was greater for females than males. . . . In contrast, more males than females were found for Caucasian top-performing students although both genders were almost evenly represented in the test-taking pool with only slightly more males than females among the Caucasian test takers.

The majority of African American and Hispanic students scored in the two lowest score ranges on the math subtest; for both males and females, more than 70% of African American students and more than 50% of Hispanic students scored in these ranges since 2000. . . .

SAT-Reading

. . . Overall, the male-to-female ratio was close to 1 for every score range on the SAT-Reading. A slightly greater number of males scored both at the low and high ends of the score distribution compared with females. . . .

Data from the 9 years demonstrated that the majority of the students in the top score range on the SAT-Reading were older and had higher family income levels. . . . [T]he majority of the top male and female students came from families with $80,000 or higher annual household income (males 64.7% to 100%, females 64.3% to 85.8%). . . . [A]mong the top scorers, Caucasian students were found in proportions comparable with their representation in the entire testing pool whereas Asian students were significantly overrepresented— by 3 to 4 times their representation in the testing pool depending on the year. . . . The underrepresentation of both ethnic groups, particularly African American students, compared with their representation in the SAT testing pool (i.e., 7% for African American, 2% for Hispanic) was considerable.

Analysis of Mean Differences on the ACT

Similar to the SAT, there were statistically significant gender differences in students' scores on each subtest of the ACT since 2000. Male students obtained higher mean scores than female students on the math . . . and science . . . subtests, whereas female students outscored male students on the reading . . . and English. . . . Although all of these differences were statistically significant, they resulted in small effect sizes ($d < .3$).

Over the 9-year period, mean scores varied significantly by grade, ethnicity, and family income level. Older students, students from families with higher household income, and Asian students tended to have the highest mean scores on each of the subtests. Among Asian and Caucasian students, there were significant differences by gender with females doing better on the reading and English subtests and males performing better on the math and science subtests for both ethnicities. Across most years, African American female students had the lowest mean scores on the math and science subtests, whereas African American male students had the lowest mean scores on the reading and English subtests. Still, each of these mean differences amounted to a small effect size.

Analysis of Proportional Differences on the ACT

ACT-Math and -Science

Significant proportional differences were found between males and females across the score ranges on the math. . . . Generally, male students were about 2 to 3 times as likely as female students to score in the range of 25 to 29 (top 12% in math, top 15% in science) or 30 to 36 (top 2% in math and science each). . . .

Students from families with higher incomes were highly overrepresented as were older students, especially ninth-graders among top scorers. . . .

Caucasians were the largest ethnic group who scored in the top range on both subtests. . . . Among top scorers however, Caucasian students were proportionally underrepresented on the ACT-Math, but on the ACT-Science, they were represented comparable to their representation. . . . Asian students were overrepresented 3 to 5 times among top scorers on the math. . . .

Most African American students had scores in the range of 1 to 14 or 15 to 19 as did Hispanic students. Both ethnic groups were highly overrepresented in these scoring categories, whereas they were severly under-represented in the highest range of 30 to 36. . . .

ACT-Reading and -English

Differences in proportions in each score range were found between genders on the reading . . . and English . . . subtests. On the ACT-Reading, a slightly greater number of female students scored in the range of 20 to 36 than male students. . . . Similarly on the ACT-English, approximately twice as many males as females scored at the lowest end of the score range, whereas females outnumbered males by 2 to 1 in the top score range (30–36) on the ACT-English.

Chi-square statistics confirmed proportional differences in each score range by students' grade in reading . . . and in English . . . ; by family annual income in reading . . . and in English, . . . and by ethnicity in reading . . . and in English. . . .

Analysis of Mean Differences on the EXPLORE

From 2000 to 2008, statistically significant gender differences were found on the subtests of the EXPLORE similar to those of the SAT and ACT. Males had higher means than females on the math . . . and science . . . subtests, whereas females had higher means than males on the reading . . . and in English. . . .

On each subtest, the combined 9-year data yielded differences in students' scores by grade, ethnicity, and family income level. With only a few exceptions, for each year of testing, the higher the students' grade and family income, the better they performed on the math, science, reading, and English portions of the EXPLORE. Overall, Asian students obtained higher means than other ethnic groups on all these subtests, and Caucasian students had the second highest means. Asian male students had the highest mean scores on the math and science subtests, followed by Asian females, Caucasian males, and Caucasian females. On the reading and English subtests, Asian females earned the highest mean scores, followed by Caucasian females or Asian males, and Caucasian males. Generally, African American males had the lowest mean scores on the science, reading, and English subtests, whereas African American females had the lowest mean scores on the math subtest most years since 2000. However, these mean differences yielded small effect sizes ($d < .3$) and were negligible on the science and reading subtests.

Analysis of Proportional Differences on the EXPLORE

EXPLORE-Math and -Science

Proportional differences were found between males and females across the score ranges on the math . . . and science . . . subtests. On the EXPLORE-Math, male students outnumbered female students for each score range except the lowest end (1–13). . . .

On both the math and science subtests, chi-square statistics showed differences by grade in math . . . and in science . . . ; by annual family income in math

. . . and in science . . . ; and by ethnicity in math . . . and in science . . . , in the proportions of students across the score ranges.
    . . .

EXPLORE-Reading and -English

The number of students scoring in each score range of the reading and English subtests varied significantly by gender. . . . Almost the same number of male and female students was found in each range of the score distribution, including the top range (23–25, top 5%) on the EXPLORE-Reading. The male-to-female ratio or the female to male ratio was virtually the same across the score ranges. Similarly, on the EXPLORE-English, almost the same or just slightly more males than females were found in the score range of 1 to 13 (male-to-female ratio = 1.1–1.3 to 1). Female students outnumbered male students among the high scorers (20–22 and 23–25) on the English subtest, and particularly at the top end (23–25, top 6%), twice as many females as males were found.

    Proportional differences across the score ranges were found by students' grade in reading . . . and in English . . . ; by annual family income in reading . . . and in English . . . ; and by ethnicity in reading . . . and in English. . . .

Summary and Discussion

Overall, this study demonstrated that for our sample of gifted students, gender differences remained steady but small in the areas of math and science and were even smaller in the verbal areas. Similar to the previous findings, we found that regardless of age (older students for the SAT or ACT and younger students for the EXPLORE), males consistently outperformed females on the math and science subtests with the most pronounced differences on the math subtests, whereas females outperformed their male counterparts on the verbal subtests. None of these differences between genders diminished over the 9-year period, but were steady with small effect sizes for the math or science subtests and negligible effect sizes for the verbal subtests.

    [It has been] reported from the SMPY that higher a "quantitative tilt" (i.e., higher math scores on the SAT compared with verbal scores) was more likely among gifted males than gifted females and was predictive of choosing math and science careers. . . .

    [In our analysis,] males were more likely to show tilted profiles toward math than females, especially on the SAT, and more females than males were likely to tilt in the direction of higher reading scores than math scores on the ACT. It is interesting that almost twice as many males and females showed a tilt toward reading versus math on the ACT than the SAT. Why this is the case is not clear but is likely attributed to subtle differences between the tests. Nevertheless, our results are generally supportive of previous findings regarding a quantitative tilt for gifted males, . . . suggest[ing] that ability profiles can underlie career choices as well as activity and course preferences, and thereby contribute to gender discrepancies in occupations such as math, engineering, and physical sciences in adulthood.

An interesting finding was that although our gifted female students obtained higher mean scores on all the verbal subtests across the various tests, an exception occurred on the reading portion of the SAT where more males than females scored at the highest end of the score ranges. We wondered if this difference had something to do with the items on the SAT versus ACT reading tests. According to the test publishers' descriptions of the tests, the reading subtests of the SAT and ACT appear very similar. . . .

The real difference between males and females in terms of verbal skills appears to be in English skills, including usage or mechanics such as punctuation, grammar and usage, and sentence structure; and rhetorical skills such as strategy, organization, and style. It is noteworthy that the 2:1 ratio, favoring females on the English subtests, was found for both younger and older students. These results support previous research that showed that males tend to score higher on verbal analogies than females, whereas females have strengths in verbal fluency.

Though gender differences were the most prominent in math for our gifted students, our results did not support the presence of more pronounced gender differences at the upper end of the score ranges previously reported in the literature. The number of males to females or females to males scoring in each range was consistently 1:1 to 3:1.

This study also confirmed the uneven profile of top-scoring students according to ethnicity, income, and grade level . . . data for each group. Particularly for ethnicity, Asian students had the highest mean scores on each of the SAT, ACT, and EXPLORE subtests and were overrepresented among the top-performing students on these tests compared with their representation in each testing pool. . . .

Another stunning finding was the unwavering differences by ethnicity and annual household income level throughout the 9-year period. Whereas Asian and Caucasian students were the two prevailing groups in the top range on each subtest, African American and Hispanic students, particularly African American students, were severely underrepresented, typically accounting for < 3% of the top-scoring students across the tests. . . . [F]or younger African American students, males were behind females, whereas the opposite was true for older African American students. Why this is the case is not readily apparent.

Students from affluent families overwhelmingly scored in the upper score ranges across gender, ethnicity, and grade level. . . . All these differences demonstrate that academic disparities by ethnicity are entangled with students' socioeconomic status from early ages, and multiple factors account for these discrepancies. These findings are disturbing because African American and Hispanic students are severely underrepresented among higher scoring students, especially on math and science subtests. All the students who participated in this study initially scored in the top 5% of students on in-grade achievement tests or state-level exams, yet of these students who are among the best in their respective schools, only a handful are African American or Hispanic students who then go on to achieve top scores on high-stakes, off-level tests. These students have hit a proverbial "glass ceiling" reaching the top in their grade or school but not proceeding further up to higher levels on criteria that will gain them entrance into supplementary educational programs and selective institutions of higher education. . . .

Our study revealed that students, regardless of gender, tended to score lower on the verbal tests compared to the math and science tests. For our sample, the math and science tests seemed to be "easier" than the verbal tests, which suggests that superior verbal ability may develop more slowly. Differences in the development and trajectories of math versus verbal abilities warrant further examination. In addition, research should continue to examine gender differences for gifted students in performances on cognitive tests, particularly in math, to see if patterns observed in our data persist or become smaller. . . .

Sara M. Lindberg et al.  **NO**

New Trends in Gender and Mathematics Performance: A Meta-Analysis

Policy decisions, such as funding for same-sex education, as well as the continuing stereotype that girls and women lack mathematical ability, call for up-to-date information about gender differences in mathematical performance. Such stereotypes can discourage women from entering or persisting in careers in science, technology, engineering, and mathematics (STEM). Today women earn 45% of the undergraduate degrees in mathematics but make up only 17% of university faculty in mathematics. We report on a meta-analysis of recent studies of gender and mathematics. We estimate the magnitude of the gender difference and test whether it varies as a function of factors such as age and the difficulty level of the test.

Stereotypes About Gender and Mathematics

Mathematics and science are stereotyped as male domains. Stereotypes about female inferiority in mathematics are prominent among children and adolescents, parents, and teachers. Although children may view boys and girls as being equal in mathematical ability, they nonetheless view adult men as being better at mathematics than adult women. Implicit attitudes that link men and mathematics have been demonstrated repeatedly in studies of college students.

Parents believe that their sons' mathematical ability is higher than their daughters'. In one study, fathers estimated their sons' mathematical IQ at 110 on average, and their daughters' at 98; mothers estimated 110 for sons and 104 for daughters. Teachers, too, tend to stereotype mathematics as a male domain. In particular, they overrate boys' ability relative to girls'.

These stereotypes are of concern for several reasons. First, in the language of cognitive social learning theory, stereotypes can influence competency beliefs or self-efficacy; correlational research does indeed show that parents' and teachers' stereotypes about gender and mathematics predict children's perceptions of their own abilities, even with actual mathematics performance controlled. Competency beliefs are important because of their profound effect on individuals' selection of activities and environments. According to an earlier meta-analysis, girls reported lower mathematics competence than boys did, although the difference was not large. In recent studies, elementary school boys still reported significantly higher mathematics competency beliefs than girls did.

A second concern is that stereotypes can have a deleterious effect on actual performance. Stereotype threat effects have been found for women in mathematics. In the standard paradigm, half the participants (talented college students) are told that the math test they are about to take typically shows gender differences (threat condition), and the other half are told that the math test is gender fair and does not show gender differences (control). Studies have found that college women underperform compared with men in the threat condition but perform equal to men in the control condition, indicating that priming for gender differences in mathematics indeed impairs girls' math performance. Stereotype threat effects have been found in children as early as kindergarten. Other research, measuring implicit stereotypes about gender and math, has found that these implicit stereotypes predict performance in a calculus course.

Stereotypes play a role in policy decisions as well as personal decision making. For example, schools and states may base a decision to offer single-sex mathematics classes on the belief that these gender differences exist.

Gender and Mathematics Performance

The stereotypes about female inferiority in mathematics stand in distinct contrast to the scientific data on actual performance. A 1990 meta-analysis found an effect size of $d = 0.15$, with men and boys scoring higher, for gender differences in mathematics performance averaged over all samples; however, in samples of the general population (i.e., national samples, classrooms—as opposed to exceptionally precocious or low ability samples), women and girls scored higher but by a negligible amount. . . . Moreover, girls earn better grades in mathematics courses than boys through the end of high school. In short, previous research showed that gender differences in mathematics performance were very small and, depending on the sample and outcome measure, sometimes favored boys and sometimes favored girls.

. . . One key moderator . . . [was] cognitive level of the test (computation was considered the lowest level, understanding of concepts was considered intermediate, and complex problem solving was considered the highest level). Girls performed better than boys at computation in elementary school and middle school, but the differences were small and there was no gender difference in high school. There was no gender difference in understanding of mathematical concepts at any age. For complex problem solving, there was no gender difference in elementary or middle school, but a gender difference favoring boys emerged in high school. This last gender difference, although small, is of concern because complex problem solving is crucial for STEM careers.

A second moderator analysis examined the magnitude of gender differences in mathematics performance as a function of the ethnicity of the sample. The striking finding was that the small gender difference favoring boys was found for Whites, but not for Blacks or Latinos.

Depth of Knowledge

Historically, researchers maintained that girls might do as well as or even better than boys on tests of computation, which require relatively simple cognitive processes. These same researchers concluded that male superiority emerged for tests requiring more advanced cognitive processing, such as complex problem solving. The 1990 meta-analysis provided some support for these ideas, although the gender difference in complex problem solving did not appear until the high school years and was not large even then.

Current mathematics education researchers conceptualize this issue of complexity of cognitive processes as a question of item demand and the depth of knowledge required to solve a particular problem. [In a] four-level depth of knowledge framework . . . , Level 1 (recall) includes the recall of information such as facts or definitions, as well as performing simple algorithms. Level 2 (skill/concept) includes items that require students to make decisions about how to approach a problem. These items typically ask students to classify, organize, estimate, or compare information. Level 3 (strategic thinking) includes complex and abstract cognitive demands that require students to reason, plan, and use evidence. Level 4 (extended thinking) requires complex reasoning, planning, developing, and thinking over an extended period of time. Items at Level 4 require students to connect ideas within the content area or among content areas as they develop one problemsolving approach from many alternatives. This depth of knowledge framework was used to rate the cognitive demands of the tests that assess mathematics performance in the studies reviewed here.

New Trends

Cultural shifts have occurred since the 1980s that call for the reexamination of gender differences in mathematics. In the 1980s, a prominent explanation of male superiority in complex problem solving beginning in high school was gender differences in course choice. Girls were less likely than boys to take advanced mathematics courses and advanced science courses. Because mathematical problem solving is an important component of chemistry and physics courses, students may learn those skills in science courses as much as in mathematics courses. Today, however, the gender gap in course taking has disappeared in all areas except physics. . . . Insofar as courses taken by students influence their mathematics performance, we expect the gender difference in complex problem solving in high school to have narrowed.

In addition, cross-national data show that the gender gap in mathematics performance narrows or even reverses in societies with more gender equality. Insofar as the United States has moved toward gender equality over the past 30 to 40 years, the gender gap in mathematics performance should have narrowed. . . .

Gender and Variability

Most of the research has focused on mean-level gender differences, but variability (variance) remains an issue even when means are similar. The greater male variability hypothesis was originally proposed in the 1800s and advocated by scientists such as Charles Darwin and Havelock Ellis to explain why there was an excess of men both in homes for the mentally deficient and among geniuses. . . . Thus, the hypothesis states that men are more likely than women to be at both the top and the bottom of the statistical distribution of mathematics performance. . . . The greater male variability hypothesis, of course, is a description of the data, not an explanation for it, but if true, it could partially account for findings of an excess of males at very high levels of mathematical performance. One goal of this meta-analysis was to reassess the greater male variability hypothesis for mathematics performance using contemporary data.

The Current Study

Several factors warrant a new meta-analysis of research on gender and mathematics performance. First, approximately 18 years of new data have accumulated since the 1990 meta-analysis. Second, cultural shifts have occurred over the last 2 decades. Specifically, girls are now taking advanced mathematics courses and some science courses in high school at the same rate as boys are, closing the gap in course choice. The magnitude of gender differences in mathematics performance is expected to be even smaller than it was in the 1990 meta-analysis; of particular interest is the gender difference favoring boys in complex problem solving in high school and whether this difference has narrowed in recent years. Third, statistical methods of meta-analysis have advanced. . . .

Our goals in these meta-analyses were to provide answers to the following questions:

1. What is the magnitude of the gender difference in mathematics performance, using the d metric?
2. Does the direction or magnitude of the gender difference vary as a function of the depth of knowledge tapped by the test?
3. Developmentally, at what ages do gender differences appear or disappear?
4. Are there variations across U.S. ethnic groups, or across nations, in the direction or magnitude of the gender difference?
5. Has the magnitude of gender differences in mathematics performance declined from 1990 to 2007?
6. Do men and boys display greater variance in scores, and if so, by how much?

Study 1 addressed these questions with traditional methods of meta-analysis that involve identifying all possible studies using article databases. Study 2 addressed the questions using an alternative method . . . , which involves the analysis of recent large, national U.S. data sets based on probability sampling. . . .

Study 1

Method

Identification of Studies. Computerized database searches of ERIC, PsycINFO, and Web of Knowledge were used to generate a pool of potential articles. To identify all articles that investigated mathematics performance, the following search terms were used: (math* or calculus or algebra or geometry) AND (performance or achievement or ability) NOT (mathematical model). These broad terms were selected to capture the widest possible range of research conducted on this topic while avoiding studies that used computational modeling methodology to study unrelated phenomena. Search limits restricted the results to articles that discussed research with human populations and that were published in English between 1990 and 2007. The three database searches identified 10,816, 9,577, and 18,244 studies, respectively, which were considered for inclusion. Given the tremendous volume of studies identified, we decided to rely solely on this method of identification, a potential limitation. . . .

Coding the Studies. If studies reported data from large data sets or longitudinal studies that were likely to create multiple publications, this was noted so as to avoid inclusion of nonindependent effect sizes.

Several characteristics of each sample were coded as potential moderators: (a) age of the participants; (b) nationality of participants (American, Canadian, European, Australian/New Zealander, Asian, African, Latin American, or Middle Eastern); (c) for U.S. samples, majority ethnic group of participants (European American, African American, Asian American, Hispanic, other; mixed; or unreported), and (d) ability level of the participants (low ability, general ability, selective, highly selective).

Several aspects of the mathematics tests were also coded as potential moderators: (a) whether the test was time-limited; (b) whether the test included each of several problem types (multiple choice, short answer, open ended); (c) which types of mathematical content were included in the test (numbers and operations, algebra, geometry, measurement, data analysis and probability); (d) depth of knowledge; and (e) whether the test was specific to the local curriculum (i.e., based on published curricular standards for the region or developed in collaboration with local teachers, textbooks, and syllabi) or was relatively independent of the curriculum. Publication year was also coded as a potential moderator. . . .

Results

Magnitude of Gender Differences. The overall weighted effect size, averaged over all studies, was $d = +0.05$, representing a negligible gender difference. . . . Heterogeneity analysis revealed that the set of effect sizes was significantly heterogeneous. . . .

Moderator Analyses. Given the heterogeneity among the effect sizes, we conducted analyses for suspected moderator variables. . . . Problem type (presence of multiple choice, short answer, and open ended questions) was the only aspect of the tests that significantly predicted heterogeneity among the effects. . . . The presence of multiple choice questions on exams predicted relatively better performance by boys, whereas the presence of short answer and open ended questions predicted relatively better performance by girls.

The magnitude of the gender difference did not depend on whether there was a time limit for the test, . . . or whether the test was curriculum-focused. . . . Similarly, there were no variations in the magnitude of the effect size as a function of problem content (numbers and operations, algebra, geometry, measurement, probability), . . . or depth of knowledge. . . .

The magnitude of the gender difference varied significantly as a function of the selectivity of the sample. . . . For samples of the general population, $d = +0.07$, but $d = +0.40$ for highly selective samples.

Nationality was not a significant predictor of effect sizes, . . . All effects were small or negligible. Among U.S. studies, effect sizes varied as a function of ethnicity. . . . Samples composed mainly of Whites showed $d = +0.13$, whereas for ethnic minority samples, $d = -0.05$. Although we would have preferred to report results from these groups separately by ethnicity, the number of samples was too small to permit this.

The analysis also indicated that age was a significant moderator. . . . Gender differences were negligible in elementary school and middle school aged children and reached a peak of $d = +0.23$ in high school. The gender difference then declined for college-aged samples and adults.

To test for trends over time from 1990 to 2007, an analog to multiple regression was performed, using year of publication to predict effect size. This analysis indicated that publication year was not a significant predictor of effect size. . . .

A final analysis explored the interaction of age and depth of knowledge. Thus, our next analysis focused on both depth of knowledge and different age groups. This analysis was limited by the fact that many articles identified in our original search provided insufficient information to be able to code depth of knowledge, so they were not useable in this analysis. Furthermore, of those that had usable information about test content, only a small proportion of tests included items that tapped complex problem solving (Level 3 or 4). Some studies located in the literature search involved problem solving at Level 3 or 4 but reported only qualitative data on students' approach to the problem, with no data on actual performance. Although these studies could not be included in the meta-analysis, they suggest the value of looking at more complex tasks. . . . Of particular interest in this analysis was whether a gender difference in complex problem solving would be seen among high school and college students. . . . Our results showed that there was a small gender difference favoring male high school students on tests that included problems at Level 3 or 4 ($d = +0.16$), but the effect was reversed among college students ($d = -0.11$). However, these findings are based on small numbers of studies and therefore cannot be considered robust.

Gender Differences in Variability.   . . . The overall weighted VR . . . [indicated] slightly larger variance for males than for females. . . .

Study 2

Method

Large United States Data Sets.   Study 1 excluded articles that reported secondary data analyses from large national data sets, because original data from those studies were acquired directly for a separate analysis, which constitutes Study 2. Data sets were included in Study 2 if they (a) included relevant information about math performance, (b) represented data collected after 1990, (c) were nationally representative with a large sample size, and (d) provided statistics for both males and females. International data sets were excluded from Study 2 because they have been thoroughly reviewed elsewhere in the literature. The following large U.S. data sets were analyzed in Study 2: the NLSY97 (Bureau of Labor Statistics), the NELS:88 (National Center for Education Statistic), the LSAY, and the NAEP (National Center for Education Statistics). . . .

Data Analysis.   Data analysis for Study 2 was similar to Study 1. All effect sizes were calculated, and a mixed effects model was used to determine whether the effect sizes within each data set were heterogeneous. . . .

Moderating variables used in Study 2 were age, publication year, percentage of each type of problem (number sense, algebra, geometry, measurement), percentage of problems in each type of format (multiple choice, short answer, open ended), and percentage of each ethnic group in the sample. Similar to Study 1, VRs were also computed. More information about sample and test characteristics was available for the large data sets than was available for the studies uncovered in the literature reviews in Study 1. Therefore, with the exception of depth of knowledge, we were able to code moderator variables with more detail, and many moderators that were coded as categorical variables in Study 1 were considered continuous variables in Study 2. . . .

Results

Across all data sets in Study 2, the average weighted effect size was $d = +0.07$. The average weighted VR across all data sets was 1.09. The effect sizes were heterogeneous. . . . Differences among the national data sets were a significant source of heterogeneity . . . therefore we describe findings from each data set in turn.

. . . [T]he mean weighted effect size for all six assessments of the NLSY was $d = +0.08$. The average weighted VR was 1.05. Effects sizes for NLSY-97 were homogenous . . .

The average weighted effect size across all eight assessments was $d = +0.10$, [and the] average weighted VR for the NELS:88 was 0.94. Effect sites within the NELS:88 were heterogeneous. . . .

Results for the LSAY indicated small or negligible gender differences for each assessment. The average weighted effect size for all six assessments was $d = -0.07$. The weighted average VR was 1.26. Effect sizes were homogenous. . . .

Results for NAEP indicated small or negligible gender differences at all grades. The average weighted effect size across all 18 assessments of the long-term trend data was $d = +0.09$. The average weighted effect size across all 18 of the main assessments was $d = +0.06$. The average weighted VR for the long-term trend data was 1.13, and for the main assessment was 1.04. Effect sizes for both the long-term trend data and the main assessment were homogenous. . . .

The heterogeneity of the effect sizes across data sets indicates that these studies are not replications of each other but rather vary along some dimension(s). We therefore conducted additional moderation analyses to examine whether sample characteristics or test characteristics could explain the heterogeneity among effect sizes across data sets. . . . The value of the moderator increases (relative advantage for males) and negative values indicating a decrease in effect size as the value of the moderator increases (relative advantage for females).

Two aspects of the tests accounted for heterogeneity among studies: problem type and mathematical content. With regard to problem type, tests with a higher proportion of multiple choice and open-ended items yielded smaller gender effect sizes, whereas tests with a higher proportion of short answer items yielded larger gender effect sizes. This finding surprised us, given that three of the big data sets (LSAY, NLSY, NELS:88) were 100% multiple choice, and only one of them had a negative overall effect size; if multiple choice items conferred a significant female advantage, we might have expected negative effects across all three of those studies. Therefore, we conducted an additional analysis looking just at the 36 NAEP effect sizes, which have variation in the proportion of multiple choice, short answer, and open-ended questions. When looking at just the NAEP effect sizes, we found a different pattern of results, such that males did better on tests with a greater proportion of multiple choice items ($\beta = +.29$), and females did better on tests with a greater proportion of short answer and open-ended items (βs $= -.32$ and $-.19$, respectively). Thus, problem type had a similar effect on gender differences in the NAEP as was found in Study 1.

With regard to mathematical content, tests with a higher proportion of algebra items yielded smaller effect sizes (females performed relatively better), and tests with a higher proportion of measurement items yielded larger effect sizes (males performed relatively better). The other three types of mathematical content were not significant predictors of effect size in this analysis.

With regard to depth of knowledge, a marginally significant trend emerged such that tests containing items at Level 3 or 4 yielded larger effect sizes (males performed better or females performed worse). All of the tests contained items at Levels 1 and 2, and therefore we were not able to examine the specific effects of items at those levels.

The ethnic composition of the samples did not have an effect on the magnitude of the gender difference in mathematics performance. However, age was a marginally significant predictor of effect size ($p = .0516$), with older samples yielding relatively larger gender differences favoring males.

Discussion

We proposed to answer six questions with these meta-analyses. We take up each question in turn.

First, what is the magnitude of the gender difference in mathematics performance, based on contemporary studies? Taking Study 1 and Study 2 together, the answer appears to be that there is no longer a gender difference in mathematics performance. . . . These results are consistent with a recent analysis of meta from state assessments of youth in Grades 2 through 11, which found that girls had reached parity with boys in math performance. . . . These results are consistent with a recent analysis of U.S. data from state assessments of youth in Grades 2 through 11, which found that girls had reached parity with boys in math performance.

Second, does the direction or magnitude of the gender difference vary as a function of the depth of knowledge tapped by the test? By itself, depth of knowledge was not a significant predictor of differences in effect sizes in Study 1. However, Study 2 indicated that there may be a modest effect of depth of knowledge on gender differences in mathematics performance, with those containing a greater proportion of items at Level 3 or 4 favoring males. . . . However, an examination of depth of knowledge and age simultaneously in Study 1 indicates a male advantage ($d = 0.16$) in Level 3 or 4 problems in high school. . . . This finding, however, is based on only three studies, so it should be interpreted with caution. Very few studies used items requiring this greater depth of knowledge, yet it is precisely the skill that is required for high-level STEM careers.

Third, developmentally, at what ages do gender differences appear or disappear? Consistent with previous meta-analyses, are gender differences larger in high school than in elementary or middle school? The data sets reviewed in Study 2 showed a marginally significant increase in effect sizes as age increased. This is consistent with the results of Study 1. . . . Again, though, it is important to consider age and depth of knowledge required by the test simultaneously.

Overall, we conclude that a small gender difference favoring boys in complex problem solving is still present in high school. Multiple factors may account for this gender gap. As noted earlier, girls are less likely to take physics than boys are, and complex problem solving is taught in physics classes, perhaps even more than in math classes. Gender differences in patterns of interest may play a role, although these patterns, too, are shaped by culture. Moreover, even in very recent studies, parents and teachers give higher ability estimates to boys than to girls, and the effects of parents' and teachers' expectations on children's estimates of their own ability and their course choices are well documented.

Fourth, are there variations across U.S. ethnic groups, or across nations, in the direction or magnitude of the gender difference? In regard to ethnicity, for Study 1, a small gender difference was found favoring males among Whites, $d = +0.13$, but for all ethnic minorities combined, $d = -0.05$. . . .

Fifth, has the magnitude of gender differences in mathematics performance declined from 1990 to 2007? Study 1 found no relation between year of publication and effect sizes, indicating no discernible trend over time toward smaller gender differences. This may be because even in 1990, gender differences were already small leaving little room for further decline.

Sixth, do males display greater variance in scores and, if so, by how much? The overall VR in Study 1 was 1.07. That is, males displayed a somewhat larger variance, but the VR was not far from 1.0 or equal variances. In Study 2, the average *VR* was 1.09, again not far from 1.0. . . .

Overall, to put these findings in a broader context, gender can be conceptualized as one of many predictors of mathematics performance. Other factors include socioeconomic status (SES), parents' education, and the quality of schooling. [In other research] the effect sizes of nine predictors of children's mathematics performance at age 10 [were compared]: birth weight, gender, SES, mother's education, father's education, family income, quality of the home learning environment, preschool effectiveness, and elementary school effectiveness. The striking finding was that gender was the weakest of these nine predictors (i.e., it had the smallest effect size). Mother's education, quality of the home learning environment, and elementary school effectiveness were far stronger predictors. . . .

Implications

Overall, the results of these two studies provide strong evidence of gender similarities in mathematics performance. The heterogeneity of the findings suggests that there are moderator variables that might clarify the pattern of effect sizes. Detecting consistent moderators of gender differences would be strengthened by measures that tap the full range of mathematical reasoning, including items that require sustained reasoning about complex problems. The existence and magnitude of gender differences in mathematics performance varies as a function of many factors, including nation, ethnicity, and age.

These findings have several policy implications. First, these findings call into question current trends toward single-sex math classrooms. Advocates of single-sex education base their argument in part on the assumption that girls lag behind boys in mathematics performance and need to be in a protected, all-girls environment to be able to learn math. The data, however, show that girls are performing as well as boys in mathematics, on the basis of 242 separate studies (Study 1) and four large, well-sampled national U.S. data sets (Study 2). The great majority of these girls and boys did their learning in coeducational classrooms. Thus, the argument that girls' mathematics performance suffers in gender-integrated classrooms simply is not supported by the data. If we wish to improve students' mathematics performance, we would do better to focus not on gender but on factors that have larger effects, such as the quality and implementation of the curriculum, as well as the quality of the elementary school and the quality of the home learning environment.

Second, the dearth of Level 3 or 4 items in assessments has a serious consequence. Given the importance of mathematics tests for school evaluation under the No Child Left Behind legislation, it is common for teachers to teach to the test. If the test fails to emphasize the skills that citizens need, American students are disadvantaged. In addition, without evidence concerning student progress on these important forms of mathematical reasoning, teachers, administrators, and policy makers cannot determine which curriculum materials or teaching strategies contribute to mathematical proficiency. Finally, tests that fail to emphasize complex problem solving or sustained reasoning communicate an inaccurate picture of mathematics to students.

These findings also have implications for dispelling stereotypes. Overall, it is clear that in the United States and some other nations, girls have reached parity with boys in mathematics performance. It is crucial that this information be made widely known to counteract stereotypes about female math inferiority held by gatekeepers such as parents and teachers and by students themselves.

EXPLORING THE ISSUE

Do Men Outperform Women in Mathematics?

Challenge Questions

1. What causes cognitive sex differences?
2. Must cognitive ability differences between the sexes, and thus societal inequalities, continue?
3. Does creating a climate that allows everyone to maximize their own potential hold risk of increasing performance differences among individuals?
4. What policies should be in place to assist students in being as competent as possible in mathematics?

Is There Common Ground?

What does it mean if we find that cognitive sex differences are more heavily accounted for by biology or by environmental reason? If individuals are differently predisposed for cognitive skill, should we and can we do something about it? If so, what? For example, evidence suggests that testosterone is implicated in spatial abilities. Should we give females more testosterone to boost their spatial abilities? Does this sound preposterous considering that thousands of athletes (predominantly males) inject themselves with steroids daily to boost their muscle mass? Feminist scholars are fearful of biological causal evidence because it renders the environment irrelevant and implies that cognitive sex differences are unchangeable. Rather, they believe that sociocultural evidence provides more hope for social change. How much truth can be found in either claim? Psychosocially caused behavior has often been very difficult to reduce or eliminate (e.g., sex and racial bias). Furthermore, biological mechanisms (e.g., hormones and brain structure) change in response to environmental input. Recent evidence shows, for example, that just as brain structures and functions have been found to impact the way people select and respond to the environment, environmental input and experience alter brain structure and function throughout the life course. If so, then a radical move like injecting females with testosterone is not necessary. Simply engaging individuals in certain activities (even the performance of cognitive tasks) can boost testosterone levels naturally. Thus, many scholars have argued for an interactionist approach to studying cognition, examining the interaction of biology and environment. Rather than think of sociocultural and biological arguments as necessarily in opposition and mutually exclusive, we must consider how they interact to explain cognitive sex differences. For example, individuals differ in

273

their genetic potential or predisposition for good spatial skills. But genetically predisposed children might select environments that provide more spatial opportunity, augmenting brain structure and further fostering the development of spatial ability. The environment also intercedes in either developing or thwarting this potential. The biological makeup of individuals in the home may also influence the family environment (e.g., parents' and siblings' biological predisposition as impacted by past experiences and environmental inputs). Likewise, individuals might recognize and directly respond to the child's predisposition for spatial ability and provide spatial experiences. Macro-level cultural influences may also act on biological predisposition (e.g., cultural prohibition of certain experiences). Scholars also urge that we need to go beyond descriptive and explanatory research to a consideration of what the differences *mean* for individuals and society, especially given differential societal valuation of the cognitive differences. Indeed, cognitive sex differences research has revealed the powerful effects of identification and reinforcement of sex role—appropriate behaviors, expectations, motivational variables, and explicit and implicit messages in cognitive sex differences. If individuals have poor mathematical or spatial skill, what does it mean to be excluded from opportunities because of these cognitive deficits (whether actual or presumed based on stereotypes)? Having cognitive deficits impacts identity and self-esteem: how we feel about our abilities, our role in society, and our potential for success. It also creates dependencies. (Think about how much more expensive life is for individuals who are not mechanically inclined.) Spending so much time in a devaluing environment provides constant reminders of the jeopardy incurred by cognitive sex differences to future income, status, and happiness. The restrictions to societal and occupational opportunities based on cognitive functioning have repercussions for individuals and also for society at large. How is society influenced by the fact that the majority of engineers, mathematicians, chemists, mechanics, and airplane pilots are male? Of course, critics point out that the sex differences in occupational representation are grossly disproportionate to the magnitude of cognitive sex differences. Thus, even if there is biological evidence for cognitive sex differences, there seem to be other social factors at work in creating this gulf.

ISSUE 13

Is Gender Related to the Use of Computers?

YES: Tim Olds, Melissa Wake, George Patton, Kate Ridley, Elizabeth Waters, Joanne Williams, and Kylie Hesketh, from "How Do School-Day Activity Patterns Differ with Age and Gender Across Adolescence?" *Journal of Adolescent Health* (vol. 44, no. 1, 2009)

NO: Susan McKenney and Joke Voogt, from "Technology and Young Children: How 4–7 Year Olds Perceive Their Own Use of Computers," *Computers in Human Behavior* (vol. 26, no. 4, 2010)

Learning Outcomes

As you read the issue, focus on the following points:

- What is the relation between age and interest in, and use of, computers? Does the age of the youth studied affect the conclusions drawn by the researchers?
- How might factors such as immigration status as well as socio-economic status affect children's attitudes toward, and use of, computers?
- What is the relation between children's attitudes toward, and perceptions of, computers and their goals for the future?
- The studies reported here were conducted in the Netherlands and in Australia. Do you think the country affects the results and would the results be generalizable to the United States?

ISSUE SUMMARY

YES: Tim Olds and his colleagues examined how much time adolescents spent in different activities during the school day and found that boys had higher levels of screen time, which included television, video games, and computer use, which peaked in the peripubertal years.

NO: Susan McKenney and Joke Voogt studied children's use of technology both within and outside school settings and found no gender differences in young children's perceptions of their own use of computers or in ability level.

Computers, and other technologies, are ubiquitous. More and more computer applications games, for educational and recreational purposes, are being developed for children. It has been claimed that children ages 8–18 are exposed to eight-and-a-half hours of digital and video sensory stimulation a day. In fact, people in their 20s and younger are now called "digital natives." They have never known a world without computers, the Internet, and cell phones. Two questions seem to dominate discussions about computers and kids. Are they good for them? Are girls at a disadvantage? As one digs to find answers to these questions, opinions and evidence abound on both the yes and no side. In general, it appears to depend on the context. On the one hand, there is concern that too much time on computers will undermine children's development of social skills. There is an amusing commercial on TV for an automobile that shows a teenager, sitting alone at her computer, bemoaning the fact that she read (online) that adults become more antisocial as they get older. So she insisted that her parents join Facebook but noted what a pathetically low number of friends they have compared to the hundreds she has. All the while in the background is an image of her parents with other adults having lots of fun that involves the car being advertised. What cultural ideas does this commercial reflect about online social networks, having fun, and age? It suggests that it is the teen with the socialization problem. On the other hand, evidence says that computers are really good for children. One study of Head Start children found that 15–20 minutes a day working on a computer with educational software substantially improved their cognitive development and school readiness, as well as visual and gross motor skills. Adding to these findings was the observation that children who used the computer at home and school showed greater improvement than the children who used the computer only at school.

Gary Small and Gigi Vorgan recently said, "Even using a computer for Web searches for just an hour a day changes the way the brain processes information." This seems to be confirmed by studies that have shown that just an hour a day on the computer affects the way the brain functions. In their 2008 article entitled "Meet your iBrain" in *Scientific American Mind*, Small and Vorgan present several findings about the "brain on technology":

- Daily exposure to high technology, including computers and video games, creates changes in the brain.
- Playing video games and other technological experiences can sharpen some cognitive abilities by altering neural networks and synaptic connections.
- Playing video games and other technological experiences can increase reactions to visual stimuli and improve many forms of attention, particularly the ability to notice images in our peripheral vision.
- The brain's plasticity allows for technology-related alterations in neural processing.
- A constant barrage of e-contacts is both stimulating and draining.
- Increased focus on technology skills shifts brain functioning away from social skills, such as reading facial expressions during a conversation.

- Frequent digital connectivity can create strain and may increase fatigue, irritability, and distraction.
- Constant monitoring of social information can lead to "continuous partial attention," a form of mental distraction (i.e., keeping tabs on lots of things but focusing on none of them).

They also described a study by cognitive psychologist Pam Briggs of Northumbria University in England, who found that Web surfers spent two seconds or less on any particular site before moving on to the next one when looking for facts about health. She suggested that many of us develop neural circuitry that is suitable for rapid spurts of directed concentration, a sort of "digital ADD."

If the "digital natives" have arrived, what does this mean for male and female natives? Are the opportunities and advantages available equally for all? Many would say no, that there is still evidence of a serious gender gap in computer use. The American Association of University Women reports that girls make up only a small percentage of students who take high-level computer courses in high school. This report also noted that girls' use of computers is more likely to be limited to activities such as word processing rather than problem solving or actually writing programs, activities boys are more likely to do. They also made the observation that girls see themselves as less competent with computers than boys and see the high-tech domain as a masculine world. Of course, such attitudes and a lack of training reduce considerably the likelihood of pursuing technology careers. In fact, girls are five times less likely to consider taking technology courses in college or pursuing a technology-related career. The seriousness of this problem is compounded by the fact that the proportion of girls considering majoring in computer and information sciences has steadily decreased relative to the proportion of boys, from 20 percent in 2001 to 12 percent in 2006. Program developers and marketers may be contributing to this problem by developing educational software that has more male than female characters and then marketing products more vigorously to boys than to girls. The situation is complicated even more by some scholars who argue that the female and male brains are actually different and therefore the impact of technology will be different. Thus, if we want to close the gender gap, we need to transform schools in gender-specific ways. This is the recommendation of Michael Gurian and Kathy Stevens of the Gurian Institute, which trains education professionals in gender difference and brain-based learning, which they call the nature-based approach. In a 2004 article they wrote for the Association for Supervision and Curriculum Development's journal *Educational Leadership*, they claim that the brains of girls and boys are different, affecting the way they learn. They suggest that PET and MRI technologies show both structural and functional differences between girls and boys that affect the way they learn. What they do not establish is which came first, the brain differences that cause the learning style differences or gender-related experiences that helped shape the brain differences. Relevant to the current discussion on gender and computer, they describe the InterCept program in Colorado Springs. This is a female-specific program for girls at risk for school failure. They argue that by helping these girls appreciate the importance of being "tech-savvy," they can reduce school failure, juvenile delinquency, and teen pregnancy. The curriculum involves a computer-based program the girls use to explore future careers. The program allows them to see what kind of education is necessary, as well as provide income projections, for various occupations. The project did not include high-risk boys, so it is not known how they would respond to similar mentoring.

YES

Tim Olds et al.

How Do School-Day Activity Patterns Differ with Age and Gender Across Adolescence?

$\mathbf{A}$n understanding of how young people use their time is important to developers of social policy, parents, and healthcare providers. For social policy issues, such knowledge should inform the development of interventions designed to target health issues, modeling consumer behavior, forward planning for services such as transport and sporting facilities, and the design of school curricula. Parents may find it of interest to have a sense of how much time children of various ages typically devote to activities such as sport, play, sleep, videogames, and television viewing. Intervention research with anything more than short-term follow-up needs to take into account typical age-related differences to interpret any incremental impacts of intervention over and above these normal age-related differences.

Activities can only be understood in the context of broader patterns of time use, taking into account interactions with peers, adults, and the media, and normal age-related differences. Between early childhood and young adulthood, it is known that sleep time and physical activity decrease. There has been a great deal of recent concern regarding the association between poor sleep and the risk of overweight and a range of psychosocial disorders. Screen time (television, videogames, computers) appears to peak around puberty. These changes probably reflect mutually reinforcing biological (maturational) and social influences. A sudden decline in play and exploratory behavior around the time of sexual maturation in mammals coincides with reductions in the dopaminergic system's activity. The evolutionary rationale for this is easy to understand. Play brings benefits (in the development of one's own skills, strength, motor abilities, and knowledge of the environment), but also risks (e.g., accidental injury and exposure to predators). As animals get older and more experienced, there is a diminishing benefit, so it is possible that the risk:benefit ratio is tilted in favor of less play. The arrival of puberty, however, also coincides with major life transitions, as the child moves from primary to secondary school. As the young person's focus is redirected toward the extrafamilial world, for example, into part-time work, biological drivers are likely to be reinforced by social and cultural changes.

Although there is general agreement on age-related differences in broad use-of-time classes (e.g., sleep and physical activity), there are fewer data on more specific classes of activities, such as passive and active transport (e.g., cars vs. bicycles), chores, phone use, and specific sports. Children's use of time is highly variable, and shows consistent variation related to geography, day of the week, type of day (school day, weekend, holiday), season, and gender.

Purpose

This study aimed primarily to describe age- and gender-related patterns in the self-reported use of time on school days in a large sample of Australian children and adolescents aged between 10 and 18 years.

Methods

Dataset and Subjects

This study analyzed 6,024 use-of-time diaries recorded by children aged 10–18 from several state and regional surveys conducted in the states of South Australia (SA) and Victoria between 2001 and 2006. . . .

Instrument

Use-of-time data were collected using a computerized activity diary, the Multimedia Activity Recall for Children and Adolescents (MARCA). The software asks young people to recall everything they did on the previous day from wake-up to bedtime. It uses a segmented day format with self-determined anchor points (e.g., meals, school bells) and multimedia cues to aid recall. Young people choose from a list of about 250 activities grouped under seven main categories (inactivity, transport, sport and play, school, self-care, chores, and other). They can recall activities in time slices as fine as 5 minutes. Each activity is associated with an energy expenditure (EE) so that an overall estimate of daily energy expenditure can be determined by multiplying the duration of each activity by the associated energy cost. Energy costs were assigned using a compendium of energy costs that contains metabolic equivalent total (MET) scores calculated from studies conducted in youth, where available. The compendium comprises 40% MET scores from studies conducted in children and 60% adult MET scores from Ainsworth and colleagues' adult compendium. However, studies . . . have concluded that the ratio of activity EE and resting EE (i.e., a MET score) appears to be similar in adults and youth. The MARCA has a same-day test–retest reliability of $r = .84-.92$ for major outcome variables (moderate to vigorous physical activity [MVPA]; physical activity level [PAL], and screen time), and a convergent validity against accelerometry of $r = .57$ in a similar age range as the current sample.

The MARCA was administered in small groups in school computer laboratories during school time, overseen by a trained research assistant. Young people recalled between 1 and 7 days according to the needs of the survey; in studies requiring more days, there was an option for young people to take CDs home and e-mail subsequent completed profiles to researchers. Where more than 1 day was recalled, 1 day only was randomly chosen so that no child was overrepresented.

Sampling Frame

Because high-resolution use-of-time data on children require more time to collect, and surveys with very large sample sizes are very expensive, it was necessary to combine data from various surveys to get an adequate coverage of children from across the age range. Although these surveys used the same instrument, the MARCA, they drew from different geographical areas (South Australia and Victoria) and used different sampling frames. The South Australian data were collected across a series of independent surveys over a 5-year period between 2000 and 2005. In most surveys (encompassing 4,676 children), schools were randomly selected from a list of all schools in the state, and all children from a particular age group were invited to participate. In these surveys, the average response rate was 69% for schools, and 92% for children within the chosen age group within each school. In a small number of cases (427 children), data were collected from students at individual schools at the invitation of the schools themselves, or as part of pilot projects. In Victoria (921 children), MARCA profiles (a "profile" is a recall of 1 day by one child) were collected as part of the third wave of a longitudinal survey, the Health of Young Victorians Study.

Because the MARCA was usually administered during school time, there were fewer recalls of nonschool days (mainly weekends, and some holidays), especially by younger children. In addition, there were scarcely any recalls of Saturdays, because the MARCA is a previous day recall. Therefore, this paper will deal only with school day recalls. Furthermore, only 5% of all profiles recalled a Friday, as opposed to 19% to 27% for each of the other weekdays. However, there were no significant differences between age-related waking time, screen time, physical activity level (or overall daily energy expenditure), or moderate to vigorous physical activity between Fridays and the other weekdays in this dataset. Because of examinations and school holidays, few data were collected in January and December, although profiles were fairly evenly distributed across the remaining months. The dataset initially consisted of 16,250 profiles, of which 474 were excluded as yielding improbably high- or low-energy expenditures (PAL <1.1 or >3.0). This was reduced to a total of 6204 profiles when only recalls of school days, and just one profile for each child, were selected.

Data Analysis

The main response variables in this study were the following activity sets.

Activity Related

PAL (the average daily rate of energy expenditure in multiples of resting metabolic rate); minutes of MVPA (participation in any activity eliciting at least three METs); organized sport and play (formal or informal structured games and school physical education classes); free play (playground games, "mucking around," unstructured activity); and active transport (walking, cycling, skateboarding etc.).

Sedentarism Related

Minutes of waking time (i.e., 1,440 minutes per 24-hour day, minus minutes spent sleeping), small screen time (i.e., time spent watching television, playing videogames, using the computer for the internet, etc.), and passive transport (riding in cars, buses, trains, etc.). Time awake rather than sleep time was used because the MARCA profiles record activities from wake-up to bedtime. The predictor variables were age at last birthday (10–17+ in 1-year increments), and gender.

Profiles were therefore divided into 16 subsets (8 ages [10–17+ years] × 2 genders). Data analysis consisted of both descriptive and comparative components. Average (mean and median) values are reported by age–gender slices for the main response variables. . . .

The time distribution of activities across the day was described by calculating the percentage of children who were engaged in each of the specified activity sets at 15-minute intervals from midnight to midnight. A 15-minute interval was chosen to minimize the time required for this computing-intensive task, and because it gives sufficient resolution to capture time-related patterns.

Results

. . . *Components of screen time and MVPA.* Overall, TV constituted about 69% of total screen time for boys, and 75% for girls; videogames made up 17% for boys and 8% for girls; and computer use made up 13% for boys and 16% for girls. On average, 70% of nonvideogame computer time was accumulated during school hours. However, the relative contribution of these different components varied with age, with the contribution of television declining from 78 (95% confidence interval [CI]: 75%–82%) at age 10 to 71 (67%–76%) at age 17, and the contribution of nonvideogame computer time increasing from 7 (5%–9%) to 16 (11%–21%).

Organized sport/play made up close to 50% of all MVPA (51% for boys, 45% for girls), and free play about 20%. The rest consisted mainly of active transport and chores. The mix differed with age, with free play in particular decreasing rapidly with increasing age. At age 10, 50 (95% CI 46%–53%) of MVPA was organized sport/play and 26 (23%–29%) free play. By age 17, these figures were 37 (31%–43%) and 8 (5%–12%), respectively.

Time distribution of activities. The time distribution of activities across the day was largely governed by the school regimen. Physical activity spiked before school, at recess, lunch, and after school. . . . Overall patterns of MVPA were fairly similar, older adolescents were less active than younger adolescents, particularly at lunch and recess, and had less MVPA during in-school hours.

Older adolescents also accumulated less screen time. There was a very large spike in screen time before school in the younger adolescents, particularly boys, and somewhat higher levels during school hours and after dinner. Peak screen time was later for older adolescents than for younger children.

Comparisons Between Genders and Across Age Groups

. . . *Activity-related variables. Age-related patterns:* PAL, MVPA, organized sport/play, and free play all declined linearly with age. PAL declined at the rate of about 2.5% per year of age. MVPA declined at the rate of 13–17 min · day^{-1} per year of age. Average daily organized sport/play declined at the rate of about 9 min · day^{-1} per year of age in both boys and girls. Free play showed a similar trend, with declines of 6–7 min · day^{-1} per year of age in both boys and girls. Active transport showed a different pattern, peaking at around age 14, before falling in later adolescence.

Gender-related patterns: Boys reported higher levels of PAL, MVPA, and organized sport/play across the age span, but similar levels of free play. The rate of age-related decline in PAL was not different between boys and girls. At every age, boys had higher levels of both MVPA (by about 30–60 min · day^{-1}) and organized play/sport (by about 15–50 min · day^{-1}). In contrast, girls had higher levels of active transport than boys, but the differences were slight (about 5 min · day^{-1}).

Sedentarism-related variables. Age-related patterns: Sedentary behavior also declined with age, particularly in late adolescence. Time awake increased (and, hence, overall sleep time decreased) approximately linearly with age, at a rate of about 13 min · day^{-1} per year of age. Screen time, television time, and computer time tended to peak at around 12–14 years, declining fairly rapidly thereafter. Daily screen time peaked at age 12, declining thereafter at the rate of 14–18 min · day^{-1} per year of age. Television time decreased between the ages of 12 and 17. Videogame time decreased across the age span in boys, but there were no trends in girls. Passive transport increased throughout the age span, with a rapid rise around age 13.

The time devoted to most activities (screen time, sleep, physical activity) decreased in late adolescence. So what do older adolescents do with their time? Their time budget is mainly filled with nonscreen sedentary activities. Homework increases from 14 min · day^{-1} at age 10 to 33 min · day^{-1} at age 17. The time spent sitting or standing and talking, including talking on the phone, increased from 38 min · day^{-1} at age 10 to 80 min · day^{-1} at age 17.

Gender-related patterns: In most sedentarism-related variables, boys had higher values than girls. There were small gender differences in time awake, with girls sleeping on average 5 min · day^{-1} longer, whereas the rates of increase with age were similar. At every age, boys exceeded girls in screen time (by 35–75 min · day^{-1}) and videogame time (by 14–32 min · day^{-1}). Boys watched somewhat more television (by 5–47 min · day^{-1}), but there were no differences in computer time. The age-related differences in total screen time were similar for boys and girls. Girls had higher levels of passive transport than boys by 5–10 min · day^{-1}.

Discussion

The data presented here provide "baseline" patterns of age- and gender-related differences in young people's time use. They may assist when making comparisons among studies on children of different ages. They may also be useful, when interventions are tracked over time, in distinguishing intervention effects from "normal" underlying age-related differences. For example, a 2-year intervention to reduce screen time in 12-year-olds might be considered "successful" if it manages to halt the age-related increase in screen time across those years of adolescence.

One striking pattern to emerge from these data is how components of various activity categories vary with age. It would be unwise, for example, to consider MVPA as a unitary concept. As children get older, a much smaller proportion of MVPA is derived from free play. Similar considerations apply when construing screen time as a single item: as children get older, television plays a lesser role, and computer time a greater role. These shifts are important when planning and monitoring interventions.

The broad patterns of age- and gender-related differences found in this study have also been found in other recent Australian and international studies [that have] found that MVPA increased and screen time decreased with age, and that boys had higher levels of both MVPA and screen time than girls. . . .

Age-Related Differences

Physical activity, as indexed by PAL, MVPA, organized sport/play, and free play, decreased with age. This has been a consistent finding in the literature. Our data suggest that much of this decrease results from lower participation in MVPA during school hours. This may reflect increasing interest in the more social aspects of school life (while fewer than 10% of 17-year-old girls were active at lunch time, almost 80% of 10-year-old boys were). Participation also declined during class hours, perhaps as a result of the crowded school curriculum in the upper years and because of the reduction in compulsory physical education classes in the upper secondary years. In Australia, physical education is compulsory in primary and lower secondary school, but often not in upper secondary school. Sport is not compulsory in government schools after Year 10.

There was no clear evidence in these data that puberty represented a watershed in physical activity patterns. The pattern of decline was generally linear from age 10 to age 17. However, pubertal stage was not assessed in this study across the relevant years, so discontinuities may be obscured by puberty occurring at different times. There were clear patterns in both active transport and screen time roughly contemporaneous with puberty, with the amount of time devoted to these activities peaking around ages 12–14. Similar patterns have been found in studies of U.S. children's media use. It is unclear whether these patterns reflect biological (puberty) or social (transition to high school) changes. . . .

Active transport plateaued at age 14, when most young people have access to bicycles and may be given road autonomy by their parents, but before they have their own driver's licences or can rely on those of their older friends. Total transport (passive plus active) increased with age. This perhaps reflects (a) the greater average distance from home to secondary school versus primary school (and, hence, the greater likelihood that the child will not walk to school), and (b) the greater social and sporting commitments of the older child, to which they may be chauffeured by their parents. The rapid increase in passive transport above the age of 15 may reflect the number of young people who get their own driver's licences around age 16. Alternatively, they may have older friends with driver's licences, and hence, have reduced reliance on walking and cycling. However, driving age varied in the different jurisdictions in this sample. Most of the age-related increase in passive transport time seems to occur before and after school, suggesting either that trips to school are longer, or that older adolescents arrive at and leave school across a wider range of times, perhaps for early classes or extracurricular commitments.

As children get older, sleep, MVPA, and screen time decline. However, other kinds of sedentary behaviors fill the time void left by these declines. Nonscreen sedentary behaviors (less active school classes, talking with friends, "hanging out," reading) rise from about 2 hours per day at age 12 to over 9 hours per day at age 17. Consequently, the age-related decline in screen time is more than compensated by increases in other kinds of sedentarism. This has implications for monitoring interventions, as screen time has often been used as a surrogate for all sedentary behaviors. Older adolescents may be sedentary in different ways, sitting and talking, for example, rather than using the videogame console.

Gender Differences

Boys had both higher MVPA and higher screen time than girls, a finding that replicates those of other studies. However, there were no differences between boys and girls in the total time committed to activities eliciting 1.0–1.5 METs (data not shown). Girls, therefore, compensated for their lower screen times with other types of sedentary behaviors (e.g., phone use, talking to friends). This, again, suggests that screen time may not be an ideal surrogate for all sedentary behaviors.

Time use showed rather stereotypical gender differences, with girls spending less time in organized sport/play and MVPA and screen time, and showing lower overall PALs. Girls also spent more time shopping, doing chores, playing with pets, and talking on the phone or texting (data not shown). The higher levels of both active and passive transport in girls may reflect either the greater willingness of parents to drive daughters to social events, or girls having older boyfriends or girlfriends who have their driver's licence, and therefore have the opportunity to travel to more distant events.

Strengths and Limitations

This dataset represents the largest and most detailed analysis of use-of-time in this group of young Australians yet conducted. The instrument used to collect data, the MARCA, uses a diary format, and therefore obliges the user to account for each minute of the day. Furthermore, the high-resolution nature of the data makes it possible to cluster activities into different activity sets. Each activity is linked to an energy cost, so that activity sets can be defined in terms of energy requirements as well as by thematic clustering.

However, this sample is not nationally representative. There will be some degree of clustering by school, and a degree of self-selection because of schools and individuals opting in or out of the various surveys, and because of drop-out of heavier and older students in the longitudinal sample. Sampling across ages in this study was not geographically homogeneous, with most of the younger children being interviewed in South Australia, and most of the older children in Victoria. These are, however, neighboring states in southeastern Australia with a similar socioeconomic and ethnic mix, including similar per-centages of overseas-born residents (SA = 21.2%; Victoria = 24.6%; national = 23.1%). South Australia has a somewhat lower socioeconomic profile than Vic-toria (the mean census-based Socioeconomic Indexes for Areas value is 973 for SA, 1,011 for Victoria, and 1,000 [SD 100] nationally). The sample described here also resembles young people of this age across Australia in height, mass, and prevalence of overweight and obesity.

A further limitation is that the data are not sampled evenly across days of the week and months of the year. Apart from January and February, the percentage of days sampled varies from 7.6% in May to 13.5% in Septem-ber. Twenty-six percent of the data were collected in autumn, 32% in winter, and 31% in spring. It is likely that school-day behaviors are different in the summer. However, the months of December and January are largely holiday months in Australia, and the error introduced in relation to school day activity patterns in likely to be modest.

The data presented here are in the form of averages. Often it is the extreme values that are of greater interest in formulating public policy (e.g., targeting "extreme users" of screen technologies). Moreover, many of these extreme behaviors (long periods of screen time, catch-up sleeping, weekend sport) occur on nonschool days, which have not been covered in this study. Furthermore, it is likely that use of time during school holidays will be quite different from both school and weekend days. An analysis of the distribu-tional characteristics of children's use of time, stratified by day type, would complement this study.

Susan McKenney and Joke Voogt  **NO**

Technology and Young Children: How 4–7 Year Olds Perceive Their Own Use of Computers

Introduction

In the past century, the introduction of new media such as films, radio and television, has spawned debate and research concerning the (educational) benefits for children versus the fears related to (over)exposure. In this millennium, the opportunities and concerns regarding widely accessible Information and Communications Technologies (ICTs) are no different. Society's perceptions of technology and expectations for its use are important. Those notions impact the use of computers at home, as well as shape the course of implementation in educational settings. While many assert that computers do not have a place at the hands of young children, others contend that those who do not embrace new media may be in danger of losing touch with the popular culture of young children and their families.

While the debate in favor of and against young children's computer use rages on, there is little dispute that today, children are using computers even before they know how to read and write. However, research is lacking on how young children use computers and what the (intentional and unintentional) effects are. This is especially true in the Netherlands. Current literature is dominated by investigations conducted in the United States. Studies involving young children and computers have increased in recent years, with greater emphasis on exploring innovative applications for this age range and only a few examining usage patterns. Of those studies that look at how children are using computers, most rely on parent and caregiver reports; and very few involve asking children directly about how they perceive their own use of computers. In analyzing the 60 structured interviews and 1852 questionnaire responses from parents and caregivers in the England, [it was] found:

- *Frequency:* 53% of the children in the 0–6 age range use computers on a typical day, usually for less than 1 hour.
- *Type:* Children's favorite type of application was playing games, either on websites (especially those associated with BBC television programs) or on CD/DVD.

From *Computers in Human Behavior*, vol. 26, no. 4, 2010, pp. 656–664. Copyright © 2010 by Elsevier Science Ltd. Reprinted by permission via Rightslink.

- *Gender:* When listing website favorites, boys' and girls' preferences were the same for the first three rankings (CBeebies, CBBC, and Nickolodeon Junior, respectively), but differed in the fourth and fifth rankings. Boys preferred Bob the Builder and Thomas the Tank Engine, while girls liked Barbie and the Tweenies.
- *Parental attitude:* Parents were overwhelmingly positive about their children using computers, noting their acquisition of computing skills as well as software-specific knowledge and skills as beneficial. Concerns about the children using computers were not expressed.

Perhaps even more problematic is the prevalence of "few facts and many opinions" about the use of computers by young children. The need for increased research into young children's computer use has been expressed by researchers and practitioners. Though early, this call is garnering response, as exemplified by programs and projects undertaken on both sides of the Atlantic such as:

- Technology and Young Children Special Interest Forum within the [American] National Association for the Education of Young Children (NAEYC); and
- Children's Awareness of Technology (CHAT) and Developmentally Appropriate Technology in Early Childhood (DATEC), sponsored by the European Union. . . .

As early as the 1990s, young children's attitudes towards computers [have been studied]. Data were collected from 1990 to 1994 and examined the impact of computer use on children in grade 1–3 (6–9 year olds) from Japan, the USA and Mexico. The results showed that computer exposure in school had a positive impact on children's attitudes towards computers and that children's perceptions of computers were not related to their home country. Studies such as this have not been conducted in the Netherlands. Therefore, the research reported in this paper focuses on computer attitudes, computer use and computer skills of pre-K–grade 2 children (4–7 year olds), an age range slightly younger than the children who were involved in the study reported above. Better insight in computer use and attitudes of young children informs the debate of the desirability of young children's exposure to computers at home as well as in educational settings.

As with an educational resource, equitable use is worthy of consideration. . . . Gender differences in attitudes towards computers for children in grade 1–3 [were not found], girls' participation in technology-related activities has been a serious concern in the last decade. Perhaps even more disquieting is the 'digital divide,' now generally defined as "situations in which there is a marked gap in access to or use of ICT devices". The digital divide usually exists when a group's access to ICT differs along one or more dimensions of social, economic, cultural, or national identity. In this study, we explore whether indications can be found for a digital divide in this age range with respect to gender, socio-economic status and (ethnic) minority versus (ethnic) majority groups in the Dutch society. Studies with older children have shown that lower-income students have less access to computers in the home, and use computers at school more often for repetitive practice; whereas higher-income students have far greater access to computers in the home and use computers at school more often for more sophisticated, intellectually complex applications. . . . Very few of the already scarce studies looking at computer use in this age range, examine the access to ICT with regard to gender and ethnic minorities. What we do know . . . [from one] study:

- Considerable inequality of access to ICT in the home: In this study, 28 children were from English families, 17 from Bangladeshi families, and 3 from another ethnic origin (African and Kosovan). 26 of the 48 households contained a computer, but only 3 of these were in Bangladeshi homes.
- Young girls are as likely as young boys to be using a home computer.
- Middle-class parents tend to be more involved in their children's computer use than lower class parents.
- No evidence that home advantages in terms of technology access directly influenced computer use at school.

The finding that girls and boys are equally likely to be using a home computer is consistent with the findings of a previous study. However, the finding that home advantages do not influence computer use at school is especially interesting, as it is contradicted by the beliefs of early years educators who responded to an earlier . . . survey.

The study reported in this article took place in the Netherlands, and speaks to the need for better insight into how children are using computers, how they experience computers, and differences associated with gender and ethnicity. With the ultimate aim of understanding how Dutch 4–7 year olds perceive their own use of computers, the following four research questions were formulated:

1. Is access to computers outside school associated with gender, age, socio-economic status or ethnic group?
2. What activities do young children do on the computer, in and out of school?
3. To what extent are they able to conduct these activities independently or with help?
4. What attitudes do young children have?
5. Are differences in the use, skills or attitudes associated with gender, age, socio-economic status and ethnic group?

Methods

Participants

Children in pre-kindergarten (pre-K) through second grade (Dutch groups 1–4) from two schools participated. In total, 167 children (82 boys and 85 girls) were involved in the study. The age range varied between 4 and 8 years. The Dutch school system starts at the age of 4 when children start in pre-K, and is compulsory from kindergarten (K) starting at age 5. In the Netherlands, 98% of all 4-year olds attend pre-K. In this study we explored in and out of school use of computers. For this reason we prefer not to use age level, but to use grade level as an indicator of age. In the Dutch school system most four year olds attend pre-K, most 5 year old attend K, the 6 year olds are in grade 1 and the most 7 year olds are in grade 2. Learning to read and to write, as well as basic arithmetic starts in grade 1, but preparatory activities are carried out in pre-K and K.

Regardless of nationality, children were classified as native Dutch or Dutch immigrants. In accordance with national guidelines, native Dutch children were defined as those whose parents were both born in the Netherlands; children of one or more parents born in another country were categorized as Dutch immigrants. Both schools were located in the same city of 150,000. One school, hereafter referred to as "Southside," is located on the outskirts of town, in an area of lower socio-economic status and many second and third generation immigrant families from Morocco or Turkey with Arab-Berber or Turkish ethnic backgrounds, respectively. Teachers in this school openly share their ongoing concerns about pupil welfare and regularly conduct home visits. 81 children from this school participated in the study. 36 were classified as Dutch natives, and can be considered as belonging to the ethnic majority; while 45 were classified as immigrants and belonging to the ethnic minorities present in this part of town. In this study, we consider the immigrants of Southside to represent ethnic minorities and compare them with the Dutch natives from Southside as a representation of an ethnic majority group.

The other school, hereafter referred to as, "Central," is located in the city center, with primarily middle class children attending. Pupil welfare issues are less common in this school, and home visits by teachers are rarely made. This school is the only school in the region that offers instruction in English for long-term visiting children whose parents work in international companies or at the local university. Children attend the English language class a few hours each day, but spend the majority of their time in their home class with the Dutch children. In addition, the school prides itself on their Early English program, teaching English as a second language to Dutch-speaking children from pre-K onwards, which is exceptional in the Dutch education system. From this school, 86 children participated, with 58 classified as Dutch natives (ethnic majority) and 33 as immigrants. It should be noted, however, that this group of immigrants is much more mixed than those from Southside, and cannot be classified as an ethnic minority group.

. . . [W]e view the Southside pupulation to represent low socio-economic status and the Central population to represent middle socio-economic status.

Both schools had similar technology facilities: one or two computers in each classroom and computer clusters in one or more hallways. Southside has a technology coordinator who manages the infrastructure and also worked with the children on a weekly basis. This school prides itself on their approach to technology integration, which begins with the pre-K groups. In contrast, Central assigns the role of technology coordinator to a regular classroom teacher, whose main task is to manage the infrastructure including, when necessary coordination with the service provider. Both schools used the same third-party provider for technology services.

Data Collection

In a preliminary study conducted in 2003, experience was acquired in collecting data with children of this age level. The data for this study were collected through one-on-one interviews with the children. The interviews contained closed questions and were designed to take less than 15 min each. They addressed five areas: demographics, computer availability/access, computer activities use, attitudes and abilities. . . .

Demographics. The demographics section included name, class, school, grade, age, gender, land of birth (of self and parents) and language spoken at home.

Computer availability, access and activity types. . . . For school and at home, the computer activities section included the following categories of activities: practicing words/math; drawing; writing letters/stories; playing games; searching for information on Internet; reading/writing e-mail; and chatting (this last one was only asked for at home, as schools do not allow this practice). . . .

Attitudes. The attitude section was based on the computer importance and computer enjoyment subscales . . . designed for first through third graders. . . .

Skills to use the computer independently. . . . Children indicated how they used each computer activity: independently, with help, or neither (meaning, not at all). . . .

Except for the demographic information, black and white icons on colored cards were used to help the learners understand and stay focused on the interview questions. For example, children were shown the school icon card and then asked, "While at school, do you use the computer?" If they said yes, then a yellow set of cards was shown. . . . Children were then told what each one meant, then asked to turn face-down the ones that represent activities they did not do. For the remaining activities, children were asked if they did this often (daily or weekly) or sometimes (less than once a week). Children were first given practice questions on how often they watch television or go to the movies. . . .

The interviews were conducted with two trained interviewers. They used the icon cards when asking each question to a child and based on the child's answer completed the questionnaire. . . .

Results

Access to Computers Outside School

While both schools have computer facilities for use by the children, we were more interested in the availability of computers for children at home. The results . . . show that the penetration of computers at home is very high. It is notable that there is a relatively low presence of computers (computers with Internet access in particular) in the homes of Dutch native children in Southside. However, the overall picture is that most children do have access to a computer, often with Internet access, in their homes.

If you ask the children where, outside school, they mainly use the computer, most of them report that they use the computer at home. A few also use the computer mainly at a friend's house or at school (after school hours). Almost 10% of children in pre-K report not using the computer outside of school. Also, (relatively few) girls report more often than boys that they do not use the computer outside school.

In and Out of School Computer Use: Activities

. . . The findings show that only a few children report never playing a computer game, but that many at this age level never search the Internet or read or write e-mail.

. . . Boys and girls do not differ a lot in the kind of use of the computer. Both boys and girls report that in school and outside the school they use the computer most often for 'playing a game.' This is followed by 'practicing words/math' (in school use) and 'searching the Internet' (out of school use). 'Reading and writing e-mail' is the least often mentioned use of the computer in this age range both in school and outside school. Although the majority of the children (both boys and girls) never chat on the computer, 'chatting' is fairly often mentioned by about 40% of the children as an activity they do on the computer.

Medium–medium effect sizes in favor of boys were found for 'drawing' 'writing a letter/story', 'playing a game', indicating that boys use the computer in school for these activities more often than girls. With regard to out of school use, a medium$^+$ effect size was found in favor of boys for 'searching the internet' and a medium effect size for 'drawing' in favor of girls.

. . . With regard to in school use, children report that 'playing games' is most often used in the lower grades (4–5 year olds), but in the middle grades (6–7 year olds) 'playing games' and 'practicing words/math' is about equally reported. The other activities are mentioned considerably less. A large effect size between pre-K and grade 2, in favor of the latter, is found for 'practicing words/math', it indicates that in the middle grades compared to the lower grades the computer is more often used for school-based activities. Also 'writing a letter/story' is mentioned considerably more in grade 2 compared to pre-K, which makes sense, because pre-K students usually do not have formal writing skills. A medium$^+$ effect size of 'playing a game' in favor of pre-K indicates that games are more often used in the lower grades.

. . . [O]utside school, an increase in use is found for all distinguished computer activities for grade 2 children compared to children in pre-K. 'Playing games' clearly is the most frequent use of the computer across grade levels. Followed by 'searching the Internet (pre-K, grade 1 and grade 2) and 'drawing' (K).

. . . The overall picture is the same: both groups use the computer most often for playing games, both in school and outside school. Concerning the use of computers in school, differences between the two groups with medium to large effect sizes for writing letter/story and playing a game, suggesting that Dutch natives at Southside use the computer in school for these activities more often than their immigrant peers. For the other activities, no differences were found between the two groups. However, out of school computer use provides a very different picture. Immigrant children seem to use the computer more often for quite a number of activities. . . . The only activity for which Dutch native children report more frequent use than their immigrant peers, is 'writing a letter/story'.

. . . The picture that emerges throughout is the use of the computer for playing games, which seems the most favorite use for children from both schools. With regard to in school use, children attending Southside use the computer more, compared to Central children, for 'drawing', while children at Central use the computer more for searching the Internet, and reading/writing e-mail. It should be noted however that e-mail use does not happen very often in both schools. The picture for computer use outside school is different. Southside children use the computer more for chatting; drawing, writing letter/story and reading/writing email compared to their peers from Central, while Central children use the computer, more for playing games.

Skills to Operate the Computer Independently

. . . The results . . . show that the majority of both boys and girls in this age range are able to play a computer game, start a computer game, make a drawing and search on the Internet alone or with some help. Differences in skills between boys and girls, with small[+] effect sizes, were found for starting a computer game (in favor of boys), writing a letter/story (in favor of girls) and searching for information (in favor of boys).

With respect to grade level, the results show that the majority of the youngest children in pre-K are already able to start and play a game (with help or alone). However, it is striking that already at this age level (most pre-K children are 4 years old) so many children report being able—often with help—to handle the computer. It far less surprising that this has changed by grade 2 (most children are then 7 years old). In grade 2, the majority is able to use the computer (with help or alone) for all the different skills that were distinguished. . . .

. . . The results show that the majority of children in both ethnic groups (Dutch natives and immigrants) are able to start and play a computer game and to make a drawing. The majority of the immigrants at Southside are also able to search for information on the Internet. . . .

With regard to socio-economic status, we did find differences . . . in favor of Southside with regard to making a drawing, reading/writing e-mail and chatting. But, Central children report being more able to write a letter/story compared to their Southside peers.

Attitudes

Overall, children express positive attitudes towards computers. Significant differences in attitudes towards computers were found for gender (in favor of boys), grade level (in favor of the older children in grade 2) and socio-economic status (in favor of the children from a lower socio-economic neighborhood, Southside).

Discussion and Conclusions

Examining how young children perceive their use of computers provides information for educators and parents, many of whom are struggling to find practical, developmentally appropriate applications of technology in classrooms and at home. This study set out to explore young children's access to computers, their perceptions of what they do on the computer (in school and outside school), their abilities to operate the computer for specific activities, and their attitudes towards computers. . . .

The findings of this study showed that most young children had access to computers, regardless of gender, socio-economic background or ethic group. . . . The findings of this study suggest that the digital divide with regard to computer access is not so much an issue anymore in the Netherlands, but more large scale studies are needed to confirm this conclusion.

Regardless of gender, age, socio-economic status and ethic group, playing games is the computer activity young children most frequently do, both at home and at school. As playing games is the most common way for children of all ages to spend their free time, it is not surprising that children report playing games as the most frequent computer activity at home both in this study and in research with older children. Next to playing games, searching the Internet is the second most-frequently reported activity for out of school computer use. The other activities are carried out less often.

It is notable that children report that they also use the computer most for playing games while at school. Children in pre-K (4 year olds) play games in school more often than their peers from grade 2 (7 year olds). These results may imply that the computer in school is used as a bonus for children who are finished with their school tasks and are allowed to play a game on the computer. However, it is also possible that especially the younger children experience their activity as a game, even though their teachers might differently describe the same software, due to its affordances with regard to, for example, learning or practice in the area of (preparatory) literacy or numeracy. Further research is necessary to better understand this finding. Next to playing games, practicing words/math is the second reported use of the computer in school. This computer activity increases with grade level. Except for drawing on the computer, the other activities are carried out less often across grade levels. For in school computer use, not many differences were found between boys and girls, nor between Dutch natives and immigrants. However, at Southside the computer is used considerably more for drawing and at Central for searching the Internet. It is not clear whether this is due to the socio-economic background of the school population or if this has more to do with other factors, such as the educational view of the school team.

It is no surprise that outside school, older children (grade 2) use the computer more often and also are more able to operate the computer for a variety of activities than younger ones (pre-K). Literature has long suggested that pupil attitudes toward computers are favorable; this is consistent with the findings from this study. In addition, this study found that older children have a more positive attitude towards computers than younger children have.

Concern about girls' lack of interest in technology has been growing in the last decade. No big differences between boys and girls out of school computer use were found. Also no gender differences were found in the ability level of using various computer activities. These findings concur with those from a recent study in which young girls and young boys were equally likely to be using a home computer as well as another in which young girls now report using home computers as often, and with as much confidence as boys. While the findings of this study revealed that boys have a comparably more positive attitude towards computers than girls have, both groups remain generally positive. . . . Children's perceptions of computers are also influenced by the software they use. [A] gender-bias content analysis of educational software for preschoolers found significantly more male characters than female characters in preschool educational software, which . . . makes it difficult for teachers to address gender diversity and suggests that girls are not as valued as boys are. Subsequent research on gender differences in computing would benefit from a deeper look at the software being used.

Literature suggests that ethnic minority children may be disadvantaged by a lack of home experience with computers. The findings of this study suggest that immigrant children have more exposure to computers out of school than Dutch children from a low socio-economic background. In addition, immigrant children seem to be better able to operate the computer for a number of different activities, searching information on the Internet in particular. An explanation put forth by Southside teachers is that, often, computer use in immigrant families is focused on communication with family members still living in the country of origin. However, more research is necessary to fully understand this finding. No differences between immigrant children and Dutch children were found in attitude towards computers. The findings of this study also suggest that children from a lower socio-economic background use the computer slightly more often outside school compared to middle class children, and have a more positive attitude towards computers. . . . Further research is necessary to understand how crucial it is that schools take it upon themselves to ensure equal opportunity for less-advantaged children to access the benefits of the more intellectually powerful uses of computer technology. . . .

It is known that the benefits of using technology with young children vary with the kind of experiences offered and how frequently the children have access to computers. . . . As our picture of how children are spending their computer time sharpens, further research should be conducted into the quality and appropriateness of those experiences. . . . Understanding children's practices and attitudes can inform educators and parents in the search for developmentally appropriate uses of technology, as well as a healthy balance between computer use and other means for children to learn and explore the world around them.

EXPLORING THE ISSUE

Is Gender Related to the Use of Computers?

Challenge Questions

1. What might be the gender implications of looking broadly at the use of a variety of technologies, such as television, video games, smart phones, and computers? In what ways are these technologies and their purposes similar and different?
2. Might there be relevant questions about gender and technology use when the various applications of the technologies are used, such as for communication (i.e., social network sites), knowledge exchange (i.e., blogging), learning (i.e., online courses), or gaming?
3. If there are meaningful gender differences in the use of computers and various technology-related skills, what are the intervention implications? Should schools have gender-specific programs?
4. Do developers and marketers of various technologies and their applications have a responsibility to address any gender-relevant consequences of their products and activities?

Is There Common Ground?

Tips for Monitoring Computer Use by Young Children

The National Association for the Education of Young Children (NAEYC) is an organization that sets standards of excellence for programs designed for children from birth through age 8. The organization bases these standards on current research in child development and on the professional opinions of early childhood educators.

NAEYC has issued the following specific recommendations regarding computer use by young children. In addition to helping your child have the best educational experience when working on a computer, these strategies may also decrease your young child's risk of fatigue-related eye strain, computer vision syndrome, and computer ergonomics problems:

- Computers should supplement, not replace, educational activities such as art, books, music, outdoor exploration, dramatic play, and socializing with other children.
- Parents should guide children's use of computers. Be on hand to help your child, answer questions, and interact with him as he works on the computer.

- Take the time to observe your child at the computer and participate in computer activities with him. Observing children working at a computer can reveal a lot about the way they think and solve problems.
- Encourage your child to work with a sibling or friend at the computer whenever possible. Using computers with others encourages important social skills, such as turn-taking and cooperation, and helps build your child's ability to speak and listen.
- Learn more about software for young children and carefully preview the software your child uses. While many high-quality products are available, some software is not appropriate for young children because it is difficult to use, highlights violent themes, or does not foster language or learning.

Additional Resources

Gary Heiting, *Kids, Computers and Computer Vision*, All About Vision. http://www.allaboutvision.com/parents/children-computer-vision-syndrome.htm

Girls and Computers. http://schoolcomputing.wikia.com/wiki/Girls_and_Computers

Girls and Computers, New York Times Opinion page. http://www.nytimes.com/1998/10/19/opinion/girls-and-computers.html

Michael Gurian and Kathy Stevens, With Boys and Girls in Mind," *Educational Leadership.* Retrieved November 2004, from http://www.ascd.org/publications/educational-leadership/nov04/vol62/num03/With-Boys-and-Girls-in-Mind.aspx

ISSUE 14

Is Cyberbullying Related to Gender?

YES: **Robin M. Kowalski, Susan P. Limber, and Patricia W. Agatston,** from *Cyberbullying: Bullying in the Digital Age* (Blackwell Publishing, 2008)

NO: **Kirk R. Williams and Nancy G. Guerra,** from "Prevalence and Predictors of Internet Bullying," *Journal of Adolescent Health* (2007)

Learning Outcomes

As you think about these issues, focus on the following points:

- What are the differences and similarities between bullying and cyberbullying?
- What are the reasons why gendered patterns of bullying and cyberbullying might be different?
- Is cyberbullying a "real" aggression? In what ways?
- How might questions about gender and cyberbullying be related to issues of gender and computer use more generally?
- When examining cyberbullying, how does the sex of the victim and perpetrator affect what is observed? And are there age differences?

ISSUE SUMMARY

YES: Social psychologist Robin Kowalski, Susan Limber, a bullying prevention expert, and Patricia Agatston, a school counselor, provide an extensive review of what is known about gender and cyberbullying and conclude that there are sex differences in cyberbullying.

NO: Criminal justice expert Kirk Williams and psychologist Nancy Guerra found that boys were more likely to bully than girls, but there were no sex differences in cyberbullying.

T here has been an explosion in the number of, and uses for, electronic technologies. As a result, virtually all aspects of our day-to-day lives are changing.

We can shop online, take virtual tours of museums, take courses, play games, and listen to music, without ever needing to leave our homes. We can be connected to the Internet 24 × 7 if we wish. Some scientists are documenting that even the wiring of the brain will actually change as young people spend more time in cyberspace. Cyberspace may also be changing our notions about ourselves as males and females. There is evidence that in massive multiplayer online role-playing games, many people engage in gender swapping. Although most online gamers are male (80 percent), females are increasingly becoming involved. Also, in many online games, the player can choose the attributes of the characters they become, including the sex of the character. One study suggested that 60 percent of gamers have played a differently gendered character; another study suggested that about half the male and two-thirds of the female gamers had gender swapped. Reasons for gender swapping included the ability to experiment with aspects of one's self in a way that would be difficult in real life and that it's just fun and different; and using stereotypic attributes of one gender or the other allows one to be treated differently, that is, a female character may be treated better and get free things—one gamer put it this way: "Nerd + Boob = Loot." One female gamer said she was tired of "creepy guys hitting on [her] female characters." Gender swappers can explore various styles of play and social interactions. Not surprisingly, if male and female gamers gender swap as a way of exploring, or exploiting, various dimensions of gender, it is not surprising that beyond the gaming environment, notions of relationships and human sexuality also are changing via the introduction of online dating, online forums, and chat rooms. Studies are beginning to examine how and why adolescents interact socially online. Cyberspace has become a common location for social interaction. Studies of social interactions online suggest that women and men may be more equal in the amount of disclosure of personal information online than in face-to-face interactions, and one study found that males are more willing than females to respond online to others' sexual disclosures, especially under conditions of anonymity. What does all this mean for gendered patterns of behavior? Will online social interactions level the "playing field" for girls and boys, women and men?

Of particular concern to parents and law enforcement is the rise in "sexting" (sex + texting: the sending of nude photos in cyberspace). Many questions arise. Is sexting a crime? Should people who send nude photos be required to register as sex offenders? What if these people are children or adolescents? The Juvenile Law Center in Philadelphia estimates that about 20 percent of adolescents have posted nude or semi-nude pictures on their computers or cell phones. It is also of concern that one can go online to learn how to sext and find recommendations of what will "work"—for example, how to attract a male's attention. According to the American Civil Liberties Union, an underage person who sends sexually explicit pictures should not be criminally charged; they feel the act should be treated as a foolish childish action. MediChat.com notes that "Sexting can be viewed as a way to express your true feelings without being face-to-face; thus there are no physically harmful consequences involved such as S.T.D.'s or unwanted pregnancies. Although sexting doesn't necessarily have physically damaging consequences, we can't say the same about the possible emotional effects; especially when it comes to teenagers." This Web site points out that the girls may be motivated to sext because they want to get the attention of a guy they like, but are afraid to say anything face to face, and also want to show off their "assets." Although males too may sext to say things they cannot in person, they are inclined to share any sext messages with others as a way of showing off their own masculinity; they may believe that being the recipient of a sext message is a marker of their status. Thus, it is often the case that sext exchanges among young people are not harmless. There is the risk of sexual exploitation that can have serious consequences for all involved. One risk is having the photo shared widely on the Internet. There is no guarantee of privacy. There can be long-lasting consequences for the individuals involved, as well as their friends and families, and may include shame and lowered self-esteem.

What are the implications of these changes in gendered behavior for the expression of aggression? Would females be more comfortable online than in the real world breaking away from cultural constraints on females' expressing aggression? Would males feel less pressure online to show they are "real men" and not behave aggressively when provoked? These are the types of questions researchers are beginning to explore as they enter cyberspace as a laboratory to explore issues of gender and aggression. In the YES and NO selections, we want to explore cyberbullying in particular, a topic that is just beginning to receive attention in the research literature. Two basic questions address whether there are gender differences in cyberbullying and why or why not. According to the Cyberbullying Research Center, cyberbullying can be defined as "Willful and repeated harm inflicted through the use of computers, cell phones, and other electronic devices." It is also known as "cyber bullying," "electronic bullying," "e-bullying," "SMS bullying," "mobile bullying," "online bullying," "digital bullying," or "Internet bullying." Some theorists suggest that cyberbullying is more akin to verbal aggression than physical aggression, and given that there are fewer sex differences in verbal than physical aggression, perhaps we might expect equivalent levels of cyberbullying in girls and boys. On the other hand, cyberbullying may be more akin to indirect and relational aggression than direct aggression, in which case we might expect more girls than boys to engage in cyberbullying. The YES and NO selections you will be reading provide some insight into these questions. Both rely on the surveys of students regarding their experiences with cyberbullying. In the excerpts from the book on cyberbullying by Robin Kowalski and her colleagues, they review the work of several researchers, as well as discussing their own work. The Williams and Guerra study also assessed for experiences with verbal and physical bullying. Thus, both selections provide a comparison of the prevalence of cyberbullying to traditional bullying. What do you think they found? Is cyberbullying or traditional bullying more common? Is the same pattern true for girls and boys?

YES ⤶   Robin M. Kowalski, Susan P. Limber, and Patricia W. Agatston

Cyber Bullying: Bullying in the Digital Age

Gender Similarities and Differences in Traditional Forms of Bullying

Although both boys and girls are frequently involved in bullying, there has been debate among researchers about which gender is more likely to engage in and experience bullying. Studies that have used anonymous, self-report measures typically have found that boys are more likely than girls to bully, but findings are less consistent when looking at gender differences in experiences of being bullied. Some studies have found that boys report higher rates of bully victimization than girls, whereas others have found no gender differences or only slight differences between boys and girls.

Probably more important than comparisons in rates of bullying between boys and girls are comparisons between the *types of bullying* in which boys and girls engage. Boys are more likely to be physically bullied by their peers, whereas girls are more likely to be bullied through rumor-spreading or through sexual comments or gestures. It also is important to note that, although boys are typically bullied by other boys (and rarely girls), girls are bullied by both boys and girls. Boys who are bullied by boys are more likely to indicate that they were physically and verbally bullied. Girls are bullied by girls more often through social exclusion (e.g., leaving another girl out of a group's social activities, and doing so in a hurtful way and on purpose). . . .

Characteristics of Children Who Cyber Bully

[C]ommon characteristics of children who bully . . . include:

- They have dominant personalities and like to assert themselves using force.
- They have a temper, are impulsive and are easily frustrated.
- They have more positive attitudes toward violence than other children.
- They have difficulty following rules.
- They appear to be tough and show little empathy or compassion for those who are bullied.
- They often relate to adults in aggressive ways.

- They are good at talking themselves out of difficult situations.
- They engage in both proactive aggression (i.e., deliberate aggression to achieve a goal) and reactive aggression (i.e., defensive reactions to being provoked).

Although it is reasonable to assume that children who cyber bully share some (or even many) of these characteristics, it is also likely that there are some important differences that will need to be explored through future research.

. . . [G]ender differences in traditional forms of bullying [suggest] that boys are more likely than girls to engage in bullying at school. When looking at similarities and differences in the types of bullying that boys and girls experience, research suggests that boys are more likely to be physically bullied by their peers, whereas girls are more likely to be bullied through some indirect forms of bullying, such as rumor-spreading, as well as through sexual comments or gestures. Interestingly, girls are more likely to report being both victims and perpetrators of cyber bullying. However, among those individuals who engage in cyber bullying, boys do so with greater frequency than girls. . . .

Because of the suggestion that socially anxious individuals might be more likely to (a) use technology as a means of communicating with others and (b) engage in cyber bullying as revenge for bullying at school, we examined the relationship between a person's dispositional tendency to experience social anxiety and their experiences with cyber bullying. [O]ur data showed that, among perpetrators, the highest levels of social anxiety were reported by 8th graders who cyber bullied others at least twice a month. The more frequent the cyber bullying, the higher the level of social anxiety, supporting our hypothesis that cyber bullying and social anxiety are linked. Importantly, however, in a comparison between individuals who cyber bully and those who are cyber bullied, social anxiety scores are higher among victims than perpetrators.

Although there are a number of other personality traits that might be shared by many children who cyber bully, there probably is no single profile of such a child. Some engage in electronic violence somewhat inadvertently without realizing that what they are doing is actually cyber bullying, particularly when they are simply responding in kind to negative comments that have been sent to them in e-mails or instant messages. Other individuals, however, cyber bully with the express purpose of hurting and humiliating their victims. Still other children and youth cyber bully because they are bored and simply think that sending threatening or demeaning messages to another person would be fun. Their focus is on alleviating their own boredom, rather than thinking about the effects that their behavior could have on their victims.

What Motivates Children to Cyber Bully?

Asking the question of "who cyber bullies?" also raises the question of "what motivates someone to engage in such a behavior?" Just as there is a variety of possible motives for engaging in traditional forms of bullying, there also is a long list of reasons why adolescents might engage in cyber bullying. Some may cyber bully as a way of asserting power or channeling their aggressive energy. Others may gain satisfaction, prestige, or other rewards from cyber bullying. Still others may bully as a way to act out aggressive fantasies online. Parry Aftab recounted a meeting with a young boy who was what some might call the "perfect child" in real life—well behaved, polite, and a good student. However, online this boy became someone completely different—violent and aggressive. When asked why, his response was, "Because I can." Nevertheless, in our focus group interviews with middle and high school students, a discrete number of motivations continued to emerge. These motives included: boredom, power, meanness, as retaliation for being bullied, for attention, looking cool and tough, and jealousy. Other key reasons included that cyber bullying was safer than traditional bullying because it was anonymous and they were less likely to get caught and it was easier because it didn't involve face-to-face confrontations. Another motive is the pleasure of inflicting pain. . . .

Gender Issues and Cyber Bullying

Over the past two to three decades, research on aggression has shown that males engage in more direct forms of aggression, such as hitting one another, and females engage in more indirect forms of aggression, such as gossiping or spreading rumors about one another. Interestingly, the definition advanced . . . for indirect aggression sounds remarkably similar to that proposed . . . for cyber bullying by proxy. [I]ndirect aggression [is a] "a kind of social manipulation; the aggressor manipulates others to attack the victim, or, by other means, makes use of the social structure in order to harm the target person, without being personally involved in attack."

A qualitative analysis of why girls are more likely than boys to engage in indirect aggression revealed some interesting insights. [Based on] focus groups with 54 teenage girls in Australia researchers concluded that girls engage in indirect aggression to eliminate boredom and because of friendship processes, including attention seeking, assuring that they are a member of the in-group as opposed to the out-group, belonging to the right group, self-protection, jealousy, and revenge.

In keeping with this, it is not all that surprising, then, that cyber bullying overall seems to occur more frequently among girls than among boys. Among the middle school students who completed our survey about cyber bullying, 25% of the girls and 11% of the boys said that they had experienced cyber bullying *at least once* in the previous two months; 5% of girls and 2% of boys indicated that they had experienced cyber bullying "2 or 3 times a month" and 3% of girls and 2% of boys said they had been cyber bullied about "once a week" in the previous two months. However, at the highest frequency level—those electronically bullied "several times a week"—boys (1.4%) slightly outnumbered girls (1.2%).

Thirteen percent of the girls and 9% of the boys said that they had perpetrated cyber bullying *at least once* within the previous two months. An equal percentage of girls and boys (1%) said they had electronically bullied others "2–3 times a month." Fewer girls (.7%) than boys (1.2%) said they had engaged in electronic bullying "once a week" in the previous two months. Twice as many boys (.8%) as girls (.4%) reported that they had electronically bullied others "several times a week."

For comparison purposes, we assessed the frequency of traditional bullying among girls and boys in our study. We found that 40% of the girls and 38% of the boys reported having been bullied at school *at least once* during the previous two months. A breakdown of prevalence rates at higher frequency levels showed that an equal percentage of girls and boys (6%) reported having been bullied "2 or 3 times a month"; 3% of girls and 4% of boys said they had been bullied "about once a week"; 3% of girls and 5% of boys indicated that the bullying occurred "several times a week."

Among perpetrators, 27% percent of the girls and 35% of the boys indicated that they had bullied someone else *at least once* within the previous two months. Observations at the higher frequency levels showed differences between girls and boys; however, these differences were not statistically significant. Three percent of girls and 5% of boys had bullied other students "2 or 3 times a month;" 1% of girls and 1% of boys had bullied others "about once a week;" twice as many boys (2%) as girls (1%) had bullied others "several times a week."

Although some studies have found no significant differences in cyber bullying between males and females, others have obtained results that parallel those in our own research. [One researcher] found that girls were significantly more likely than boys to be cyber bullied. In terms of specific methods, they found that incidence rates for girls surpassed those for boys for all methods except for Web pages and picture editing.

Data from the Fight Crime surveys with preteens and teens (www.fightcrime .org) show mixed findings regarding gender differences. In the preteen survey, no significant differences in the frequency of experiencing cyber bullying were observed between boys and girls. Fifteen percent of the boys and 19% of the girls reported having been cyber bullied within the previous year. Among teens, however, a significant difference was obtained. Almost twice as many females (44%) as males (28%) reported having been cyber bullied within the previous year.

Participants in our focus groups acknowledged the link between gender and cyber bullying. When asked what can be done to prevent cyber bullying, respondents in one of our focus groups said the following: "It depends on if it's a guy or a girl or how mean they are. Some people are just going to do it anyway. Girls are harder to stand up to. Cause like guys can be like 'stop bothering me.' I'm not afraid that a guy is going to hit me, but girls are like catty. They get back at you in a more subtle way."

In keeping with this, a male focus group respondent, when asked what he would do if he were cyber bullied at home by a student, said he would "print out the pages and say—'what's up, man?'" Another male student responded similarly: "Just go up to them and be like 'how come you didn't say it to my face?'" None of the female focus group respondents indicated a similar response.

As some of these data show, in examining gender differences in cyber bullying, it is important to bear in mind the method by which the cyber bullying is executed. Even though females may outnumber males in terms of the overall frequency with which cyber bullying occurs, . . . variations also occur with the method used.

Arizona, California, Illinois, Maine, Minnesota, New Hampshire, New York, Virginia address bullying but fail to define the term, and . . . Maryland and Nevada address "harassment or intimidation" but not specifically bullying. Georgia's bullying law focuses only on conduct of a physical nature ("[a]ny willful attempt or threat to inflict injury on another person, when accompanied by an apparent present ability to do so"), and, therefore, likely does not include cases of cyber bullying (unless perhaps the perpetrator was in the victim's presence when the victim received the message). . . .

Under What Circumstances May School Personnel Be Held Liable for Failing to Address Cyber Bullying?

School personnel have a duty to protect students in their care and to ensure that there is no substantial interference with their rights to receive an education. School districts may be held liable for failing to stop bullying (and, specifically, cyber bullying) if personnel are found to have acted negligently or if they violate provisions of relevant federal or state statutes.

Statutory Liability
Although there currently is no federal law against bullying per se, victims and their parents may, depending on the circumstances, sue for damages under a number of federal laws that prohibit harassment against protected classes of individuals. The federal laws that are most often implicated in such cases relate to sexual- or gender-based harassment, racial harassment, and disability harassment.

Claims of sexual harassment or gender discrimination usually rely on Title IX of the Education Amendments Act of 1972. [Under what circumstances may school personnel be held liable for failing to address cyber bullying?]. . .

[O]ur review of the research indicates that cyber bullying is a form of bullying behavior that is on the rise and peaks during middle school. It is important to recognize that, as with traditional bullying, young people are more likely to engage in cyber bullying if they believe that adults and bystanders are unlikely to intervene. This same research indicates that students perceive adults as least likely to intervene in bullying that occurs over the Internet, which may help explain the increases we are observing in cyber bullying behavior.

The research also suggests that females are more likely than males to both engage in cyber bullying others and to be a target of cyber bullying behavior at certain grade levels, unlike some specific forms of traditional bullying behavior (e.g., physical bullying) and overall rates of traditional bullying. This is consistent with research showing that females are more likely than males to engage in indirect forms of aggression. However, fewer girls than boys reported engaging in the highest frequencies of cyber bullying (i.e., several times a week).

Though in its infancy, research on cyber bullying has spanned several countries. [Al]though the prevalence rates and methods of cyber bullying vary slightly from one country to another, most, if not all, developed countries are being forced to deal with this phenomenon. As attention to cyber bullying continues to increase, it will be important that researchers and policy-makers adopt an interdisciplinary and multicultural approach to the topic.

While we are learning more about cyber bullying, there is still much that is unknown about this new form of bullying. The research on traditional bullying provide[s] a context for examining how cyber bullying is similar to and different from traditional bullying. The definition of traditional bullying that is widespread involves behavior that is repeated, intentionally aggressive and based on an imbalance of power. Cyber bullying often meets the definition of intentionally aggressive behavior. Although cyber bullying shares these characteristics, questions may be raised about the repetitiveness of actions online. Might repeated viewings of a one-time posting of an aggressive message constitute cyber bullying? This issue needs further clarification and research. Similarly, the nature of an online power imbalance also warrants further attention.

**Kirk R. Williams and
Nancy G. Guerra**

 **NO**

Prevalence and Predictors
of Internet Bullying

Bullying is a form of aggression involving intentional and harmful behavior marked by repeated engagement and an asymmetric physical or psychological power relationship. The specific type of harmful behavior can vary considerably; previous studies of children's bullying have considered a range of diverse behaviors, including name calling, saying mean things, destruction or taking of property, demanding money, social exclusion, hitting, and kicking. What brands these behaviors as bullying rather than aggression is that they occur repeatedly, typically involving a weaker victim within the context of an ongoing social interaction. As such, research examining the prevalence, predictors, and prevention of bullying largely has examined this behavior as it unfolds within a specific social context. For children, schools have been the primary context for studying bullying behavior.

Over the last decade, interest in understanding and preventing bullying among school children in the U.S. and internationally has surged. Such interest coincides with a growing awareness of the detrimental consequences of being bullied on children's well-being as well as the recognition that bullying is a significant problem in schools. Still, prevalence rates vary as a function of how bullying is measured, what type of bullying (e.g., physical vs. verbal) is assessed, the age of respondents, and the country where the study takes place. Reported perpetration and victimization rates typically range from 10% of students reporting physical bullying or victimization to more than 50% reporting indirect bullying or victimization involving teasing, name calling, spreading rumors, or verbal aggression.

Because bullying has been framed as a schoolyard issue, the focus of research has largely been on bullying in schools—whether in the classroom, locker room, hallway, or bathroom—based on the assumption that personal contact is a prerequisite to bullying. Yet, in recent years, technology has transformed the landscape of children's social lives. With an estimated 45 million children between the ages of 10 and 17 in the U.S. alone using the Internet every day, social interactions have increasingly moved from personal contact in the school room to virtual contact in the chat room, and Internet bullying has emerged as a new and growing form of social cruelty. Such bullying

From *Journal of Adolescent Health*, vol. 41, no. 6, pp. S14–S21. Copyright © 2007 by Elsevier Health Sciences. Reprinted by permission.

is clearly not physical in nature and has more in common with verbal bullying. Intimidation is quickly being augmented by humiliation, destructive messages, gossip, slander, and other virtual taunts communicated through e-mail, instant messaging, chat rooms, and blogs. The Internet has become a new arena for social interactions, allowing children and youth to say and do things with a certain degree of anonymity and limited oversight by adult monitors. Internet bullying, as defined here, refers to the willful use of the Internet as a technological medium through which harm or discomfort is intentionally and repeatedly inflicted through indirect aggression that targets a specific person or group of persons.

The purpose of the present study is to contrast the prevalence of Internet bullying with physical and verbal bullying among 5th, 8th, and 11th grade boys and girls and to examine whether key predictors of physical and verbal bullying also predict Internet bullying. The focus is on youth involvement in such bullying as perpetrators, not victims. Perhaps because this type of bullying has unfolded on the fringes of the adult radar screen, it has only recently been considered in studies of bullying among children and youth. Relatively little is known about the prevalence of Internet bullying and how this compares with other types of bullying for boys and girls across different ages. Little is also known about whether Internet bullying is predicted (and potentially prevented) by the same types of factors that have been linked to physical and verbal bullying in schools. To date, information on the prevalence of Internet bullying comes primarily from anecdotal reports and a limited number of youth surveys. Findings suggest that Internet bullying and victimization rates are around 25%. This is higher than physical bullying rates but lower than indirect bullying rates from most school-based prevalence studies. Very few studies have examined age and gender differences for Internet bullying, although overall bullying appears to peak during early adolescence, with verbal bullying remaining high throughout the adolescent years. Furthermore boys are more likely to engage in physical bullying than girls.

Even fewer studies have examined the correlates and predictors of Internet bullying and whether these are similar or distinct from factors linked to bullying in schools. Overall, predictors of physical and verbal bullying are quite similar to predictors of aggression more generally. However studies of the etiology and prevention of bullying have emphasized a smaller set of predictors reflecting the social and normative context of bullying within peer networks and school settings. Two important predictors linked to bullying in both prediction and prevention studies are student perceptions of the acceptability (or moral approval) of bullying and student perceptions that school is an unsupportive context in which peers and adults cannot be trusted.

Bullying is behavior that is harmful to others and falls within the domain of behaviors with moral consequences: endorsement of the acceptability of bullying is akin to moral approval because harm to others is considered to be a key element of moral reasoning. A consistent finding in both the aggression and bullying literature is that children who endorse normative beliefs supporting such behavior are more likely to be perpetrators. A peer and school culture that supports bullying is more likely to have individuals who view this behavior as acceptable, further increasing normative support for bullying. Indeed a primary emphasis of many school-based bullying prevention programs is to change the normative climate so that bullying is seen as unacceptable.

Besides normative climate, several studies have examined the impact of various contextual characteristics of schools on bullying perpetration and victimization. For example, increases in student bullying over time are more likely in high-conflict, disorganized schools than in low-conflict, harmonious schools. Low levels of supervision within school settings have also been associated with higher rates of bullying. Disciplinary harshness, safety problems, and negative peer interactions have also been linked to behavior problems and bullying. The influence of peers is particularly noteworthy. Within the school setting, peers can escalate bullying through encouragement and validation. However, just as peers can enable bullying, they can also provide a supportive social context that encourages acceptance, belonging, and trust; many effective bullying prevention programs encourage students helping other students to form positive peer support systems.

If students believe that bullying is acceptable and if they feel disconnected and unsupported at school and by peers, they should be more likely to engage in all types of bullying behavior, including Internet bullying. However because both verbal and Internet bullying can occur behind the victim's back with a greater degree of anonymity than with physical bullying, both the prevalence and predictors of Internet bullying are expected to be more similar to verbal bullying than to physical bullying.

Methods

Data for the present research were collected as part of a larger study evaluating a statewide initiative in Colorado to strengthen the skills and willingness of youth and adults to intervene in bullying situations. The Bullying Prevention Initiative (BPI) is a 3-year, $8.6-million initiative funded by The Colorado Trust, a private grant-making foundation in Denver, Colorado. The grantees funded by this initiative represent school districts, individual schools, or community-based organizations, evenly split between rural and urban areas of the state and responsible for implementing bullying prevention programming in 78 schools across 40 of Colorado's 64 counties.

The larger BPI evaluation will provide an empirically based understanding of bullying and bystander behavior among youth, including an increased awareness of this behavior, social cognitive processes involved in the prevention of bullying, the social context surrounding bullying incidents, and the involvement of adults and youth in preventing such incidents. These issues are being addressed by collecting survey data from youth and adults in schools, collecting data from grantees concerning program implementation, and conducting a supplemental qualitative study seeking to acquire in-depth information from adults about challenges and successes in program implementation and from youth in terms of their awareness of the bullying prevention programs and their perceived effectiveness. A pre–post survey design collects data from youth in the fall and the spring of 3 academic years (2005–2006, 2006–2007, and 2007–2008) within the 78 schools. This design allows the assessment of single year changes in individual youth and contextual (school level) changes over the full 3 years of the BPI. All instruments developed to collect data from youth were piloted in the summer of 2005 before full implementation in the fall of that year, with all indices having acceptable reliabilities. . . .

Participants in the Present Study

The first year of the BPI was a start-up period for both the prevention programming as well as the evaluation study in refining its data collection instruments and procedures. During this year, 3,339 youth completed questionnaires in the 78 school sites during the fall of 2005, and another 2,293 youth in that original sample participated in a follow-up survey in 65 school sites in the spring of 2006. Data were collected in 5th, 8th, and 11th grades, representing transition years in elementary, middle, and high schools. All data collection was conducted in compliance with the protocol approved by the human subjects review board, including acquiring informed parental consent and youth ascent. To ensure the quality of data and that school samples are representative, a subsample of these first-year participants was selected for the present analysis based on two criteria: (1) schools must have successfully completed both fall and spring data collection, and (2) consent and completion rates at those schools must be 50% or greater. Applying these selection criteria yielded a subsample of 1,519 youth participating in both the fall and spring data collection, representing 46 school sites. The subsample has a greater percentage of rural participants, compared with the total first-year sample, and a greater percentage of 5th grade but a lower percentage of 11th grade participants, compared with the total first-year sample. The percentages for the remainder of the demographic characteristics are very similar between the subsample and the total first-year sample.

Procedures

Data were collected using two different electronic methods, with the choice of methods negotiated with schools in terms of what was deemed best for their students. However paper questionnaires were used by a small percentage of youth absent the day for which data collection was scheduled (4% of the total first-year sample and 1.6% of the subsample analyzed here). First, data collectors used a liquid crystal display projector to present questionnaire items in classrooms of approximately 30 students or less (used by 61.7% of the students in this subsample). After the data collectors read each question aloud, youth used a wireless response pad to enter their answers, which were automatically recorded in an electronic database and linked to the student identification code. The questionnaire was administered in English or Spanish as needed, using standard back-translation methods. Second, the questionnaire was adapted to a web-based format linked to the electronic database (36.7% of students in this subsample used this method). The youth web-based questionnaire was administered in school computer laboratories. Data collectors assisted youth in logging on to the password-protected questionnaire and were available for assistance as youth answered questions at their own pace. No evidence was found that these different data collection procedures influenced responding.

Measures

Bullying perpetration. Items bearing on the perpetration (not victimization) of different types of bullying were used. Youth were asked to respond to the following four items: "I pushed, shoved, tripped, or picked fights with students I know are weaker than me"; "I teased or said mean things to certain students"; "I spread rumors about some students"; and "I told lies about some students through e-mail or instant messaging." Numeric coding (in parentheses) and response options included (1) never, (2) one or two times, (3) several times, and (4) a lot. The first item was used to measure physical bullying perpetration, and the second and third items were combined to measure verbal bullying perpetration. Internet bullying perpetration was measured by the fourth item. . . .

As mentioned below, the appropriate temporal ordering between the predictors examined in this empirical analysis and these types of bullying perpetration requires using data collected in the fall of 2005 for the predictors and data gathered in the spring of 2006 for bullying perpetration. Therefore, the reference period for the four bullying items was "since the school year began." The distributions for these variables are highly skewed, with a high concentration of participants scoring one (i.e., never) and a precipitous decline in the distribution of participants across the higher scores. Hence these variables were dichotomized, with comparisons made between those participants who reported never engaging in these types of bullying (scoring 1) with those who reported doing so one or more times during the school year (scoring 2–4).

Moral approval of bullying. Moral beliefs about bullying perpetration and bystander involvement in bullying situations were assessed by asking participants to evaluate six different items on a four point Likert-type scale ranging from "really wrong" to "perfectly ok." These items were taken from the Normative Beliefs About Aggression Scale and were modified slightly to refer to bullying instead of aggression. The items included bullying perpetration as mentioned above (including Internet bullying), in addition to items pertaining to negative bystander involvement, such as encouraging others to fight smaller students or spread lies and rumors about them. These six items were summed to construct a summary additive index. . . . The distribution on the index was positively skewed, but it had a clustering of cases at the high end of the continuum of scores. The distribution of this measure was adjusted by sub-dividing it into six categories having approximately equal distributions. High scorers indicate participants who approve bullying perpetration and negative bystander behavior in general, not behavior-specific approval. Participants scoring low on this index disapprove of bullying and negative bystander behavior in general. This measure is appropriate given the emphasis on capturing the normative orientation of students about bullying overall, not behavior-specific moral beliefs.

School climate. Student perceptions of school climate were assessed using the California School Climate Scale. This measure contains nine items about teachers, school staff and administrators, school policy, and a student's perceived personal connection to the school. For example, participants were asked whether they disagree or agree with statements like "My teachers respect me," "My teachers are fair," or "Teachers at my school are nice people." Other items addressed whether the principal in their school listens to the ideas of students, whether students who break school rules are treated fairly, and whether teachers and staff are doing the right things to prevent bullying in general, not specific forms of bullying in the school. The nine items were summed to form an additive index . . . with scores ranging from 9 to 36, given the response categories of the individual items. Respondents with high scores perceived a positive school climate, whereas those with low scores perceived a more negative school climate.

Perceived peer support. This four-item scale focused on positive and negative qualities of peers as a source of social support. It was adapted from the Generalized Perception of Peers Scale. Regardless of social context (e.g., schools), participants were asked to assess whether "students their age" care about what happens to them, will help them in time of need, can be trusted, and are sensitive to their feelings. Response options range from "no, not at all" to "yes, completely." The four items were summed to form an additive index, with scores ranging from a low of 4 to a high of 16, given the response categories for each of the individual items. High scores indicated higher perceptions of peers as supportive, whereas low scores indicated the opposite view. . . .

Results

The results presented below are arranged according to the two primary research objectives of this analysis: (1) to determine the prevalence of Internet compared with verbal and physical bullying perpetration in this sample of youth, and (2) to determine whether predictors of Internet bullying perpetration are similar to predictors of verbal and physical bullying perpetration. The first objective is addressed simply by tabulating the distributions of the three forms of bullying and examining whether these distributions vary by gender and grade level (5th, 8th, and 11th grades). The empirical examination by gender and grade was done by estimating their effects on each form of bullying perpetration through logistic regression, given the dichotomous bullying measures used.

The second objective is addressed by estimating the bivariate relations between each of the three predictors and the three forms of bullying perpetration. As noted above, these behavioral measures are dichotomized, differentiating between participants who report never perpetrating such behavior and those reporting they did so one or more times during the school year. . . .

Prevalence of Bullying

. . . Verbal bullying is clearly most prevalent for the total sample, followed by physical bullying and then bullying via e-mail or instant messaging. In short,

Internet bullying was a part of the behavioral repertoire of only a minority of youth in this sample during the last school year, but its prevalence is non-trivial. These three types of bullying perpetration are clearly interrelated, with ordinal associations (gamma coefficients) ranging from .66 for the relation between Internet and physical bullying to .87 for the relation between Internet and verbal bullying. However, distinctions remain, as suggested by 24.8% of the sample refraining from any type of bullying, 37.9% engaging in only one type, 30.7% perpetrating two types, and only 6.6% self-reporting involvement in all three types.

. . . No gender differences were found for Internet and verbal bullying, although such differences were pronounced for physical bullying, with males being more than twice as likely as females to report perpetrating such behavior. . . . Grade was significantly related to all forms of bullying perpetration, with the estimated effect being literally identical between Internet and verbal bullying . . . but substantially smaller for physical bullying. . . .

. . . About one third of 5th-graders reported engaging in verbal bullying in the past school year, with the prevalence rates then peaking in 8th grade and dropping off only slightly by 11th grade. A similar pattern holds for physical bullying as well, although the prevalence rates are lower than verbal bullying, especially among 5th and 11th-graders. A relatively small percentage of 5th-graders reported engaging in Internet bullying, with the distribution peaking in 8th grade and again declining slightly among 11th-graders.

Predictors of Bullying

Moral approval of bullying. . . . The results show that this predictor is significantly and positively related to all three forms of bullying as expected; that is, beliefs endorsing bullying and negative bystander behavior are associated with self-reported involvement in verbal, physical, and Internet bullying. Specifically, an increase in one of the six ordinal categories of the moral beliefs measure (see description of measure above) is associated with a 43% increase in the odds of verbal bullying . . . , a 27% increase in the odds of physical bullying . . . and a 24% increase in the odds of Internet bullying. . . . However, the estimated effects for verbal bullying are significantly greater than those of both physical and Internet bullying . . . , but the difference between the estimated effects for physical and Internet bullying is not statistically significant. In short, although moral beliefs approving of bullying and negative bystander behavior are significantly and positively related to all three forms of bullying perpetration, the estimated effects for Internet bullying appear to be significantly lower than for verbal bullying.

Perceived school climate. . . . The more youth perceive themselves as connected to their schools, with the climate being trusting, fair, pleasant, etc. (i.e., a positive school climate), the lower is their self-reported involvement in verbal, physical, and Internet bullying perpetration. An increase of a single unit on the 9–36-point perceived school climate index (see description of measure above) is associated with a 7% decline in the odds of physical bullying . . . a

9% decline in the odds of Internet bullying . . . , and a 10% decline in the odds of verbal bullying. . . . Moreover, the difference between the estimated effects for Internet bullying and either physical bullying or verbal bullying is not statistically significant.

Perceived peer support. Youth perceptions that friends their age are trustworthy, caring, and helpful are significantly associated with lower self-reported participation in verbal, physical, and Internet bullying. Again, these empirical relations were anticipated. A single unit increase on the 4- to 16-point index of perceived peer support (see description of measure above) is associated with a 7% decline in the odds of physical bullying . . . , with the estimated effects being greatest for Internet . . . and verbal . . . bullying. Similar to the empirical relations between perceived school climate and these three forms of bullying perpetration, the estimated effects for Internet bullying are not significantly different from those of verbal or physical bullying.

Summary and Conclusion

The findings on the prevalence of bullying perpetration suggest that distributions vary by type, with verbal being most prevalent, followed by physical and then by Internet bullying. Physical and Internet bullying peaked in 8th grade and declined in 11th grade, whereas verbal bullying peaked in 8th grade and remained relatively high in the 11th grade. Males were more likely than females to report physical bullying perpetration. Consistent with the expectation that Internet bullying and verbal bullying would share common features, no gender differences were found for prevalence of Internet and verbal bullying.

Three predictors of bullying were empirically examined. One reflects an individual's normative orientation about the moral acceptability of bullying—that is, whether such behavior is right or wrong. However, the other two predictors capture perceptions of either the context in which youth regularly participate (i.e., schools) or the nature of peers with whom youth regularly interact (i.e., students their age). Regardless, Internet bullying was significantly related to all three predictors, and these empirical relations were similar to those of physical and verbal bullying, with the one exception of moral beliefs having a significantly greater positive estimated effect on verbal bullying than on Internet bullying. These findings suggest that the causal pathways to Internet bullying may not be unique; rather, it appears to share common causal pathways with other forms of bullying, particularly verbal bullying.

Technological advances (e.g., Internet e-mail, web sites, and blogs) merely provide yet another venue through which bullying among youth can occur. Indeed a limitation of the current study is that we did not consider a wider range of electronic bullying methods such as picture cell phones and text messages. However preliminary evidence from the second year of the larger study suggests that expanding the scope of the Internet question does not make a major difference. Specifically, the second-year student survey added cell phone text messaging and bullying on various websites. The result was an Internet bullying prevalence rate of 13.6% for the full pre-tested sample in year two, compared with 12.0% for the full pre-tested sample in year 1. These rates are comparable to more recent estimates of Internet bullying (13.1%) based on only 84 adolescents 13–18 years of age.

The present study highlighted common predictors of different types of bullying, including Internet bullying. The findings suggest that preventive interventions can impact these diverse types of bullying by changing normative beliefs about the acceptability of bullying while simultaneously considering how to increase trust and support among peers and within the school setting. For schools, this suggests a "whole school" approach to bullying prevention that facilitates changes in beliefs and behaviors toward greater support, trust, and cohesion. Furthermore, it is important to consider additional potential predictors uniquely linked to the anonymous nature of bullying via the Internet or other communication technologies (e.g., cell phone cameras, text messaging) that may further enhance an understanding of this behavior and thus preventive efforts in this domain. Once again, however, the findings reported here underscore a critical point of this paper: Common social forces influence the various ways in which bullying is expressed—through physical aggression, verbal aggression, or aggression perpetrated through new communication technologies.

EXPLORING THE ISSUE

Is Cyberbullying Related to Gender?

Challenge Questions

1. What are the various forms cyberbullying can take? Are they equally harmful?
2. Is being the victim of cyberbullying the same as being the victim of bullying or other forms of aggression?
3. Do you think that girls and women may be more comfortable online than in the real world breaking away from cultural constraints on females' expressing aggression?
4. Do you think boys and men may feel less pressure online to show they are "real men" and not behave as aggressively when provoked as they would in the "real" world?
5. Can sexting be a form of cyberbullying?

Is There Common Ground?

Because of the notion that aggression is a predominantly male attribute, researchers have disproportionately used male as opposed to female participants in their research studies. Even when female aggression has been the research focus, the conceptualization of aggression has stemmed from the "male" perspective on aggression. For example, much of the research on aggression has focused specifically on physical aggression using the teacher–learner paradigm. In this paradigm, the participant, acting as teacher, punishes the "learner" with electric shocks for incorrect responses. Research has shown, however, that women perceive electric shock more negatively and a less effective deterrent than do men; thus, they are more reluctant than men to administer it. Research demonstrating gender differences in aggression might be reflecting gender differences in a willingness to behave physically aggressively rather than the potential for aggression. A continued focus on types of aggression in which men consistently emerge as more aggressive than women fails to examine those situations in which women might aggress and the modes of aggression they might adopt. Cross-cultural analyses suggest that despite tremendous cross-cultural variation, men tend to be more physically aggressive, but women may use more indirect aggression. Men are more likely to use aggression that produces pain or physical harm, whereas women are more likely to use aggression that produces psychological or social harm. Because the majority of researchers have been male, they may have chosen questions and contexts regarding aggression of greatest personal relevance. As the use of the Internet increases at exponential rates, questions about gender behavior in cyberspace abound. Research on how girls and boys, women and men, use the Internet as a tool for harm-doing is just beginning. Some work that explicitly addresses gender differences suggests that patterns of cyberbullying parallel patterns of traditional bullying, with boys more likely to be perpetrators than girls, and female victims more likely to report the bullying to adults than boys. Williams and Guerra, using a slightly older sample of students, find no differences in Internet or verbal bullying between girls and boys, although boys were more than twice as likely to engage in physical bullying. Reconciling the differences between these various studies remains a task for future research. However, results of these and future studies hold the potential to both challenge time-honored assumptions about gender and aggression and allow us to more fully explore how the expressions of gender and aggression mutually define each other. Thus, when asking questions about gender and aggression, aggression should be defined as any behavior directed toward another person or a person's property with the intent to do harm, even if the aggressor was unsuccessful. The behavior could be physical or verbal, active or passive, direct or indirect (i.e., aggressor may remain anonymous), occur in real space or cyberspace, and the consequence for the target could be physical or psychological. All forms of harm-doing behavior, including self-defense, should be considered because in some cases, such as domestic violence, it is difficult to distinguish retaliative motives from self-defense motives. Also, aggression, broadly defined, allows us to examine more fully the broad range of harm-doing behaviors available to human beings. Thus, rather than asking who is more aggressive, it might be more productive to ask what are the forms and functions of aggression for women and men, and to what degree is the expression of aggression shaped by cultural expectations regarding masculinity (power, dominance, strength) and femininity (nurturing, passive, weak).

Internet References . . .

Work and Family: National Partnership for Women and Families

This public education and advocacy site aims "to promote fairness in the workplace, quality health care, and policies that help women and men meet the dual demands of work and family." This site includes a wealth of information about relevant public policy issues, including the Family Medical Leave Act.

http://www.nationalpartnership.org

About Women's Issues

This Web site addresses a number of issues related to gender and the world of work

http://womensissues.about.com/od/genderdiscrimination/i/isgendergap.htm

International Labour Organization (ILO)

The ILO is dedicated to reducing poverty and promoting opportunities for women and men to obtain decent and productive work. This Web site provides a comprehensive bibliography of materials related to gender issues and women at work.

http://www.ilo.org

Gender at Work

The Web site for Gender at Work was created in June 2001 by AWID (Association for Women's Rights in Development), WLP (Women's Learning Partnership), CIVICUS (World Alliance for Citizen Participation), and UNIFEM (United Nations Fund for Women). They state, "We aim to develop new theory and practice on how organizations can change gender-biased institutional rules (the distribution of power, privileges and rights), values (norms and attitudes), and practices. We also aim to change the political, accountability, cultural and knowledge systems of organizations to challenge social norms and gender inequity."

http://www.genderatwork.org

Advancing Women

This Web site offers advice on career and business strategies; provides tools and resources to support one's career, business, and leadership goals; and features a targeted, diversity job board.

http://www.advancingwomen.com/

From 9 to 5: Gender in the World of Work

*T*here are few places other than the workplace where gendered patterns are more apparent. There are sex-segregated jobs: "pink" collar jobs for women and "blue" collar jobs for men. Within occupational categories, there is sex stratification, with men more often holding the higher, more prestigious and better-paying positions, such as anesthesiologist versus pediatrician, or corporate lawyer versus family lawyer. Women on average make $.75 for each man's dollar; this holds across race, ethnicity, social class, educational level, and work status (full-time or part-time). Such disparities provoke heated discussion. Are they the result of discrimination against women in the workplace, or are they justifiable differences based on natural talents? How does gender influence women's and men's efforts to balance work and family interests and responsibilities? Why do we ask the question about the impact on children of mothers working outside the home but never the question of the impact of fathers working? What are the ramifications of this question for poor people, especially women? Are these women to be blamed for their status as single mothers on welfare? Given the economic downturn, workplace issues have taken on a new urgency and have differential consequences for women and men. As you explore the issues raised in this unit consider the competing, or perhaps complementary, explanations for gender differences in the workplace: biologically based differences that lead to differences in interests, motivations, and achievement level and/or culturally based differences, such as discrimination in hiring and promotion practices, the devaluing of women's work, the social rejection of competent women, and the lack of role models and mentors. Are biologically based explanations justified in the face of differential experiences in the workplace based on race, ethnicity, class, culture, and other status-defining attributes, such as disability status or sexual orientation? How do media images of the workplace affect our understanding of the workplace?

- Is the Gender Wage Gap Justified?

- Has the Economic Recession Been Harder on Women's Employment Than Men's Employment?

- Do Social Policies Improve Gender Inequalities in the Workplace?

- Are Barriers to Women's Success as Leaders Due to Societal Obstacles?

ISSUE 15

Is the Gender Wage Gap Justified?

YES: J. R. Shackleton, from "Explaining the Overall Pay Gap," in *Should We Mind the Gap? Gender Pay Differentials and Public Policy* (The Institute of Economic Affairs, 2008)

NO: Hilary M. Lips, from "The Gender Wage Gap: Debunking the Rationalizations," *Expert Advice for Working Women*, http://www.womensmedia.com

---

Learning Outcomes

As you read the issue, focus on the following points:

- What are the criteria for deciding that the work skills associated with two different jobs are comparable?
- How can educational and career choices be shaped by gender expectations?
- Do cultural expectations make it difficult for women and men to freely choose their work and career?
- How might explanations of the gender wage gap at the individual level of analysis and at the sociocultural level lead to different conclusions regarding its justification?

ISSUE SUMMARY

YES: John Shackleton, a professor of economics and dean of the Business School, University of East London, suggests that the gender gap is largely due to nondiscriminatory factors; most notable are those associated with compensation for the differential value associated with women's choices due to lifestyle, preferences, attitudes, and expectations.

NO: Hilary Lips, a professor of psychology and the director of the Center for Gender Studies at Radford University, documents the continuing gender gap in wages and argues that a continuing undervaluing of women's work, whatever it happens to be, due to stereotypes and prejudice maintains the wage gap. She argues that the language of "choice" is deceptive.

"**E**qual pay for equal work" and "Equal pay for comparable work": These two phrases have been hallmarks of the women's movement's list of rights to which women are entitled. And there are several federal laws, enforced by the U.S. Equal Employment Opportunity Commission (EEOC), that are supposed to protect women from discrimination in their compensation. The Equal Pay Act states, "Employers may not pay unequal wages to men and women who perform jobs that require substantially equal skill, effort and responsibility, and that are performed under similar working conditions within the same establishment," but the act does allow for differences in pay under certain conditions: "Pay differentials are permitted when they are based on seniority, merit, quantity or quality of production, or a factor other than sex." These are known as "affirmative defenses," and it is the employer's burden to prove that they apply. Questions arise from these declarations. What constitutes "substantially equal"? By what criteria are judgments of "merit, quantity and quality of production or a factor other than sex" made? Classic studies in social psychology have shown repeatedly that the same work, whether it is an essay, a painting, or a resume, when attributed to a man receives a more favorable evaluation than when attributed to a woman. In these studies, research participants are presented with an exemplar of a person's work. Half are told it is the work of a man and half are told it is the work of a woman. In almost all cases, when the work was assumed to be the product of a man it was more highly rated. The only exception was when participants were told that a panel of experts had already judged it the best.

Women account for about 47 percent of the workforce in the United States and work approximately the same number of hours as men (35–50 hours/week); 60 percent of all women over age 16 are in the workforce. However, women earn less than men on average; this is true across full-time and part-time work, as well as across race, class, and educational levels. One explanation for the earning discrepancy is that women experience more job discontinuity due to family obligations, such as taking time off for childbirth, as well as dual-career conflicts, such as following a spouse who relocates to improve his job status. That is, women are expected to choose family over career in any work–family conflicts. Job interruptions and lower wages can result in women experiencing lower self-esteem and a reduced sense of accomplishment. Often these patterns are attributed to women's own choices and that they "deserve" less. However, others have suggested that society would benefit from recognizing that the childbearing years are also the years during which one is most likely to make the greatest career advancements. Thus, if women get off the career track to have children, they begin to lag and struggle to ever get back on the track. As a solution to this problem, the "mommy track" was proposed in 1989, a phrase coined in the *New York Times* to describe a "career and family" path that would serve as a viable alternative to the traditional "career primary" path typically followed by men. The "career and family" path was intended to offer women—only temporarily— flexible schedules, with reduced salaries and less responsibilities, while they tended to family matters, with the opportunity to return later to the fast track. A debate ensued as to whether the mommy track adequately allows for a temporary delay in women's career trajectory or if it really is a dead end. Skeptics question whether it is ever possible to truly get back on the fast track following a timeout for family. Although the concept of the mommy track was to prevent women from being unfairly treated, current research suggests that all it has done is perpetuate the stereotype that women who choose, even temporarily, family over career, are not really committed to the workplace. As recently as July 2007, a *U.S. News & World Report* article was focused on how the mommy track can derail a career.

Attributions for success and failure have also been implicated in individuals' academic and career choices. Additionally, the attributions that others make about the reasons for someone's success or failure can affect the opportunities for advancement they afford that person. For example, promotions are more likely to be given to individuals employers believe have the ability to take on more responsibility and more difficult tasks, whereas bonuses, without a promotion, are more likely if someone worked hard (i.e., put in a great deal of effort) on a particular task. In general, the reasons for success or failure may be attributed to stable internal causes (such as ability), or unstable internal causes (such as effort), or stable external causes (such as a very difficult task), or unstable external causes (such as luck). Although gender-related patterns in attributions for success and failure are not always found, when they are both women, they themselves as well as others are more likely to attribute their success to effort or luck and their failure to lack of ability, whereas men as well as others tend to attribute their success to ability and their failure to being faced with a tough task or bad luck. Recent studies suggest that this gendered pattern show up even among children, and that with age there is an increased likelihood of making internal attributions. Imagine what implications such patterns of attributions have if during high school girls and boys are already explaining their successes and failures in the classroom differently, and how the consequences will be compounded if teachers also embrace gender-related attributions.

Decisions are made on a daily basis regarding who gets hired, who gets a pay raise, and who gets a promotion. To what extent do women's personality, interests, and choices affect these decisions and to what extent do sexism and discrimination affect these decisions? Is the world of work so constructed that its practices and policies result in discrimination against women? These practices might include policies that require out-of-town travel to get a promotion and for the single mother in particular to have adequate child care. Or these practices might include tolerance for sexual harassment that forces a woman to quit her job or suffer in silence because she cannot afford to lose her job. Or perhaps there are policies that are intolerant of a single mother missing work because she has a sick child. So, under such institutional barriers to success, women may be forced to forego certain careers and occupations, "choosing" those more compatible with the gender roles society expects them to fulfill. Or, alternatively, perhaps it is the way women are constituted that makes the difference. Are women by nature less ambitious, less competitive, less assertive, and as a consequence less effective leaders? If so, they may freely choose careers and occupations that are more suited to their nature, careers, and occupations that just happen to pay less. In the YES selection, John Shackleton argues that women make employment choices that ultimately determine their wages. He suggests that the division of labor in the home plays a large role in the choices women make and that discriminatory factors are negligible. Hilary Lips could not disagree more. In the NO selection, Lips argues that the continued undervaluing of women's work and prejudice against women in the workplace result in a continuing unjustifiable gender wage gap.

YES

J. R. Shackleton

Should We Mind the Gap? Gender Pay Differentials and Public Policy

In this chapter various possible explanations for the differences in male and female earnings are examined.

We should begin by asking what determines pay, in general terms, in a competitive market. In such a market we would not expect everybody to earn the same. In the short run, wages are determined simply by supply and demand. If there is a sudden increase in the demand for construction workers because a new underground line is being built, and a limited supply of those with the necessary skills, wages will rise. But in the longer term, more workers will be attracted into construction, perhaps from abroad, or workers in other occupations will retrain. Longer term, it is possible that big pay differentials can persist if people possess unique skills or talents in high demand. . . .

Compensating Differentials

Even where people are free to enter a well-paid field of employment, however, they may not choose to do so. Long ago Adam Smith, in his *Wealth of Nations*, spelled out several reasons why some workers consistently earn more than others. His reasoning forms the basis for the modern idea of "compensating differentials"—where jobs that are unattractive may have to be rewarded with higher pay if they are to attract sufficient workers.

One factor is what Smith called "the difficulty and expense" of learning a job. Some forms of employment require years of training, education, and work experience—generically classed as human capital. The acquisition of human capital typically involves some cost to the trainee in terms of time and forgone earnings, even if the direct costs are paid by the state or the employer, and the worker will expect to be compensated by higher pay. This is clearly relevant to discussion of the gender pay gap, because women are likely to differ from men in relation to their human capital.

Note, however, that the amount of extra pay required will vary, Smith argues, with the "agreeableness or disagreeableness" of the job. Apparently an academic job in a high-ranking research department at Oxford carries sufficient kudos to offset the higher salary obtainable in other universities. By

From *Should We Mind the Gap? Gender Pay Differentials and Public Policy,* Institute of Economic Affairs, 2008, pp. 45–66. Copyright © 2008 by Institute of Economic Affairs. Reprinted by permission.

contrast, a cook on a North Sea oil rig, for example, will normally be paid more than a similarly skilled cook working in a city. But whether a premium is paid, and its size, will depend on the tastes and preferences of individuals. If, over time, Oxford becomes overcrowded and less attractive as a city, the university will have to pay more to attract the best academics. If lots of cooks develop a taste for working at sea, their premium will diminish or disappear. This is pertinent to discussion of the pay gap, for women's preferences in relation to jobs may differ systematically from those of men, as we shall see.

It is rarely discussed in the debate over the pay gap, but part of the explanation for men's higher average pay could well be that there is a compensating differential for less attractive working conditions. Men are more likely to work outside in all weathers. They are more likely to work unsocial hours. Thirty-six percent of male managers work more than 48 hours a week; the figure for women managers is only 18 percent. Men suffer much higher rates of industrial injury.

Looking at the economy as a whole, we see that women's jobs are less at risk: in the three months from November 2007 to January 2008, there were 3.4 redundancies per thousand female employees; the figure for men was 5.3. Women are more likely to get employer-provided training: 13.6 percent of females had received job-related training in the last four weeks in the third quarter of 2007, as against 11.3 percent of males. They have a shorter commuting time to work and take more time off work. No wonder, perhaps, that they report greater job satisfaction than men.

The implication of this is that the "true" gender pay gap may be less than the measured one, as male pay may include an element of compensation for less attractive working conditions. This is ignored in many empirical studies, and it is a serious omission.

Discrimination

Discrimination is often seen as an important explanation of the gender pay gap. The concept needs some clarification before we assess this belief.

Discrimination is a word that has changed its common meaning. Whereas once it was seen as something worthy of praise—as in somebody displaying "a fine discrimination" between paintings or pieces of music—it now usually means something unfair, unacceptable, and, in an increasing number of cases, illegal.

Economic analysis of the subject effectively began with the work of Gary Becker in the 1950s. In Becker's analysis, employers, fellow employees, and governments may engage in discrimination, which he interprets as an economically unjustified preference for one group over another, such that members of the favoured group would be more likely to be given a job, to be paid more, or otherwise treated better than another group or groups. Becker's particular insight was that this preference, this "taste for discrimination," could be seen as an end in itself, something that therefore entailed a "cost" to the discriminator. For example, employers might prefer to hire male rather than female workers even if this were more expensive. In this respect Becker differed fundamentally from Marxists and other critics of capitalism who saw discrimination as a means of exploiting subordinate groups to the benefit of the discriminator.

If this taste for discrimination exists, it *may* be manifested in the existence of a pay gap. This is not necessarily the case, however. If rigorous laws prevent women being paid less than men, discriminating firms may simply hire fewer women, but they will be paid the same as men. So Becker's analysis supports the point made earlier in relation to Italy and Spain: the size of the pay gap in itself does not say very much about the extent of discrimination.

From Becker's analysis, originally applied to racial differences, it followed that discriminating firms would hire white workers, or pay them a higher wage, rather than black workers of identical or superior productivity characteristics. But, he reasoned, this behaviour would raise costs. If other employers who were "colour-blind" entered the market, they would be able to undercut the discriminators and gain a competitive edge.

From this, Becker argued that, in a competitive market where non-discriminators were free to enter, discrimination would be unlikely to persist for long. It could be found where firms had monopsony power;[1] it could also be found where trade unions exercised power to protect white workers against blacks, or, in our context, men against women. But Becker, as a Chicago economist, argued that market power to sustain discrimination is unlikely to persist for any extended period if free entry of firms is allowed and union power is limited. Therefore any sustained discriminatory power is to be attributed to government interference in the free market. Apartheid South Africa is an obvious example. And in the USA, the so-called "Jim Crow" laws in the South sustained labour market discrimination for many years: when they were abolished there was a big increase in the relative pay of black workers—the reduction in the white/black pay gap since then has been relatively modest.

In our current context, it should be remembered that government discrimination against women was often quite explicit in the UK until the mid-twentieth century, with different pay rates for men and women civil servants and teachers, requirements to resign on marriage, and prohibitions on working at all in certain jobs.

A quite different approach to the economics of discrimination was taken by Arrow and Phelps. In their view, employer discrimination was not the result of "tastes" or simple prejudice. Rather, it was a rational response to imperfect knowledge about the characteristics of individual job applicants. This led risk-averse employers to operate with stereotypes, which might be accurate or inaccurate, of common group characteristics. Suppose—and this is true, whatever its cause—that women on average take more time off work than men for sickness, employers might hold this against a female job applicant even if, unknown to the employer, she as an individual had a low sickness risk. Such "statistical discrimination" would be economically rational even if unfair to individuals in particular cases.

As in Becker's reasoning, however, free competition ought to reduce discrimination. Some firms might find it easier than others to acquire more information about individuals, or would be prepared to take a chance on them, because they faced different cost and demand conditions. Not all firms, there-fore, will behave in the same way. Furthermore, individuals are not passive. They can signal more information about themselves and market themselves more effectively to potential employers. One way they could in principle do this is to offer to work for less pay during a trial period. In most developed countries, however, such trial arrangements are difficult if not impossible because of legislation on equal pay, minimum wages, and employment pro-tection. Again, governments may be part of the problem.

Some support is given to the common Becker and Arrow/Phelps thesis that free competition tends to eliminate discrimination, while some forms of government intervention assist it, countries with greater economic com-petition, as measured by the Economic Freedom Index, display lower gender pay gaps. The OECD has recently reached similar conclusions, with the added insight that product market regulation may be an important factor, by pro-tecting disproportionately male "insiders" from new entrants. It finds that "regulatory barriers to competition explain between 20% and 40% of the cross country/time series variation in the gender wage gap."

As overt discrimination is now illegal, direct evidence of its existence is hard to come by. Some studies have used "correspondence tests," where there is some limited evidence that matched job applications from females and males elicit more interview offers for males. Another example is that of "blind" musi-cal auditions which suggest women do better if only their playing is heard. And careful documentation of practices in, for instance, construction indicates prejudice against female employees. But this sort of evidence is sparse.

Those seeking evidence of discrimination might also point to the large number of employment tribunal cases over sex discrimination and equal pay issues as evidence of the problem. It is certainly true that the number of such cases has risen recently: between 2004/05 and 2006/07, the number of sex dis-crimination cases accepted by tribunals rose from 11,726 to 28,153, while equal pay cases rose from 8,229 to a massive 44,013. There has been little detailed analysis of the growth of these cases, but it is known that there were special factors associated with changes in the law, and with the advent of "no-win, no-fee" lawyers. It is interesting, incidentally, that a disproportionate number of these cases are against public sector employers, although as we have seen, the gender pay gap is much smaller in the public sector. The majority of these claims were multiple claims brought against local authorities and the NHS, paradoxically as a result of the introduction of Job Evaluation Schemes aimed at closing the pay gap.

Looking at the private sector, though, it is clear that only a small pro-portion of equal pay and sex discrimination claims succeed. The Women and Work Commission examined all private sector equal pay claims from 2000 to 2004 and found that only 25 reached the decision stage, with applicants win-ning in only five cases.

Despite their growing numbers, tribunal cases are brought by only a tiny proportion of the workforce and cannot really do much to explain the aggre-gate phenomenon of the overall gender pay gap. They often concern procedural issues rather than more fundamental matters: in the case of sex discrimination tribunal claims, they are often about issues such as sexual harassment, bullying, and other offences rather than issues directly related to pay.

Econometric Analysis of the Pay Gap

Given the limited evidence of direct discrimination, in trying to analyse pay inequality researchers have increasingly concentrated on econometric work.[2] A substantial literature is concerned with separating out that part of the overall gender pay gap that can be accounted for by relevant economic characteristics and that residual part which could possibly be attributable to discrimination—defined as paying different amounts to men and women for identical skills and abilities, and usually seen as conscious or unconscious behaviour by misguided employers.

The large number of studies that have been made of pay gaps in many different countries vary considerably in methodology and conclusions, but there are some common threads. Most studies use a statistical technique first developed more or less simultaneously by Oaxaca and Blinder. This decomposes the gender pay gap into two parts. The first component is the difference in pay associated with differences in observable characteristics such as experience and education. The second is the "residual," which may partly result from discrimination.

The procedure involves first estimating a wage equation, which relates the logarithm of wages to years of education, work experience, and a range of other productivity-related characteristics that are available in the particular dataset the researcher is using. In effect the coefficients of the estimated equation indicate how much the labour market pays for these characteristics. One equation may be estimated for males, and then the regression coefficients are used to calculate what women would have earned had their characteristics been rewarded at the same pay rate as men. This typically reduces the pay gap between men and women quite significantly, leaving the "unexplained" element as the differences in returns to productivity-related characteristics for males and females.

Another wage equation may be estimated from data on women's earnings; the coefficients in this regression can then be applied to see what men would have earned if their characteristics had been paid at the same rate as those of women. This can then be used to give another possible estimate of the proportion of pay explained by worker characteristics, together with the residual potentially attributable to discrimination. Alternatively a pooled regression may be used.

Since the early studies, more sophisticated modelling has developed. One problem with the Oaxaca–Blinder approach is sample selection bias. When calculating the gender pay gap, researchers are using data on men and women who are in employment. Many women, however, especially those with lower levels of skills and qualifications or with less interest in careers, may drop out of the workforce and live on benefits and/or intra-household transfers from partners. So women who work may be untypical of all women—they are the more skilled and committed females, while employed men will cover a far wider spectrum of ability and commitment. The size of the underlying wage gap—between what men and women could earn—may therefore be underestimated, and the statistical explanation of the gap erroneous. The "Heckman correction" gets round this problem by using other variables to estimate the probability of employment of men and women and uses this as a further explanatory variable in the wage equation.

Other refinements have involved the development of international comparisons through the Juhn, Murphy and Pierce methodology. This approach assumes an "institutionalist" view that the structures of pay (including collective bargaining systems) affect gender differentials. It involves decomposing down cross-country differences in the gender pay gap by taking one country as a benchmark, and analysing pay gaps in other countries with reference to the pay structure of that country. So the decomposition involves explaining differences in pay gaps by reference to gender differences in observed characteristics, to a component associated with cross-country differences in wage structures, and to an unexplained element. Some interesting work has been done with this approach.

It is worth emphasising again that analysts are not unanimous in their choice of modelling strategy. And the quality and coverage of the data used in different studies often leave much to be desired. While most studies suggest that there is a sizeable unexplained residual pay gap, this varies considerably in size, as does the proportion of the explained gap associated with relevant individual and job characteristics.

A rather different approach to decomposition is used in work done by Wendy Olsen and Sylvia Walby for the Equal Opportunities Commission. As this has been widely quoted in UK debates, it is worth describing in some detail. Olsen and Walby adopt a novel approach which avoids some of the problems they perceive with the Oaxaca–Blinder technique. They prefer to estimate a single equation for men and women which produces estimates of coefficients on a range of explanatory variables. They then bring out the sizes of the main components of the pay gap by "simulating the hypothetical changes which would be needed to bring women's levels of these components into line with those of men." They use data from the British Household Panel Survey.

How does their approach work? Their wage equation shows a significant relationship between hourly earnings and, for example, the proportion of men in an occupation. This proportion is an indicator of "gender segregation" at work, which is believed by many to be an element in perpetuating pay inequality. The coefficient on this variable is 0.13, which means that, other things being equal, pay rises by 1.3 percent for every 10 percent more males in an occupation. So Olsen and Walby simulate the effect of increasing the proportion of men in every female-dominated occupational category to 50 percent. This is what they mean by an "unsegregated" workforce. If this were to be done, they find, earnings in these categories would rise by an average of 2.5 percent, or about 10 percent of the measured pay gap in their study.

This careful study still shows a largish "unexplained" pay gap, although it's a good deal smaller than some earlier studies, where only tiny proportions of the gap were explained. The large size of the unexplained gap in some of these studies is often the result of poor or proxy data. For example, work experience is used in estimating wage equations, but information on work history is often missing or incomplete, and some studies use the difference between current age and age at (assumed) completion of schooling as a proxy for this. For many women, and some men, with periods outside the workforce, this will exaggerate the true extent of their work experience. This in turn will lead to the role of experience in explaining the pay gap being underestimated because the differential in experience between men and women is inaccurately measured. Moreover, another key explanatory variable in wage equations, education, is often just measured by years of schooling, when it is known that the type and especially the subject of qualification are important, particularly in higher education. Women tend not to study the same subjects as men at university. Overall, in 2006, women accounted for 58.9 percent of the UK student population, but the proportion of women in the major subject areas shown varies considerably. Women are startlingly under-represented in some subjects and over-represented in others.

This in itself might not matter if different subjects were rewarded equally in the labour market, but this is not the case. For example, a study for the Royal Society of Chemistry showed that individuals' rates of return on more narrowly defined degrees varied widely. Engineering, chemistry, and physics, where women are seriously under-represented in the student population, offer rates of return significantly above average. By contrast, psychology degrees (where almost 80 percent of the 66,000 students in 2006 were female) and linguistics, English literature, and Celtic studies (where 72 percent of over 70,000 students were female) give returns that are markedly less than the average.

Variations in rates of return might reflect discrimination or the systematic undervaluing of the jobs of graduates in areas where women dominate. But there are some obvious structural factors at work. One is the sector in which different types of graduates are likely to work. Over a quarter of all women in higher education are studying nursing or education. The vast majority of graduates in these areas will work in the public sector: there are relatively few highly paid jobs in government employment.

Lifestyles, Preferences, Attitudes, Expectations

After allowing for these factors, is that part of the pay gap left unexplained attributable to discrimination, as many claim? Well, possibly, but in addition to [various] factors [such as amount of full-time experience; interruption in employment; education; years of part-time experience, etc.] there is also what econometricians call "unobservable heterogeneity." Here this means differences in attitudes, preferences, and expectations which can cause apparently similarly qualified and experienced individuals to behave very differently.

Catherine Hakim, a sociologist whose work on "preference theory" has created some controversy, claims that, in countries such as the UK, women now have a wide range of lifestyle options and that they can be classified into three relatively distinct groups by their preferences—those who are home-centred, those who are work-centred, and those who are "adaptive."

The first group, which she estimates to be approximately 20 percent of UK women, prioritise family life and children, and prefer not to work in the labour market (though they do so, they are not career-driven). Work-centred women, again about 20 percent, are likely to be childless, committed to their careers, and with a high level of investment in qualifications and training. The largest group, the "adaptives," around 60 percent of UK women, want to work, but they also want families. Their careers tend to be more erratic.

Hakim carried out a national survey which indicated that women's expressed preferences were good predictors of their employment status, whereas, perhaps surprisingly, their educational qualifications were not: some well-qualified women were in the "home-centred" camp. She argues that her preference theory "explains continuing sex differentials in labour market behaviour (workrates, labour turnover, the choice of job etc) and hence also in the pay gap."

Hakim's assertion receives some support from the work of Arnaud Chevalier, who uses data on attitudes and expectations to demonstrate how standard econometric analysis of the gender pay gap often misleads by leaving a large unexplained pay gap which is then too easily attributed to discrimination.

His work is based on a survey that covers more than 10,000 UK graduates who left university in 1995 and provides data on the 42 months following graduation. Unusually, in addition to information on wages, educational attainment, and job history, it provides data on family background, subject of degree, and, most importantly, attitudes and expectations. The survey asked twenty questions, coded on a five-point scale, about character traits, motivation and expectations.

The data indicated a mean raw gender pay gap of 12.6 percent for this group of young graduates. Chevalier's meticulous multistage process illustrates very clearly that the large residual pay gap found in many studies is likely to be the result of model misspecification because of the omission of explanatory variables.

What Chevalier does is fascinating. In essence he recapitulates the development of work on pay gaps in various stages, to show how adding information about individuals can explain more and more of the difference in earnings. His first step is to use a very basic specification using labour market experience, age at graduation, ethnicity, and region of residence as explanatory variables. Many widely cited studies of gender pay gaps tend to be confined to a few variables such as these. As might be expected, given that the group is fairly homogeneous in view of them having a degree and being relatively young, the simple model explains very little, only about 20 percent, of the observed pay gap between men and women.

He then goes on to include further explanatory variables such as A-level score, degree results, type of higher education institution and postgraduate qualifications. These indicators add a little, but not very much, to the explanatory power of the model. Adding in controls for the subject in which these young people graduated, however, increases the explanatory power of the model very significantly, with over 50 percent of the pay gap now accounted for.

A further iteration extends the model to include other objective data such as the characteristics (size and sector) of the workplace, the type of contract, and the "feminisation" of the occupation. This raises the proportion of the wage gap which is explained to 65 percent. The addition of data on the number of jobs held since graduation—a measure of mobility—adds another minor increment to the specification's explanatory power.

The final specification includes information on the values that graduates attach to jobs and their career expectations. Men and women differ significantly with regard to these characteristics: men are more likely to state that career development and financial rewards are very important, and are much more likely to define themselves as very ambitious, while women emphasise job satisfaction, being valued by employers and doing a socially useful job. Two-thirds of women in this sample expect to take career breaks for family reasons; 40 percent of men expect their partners to do this, but only 12 percent expect to do it themselves.

When these attitudinal variables are added to the specification, the result is that 84 percent of the wage gap can now be explained. This suggests that many of the models that generate large "unexplained" wage gaps, and from which non-specialists frequently infer a significant element of employer discrimination, are simply misspecified. They just don't incorporate sufficient explanatory variables for a satisfactory analysis of the causes of the gender pay differential.

How exactly do these attitudes and values lead to women being paid less than men? One way is through different individuals' choices of potential employers. A recent survey of young graduates shows that women's choices of preferred employers are very different from those of men. Of the top 25 ideal employers for women, twelve were in the public or voluntary sectors, as against only four out of 25 for men. The top three ideal employers for women graduates were all in the public sector.

Such preferences mean that many bright women are deliberately choosing jobs where really high earnings are impossible or unlikely. They clearly regard other aspects of the job—a greater sense of moral purpose, perhaps? Or maybe greater job security, less stress, and relatively generous pension provision—as offsetting the reduced chance of very high earnings. This is the compensating differential principle touched on earlier.

Another way in which employee attitudes influence earnings outcomes may be through different approaches to pay negotiations and promotion applications. Particularly at more senior levels, the pay offer an employer makes may be negotiable—if, that is, the employee chooses to negotiate. In their book *Women Don't Ask: Negotiation and the Gender Divide,* American academics Linda Balcock and Sara Laschever claim that women are very reluctant to negotiate over salaries. In one US study eight times as many men as women graduating with master's degrees negotiated their salaries, adding an average of 7.4 percent to their starting pay. This initial gap is likely to persist and grow over time. This is partly because women may have lower expectations: women's salary expectations for their first job are significantly lower than those of men going for similar jobs.

In the UK, an analysis of the pay gap among academic economists indicates that men receive more promotions and higher placings on pay scales, and one of the factors associated with this is the receipt of outside offers. Men receive more outside offers than women and are thus able to negotiate their pay upwards. They also make more pay-oriented moves between jobs than women.

So the conclusion we can draw from empirical analysis of the full-time pay gap is that a high proportion of this gap can be accounted for, given sufficient information on individual and job characteristics and the attitudes and expectations of employees. Males and females make different choices in the labour market, in terms of the trade-off between pay and other job characteristics, choice of education, choice of occupation, and attitudes to work. These strongly influence earnings. Employer attitudes and discrimination seem not to be nearly as important as politicians and lobbyists have suggested.

Summary

There is a sizeable gap between the average hourly earnings of UK men and women working full time: this is the gender pay gap. The gap has, however, declined over time and is expected to decline further given demographic trends and changes in women's qualifications. It could even go into reverse.

The view that the UK has a particularly large gender pay gap by international standards is misleading. The gap is anyway only one indicator of women's economic status. Its size is not necessarily related to other indicators of sex discrimination and it can increase or decrease for reasons that have nothing to do with employers' behaviour.

The pay gap may partly reflect compensating differentials: men's jobs may typically have disadvantages that are reflected in higher pay. Women report greater job satisfaction than men.

There is little evidence of direct discrimination by employers against women. Discrimination is often inferred from the unexplained residual in econometric analyses of the causes of the gender pay gap.

When attitudes and preferences, as well as objective characteristics such as work experience and qualifications, are brought into the picture, however, most of the pay gap can be explained without reference to discrimination.

Notes

1. Where a firm is the dominant employer in an area, it may be able to segment the job market and pay different rates to different groups of workers without being undercut by other firms. Such a situation could also arise if gender segregation occurred as a result of employee job choice.

2. Econometrics uses statistical methods to analyse and test relationships between economic variables.

Hilary M. Lips

The Gender Wage Gap: Debunking the Rationalizations

Last year, a labor economist from the Economic Policy Institute made the widely-quoted estimate that the gender pay gap would be closed within 30 years. Other commentators state confidently that the gap does not reflect discrimination, but other factors, such as the high wages of a few white men, and gendered patterns of occupational and educational choice and work experience. The effect of such assertions is to make women feel complacent about the wage gap—and perhaps to feel that they can avoid its impact by making the right educational, occupational, and negotiation-related choices. Such complacency is unwarranted.

The Wage Gap Exists within Racial/Ethnic Groups

White men are not the only group that out-earns women, although the wage gap is largest between white men and white women. Within other groups, such as African Americans, Latinos, and Asian/Pacific Islanders, men earn more than women (Source: U.S. Census Bureau).

What Difference Does Education Make?

Higher levels of education increase women's earnings, just as they do for men. However, there is no evidence that the gender gap in wages closes at higher levels of education. If anything, the reverse is true: at the very highest levels of education, the gap is at its largest.

The Wage Gap Exists within Occupations

Some people think that if women move into male-dominated occupations in larger numbers, the wage gap will close. However, there appears to be a gender-related wage gap in virtually every occupational category. In researching this issue at the Center for Gender Studies, we found only four occupational categories for which comparison data were available in which women earned even a little more than men: special education teachers, order clerks, electrical and electronic engineers, and miscellaneous food preparation occupations (Source: Bureau of Labor Statistics).

The movement of women into higher paid occupations, whether male-dominated or not, may not have the impact of narrowing the earnings gap. Social psychologists have demonstrated repeatedly that occupations associated with women or requiring stereotypically feminine skills are rated as less prestigious and deserving of less pay than occupations associated with men and masculine skills. Thus, as more and more women enter an occupation, there may be a tendency to value (and reward) that occupation less and less.

Do Women Earn Less Because They Work Less?

Women are more likely than men to work part-time. However, most gender wage comparisons leave out part-time workers and focus only on full-time, year-round workers. A close look at the earnings of women and men who work 40 hours or more per week reveals that the wage gap may actually widen as the number of hours worked increases. Women working 41 to 44 hours per week earn 84.6% of what men working similar hours earn; women working more than 60 hours per week earn only 78.3% of what men in the same time category earn (Source: Bureau of Labor Statistics). Furthermore, women may work longer to receive the promotions that provide access to higher pay. For example, among school principals, women have an average of 3 years longer as teachers than men do (Source: National Center for Education Statistics). So it is hard to argue that women's lower earnings are simply a result of women putting in fewer hours per week, or even fewer years than men.

Is the Wage Gap Closing?

The U.S. Census Bureau has made available statistics on women's and men's earnings for several decades. By examining this time series of data, it is possible to get a feel for the changes and trends in earnings. One thing revealed by a simple visual examination of the series since 1960 is how closely the shapes of the two lines parallel each other. The dips and bumps in women's and men's earnings seem to move in tandem. Clearly, similar economic and social forces are at work in influencing the rise and fall of earnings for both sexes. Men's earnings do not stand still and wait for women's to catch up.

Another thing that is apparent is that there is some minor fluctuation in the size of the wage gap. For example, the gap widened in the 1960s, closed a little in the 1980s, and widened slightly in the late 1990s. Thus, depending on which chunk of years one examines, it may be possible to conclude that the gap is either widening or narrowing. The only way to get a clear picture of what is happening is to examine the whole series rather than a few years at a time.

The series of data points from 1960 onward provides a basis for a forecast of the future, although such forecasts are always estimates rather than hard certainties. When we used forecasting analyses to project the earnings of women and men into the future, to the year 2010, we found no evidence on which we could base a prediction for a closing (or widening) wage gap. The forecast was, in essence, for the two lines to remain parallel, although the 90% confidence intervals (the range within which we are 90% certain the actual future earnings will fall) do overlap a little.

A Question of Value

As women and men left their jobs this spring because they were called up for military duty, employers scrambled to make sure that these workers did not suffer losses of salary and benefits. In a number of cases, organizations made up the difference between their employees' military pay and their normal pay, held jobs open, and made sure that benefits continued during workers' absence. At the same time, the media made a hero out of a father who chose to ship out with his military unit rather than stay home with his infant son who was awaiting a heart transplant. The message about what we as a society consider important is clear:

- When something perceived as very important needs to be done out-side of the workplace, employers feel obligated to provide support for their employees to go and do it.
- In the eyes of society, or at least many employers, family concerns and the care of children do not fall into the category of "very important"—certainly not as important as military duty.

Are these the values we want to live by? If women and men continue to accept the notion that the domestic and caretaking work traditionally classified as "women's work" is not important enough for employers to accommodate, the gender gap in wages will never close. A few individual women may be able to evade the gap by choosing to be childfree, being fortunate enough to have a supportive spouse, and carefully following a model of career advancement that was developed to fit men's needs. However, to make the wage gap disappear will require that we stop buying into the idea that the rules are gender-neutral and that men just follow them better than women do. One by one, employers must be convinced to re-examine assumptions that unwittingly place higher value on the type of work men do than on the type of work women do. The most important step in closing the wage gap is for all of us to give up the notion that, to be paid fairly, a woman must "make it in a man's world."

Blaming Women's Choices for the Gender Pay Gap

A 2006 article in the *New York Times* cited Labor Department statistics that, for college-educated women in middle adulthood, the gender pay gap had widened during the previous decade. The phenomenon was attributed partly to discrimination, but also to "women's own choices. The number of women staying home with young children has risen . . . especially among highly edu-cated mothers, who might otherwise be earning high salaries."

A 2007 report from the American Association of University Women sounded the alarm about a continuing wage gap that is evident even in the first year after college graduation. The authors noted, however, that individual choices with respect to college major, occupation, and parenthood have a strong impact on the gap. Accepting the idea that much of the pay gap can be accounted for by such neutral factors as experience and training, they concluded that, in the first year after college graduation, about 5 percent of the pay gap is unexplained by such factors—and it is that 5 percent that represents the impact of discrimination.

The language attributing women's lower pay to their own lifestyle choices is seductive—in an era when women are widely believed to have overcome the most serious forms of discrimination and in a society in which we are fond of emphasizing individual responsibility for life outcomes. Indeed, it is possible to point to a variety of ways in which women's work lives differ from men's in ways that might justify gender differences in earnings. Women work in lower-paid occupations; on average they work fewer paid hours per week and fewer paid weeks per year than men do; their employment is more likely than men's to be discontinuous. As many economists with a predilection for the "human capital model" would argue, women as a group make lower investments in their working lives, so they logically reap fewer rewards.

At first blush, this argument sounds reasonable. However, a closer look reveals that the language of "choice" obscures larger social forces that maintain the wage gap and the very real constraints under which women labor. The impact of discrimination, far from being limited to the portion of the wage gap that cannot be accounted for by women's choices, is actually deeply embedded in and constrains these choices.

Do Women Choose Lower-Paid Occupations?

Women continue to be clustered in low-paid occupational categories: office and administrative support and various service jobs. While they now make up a majority of university students, they are concentrated in academic specialties that lead to lower paid occupations: education rather than engineering, for example. If women persist in choosing work that is poorly paid, shouldn't the responsibility for the wage gap be laid squarely at their own doorstep?

Actually, within groups graduating with particular academic majors, women earn less than men, as illustrated in the AAUW report cited above. And within occupational categories, women earn less than their male counterparts, as revealed in this chart.

Furthermore, there is a catch-22 embedded in women's occupational choices: the migration of women into an occupation is associated with a lowering of its status and salary, and defining an occupation as requiring stereotypically masculine skills is associated with higher prestige, salary, and discrimination in favor of male job applicants. So convincing women in large numbers to shift their occupational choices is unlikely to obliterate the earnings gap.

As well, using the language of choice to refer to women's career outcomes tacitly ignores the many subtle constraints on such decisions. From childhood

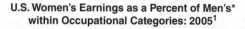

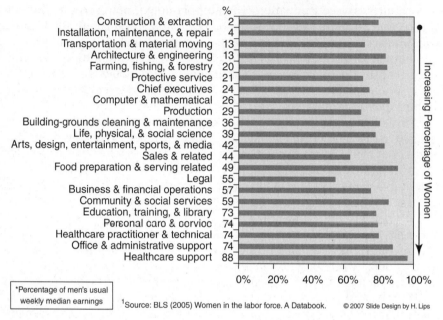

U.S. Women's Earnings as a Percent of Men's* within Occupational Categories: 2005[1]

Occupational Category	%
Construction & extraction	2
Installation, maintenance, & repair	4
Transportation & material moving	13
Architecture & engineering	13
Farming, fishing, & forestry	20
Protective service	21
Chief executives	24
Computer & mathematical	26
Production	29
Building-grounds cleaning & maintenance	36
Life, physical, & social science	39
Arts, design, entertainment, sports, & media	42
Sales & related	44
Food preparation & serving related	49
Legal	55
Business & financial operations	57
Community & social services	59
Education, training, & library	73
Personal care & service	74
Healthcare practitioner & technical	74
Office & administrative support	74
Healthcare support	88

Increasing Percentage of Women

*Percentage of men's usual weekly median earnings

[1]Source: BLS (2005) Women in the labor force. A Databook.   © 2007 Slide Design by H. Lips

onward, we view media that consistently portray men more often than women in professional occupations and in masculine-stereotyped jobs. Not surprisingly, researchers find that the more TV children watch, the more accepting they are of occupational gender stereotypes. Why does the acceptance of gender stereotypes matter? Gender-stereotyped messages about particular skills (e.g., "males are generally better at this than females") lower women's beliefs in their competence—even when they perform at exactly the same level as their male counterparts. In such situations, women's lower confidence in their abilities translates into a reluctance to pursue career paths that require such abilities.

So, there are many problems with treating women's occupational choices as based purely on individual temperament and as occurring within a static occupational system that is unaffected by such choices. Women's employment choices are systematically channeled and constrained—and when women elude the constraints and flow into previously male-dominated jobs, the system apparently adapts to keep those jobs low-paid.

If Women Chose to Work More Hours, Would They Close the Gap?

Women work fewer paid hours per week than men do, but among workers who labor more than 40 hours per week, women earn less than men. Indeed, among workers working 60 hours or more per week at their primary job, women earned only 82% of men's median weekly earnings in 2006. Furthermore, women do not necessarily choose to work fewer hours than men do. One researcher found that 58% of workers want to change their work hours in some way—and that 19% of women report they want the opportunity to work more hours. Also, women have recently brought lawsuits against corporations such as Boeing and CBS claiming discrimination in access to overtime. Thus, in the realm of hours worked for pay, it is probably a mistake to use the number of hours worked as a simple indicator of women's (or men's) choices. As in the case of occupational segregation by gender, the number of hours worked reflects some systematic constraints.

Choosing Parenthood Means Lower Wages Only for Women

For women, having children has a negative effect on wages, even when labor market experience is taken into account. This may be due to mothers' temporary separation from the workforce and/or the loss of the benefits of seniority and position-specific training, experience, and contacts. Among married persons working full-time, the ratio of women's to men's median weekly earnings is 76.4% for those with no children under the age of 18, but only 73.6% for those with children. And when women and men of all marital statuses are considered together, women with children under 18 earn 97.1% of what women without children earn, whereas men with children under 18 earn 122% of what men without children earn.

So, the choice to have children is associated with very different earnings-related outcomes for women and men. In terms of children, it is not that women and men are making different choices, but that the same choices have very different consequences for the two groups. Those consequences reflect society's failure to value the work of parenting. Yet, if most women decided to forego motherhood, the declining birthrate already causing concern in some parts of the developed world would soon become catastrophic.

Women's Choices Are Not the Problem

Individual women can sometimes evade the effects of the gender pay gap by making certain kinds of choices, such as selecting male-dominated occupations, working more hours, avoiding parenthood. However, these choices occur in an environment suffused with subtle sexism and discrimination: there are more barriers for women than for men to making certain choices, and the consequences of some choices are starkly different for women and men.

Moreover, these individual solutions are not effective on a societal level; they work only if the women enacting them remain in a minority. For example, if most women moved into jobs that are now male-dominated, signs are that the salaries associated with those jobs would likely drop. But, by making it difficult to go against the tide, the forces of discrimination ensure that most women don't move into such jobs. And as long as a few women get past the barriers, the illusion persists that any woman could do it if she wanted to—it's a matter of free choice. However, women's choices will not be free until their abilities and their work are valued equally with men's, and until women and men reap equivalent consequences for their choices in the realm of work and family.

EXPLORING THE ISSUE

Is the Gender Wage Gap Justified?

Challenge Questions

1. Is it possible for women's and men's labor to be equally valued?
2. Are women by nature less ambitious, less competitive, less assertive, and as a consequence less effective laborers and leaders?
3. To what extent do women and men have true career choices?
4. How do race, ethnicity, and class affect career choices?

Is There Common Ground?

The irony of the mommy track–fast track debate had its basis on the assumption that women have a choice regarding work. In fact, most women have no choice. They are either single parents or part of a family that needs two paychecks to meet the family's financial needs. Thus, for large numbers of working women, this was a meaningless debate. Choice is reserved for the educational elite, according to Mary Blair-Loy in *Competing Devotions*. Rather, the debate served to perpetuate stereotypes regarding women's commitment to family over work. The reality is that most working women have little control over the hours they work. Indeed, for the lowest income jobs, working hours are not family-friendly hours. Consider the schedules of waitresses and housekeeping staff, for example. It is worth noting that the family–career conflict that is receiving so much attention currently is in fact a rather current phenomenon. Claudia Goldin (2004) has suggested that this "conflict" has changed over time. For women graduating from college in the early 1900s, the choice was clear: family or career. From 1920 to 1945, many women opted for a "job then family" model. From about 1946 to the 1960s, the pattern was reversed to "family then job." In the late 1960s, the language shifted from "job" to "career," with a pattern of "career then family" dominating through the 1980s. Since then the trend has been toward "career and family." Goldin contends that these shifts have been possible due largely to increased career opportunities for women, especially white collar jobs, with improved contraceptive methods also making it easier for women to control their fertility. Some scholars have suggested that it is the issue of caregiving that needs to be rethought in our society. If society as a whole were committed to the well-being of children, then conceptualizations of child care might well rest on a foundation of shared community support, freeing up all parents to provide quality care to their children. No longer would the parent who wants/needs to stay home with a sick child or attend preschool graduation be looked upon as less than the ideal worker. A shift in perceptions of who is responsible for child care is necessary in order for women to gain more equality in the workforce and to have their labor judged by the same criteria as those of men.

ISSUE 16

Has the Economic Recession Been Harder on Women's Employment Than Men's Employment?

YES: **Government Equalities Office**, from "The Economic Downturn—The Concerns and Experiences of Women and Families" (March 2009), http://www.ipsos-mori.com/researchpublications/researcharchive/2359/Impact-of-the-economic-downturn-on-women.aspx

NO: **Teri Fritsma**, from "Minnesota's He-Cession: Are Men Bearing the Brunt of the Economic Downturn?" *Minnesota Economic TRENDS* (September 2009), http://www.positivelyminnesota.com/Data_Publications/Economic_Trends_Magazine/September_2009_Edition/Minnesota%27s_He-cession.aspx

---

Learning Outcomes

As you read the issue, focus on the following points:

- Has the recession been equally harmful for women and men?
- Have the effects of recession been similar across all ages, races, ethnicities, and social classes?
- What are the indicators of being affected by the economic downturn?
- What is the role of regional and national differences in understanding the effect of the economy on families?

ISSUE SUMMARY

YES: The Government Equalities Office presents data suggesting that women are experiencing more challenges than men due to the economic recession.

NO: Teri Fritsma, in an analysis of data based on employment patterns in Minnesota, suggests that men are being more negatively affected by the recession than are women.

Historically, poor women have always worked, perhaps as a housekeeper or a nanny or a seamstress in a sweatshop. In recent U.S. history, women were most likely to enter the workforce in masses during times of war. Their presence was needed to compensate for the lack of male laborers. Rosie the Riveter became the patriotic role model. However, after each of the two major world wars, women were encouraged to return to their rightful place in the home with as much enthusiasm as they had been encouraged to leave the home. Suzi Homemaker became the new cultural icon for women. Issues of women's equal treatment in the workplace did not really come to the forefront for debate until large numbers of women entered higher education and participated in the civil rights movement and the antiwar movement of the 1960s. The second wave of the women's movement was the result. Many believed that as more women obtained more education and began to climb the career ladder, gender inequities would begin to dissipate. However, although in 40 years there has been progress at the entry level for women, women at the top find themselves in a minority. Ironically, during the 2008–2009 recession, men held 78 percent of the jobs lost. As a result, women may actually be faring better by comparison. But are they? Women now hold almost 50 percent of all jobs today (compared to 36 percent 40 years ago). But once again, in the words of Lisa Belkin, "The history of women in the workplace (both their leaps forward and then slips back) is a reaction to what was happening to men." Women currently are returning to the workforce because they have to and they are cheaper to hire than are men. The glass ceiling has not been broken. Some have suggested that women no longer "want it all"—career and family; rather, women are willingly choosing to opt out of the fast-paced, competitive rat race to be stay-at-home moms. There is evidence that some women with advanced degrees from some of the most prestigious institutions in the United States have done this. However, these women are married to highly successful men who generate enough income to maintain an upper-middle-class lifestyle. Other women have opted out of the corporate race to the top because they realized they were not going to break through the glass ceiling. Women are a fast-growing group to start their own businesses. However, such examples ignore the fact that the vast majority of people (women and men) do not have the resources to begin their own businesses, nor can they maintain a comfortable lifestyle without two incomes; and for single mothers, it is not a question of lifestyle but a matter of survival. Economists have evaluated the notions of the mommy track and the fast track (see Issue 15). The mommy track had originally been proposed as a career path that recognized women's role as child-bearers; the idea was that a woman's career trajectory would be adjusted to allow for this reality without jeopardizing her chances of advancement. It did not work. Such a choice by women has resulted in subtle discrimination. A self-fulfilling prophecy occurred. An employer is more likely to put a male than a female employee on the fast track, believing that he will not be distracted by child-care responsibilities like a female employee. As a result, effort rather than talent is being rewarded. The man is expected to be on the fast track and to put forth more effort than his partner who is on the mommy track. Only permanent changes in public policy will remove the discrimination.

In the current economic climate, it is necessary to consider a host of factors that likely interact with gender to understand fully the impact of the downturn. For example, one recent analysis suggested that both older employed women and men who have an employed spouse have more financial capability (i.e., making ends meet and managing money) than other groups of individuals; young, currently unemployed adults have the least capability. Furthermore, the economic climate affects factors other than financial capability. For example, in a recent 2008 *Journal of Men's Health* article, Siegfried Meryn of the International Society of Men's Health reported that the economic downturn is taking a serious toll on men's health, especially men of color. He noted that men's mortality is higher than women's and that decreases in health budgets will only exacerbate the health problems that are emerging.

Because we are currently in the middle of an economic crisis, it is difficult to assess its full long-term impact. However, scholars have studied the impact of past economic downturns and have findings that may offer insights into the current situation. Sociologists have suggested that there is typically social and political mobilization in the face of economic restructuring and the household is often the site of the day-to-day coping with economic stress. One study of farm families in the Midwest during the 1980s observed that women exerted a more radicalizing influence on their spouses than did men, at least among women who joined political organizations. The study looked at the family as a source of adaptive strategy and found that women were more likely than men to join political activist groups and when they did, it affected their husbands' activism. They stated that "women's distinct roles in farming, household reproduction, and as mediators between household and community suggest that farm women . . . may have a 'moral framework of public life'. . . that differs from men." In a recent *Washington Post* article, Ezra Klein raised the question of women in the current Tea Party movement. Does the study of women, political mobilization, and the economic crisis among Midwestern farmers in the 1980s offer any insight into the extent to which women are welcomed and comfortable in the newest political movement? Only time will tell.

Of importance in the discussion of who is suffering the most as the result of the recession is the question of who is the focus of discussion and what are the criteria for determining a negative impact. For example, the Institute for Women's Policy Research reported that women, and single mothers in particular, have been experiencing the highest rates of financial strain and are having the most difficulties on a day-to-day basis. They noted that these women are recovering from a "mancession." In contrast the Women's Enterprise Task Force, set up in the United Kingdom by the government, found that women were losing their jobs at a slower pace than men. They also found that female entrepreneurs in particular were faring fairly well, did not see themselves as victims, and were not having difficulty accessing financing. Such contrasting reports underscore the importance of paying close attention to which segments of the population and where in the world they are located are being studied before sweeping conclusions can be made. For example, the report in the YES selection suggesting greater hardships on women and families is based on data from Great Britain, whereas the data in the report in the NO selection suggesting a greater negative impact on men is from the state of Minnesota.

YES

Government Equalities Office

The Economic Downturn—The Concerns and Experiences of Women and Families

Background

The Government Equalities Office (GEO) commissioned Ipsos MORI to undertake qualitative and quantitative research on the impact of the economic downturn on women and families. In particular, the research examines how the downturn has influenced women's fears, their finances, working and caring arrangements, family life, future plans and wellbeing. Comparative research was undertaken among men as well, to look for similarities and differences.

The research comprised both qualitative and quantitative elements. The qualitative work consisted of 10 discussion groups (seven among women and three among men) in three locations in England (London, Northampton and Newcastle) in January and February 2009. In addition, two quantitative telephone surveys were administered to representative samples of British adults to test the extent to which the views of participants in the qualitative research were indicative of wider public opinion.

The survey research, or quantitative work, was designed to provide robust data that is representative of the views of the British population as a whole. The focus group work, or qualitative research, is not statistically robust or representative, but rather was designed to illustrate and explore participants' understanding of and reasoning about the issues at hand.

Key Concerns About the Impact of the Downturn

Three-quarters (75%) of British adults were concerned about the impact of the economic downturn on their family life, with 80% of women concerned compared with 70% of men. This is a trend felt throughout this research project, which finds women more concerned than men on a range of subjects, especially those that centre around family and caring. Many women in the discussion groups expressed deep-seated concerns about job prospects, the threat of redundancy for themselves and/or for their partners, and the pressure both on the individual and [on the] household.

From *Impact of the Economic Downturn on Women,* March 2009.

Men in the discussion groups tended to focus primarily on concern about job loss per se, as opposed to overall effect on their family, and were much more expressive on the *causes* of the downturn than on the effects. The discussion groups with men tended to focus more on who to blame for the downturn rather than dealing with the aftermath.

It is important to note, however, that opinions were not universal across group participants, and also that there were notable differences in attitudes between women (and men) of different ages and social grades. It may also be the case that the type of industry an individual works in affects their level of concern about job loss; the group discussions found that people in industries they perceived to be less stable showed more concern about losing their jobs (for example, the service industries).

From the survey, and mirrored by the opinions of discussion group participants, one of the most immediate concerns for the public was losing their jobs, or someone in their household losing their job. A third (33%) of men were worried about unemployment, compared with four in 10 (40%) women. In addition, Ipsos MORI's monthly Issues Index which asks an open-ended question about the most important issues facing the country, shows that in January 2009 public levels of concern about unemployment reached a 10-year high, with 24% of Britons naming unemployment as one of the main issues facing Britain today, an increase of 9 percentage points since December 2008. There was no difference in concern between men and women on this measure.

Participants' other concerns centred around bills and family worries, although these often differed depending on the individual's life stage and socio-demographic profile. Mid-life participants (middle-aged, and often with children), for example, were more concerned with paying their mortgages and the welfare of their children. Many older participants seemed resigned to the recession—some had lived through rationing—and, though they were upset about their (often) reduced income and certainly felt pessimistic about the future, they did not demonstrate the same levels of anxiety and confusion as younger participants who had not lived through a recession before.

Younger participants under age 30 tend to have fewer commitments and thus fewer concerns, but where there was anxiety about their finances, it was associated more with "lifestyle" costs (clothes, the cost of a night out, etc.) rather than concerns about job loss or family members. This group also displayed more confusion and uncertainty about the future, especially when contrasted with the more "resigned" attitudes of the older group participants.

The oldest and youngest participants in the discussion groups seemed to be concerned about each other, but less about themselves. Younger participants often expressed concern for older individuals who lived with fixed incomes, worrying that savings and/or pensions losses would impact adversely on older people's lives. Participants over age 65, while they did feel concern about issues such as loss of personal savings, were also less worried for themselves because they felt that they had previous experience of living with a limited income (living through past recessions), or at least felt themselves more able to adjust to a more limited income. They expressed concern both for people struggling to raise children, as well as for younger generations in general who they felt would experience a real "shock" at the limitations a recession would impose on them (never having experienced one before).

Concerns About Finances

From the quantitative research, the age group most likely to think that their personal financial circumstances would worsen over the coming years were those over age 65, almost half (46%) of whom felt that their circumstances would get worse—compared with a quarter (27%) of those age 16–34 who said the same. This finding was strongly reflected in the qualitative research, where the groups that unanimously and immediately mentioned feeling real effects due to the economic downturn (though not necessarily worrying as much about them) were the older (65+) individuals. These men and women stated that they had felt the effects of the downturn already, in their savings and pensions accounts—and also, as a result, in their ability to pay bills.

When asked about general experiences and worries, concerns such as the price of food and utilities were more frequently mentioned by the female group participants (particularly those over age 25) than the male ones. Participants' concern levels were high enough that they were genuinely cutting back on their spending—some because they needed to financially, while others were doing so pre-emptively because they felt they needed to start saving or cutting back now.

Women with children and/or families, as well as those with caring responsibilities of any kind were among the most worried groups of women. Those who felt more at risk of job losses within the family were especially anxious about issues such as arrears and repossession (although very few were at risk of it at the time the groups were conducted).

Concerns About Working and Caring

Just under half (48%) of men and women said that the downturn has had no effect on their working hours. However, many women—especially those with children or those in part-time work—expressed concern about their jobs and balancing their work lives and home lives.

People with mortgages and/or children to support said that they felt the impacts of the downturn on their family life most strongly. Worries about job security, income and problems at work due to the downturn were all cited as reasons by some people for tension in their family relationships, especially in relationships with partners. Some group participants said their family life had been made more difficult by the need to live within a tighter budget, due to either a decrease in income or an increase in the amount spent on bills.

Many women in the groups felt that the loss of men's jobs would affect their lives deeply, as they and their families were, in many cases, partly or fully dependent on the more significant incomes of their partners. This view was widely held across the groups, although least strongly in the youngest groups and most strongly in the middle-aged groups of women of lower social grades (C2DE).

A number of mothers in the groups noted that their childcare costs were rising. This affected all types of care, both formal and informal, with parents finding nursery and childminders' fees rising, and increasing costs related to informal care, such as the cost of groceries and simple medical supplies. Women whose working hours had increased in the last few months reconsidered care provision in the family, with greater reliance on informal care, such as grandparents and elder siblings.

 **NO**

Minnesota's He-Cession:
Are Men Bearing the Brunt
of the Economic Downturn?

Several recent articles in the popular press have suggested that men are taking it on the chin during this economic downturn. A recent *New York Times* article reported that more than four out of five jobs lost since 2007 were held by men. The executive editor of *The Nation* is blogging about the new gender gap in unemployment, and the *Los Angeles Times* dubbed this a "he-cession."

The current economic slump isn't unique in this regard. Men's job losses have dramatically outpaced women's in each of the last five recessions. What's behind this phenomenon? And do Minnesota patterns parallel the national trends?

The unemployment rate for men and women shows a clear disparity and suggests that men are far more vulnerable to layoffs these days both nationally and in Minnesota. The male and female unemployment rates have both increased over the past year, but while female unemployment rose fairly modestly, male unemployment nearly doubled. Sex differences in unemployment are even more pronounced in Minnesota than they are nationally. Male unemployment in Minnesota rose by 5 percent, while female unemployment edged up by less than 0.5 percent over the past year.

Why is the risk of unemployment so much greater for men? There are probably a combination of reasons, but most analysts and commentators point to one major factor: the employment patterns of men and women. While many men are employed in the hard-hit construction and manufacturing industries, women are more likely to work in the relatively stable government, health care and education services industries. How accurate is this claim and how much can these differences account for the sex gap in unemployment?

No Hard Hats for Women?

A large body of research is devoted to studying sex differences in industry or occupational employment. What this research makes clear is that women and men generally occupy different space in the labor market. And while men frequently benefit from these differences in the form of higher average pay, they also appear to be far more exposed to layoffs during economic downturns.

[In] Minnesota, . . . we see . . . that two male-dominated industries—construction and manufacturing—were responsible for about half of all unemployment claims in March 2009. Meanwhile, the two most female-dominated industries in Minnesota—health care and education services—together made

From *Minnesota Economic Trends*, September 2009.

up less than 5 percent of all UI claims. It's worth noting that there were many industries that didn't fit this pattern. Three heavily male-dominated industries—agriculture, mining, and transportation and utilities—were each responsible for less than 3 percent of unemployment claims, and two industries that are almost 50 percent female (wholesale and retail trade, and information) each accounted for more than 10 percent of UI claims.

The Role of Industry Sex Composition

Suppose you could take all people in the labor market and randomly assign them to industries so that women were just as likely as men to be employed in the hard-hit construction and manufacturing industries. Then imagine you computed a new, hypothetical unemployment rate for women. The difference between that hypothetical rate and the true rate is the share of unemployment that can be attributed to the different industry employment patterns. For example, suppose the true unemployment rate for women and men is 6.5 and 9 percent, respectively. Then suppose the hypothetical rate for women is 8.5 percent. This means that the different employment patterns can account for 2 percentage points, or about 80 percent (2/2.5) of the total gap in unemployment.

As it turns out, this type of "what if" analysis is possible with specialized statistical techniques developed by sociologists studying the labor market. We used this methodological approach for the following analyses to better understand the relationship between men's and women's industry composition and the risk of unemployment. . . .

[Comparing] the true U.S. unemployment rate for men and women from March 2008 through April 2009 [with] the hypothetical unemployment rate for women that would result if they were as likely as men to be employed in the male-dominated sectors of the economy, [we] document, again, that the true unemployment rates for men and women have both risen, with the male rate rising more dramatically than the female rate. However, the hypothetical rate for women from March through September 2008 actually exceeds the true male rate—meaning that if women and men were equally likely to be employed in the hard-hat industries like construction and manufacturing, women's unemployment would actually have been higher than men's by a few percentage points during those months.

Beginning in December 2008, and continuing through April 2009, the true male and hypothetical female unemployment rates merge—meaning that men['s] and women's different employment patterns currently account for the entire gap in unemployment. That is, if we could rearrange people so that women and men were employed in the same industries at the same rate, their unemployment rates would be almost identical.

[A]t the state level, . . . we see that while the male rate has jumped to 10.4 percent since September 2008, the female unemployment rate has barely moved. Furthermore, the hypothetical female rate is consistently about 1 to 2 percent higher than the true female rate. In April 2009, the different employment patterns of men and women in Minnesota accounted for 2.2 percentage points, or just over 40 percent, of the total gap in unemployment. That is, if we rearranged men and women in the labor market so that women's concentration in construction and manufacturing was the same as men's, the male/female unemployment gap would be 40 percent smaller in Minnesota.

Conclusion: Stay Tuned

The analysis above suggests that there are some substantial differences between Minnesota and U.S. patterns. The first difference is the female unemployment rate: While the national female unemployment rate has risen (albeit modestly, compared to men's) the Minnesota female unemployment rate has stayed more or less constant over the last 12 months.

Secondly, the industry employment concentration accounts for essentially the entire unemployment gap at the national level, but it explains only 40 percent of the unemployment gap at the state level.

What can account for these differences? What is unique about Minnesota? Time and space limitations preclude us from answering these questions in this article. . . .

Who Has It Better?

What's clear from this study is that Minnesota men are indeed taking the lion's share of job losses in the recession, primarily because men and women are concentrated in different industries.

What the analysis can't answer, however, is the more subjective question of which sex has it "better" or "easier" these days. It might be tempting to assume from the patterns of job loss that men alone are affected by this recession. Before jumping to that conclusion, however, consider the following:

First, when any member of a household is laid off, the whole household is impacted—and the impact may be greater when the salary lost is the man's. Working women still earn less than men. According to the U.S. Bureau of Labor Statistics, men out-earned women in every age, race, major occupational group and state in 2007. (In Minnesota, the average woman's earnings were 76.9 percent of the average man's.) This means that making ends meet on one woman's salary is likely to prove more challenging for a household or family accustomed to relying on both a male and female salary.

Second, nonworking men and women tend to spend their time in different ways. According to data from the 2003–2006 American Time Use Survey, married fathers who were not employed spent an average of 2.32 hours on housework and 1.26 hours on child care each day. Married mothers who were not employed spent nearly double the time on these same activities: 3.64 hours on housework and 2.48 hours on child care. And full-time working moms? They spent almost as much time as nonemployed dads on household and child care activities (2.05 and 1.22 hours, respectively).

One can always find exceptions to these broad trends—and it's likely that men's and women's salaries and time-use will continue to edge toward parity. Still, it's worth keeping in mind that the women who remain in the labor market during this recession are, on average, working for less money and putting in nearly the same hours at home as their unemployed male counterparts.

EXPLORING THE ISSUE

Has the Economic Recession Been Harder on Women's Employment Than Men's Employment?

Challenge Questions

1. Are there some indicators that suggest a greater impact of the economic downturn on women and some that suggest a greater impact on men?
2. Is it wise to consider factors other than employment status and income in assessing the impact of the economic climate, dimensions such as mental and physical health, educational opportunities, and crime rates?
3. Regardless of whether it is women or men who are more affected, what about the impact on families, and on society?
4. How might gender roles contribute to the effect of the economic downturn?
5. What are the implications of the economic downturn for women breaking the glass ceiling? Will it be easier or more difficult?

Is There Common Ground?

It seems that if one looks hard enough it is possible to find evidence that supports contradictory claims that the economic downturn is harder on women than men and vice versa. However, in reality the sum total of evidence suggests that just about everyone is suffering by some measure, be it economic, psychological, or societal. Overall, according to the Bureau of Labor Statistics as of September 2011, unemployment was just over 9 percent, with real earnings dropping, although there is great variability across region and various demographic categories. Some analysts say these numbers are too low because they do not take into account the huge numbers of people who are underemployed and who are no longer even looking for work because they have just given up. This last point is one of great concern. To the extent that one gives up, the consequences can have cascading negative effects. For example, there is an increased risk of depression, with all the other serious problems that are often associated with this and other serious mental health problems. It has been estimated that the rate of suicide is two to three times higher among the unemployed than the employed. Furthermore, according to the National Institute for Justice, unemployment has been associated with increases in violence, including domestic violence. It has been estimated that the rate of domestic violence is 12.3 percent for men who have been unemployed two or more periods, but only 4.7 percent when employed. The problem is compounded by the finding that lack of money is one of the major reasons a female victim does not leave an abusive partner.

ISSUE 17

Do Social Policies Improve Gender Inequalities in the Workplace?

YES: Hilda Kahne and Zachary Mabel, from "Single Mothers and Other Low Earners: Policy Routes to Adequate Wages," *Poverty and Public Policy* (vol. 2, no. 3, 2010)

NO: Hadas Mandel, from "Configurations of Gender Inequality: The Consequences of Ideology and Public Policy," *The British Journal of Sociology* (vol. 60, no. 4, pp. 693–719, 2009)

Learning Outcomes
As you read the issue, focus on the following points: • Does gender ideology, that is, beliefs about the role of women and men in the family and society, shape public policy, or does public policy shape and reflect societal values regarding gender?   • Should public policies be affected by gender-related issues?   • Are there some policies that increase women's access to entry-level jobs but actually inhibit movement up the employment ladder?   • Are there some policies that increase women's movement up the employment ladder but actually inhibit access to entry-level jobs?   • How relevant to discussions of gender equalities in the workplace is it to focus on employment rates of women in contrast to what women who are employed can accomplish?

ISSUE SUMMARY

YES: In contrast, Hilda Kahne, professor emerita at Wheaton College in Massachusetts, and Zachary Mabel, research analyst with the Center for Education Policy Research at Harvard University, make the argument that incomplete education and few training programs, rather than gender discrimination, make it more difficult for low-age single mothers to raise their earnings. They advocate for policies that foster economic advancement.

NO: Hadas Mandel of the Department of Sociology and Anthropology at Tel Aviv University reviews extensive data from 14 countries and concludes that social policies have the counterintuitive impact of decreasing women's opportunities for access to more desirable and powerful positions. His analyses show distinct profiles of gender inequality and their relations to ideology and public policy.

According to the U.S. Census Bureau, there were an estimated 11.4 million single mothers in the United States in 2005, a number that had increased dramatically in the past 25 years. Approximately 79 percent of them were employed at least part-time. As of 1998, there were an estimated 948,000 teen mothers age 15–19. About five-sixths of all single parents are women. Approximately 42 percent of single mothers have never married. From 1960 to 1980, the rate of divorce doubled, and although the rate has leveled off since, an increasing number of women find themselves in the role of single mother. Children, because they usually live with their mothers, are affected. Approximately two-thirds of divorces involve children and over one-half of children in the United States will experience parents' divorce. For these children, their standard of living declines 30–40 percent, and 25 percent of divorced mothers will fall into poverty within 5 years. Contributing to this poverty is the likelihood of not receiving child support even when entitled to it. Factors contributing to divorce, as well as single parenthood, for women include younger age of marriage, social attitudes more accepting of divorce, cohabitation and single-parenthood, as well as women's greater independence because of more opportunities in the workforce. At the same time, and perhaps ironically, the employment rate for single mothers has decreased from 73 percent in 2000 to 69.8 percent in 2003, and the steepest loss has been for black mothers. Numerous debates surround these numbers. Issues being discussed include teen sexuality and unintended pregnancy as well as marriage initiatives. There is a strong belief among religious conservatives as well as economists that there is a relation between marital stability, job stability, and earnings.

A related controversy surrounds the incidence of conception and childbirth while the mother is a welfare recipient (i.e., "subsequent births"). Traditionally, welfare policies grant monetary benefits to families based on the number of children. Thus, the birth of another child would earn the family increased financial support. Critics charge these women with intentionally having additional children to increase their financial benefit and view them as irresponsible and promiscuous (though, on average, welfare recipients have fewer children than individuals not on welfare). Critics fear that subsequent births will promote long-term dependency on federal aid. The 1996 federal welfare reform law allows states discretion to adopt strategies for inhibiting subsequent births. States have adopted a variety of programs that operationalize supposed solutions to the subsequent birth problem. Efforts include family caps on welfare benefits, enhanced family-planning services, directive counseling (telling mothers they should not have another baby and instructing them in how to prevent pregnancy), and financial incentives for young mothers who do not become pregnant. Additional incentives and programs aimed at keeping women from having additional children and keeping young women from having sex include the "Illegitimacy Bonus," which rewards states that reduce their out-of-wedlock birthrate while also reducing abortion rates for all women, not just those on welfare; the "Abstinence-Only Standard," which offers financial incentives to states that teach abstinence as the expected or only standard; requiring unmarried mothers under the age of 18 to live with their parents; and enforcing child support by performing paternity tests to identify biological fathers and forcing women to turn in fathers of their children or lose benefits, regardless of the risk of physical or emotional harm to the woman or her children. Most controversial are family cap provisions, which preclude a welfare recipient from receiving additional case benefits for a child conceived while the recipient parent was on welfare (albeit the child would be eligible for Medicaid coverage and other benefits). The desired outcome of family cap provisions would be fewer out-of-wedlock births. Supporters of family caps believe that the traditional rule that welfare benefits are determined on the basis of the number of children in a family actually provides a financial incentive to have children while on welfare. Therefore, family caps are implemented to send a message to these women that they should not have more children until they can support them.

Opponents of family caps consider them to be in violation of a mother's right to determine whether or when to have children. Others fear that family caps will increase welfare families' hardship and abortion rates. Interestingly, some evaluation studies of such programs also look for higher abortion rates as an outcome signifying program success. In fact, program evaluation research to date has been underwhelming, resulting frequently in inconclusive or disappointing results. Another criticism is that efforts at the "rational econometric control" of reproduction are ignorant of the complexities involved in becoming pregnant. Typically, two individuals are involved in a social interaction that is not always volitional and often includes an array of pressures. To what degree can reproduction be controlled by incentive pressures? It is also noteworthy that males' role in fertility is largely ignored in programs aimed at reducing subsequent births. Welfare legislation and statistics raise serious questions about gender dynamics and differentials. Why are most welfare recipients women? How is the societal construction of "mother" and "father" related to welfare statistics and policies? How is socioeconomic class associated with women's reproductive rights and freedoms? How do existing gender inequalities contribute to single mothers' low-income status? How does racism amplify the problems for women of color?

In the YES selection, Mandel argues that although policies have indeed increased women's entry into the job market, very often they have failed to give women increased access to higher paying, more attractive jobs. This would suggest that current policies may actually contribute to gender-related inequalities in the world of work. In contrast, in the NO selection, Kahne and Mabel suggest that wage-related social policies should be developed to improve educational and training opportunities for low-wage single mothers, thereby increasing their earning potential. That is, they argue that policy changes can help women overcome gender inequalities in the workplace.

YES    Hilda Kahne and Zachary Mabel

Single Mothers and Other Low Earners: Policy Routes to Adequate Wages

"Things are seldom what they seem," as Gilbert and Sullivan stressed in *H.M.S. Pinafore*, and rarely do they stay the same. And so it is that technological advancements and increasing family life demands over the past several decades have changed the nature and skill requirements of work, and call for new policy approaches to improve the earnings and advancement prospects of single mothers and other low-wage workers. Developers of workforce policies in private enterprise and the public sector are finding ways simultaneously to advance worker skills and earnings, thus raising economic productivity and creating benefits for businesses, employees, and consumers in the form of improved product quality and price.

This paper, based on a broad and extensive literature review, describes the employment environment within which low-wage single mothers and other low-wage earners work. It also examines policy approaches to improve their earning ability so that they can better provide for their families over the course of their working lives. The first section describes the characteristics of low-wage, single-mother families. The second section spells out the labor market aspects that distinguish low-wage jobs from more highly skilled work, and the resulting differentiation in income protection under current unemployment policy. The third section explores longer run influences on job and wage characteristics for low-wage workers. The final section discusses new opportunities to extend and integrate policies that promise to improve worker skills, increase their job continuity, and provide more opportunities for upward career mobility to ensure that single mothers and other low-wage workers acquire family-sustaining earnings and have continuing opportunities for job and wage advancement. Joint public and private sector development of programs can establish resource efficiencies and maximize resulting benefits.[1]

Single Mothers: Changing Family Structures and Single-Mother Characteristics

The family unit is represented in an increasing variety of forms today, a number of which are not yet accounted for in government data.[2] But however it is defined, we can all agree that the concept of "family" is an anchor of our

From *Poverty & Public Policy*, vol. 2, no. 3, 2010. Copyright © 2010 by Hilda Kahne and Zachary Mabel. Reprinted by permission of the authors.

social lives. Although a feminist economic definition of family might focus on attributes of "community," "interdependency," and "the provisioning of goods and services for family use and exchange,"[3] in the United States it is "structure" and relationships that statistically define the family unit. The U.S. Census, for example, perceives family data as a subdivision of household data. According to the Census, a family household consists of two or more persons related by birth, marriage, or adoption who reside together.

In recent years, within the Census category, the proportion of single-parent households with children under age 18 has increased, and in 2009 roughly 53.2% of all single-family householders are also single parents.[4]

A few additional figures will place this proportion in clearer perspective. In 2009, 75% of family households with children under age 18 (own, step, or adopted) were married-couple family households. In that year, 23.5% of family households with such children were maintained by a single mother with no husband present (a rise from 18.6% in 1990), and 5.9% of those households were maintained by a single father with no wife present. In Spring 2008, the U.S. Census estimated there were 11.4 million single-mother households with children under age 21.[5]

Labor force participation of single mothers with children under age 18 has also risen—from 67.9% of the category in 1990 to 76.6% in 2009.[6] In 2009, more than three-fourths of single mothers with children under age 18 were members of the paid labor force.

By way of contrast, the U.S. Bureau of Labor Statistics uses the term "single" to describe women in several different situations. The term is some-times used to refer to single women (with and without children), sometimes it applies to single mothers with one or more children (including step or adopted children), and sometimes it applies to single-female householders (who may or may not have children).[7] If a single mother with children is living in her mother's home, she may be excluded from a single-family head accounting.[8] Thus, to understand the work environment experienced by single mothers, a discussion about families with female heads must be carefully defined and described.

A demographic portrait of single mothers is provided by two studies, based on a national sample of mothers who had children under age 18. What follows is a description of some of the findings about them in the year 2000.[9] The first study compared the demographic characteristics of a sample of married and single mothers between the ages of 18 and 44. Data showed that in 2000, mothers who were single were more likely than married mothers to be between the ages of 18 and 29 (38.8% vs. 20.9%). Almost one-third of single mothers were Black, non-Hispanic (31.9%), compared with 7.8% of married mothers. Interestingly, for both single and married mothers, the number of children in the family (1.7 and 2.0 respectively) and the proportions of children younger than age 18 (81.9% and 79.2% respectively) were similar. There was, however, a major difference in the educational achievement of mothers between the two groups. A higher proportion of single than married mothers reported less than high school completion in their backgrounds (19.9% vs. 11.1%), and a much smaller proportion of single than married mothers were college graduates (9.6% vs. 26.4%). These educational differences help to explain why 35.9% of families headed by a female lived in poverty in 2004, compared with only 7.0% of married-couple families in the same year.[10] As a result of limited educational experience, many single mothers' work lives are disadvantaged by the poor quality of low-skill jobs to which they are confined.

In the second study, characteristics of single-mother welfare and non-welfare recipients also differed.[11] Here the data showed that a higher proportion of the younger cohort (ages 18–29) were welfare recipients compared with the older women ages 30–44 (55.7% vs. 35.7%) and a higher proportion of the younger cohort were Black, non-Hispanic (40.9% vs. 30.3%). For welfare single mothers it was also more common for the youngest child in the family to be under the age of 6 than was true for non-welfare single mothers (69.9% vs. 44.2%). Similar to the first study, educational differences again divided the welfare and non-welfare groups. The highest level of education attained by 77.8% of single-mother welfare recipients was a high school diploma, compared with only 55.8% for non-welfare single mothers. Twice as many non-welfare single mothers (44.2% vs. 22.0%) had received a college degree or spent some time in college compared with single mothers on welfare. Higher educational levels appear to have a strong connection to attainment of higher family income among single-mother households, although by no means is it the sole determining factor. Other factors such as labor market structure and job availability, as well as worker health and other personal characteristics, also play important roles in this determination.

Labor Market Aspects: The Link Between Low-Wage Jobs and Poverty Income[12]

Only a fine dividing line exists between a level of family income adequacy provided by a low-wage job and the need to receive public assistance, either due to the lack of any income or due to inadequate or intermittent family sustainable income. These factors explain why low-skilled single mothers frequently cycle between welfare and low-wage work in an effort to meet their family's financial needs.

Although no single standard defines a low-wage job, empirical studies often use a wage standard that approximates the poverty level as a measure of income adequacy. The federal poverty threshold in 2005 was almost $16,000 for a family with one adult and two children. This estimate does not include actual costs for items such as housing, child care, or out-of-pocket medical expenses, nor does it adjust for regional cost variations.[13] The figure is widely acknowledged to be an inadequate standard of need. It is used, however, as a rough estimate to measure the share of single-mother families who are poor or "near poor." In 2005, 67% of single-mother families had incomes below 200% of the poverty line, a considerably higher proportion than for all families (31%).[14] The National Center for Children in Poverty (NCCP) estimates that, on average, an annual income of $40,000 representing an hourly wage of $19.28 is required to cover all needs of a single-earner family with one pre-school child and one school-aged child, including child care and health insurance.[15] In conceptualizing the magnitude of low-wage work in the United States at present, the Manpower Demonstration Research Corporation (MDRC) notes that in 2005 one quarter of all U.S. workers earned $9.46 or less an hour (just above the official poverty level for a family of four), and fully one half earned less than $14.15 per hour.[16] These low-wage jobs are disproportionately held by women, people of color, non-college educated, and young workers.

Supplementing welfare and low wages, the federal government provides several forms of work-related assistance, including the Earned Income Tax Credit, child care and child health benefits, and food stamps. But poverty, always hovering in the background for low-wage earners, underlies the concern families have about whether income is sufficient to provide food, clothing, healthcare, work transportation, and child care for themselves and their family members.

Employment and Unemployment in Low-Wage Jobs

As Jacob Mincer first demonstrated in the 1970s in U.S. Census studies that related education and on-the-job training to annual earnings, we know that educational attainment is one important factor in determining access to jobs with adequate income, and that lack of education leads some low-skill workers with low educational levels to seek public assistance.[17] But also important for employment is an availability of unfilled jobs with adequate earnings that create a demand for workers.[18] Thus, whether due to the lack of adequate education that limits the supply of labor for skilled work or due to a lack of labor demand, low-skilled workers lose out. They tend to experience more and longer periods of unemployment than do their more skilled counterparts. From 1995 to 2000, with a prosperous economy and a relatively generous level of assistance and supports for low-wage working families, the proportion of single mothers who were employed grew from 61.7% to 73.0%, a gain of 11.3 percentage points. By the end of the decade single mothers were working more hours per year than were married mothers.[19] This trend was reversed, however, by the decline in low-skilled labor demand in the early 2000s.[20]

With the economic reversal that took place at that time, more than one-fourth of the prior employment increase was lost; the overall employment rate of single mothers fell to 69.8%. For Black single mothers the decline was greater than for White single mothers—4.0 percentage points compared with 2.8 percentage points for White single mothers. The overall unemployment rate among single mothers rose from 7.5% in 2000 to 10.2% in 2003. Across all workers the unemployment rate was much lower and increased less. It rose from 4.0% in 2000 to 6.0% in 2003. Single mothers with less education and fewer skills than other workers were much more affected by the recession than were more skilled working parents, college-educated adults, or the population as a whole.[21] Not only was the incidence of unemployment greater for them, but its duration was also longer than for more highly educated and skilled groups. Moreover, the availability of unemployment benefits was often restricted for them either because they failed to meet benefit eligibility requirements or because they exhausted their benefit coverage before securing a new job.[22] As a segment of low-wage workers where the employment rate rose more slowly and began to fall earlier than for other jobs during job market fluctuations, their employment security was more compromised than that of higher earning, more skilled married workers.[23]

Low-Wage Jobs and Unemployment Benefits

Having a desire to be employed does not ensure finding an appropriate job that offers stability and adequate income with no gender wage penalty.[24] Nor does it protect workers against the pitfalls of unemployment. The federal/state unemployment insurance system is designed partially to replace earnings for qualified workers who meet eligibility requirements of engaging in paid work in employment covered by the program but who become unemployed through no fault of their own (i.e., they do not voluntarily leave a job).

Unemployment benefit levels are set by the 50 states and vary widely. Typically, in the past, benefits have replaced about one-half of a worker's past earnings and have provided a maximum benefit length of up to 26 weeks. In recent years, however, volatility of income and employment uncertainty has grown. The annual benefit replacement rate is now close to one-third, not one-half, of past wages. And in 2004, 46% of claimants remained unemployed beyond the maximum benefit time allowed under the state laws.[25] Moreover, permanent job displacement rather than time-limited layoff has become more frequent than in the past, making paid work continuity more difficult to attain.[26]

The situation is even less favorable for low-wage workers than this overall average might suggest—because earnings on which unemployment compensation is based are low, unemployment when it occurs is for longer periods, job turnover is greater than for more skilled workers, and full-time work and employment continuity are less common. Each of these factors can result in reducing eligibility or lowering benefit levels or their duration for low-wage workers. An Urban Institute study found that between 2000 and 2003, single-parent households accounted for 37% of the loss in full-time, full-year employment but received only 8% of the increase in unemployment insurance paid during the period.[27]

Low-wage single mothers must pay attention to both employment characteristics of job continuity and the potential for career progress, while continuing to meet the pressures brought to the many family-related demands on their time and energy. Both workers and employers must accurately judge worker aptitudes and skill growth potential in order to successfully navigate the labor market. Both groups of work participants can benefit from financial and other support as they traverse this rocky road of employment complexities accompanying production decisions relating to company progress.

A Longer Run Perspective

In concluding this discussion of the circumstances affecting the economic well-being of low-wage single-mother families, we take note of some longer run changing trends in the workforce experience of low-wage earners as background for the discussion that follows of new and improved policies to foster sustained income adequacy for this group of single mothers and other low earners over the long run.[28]

Unfavorable Trends Affecting Low-Wage Workers

As we are all aware, the national incidence of unemployment has changed dramatically over the past months. Between 1975 and 1994, for example, it fell on average a little over 7% annually. In 2006, the unemployment rate was 4.6%; it was 4.5% in the early months of 2007. But by the end of 2007, unemployment began to rise, reaching 5.5% in May 2008, and its negative effects were reinforced in some areas by a reduction in working hours.[29] An uncertain and increasingly negative employment outlook beginning in December 2007 and extending into 2010 raises a number of questions about long-term as well as cyclical stability of all jobs, and is being addressed by both public and private sector policies.

Earning trends have also followed a changing trajectory. After rising from the post–World War II period through the early 1970s, the upward trend of real weekly earnings of private sector non-farm, non-supervisory production workers has ceased. This has had negative consequences on wages across sectors in both high- and low-wage occupations, and on the poverty rate, which has held relatively steady since the early 1970s.[30]

The impact of market globalization on production costs, competitiveness, and the inevitable evolutionary changes in technology have added to the negative effects on the labor market and on consumer prices.[31] Moreover, the weakening of protective labor legislation and the decline of trade unions, representing only 12% of American workers in 2006 paying union dues compared with 24% in 1973, has weakened workers' bargaining power and their resistance to downward earnings pressure.[32]

The absence and lag in wage improvement for low earners, despite rising economic productivity since 2001, spurred by technological advances and increased computer use at work, has gradually contributed to another worrisome change—an increase in inequality in income distribution with further negative consequences for the least well off in society.[33] Although the economy's real output in relation to its total labor input has risen in the recent past (i.e., rising productivity), providing the potential for a higher standard of living for those who have contributed to its growth, these benefits have not been equitably shared among all labor market contributors. That is, "the rising tide" (of production) has not "lifted all boats" (income). The innovation and increased efficiency that has occurred has been accompanied by a growing inequality in the distribution of income. Thus, in the 10 years between 1995 and 2005, annual productivity growth measured almost 2.5% higher than in the 20 years that preceded it.[34] But the positive effects of productivity growth on the relative distribution of income after taxes, especially since 2002, have been reflected in gains accruing disproportionately to higher income earners but much less to low-wage workers in jobs where many of the improvements in information and communication technology have actually taken place.[35]

The combined effect of these factors has been that after-tax income has risen more since 1929 for the highest income groups than for the lowest and middle earners.[36] In 2004, for example, the poorest 20% of all families received only 4% of aggregate family income in the country, while the top 5% received 20.9%.[37] Concentration of income continued, and by 2006 income concentration for the top 1% was at its highest level since 1928.[38] A lack of sharing in the reported productivity gains that have been generated by all labor force participants has serious negative consequences for societal well-being. And, as stated by Ben Bernanke, Chair of the Federal Reserve Board, a lack of visible skills is likely "the single greatest source of the long-term increase in income inequality."[39]

In summary, single mothers and other low-wage workers have often been a casualty of a labor market buffeted by trends of an uncertain and changing economy.[40] With limited skills they have lost out in sharing the benefits of rising worker productivity. Extended availability of education and skill training support for low-earning single mothers and others with minimal skills could help reverse this trend while simultaneously improving productive business efficiency as well as consumer product satisfaction.

Some Heartening Signs

But despite these worrisome trends affecting low earners, there have also been a few heartening signs of improved policies and trends. Important progress moving low earners towards self-sufficiency has occurred, for example, with the raising of the federal minimum wage in May 2007 from $5.15 per hour, which, at that time, was only two-thirds of the federal poverty level for a family of three with one full-time worker, and less than one-third of the average hourly wage for private sector non-supervisory workers. The current minimum hourly wage is now $7.25, reached in three period raises on July 24, 2007 (from $5.15 to $5.85), on July 24, 2008 (from $5.85 to $6.55), and on and after July 24, 2009, when the wage became $7.25/hour.[41] Because of their low wages, single mothers particularly benefit from the recent increases in the minimum wage.[42]

Moreover, a recent stirring of employment gain and stimulation of production provide optimism about improvement in the economy in the near future. Labor economists Holzer and Lerman foresee increased growth in demand for some "middle-skill" jobs that require post–high school education, though not necessarily receipt of a four-year college degree, that offer career opportunities and higher wages reflecting a higher level of worker productivity.[43] The next sections describe specific private and public sector programs and the positive benefits that can result from their implementation for workers, employers, and our society as a whole.

New Policy Approaches to Enhancing Adequacy and Advancement

Disappointing economic gains achieved by low-wage single mothers through existing workforce policy call for new approaches to improve their economic and advancement prospects, and at the same time ensure greater productivity and efficiency for employers. It is worth noting also that although policy improvements are discussed within a frame of family and work needs of low-wage single mothers, they are relevant for all low earners whose work skills can also benefit from skill-enhancing programs that meet the challenges and needs of an evolving society.[44]

We conclude this paper with a series of suggestions for improving American workforce policy to benefit low-wage single mothers and other low earners while maintaining high levels of productivity in the American economy.

The Path Dependency of Policy Development

Critical to any assessment of prospective policy development is understanding that new approaches are constrained by established political and cultural foundations. The historical context within which policy exists limits the degree to which new approaches can dramatically diverge from past policies. This notion of "path dependency" dictates that new strategies must build upon the core values of earlier policy to ensure political feasibility.[45]

It is important to understand the cultural and political context surrounding the existing employment and training services available to single mothers in order to understand the specific constraints to change in the workforce arena. Two key lessons emerge from the history of workforce development policy. First, public institutions in the United States responsible for addressing labor force issues have not adequately promoted training and advancement activities to benefit low-wage earners.[46] This is partly because workforce policy in the post–World War II era assumed that most workers would hold one stable, full-time job over the course of their career, and would gain access to career and economic advancement opportunities through their employer. Changes in the economy over the past several decades have changed the nature of the traditional employment contract by making long-term employment with one firm an anomaly. As a result, employers today are often reluctant to assume responsibility for the provision of vocational training when workers are unlikely to remain employed with the particular firm over the course of their lifetime.[47]

Secondly, new workforce policy is constrained due to the questionable outcomes generated by large-scale public job training programs to date. Indeed, critics of public workforce efforts can point to over 40 years of outcomes from earlier national workforce programs—including the Vocational Rehabilitation Act of 1973, the Job Training Partnership Act of 1982, and the Workforce Investment Act (WIA) of 1998 (in its first nine years of implementation)—that had negligible effects on increasing the household incomes of low-wage workers and alleviating their severe economic hardship.[48] Although past results do not legitimize calls to redirect federal funds away from public workforce programs, the history of public financing in the United States tells us that, all too often, politicians are inclined to curtail public spending on job training efforts in order to focus funds on competing national priorities.[49] The harsh reality is that these employment and training programs have often borne the brunt of cost containment efforts, especially when sizeable budget deficits have demanded stringent prioritization of federal resources. New policy approaches will need to address critics' doubts by providing sufficient evidence that future public employment and training initiatives will diverge from previously weakened programs.

The factors discussed above significantly affect future workforce policy changes in the United States. No doubt, the public sector must play a formidable role in the development and implementation of future workforce policies. Government, after all, is best positioned to establish career advancement as a national priority and allocate targeted federal resources to achieve this goal. Nevertheless, some policymakers are reluctant to expand existing public programs to increase the mobility prospects of low-wage earners.

In response to the current political landscape, leaders in the workforce development arena are turning to policy approaches that couple the expertise of government and the private sector to implement effective employment and training efforts. This focus on public/private collaboration has increased government contracting with nonprofit organizations and for-profit service providers to respond to gaps in social provision where the public sector has not responded adequately. Current trends suggest that new workforce policies promoting career advancement for single mothers will likely take the form of public/private partnerships, through which private actors will be required to play a leadership role in both securing resources and providing direct services for such use.

The Role of Workforce Intermediaries

The growing demand for private sector involvement in the U.S. social policy arena creates opportunities for workforce intermediaries to provide career advancement services to single mothers at greater scale nationwide. Workforce intermediaries are private and nonprofit organizations whose primary mission is to create long-term career advancement opportunities for low-skilled workers, while also increasing business productivity. In this capacity, workforce intermediaries serve two distinct clients—low-wage workers and employers. Effective intermediaries obtain high-impact results by (1) identifying targeted job opportunities with employers in high-wage sectors, (2) providing workers with a range of basic job readiness training as well as occupational skills, (3) providing ongoing counseling services to help individuals manage their competing family and work obligations, and (4) connecting workers to job retention services and income-enhancing work supports such as the Earned Income Tax Credit, affordable health insurance, and child care subsidies.

As of 2004, it was estimated that over 250 workforce intermediaries were in operation throughout the United States.[50] One example of an intermediary with proven outcomes around career and economic advancement is the Milwaukee-based Wisconsin Regional Training Partnership (WRTP). The WRTP has developed an innovative training program that links low-wage workers to employers in Milwaukee's high-growth manufacturing sector. The WRTP also operates career advancement programs in construction, healthcare, hospitality, technology, transportation, and utilities. It focuses its efforts on developing occupational training programs that leverage expertise from the business community, while also servicing the job retention and advancement needs of low-income and unemployed jobseekers. As a result of its efforts, the WRTP has recruited 125 employer partners into its collaborative partnership. Between 1995 and 2000, these businesses contributed more than $100 million towards education and training, thereby creating 6,000 new jobs and placing 1,400 low-income residents into employment with starting wages of at least $10 per hour and fringe benefits, including health insurance and pensions. As a testament to the success of the WRTP's program model, in just their first year of work after completing training, program participants experienced an average annual earnings increase of 155%, from $9,000 to $23,000 in household earnings per year.[51]

Despite the results achieved by the WRTP and others over the past decade, workforce intermediaries remain largely localized entities and receive limited public resources to support their efforts. The emphasis that these organizations place on assembling partnerships with institutions across the public and private sector, however—including low-skilled workers, the business community, educational institutions, and government agencies—positions them to assume a greater degree of responsibility in developing effective training programs on behalf of single mothers.

Of critical importance, the focus workforce intermediaries pay to career advancement and business development stands in stark contrast to the traditional work-first policies advanced by current workforce policy.[52] Workforce intermediaries go beyond placing low-skilled workers in entry-level jobs by maintaining long-term contact with their clients to ensure that they advance along career and earnings trajectories. The effectiveness of their long-term engagement practices is proven. Survey results from the National Network of Sector Partners' (NNSP) 2002 analysis of 243 workforce intermediaries found that over half of all low-wage workers served by workforce intermediaries earned over $9.50 per hour (equivalent to $20,000 per year in earnings when employed continuously in a full-time job throughout the year) in their first job after participating in workforce intermediary advancement programs, and nearly one-third of clients earned over $11.00 per hour (equivalent to $23,000 per year in earnings when employed continuously in a full-time job throughout the year).[53] Comparatively, the average low-wage worker in the United States without access to workforce intermediary services earns between $5.15 per hour and $7.50 per hour (equivalent to $11,000 and $15,500, respectively, per year in earnings when employed continuously in a full-time job throughout the year). Although workers' earnings may fluctuate annually given the strength of the economy, it is estimated that fewer than 30% of low-wage workers advance enough over time to regularly earn more than $15,000 per year.[54]

That intermediaries significantly improve the advancement prospects of single mothers is not the complete story. These organizations also strengthen the competitiveness of the business community by encouraging economic efficiency, productivity, and growth. Employers working with workforce intermediaries reap several benefits from the partnership. First, employers looking to fill job slots gain access to a new source of skilled job applicants, thereby reducing recruitment costs. Over the next decade and beyond, many employers are expected to encounter difficulties hiring qualified applicants for "middle-skill jobs" that require some education beyond high school but less than a college degree, largely due to the impending retirement of baby boomers and their replacement in the labor force by currently under-skilled and undereducated immigrant workers.[55] Education and training efforts spearheaded by workforce intermediaries can create a new pipeline of middle-skilled workers that employers will rely on to remain competitive in the global economy. Additionally, workers connected to intermediaries often have access to supportive services that increase their job retention rates, thereby reducing employers' costs related to job turnover. Employers are also eligible for special tax credit savings that reduce their overall operational costs when hiring low-wage workers. These gains provide a real opportunity for workforce intermediaries to garner increased support from the business community and government. Recognizing that the benefits attributed to improving the advancement prospects of low-wage workers may resonate less in the ears of some policymakers than those associated with strengthening the economy, increased efforts must be taken to publicize the positive impact of workforce intermediaries on employers' bottom-line results. With this information more widely disseminated, policymakers can reconcile the seemingly contradictory demands of successfully building skills and income among low-wage workers, while also enhancing long-term economic growth and productivity.

Policy Recommendations

Public Finance Reform and Tracking

There are several steps policymakers can take to increase the scope and impact of workforce intermediaries. First, they can allocate more federal funding specifically for the purposes of educating and training low-wage workers. Despite current fiscal constraints, it is imperative that federal and state agencies maintain current levels of funding for workforce development, regularly increase those levels to compensate for inflationary effects, and authorize a growing portion of such funds for the provision of career advancement services to single mothers.

To ensure that workforce intermediaries achieve greater scale and leverage the resources of the private sector, the federal government could require that all public grants receive matching private sector support. For every dollar of public funds allocated to workforce intermediaries, for example, the federal government could require a one-dollar matching contribution from private foundations, $2.50 from employers, and $0.50 in participant tuition fees. In this example, one dollar of federal support would yield an additional $4 in private sector investment, with a majority of private resources coming from employers that stand to benefit directly from an increased investment in low-skilled workers. If the federal government were to appropriate $100 million for such an initiative, a $500 million fund would be created to increase the scale and impact of workforce intermediaries across the country. Based on the out-comes generated by WRTP to date, this $500 million fund would likely enable over 7,000 low-wage workers to secure employment paying $10 or more per hour, and create 30,000 new jobs across the country.[56]

In addition to public finance reform, the federal government should establish more uniform funding and tracking measures across the disparate public workforce funding sources. Aligning these requirements will provide workforce intermediaries and other service providers with greater freedom to develop career and economic advancement initiatives that provide low-wage workers with a continuum of services essential to securing advancement.

Private Sector Reform

The private sector can also play an active role in developing the capacity of workforce intermediaries. National and regional foundations dedicated to advancing opportunities for single mothers can provide workforce interme-diaries with a larger share of funding for organizational capacity-building purposes, thereby fostering innovation in workforce development activities and eliminating advancement barriers facing low-wage workers. These fund-ing sources are critical to intermediaries since government restrictions often disallow the use of public resources for organizational capacity-building. An increased effort on the part of foundations to provide such funding will go a long way towards expanding the number of effective workforce intermediaries nationwide. Lastly, workforce intermediaries themselves should explore fee-for-service financing models to ensure their long-term financial sustainability. Such models could take the form of tuition payments, employer contributions/fees, or union-management training funds.[57] These private sector strategies could supplement available public resources to support career advancement programs.

By developing the capacity of workforce intermediaries to address the nation's high-skilled labor needs, the proposed reform measures also prom-ise to increase business productivity. Increasing the presence of workforce intermediaries nationwide will therefore generate employer efficiencies while simultaneously improving advancement opportunities for thousands of single mothers nationwide.

The Role of Community Colleges

New workforce policy must also promote the role of community colleges in training and educating single mothers. Not only are community colleges seen as a primary component of workforce policy and occupational training, but nationwide the system is designated as the lead agency to provide workforce training in 19 states.[58] Each year community colleges engage 5.5 million stu-dents in higher education, of whom over 40% are students enrolled in non-credit, job-related training programs.[59]

Single mothers who participate in community-college-based occupa-tional training programs gain opportunities to increase their long-term earning capacity. Research has shown that individuals who attend one year of community college experience an average annual income gain of 6% in the year following coursework, and in 2004, workers with at least some college experience earned, on average, 20% more than their counterparts who held only a high school diploma.[60] Even those who attend community college to take remedial education courses tend to become more productively employed than other low-wage workers, with over 50% of students securing midlevel, white-collar, or technical positions and fewer than 10% remaining in unskilled or low-skill work upon course completion.[61] The challenge community colleges face when it comes to promoting career advancement is not how to endow students with marketable skills that yield an increase in earnings potential; rather, the difficulty lies in ensuring that working adults complete their studies so they can reap the earnings gains that result from completion of certificate and degree programs.

Engaging low-wage working adults over the long term to ensure that they complete their course of study is an ongoing struggle. Although the system has little difficulty enrolling students initially, data show that only a slim majority complete their intended coursework. One longitudinal study of high school graduates in 1992 found that by 2000 roughly 60% had not yet received a community college certificate. Those students who entered community college but did not complete requirements for an associate's degree received, on average, only 16% of the necessary credits to obtain a full year's worth of community college credit.[62]

Two major impediments stand out as the primary causes of student attrition—family life responsibilities and the cost of attending college. Nontraditional students make up the majority of students at community colleges, and working adults—especially single mothers—often struggle to find the time to attend classes. Indeed, a majority of students enrolled in occupational training programs at community colleges are adults, aged 24 or older; nearly two-thirds attend school part-time; 80% work at least part-time; and nearly 40% spend more than 11 hours per week caring for dependents.[63] As a result, many of these students do not complete their intended studies due to their family and other life responsibilities. Furthermore, among the student respondents to the 2005 Community College Survey of Student Engagement, 45% reported a lack of finances as a primary reason for possibly not returning to school in the future.[64] Thirty-seven percent and 29% of respondents, respectively, also cited working full-time and caring for dependents as major constraints to continuing their educational pursuits.

Policy Recommendations

Increasing program completion rates among low-wage working adults attending community college requires three key service improvements: (1) more closely integrating community college funding streams to create better structured career pathways for working parents, (2) developing targeted engagement strategies in training programs with high dropout rates, and (3) restructuring the federal financial aid system to make school more affordable.

Integrating Funding Streams

Community colleges struggle to connect their remedial course offerings, such as GED preparation courses, with more advanced education and training programs due to the separate funding silos that support these disparate efforts.[65] Students with greater educational deficiencies, as a result, struggle to advance beyond basic education classes and into more advanced occupational training programs that provide the most potential for economic advancement. By integrating their funding streams, community colleges will be better able to align their service offerings and create more structured pathways for single mothers to achieve career and economic progress.

Portland Community College (PCC) is an exemplary model of a community college that successfully pools its resources to create sequential career-building programs for low-skilled adults. Students at PCC are able to build upon their previous educational investments by transitioning into more advanced career pathway modules, and the program model is designed with multiple entry and exit points to provide working adults with much needed flexibility when pursuing higher education. Similar to the efforts of workforce intermediaries, PCC works closely with local employers in each career pathway module to ensure that the needs of the business community are met, and to ensure that students who have completed a training program and are entering the labor market reap immediate economic payoffs through employment.[66]

Matched Private Support

In addition to integrating funding streams, the federal government and states could also require greater matched private support for community colleges. By leveraging public financing to generate greater private sector collaboration, community colleges will be more likely to build career advancement initiatives into their service offerings. Leveraging the efforts of the private sector through public finance reform will also ensure that community-college-based training and advancement programs specifically address the needs of local employers best positioned to hire participants upon completion of their training.

Developing Targeted Engagement Strategies

To increase program completion rates, community colleges must develop more targeted engagement strategies that address the family/life responsibilities of single mothers. An analysis of the national student-to-counselor ratio at community colleges, which currently stands at 1,000 to 1, indicates that the system today does not allocate enough resources for counseling and supportive services to prevent attrition.[67] Engagement strategies need to be integrated into the design of training programs to ensure that students at high risk of dropout are aware of, and utilize, available school retention services. Additionally, more family services—such as on-site child care services—must be made available to parents attending college to reduce attrition rates. With these supportive services established and made widely accessible, more single mothers will find ways to juggle their many responsibilities and address those barriers to success in the classroom.

Examples of innovative engagement strategies employed by community colleges include the development of academic and family advising to help students with children identify their professional goals; the introduction of career counselors into degree/certification programs to help students make the connection between their academic and professional pursuits; and the provision of specialized faculty training to encourage active and collaborative learning in the classroom.[68] Recent research about performance-based student scholarships, which make financial aid contingent upon maintaining enrollment and/or a minimum grade-point average, also suggests that they can have a large, positive effect on academic achievement among single-mother student populations that face multiple barriers to completing college.[69] Additionally, distance-learning strategies can be employed so that working parents are able to complete their coursework remotely. These measures can further reduce barriers to program completion as a result of parenting or work responsibilities, or poor access to transportation.

Restructuring Federal Financial Aid

College affordability is a critical and growing problem precluding many low-wage workers from attending institutions of higher education. Over the past two decades, the cost of tuition at community colleges has risen by 85%, from $1,227 in 1986 to $2,272 in 2006, largely due to significant decreases in per-pupil state spending on public education.[70] Although student tuition fees have increased over the past 20 years, the federal government has simultaneously adjusted the distribution of federal financial aid to heavily favor loans instead of grant-based assistance. In the 2003–2004 school year, for example, only 21% of the $91 billion in federal financial aid took the form of student grants, whereas loan-based aid accounted for over 70% of total federal assistance.[71] In comparison, grant assistance in 1980 constituted 55% of total federal student aid expenditures; loans stood at only 41%.[72] The result of this distributional shift is that as the cost of higher education rises, students are finding it increasingly difficult to pay for their studies. This issue is of particular concern to single mothers, as they often do not receive grant-based aid because of their part-time student status. In 2000, only 3.5% of working adults attending school less than half time received Federal Pell Grants, the largest form of means-tested grant assistance for low-income students pursuing higher education.[73] The lack of financial assistance available to these students has resulted in the accrual of significant debt, averaging nearly $9,000 for a former community college student.[74] This debt threatens to offset the economic gains single mothers can obtain by enrolling in community-college-based occupational training programs.

Making college-based occupational training programs financially viable for single mothers requires that the federal government allocate more grant-based assistance to those in need. The federal government should also make Pell Grants more widely available to low-income individuals attending school part-time, and to working adults who are enrolled in certificate rather than degree-based programs. At the state level, policymakers should maintain their current levels of appropriation to public institutions of higher education (and adjust them for annual increases in inflation) to counter the trend of rising student tuition. Enacting these measures will make it more likely that students will maintain engagement in training; these strategies may also encourage other single mothers who otherwise might not enroll in school-based training to realize the economic payoffs available to them if they enroll and complete an occupational training program at a local community college.

The Role of Income-Enhancing Work Supports

If the objective of new workforce policy is to ensure that low-wage workers achieve economic adequacy and develop the capacity to attain long-term upward mobility, then the development of effective career advancement initiatives is only part of the solution. Although workforce intermediaries and community colleges can play a significant role in enhancing the employment and earnings prospects of single mothers, they are not, in and of themselves, the consummate solution to increasing opportunities for economic advancement. And although it is true that low-wage workers assisted by workforce intermediaries and community colleges earn, on average, several more dollars per hour than the typical low-skilled worker, a closer analysis of their earnings prospects indicates that they still fall far shy of the estimated $40,000 in annual income needed to attain economic self-sufficiency for a single earner with two children.[75] Given the difficulty single mothers face in achieving economic self-sufficiency, many require further help to increase their skills and earnings.

Integrating existing work supports into structured career advancement programs, and providing facilitated access to these income-enhancing resources, is one way to further buttress family income. Work supports over the past decade have become an integral component of our nation's policy for aiding low-income earners and discouraging long-term reliance on welfare. In conjunction with the passage of welfare reform in the late 1990s, increased availability of work supports—including the Earned Income Tax Credit, food stamps, affordable health insurance, and child-care subsidies—has significantly supplemented the low hourly wages of entry-level, low-skilled work. But despite the fact that greater attention has been paid to work supports over the past decade, low-wage workers are not fully utilizing the supports to which they are entitled. For some programs, such as food stamps and child-care subsidies, fewer than half of all eligible workers access these benefits, and fewer than 10% of workers nationwide access the full range of work supports to which they are entitled.[76] Low take-up is often the result of onerous application procedures, the perceived stigmatization of supports administered through local welfare offices, a general lack of awareness that such resources exist, and concerns among many immigrant populations that they or their children do not qualify for, or may even face negative legal consequences as a result of seeking public assistance.[77]

Encouraging work support utilization in the United States provides a major opportunity to activate existing policy that has been specifically designed to increase the household income of single mothers. Although the benefit package available varies across states and municipalities based on levels of perceived need, in many locations families could double their household income by simply accessing the full range of work supports to which they are entitled.[78] In addition to increasing income, greater benefit utilization also advances the goal of existing workforce policy—namely to empower single mothers to advance on their own accord as productive members of the labor force. Rigorous program evaluations over the past decade have found the most effective career advancement initiatives to be those that connect individuals not only to employment and training, but also to other supportive services and benefits—including income-enhancing work supports that encourage individuals to remain engaged in training and retain a long-term connection to the labor market.[79]

Policy Recommendations

Managing Benefits

Increasing the take-up of work supports will require new strategies that make applying for and managing benefits easier. Significant efforts must also be taken to de-stigmatize work supports so that individuals do not view them as an extension of the welfare system. Both these efforts can be achieved by integrating work supports into the existing structure of One-Stop Career Centers (One-Stops) across the country. One-Stops, established and federally funded through the Workforce Investment Act (WIA), serve as a single point of contact for employed workers and jobseekers in search of job readiness, training, and placement assistance. Specifically, One-Stops were created to ensure that a universal population of workers and jobseekers could easily navigate and access various employment services through one multipurpose agency. As such, they can significantly reduce the level of stigmatization single mothers associate with work support programs, given that the system is designed to serve a broad range of individuals with varying levels of education and skill.

Making work supports available at local One-Stops also promises to increase the take-up of those resources, by enabling individuals to access benefits at a central facility. Presently, workers are often required to apply for different work supports at separate welfare offices. This process is inconvenient at best, and sometimes not even possible for working parents who already struggle with time to manage their work and family obligations, leaving little leftover time to navigate the intricacies of the work support system. Establishing a central work support hub through the One-Stop system can ensure greater efficiency and convenience for single mothers in accessing available resources. To further encourage benefit access, policymakers should also consider utilizing new technologies to centralize application procedures and encourage the bundling of work support programs. For example, the electronic filing of benefits could take place from home, work, or a public library by accessing the

Internet. This would reduce time pressures on overburdened single mothers and other low-wage applicants juggling work and parental responsibilities.

One of the most promising efforts currently being made to bundle career advancement and work support services through the One-Stop system is the Work Advancement and Support Center (WASC) Demonstration Project, developed by MDRC. WASC augments the traditional provision of job readiness and placement services at participating One-Stops by providing low-wage workers with facilitated access to financial work supports and a more targeted job retention and advancement orientation.[80]

Within WASC's program model are innovative service strategies to ensure that program participants increase their household earnings and receive the skills and support necessary to achieve economic adequacy and advancement over the long term. These services include individualized career coaching; employer intervention assistance to deal with participants' job-related problems; assistance with the development of transportation and child-care plans; and facilitated access to community-based organizations with expertise in addressing acute barriers to employment around substance abuse, legal issues, and mental illness. And most relevant to this discussion of bundling work supports and career advancement services, WASC provides low-wage workers with facilitated access to work supports through (1) the development of simplified enrollment and recertification procedures, (2) the dissemination of benefit eligibility information through the WASC income calculator, and (3) the provision of guaranteed child-care subsidies to parents with children.[81]

Early analysis of WASC suggests that the project is enabling low-wage workers to access substantially more integrated services than they would otherwise receive. Although MDRC is still in the early stages of assessing WASC's impact on the advancement prospects of program participants, the demonstration project will provide a better understanding of the best practices policymakers and practitioners can adopt to improve the economic prospects of single mothers and other low-wage earners. Additionally, as a joint public/private initiative, WASC will provide insight for future career advancement initiatives to identify best practices around the development of collaborative partnerships to achieve economic progress on behalf of low-wage workers. If WASC proves successful, more efforts should be taken to replicate the program model.

Conclusion

The number and proportion of single mothers in the labor force is growing, and many continue to work in a low-income category even though three-fourths of them are now members of the paid labor force. If low-wage single mothers are to share more equitably in the gains from rising productivity, they will require greater access to career and economic advancement opportunities through education, marketable skills training, and income-enhancing work supports. Such interventions offer single mothers and other low-wage workers the best opportunities to acquire family-sustaining wages.

There is no doubt that steep challenges exist to implementing new workforce policies that provide greater career and economic advancement opportunities for single mothers and other low-wage workers. Low-wage earners appear to experience low and diminishing rewards for their contribution to productivity growth, more frequent and longer periods of unemployment, less access to fringe benefits, and fewer built-in programs fostering advancement. They are susceptible to the effects of global competition and without training are less resilient than higher earners to the effects of technological change. Collaborative public/private partnerships intended to strengthen business operations and career opportunities would give both workers and management a voice in designing more effective twenty-first-century careers, especially given the fragmented nature of the workforce system in the United States.

Reaching our collective potential requires that the roles of public and private actors be more clearly articulated and integrated. The federal government must identify the strategic goals of advancement to be achieved, and earmark public resources to make the attainment of these targets possible. States and municipalities must ensure that local efforts reinforce these federal priorities. Private sector stakeholders must increase their direct service capacity to provide targeted services where needed, and to fill gaps in the public workforce system that thwart advancement. Such collaboration can help establish a more effective workforce system that strengthens employer efficiency and productivity, while making economic advancement for single mothers and other low-wage workers a national priority.

Notes

1. We focus on only one aspect of single mothers' lives—economic hardship—that underlies many of their activities. Their work also involves emotional support of family members and their physical well-being, household provisioning, as well as everyday caring for and raising of children and providing for their education. Single-parent responsibilities and demands on their time and energies are multiple. See Jacqueline Anderson, Linda Kato, and James Riccio, *A New Approach to Low-Wage Workers and Employers: Launching the Work Advancement and Support Center Demonstration* (New York: MDRC, March 2006).

2. For example, official family data do not regularly report on gay and lesbian families, nor do they report on cohabiting families, although the latter have grown from 3 to 5.5 million between 1990 and 2000. No regular account is taken of the growing number of blended families as a category, not infrequently composed of two or more clusters of stepchildren. Sometimes single mothers and children live in a grandparent household—grandparents are often the parental figures here. "Non-family households" composed of unrelated individuals, a form that has grown twice as fast as family households, sometimes fulfill the role of family.

3. J. Nelson, "On Feminist Definition of Family," work in progress, 2003.

4. U.S. Department of Commerce, Bureau of the Census, *U.S. 2009 Current Population Survey* (Washington, DC: 2010); A. Bakis, personal communication, 2010.

5. Timothy S. Grall, *Custodial Mothers and Fathers and Their Child Support: 2007* (Washington, DC: U.S. Department of Commerce, Bureau of the Census, 2009).

6. U.S. Department of Commerce, Bureau of the Census, *U.S. 2009 Current Population Survey* (Washington, DC: 2009).

7. The Bureau of Labor Statistics estimates that in March 2006, 19% of all families in the United States were maintained by women without spouses, whether or not they had children, an increase from 11% in March 1970. In March 2006, they represented 46% of Black families, 23% of families of Hispanic or Latina ethnicity, 14% of White families, and 12% of Asian families. In that period, the proportion of families maintained by men without spouses also rose—from 2% to 7%. See S.P. Cromartie, "Labor Force Status of Families: A Visual Essay," *Monthly Labor Review* 130, nos. 7 and 8 (July–August 2007): 35–41.

8. K. Kosanovich, C. Gillham, and A. Rizzolo (Economists, U.S. Department of Labor, Bureau of Labor Statistics), personal communication, 2002 and 2010.

9. J. O'Neill and M.A. Hill, "Gaining Ground, Moving Up: The Change in the Economic Status of Single Mothers under Welfare Reform," Civic Reports 34 and 35, Center for Civic Innovation at the Manhattan Institute (July 2001; March 2003).

10. L. Mishel, J. Bernstein, and S. Allegretto, *The State of Working America, 2006–07* (Ithaca, NY: ILR Press, 2006), 285.

11. J. O'Neill and M.A. Hill, "Gaining Ground, Moving Up: The Change in the Economic Status of Single Mothers under Welfare Reform," Civic Reports 34 and 35, Center for Civic Innovation at the Manhattan Institute (March 2003).

12. Much of this paper was drafted prior to December 2007, when the current recession, the longest since World War II, officially began. The unemployment rate, 4.9% at that time, reached 9.7% by the first quarter of 2010, reflecting the severe drop in demand for goods and services. For married mothers, although their labor force participation rate increased between 2007 and 2009 as their job search rate rose, their employment rate fell over the period—from 66.7% to 65.5%—indicating that fewer married mothers had a job. The employment experience of single mothers was less favorable, despite their higher labor force participation rate of 76.5% in 2007. Their participation rate dropped to 75.8% by 2009, probably reflecting the fact that some single mothers had dropped out of the labor force because they could not find work. In 2009, the unemployment rate among single mothers with children under age 6 registered at 17.5% (U.S. Congress, Joint Economic Committee, May 2010). Workers have recently (as of April 2010) been returning to the labor force, and it is hoped that increasing demand for workers will be sustained to provide jobs for the unemployed as well as for new entrants who join the labor force over time. In recent articles (Holzer and Lerman 2007, 2009; Holzer 2010), the authors reinforce their view that some "middle skill" jobs requiring post–high school training but less than a college degree will offer specialization and increased career opportunities at higher earnings for the currently unemployed and new entrants. For a detailed discussion of a range of labor market issues, see H.J. Holzer and D.S. Nightingale, eds., *Reshaping the American Workforce in a Changing Economy* (Washington, DC: Urban Institute Press, 2007).

13. U.S. Department of Health and Human Services (USDHHS), *Report on Low Wages* (Washington, DC: January 2006), 7.

14. R. Blank and B. Kovak, *The Growing Problem of Disconnected Single Mothers* (Madison, WI: Institute for Research on Poverty, Fall–Winter 2007–08).

15. National Center for Children in Poverty, *When Work Doesn't Pay: What Every Policy Maker Should Know* (New York: Columbia University, June 2006).

16. U.S. Bureau of Labor Statistics data quoted in Manpower Demonstration Research Corporation (MDRC), "Climbing the Economic Ladder and Rising Out of Poverty," Issue Focus, October 24, 2006.

17. J. Mincer, *Schooling Experience and Earnings* (New York: Columbia University Press, 1974).

18. H. Boushey and D. Rosnick, *For Welfare Reform to Work, Jobs Must Be Available* (Washington, DC: Center for Economic Policy Research, April 2004).

19. L. Mishel, J. Bernstein, and S. Allegretto, *The State of Working America, 2004–05* (Ithaca, NY: ILR Press, 2005), 326.

20. Ibid., 327–329.

21. A. Sherman, S. Fernstad, and S. Parrott, *Employment Rates for Single Mothers Fell Substantially During Recent Period of Labor Market Weakness* (Washington, DC: Center on Budget and Policy Priorities, June 22, 2004), 2.

22. H. Kahne, "Low-Wage Single-Mother Families in This Jobless Recovery: Can Improved Social Policies Help?" *Analysis of Social Issues and Public Policy* 4 (1): 50–51.

23. J. Bernstein, *Economic Snapshots* (Washington, DC: Economic Policy Institute, July 27, 2005).

24. See E. Murphy and E.J. Graff, *Getting Even: Why Women Still Don't Get Paid Like Men and What to Do About It* (New York: Simon and Schuster, 2005). Also look at F. Blau, "Recent Trends in Women's Earnings," *The New York Times*, December 24, 2006.

25. See W. Vroman, *An Introduction to Unemployment and Unemployment Insurance.* "Low-Income Working Families Brief 1" (Washington, DC: The Urban Institute, 2005). Also check Golden et al., *Framework for a New Safety Net for Low-Income Working Families* (Washington, DC: The Urban Institute, June 2007); J.S. Hacker, *Universal Insurance: Enhancing Economic Security to Promote Opportunity* (Washington, DC: The Hamilton Project, Brookings Institution, September 2006); L.G. Kletzer and H.F. Rosen, *Reforming Unemployment Insurance for the Twenty-First Century Workforce* (Washington, DC: The Hamilton Project, Brookings Institution, September 2006); and J.R. Kling, *Fundamental Restructuring of Unemployment Insurance: Wage-Loss Insurance and Temporary Earnings Replacement Accounts* (Washington DC: The Hamilton Project, Brookings Institution, September 2006).

26. A series of monographs evaluating current unemployment insurance policy and recommending improvements have been published under the Hamilton Project of the Brookings Institution (*U.S. News Wire*, September 2006). Proposals for improvement of the unemployment insurance program include greater uniformity of provisions among states through federal guidelines for eligibility and benefits, an extension of coverage to a broader group of workers, and establishment of a system of personal accounts for the self-employed, including matching federal contributions and introduction of wage insurance for low-wage workers who find that changing jobs often results in reduced wages. Higher expenditures would be covered by an increase in the federal unemployment tax—a tax that has not been raised in over 20 years (see Hacker, *Universal Insurance*; Kletzer and Rosen, *Reforming Unemployment Insurance*; and Kling, *Fundamental Restructuring*).

27. G. Acs, H.J. Holzer, and A. Nichols, "How Have Households with Children Fared in the Job Market Turndown?" *Assessing the New Federalism.* Policy Brief A-67 (Washington, DC: The Urban Institute, 2005). See also Golden et al., *Framework for a New Safety Net.*

28. See G.L. Berlin, "Congressional Testimony on Solutions to Poverty," MDRC, April 26, 2007; Holzer and Nightingale, eds., *Reshaping the American Workforce*; and S. Zedlewski et al., *A New Safety Net for Low Income Families* (Washington, DC: The Urban Institute, July 2008).

29. J. Wallace, "A Vision for the Future of the Workforce Investment System," Address to the National Workforce Association, St. Petersburg, Florida, December 4, 2006 (Oakland, CA: MDRC, January 2007).

30. MDRC. *Why Has the Poverty Rate Not Fallen Since the Early 1970s?* (Oakland, CA: Fast Fact, June 13, 2007).

31. A. Blinder, "Fear of Offshoring," Princeton University, Center for Economic Policy Studies (CEPS), Working Paper No. 119, December 2005.

32. J. Visser, "Membership Statistics in 24 Countries," *Monthly Labor Review* 124 (1) (January 2006): 38–49.

33. *Monthly Labor Review*, "Productivity Gains: Who Benefits?" 130(5) (May 2007): 57.

34. R.A. Anderson and K. Kliesen, "The 1990s Acceleration in Labor Productivity: Causes and Measurement." Federal Reserve Bank of St. Louis *Review* (May/June 2006): 182–202.

35. Ibid. See also Mishel, Bernstein, and Allegretto, *The State of Working America, 2006–07*, 107ff; A. Sherman and A. Aron-Dine, *New CBO Data Show Income Inequity Continues to Widen* (Washington, DC: Center on Budget and Policy Priorities, January 23, 2007); and J. Bernstein, C. Brocht, and L. Mishel, *Any Way You Cut It—Income Inequality on the Rise* (Washington, DC: Economic Policy Institute, 2000).

36. Anderson and Kliesen "The 1990s Acceleration," 56. See also Mishel, Bernstein, and Allegretto, *The State of Working America, 2006–07*, 107-113; and J. Bernstein, E. McNichol, and K. Lyons, *Pulling Apart: Income Inequality Grew Across the Country over the Past Two Decades: A State by State Analysis of Income Trends* (Washington, DC: Economic Policy Institute, Center on Budget and Policy Priorities, January 29, 2006).

37. Mishel, Bernstein, and Allegretto, *The State of Working America, 2006–07*, 57.

38. N.J. Wollman, "Decade-Long Trend of Lessening Violence and Harm in the U.S. Stalls," December 18, 2007. See also Center on Budget and Policy Priorities (CBPP), *Average Income in 2006 up $60,000 for Top 1 Percent of Households Just $430 for Bottom 90 Percent* (Washington, DC: July 30 and 31, 2008).

39. "Bernanke Suggests How to Narrow Wage Gap," *New York Times*, February 7, 2007, sec. B.

40. E. Appelbaum, A. Bernhardt, and R. Murname, eds., *Low Wage America: How Employers Are Reshaping Opportunity in the Workplace* (New York: Russell Sage Foundation, 2003).

41. Anderson, Kato, and Riccio, *A New Approach*. See also J. Bernstein and I. Shapiro, *Nine Years of Neglect: Federal Minimum Wage Revisions—Unchanged for Eight Straight Years, Falls to 56 Year Low Relative to the Average Wage* (Washington, DC:

Economic Policy Institute, Center on Budget and Priorities); and USDHHS, *Report on Low Wages*.

42. The Urban Institute estimates that the increase in the minimum wage will raise the incomes of more than 4.5 million poor workers and 9 million other persons whose incomes are just above the poverty level (*New York Times* April 25, 2007). Also see Mishel, Bernstein, and Allegretto, *The State of Working America, 2006–07*, 109; and U.S. Department of Labor, *E-Laws Fair Labor Standards Act* (Washington, DC 2010).

43. H.J. Holzer and R.I. Lerman, *America's Forgotten Middle-Skill Jobs: Education and Training Requirements in the Next Decade and Beyond* (Washington, DC: The Urban Institute, November 2007). Also see H.J. Holzer and R.I. Lerman, *The Future of Middle Skill Jobs* (Washington, DC: The Brookings Institution, 2009).

44. U.S. Executive Office of the President, Council of Economic Advisers, Preparing the Workers of Today for the Jobs of Tomorrow (Washington, DC, July 2009).

45. J.S. Hacker, *The Divided Welfare State: The Battle over Public and Private Social Benefits in the United States* (Cambridge, UK: Cambridge University Press, 2002).

46. H.J. Holzer, "Economic Costs of Inadequate Investments in Workforce Development," Testimony submitted to the U. S. House Subcommittee on Labor, Health, and Human Services, Education and Related Agencies Committee on Appropriations (Washington, DC: U.S. House of Representatives, February 26, 2008).

47. J. Lotto-Casner and M.W. Brenner, *Are They Really Ready to Work: Employers' Perspectives on the Basic Knowledge and Applied Skills of New Entrants to the 21st Century Workforce* (Washington, DC: Corporation Voices for Working Families, The Conference Board. The Partnership for 21st Century Skills, and The Society for Human Resource Management, September 29, 2006).

48. The Workforce Investment Act of 1998 (WIA) is a major federal workforce program. WIA offers job placement assistance, case management, and occupational or on-the-job training to jobseekers through more than 600 local One-Stop Career Centers. Because it does not assign any priority to specific hardship groups such as the hard-to-employ, WIA's impact on the working poor is limited. Training, when offered, is limited and fails to target those most in need of assistance, including poor single mothers and other low-wage workers. See V. Galetto and G.P. Green, "Employer Participation in Workforce Development Networks," *Economic Development Quarterly* 19 (3) (August 2005): 225–231.

49. Indeed, since 1985 the U.S. Department of Labor has decreased its inflation-adjusted investments in worker training by nearly 30%, despite the fact that educational and training programs across the country only serve an estimated 25% to 30% of the 20 million low-wage workers (Colborn 2005; Carnevale and Desrochers 2004). It is estimated that only $50, on average, is available per year per low-educated, non-employed adult for federally financed employment services and/or job training (Holzer and Waller 2003).

50. C. Marano and K. Tarr, "The Workforce Intermediary: Profiling the Field of Practice and Its Challenges," in *Workforce Intermediaries for the Twenty-First Century*, ed. Robert P. Giloth (Philadelphia, PA: Temple University Press, 2004).

51. Center on Wisconsin Strategy, *The Wisconsin Regional Training Partnership: Developing a Highly Qualified Workforce for the Milwaukee Metropolitan Area* (Madison, WI: February 2003).

52. The Personal Responsibility and Work Opportunity Reconciliation Act of 1996 (PRWORA) replaced a 60-year-old welfare program, Aid for Families with Dependent Children (AFDC) with the Temporary Assistance for Needy Families (TANF). Welfare recipients are no longer entitled to cash assistance strictly on the basis of need. TANF limits recipients to five years of benefit over their lifetimes, and only provides economic support to individuals who are actively engaged in job training or work. A service "work-first" approach focuses on placing TANF recipients in jobs to give them the experience of working in paid employment. Through "work-first," TANF recipients gain an understanding of the customs, obligations, and experience of paid work. Although numerous studies document the positive effects of education and training on job quality and earnings (Ganzglass 2006), the results of post-welfare employment experience grounded in the "work-first" philosophy reflect sporadic job continuity and low wages among welfare leavers

53. Marano and Tarr, "The Workforce Intermediary."

54. H.J. Holzer, *Encouraging Job Advancement Among Low-Wage Workers: A New Approach,* Welfare Reform and Beyond Policy Brief #30 (Washington, DC: The Brookings Institution, May 2004).

55. Holzer and Lerman, *America's Forgotten Middle-Skill Jobs.*

56. Another proposal to encourage, facilitate, and reward work is being extended by Harry Holzer of the Georgetown Public Policy and Urban Institutes. Holzer proposes that the federal government provide $5 billion in matching funds for increases in state, local, and private expenditures on career advancement projects (Brookings Institution 2007). The proposed Worker Advancement Grants for Employment in States (WAGES) would identify, expand, and replicate successful career advancement strategies by rigorously evaluating programs and disseminating data on effective program models. Over the course of one decade it is expected that WAGES would serve about 7 million low-wage workers and generate $160 billion in benefits for them (Brookings Institution 2007). These fiscal reforms are designed to ensure that targeted federal resources and matching private sector support will enable workforce intermediaries to achieve significant results that simultaneously serve the needs of low-wage workers and the business community.

57. D.J. Fischer, *Workforce Intermediaries: Powering Regional Economies in the New Century* (Baltimore, MD: The Annie E. Casey Foundation, May 2005).

58. K. Boswell and D. Jenkins, *State Policies on Community College Workforce Development: Findings from a National Survey* (Denver, CO: Education Commission of the States, Center for Community College Policy, September 2002).

59. Demos, *Higher and Higher Education: Trends in Access, Affordability, and Debt* (New York: Demos Young Adult Economic Series Part 1, Winter 2007).

60. P. Osterman, "Employment and Training Policies: New Directions for Less-Skilled Adults," in *Reshaping the American Workforce in a Changing Economy,* eds. H.J. Holzer and D.S. Nightingale (Washington, DC: Urban Institute Press, 2007). See also T. Draut, "Higher Education, Higher Cost and Higher Debt: Paying College in the Future," Testimony of Tamara Draut before the

United States Senate Committee on Health, Education, Labor and Pensions (New York, NY: Demos, February 2007).

61. Community College Leadership Program, *Community College Survey of Student Engagement, 2005 Findings: Engaging Students, Challenging the Odds* (Austin, TX: University of Texas at Austin, 2006). Osterman, "Employment and Training Policies."

62. Ibid.

63. See Osterman, op. cit.; and Community College Leadership Program, *Community College Survey of Student Engagement, 2005 Findings.*

64. Community College Leadership Program, op. cit.

65. Osterman, "Employment and Training Policies."

66. Ibid.

67. Ibid.

68. E. Ashburn, *Living Laboratories: 5 Community Colleges Offer Lessons That Have Produced Results* (Washington, DC: *The Chronicle of Higher Education,* October 2006). See also Community College Leadership Program (2006).

69. L.R. Hayes, *Helping Low-Wage Workers Persist in Education Programs: Lessons from Research on Welfare Training Programs and Two Promising Community College Strategies* (New York: MDRC, February 2008).

70. Draut, "Higher Education, Higher Cost and Higher Debt."

71. Ibid.

72. Ibid.

73. Osterman, "Employment and Training Policies."

74. Demos, *Higher and Higher Education.*

75. National Center for Children in Poverty (NCCP), *When Work Doesn't Pay: What Every Policy Maker Should Know* (New York: Columbia University, June 2006).

76. Wallace, "A Vision for the Future of the Workforce Investment System."

77. Ibid.

78. Ibid.

79. N. Poppe, J. Strawn, and K. Martinson, "Whose Job Is It? Creating Opportunities for Advancement," in *Workforce Intermediaries for the Twenty-First Century,* ed. Robert P. Giloth (Philadelphia, PA: Temple University Press, 2004).

80. Anderson et al., *A New Approach to Low-Wage Workers and Employers.*

81. Ibid.

Hadas Mandel  **NO**

Configurations of Gender Inequality: The Consequences of Ideology and Public Policy

The role of the state in reproducing gender stratification has been central to feminist discussions of the welfare state. In parallel, extensive empirical research has demonstrated the impact of welfare policy on various forms of gender inequality, particularly the massive entry of women into the labour market over the last half century. With the increase of women's labour force participation, significant cross-country variations have emerged in their patterns of integration within labour markets and in the nature of gender stratification. Empirical studies that focus on these variations have yielded contradictory conclusions concerning the implications of welfare states for gender stratification. While progressive welfare states were generally found to be those with the highest women's labour market participation rates, and thus the lowest levels of women's economic dependency and poverty rates, they were also found to be those with the lowest women's occupational and earnings attainment. The prediction of gendered outcomes from patterns of state intervention very much depends on the dimension of gender inequality in focus.

While previous studies tend to base their conclusions on a single dimension of gender inequality or several dimensions treated serially, this paper favours a holistic perspective by analysing relations between dimensions. This shift is significant because only when multiple aspects of gender inequality are simultaneously mapped is it possible to see that all societies exhibit both gender-egalitarian and inegalitarian features. Rather than viewing some contexts as more inegalitarian than others, the paper highlights configurations of inequality and bases its discussion on the inherent tradeoffs between them. These unique configurations are then analysed and understood within their distinctive institutional and ideological context.

Analysing configurations of gender inequality rather than single outcomes opens a wider perspective on gender stratification, and suggests a different outlook for understanding the implications of welfare states on it. The interpretative framework developed in this paper views the uneven record of achievement and failure that characterizes welfare regimes as products of welfare state interventions and intentions. Thus, what could be interpreted

From *The British Journal of Sociology*, vol. 60, no. 4, 2009, pp. 693–719. Copyright © 2009 by Wiley-Blackwell. Reprinted by permission via Rightslink.

as a paradoxical consequence of welfare state activity when highlighting one dimension is viewed here as a by-product which might be considered justifiable, or even worthwhile, within its particular ideological and institutional context.

Identifying configurations of gender inequality rather than configurations of welfare policies provides a counterpoint to mainstream studies which have been primarily interested in the welfare state, and investigated gender inequality as a way of exemplifying its significance for various forms of stratification. . . . As the main concern of this paper is gender, it identifies profiles of gender inequality and places them in context rather than the other way around [looking at the patterns of welfare policy first].

The article begins by pointing to the different conceptions of gender equality—based on either similarity or difference—which, throughout the history of welfare states, have served as the basis for demands for social protection for women. Its first section exposes the affinity between these conceptions and the distinctive strategies of state interventions found in different welfare regimes. The second section provides empirical evidence, which establishes the association between configurations of policies and configurations of outcomes. The theoretical discussion that follows it offers an interpretive framework for understanding the unique form of gender stratification in each regime, by referring to both the institutional characteristics and the dominant gender ideologies that characterize it. Configurations of inequality are identified through cluster analysis—a statistical method for discovering affinities between cases—on the basis of a wide range of indicators of gender economic inequality for fourteen advanced societies.

Gender Ideology and Welfare Regime

Advocates of gender equality are committed to a variety of different ideals. Nevertheless, demands to empower women by allowing them to set up an independent household, calls for an equal division of labour between spouses, and the protection of women's economic independence are among the requirements consistently voiced as conditions for the attainment of equality between women and men. The economic and social importance of the labour market has led both mainstream and feminist researchers to see women's participation in it as a principal and essential condition for meeting those demands. Because labour market attainments are the most important determinant of life chances, the gendered division of labour between breadwinner and housewife not only makes women economically dependent on their spouses in the immediate present, but also prevents their equal access to social rights that are tied to paid labour in the long term. Moreover, because employment is the main source of self-realization and social status as well as income and social protection, labour market activity has become a necessary condition for equality in contemporary societies.

In the liberal approach to gender equality, this outlook is taken to its extreme. As an economic ideology, liberalism regards paid work in a free market as properly being the almost exclusive determinant of individual life chances.

The USA is the closest empirical approximation to a political economy in which the state supports an uninhibited market that is not only the dominant mechanism for service provision, but also the primary source of social protection. Consequently, care services that facilitate women's employment, such as daycare, are mostly purchased in the market, with price determining their quality. Likewise, paid maternity leave is not provided universally by the state, but rather is conditional on each mother's terms of employment. The state takes no practical responsibility for the special needs of women as childbearers and mothers. In the liberal belief that there is no better alternative to the labour market for attaining economic independence, women, like men, are seen as potential earners, and the grounds for achieving gender equality rest clearly on similarity rather than difference.

Although participation in the labour market is seen as a choice made privately by the individual, rather than as a public responsibility, the liberal state is committed to enabling the market to work efficiently and without interference. Accordingly, it seeks to remove obstacles by legislating against discrimination, with the aim of ensuring equal competition for jobs and earnings. In keeping with this ideology, liberal-feminist calls for gender equality are based on women's status as workers rather than as mothers. . . . [T]he liberal regime is committed to formal egalitarianism, rather than the substantive egalitarianism that characterizes settings in which the state actively intervenes in the stratification process by providing public services and cash transfers.

The notion of gender difference underlies the alternative to the liberal emphasis on equality of access. This alternative view rejects the idea that women need to compete with men in the labour market in order to attain equal rights and social recognition, and makes claims on women's behalf that rest on their status as mothers and caregivers. Instead of aspiring for equality of equals, this ideology ties social rights to motherhood as an alternative mechanism for economically empowering women. A key claim is that if caregiving were to accrue social and economic rewards, this would improve the chances of both sexes participating in both paid and unpaid forms of work.

Translated to existing family policies, the ideology of difference legitimates financial support to mothers in preference to employment-supportive policies. Such financial support has been adopted mainly in the conservative welfare states of continental and southern Europe. . . .

It is important to note that although economic support for non-working mothers may have the potential to advance women's economic independence, in practice that was never their intention. In contrast to income-related benefits, cash benefits for mothers that are not conditional on employment are provided on a flat-rate basis. At best, they barely reach one third of the average wage. Such limited allowances are insufficient to independently run a household, and are therefore only effective when accompanied by the protection of an institutionalized marriage. . . .

The contrast drawn here between the liberal principle of similarity that links equality to free competition in labour markets, and the principle of difference that ties social rights to unpaid care work, reflects extreme attitudes. In practice, with the entrance of women into the labour market and the rise of dual-earner families, women began to benefit from the social rights associated with employment in an increasingly independent manner. As a result, demands based on difference and similarity began to be mixed together. This mix between contrasting principles reflects the importance of the labour market as a means of attaining gender equality, on the one hand, and on the other the state's obligation to assist women to reconcile paid employment with their roles as child-bearers and mothers. . . .

Policies in the social-democratic nations clearly reflect an assumption that women's advance in the labour market is impossible without active efforts by the state to protect their rights as mothers, and to provide them with comfortable terms of employment and support services. Foremost among the latter is an extensive supply of high-quality public daycare facilities subsidized by the state, in addition to flexible terms of employment, long maternity leaves, and paid leave to care for sick children. . . .

Profiles of Inequality: Empirical Evidence

This section provides empirical support for establishing the association between configurations of policies and configurations of outcomes. It shows that the different models of gender equality—based on the analytical axis of difference vs. similarity—not only underlie different patterns of state intervention, but also correlate with the diverse patterns of gender stratification found in rich democracies. In order to cover the major expressions of gender economic inequality, I have gathered a wide range of indicators that encompasses most aspects of women's economic activities in comparative research. To cover a broad spectrum I chose indicators that reflect different dimensions of gender inequality (like access to paid work on the one hand, and the economic attainments of those who work on the other), and included indicators that pertain to economic position of women in different class situations (like access to managerial positions at the top and poverty rates at the bottom). As different measures tend to suffer from different biases and to emphasize different nuances, I deliberately utilized multiple indicators of each major dimension of inequality.

. . . The importance of this analysis lies in its potential to highlight the tradeoffs between these different dimensions and to establish their connection to the diverse modes of state intervention found in the countries under study. . . .

The connection between these configurations and welfare state strategies lies on the assumption that countries with similar welfare state strategies should also resemble each other in their patterns of gender stratification. Therefore the fourteen OECD countries . . . included in the analysis are all countries with familiar institutional context. . . .

According to Esping-Andersen's classification Sweden, Denmark, Norway, and Finland are the typical social-democratic welfare states; the USA, the UK, Canada and Australia are liberal welfare states; Germany, the Netherlands, France, Belgium and southern European Italy and Spain are all regarded as conservative welfare states. . . .

[T]he purpose of the present research is not to validate any particular welfare state typology, but to link welfare state strategies to their gendered outcomes. On the assumption that welfare state strategies affect patterns of gender stratification, if countries within each regime share a similar institutional context they are also expected to resemble each other in their patterns of gender stratification. Deviations from general patterns are also expected to be reflected in outcomes. Thus, I will try to benefit from such deviations in order to better explain the fit between welfare regimes and their presumed outcomes. . . .

Cluster Characteristics

. . . The first and most fundamental dimension of equality or inequality, which is also the one most obviously influenced by state intervention, is women's economic activity. . . . [Results] strongly confirm the effectiveness of the social-democratic model in raising women's participation rates, most notably among mothers of young children. High rates of paid activity among women and mothers are also indicated by the centrality of the dual-earner family model and the tiny proportion of couple-headed households in which the man is the sole earner. The commitment of the social-democratic welfare regime to promoting women's labour force participation is also reflected in the continuous involvement of mothers in paid work. Three-quarters of married women continue to work after birth and during the childrearing period. The continuous access of women to an independent income significantly reduces their economic dependency on their partners, as seen by the low level of women's earning dependency in the social-democratic regime. Although earnings dependency is primarily influenced by access to a paycheck, it also reflects differences between the spouses' income, as it is measured by the gap (in favour of the husband) between the relative contributions of the two spouses to the household income.

In sharp contrast to the social-democratic model, the conservative cluster is characterized by low proportions of working women and a large number of households with only a male wage-earner. The more familistic southern European countries (separate averages shown in parentheses) are the only ones in which male-breadwinner households are more common than dual-earners. . . .

The restricted access of women in general and mothers in particular to sources of independent income in the conservative countries increases women's economic dependence on their partners, as illustrated by the dependency index. . . .

The impressive entry of women into the labour market of social-democratic countries and the relative economic autonomy that they enjoy from their partners have not, however, been accompanied by gender convergence in labour market attainments. On the contrary, in the protected labour markets of social-democratic welfare regimes women are concentrated in high proportions in female-typed jobs within the public sector and, compared to other countries, have less access to positions of power and prestige and enjoy lower economic rewards. . . .

Compared to the other welfare regimes, the social-democratic cluster has the highest rate of occupational sex segregation and the lowest proportion of women in managerial positions. Given the high rewards that usually accompany managerial positions and the comparatively low pay typical of female-typed occupations, women's position in the occupational structure has tangible consequences for their economic achievements. . . .

In social-democratic countries . . . , the equality implied by measures of women's employment rates is replaced by inequality when we turn to the achievements of working women. In the conservative cluster, particularly in Italy and Spain, the picture is reversed: low participation of women in paid work is parlayed into relatively favourable attainments for those who do enter the labour market. This is something of a surprise for societies with a conservative tradition. One plausible explanation is that women who enter an economy dependent on highly-committed male labour tend to be highly qualified. They are a relatively select group able to compete with men in a labour market that is not adapted to women and does not offer them preferential terms of employment.

. . . [T]wo factors that most influence women's employment—motherhood and education—substantiate this selectivity, particularly in Italy and Spain. Only in the social-democratic countries are there virtually no barriers to employment—even in the most vulnerable group, low-educated mothers of preschool children, almost 80 per cent of women work. Motherhood and low education, however, play a significant role in women's decisions to enter the labour market in both liberal and conservative regimes, but more so in the latter. . . .

In notable contrast to the social-democratic cluster, labour markets [in conservative countries] are less gender-segregated both horizontally and vertically. General levels of occupational segregation are comparatively low, and women have also succeeded in penetrating privileged positions. Thus, at first sight it seems that the liberal version of the dual-earner model has managed to avoid the failures of the social-democratic and conservative welfare regimes, succeeding in both bringing women into the labour market and providing them with access to senior positions. However, these successes have not come without their costs, which are paid primarily by disadvantaged groups.

The lack of regulation of employment conditions and earnings—a central characteristic of the liberal labour markets—erodes the wages of the weaker groups, in which women are overrepresented. This is held to be the main explanation for the large wage gaps between men and women in liberal markets in general, and the USA in particular. . . .

The class stratification that characterizes the liberal markets is translated into class differentiation among women themselves[, as] indicat[ed] by the wage gap between high- and low-educated women. . . . [T]he average wage of high-educated women in the liberal labour markets is more than double the wage of the low-educated (a 50 per cent gap would be double). This gap is twice as high as the gap in the social-democratic cluster, and is also substantially higher than in the conservative cluster. It would therefore be mistaken to interpret the impressive success of American women in entering managerial positions as representing success for women as a whole. For most women, attaining economic independence without protective social rights implies a significant disadvantage.

. . . [M]otherhood continues to constitute an obstacle to employment in the liberal countries, even among educated women. But while married mothers who withdraw from the labour market are protected by their husbands' income, this is not the case for the unmarried. The limited support for mothers in market-oriented welfare regimes—either in terms of cash transfers or public services that facilitate their employment—is a central factor behind the high rates of poverty among women in general, and lone mothers in particular. The . . . average rate of poverty among lone mothers is 8 times higher in the liberal cluster than in the social-democratic, and twice as high as in the conservative cluster. . . . [A]lmost 80 per cent of non-working lone mothers in the liberal countries live in poverty, as do more than a third of those who work. . . . Bearing in mind that more than one fifth of all households in the liberal cluster are lone-parent families, and that the vast majority of these families live in poverty, it would appear that equal opportunity legislation is ultimately of little help to a considerable portion of women.

Social-democratic conditions for lone mothers are almost the mirror-image of those in the liberal countries. [P]overty rates among both working and non-working lone mothers are relatively low in the social-democratic countries, compared to all the other clusters, especially the liberal. . . .[T]he best economic protection for mothers in all regimes—including the conservative—is participation in the labour market. . . .

Ideology, Policy and Inequality Tradeoffs

The findings above reveal that multiple indicators of the economic position of women combine to form distinctive patterns of gender stratification. These patterns are qualitatively different across welfare state regimes, and each one of them implies different tradeoffs for women. These tradeoffs become readily interpretable once gender politics are taken into account, in the form of the different conceptions and ideals of gender equality that prevail in different welfare regimes.

Substantively, it is often the case that the very success of one element of a welfare regime is the source of the inadequacies of another. The gender segregation characteristic of the labour market in Scandinavia indirectly results from the state's success in eliminating the gender gap in labour force participation. In the conservative countries, women's relative success in penetrating positions of power is explained by the selectivity of the female work force, that is, the barriers that discourage many women from entering the labour market in the first place. In the liberal context, the burden placed on economically disadvantaged women is the consequence of the very same policy that has enabled relatively advantaged women to attain high rewards in the labour market.

Patterns of inequality in countries with a social-democratic welfare regime reveal a particularly clear tradeoff. Aiming to encourage mothers to join the labour market, the state passes laws that protect their jobs and provide them with convenient terms of employment. Similar effects result from the state's direct role as an employer. These interventions knowingly bring women with a weaker attachment to work into the labour market. They also channel the female workforce into gender-specific occupations within the public sector and heighten the reluctance of private sector employers to hire women. The labour market in social-democratic countries thus becomes more gender-segregated the more that the state attains its goal of high rates of employment among all women.

. . . The assumption at the basis of the 'productivist' social-democratic regime, one based on emploment rather than financial transfers, is that it is better to over-employ, or at least to provide non-profitable jobs, than to financially support non-workers. As a consequence, while the benefits accruing to working mothers render female job applicants less attractive to private employers, this is justified by the higher aim of full employment. Women's entry into the labour market, even at the price of their concentration in feminized ghettoes and their relative exclusion from positions of economic power, is seen as an important step towards equality in that it provides more women with the elementary right to independence: liberation from long-term dependency on their spouses and families on the one hand, or the state's welfare institutions on the other. From this perspective, part-time work and a high concentration of women in education and care services are legitimate means to the end of narrowing gender inequality by supporting women's employment. The by-products—unusually gender-segregated working patterns and a relatively low glass ceiling—are justified by social-democratic ideology, which in sharp contrast to the liberal faith in markets forces, actively aspires to advance equality on a universal basis, even at the expense of hampering the attainments of the advantaged. . . .

The limits of social-democratic policies have different parallels in the other welfare regimes. While . . . segregated labour markets are a by-product of successful attempts to provide more women with a source of independent income, in conservative settings the picture is reversed: a relatively egalitarian labour market within a non-egalitarian society. . . . [W]omen who work are able to attain high salaries, as reflected in more egalitarian wage ratios between men and women. . . .

The traditionalist gender role ideology that animates family policy in the conservative welfare regime receives clear expression in the comparatively low proportion of working mothers and limited support for lone mothers. In most conservative countries the male breadwinner model rests on two mutually reinforcing foundations: sparse provision of public care services and extensive protection of male wage-earners, based on the assumption that they bear sole responsibility for the economic wellbeing of the household. This has freed married women from financial pressure to support their family, and allowed their selective entry into the labour market with a bias in favour of women with high levels of human capital. On the other hand, the limited aid available to lone mothers has forced them to participate in the labour market at considerably higher rates.

Given the role of selectivity, continuing increases in female labour force participation in conservative countries can be expected to undermine gender equality within the labour market. The decline in fertility rates, which especially characterizes central and southern Europe and which has been convincingly linked to the difficulties experienced by mothers in these countries in combining paid and unpaid work, may create pressure on conservative states to assist women to integrate work and family. . . .

The liberal model—especially its exemplar, the USA—is similar to conservative settings in that the state plays a passive role regarding women's employment. However, unlike the interventionism of conservative states in regulating working conditions and providing social protection, the liberal state largely refrains from interfering with class stratification. High participation rates of women are, therefore, the joint result of market-based provision of care services and the sheer necessity of working due to miserly income guarantees. The prevailing ideologies of non-intervention and gender neutrality reflect the liberal faith in markets. However, given the burdens placed on women as primary caregivers, and the consequent unequal division of labour within the family, mothers cannot compete with men on equal terms.

The consequences of the liberal model are evident in the contrasting impacts of women's employment on their economic wellbeing in the liberal and social-democratic regimes. While in the la[t]ter women's high rates of participation coincide with a relatively high wage floor and publicly subsidized care services, in the former high rates of employment have not succeeded in reducing the substantial risk of poverty among women. In a market-oriented economy where success is determined mainly by personal characteristics and skills, women's ability to escape poverty largely depends on the amount of time they can allocate to paid employment. Most women would therefore benefit from policies that ease the family burden and help them combine their caregiving obligations with commitments to the workplace. The absence of such policies is a substantial barrier against equal competition between men and women, and laws that promise equality of access to employment are not enough to overcome this barrier.

State passivity not only explains women's average disadvantage in relation to men, but also contributes to pronounced diversity among women because of the contradictory effects of non-intervention on different classes. For advantaged women, whose skills enable them to successfully compete with men without assistance from the state, the liberal labour market provides conditions that facilitate success. They benefit from the state's insistence on gender neutrality, with the absence of legislation mandating paid maternity leave being the most significant example, as it reduces employers' tendencies to discriminate against women on the basis of gender. In any case, many of the women who work in higher-status and well-paid jobs have access to maternity leave by virtue of private arrangements with employers. They are also able to consume relatively cheap childcare services, given that the state refrains from regulating the qualifications and employment conditions of caregivers. Consequently, they do not need help from government in entering the labour market and are not harmed by the potentially negative consequences of such policies, as in the social-democratic case. The liberal assumption that free competition will advance equality without state interference is therefore substantiated in the case of higher-class women. Moreover, state interventions in ensuring free competition in the labour market through equal opportunity laws are mainly likely to benefit these women.

Conditions for working women who are less skilled and educated are very different. The non-compulsory character of paid maternity leave excludes most of them from this form of support. Likewise, the limited scope of public financial assistance for families with children and public provision of care services render the child penalty especially burdensome for these women. Finally, the same unregulated market that enables higher-class women to purchase care services relatively cheaply denies their lower-class counterparts economic security. For these women, therefore, class inequality looms much larger than gender discrimination as a source of disadvantage in the labour market.

Conclusions

This article has argued that the nature of gender stratification varies across countries in accordance with different modes of welfare state intervention and divergent ideological approaches to gender stratification. In theory, the principles of similarity and difference constitute two alternative paths to gender equality. In practice, neither paying women to mother their children, nor providing them with benefits designed to ease work/family conflicts, have succeeded in eradicating women's economic disadvantage, mainly because both approaches take traditional gender roles for granted.

The solution favoured by conservatives, income replacement for mothers, could potentially empower women economically without requiring their participation in the labour market. But existing childcare allowances have not provided women with financial independence and do not constitute a viable alternative to the protection afforded by marriage. Consequently, policies based on the assumption that there is no real alternative to paid employment contribute more effectively to women's economic autonomy. However, both the liberal and social-democratic paths to incorporating women into the labour market have seriously inegalitarian consequences. On the one hand, ignoring the traditional division of labour within the household and attempting to sustain gender neutrality places a greater burden on women, especially those who are less privileged. On the other, efforts at making the labour market friendlier to women by recognizing their special needs as child-bearers and mothers transfer the traditional division of labour from the family to the labour market and encourage gender discrimination by private employers.

The attempt made in this article to identify the contextual sources of different patterns of gender inequality emphasizes the pivotal role of state action or inaction and stresses the different challenges that different contexts pose to overcoming gender inequality. Each pattern of state intervention, and the configuration of gender stratification which it promotes, operates in a deeply-rooted ideological and cultural context. As a result, solutions cannot easily be imported from one context to another. Nevertheless, this does not imply that forward movement is impossible. Based on past experience, the most likely scenarios for increased gender equality will entail processes of change that evolve within specific contexts.

An example of such a process is provided by the development of policies towards women's paid and unpaid labour in Scandinavia during the last half century. In the late 1940s state support for motherhood was aimed at facilitating a two-stage career, starting before women had children and continuing after they began school. Twenty years later, the dual-earner model offered support for the employment of mothers of preschool children in order to integrate work and family throughout the life cycle. The reforms of the 1970s indeed changed the position of women, but left that of men relatively intact. Recognizing that women's entry to the labour market is not a sufficient condition for them to advance within it so long as the burden of care remains on their shoulders is what prompted feminist calls for a dual-earner/dual-carer model.

These paradigm shifts have received concrete expression in changing parental leave policies in Sweden, and most other Scandinavian countries—a shift from maternity leave to parental leave, and the introduction of daddy quota. In 1974 traditional maternity leave was replaced by a parental leave scheme covering fathers as well. Subsequently in 1995 an additional month of leave was offered solely to fathers. True, apart from this innovation the dual-earner/dual-carer model has still largely to be translated into substantive policies, and in the 2006 election campaign the social-democratic party chose not to advocate further enlargement of the quota reserved for fathers. Nevertheless, in the new millennium the existing quota (which was raised to two 'daddy months' in 2002) was increasingly utilized, with fathers' share of total leave rising rapidly to reach one-fifth by 2006. Notably, while the initial transition to gender-neutral parental leave had very little effect on the behaviour of fathers, this is not the case for the 'use it or lose it' system adopted at a later stage. The lesson is that when states offer strong incentives to men to participate in care work, they are able to powerfully influence their actions.

EXPLORING THE ISSUE

Do Social Policies Improve Gender Inequalities in the Workplace?

Challenge Questions

1. Can policy changes alone change societal gender inequalities?
2. Is it possible to have a set of policies that simultaneously creates access to entry-level jobs, encouraging movement up the employment ladder, and supports individual agency to set goals and strive to improve oneself?
3. Does the increase in the number of celebrities having children outside of marriage have an impact on public opinion and does this affect social policies?
4. Do programs such as *Teen Mom* and *16 and Pregnant* have an effect on most teens' attitudes toward sex, pregnancy, and parenthood? Could these shows also affect public opinion and social policies regarding education and employment of single mothers?

Is There Common Ground?

One dimension of these debates about gender inequalities in the workplace relates to whether welfare and work policies should be gender sensitive. There are stereotypes of welfare recipients, typically women, as lazy and irresponsible. Why are so many welfare recipients women and children? However, stories of individual welfare recipients call welfare recipient stereotypes into question. In fact, it is common for poor women to combine welfare with work or to get welfare benefits between jobs. Many women use welfare to help them get more education—a critical factor in moving out of poverty. Many factors conspire against poor women: they can't find employment; they can't secure high enough pay, particularly if they have children in their care; they are financially penalized if they marry; and they have to endure public condemnation and discrimination. Nevertheless, stereotypes of welfare mothers remain rigid and condemning. These stereotypes reflect three dominant perspectives or beliefs about the causes of poverty and wealth: (1) Individualism contends that individuals are responsible for their own lot in life. Those who are motivated and work hard will make it. Those who do not make it (i.e., welfare recipients) have only themselves to blame. (2) Social-structuralism asserts that due to economic or social imbalances (e.g., in education, marriage and family life, and even welfare programs themselves), opportunities are restricted for some people, overriding individual agency and affecting the likelihood of success; and (3) "culture of poverty," most often associated with African Americans who are thought to have developed a culture—some would say counterculture—of poverty with values, traits, and expectations that have developed from the structural constraints of living in poverty and that may be intergenerationally transmitted. Such logic demonstrates what social psychologists call the "fundamental attribution error," that is, the tendency to blame individuals for their outcomes while ignoring the situational context. A focus on social structural factors leads to a discussion of the effectiveness of social policies. Can social policies help lift women from poverty?

ISSUE 18

Are Barriers to Women's Success as Leaders Due to Societal Obstacles?

YES: **Alice H. Eagly and Linda L. Carli**, from "Women and the Labyrinth of Leadership," *Harvard Business Review* (pp. 1–11, September, 2007)

NO: **Mark van Vugt and Anjana Ahuja**, from *Naturally Selected: The Evolutionary Science of Leadership* (Harper Business, 2011)

Learning Outcomes

As you read the issue, focus on the following points:

- What is an evolutionary explanation of leadership styles that accounts for gender-related patterns? Is there evidence for hard-wiring for differences?
- What are the strengths and weaknesses of the glass ceiling and labyrinth analogies in describing women's barriers to success as leaders?
- What is the value of focusing on "how" gender-related patterns in leadership styles come about rather than focusing on "why"?
- How would Eagly and Carli explain the Savannah Hypothesis?

ISSUE SUMMARY

YES: Alice Eagly and Linda Carli contend that barriers exist for women at every stage of their career trajectories, resulting in, not a glass ceiling, but a labyrinth.

NO: Mark van Vugt and Anjana Ahuja assert that the division of labor by sex is rooted in biologically based differences between women and men. Evolutionarily based natural selection has led to inclinations that make women and men better suited for different types of jobs.

Women continue to face career barriers. Although women hold 40 percent of managerial positions in the United States today, only 2 percent of *Fortune 500*

CEOs are women. The question remains as to why. Explanations tend to fall into one of two camps: human capital theory and discrimination theory. Human capital theories focus on obstacles from within the person. These theories focus on explanations such as differences in women's and men's abilities, interests, education, qualifications, personal investment in their careers, and leadership style, as well as choices related to family–work conflicts that are more likely to result in job discontinuity and turnover for women than for men. On the other hand, discrimination theorists focus on sociocultural factors that result in differential treatment of women and men. Three forms of employment discrimination have been identified. *Within-job wage discrimination* occurs when there are disparities within the same job or unequal pay for equal work. *Valuative discrimination* is associated with lower wages in female- than male-dominated fields. Finally, *allocative discrimination* occurs when there are biases in hiring, promotion, and dismissal. This latter form of discrimination has evoked various descriptors of discrimination, including the "glass ceiling," "concrete wall," "sticky floor," and "glass escalator." The image of the glass ceiling suggests that women ascend the career ladder with the top in sight, but at some rung on that ladder they hit the "glass ceiling." This image was transformed to that of a "concrete wall" to describe the even greater challenges faced by ethnic minority women. The "glass elevator" was a term coined to express the rapid career advancement of men who enter nontraditional, historically female-dominated fields, such as nursing. The "sticky floor" refers to the finding that when there is a critical mass of members of a particular under-valued group in the workplace, one of their own may be more likely to achieve a position of mid-management, but it is very difficult to rise higher.

Power operates as a social structure that affects how people respond to female leaders. Hilary Lips has identified four ways in which women are responded to differently and which can undermine their effectiveness as leaders: (1) Women are expected to combine leadership with compassion; (2) people do not listen to or take direction from women as comfortably as from men; (3) women who promote themselves and their abilities reap disapproval; and (4) women require more external validation than do men in some contexts. Furthermore, women in leadership positions are quite aware of these reactions. Some are more comfortable than others taking on the negative reactions of others if they are seen as too bossy, aggressive, or domineering. They also realize the double-bind created if they try to counter such judgments by toning down their actions, actions that may ultimately undermine their authority. Lips has noted that women cope with this conundrum by finding rewards in their leadership roles. She says these rewards include a sense of competence and of positive impact and the opportunity to empower others. She further suggests that organizations committed to supporting female leaders can do so by not isolating women as tokens in male-dominated departments; by endorsing and legitimating them; and by ensuring that differential standards are not used to evaluate male and female leaders. These issues raise questions about what women should do if they wish to continue to strive for higher levels of leadership. Is there some leadership style that is most likely to ensure success?

Research has identified several different leadership styles. Autocratic leaders exercise a great deal of personal control whereas democratic leaders involve group members in the decision-making process. At one extreme, laissez-faire leadership entails a hands-off approach in which the followers are expected to solve problems and make decisions on their own. Management by exception is the style wherein the leader allows the group to handle routine matters and gets involved only with matters that are non-routine. In contrast, transactional leadership involves interactions with group members, but ultimately the leader makes the decisions and is very focused on rewards and punishments. Transformational leaders provide yet another contrast. They are focused on the goals of individuals and organizations and lead in ways that result in change (transformation) within the organization. Their goals are to inspire and be a role model. There are numerous stereotypical beliefs, both descriptive and prescriptive, about women and leadership than have implications for which leadership style(s) might be best suited for women who are interested in being successful. Given that stereotypically men are seen as agentic and women as communal, it is not surprising that stereotypes about leadership styles reflect this distinction. In general, people believe that women are more transformational and use more contingent rewards than men, whereas men are thought to lead in a more laissez-faire style and use more management by exception than do women. Furthermore, it appears that the leadership style used by women and men leaders affects the likelihood that they are judged worthy of promotion. Alice Eagly and her colleagues conducted a study in which they found that of all the various dimensions of transformational leadership, only inspirational motivation (i.e., being optimistic and excited about goals and the future) was judged more important for male than female leaders as a criterion for promotion, especially promotion to CEO. For females leaders, while inspirational motivation was seen as relevant, so too was individualized consideration (i.e., paying attention to the needs and goals of individuals), which is another component of transformational leadership. This was seen as particularly relevant for promoting women to senior management positions. Eagly and her colleagues concluded that for women the inclusion of individualized consideration into their leadership style, along with inspirational motivation, may enable them to "to fulfill prescriptive gender norms and avoid backlash."

In contrast, Eagly and Carli's selection represents a discrimination theory perspective. In addition to describing all the various ways in which women can be targets of discrimination in the workplace, they coin a new term for allocative discrimination, the "labyrinth." That is, women must navigate a maze of obstacles to succeed. In the selection that follows, the excerpt from Mark van Vugt and Anjana Ahuja is an example of an explanation from the human capital perspective in which they argue that by nature women and men have different interests and talents that better suit them for different jobs. They argue from an evolutionary perspective that women and men are designed to lead differently.

YES

Alice H. Eagly and
Linda L. Carli

Women and the Labyrinth of Leadership

If one has misdiagnosed a problem, then one is unlikely to prescribe an effective cure. This is the situation regarding the scarcity of women in top leadership. Because people with the best of intentions have misread the symptoms, the solutions that managers are investing in are not making enough of a difference.

That there is a problem is not in doubt. Despite years of progress by women in the workforce (they now occupy more than 40% of all managerial positions in the United States), within the C-suite they remain as rare as hens' teeth. Consider the most highly paid executives of *Fortune 500* companies—those with titles such as chairman, president, chief executive officer, and chief operating officer. Of this group, only 6% are women. Most notably, only 2% of the CEOs are women, and only 15% of the seats on the boards of directors are held by women. The situation is not much different in other industrialized countries. In the 50 largest publicly traded corporations in each nation of the European Union, women make up, on average, 11% of the top executives and 4% of the CEOs and heads of boards. Just seven companies, or 1%, of *Fortune* magazine's Global 500 have female CEOs. What is to blame for the pronounced lack of women in positions of power and authority?

In 1986 the *Wall Street Journal's* Carol Hymowitz and Timothy Schellhardt gave the world an answer: "Even those few women who rose steadily through the ranks eventually crashed into an invisible barrier. The executive suite seemed within their grasp, but they just couldn't break through the glass ceiling." The metaphor, driven home by the article's accompanying illustration, resonated; it captured the frustration of a goal within sight but somehow unattainable. To be sure, there was a time when the barriers were absolute. Even within the career spans of 1980s-era executives, access to top posts had been explicitly denied. . . .

Times have changed, however, and the glass ceiling metaphor is now more wrong than right. For one thing, it describes an absolute barrier at a specific high level in organizations. The fact that there have been female chief executives, university presidents, state governors, and presidents of nations gives the lie to that charge. At the same time, the metaphor implies that women

From *Harvard Business Review,* September 2007, pp. 63–71. Copyright © 2007 by Harvard Business School Publishing. Reprinted by permission.

and men have equal access to entry- and mid-level positions. They do not. The image of a transparent obstruction also suggests that women are being misled about their opportunities, because the impediment is not easy for them to see from a distance. But some impediments are not subtle. Worst of all, by depicting a single, unvarying obstacle, the glass ceiling fails to incorporate the complexity and variety of challenges that women can face in their leadership journeys. In truth, women are not turned away only as they reach the penultimate stage of a distinguished career. They disappear in various numbers at many points leading up to that stage.

Metaphors matter because they are part of the storytelling that can compel change. Believing in the existence of a glass ceiling, people emphasize certain kinds of interventions: top-to-top networking, mentoring to increase board memberships, requirements for diverse candidates in high-profile succession horse races, litigation aimed at punishing discrimination in the C-suite. None of these is counterproductive; all have a role to play. The danger arises when they draw attention and resources away from other kinds of interventions that might attack the problem more potently. If we want to make better progress, it's time to rename the challenge.

Walls All Around

A better metaphor for what confronts women in their professional endeavors is the labyrinth. It's an image with a long and varied history in ancient Greece, India, Nepal, native North and South America, medieval Europe, and elsewhere. As a contemporary symbol, it conveys the idea of a complex journey toward a goal worth striving for. Passage through a labyrinth is not simple or direct, but requires persistence, awareness of one's progress, and a careful analysis of the puzzles that lie ahead. It is this meaning that we intend to convey. For women who aspire to top leadership, routes exist but are full of twists and turns, both unexpected and expected. Because all labyrinths have a viable route to the center, it is understood that goals are attainable. The metaphor acknowledges obstacles but is not ultimately discouraging.

If we can understand the various barriers that make up this labyrinth, and how some women find their way around them, we can work more effectively to improve the situation. What are the obstructions that women run up against? Let's explore them in turn.

Vestiges of prejudice. It is a well-established fact that men as a group still have the benefit of higher wages and faster promotions. In the United States in 2005, for example, women employed full-time earned 81 cents for every dollar that men earned. . . .

One of the most comprehensive of these studies was conducted by the U.S. Government Accountability Office. The study was based on survey data from 1983 through 2000 from a representative sample of Americans. Because the same people responded to the survey repeatedly over the years, the study provided accurate estimates of past work experience, which is important for explaining later wages.

The GAO researchers tested whether individuals' total wages could be predicted by sex and other characteristics. They included part-time and full-time employees in the surveys and took into account all the factors that they could estimate and that might affect earnings, such as education and work experience. Without controls for these variables, the data showed that women earned about 44% less than men, averaged over the entire period from 1983 to 2000. With these controls in place, the gap was only about half as large, but still substantial. The control factors that reduced the wage gap most were the different employment patterns of men and women: Men undertook more hours of paid labor per year than women and had more years of job experience.

Although most variables affected the wages of men and women similarly, there were exceptions. Marriage and parenthood, for instance, were associated with higher wages for men but not for women. In contrast, other character-istics, especially years of education, had a more positive effect on women's wages than on men's. Even after adjusting wages for all of the ways men and women differ, the GAO study, like similar studies, showed that women's wages remained lower than men's. The unexplained gender gap is consistent with the presence of wage discrimination.

Similar methods have been applied to the question of whether discrimi-nation affects promotions. Evidently it does. Promotions come more slowly for women than for men with equivalent qualifications. . . . Even in cultur-ally feminine settings such as nursing, librarianship, elementary education, and social work, men ascend to supervisory and administrative positions more quickly than women.

The findings of correlational studies are supported by experimental research, in which subjects are asked to evaluate hypothetical individuals as managers or job candidates, and all characteristics of these individuals are held constant except for their sex. Such efforts continue the tradition of the Goldberg paradigm, named for a 1968 experiment by Philip Goldberg. His simple, elegant study had student participants evaluate written essays that were identical except for the attached male or female name. The students were unaware that other students had received identical material ascribed to a writer of the other sex. This initial experiment demonstrated an overall gender bias: Women received lower evaluations unless the essay was on a feminine topic. Some 40 years later, unfortunately, experiments continue to reveal the same kind of bias in work settings. Men are advantaged over equivalent women as can-didates for jobs traditionally held by men as well as for more gender-integrated jobs. Similarly, male leaders receive somewhat more favorable evaluations than equivalent female leaders, especially in roles usually occupied by men.

. . . [A] general bias against women appears to operate with approxi-mately equal strength at all levels. The scarcity of female corporate officers is the sum of discrimination that has operated at all ranks, not evidence of a particular obstacle to advancement as women approach the top. The problem, in other words, is not a glass ceiling.

Resistance to women's leadership.   What's behind the discrimination we've been describing? Essentially, a set of widely shared conscious and unconscious mental associations about women, men, and leaders. Study after study has affirmed that people associate women and men with different traits and link men with more of the traits that connote leadership. . . .

In the language of psychologists, the clash is between two sets of associations: communal and agentic. Women are associated with communal qualities, which convey a concern for the compassionate treatment of others. They include being especially affectionate, helpful, friendly, kind, and sympathetic, as well as interpersonally sensitive, gentle, and soft-spoken. In contrast, men are associated with agentic qualities, which convey assertion and control. They include being especially aggressive, ambitious, dominant, self-confident, and forceful, as well as self-reliant and individualistic. The agentic traits are also associated in most people's minds with effective leadership—perhaps because a long history of male domination of leadership roles has made it difficult to separate the leader associations from the male associations.

As a result, women leaders find themselves in a double bind. If they are highly communal, they may be criticized for not being agentic enough. But if they are highly agentic, they may be criticized for lacking communion. Either way, they may leave the impression that they don't have "the right stuff" for powerful jobs.

Given this double bind, it is hardly surprising that people are more resistant to women's influence than to men's. . . .

Studies have gauged reactions to men and women engaging in various types of dominant behavior. The findings are quite consistent. Nonverbal dominance, such as staring at others while speaking to them or pointing at people, is a more damaging behavior for women than for men. Verbally intimidating others can undermine a woman's influence, and assertive behavior can reduce her chances of getting a job or advancing in her career. Simply disagreeing can sometimes get women into trouble. Men who disagree or otherwise act dominant get away with it more often than women do.

Self-promotion is similarly risky for women. Although it can convey status and competence, it is not at all communal. So while men can use bluster to get themselves noticed, modesty is expected even of highly accomplished women. . . .

Another way the double bind penalizes women is by denying them the full benefits of being warm and considerate. Because people expect it of women, nice behavior that seems noteworthy in men seems unimpressive in women. For example, in one study, helpful men reaped a lot of approval, but helpful women did not. Likewise, men got away with being unhelpful, but women did not. . . .

While one might suppose that men would have a double bind of their own, they in fact have more freedom. Several experiments and organizational studies have assessed reactions to behavior that is warm and friendly versus dominant and assertive. The findings show that men can communicate in a warm or a dominant manner, with no penalty either way. People like men equally well and are equally influenced by them regardless of their warmth.

It all amounts to a clash of assumptions when the average person confronts a woman in management. . . . In the absence of any evidence to the contrary, people suspect that such highly effective women must not be very likable or nice.

Issues of leadership style.   In response to the challenges presented by the double bind, female leaders often struggle to cultivate an appropriate and effective leadership style—one that reconciles the communal qualities people prefer in women with the agentic qualities people think leaders need to succeed. . . .

It's difficult to pull off such a transformation while maintaining a sense of authenticity as a leader. Sometimes the whole effort can backfire. In the words of another female leader, "I think that there is a real penalty for a woman who behaves like a man. The men don't like her and the women don't either." Women leaders worry a lot about these things, complicating the labyrinth that they negotiate. For example, Catalyst's study of *Fortune* 1000 female executives found that 96% of them rated as critical or fairly important that they develop "a style with which male managers are comfortable."

Does a distinct "female" leadership style exist? There seems to be a popular consensus that it does. . . .

More scientifically, a recent meta-analysis integrated the results of 45 studies addressing the question [comparing three leadership styles]. . . . Transformational leaders establish themselves as role models by gaining followers' trust and confidence. They state future goals, develop plans to achieve those goals, and innovate, even when their organizations are generally successful. Such leaders mentor and empower followers, encouraging them to develop their full potential and thus to contribute more effectively to their organizations. By contrast, transactional leaders establish give-and-take relationships that appeal to subordinates' self-interest. Such leaders manage in the conventional manner of clarifying subordinates' responsibilities, rewarding them for meeting objectives, and correcting them for failing to meet objectives. Although transformational and transactional leadership styles are different, most leaders adopt at least some behaviors of both types. The researchers also allowed for a third category, called the laissez-faire style—a sort of non-leadership that concerns itself with none of the above, despite rank authority.

The meta-analysis found that, in general, female leaders were somewhat more transformational than male leaders, especially when it came to giving support and encouragement to subordinates. They also engaged in more of the rewarding behaviors that are one aspect of transactional leadership. Meanwhile, men exceeded women on the aspects of transactional leadership involving corrective and disciplinary actions that are either active (timely) or passive (belated). Men were also more likely than women to be laissez-faire leaders, who take little responsibility for managing. These findings add up to a startling conclusion, given that most leadership research has found the transformational style (along with the rewards and positive incentives associated with the transactional style) to be more suited to leading the modern organization. The research tells us not only that men and women do have somewhat different leadership styles, but also that women's approaches are the more generally effective—while men's often are only somewhat effective or actually hinder effectiveness.

Another part of this picture, based on a separate meta-analysis, is that women adopt a more participative and collaborative style than men typically favor. The reason for this difference is unlikely to be genetic. Rather, it may be that collaboration can get results without seeming particularly masculine. As women navigate their way through the double bind, they seek ways to project authority without relying on the autocratic behaviors that people find so jarring in women. A viable path is to bring others into decision making and to lead as an encouraging teacher and positive role model. . . .

Demands of family life.   For many women, the most fateful turns in the labyrinth are the ones taken under pressure of family responsibilities. Women continue to be the ones who interrupt their careers, take more days off, and work part-time. As a result, they have fewer years of job experience and fewer hours of employment per year, which slows their career progress and reduces their earnings. . . .

There is no question that, while men increasingly share housework and child rearing, the bulk of domestic work still falls on women's shoulders. We know this from time-diary studies, in which people record what they are doing during each hour of a 24-hour day. So, for example, in the United States married women devoted 19 hours per week on average to housework in 2005, while married men contributed 11 hours. That's a huge improvement over 1965 numbers, when women spent a whopping 34 hours per week to men's five, but it is still a major inequity. And the situation looks worse when child care hours are added.

Although it is common knowledge that mothers provide more child care than fathers, few people realize that mothers provide more than they did in earlier generations—despite the fact that fathers are putting in a lot more time than in the past. . . . Thus, though husbands have taken on more domestic work, the work/family conflict has not eased for women; the gain has been offset by escalating pressures for intensive parenting and the increasing time demands of most high-level careers.

Even women who have found a way to relieve pressures from the home front by sharing child care with husbands, other family members, or paid workers may not enjoy the full workplace benefit of having done so. Decision makers often assume that mothers have domestic responsibilities that make it inappropriate to promote them to demanding positions. . . .

Underinvestment in social capital.   Perhaps the most destructive result of the work/family balancing act so many women must perform is that it leaves very little time for socializing with colleagues and building professional networks. The social capital that accrues from such "nonessential" parts of work turns out to be quite essential indeed. One study yielded the following description of managers who advanced rapidly in hierarchies: Fast-track managers "spent relatively more time and effort socializing, politicking, and interacting with outsiders than did their less successful counterparts . . . [and] did not give much time or attention to the traditional management activities of planning, decision making, and controlling or to the human resource management activities of motivating/reinforcing, staffing, training/developing, and managing conflict." . . .

Even given sufficient time, women can find it difficult to engage in and benefit from informal networking if they are a small minority. In such settings, the influential networks are composed entirely or almost entirely of men. Breaking into those male networks can be hard, especially when men center their networks on masculine activities. The recent gender discrimination lawsuit against Wal-Mart provides examples of this. For instance, an executive retreat took the form of a quail-hunting expedition at Sam Walton's ranch in Texas. Middle managers' meetings included visits to strip clubs and Hooters restaurants, and a sales conference attended by thousands of store managers featured a football theme. One executive received feedback that she probably would not advance in the company because she didn't hunt or fish.

Management Interventions That Work

Taking the measure of the labyrinth that confronts women leaders, we see that it begins with prejudices that benefit men and penalize women, continues with particular resistance to women's leadership, includes questions of leadership style and authenticity, and—most dramatically for many women—features the challenge of balancing work and family responsibilities. It becomes clear that a woman's situation as she reaches her peak career years is the result of many turns at many challenging junctures. Only a few individual women have made the right combination of moves to land at the center of power—but as for the rest, there is usually no single turning point where their progress was diverted and the prize was lost.

What's to be done in the face of such a multifaceted problem? A solution that is often proposed is for governments to implement and enforce antidiscrimination legislation and thereby require organizations to eliminate inequitable practices. However, analysis of discrimination cases that have gone to court has shown that legal remedies can be elusive when gender inequality results from norms embedded in organizational structure and culture. The more effective approach is for organizations to appreciate the subtlety and complexity of the problem and to attack its many roots simultaneously. More specifically, if a company wants to see more women arrive in its executive suite, it should do the following:

> **Increase people's awareness of the psychological drivers of prejudice toward female leaders, and work to dispel those perceptions.** . . .
>
> **Change the long-hours norm.** . . . To the extent an organization can shift the focus to objective measures of productivity, women with family demands on their time but highly productive work habits will receive the rewards and encouragement they deserve.
>
> **Reduce the subjectivity of performance evaluation.** . . . To ensure fairness, criteria should be explicit and evaluation processes designed to limit the influence of decision makers' conscious and unconscious biases.

Use open-recruitment tools, such as advertising and employment agencies, rather than relying on informal social networks and referrals to fill positions. . . . Research has shown that such personnel practices increase the numbers of women in managerial roles.

Ensure a critical mass of women in executive positions—not just one or two women—to head off the problems that come with tokenism. Token women tend to be pegged into narrow stereotypical roles such as "seductress," "mother," "pet," or "iron maiden." . . . When women are not a small minority, their identities as women become less salient, and colleagues are more likely to react to them in terms of their individual competencies.

Avoid having a sole female member of any team. Top management tends to divide its small population of women managers among many projects in the interests of introducing diversity to them all. But several studies have found that, so outnumbered, the women tend to be ignored by the men. . . . This is part of the reason that the glass ceiling metaphor resonates with so many. But in fact, the problem can be present at any level.

Help shore up social capital. As we've discussed, the call of family responsibilities is mainly to blame for women's underinvestment in networking. When time is scarce, this social activity is the first thing to go by the wayside. . . . When a well-placed individual who possesses greater legitimacy (often a man) takes an interest in a woman's career, her efforts to build social capital can proceed far more efficiently.

Prepare women for line management with appropriately demanding assignments. Women, like men, must have the benefit of developmental job experiences if they are to qualify for promotions. . . .

Establish family-friendly human resources practices. These may include flextime, job sharing, telecommuting, elder care provisions, adoption benefits, dependent child care options, and employee-sponsored on-site child care. Such support can allow women to stay in their jobs during the most demanding years of child rearing, build social capital, keep up to date in their fields, and eventually compete for higher positions. . . .

Allow employees who have significant parental responsibility more time to prove themselves worthy of promotion. This recommendation is particularly directed to organizations, many of them professional services firms, that have established "up or out" career progressions. People not ready for promotion at the same time as the top performers in their cohort aren't simply left in place—they're asked to leave. But many parents (most often mothers), while fully capable of reaching that level of achievement, need extra time—perhaps a year or two—to get there. . . .

Welcome women back. It makes sense to give high-performing women who step away from the workforce an opportunity to return to responsible positions when their circumstances change. . . .

Encourage male participation in family-friendly benefits. Dangers lurk in family-friendly benefits that are used only by women. Exercising options such as generous parental leave and part-time work slows down women's careers. More profoundly, having many more women than men take such benefits can harm the careers of women in general because of the expectation that they may well exercise those options. Any effort toward greater family friendliness should actively recruit male participation to avoid inadvertently making it harder for women to gain access to essential managerial roles.

Managers can be forgiven if they find the foregoing list a tall order. It's a wide-ranging set of interventions and still far from exhaustive. The point, however, is just that: Organizations will succeed in filling half their top management slots with women—and women who are the true performance equals of their male counterparts—only by attacking all the reasons they are absent today. Glass ceiling-inspired programs and projects can do just so much if the leakage of talented women is happening on every lower floor of the building. Individually, each of these interventions has been shown to make a difference. Collectively, we believe, they can make all the difference.

The View from Above

Imagine visiting a formal garden and finding within it a high hedgerow. At a point along its vertical face, you spot a rectangle—a neatly pruned and inviting doorway. Are you aware as you step through that you are entering a labyrinth? And, three doorways later, as the reality of the puzzle settles in, do you have any idea how to proceed? This is the situation in which many women find themselves in their career endeavors. Ground-level perplexity and frustration make every move uncertain.

Labyrinths become infinitely more tractable when seen from above. When the eye can take in the whole of the puzzle—the starting position, the goal, and the maze of walls—solutions begin to suggest themselves. This has been the goal of our research. Our hope is that women, equipped with a map of the barriers they will confront on their path to professional achievement, will make more informed choices. We hope that managers, too, will understand where their efforts can facilitate the progress of women. If women are to achieve equality, women and men will have to share leadership equally. With a greater understanding of what stands in the way of gender-balanced leadership, we draw nearer to attaining it in our time.

Mark van Vugt and
Anjana Ahuja

 **NO**

Naturally Selected: The Evolutionary Science of Leadership

Our brand new theory of leadership [is] grounded in evolutionary science.... [W]hen viewed in the context of this theory, much of human behaviour—the leadership styles we prefer, and those we abhor—begins to make sense: why we don't like middle managers, why we prefer the political devil we know to the angel we don't, why we bristle at extravagance among leaders, and why there is universal interest in the domestic minutiae of political figures. Our theory accommodates all the familiar features of the leadership landscape—charisma, personality traits, alpha males, the glass ceiling for women, nature versus nurture—but, unlike other leadership theories, brings them together in a way that makes sense.

We have a name for this bigger picture: evolutionary leadership theory (ELT). Its name reflects our contention, backed up by observations and experiment, that leadership and followership emerged during the course of human evolution and that their foundations were laid long before humans evolved. We call them adaptive behaviours. When scientists use the word 'adaptive' to describe a behaviour, they mean that it emerged during the course of evolution in order to enhance an organism's chances of reproduction by enabling it to adapt to the environment. Evolution selected for a combination of leaders and followers in human society; a template for these behaviours eventually became 'hard-wired' into the human brain. As you'll see, there is an abundance of evidence that leadership and followership are automatic and (usually) beneficial. Groups of strangers speedily and spontaneously arrange themselves into a led group when asked to carry out a task, and led groups invariably fare better than groups without leaders. There is, as all of us already know, something instinctive and unforced about human leadership. The ubiquity of leadership and followership in the hierarchy of life—from fish to bees to humans—also suggests that tagging behind a competent leader is a smart way for any species, not just *Homo sapiens*, to prosper.

This brings us to the distinctive and unique feature of evolutionary leadership theory. We tackle leadership by doing something startlingly simple: turning back the clock and revisiting its origins. Human leadership as we know it had to start somewhere, and it began more than two million years ago on the African savannah with the birth of the species *Homo*. Our ancestors teamed up to hunt, to fight, to live, to love—and, because tribes showing strong leadership thrived, leadership and followership came to be part of the fabric of human life. This perspective makes *Naturally Selected* very different from most of the other books on leadership psychology, which often start by scrutinising a great leader and then combing through his background to fathom what makes him tick (no apologies for the male bias here; accounts of successful female leaders are rare, and we'll explain why later on). Such biographies, while making compelling reading, rarely provide insight beyond the psychology of the lantern-jawed hero gazing out assertively from the front cover.

Naturally Selected, on the other hand, applies to each and every one of us. It goes back to basics. It transports us back to the beginning, to trace how leadership emerged and changed over an evolutionary time period of several million years. If there is any central figure in the book, it is evolution's Everyman. Conceptually, we believe that the psychology of leadership and followership emerged in our species (as well as in many others) as a response to the challenges of survival and reproduction, which are the ultimate aim of any organism. We should note here that we are adopting an evolutionary perspective which applies insights from evolutionary biology and evolutionary psychology to questions concerning leadership. An evolutionary perspective assumes that certain cognitive capacities, such as language, evolved to solve certain problems that would have preoccupied our ancestors, such as finding shelter and food. . . . Combining and integrating insights about leadership from psychology, biology, neuroscience, economics, anthropology and primatology, evolutionary leadership theory investigates what those evolutionary pressures may have been, how they might have prompted differing leadership styles throughout human history, and, finally, attempts to cast some light on what this means for us today. . . .

You'll discover that, when it comes to the workplace, the pinstripes conceal an ancient brain. That statement is not intended as an insult either to you or your ancestors; it's a fact. First, evolution works on such long timescales that all of us have, more or less, the brains that our African ancestors did, even if your entire white-skinned family has blond hair and blue eyes. Second, we are not entitled to disrespect our forebears: it is thanks to their resourcefulness that *Homo sapiens* has risen to become the most successful species on earth. Whether your distant African relatives were despots or peacemakers, you would not exist were it not for their instinct for survival. Still, the fact is that we are ancient brains trying to make our way in an ultra-modern world; when shiny new corporate ideas rub up against our creaking millennia-old psyches, the clash can make us feel uneasy. . . .

We survey evidence that voters prize traits such as height, physique, facial structure, oratorical skill—and a Y chromosome. These make little sense from a political theorist's point of view, because none of these traits (except the power of oratory, which is correlated with intelligence) is obviously linked to being able to govern well. They fit neatly, however, with what we would expect from evolutionary leadership theory. We show that our ancestral biases towards tall men with square jawlines, who look like 'one of us', often exclude better-qualified candidates. We yearn for personal information about potential leaders too—in the absence of CVs and job appraisals, this is how our ancestors gauged the quality of potential leaders within their tribes. . . .

Often, the shared objective is the leader's objective. So becoming a leader is a good way of achieving whatever it is you want to achieve, whether it is building a well or building up support for an ideology. Not only that, but leaders reap benefits, both financial (top executives get paid more than middle-ranking ones) and sexual, because (generally male) leaders appear to get their pick of (female) followers. They also enjoy an elevated social status. We will call these perks the three S's—representing salary, status and sex—and that this triumvirate of factors drives power-seeking behaviour, because they enhance the reproductive potential of the (usually) men who pursue them. Political leaders, for example, have a long and ignoble history of polygamy and infidelity.

In fact, the three S's have a clear relationship to each other, and to ELT: the ultimate evolutionary aim is reproductive success, which must be achieved through sex, which means catching the eye of sexual partners, which means being a man of status. And how is status signified today? Through salary. And so, thanks to evolutionary leadership theory, we have a thread linking money to power to sex.

This has to be one explanation for the preponderance of books about leadership: people buy them in the hope they can achieve leadership positions, and an accompanying helping of the three S's. This would suggest there are hundreds of authors who understand what leadership is about. If this is true, why do we still have so many leaders in business and politics made of the wrong stuff? Why do half of chief executives fail in their jobs? Why do political leaders lead us into unwinnable wars? Why do incompetence and immorality so often come as part of the whole human leadership package.

For the answers, we do something that no other students of leadership have yet done: travel back in time to explore the origins of human leadership. *Naturally Selected* is about how and why leadership evolved in our species. The 'why' of leadership is very rarely addressed: despite the trillions of words on the different forms leadership can take, and whether people are born to lead or can be schooled for greatness, few have paused to ask why we bother with leaders at all. Why is it that almost every social grouping—from countries to companies, councils to cults—has a figurehead out in front? Why don't individuals break from the crowd and do their own thing? This gaping hole must be plugged if we are to truly understand the human instinct to lead and the accompanying instinct to follow.

Naturally Selected is that intellectual stopper—by stepping back deep into human history, into the societies inhabited by our ancestors, we can arrive at a deeper, more complete and pleasingly concise understanding of how the twin phenomena of leadership and followership evolved in our own and other species. It allows us to identify the ingredients of good leadership ('good' in the sense of both competent and moral; as we know from the besieged financial world, leadership is frequently amoral, even immoral, and incompetent)—and to understand why bad leadership flourishes. Evolutionary leadership theory proposes a brand-new framework for answering the 'why' question: it contends that, since humans are evolutionarily adapted to live in groups, and since groups with leaders do much better than groups without leaders, it follows that leadership and followership became prerequisites for reproductive success (which is the only kind of success that matters when it comes to evolution). Simply, groups without effective leaders died out. All of us who live today carry the psychological legacy gifted to us by our forebears: we are programmed to live in led groups and, most of the time, be obedient group members. . . . We . . . discover that when we select our leaders, we consistently favour tall, fit-looking males. We call this the Savannah Hypothesis, and it contends that we still choose our leaders as if we are appointing Big Men to protect us from aggressors and predators on the savannah. . . . Sometimes we want our leaders to look warm, sometimes steely. All those traits that we pay close attention to—height, age, perceived masculinity, gender and reputation—can be thought of as 'savannah traits' of leaders. We have folded the Savannah Hypothesis into the Mismatch Hypothesis . . . because focusing on savannah traits can blind us to better candidates with proven competence, and ranks as an obvious example of a mismatch. . . .

Mismatch is a concept from evolutionary science. All organisms, indcluding people, possess traits (biological and behavioural) that have been passed down through generations through natural selection. . . .

[But] traits that were adaptive, or useful, in ancestral times are no longer necessarily adaptive in these new, different surroundings. As the experimental psychologist Steven Pinker writes: '. . . our ordeals come from a mismatch between the sources of our passions in evolutionary history and the goals we set for ourselves today'. Witness, for example, the rising rate of obesity in the West, where energy-dense foods are widely and cheaply available. Our ancestors did not live in a time when food was so plentiful; when they came across such bounty, they made the most of it. Unfortunately, we still carry the ancestral propensity to tuck into fatty, sugary foods whenever we can. Couple that with a more sedentary way of life today, and it is no wonder that our waistlines are expanding. . . .

An important aspect of Big Men leadership is that they exercise influence through persuasion rather than coercion. Big Men would be foolish to throw their weight around members of hunter-gatherer societies don't like being bossed around and, it is not unknown for them to ignore, disobey or even kill a person who assumes too much power and authority (murder is thousands of times more common in these tribes than in modern society). In an echo of our ancestral past, we still dislike bossy, self-centred and corrupt leaders today. The GLOBE project data are useful here. Dominance, despotism and selfishness are universally loathed, as are leaders regarded as arrogant, vindictive, untrustworthy, emotional, compulsive, over-controlling, insensitive, abrasive, aloof, too ambitious, or unable to delegate or make decisions.

The challenge, then, for any evolutionary framework, is to explain why leaders with these attributes still make it to the top. One possibility is that they appear benign when angling for power but show their true dictatorial colours once in office. This is where, we suggest, the Dark Triad comes into play: men who score highly on all three traits—narcissism, Machiavellianism and psychopathy—often rise to leadership positions because their cunning allows them to present a likable face to the world. Only once enthroned do they unveil their manipulative, selfish and power-hungry personalities.

In the absence of a personality test result, we do not know for sure whether Robert Mugabe, who started life as a freedom fighter in Zimbabwe against British colonialists, is a member of the Dark Triad fraternity, but we can be certain he is no longer seen as a noble liberator of his people. In 2009, while Zimbabwe starved, Mugabe ordered tons of lobster, champagne and chocolates to be flown into the country for his 85th birthday celebrations. Today, despotic leaders such as Mugabe can stay in power with the help of the army (because armies benefit from being 'in' with the ruler) and maintain the monopoly on violence. In traditional societies, such behaviour would not be tolerated for long. . . .

Women

[The] innate favouritism for 'people like us' can work against success. . . . Sometimes, the most competent leader is a different colour, a different gender or a different social class from us; and yet our evolved psychology prevents us from fully embracing this fact. For example, there are very few women directors on the boards of companies (and even fewer CEOs). A study of the 500 top US companies in 2006, however, as listed by *Fortune* magazine, showed that those with women directors are more profitable than those with no women on the board. The women-friendly companies are especially strong on corporate governance. A study from Leeds University Business School has found the same phenomenon: the data suggest that a 50:50 ratio of men and women on a board makes for a healthy balance sheet. All male boards are not good: adding just one female director cuts the risk of bankruptcy by 20 per cent. The Savannah Hypothesis will show how our gender bias is very probably a consequence of the time our species spent on the savannah. . . .

Tall, Fit, Male Leaders (or the Savannah Hypothesis)

The Savannah Hypothesis is the conceptual cocktail you get when you blend evolutionary leadership theory with the Mismatch Hypothesis. And we can give you an inkling of what we mean by asking you to consider the word 'statesmanlike'. What does it mean? You could answer: it means looking or acting like a statesman. We have certain expectations of a 'statesman': he should be male, authoritative, wise, benevolent. But to earn this epithet a leader must also have a special demeanour or even physique about him. It is hard for a nervy beanpole who stutters to look statesmanlike; a short, tubby fellow with a high-pitched voice would be similarly challenged. Where do we get this mental image of what a statesman should be like?

The truth is, voters approve of candidates who look, sound and behave in a certain way. Height, physique and attractiveness matter. Political scientists have consistently noted that taller presidential candidates are more likely to be voted in; rotund hopefuls are extremely unlikely to become wedged behind the desk in the Oval Office (the last overweight candidate to roll into the White House was William Howard Taft, in 1909). Voters also generally favour mature leaders over young ones. Barack Obama bucked the maturity trend, partly because some voters thought that, at 72, John McCain was a little too mature to start ruling. Not that Obama coveted the gift of youth: there were rumours that the dynamic lawyer dyed his hair grey in order to heighten his air of authority.

Traditional leadership theories have some difficulty explaining the seemingly irrelevant correlations with age, height, weight, health and gender, and tend to see them as spurious (and the preference for male leaders as an example of social conditioning). After all, ruling is more of a cerebral activity than a physical one. But view these same correlations through the lens of evolutionary leadership theory, and these preferences begin to make sense. In ancestral environments, choosing a poor leader was potentially so costly that any notable personal trait would be folded into the selection process. After all, hunter-gatherer tribes didn't do interview boards, leaving physical appearance and personality as the only viable metrics for competence. For leadership activities requiring physical strength and stamina, such as group hunting or warfare, our ancestors would have wanted the physically fittest man for the job (in retrospect, a wise judgement, because you are testament to their success). Height, weight and health would have pointed to fitness. Evolutionary leadership theory explains it like this: evolution has burned into our brains a set of templates for selecting those who lead us, and these templates are activated whenever we encounter a specific problem requiring coordination (such as in times of war or recession). The Savannah Hypothesis spells out what those criteria, or savannah traits, are.

Our Savannah Hypothesis contains four broad ingredients. First, it proposes that individuals with a particular set of physical features and psychological traits were more likely to emerge as leaders in ancestral societies. To the extent that these traits were reliable predictors of effective leadership, followers started to pay closer attention to these cues. Over time, using these cues, followers built up cognitive profiles or prototypes of good leadership, and individuals who slotted most closely into these moulds were more likely to be accorded leadership status.

Second, the Savannah Hypothesis maintains that these cognitive ancestral leader prototypes (let's call them CALPs for short) varied according to the task in hand. For instance, the CALP of a peacetime leader would look very different from the CALP of a war leader, because different leadership traits are required for fighting wars and maintaining peace.

A third plank of the hypothesis is that, over time, these CALPs became hard-wired in our brains. This is how it works: if a particular action (say, following Thor to go hunting) is consistently associated with a particular, positive outcome (say, filling one's belly), the mental association between action and outcome becomes reinforced over time. So, whenever Thor dons his hunting boots, he attracts followers. This cognitive association can then be generalised to other situations in which Thor wants to take the lead—such as going into battle with another group—as well as to situations in which people who look or behave like Thor want to take the reins. Over many generations, this reinforced association becomes a cognitive template. So, people lacking in experience might still become leaders simply because they fit the CALP template.

A fourth and final implication is that we still spontaneously evaluate aspiring leaders based on these CALPs, even though the templates are no longer relevant (because most of us don't need to hunt for food). Think of the automatic fear response towards snakes and spiders. Although they hardly threaten modern humans, these creatures—and even pictures of them—consistently elicit a powerful fear response. We don't respond in anything like the same way to cars, which are much more threatening to human survival in terms of the number of genetic lines they bring to a premature end. So, our brains seem to be primed to instantly respond to dangers that were lethal in ancestral times, rather than to modern killers; and we are similarly psychologically primed to this day to seek out leaders who would have surpassed themselves on the savannah. Astonishingly, young children who are shown photographs of election candidates are extremely accurate at forecasting the winner, even though they base their judgements on looks alone. [T]he savannah traits that appear to influence the perception of leadership potential . . . [include] overall health, height, age, a masculine appearance, gender, reputation and, finally, charisma. . . .

Gender

. . . We invited four people at a time to our laboratory to play an investment game. Half the groups were told that the aim of the game was 'to earn more money with your team than the other teams in the game' (we call this the war scenario, because teams are pitted against one another). The other half were told that the aim of the game was 'to earn more money than the other players in your team' (the peace scenario).

Each group was then asked to choose a leader from two candidates, described like this: 'Sarah, a 21-year-old university student in law. Her hobbies are exercise, travelling, and going out with friends' and 'Peter, a 20-year-old university student in English literature. His hobbies are reading, music, and attending parties.' In other words, the only salient difference between the two leaders was gender. Predictably, most players (78 per cent) voted for Peter in the war scenario, and there was an overwhelming preference for Sarah (93 per cent) as leader in the peace scenario. Furthermore, these leaders were also more effective in the situations that members thought them most suited to; Peter raised more contributions in the war scenario and Sarah in the peace scenario.

Interestingly, there was also a version of the game which combined elements of both war and peace. The players were told that the goal was 'to earn more money than other teams and to earn more than the other players in your team'. In these hybrid cases the players preferred Sarah to lead (75 per cent). There is some evidence from other research that women have a more flexible leadership style, making them exceptionally capable of dealing with situations involving high degrees of complexity, such as when there are simultaneous opportunities for conflict and collaboration (and those women diplomats come to mind again).

Our relative reluctance to choose women leaders explains their absence in the top echelons of politics and business; only a third of the FTSE100 companies boast women directors, and most of those are non-executive. Just 3 percent of executive directors are female. Female presidents and prime ministers are few and far between, and tend to be daughters or widows of previous leaders (Benazir Bhutto and Corazon Aquino, for example). Where does this reluctance come from? In hunter-gatherer societies, leadership often includes a physical component. Duties include spearheading group hunts, organising raids and breaking up group fights. Because men are usually bigger and stronger than women, they are more likely to rise to prominence.

We must also remember that the perks of leadership—salary, status and sex—militate against women. Men hunger for high-status positions because it makes them more desirable to women (Darwinian logic explains the sexual allure of rich men: women know their babies will be well provided for). Women don't benefit evolutionarily from acquiring personal status and riches in quite the same way: they can best serve evolution's end (which is the propagation of the species) by nurturing their children rather than chasing a promotion or salary increase (in fact, there is some indication that career women have fertility problems because of job-related stress). These evolved differences in the way men and women view status—men care about it much more than women do—might be responsible for strengthening the already robust bias towards male leaders.

Some women do make it the top but they seem to be penalised for excelling at stereotypically masculine tasks. Carly Fiorina, the former CEO of Hewlett Packard, has often remarked on how sexist the coverage of her tenure was. It is true: we don't ask male CEOs what it's like to be a man at the top.

Society tends to assume it is the natural order of things; a woman wielding great power is still somehow seen as unnatural, especially if she is of childbearing age. We find it hard to shake the feeling that she should be at home looking after her brood. Post-menopausal women, however, appear to be taken more seriously in politics and business. Angela Merkel, the Chancellor of Germany, Hillary Clinton and Kraft CEO Irene Rosenfeld are all highly respected. In *Fortune's* 2009 ranking of America's leading businesswomen, only two were under 40. . . .

To recap, we hope we've convinced you that the way we choose our leaders owes much to our time on the savannah, where our psychology evolved to help us operate in small hunter-gatherer tribes. But, because society today is much larger and socially more complex, we've become wedged in the gap between savannah and suburbia. However much we may employ our intellect, our brains have tunnel vision when it comes to leadership psychology. And we have been in that evolutionary tunnel for perhaps two million years since the emergence of the genus *Homo:* the 13,000 years since agriculture, which fuelled the growth of large settlements, don't even register on our evolutionary radar. And so we still hanker after certain leader prototypes: we like to be led by tall, strong, lantern-jawed men who know us personally. They must possess self-belief but not self-regard; they should be charismatic, but not charlatans. These revered figures should receive extra rewards and privileges, but not too many. Today, though, leadership is very rarely about foraging and fighting in 100-strong tribes of blood relatives; it's about ruling nations of millions (a billion, in the case of China), running multinational corporations with thousand of employees, and rubbing along in a global village where people don't look and behave the same way as you do. Is it any wonder that the leaders we choose today so often disappoint?

. . . What does this mean for leadership and followership? As evolutionary leadership theory explains, our psychology has been sculpted to thrive in small, flattened communities. So, we make the kind of instinctive judgements that our ancestors made. We follow people with charisma because we use it as a proxy for competence, but we often find out to our cost that a charismatic exterior can conceal a vacuous, even vindictive, nature. We vote for tall, fit men because those are the kind of people whom our ancestors sought out to provide tribal protection. We tend to exclude women (because they were confined to traditional roles in tribal life) and minorities (because we instinctively feel suspicious of people who are not like us). Today, there is no rational reason why height, age, weight, colour and gender should be used as sole qualifications for jobs or roles. Yet these savannah instincts continue to prevent us from picking the best person to fill a particular role, which we hypothesise contributes to the substantial failure rate of managers in corporate America. . . .

Again, although male leadership is the norm in preindustrial societies we should be wary of excluding women. In today's global village, business and politics bring people of different cultures together. Interpersonal skills and network-building are supremely valuable abilities. There is good evidence that women leaders, armed with superior empathic and verbal skills, cope better in these novel environments. While our 'think leader think male' bias might be difficult to overcome, we should be aware that it might prejudice our consideration of talented women candidates.

Status is a major factor in the gender debate: evolution has selected men to be more ambitious and status-obsessed than women because, for them, these behaviours translated into ancestral reproductive success. When men and women work together, men are quicker to assume the position of a leader even when a better-qualified woman is present. Illuminatingly, Charles A. O'Reilly III, a Stanford University business professor, concludes it is not gender per se which leads to the glass ceiling for women, but the overwhelming male desire to compete. It is an interesting rewording of the evolutionary imperative we've already discussed (and he found it was the most masculine men who excelled). . . .

EXPLORING THE ISSUE

Are Barriers to Women's Success as Leaders Due to Societal Obstacles?

Challenge Questions

1. Are leaders born or made?
2. How do circumstances help determine the attributes most likely to portend success?
3. Should women deliberately adjust their leadership style to achieve promotion in the workplace?
4. What strategies should workplaces adopt to ensure that the best leaders, women and men, make it to the top?
5. Are workplaces better for having a diversity of people in various leadership roles?

Is There Common Ground?

Women's leadership style has been cited frequently as a barrier to success at the top of the corporate ladder. Leadership can be viewed from either the human capital perspective or the discrimination perspective. The human capital view would suggest that women, due to their natures, simply do not have the dominance-related and assertive dispositions that are presumed to be correlates of leadership. From a discrimination perspective, one can argue that women have not been given opportunities to learn and practice leadership skills. Furthermore, research shows that many people prefer a male to a female boss. The irony is that much of the research suggests that women's leadership styles, when they differ from those of men, can be more effective, although the job description rather than the sex of the person usually better predicts what type of leadership style one will use. How can the contradictions between women being effective leaders and still having difficulty exercising leadership be resolved? Alice Eagly has suggested that the view of female leadership is complex and is a mixture of advantage and disadvantage. On the one hand, women's styles have been described as transformative, in that they promote innovation, trust, and empowerment in followers. On the other hand, expectations regarding competitiveness and toughness, coupled with old-fashioned prejudice against women, can interfere with effective leadership, especially in male-dominated domains.

Additional Resources

Hilary Lips, "Women and Leadership: Delicate Balancing Act," *Womens Media* (April, 2009): http://www.womensmedia.com/lead/88-women-and-leadership-delicate-balancing-act.html

Worldwide Guide to Women in Leadership: http://www.guide2womenleaders.com/

Internet References . . .

Advocates for Youth

This Web site, established in 1980 as the Center for Population Options, works to help young people make informed and responsible decisions about their reproductive and sexual health, fostering a positive and realistic approach to adolescent sexual health.

http://www.advocatesforyouth.org/%20%09%20index.php?option=com_content&task=view&id=46&Itemid=75

American Psychological Association

This section of the APA Web site provides definitions of transgender and related concepts and answers a number of questions about development and mental health.

http://www.apa.org/topics/sexuality/transgender.aspx

WebMD Sexual Health Center

This Web site provides information from a medical perspective on gender identity disorder.

http://www.webmd.com/sex/gender-identity-disorder

Information for Health

The INFO Project (Information and Knowledge for Optimal Health Project), based at the Johns Hopkins University Bloomberg School of Public Health's Center for Communication Programs, is focused on understanding how knowledge and information can improve the quality of reproductive health programs, practice, and policies.

http://www.infoforhealth.org/

Gender Talk

Gendertalk.com is a resource for trans persons and folks interested in learning about trans persons. Gendertalk.com provides comprehensive access to GenderTalk Radio, the leading radio program on transgender issues.

http://www.gendertalk.com/radio/about.shtml

Go Ask Alice!

Go Ask Alice! is a health question-and-answer site sponsored by Columbia University's health education program. The mission of this site is to provide in-depth, factual, and nonjudgmental information to assist individuals' decision making about their physical, sexual, emotional, and spiritual health. Questions about sexuality, sexual health, and relationships are frequent. This site includes hundreds of relevant links.

http://www.goaskalice.columbia.edu/

Susan's Place for Transgender Resources

This Web site provides access to a wealth of information for transgendered persons, including information on health sex reassignment surgery, links to various support groups, activism, and spirituality.

http://www.susans.org/

Gender and Sexuality: Double Standards?

*M*any contemporary scholars view sexuality as a cultural construction. Cultures provide individuals with knowledge and "lenses" that
structure institutions, social interactions, beliefs, and behaviors. Through
cultural lenses or meaning systems, individuals perceive the "facts" of sex
and gender. Conceptualizations of sex and gender and the importance of
sex and gender as social categories vary from culture to culture. However,
within a particular culture, because individuals are usually limited to
their own cultural lens, definitions of sex and gender seem fixed or even
natural. In fact, cultural scholars argue, culture so completely defines us
that we are usually oblivious to its presence in our own society. We think
of culture as something that other societies have. How do adolescents first
experience sexual attractions—developing a "crush," falling in love, making the decision to "go all the way"? How does a child grow into a sexual
being? What does it mean to be sexual? How does a child learn to think
about his or her own genitals? These are profoundly personal and important questions, the answers to which are shaped by our cultural understanding of sexuality. In this unit, we examine cultural constructions of
sex, gender, gender identity, and sexuality, especially messages sent to
children and adolescents. Specifically, how are cultural institutions and
mores structured by cultural definitions of the importance of sex and gender and by cultural gender proscriptions? What does culture dictate about
the significance and characteristics of the social categories, "male" and
"female"? Where is there space for people who identify as other than
male or female? Does one's standpoint or location within the culture
prescribe one's sexual experiences? Consider how assumptions about the
biological basis of sexuality as a prime force in human behavior influence
how cultures attempt to control sexuality through various sex education
strategies. Does the assumption that the expression of sexuality is based
on biological drives affect messages that are delivered via the media? How
can media images of sexual expression operate as both informational and
normative sources of influence? Is it possible to resist media images?

- Is There Something Wrong with the Content of Comprehensive Sex
  Education Curricula?

- Is "Gender Identity Disorder" an Appropriate Psychiatric Diagnosis?

- Should Transgender Women Be Considered "Real" Women?

ISSUE 19

Is There Something Wrong with the Content of Comprehensive Sex Education Curricula?

YES: The Administration for Children and Families (ACF), Department of Health and Human Services (HHS), from "Review of Comprehensive Sex Education Curricula" (Washington, DC: U.S. Government Printing Office, 2007)

NO: Elokin CaPece, from "Commentary on the *Review of Comprehensive Sex Education Curricula* (2007)," *American Journal of Sexuality Education* (vol. 3, no. 3, 2007)

Learning Outcomes

As you read the issue, focus on the following points:

- Should the public be responsible for sex education or is it parents' responsibility?
- What are the criteria for determining that a sex education program is comprehensive and effective?
- To what extent do sex education programs address issues of gender and sexual orientation? Should they?
- What insights might be gained from examining the words that appear in a curriculum? Is such an examination a reasonable barometer for programs' contents?

ISSUE SUMMARY

YES: The Administration for Children and Families, Department of Health and Human Services, presents their findings in a critical analysis of comprehensive sexuality education curricula.

NO: Elokin CaPece disputes the research methods used and the findings of the report, highlighting what she sees as bias in the overall findings.

In 1996, President Clinton signed the welfare reform law. Attached to this law was a federal entitlement program allocating $50 million per year over a five-year period to abstinence-only-until-marriage educational programs. This Act specified that a program is defined as "abstinence-only" education if it:

- has as its exclusive purpose teaching the social, psychological, and health gains to be realized by abstaining from sexual activity;
- teaches that abstinence from sexual activity outside of marriage is the expected standard for all school-age children;
- teaches that abstinence from sexual activity is the only certain way to avoid out-of-wedlock pregnancy, sexually transmitted diseases, and other associated health problems;
- teaches that a mutually faithful monogamous relationship in the context of marriage is the expected standard of sexual activity;
- teaches that sexual activity outside the context of marriage is likely to have harmful psychological and physical side effects;
- teaches that bearing children out of wedlock is likely to have harmful consequences for the child, the child's parents, and society;
- teaches young people how to reject sexual advances and how alcohol and drug use increases vulnerability to sexual advances; and
- teaches the importance of attaining self-sufficiency before engaging in sexual activity. *(Section 510(b) of Title V of the Social Security Act, P.L. 104-193).*

To access these funds, an entity must agree to teach all of these points, not just a few. Failure to do so would result in loss of the funding. Those who support the teaching of comprehensive sexuality education have disagreed with the tenets that abstinence-only-until-marriage (AOUM) supports. They presented research that demonstrated how comprehensive sexuality education programs help young people to delay the onset of risky sexual behaviors, and to use contraceptives more effectively once they do start engaging in these behaviors. Some argue that AOUM is exclusionary, excluding nonheterosexual youth, is fear- and shame-based, and is wildly out of touch with the reality in which young people are living. They are quick to point out that AOUM supporters have yet to provide empirical evidence that their programs "work." AOUM supporters believe that comprehensive sexuality education programs teach "too much, too soon." They believe strongly that providing information about abstinence, along with safer sex information, confuses teens and gives them permission to become sexually active when the potential consequences for sexual activity are much more serious. Take a look at the language of the legislation. The language refers to "sexual activity." We know that for many people "having sex" means only sexual intercourse. It does not include oral or anal sex, for example. We know that many teens are having sexual intercourse outside of marriage, and although this number is going down, the number of youth engaging in oral and anal sex is increasing. What does "sexual activity" mean to you? Would you be able to support the legislation if it included some behaviors, but not others?

AOUM programs forbid providing accurate information about the use of contraceptives and condoms to prevent unplanned pregnancy and sexually transmitted infections, respectively. Concurrently, the federal government had also elected *not* to fund comprehensive sex education, which would have provided safer sex and contraceptive information, as well as other expert suggested age-appropriate information. Initially, criticism of comprehensive sex education was largely ideological. AOUM advocates would argue. "Why subject children to explicit information about sex when they should be waiting for marriage?" Proponents of comprehensive sex education counter with the argument "Why fund programs that withhold critical, potentially life-saving information from teens?" There were also concerns about using public funds—and public schools—to establish a singular moral (and, in some cases, religious) standard sexual behavior: sex *only* in monogamous, heterosexual marriages. As the battle waged, money continued to pour in for AOUM programs. The annual spending more than doubled during the administration of George W. Bush, rising from $97.5 million per year at the time of his election to $242 million in his last year in office. This enormous amount of spending surprised many, and American taxpayers who overwhelmingly support sexuality education were chagrined as the national economy tanked. During the administration of Barack Obama, AOUM funding continued but was substantially reduced. Obama also signed the Consolidated Appropriations Act of 2010, which marked the first time that the U.S. government funded teen pregnancy prevention programs and projects, and included $114.5 million in federal funds for the Teen Pregnancy Prevention Initiative (TPPI). In the midst of the perennial debate over AOUM funding, a federally commissioned review of 13 AOUM curricula found that 80% of the curricula material provided "false, misleading, or distorted information about sexual health" (United States House of Representatives Committee on Government Reform, 2004). In some cases, the distortions were without reference, such as the assertion of one curriculum that "girls who have sex before marriage are six times as likely to commit suicide than virgins." Research also found the programs to be ineffective. The independent research group Mathematica Policy Research, Inc. found that teens who participated in AOUM programs "were no more likely than control group youth to have abstained from sex." Doug Kirby, one of the nation's most respected researchers on adolescent sexual health, also found no impact of AOUM programs on teen sexual behavior. Two researchers found that AOUM programs were ineffective and potentially harmful. In a study of virginity pledge programs, the researchers found that 88% of those who made a pledge failed to keep that pledge, and one-third were less likely to use a condom during intercourse. There was a backlash among conservatives who championed AOUM programs all along. As evidence documenting the failure of AOUM programs grew (and a number of states—17 to date—actually began *rejecting* the federal funds), Senator Tom Coburn (R-Oklahoma) and former Senator Rick Santorum (R-Pennsylvania) commissioned a new federal study to scrutinize the content of comprehensive sexuality education programs. Under their direction, the Administration for Children and Families of the U.S. Department of Health and Human

Services sought to similarly discredit sexuality education, focusing primarily on the types of words that appear in the text of sexuality education curricula. The YES selection that follows is an excerpt from the report. In response, sexual health educator Elokin CaPece criticizes the report as "irresponsible research" and critiques its research methods and findings. She criticizes the report for its clear and inappropriate bias against the subject examined, and for its unreasonable criteria to describing the "failure" of sexuality education programs.

YES

The Administration for Children and Families (ACF), Department of Health and Human Services (HHS)

Review of Comprehensive Sex Education Curricula

Introduction

"Comprehensive Sex Education" curricula for adolescents have been endorsed by various governmental agencies, educational organizations, and teenage advocacy groups as the most effective educational method for reducing teenage pregnancy and helping prevent the spread of sexually transmitted diseases (STDs) among America's youth. The National Institutes of Health (NIH) defines Comprehensive Sex Education (CSE) as "teaching both abstinence and the use of protective methods for sexually active youth"; NIH states that CSE curricula have been "shown to delay sexual activity among teens." Non-governmental groups that support CSE have also made statements linking CSE curricula to abstinence as well as reduction of pregnancy and sexually transmitted infections (STIs).

The Administration for Children and Families, within the Department of Health and Human Services undertook an examination of some of the most common CSE curricula currently in use. The purpose of this examination was to inform federal policymakers of the content, medical accuracy, and effectiveness of CSE curricula currently in use.

Background

In 2005, Senators Santorum and Coburn requested that the Administration for Children and Families (ACF) review and evaluate comprehensive sex education programs supported with federal dollars. The Senators wrote to the Assistant Secretary for Children and Families,

> In particular, we would appreciate a review that explores the effectiveness of these programs in reducing teen pregnancy rates and the transmission of sexually transmitted diseases. In addition, please assess the effectiveness of these programs in advancing the greater goal of encouraging teens to make the healthy decision to delay sexual activity. Please also include an evaluation of the scientific accuracy of the content of these programs. Finally, we would appreciate an assessment of how the actual content of these programs compares to their stated goals.

From a report published by Administration for Children & Families (ACF)/U.S. Dept. of Health and Human Services. May 2007, pp. 3–12. http://www.acf.hhs.gov/programs/fysb/content/docs/comprehensive.pdf

In response, ACF contracted with the Sagamore Institute for Policy Research to review some of the most common CSE curricula currently in use. ACF also requested and received comments on these reviews from the Medical Institute for Sexual Health (MISH).

Research Questions and Methodology

In response to the request from Senators Santorum and Coburn, the curriculum reviews evaluated four questions:

1. Does the content of the comprehensive sex education curricula mirror the stated purposes?
2. What is the content of comprehensive sex education curricula?
3. Do comprehensive sex education curricula contain medically inaccurate statements?
4. Do evaluations of these curricula show them to be effective at (a) delaying sexual debut and (b) reducing sex without condoms?

The initial charge of this project was to evaluate the content and effectiveness of the "most frequently used" CSE curricula. After a thorough search, which included contacting publishers, researchers, distributors, and advocacy groups, it was determined that a list ranked by "frequency of use" or "number of copies purchased" was not in existence nor could one be produced.

Instead, curricula were chosen for this study based on the frequency and strength of endorsement received from leading and recognized sexuality information organizations and resources. A curriculum was considered to be "endorsed" if a source recommended it or promoted it as a "program that works." The curricula mentioned most frequently were chosen for this study if they were school-based (i.e., not solely for community organizations), widely available, and described by at least one source as "comprehensive" or "abstinence-plus." Additional weight was given to curricula described as evidence-based or as a "program that works."

It should be noted that some of the curricula reviewed do not state in their materials that they have an abstinence focus—i.e., that they are "comprehensive sex education," "abstinence plus," or in some other way focused on abstinence. However, if a curriculum were endorsed as "comprehensive" or "abstinence plus" by a leading sexuality information organization and resources, it was assumed that the curriculum would be purchased and used for the purpose of providing comprehensive sex education. Additionally of note, some of the curricula have recently published revisions with added abstinence components. In every case, the most recent version of the curricula available was studied.

Nine curricula met the criteria for this study and were subsequently reviewed:

1. *Reducing the Risk: Building Skills to Prevent Pregnancy, STD & HIV (4th Edition)*, by R. Barth, 2004.
2. *Be Proud! Be Responsible!*, L. Jemmott, J. Jemmott, K. McCaffree, published by Select Media, Inc. 2003.

3. *Safer Choices: Preventing HIV, Other STD and Pregnancy (Level 1)*, by J. Fetro, R. Barth, K. Coyle, published by ETR Associates, 1998; and *Safer Choices: Preventing HIV, Other STD and Pregnancy (Level 2)*, by K. Coyle and J. Fetro, published by ETR Associates, 1998.
4. *AIDS Prevention for Adolescents in School*, by S. Kasen and I. Tropp, distributed by the Program Archive on Sexuality, Health, and Adolescence (PASHA), 2003.
5. *BART=Becoming a Responsible Teen (Revised Edition)*, by J. Lawrence, published by ETR (Education, Training, Research) Associates, 2005.
6. *Teen Talk: An Adolescent Pregnancy Prevention Program*, by M. Eisen, A. McAlister, G. Zellman, distributed by PASHA, 2003.
7. *Reach for Health, Curriculum, Grade 8*, by L. O'Donnell, et al., by Education Development Center, Inc., 2003.
8. *Making Proud Choices*. L. Jemmott, J. Jemmott, K. McCaffree, published by Select Media, Inc., 2001, 2002.
9. *Positive Images: Teaching Abstinence, Contraception, and Sexual Health*, by P. Brick and B. Taverner, published by Planned Parenthood of Greater Northern New Jersey, Inc., 2001.

The curriculum review consisted of four components. First, each curriculum underwent an extensive content analysis, i.e., a word-by-word count of instances in which certain words or themes (e.g., condoms, abstinence) are mentioned. Content analyses offer insight into the weight respective curricula give to key themes. Appendix A contains the complete content analysis for each curriculum reviewed.

Second, the stated purposes of the curricula were compared to the actual emphases of the curricula, as demonstrated by the content analysis.

Third, curriculum content was evaluated for medical accuracy, primarily the accuracy of statements about condoms (including statements on a common spermicide, nonoxynol-9, that was previously recommended to be added to condoms).

Lastly, evaluations of each curriculum—which offer insights into curriculum effectiveness at delaying sexual debut and increasing condom use—were located and summarized.

Appendix B contains a curriculum-by-curriculum review of the each curriculum's content, medical accuracy, and evaluations of each curriculum.

Findings

The curriculum reviews yielded the following findings:

- **Does the content of the curricula mirror their stated purposes?** While the content of the curricula reviewed adheres to their stated purposes for the most part, these curricula often do not spend as much time discussing abstinence as they do discussing contraception and ways to lessen risks of sexual activity. Of the curricula reviewed, the curriculum with the most balanced discussion of abstinence and safer-sex still discussed condoms and contraception nearly seven times more than abstinence. Three of the nine curricula reviewed did not have a stated purpose of promoting abstinence; however, two of these three curricula still discussed abstinence as an option (although, again, discussion of condoms and safer sex predominated). As a last note, it is important to recognize that, although some of the curricula do not include abstinence as a stated purpose, some sexuality information organizations and resources recommend these curricula as comprehensive sex education.

- **What is the content of comprehensive sex education curricula?** As mentioned in the previous paragraph, these curricula focus on contraception and ways to lessen risks of sexual activity, although abstinence is at times a non-trivial component. Curriculum approaches to discussing contraception and ways to lessen risks of sexual activity can be grouped in three broad areas: (1) how to obtain protective devices (e.g., condoms), (2) how to broach a discussion on introducing these devices in a relationship, and (3) how to correctly use the devices. Below are a few excerpts from the curricula in these three areas.

  - **How to obtain protective devices:** "How can you minimize your embarrassment when buying condoms? . . . Take a friend along; find stores where you don't have to ask for condoms (e.g., stocked on open counter or shelf); wear shades or a disguise so no one will recognize you; have a friend or sibling who isn't embarrassed buy them for you; make up a condom request card that you can hand to the store clerk (Show example)" (*AIDS Prevention for Adolescents in School*, p. 63).
  - **How to broach a discussion on introducing these devices in a relationship:** "Teacher states: 'Pretend I am your sexual partner. I am going to read more excuses (for not using condoms) and I want you to convince me to use a condom' (*Making Proud Choices*, p. 157).
  - **How to correctly use the devices:** "Have volunteers come to the front of the room (preferably an equal number of males and females). Distribute one card to each. Give them a few minutes to arrange themselves in the proper order so their cards illustrate effective condom use from start to finish. Non-participants observe how the group completes this task and review the final order. When the order is correct, post the cards in the front of the room. CORRECT ORDER: (Sexual Arousal, Erection, Leave Room at the Tip, Roll Condom On, Intercourse, Orgasm/Ejaculation, Hold Onto Rim, Withdraw the Penis, Loss of Erection, Relaxation). Ask a volunteer to describe each step in condom use, using the index and middle finger or a model of a penis" (*Positive Images*, p. 102).

- **Do the curricula contain medically inaccurate statements?** Most comprehensive sex education curricula reviewed contain some level of medical inaccuracy. Of the nine curricula reviewed, three had no medically inaccurate statements. The most common type of medical inaccuracy involved promotion of nonoxynol-9, a common spermicide; three curricula had medical inaccuracies involving nonoxynol-9. While condoms with nonoxynol-9 (N-9) had previously been recommended for reducing the risk of HIV and other STD in the 1990s, research over the last decade has demonstrated that nonoxynol-9 is at best ineffective against STDs and HIV, and at worse increases risk.

Other inaccuracies included: (a) one curriculum that used the term "dental dam" instead of the FDA-approved "rubber dam"; (b) one curriculum that quoted first year condom failure rates for pregnancy at 12%, when the correct statistic is 15%; and (c) one curriculum that stated that all condoms marketed in the United States "meet federal assurance standards" (which is not true).

In terms of inaccurate statistics related to condom effectiveness, eight of the nine curricula did not have any inaccuracies. The one curriculum which did have inaccuracies, *Making Proud Choices,* had three erroneous statements.

Although there were few inaccurate statements regarding condom effectiveness, the curricula do not state the risks of condom failure as extensively as is done in some abstinence-until-marriage curricula, nor do they discuss condom failure rates in context. Indeed, there were misleading statements in every curriculum reviewed. For example, one curriculum states, "When used correctly, latex condoms prevent pregnancy 97% of the time." While this statement is technically true, 15% percent of women using condoms for contraception experience an unintended pregnancy during the first year of "typical use," and 20% of adolescents under the age of 18 using condoms for contraception get pregnant within one year.

For perspective, it may be helpful to compare the error rate reported here with statistics cited in the December 2004 report entitled "The Content of Federally Funded Abstinence Education Programs," which is typically called the Waxman Report. This report found that, of thirteen abstinence-until-marriage curricula reviewed, eleven contained medically inaccurate statements; in all thirteen curricula (nearly 5,000 pages of information), there were 49 instances of questionable information. It could easily be argued that the comprehensive sex education curricula reviewed for this report have a similar rate of error compared with abstinence-until-marriage curricula.

• **Do evaluations of these curricula show them to be effective at (a) delaying sexual debut and (b) reducing sex without condoms?** According to the evaluations reviewed, these curricula show some small positive impacts on (b) reducing sex without condoms, and to a lesser extent (a) delaying sexual debut. Specifically, there were evaluations for eight of the nine curricula reviewed. Of those eight curricula, seven showed at least some positive impacts on condom use; two showed some positive impacts on delay of sexual initiation. One curriculum (*Teen Talk*) showed the only negative impact: for sexually inexperienced females, there was a negative impact on first intercourse and on consistent use of contraceptives. Often the impacts observed in evaluations are small, and most often the impacts do not extend three or six months after a curriculum has been used. It is important to note that evaluations of the curricula do have limitations. All curricula were evaluated by the curriculum authors themselves (although all evaluations were peer-reviewed and published in established journals). Also, the sample sizes are small in some of the evaluations, and research design issues decrease the ability to draw conclusions from some of the evaluations. Appendix B contains details on the evaluations of these curricula.

Conclusion

Research on the effectiveness of nine commonly used comprehensive sex education curricula demonstrates that, while such curricula show small positive impacts on increasing condom use among youth, only a couple of curricula show impacts on delaying sexual debut; moreover, effects most often disappear over time. The fact that both the stated purposes and the actual content of these curricula emphasize ways to lessen risks associated with sexual activity—and not necessarily avoiding sexual activity—may explain why research shows them to be more effective at increasing condom use than at delaying sexual debut. Lastly, although the medical accuracy of comprehensive sex education curricula is nearly 100%—similar to that of abstinence-until-marriage curricula—efforts could be made to more extensively detail condom failure rates in context.

Appendix A: Content Analysis

Provided below is a word-by-word count of the number of times specific words or themes appears in each of the reviewed curricula.

      RTR = Reducing the Risk
      Be Proud = Be Proud, Be Responsible
      SC1 = Safer Choices 1
      SC2 = Safer Choices 2
      AIDS = AIDS Prevention for Adolescents in School
      BART = Becoming A Responsible Teen
      Teen Talk
      Reach = Reach for Health
      MPC = Making Proud Choices
      PI = Positive Images

	RTR	Be Proud	SC 1	SC 2	AIDS	BART	Teen Talk	Reach	MPC	PI
100% safe/effective	4	22	7	1	4	0	5	12	1	7
abortion/termination/ interruption	1	0	0	1	0	0	8	0	0	18
abstinence/abstain	90	50	5	5	0	19	32	15	18	87
alcohol	3	14	2	3	5	12	2	0	18	21
alternatives to sexual intercourse	45	10	64	40	1	7	0	5	12	16
anal sex	11	33	10	2	4	16	0	1	57	8
avoid/avoiding (behaviors/consequences)	20	9	24	1	0	14	11	9	42	18
birth control	27	5	25	25	9	5	58	10	37	37
boyfriend (s)	24	13	1	3	11	8	2	11	23	7
casual sex	0	0	0	0	0	0	0	0	0	0
cervical cap	0	0	1	0	0	0	8	0	5	15

(continued)

	RTR	Be Proud	SC 1	SC 2	AIDS	BART	Teen Talk	Reach	MPC	PI
chlamydia	5	0	16	7	1	0	5	2	6	1
committed relationship	0	2	0	0	0	1	0	1	0	1
condom/contraceptive failure	1	3	5	5	0	0	0	0	2	7
condom/condoms	183	495	383	389	136	262	22	8	650	235
contraception/ contraceptive	18	3	31	38	2	0	131	3	39	381
diaphragm	0	0	3	2	0	0	31	0	7	26
douche/douching	8	0	11	10	0	0	14	5	10	2
drug/drugs	32	58	20	8	36	45	2	2	81	75
ejaculate (tion, s, ed, "cum")	6	14	10	11	0	5	9	18	24	12
emotional (consequences)	2	0	0	0	0	0	1	2	1	0
erection (erect)	1	12	9	9	3	0	8	7	15	19
fantasy (ies, ize)	0	3	0	0	0	0	2	9	5	0
French kissing	2	1	1	0	0	0	0	0	1	1
fun (of sex)	0	24	0	1	0	0	0	0	19	0
genital warts/warts	1	0	8	4	0	0	6	1	11	1
girlfriend	31	13	3	3	6	8	3	6	24	3
gonorrhea	5	1	16	7	2	0	12	3	20	2
health/healthy	27	39	58	60	16	72	77	54	35	180
healthier/healthiest	2	2	0	0	0	1	0	1	3	1
Herpes	4	1	15	6	0	0	20	5	18	1
HIV/AIDS	451	477	369	253	28	473	20	7	210	48
IUD	0	0	4	6	0	0	0	0	0	5
kiss, kissing, kissed, kisses	29	30	15	14	2	8	0	4	33	6
love, loved, loves	51	9	35	19	6	16	0	14	22	14
lovers	1	1	0	0	0	0	0	0	1	1
making love (love making)	0	0	1	1	0	0	0	0	1	1
marriage	3	0	4	1	0	0	0	1	0	9
marry, married	3	0	0	5	1	0	4	0	0	4
masturbation, masturbate	4	5	0	0	0	3	8	2	9	13
masturbation: mutual/ partner	1	2	0	0	0	0	1	0	3	0
maximum protection	0	1	0	0	0	0	0	0	0	0
morning after pill (emergency contraception)	0	0	6	12	0	0	1	0	0	24
negative, negatively, (ism)	2	18	12	27	6	10	4	22	14	18
negotiation (to use condoms)	1	37	4	1	14	35	1	0	52	1
no risk	0	0	0	0	0	2	0	0	3	1
not having sex	8	0	7	7	7	1	2	3	0	0
oral sex	10	36	9	2	3	13	0	2	73	4
orgasm	1	15	0	0	0	0	6	1	8	11
outercourse	0	2	0	0	0	0	0	0	0	13
parents/parenthood	104	0	97	118	5	34	11	13	13	65

	RTR	Be Proud	SC 1	SC 2	AIDS	BART	Teen Talk	Reach	MPC	PI
pill (contraceptive)	45	13	37	35	7	4	27	3	31	59
pleasure, able, ing (re: sex)	0	31	2	1	1	0	3	3	8	8
practice (s, ed, ing) (techniques, skills, using condoms)	2	5	13	14	0	6	19	47	70	20
pregnant, pregnancy	348	30	167	242	3	8	155	113	184	241
prophylactics	1	0	1	1	0	0	2	0	0	0
protect (s, ed), protection	254	25	314	145	7	24	7	20	82	80
protective (products)	1	10	6	0	0	0	0	0	0	1
purchasing (buying) condoms	2	6	11	12	8	10	4	0	12	5
rape	0	1	0	0	0	0	0	0	2	3
rape: date	0	0	0	0	0	0	0	0	2	1
refuse, refusal (skills)/ delaying sex tactics	110	11	84	76	1	13	2	48	46	0
reproductive, reproduction	0	0	5	4	0	0	33	18	2	80
risk reduction	0	0	0	1	0	2	0	0	3	0
risk (high)	4	4	0	0	4	5	4	0	5	3
risk (low, lower)	1	0	0	0	0	1	1	0	1	2
risk, risks, risking	273	166	133	112	32	149	31	38	118	140
riskier	0	0	0	0	0	2	0	0	0	0
risky	8	25	9	5	21	42	2	2	18	2
rubber (s)	8	3	2	2	0	5	24	0	4	4
safe, safely	11	41	8	7	3	67	8	4	40	12
safer	0	74	297	345	2	55	0	0	61	38
safest	6	1	45	26	2	0	1	0	1	0
sex	290	334	442	287	64	168	91	168	440	83
sexual	71	152	106	81	101	94	78	116	146	232
intercourse (sexual)	46	47	81	46	77	23	22	28	58	237
sexual orientation (gay, lesbian, homosexual, same sex)	5	19	7	2	0	6	1	2	9	13
sexuality	18	0	17	19	1	3	32	115	1	98
sexually	47	46	18	23	11	33	38	49	60	85
sexy	2	1	0	1	1	0	0	4	2	0
spermicide (s, dal)	14	11	35	19	4	15	25	4	43	23
sponge	0	0	0	0	0	0	4	0	0	28
STD (s)	230	44	221	178	2	8	47	77	281	2
STI	0	0	0	0	0	0	0	0	0	64
syphilis	0	2	15	4	2	0	12	0	17	1
unprotected sex/ intercourse	54	26	43	0	0	23	13	8	30	5
contraceptive film	3	0	6	5	0	0	0	0	6	4
venereal disease (VD)	0	0	0	0	0	0	3	0	0	0
withdrawal (withdraws, pull out)	10	3	12	0	0	6	9	4	13	17

Elokin CaPece  **NO**

Commentary on the *Review of Comprehensive Sex Education Curricula* (2007)

In the last several years research on the effectiveness of sex education programs that target preteens and teens has evolved into a very sophisticated and professional discourse. In 2002, a review of 73 studies of programs (including but not limited to comprehensive sex education programs) pulled out a set of characteristics that were found in programs that reduced sexual risk-taking, promoted condom use, and/or delayed sexual onset. These programs focused on behaviors that prevented unintended pregnancy or sexually transmitted infection (including HIV), utilized already-established practices for reducing risk-taking behaviors, gave a clear message that emphasized the prevention behaviors and frequently reinforced that message, provided basic and accurate information, included modeling, role-playing, and refusal skills practice, employed a high degree of student participation in a wide range of educational styles, were tailored to the age, culture, and sexual experience of their audience, lasted a sufficient length of time, and were taught by facilitators who had adequate training and believed in the program's effectiveness. This same review attempted to include abstinence-only program studies in its analysis but found that only three published studies met the criteria for his review and two of these had "important methodological limitations." The article did not make any claims about the effectiveness or ineffectiveness of such programs (due to the lack of reliable research and the wide variance in program formats), but concluded that the characteristics found common in effective comprehensive sex education programs should be considered best practices for abstinence-only programs of comparable design as well (Kirby, 2002, 51–54).

In 2004 a federally funded and commissioned review of 13 abstinence-only curricula (representing two-thirds of the programs funded by abstinence-only federal money at the time of the review), commonly known as the Waxman Report, found that 80% of the curricular material reviewed contained "false, misleading, or distorted information about reproductive health (United States House of Representatives Committee on Government Reform [United States Committee on Govt. Reform], 2004, i)." The most common inaccuracies were an exaggeration of contraceptive failure rates, inaccurate information

From *American Journal of Sexuality Education*, September 2008, pp. 295–312. Copyright © 2008 by Routledge/Taylor & Francis Group. Reprinted by permission via Rightslink.

about the risks of abortion, the stating of religious belief as scientific fact, the treatment of gender role stereotypes as scientific fact, and general scientific errors (United States Committee on Govt. Reform, 2004, i–ii).

In 2007 Mathematica Policy, Inc. released a study of four federally funded abstinence-only programs. These programs were chosen because they represented the wide range of types of educational programming that fell under the banner of abstinence-only and because they served rural and urban communities in every region of the United States The report found that these programs had just as much of an impact on teens as no sex education programming at all had. Teens in the abstinence-only programs behaved in statistically similar ways to teens in the control group (who were receiving no sex education programming) (Mathematica Policy Research, 2007, 59–60).

These reviews represent the macro-level of sex education research. On the micro-level there are individual program evaluations, the quality of which has been transformed in the last ten years. In 1997 SIECUS published a manual written by researchers critiquing the research done on sex education programs as poorly designed, weakly implemented, and not well funded (Haffner & Goldfarb, 1997, 4). In 2002 Doug Kirby noted that while very few program evaluations had experimental or quasi-experimental designs and rarely were evaluations replicated in the late 1990s, by 2000 he had enough well-researched material to examine comprehensive sex education programs, reproductive health clinic services, service learning programs, and Children's Aid Society Carrera programs (Kirby, 2002). Today, the research standards put forth by SIECUS influence how many sex education programs are designed, implemented, and evaluated.

Background Information on the 2007 Comprehensive Sex Education Review

The 2007 *Review of Comprehensive Sex Education Curricula* was commissioned by Rick Santorum, former United States senator from Pennsylvania and Tom Coburn, United States senator from Oklahoma and conducted by The Administration for Children and Families (ACF) and The Department of Health and Human Services (HHS). Like the 2003 Waxman Report (commissioned by Representative Henry Waxman from California), the new report was commissioned with the intention of helping political leaders make informed decisions about sex education funding. Nine curricula were reviewed, and they were chosen by the "frequency and strength of endorsement" by sexuality and sexual health organizations (The Administration for Children and Families [ACF] & The Department of Health and Human Services [HHS], 2007, 4). These curricula were evaluated for four criteria: whether the content mirrored the curricula's stated purpose, the content itself, whether the content was medically accurate, and whether evaluations of these curricula demonstrated that they were effective at delaying sexual onset and reducing sex without condoms (ACF & HHS, 2007, 4). [See Table 1 at the end of this section for a list of the reviewed curricula.]

The remaining sections of this article will focus on the content of the review (and its appendices), specifically looking at instances of clear and interfering bias, the use of research methodologies that are not in line with presented findings, inappropriately critical benchmarks for failure, and inaccurate referencing of outside works.

Table 1

CURRICULA REVIEWED IN THE 2007 REVIEW		
Title	Author	Year
Reducing the Risk: Building Skills to Prevent Pregnancy, STD, & HIV (4th Edition)	R. Barth	2004
Be Proud! Be Responsible!	L. S. Jemmott & J. B. Jemmott	2003
Safer Choices: Preventing HIV, Other STD and Pregnancy (Level 1 & Level 2)	J. Fetro, R. Barth, K. Coyle	1998
AIDS Prevention for Adolescents in School	S. Kasen & I. Troop	2003
BART = Becoming a Responsible Teen (Revised Edition)	J. Lawrence	2005
Teen Talk: An Adolescent Pregnancy Prevention Program	M. Eisen, A. McAlister, G. Zellman	2003
Reach for Health Curriculum, Grade 8	L. O'Donnell, et al.	2003
Making Proud Choices	L. Jemmott, J. Jemmott, K. McCaffree	2002
Positive Images: Teaching Abstinence, Contraception, and Sexual Health	P. Brick & B. Taverner	2001

Clear and Interfering Bias

The first criterion used to evaluate the selected comprehensive sex education curricula highlighted whether or not these curricula do what they say they will. The content of each of the curricula was compared to that curriculum's stated objectives. In several places the authors express dissatisfaction with their own measure primarily because that measure privileges ideologies they hold a bias against. Right off the bat the authors issue a warning that most of the curricula do not claim to be abstinence-based or to exclusively privilege abstinence over other safe sex practices (ACF & HHS, 2007, 4). This does not stop them from later critiquing the examined curricula for just that. They gloss over their stated measure (whether the curricula content mirrors its purpose) in favor of discussing an underlying measure:

> While the content of the curricula reviewed adheres to their stated purposes for the most part, these curricula do not spend as much time discussing abstinence as they do discussing contraception and ways to lessen sexual activity . . . As a last note, it is important to realize that, although some of the curricula do not include abstinence as a stated purpose, some sexuality information organizations and resources recommend these curricula as comprehensive sex education (ACF & HHS, 2007, 6).

This is one place where the clear bias of the authors (toward curricula that privilege abstinence exclusively over other forms of contraception) interfered with their stated goals. If you set out to measure whether a curriculum stuck to its stated purposes, and it did, then that's a passing measurement.

A second place where clear and interfering bias presented itself was in the content section of the review. Incredibly, the content analysis for all nine curricula could be summed up in four paragraphs, all of which were related to condom use. In the section that is supposed to describe the content of the curricula, there is no discussion of abstinence, other forms of contraception, STIs, HIV, or healthy relationship programming. Instead, the authors explain that "these curricula focus on contraception and ways to lessen risks of sexual activity," then that is boiled down to three main foci: how to get condoms, how to integrate condom use into a relationship, and how to use condoms. The three subsequent paragraphs are excerpts from curricula in these three main areas. All in all, the section succeeded in likening the promotion of condom use with the marketing of cigarettes to children (ACF & HHS, 2007, 6–7).

A third place where bias creeps into the review is in the section on medical inaccuracy. In the section on condom failure rates a curriculum that uses a correct statistic on the failure rate of a condom with perfect use is considered "misleading":

> Indeed, there were misleading statements in every curriculum reviewed. For example, one curriculum states, "When used correctly, latex condoms prevent pregnancy 97% of the time." While this statement is technically true, 15% percent [sic] of women using condoms for contraception experience an unintended pregnancy during the first year of "typical use" and 20% of adolescents under the age of 18 using condoms for contraception get pregnant within one year. (ACF & HHS, 2007, 7–8)

The curriculum excerpt they chose for this part of the medical inaccuracy section is . . . accurate. According to *The Essentials of Contraceptive Technology,* 1997 [which they would have been using for their failure rates in *Safer Choices* (1998)] condoms do have a 3% failure rate with perfect use (Hatcher, 1997, 4–19). In addition, they quote *Contraceptive Technology* (2005)'s rate for "typical use" (which is clearly different from perfect use) and then throw in a statistic from a longitudinal study from 1986 (ACF & HHS, 2007, 7–8). While a longitudinal study is a great place to see a "typical use" rate in action, the authors are clearly comparing apples to oranges in a biased fishing expedition to find medical inaccuracies.

Use of Research Methodologies That Do Not Match Their Findings

The first two research questions use evidence from a keyword content analysis. The keywords used in the content analysis and how often they were found in each of the curricula are provided for the reader (ACF & HHS, 2007, 10–12).

The content analysis is a valid methodology in sociology, provided it is done properly and that it only generates findings that are within its limits. According to Bernard Berelson, content analysis can be used to compare the content of communication to specific objectives, construct and apply communication standards, make assumptions about the intentions and/or beliefs of the communicators, and to reveal the focus of attention in a communication (Krippendorff, 2003, 44–47). That said, it is easy to see the difference between a methodologically sound content analysis and the content analysis in the 2007 Review.

The 2007 review was chiefly concerned with the treatment of abstinence in sex education curricula and, specifically, whether it got more time and was privileged over other sex risk-reduction strategies:

> While the content of the curricula reviewed adheres to their stated purposes for the most part, these curricula do not spend as much time discussing abstinence as they do discussing contraception and ways to lessen sexual activity (ACF & HHS, 2007, 6).

This assertion, that the studied curricula do not contain as much information about abstinence as they do about contraception is supported by the key word content analysis:

> The content analysis counted words used in each curriculum. Of the words counted, variations on the word "condom" occurred 235 times and variations on the word "contraception" occurred 381 times, while variations on the word "abstinence" occurred 87 times (ACF & HHS, 2007, 6, in footnote).

While content analysis can be used to highlight the focus of a communication, the construction of the analytical tool is critical for usable results. The 2007 review content analysis tool was designed in such a way that it could not help but indicate that condoms/contraceptives were more discussed than abstinence. A breakdown of the keywords used with attention placed on what would count as an "abstinence reference" versus a "condom/contraceptive reference" reveals:

- 21 keywords explicitly related to condoms/contraceptives
- 2 keywords explicitly related to abstinence
- 8 keywords were ambiguous but could have been tied to one or the other
- 3 keywords were conversation descriptors were condoms were designated as the subject (for example: "negotiation (to use condoms)"
- 0 keywords had abstinence designated as the subject (ACF & HHS, 2007, 10–12)

The keywords notably did their own injustice to abstinence by not looking for it in as many ways as they looked for condoms. There was the keyword "negotiation (to use condoms)" but not "negotiation (to abstain from sex)", and similarly "practice (s, ed, ing) (techniques, skills, using condoms)" but no "practice (s, ed, ing) (techniques and skills for abstaining)."

That said, even if the keyword search had been carefully designed to balance abstinence and condom terminology, it still would not have been an appropriate assessment tool for curricula. When looking at teaching tools, it is important to remember that often the themes and "take home" messages in a lesson are not completely spelled out. One example of this can be found in *Positive Images,* one of the reviewed curricula. In a lesson titled "Choices and Consequences", this scenario is described:

> Jerome's family has strong values, including the belief that intercourse should be saved for marriage. Jerome respects both his parents and his religion (Brick & Taverner, 2001, 51–56).

This scenario is part of an activity where students are urged to advise Jerome on the contraceptive option best for him where the best answer is clearly abstinence. Activities like this get no acknowledgement as abstinence-promoting lessons when content analysis is used. Often in educational tools the use of a word in a lesson plan is not nearly as effective as the use of a theme. The measurement tool did not take into account the language and treatment of abstinence in comprehensive sex education before trying to measure it. With this measuring tool, there was no way abstinence would have come out ahead.

Inappropriately Critical Benchmarks for Failure

It is obvious from the tone of the review that the authors were looking for their chosen curricula to fail. Frequently in an effort to achieve that goal the article contains inappropriately critical benchmarks for failure. The main place this occurs is in the section on medical inaccuracies. This section starts out with the sentence, "Most comprehensive sex education curricula reviewed contain some level of medical inaccuracy (ACF & HHS, 2007, 7)." From there they break down exactly which curricula contained what inaccuracies:

- One-third of the curricula contained no medical inaccuracies.
- One-third of the curricula had errors in their discussion of nonoxyl-9 (N-9).
- One of the curricula called a "rubber dam" a "dental dam". This curriculum was one of the three with an N-9 error.
- In the last one-third (the 3 that had "medical inaccuracies", but none related to N-9), one was a 1998 curriculum whose condom failure rate did not match the rate quoted in *Contraceptive Technology* 2006, and the other (which they footnoted as *Positive Choices* but which they corrected in their appendix as *Positive Images*) was quoted as saying that all condoms marketed in the United States today meet federal quality standards.
- Eight out of the 9 curricula did not contain incorrect condom failure rates. The one that the reviewers cited as having an incorrect rate was a 1998 curriculum compared to a 2006 failure rate (ACF & HHS, 2007, 7–8).

Some of these "medical inaccuracies" are themselves inaccurate. "Dental dam" is an acceptable name for a "rubber dam" and is used by both health educators and contraceptive suppliers. One of the most popular "rubber dam" products in the United States, the Trustex/LIXX Dental Dam, has "dental dam" on the box (Total Access Group, 2005–2006, 1, 9). Another "medical inaccuracy" that can be dismissed is the erroneous condom failure rate in *Safer Choices* (1998). A curriculum can only be expected to be accurate according to the information available at least a year before its release, so *Safer Choices* statistics should only be compared with the condom statistics available in 1997 or before. In *The Essentials of Contraceptive Technology* (1997), which is the correct reference for this curriculum, the statistic is 14%, so *Safer Choices* was off by one, but so was the Review (Hatcher, 1997, 4–19).

When these are dismissed, 4 out of 9 of the curricula have one medical inaccuracy each. Those involving nonoxynol-9 are serious, but as they involve developing research on the subject that was not confirmed by the CDC until 2002 (and even then this confirmation only led to a recommendation to no longer purchase N-9 products) this does not constitute what the authors cite as a "serious medical error" (Centers for Disease Control and Prevention [CDC], 2002, 3–4; ACF & HHS, 2007, 18). This also does not take into account the live teaching of these curricula by trained professionals. It is reasonable to assume that, when reproductive health care clinics were advised to use up their stores of N-9 condoms and then stop purchasing more, that reproductive health educators would either omit or modify the N-9 phrase in their curricula to the new guidelines (CDC, 2002, 3–4). This leaves *Positive Images,* which states that all condoms marketed in the United States are federally approved. Though there are products marketed as condoms that are not federally approved for pregnancy and disease prevention (e.g. condoms made of lambskin), the majority of condoms readily available to the general public, even those with novelty enhancements, do follow FDA guidelines for pregnancy and disease prevention. Again, this is another instance where it can be assumed a trained curriculum implementer would elaborate based on knowledge and experience. That said, it is uncertain whether condom product sales can even count as "medical inaccuracy."

When critically examined, 5 out of the 9 curricula had no reasonable medical inaccuracies, and 4 of the 9 had one to two sentences of technical inaccuracy, medical or otherwise, in their entire content. Compared to textbooks on other subjects geared towards middle and high school age American children, this is an amazing level of accuracy (for common inaccuracies in middle and high school textbooks see Beaty, 2007; Loewen, 1996).

Medical inaccuracies were addressed in the appendices as well, and there "inaccuracy" was expanded to include content excerpts that did not make it into the executive summary findings. The appendix entry for *Reducing the Risk* was an excellent example of this. It had three quotes from the curriculum on condom failure rates. Two of the three stated that when condoms were used "correctly and consistently" or "correctly . . . every time a couple has sex" they "provide good protection" or "work almost all of the time" (ACF & HHS, 2007, 14–15). The authors followed the quotes with the statement that,

" 'Good,' 'almost all the time,' and 'very effective' are subjective terms (ACF & HHS, 2007, 15)." Even with an explicit reference to perfect use and admittance that condoms were not 100% safe or effective, these descriptors were still picked out for failure. The third quote stated that condoms were "very effective" at preventing STI transmission, including "gonorrhea, chlamydia and trichomoniasis", but they added that "further studies are being done in this area (ACF & HHS, 2007, 14)." Even after the caveat, the authors criticized this quote for not acknowledging a specific 2001 study that did not find enough evidence to claim that condoms reduced trichomoniasis risk (ACF & HHS, 2007, 15). All of this fell under a statement claiming that these quotes "did not provide explicit details of condom failure rates". When reading a review, one assumes that quotes pulled from the text are the best representation in that text of the subject under discussion. However, someone reading this who was unfamiliar with *Reducing the Risk* would have no idea that the curriculum has a whole appendix dedicated to the subject of "Condom Use Effectiveness" (Barth, 2004, 23–24). These extremely critical benchmarks appear in every curriculum entry in the appendix. In *Reach for Health* (2003), a quote giving an incidence rate for HPV was deemed inaccurate because it did not match a report that came out in 2004, a *year after it* (ACF & HHS, 2007, 32).

Inappropriately critical benchmarks for failure went beyond the medical inaccuracies sections. The first two research questions, 1) comparing curriculum content to its stated purpose and 2) examining the content on its own, both contained failure language because the curricula did not place enough of an emphasis on abstinence. From the language, "enough of an emphasis" for the authors was at least more content on abstinence than on contraceptive methods. As discussed in the section on methodology, it is inappropriate to consider the content of these curricula as inadequate solely from the results of the keyword content analysis.

The final research question, whether evaluations of the curricula demonstrated that they were effective at delaying sexual onset and increasing condom use, also suffered from inappropriately critical analysis. This section also only merited one paragraph, which started with a summary of the research findings:

> According to the evaluations reviewed, these curricula show some small positive impacts on (b) reducing sex without condoms and to a lesser extent (a) delaying sexual debut (ACF & HHS, 2007, 8).

According to their appendices, here is a breakdown of the reviewed research results for the 8 curricula that had research:

- 6 out of the 8 had positive impacts at their first review
- 4 out of 8 had one or more subsequent reviews
- 4 out of the 4 with subsequent reviews still had positive impacts (though 2 of the 4 had greatly diminished impacts at the time of second review)

- 2 of the 8 had positive impacts on delaying sexual initiation
- 6 of the 8 had positive impacts on condom use (ACF & HHS, 2007, 10–40)

Left out of this analysis was the range of other risky behaviors that many of these curricula were shown to reduce, including number of sexual partners, frequency of sex, and increased knowledge about contraceptives and HIV (ACF & HHS, 2007, 13–40). The authors summarized these impacts as "often . . . small, and most often the impacts do not extend three or sex months after a curriculum has been used," though they immediately footnoted that with examples of 2 curricula that had demonstrated positive impacts after three months (of which there were four) and neglected to note that only 4 of the curricula studied had subsequent studies (which means that it is impossible to say that the remaining 5 out of 9 did not have enduring impacts) (ACF & HHS, 2007, 8). They followed up with a comment on the limitations of the research, specifically that "all curricula were evaluated by the authors themselves (ACF & HHS, 2007, 8)." This makes it sound like all of the evaluations were done only by the authors, when the reality was much more complex:

- 4 out of 8 only had research that was solely conducted by one or more of the authors
- 3 out of 8 had research that was conducted by one or more of the authors plus one or more independent researchers
- 2 out of 8 had at least one published research study conducted solely by independent researchers
- 4 out of 8 had research where independent researchers were represented either in a study collaborating with one or more of the authors or in a study without an author on the research team (ACF & HHS, 2007, 10–40)

A detailed look at their appendices revealed that at least half of the curricula had some sort of outside input in the research, and one-fourth had at least one study conducted by a completely unaffiliated research team (with "affiliated" meaning they were not a part of the curriculum's design). To represent this with the phrase "conducted by the curriculum's author", which appears in some permutation in every appendix with a research section, is inappropriately critical, not to mention misleading and technically inaccurate. Furthermore, it is important to note that having a curriculum designer on its research team, or having a researcher on a curriculum design team, is not necessarily a bad thing. Sex education curricula benefit when researchers are on board in the design phase to make sure they reflect current best practices, and research on sex education benefits when curriculum designers work with researchers to ensure that all of the curriculum's target behavior goals are measured.

All-in-all, every section of the review contained some example of inappropriately critical benchmarks for failure. But while the reviewers apparently went through selected portions of each curriculum with a fine tooth comb, their reading of outside sources was not as detailed.

Inaccurate Referencing of Outside Works

Often in the 2007 Review outside sources were brought in to prove the inaccuracy of the studied curricula. The bringing in of outside sources also went hand-in-hand with inaccurate referencing. Take this excerpt from the section on medical inaccuracy:

> For example, one curriculum states, "When used correctly, latex condoms prevent pregnancy 97% of the time." While this statement is technically true, 15% of women using condoms for contraception experience an unintended pregnancy during the first year of "typical use" and about 20% of adolescents under the age of 18 using condoms for contraception get pregnant within one year (ACF & HHS, 2007, 7–8).

Contraceptive technology has always used two measures to capture how effective contraceptive methods are in real-life situations: "perfect" and "typical". "Perfect" refers to how effective a particular method is when that method is employed consistently and correctly. "Typical" refers to how effective that method is when it is employed inconsistently or when user-error is taken into account (Hatcher, 2004, 225–228). "When used correctly" or "When used correctly and consistently" are reasonably clear and accurate ways to explain "perfect use" statistics to preteens and teens according to the Centers for Disease Control (CDC, 2003, 2). Proving a "perfect use" statistic wrong with a "typical use" statistic, especially in a context when the potential condom users are being taught how to use condoms correctly and how to obtain them consistently (and thus prepared to be "perfect" users) is both an instance of inaccurate referencing and an inappropriately critical benchmark for failure.

A second instance of inaccurate referencing compared the "medical inaccuracies" of selected comprehensive sex education curricula found in the 2007 Review with those found in selected abstinence-only curricula in the 2004 Waxman Report:

> For perspective, it may be helpful to compare the error rate reported here with statistics cited in the December 2004 report entitled "The Content of Federally Funded Abstinence Education Programs," which is typically called the Waxman Report. This report found that, of the thirteen abstinence-until-marriage curricula reviewed, eleven contained medically inaccurate statements; in all thirteen curricula, (nearly 5,000 pages of information), there were 49 instances of questionable information. It could easily be argued that the comprehensive sex education curricula reviewed for this report have a similar rate of error compared with abstinence-until-marriage curricula (ACF & HHS, 2007, 8).

This reference to the 2004 Waxman Report is brought up again in the conclusion:

> Lastly, although the medical accuracy of comprehensive sex education curricula is nearly 100%—similar to that of abstinence-until-marriage

curricula—efforts could be made to more extensively detail condom failure rates in context (ACF & HHS, 2007, 9).

At the beginning of this article, the 2004 Waxman Report itself was quoted stating that 80% of the curricular material reviewed contained "false, misleading, or distorted information about reproductive health" (United States House of Representatives Committee on Govt. Reform, 2004, i). These quotes ignore the fundamental differences in the quality and quantity of errors found in the Waxman Report versus the 2007 Review. These quality and quantity differences can be broken down into several categories:

- **Quantity:** The inaccuracies cited in the 2007 Review curricula were one to two sentences at most, while the inaccuracies cited in the Waxman Report were often whole blocks of text or reoccurring themes in the text (ACF & HHS, 2007, 7–8; United States House of Representatives Committee on Govt. Reform, 2004, 8–22).
- **Reference Use:** In the 2007 Review curricula, inaccuracies in the curricula were either instances where the reviewers were not satisfied with specific phrasing or where statistics and details did not match current research either because the research was published right at or after the curriculum, or because the body of research had still not come to a satisfactory consensus. In the Waxman Report, inaccuracies were consistently defended with research that was either extremely outdated or rejected by federal bodies at large (ACF & HHS, 2007, 7–8; United States House of Representatives Committee on Govt. Reform, 2004, 8–22).
- **Ability of Implementer to Circumvent:** The inaccuracies in the 2007 Review curricula were the types of errors that could be corrected by a trained professional implementer (for example: when studies consistently showed that N-9 was ineffective, a trained implementer could easily leave out N-9 info or give updated, correct information for N-9). While some of the inaccuracies of the Waxman Report were of that type, most were thematic, making them impossible for a trained implementer to completely eliminate (for example, repeated emphasis on exaggerated condom failure rates throughout curricular materials in statistics, phrasing, and activities) (ACF & HHS, 2007, 7–8; United States House of Representatives Committee on Govt. Reform, 2004, 8–22).

Any assumption of similarity between the reviewed abstinence-only curricula and the reviewed comprehensive sex education curricula is, at best, wishful thinking on behalf of those who wish to debunk comprehensive sex education. Of the six inaccuracies cited in the 2007 Review's executive summary, three were N-9 statements (one to two sentences) that reflected the research at the time of publication (where the curricula was a few years old or N-9 statements were still not conclusive across the body of research), one was the use of manufacturer and layman terminology instead of FDA terminology, one was a condom failure rate that was correct when compared with a referent published before the curriculum, and one was a condom accessibility statement that could easily be corrected by the implementer. In addition, there were several instances of phrasing and statistic use around condom failure rates that were technically correct and used CDC-approved language about condom effectiveness, but that the authors took issue with.

The errors found by the Waxman Report for abstinence-only curricula were fundamentally different. The treatment of condom use is an excellent example of this fundamental difference. Studied abstinence-only curricula consistently used a 1993 study (commonly referred to as the Weller Study) which was rejected by the Department of Health and Human Services in 1997. Of the studied curricula, only one was put out at a time where use of the Weller Study might have been acceptable (*Sex Can Wait,* published in 1997). Even so, the Weller Study was a poor reference for condom failure rates when compared with the primarily used and endorsed *Contraceptive Technology,* which was available before 1997. Several abstinence-only curricula had activities which explicitly taught students that condoms did not work and had holes big enough for STIs to pass through. Many included erroneous research that STI rates have not fallen as condom use rates rose. STI risks were exaggerated in many curricula alongside exaggerated condom failure rates (United States House of Representatives Committee on Govt. Reform, 2004, 8–11, 21). For pregnancy prevention, curricula confused "perfect" and "typical" use and had activities designed to convince preteens and teens that condoms do not work to prevent pregnancy. Some have gender role lessons that imply that contraceptive use is a man's decision and that if women make demands in relationships (contraceptive demands included) that they will lose their partners (United States House of Representatives Committee on Govt. Reform, 2004, 11–12, 17–18). These types of errors were designed to scare teens to abstinence, but as a consequence create a dangerous false consciousness about condoms and contraceptive use in relationships that is too pervasive for an implementer to single-handedly correct.

In light of a careful reading of the 2007 Review and the 2004 Waxman Report, any comparison between the results of the two is both inaccurate and misleading. Abstinence-only programs benefit from their counterparts' exceptional performance in terms of medical accuracy. Comprehensive sex education programs are pulled down by the assumption that they are "similar to that of 'abstinence-until-marriage curricula'" (ACF & HHS, 2007, 9).

Conclusion

The 2007 *Review of Comprehensive Sex Education Curricula* was a timely addition to the current sex education discourse. As such, the Review garnered press attention and its conclusions were put out to the public at large. But the real impact of this study was not the attention it received from the press, but the ability it gave to supporters of abstinence-only education to say that comprehensive sex education did not work. One example of this comes from Project Reality, a publishing company that puts out two abstinence-only curricula, *A.C. Green's Game Play* and *Navigator,* both products which received negative reviews in the Waxman Report. Project Reality covered the 2007 Review's release, and has a handy fact sheet to help people browsing its website understand the findings of the Review. Its summary of the "overall findings of interest" included:

> Of the curricula reviewed, the curriculum with the most balanced discussion of abstinence and safer sex still discussed condoms and contraception nearly **seven times more than abstinence.** (their emphasis)
>
> Every curricula reviewed contained misleading statements about condom effectiveness—leading teens to believe condoms are more effective than they actually are.
>
> All curricula were evaluated by the program authors themselves.
>
> **Seven of the nine curricula reviewed instructed and encouraged teens to shop for condoms themselves.** (their emphasis)
>
> **THERE WAS NO REFERENCE IN ANY OF THESE COMPREHENSIVE SEX ED CURRICULA TO THE EMOTIONAL RISKS ASSOCIATED WITH SEXUAL ACTIVITY.** (their emphasis) (Project Reality, 2007)

Irresponsible research on the federal level affects how people on the local level chose what sex education is appropriate for their youth. The 2007 *Review of Comprehensive Sex Education Curricula* is not responsible research for all the reasons stated. The sooner it can be removed from the discourse and replaced with research that is less biased, uses reasonable benchmarks for success and failure, and which appropriately references other works, the better.

EXPLORING THE ISSUE

Is There Something Wrong with the Content of Comprehensive Sex Education Curricula?

Challenge Questions

1. What is the impact of ignoring gender and sexual orientation in sex education programs?
2. Think about any sexuality education classes you may have had—do you think they should have taught you more? Less?
3. What's your opinion of the content of the sexuality education curricula examined?
4. Should sex education programs, whether abstinence-only or comprehensive, include more information on the development of romantic relationships?
5. What is "real" sex?

Is There Common Ground?

The *Healthy People 2010: Understanding and Improving Health* report suggests that as many as 50 percent of all adolescents are sexually active. The *National Youth Risk Behavior Survey* reported similar findings, with rates higher for boys than girls, and with 7.1 percent of youth having sexual intercourse before age 13. Approximately 35 percent of students surveyed had had sexual intercourse in the three months before the survey, and only 61.5 percent used a condom during the most recent sexual intercourse. The *National Survey of American Attitudes on Substance Abuse XIV: Teens and Parents* found strong relations among teen drunkenness, marijuana use, and harmful sexual behaviors. The high rates of sexual activity among young people are especially troubling, given that a large and disproportionate percentage of sexually transmitted diseases and unintended pregnancies occur among adolescents. In March of 2008, the Centers for Disease Control released results of a survey of teens that indicates that at least 25 percent of teen girls have a sexually transmitted disease (STD), in spite of the fact that many claimed they had not had sexual intercourse. Among those who admitted to sexual intercourse, 40 percent had an STD. The discrepancy is likely due to the fact that some STDs are oral, and many youth do not consider oral sex as "real" sex. There is no doubt that STDs have become a serious public health issue among teens. In reality we know that during the teen years, young people go through many powerful hormonal, emotional, and social changes. They discover sexual feelings without fully understanding their meaning or what to do with them. They often end up engaging in sexual activity that is not pleasant (especially females) and often do not practice safe sex (using condoms or dental dams, for example). There are powerful gender-related dating and sexual scripts that make it more difficult for adolescents to negotiate their sexual experiences. These scripts guide expectations: notions of "real" sex, who is supposed to initiate, and what the experience is supposed to be like (e.g., an ideal), as well as the consequences for engaging (or not) in sexual activity. Males may feel like they have to be sexually active to be seen as a "real" man and run the risk of being called "gay" if they refrain. Females have to deal with the stereotypes of "prude" or "slut." Many adolescent girls report they engage in oral sex to be popular. Each side of the sexuality debate is working with what it considers to be a logical presumption. For AOUM proponents, the surest way to avoid an unintended pregnancy or STI is to not do anything sexually until in a committed, monogamous relationship—which, to them, is only acceptable within the context of marriage. If people do not engage in the behaviors, they cannot be exposed to the negatives. Since AOUM supporters also believe that marriage is a commitment that is accompanied by a promise of monogamy, or sexual exclusivity, it is, for them, the only appropriate choice for teens. For comprehensive sexuality education proponents, the logic is that sexual exploration is a normal part of adolescents' development. They believe that the "just say no" approach to sexual behaviors is as unrealistic as it is unhealthy. Rooted in education, social learning, and health belief theories, comprehensive sexuality education programs believe that youth can make wise decisions about their sexual health if given the proper information. Comprehensive programs can address the psychosocial issues and the role of gender-role expectations in ways that AOUM cannot. Organizations supporting abstinence-only-until-marriage (AOUM) programs lauded the government's report and seized on the opportunity to criticize sexuality education. One AOUM-promoting organization, Operation Keepsake, based in Twinsburg, Ohio, complained that the word "abstinence" or "abstain" was mentioned only 321 times in sexuality education curricula, compared to 928 mentions of the word "protection." The conservative group Concerned Women for America responded to the report by calling sex education "Rated X." Most conservative organizations expressed alarm that the words "condoms" and "contraceptives" were mentioned more frequently than abstinence. Several organizations, including the National Abstinence Education Association, responded to the report by taking aim at *Making Sense of Abstinence*, a manual that was not even among those curricula examined. Meanwhile, organizations supporting sexuality education rose to the defense of these programs. The Guttmacher Institute, which publishes the peer-reviewed journal *Perspectives on Sexual and Reproductive Health*, said, "The analysis was poorly conducted and would never pass peer review by an established journal. Its findings should not be viewed or described as a credible or unbiased assessment of the content of sexuality education curricula."

ISSUE 20

Is "Gender Identity Disorder" an Appropriate Psychiatric Diagnosis?

YES: Mercedes Allen, from "Destigmatization versus Coverage and Access: The Medical Model of Transsexuality," http://dentedbluemercedes .wordpress.com/2008/04/05/destigmatizationversus-coverage-and-access-the-medical-model-of-transsexuality/ (2008)

NO: Kelley Winters, from "GID Reform Advocates: Issues of GID Diagnosis for Transsexual Women and Men," http://www.gidreform.org/ GID30285a.pdf (2007)

Learning Outcomes

As you read the issue, focus on the following points:

- What is a psychiatric diagnosis? What criteria must be met?
- Why are psychiatric diagnoses stigmatizing?
- Would not treating transsexualism as a psychiatric disorder remove stigma?
- How might race, ethnicity, class, and culture interact to affect the experience of transgenderism?
- Might the form in which transgenderism is expressed affect whether it is labeled as a gender identity disorder?

ISSUE SUMMARY

YES: Mercedes Allen recognizes the bias in the DSM's classification of Gender Identity Disorder as a mental disorder but argues that changes run the risk of leaving the trans community at risk of losing medical care and treatment.

NO: Kelley Winters argues the inclusion of gender identity disorder in the DSM adds to the stigma faced by transpersons and that reclassification is necessary to adequately address the population's health care needs.

Gender identity is one's sense of self as belonging to one sex: male or female. Gender identity can be a difficult concept to describe. Many people have probably never given much thought to questions regarding how they feel about themselves in terms of maleness or femaleness. It is assumed that most people have a gender identity that is congruent with their anatomical sex. While some men may feel more (or less) masculine than others, the majority strongly *identify* as male. The same could be said for most women—regardless of how feminine they feel (or don't feel), the majority *identify* as women. If asked, most women would probably say they feel like a woman. Most men simply feel like a man. But what does it mean to "feel" like a woman or a man? What is it to "feel" feminine or masculine? Is there only one type of femininity? Is there only one type of masculinity? And what about those who feel that their gender identity, their feelings of maleness or femaleness, doesn't match their birth sex? For those whose gender does not match societal expectations for a person of their anatomical sex, gender identity can be hard to ignore. Their gender identities do not fit the binary gender system that is firmly in place in American society. Because of this, a diagnosis of Gender Identity Disorder has been applied to those who identify as transgender or transsexual.

Gender identity disorder (GID) is defined as a strong psychological identification with the opposite sex and is signaled by the display of opposite sex-typed behaviors and avoidance or rejection of sex-typed behaviors characteristic of one's own sex. It is not related to sexual orientation. Distress or discomfort about one's status as a boy or a girl frequently accompanies these behaviors. The age of onset is 2–4 years. Some children self-label as the opposite sex, some self-label correctly but wish to become a member of the opposite sex. Other children do not express cross-sex desires but exhibit cross-sex-typed behavior. Some children cross-dress, sometimes insistently. Less characteristic are cross-sex-typed mannerisms (e.g., body movements, voice, pitch, etc.). Cross-sex peer affiliation preferences, poor peer relations, and alienation are typical.

The GID diagnosis can be found in the *Diagnostic and Statistical Manual of Mental Disorders*, commonly referred to as the DSM, published by the American Psychiatric Association. In 2012, an updated, fifth edition of the DSM will be published. Over the years, new editions have been greatly anticipated to see what changes occur. With each edition, new disorders have been identified, adding to the list of mental illnesses. Diagnostic criteria for others have been refined, and some behaviors, once defined as disordered, have been removed because they no longer meet the criteria for diagnosis as a mental illness. An example of this is homosexuality. In the DSM-II, published in 1968, homosexuality was considered a mental illness. The 1973 publication of the DSM-III did not list homosexuality as a disorder. This declassification erased some of the stigma associated with same-sex attraction and provided a boost to the gay rights movement in the United States. As the release of the DSM-V draws closer, experts from various fields, appointed to an array of work groups, are holding meetings to discuss what should be added, revised, or removed. For those interested in the field of human sexuality, much attention is being given to the status of GID. There has even been controversy over those appointed to the Sexual and Gender Identity Disorders Work Group. The changes made to the upcoming DSM-V concerning GID, or the lack thereof, could have great impact on the lives of transgender individuals.

There is considerable debate over a variety of terms associated with people who do not identify their gender in a way that is totally congruent with their anatomy. These terms include androgynes, genderqueer, cross-dressers, transvestites, drag kings, drag queens, transsexual, and transgender. Each of these terms indicates something different about how the person experiences gender identity and how he/she behaves. The terms androgynes and genderqueer are the most general and inclusive. Androgyne comes from the word androgyny, which means a combination of the masculine and feminine. It is a general term than can reflect a wide variety of ways to combine the masculine and feminine. Similarly, genderqueer is a catch-all term that covers all categories rather than the binary man-woman. In contrast, cross-dressers are persons who at least occasionally wear clothing and accessories typically associated with the other sex; however, in most cases these individuals are not transgender people and are often heterosexual. Their gender identity is congruent with their anatomy. They know they are a man or woman and feel so, but opt to alter their exterior appearance by dressing as the other sex. Similarly, terms such as transvestite, drag king, and drag queen refer to individuals who cross-dress, but primarily for the purpose of entertainment or performance, without a necessary reflection of their gender identity. There is considerable political contention in the trans-community around the terms transsexual and transgender. Initially transsexualism was coined by Harry Benjamin and viewed from a medical perspective with a primary focus on the type of medical intervention necessary, and includes intersex individuals (people with genitalia or other anatomical characteristics of the other sex). Many people prefer the term transgender. However, there is considerable variation in how people express their transgender identity, including surgery to change their anatomy to fit their psychologically experienced gender. The term trans woman refers to male-to-female (MtF or M2F) transgender people, whereas trans man refers to female-to-male (FtM or F2M) transgender people. Recent evidence suggests that there are approximately as many trans women as there are trans men.

In the YES selection, Mercedes Allen argues that the removal of Gender Identity Disorder from the DSM would put access to mental health care, hormonal treatments, and surgeries needed by some transsexual individuals at risk of being denied. Kelly Winters, in the NO selection, argues that the inclusion of GID in the DSM only serves to stigmatize the transgender and transsexual community, while failing to promote hormonal or surgical treatments as medical necessities.

Mercedes Allen

Destigmatization versus Coverage and Access: The Medical Model of Transsexuality

In recent years, the GLB community has been more receptive to (and even energized in) assisting the transgender community, but regularly asks what its needs are. One that is often touted is the "complete depathologization of Trans identities" (quoting from a press release for an October 7, 2007, demonstration in Barcelona, Spain) by removing "Gender Identity Disorder" (GID) from medical classification. The reasoning generally flows in a logic chain stating that with homosexuality removed from the Diagnostic and Statistical Manual (DSM, the "bible" of the medical community) in 1974, gay and lesbian rights were able to follow as a consequence—and with similar removal, we should be able to do the same. Living in an area where GRS (genital reassignment surgery) is covered under provincial Health Care, however, provides a unique perspective on this issue. And with Presidential candidates proposing models for national health care in the U.S., it would obviously be easier to establish GRS coverage for transsexuals at the ground floor, rather than fight for it later. So it is important to note, from this "other side of the coin," how delisting GID could do far more harm than good.

Granted, there are concerns about the current classification as a "mental disorder," and certainly as a transgender person myself, it's quite unnerving that my diagnosis of GID puts me in the same range of classification as things such as schizophrenia or even pedophilia. And when the emotional argument of "mental unfitness" can lead to ostracism, discrimination in the workplace or the loss of custody and/or visitation rights of children, there are some very serious things at stake. But when the lobbies are calling for a reclassification— or more dramatically a total declassification—of GID, one would expect that they had a better medical and social model to propose. They don't.

Basic Access to Services

The argument for complete declassification is a great concern, because unlike homosexuals, transgender people—especially transsexuals—do have medical needs and issues related to their journey. Genital reassignment surgery (GRS), mastectomies and hysterectomies for transmen, tracheal shave, facial hair removal and breast augmentation for transwomen . . . there are clear medical applications that some require, even to the point of being at risk of suicide from the distress of not having these things available (which is an important point to keep in mind for those in our own communities who assume that GRS is cosmetic surgery and not worthy of health care funding). And we need to use caution about taking psychiatry out of the equation: GID really does affect us psychologically, and we do benefit from having a central source of guidance through the process that keeps this in mind, however flawed and gated the process otherwise might be.

Declassification of GID would essentially relegate transsexuality to a strictly cosmetic issue. Without being able to demonstrate that GID is a real medical condition via a listing in the Diagnostic and Statistical Manual (DSM), convincing a doctor that it is necessary to treat us, provide referrals or even provide a carry letter that will enable us to use a washroom appropriate to our gender presentation could prove to be very difficult, if not impossible. Access to care is difficult enough *even with* the DSM-IV recommending the transition process—imagine the barriers that would be there without it weighing in on that! And with cases regarding the refusal of medical services already before review or recently faced in California, Ontario and elsewhere, the availability of services could grow overwhelmingly scarce.

A Model of Medical Coverage

And then there is health care coverage, which often causes a lot of issues of itself, usually of the "not with my tax money" variety. But no one just wakes up out of the blue and decides that alienating themselves from the rest of the world by having a "sex change" is a good idea. Science is developing a greater understanding that physical sex and psychological gender can, in fact, be made misaligned, causing a person to be like a stranger in their own body. In extreme cases (transsexuals), this often makes it impossible to function emotionally, socially, sexually, or to develop any kind of career—and often makes one constantly borderline suicidal. The medical community currently recognizes this with the existing medical classification, which is why GRS surgery is the recognized treatment, and why it (GRS, that is, and usually not things like breast augmentation) is funded by some existing health plans.

Canada provides an interesting model on this, as the nation has universal health care, and several provinces fund GRS with some limitations (British Columbia, Newfoundland, Saskatchewan and Quebec fund vaginaplasty, hysterectomy and breast reduction for FTMs, Alberta funds those plus phalloplasty, and Manitoba funds 60% of GRS-related costs). Funding may be restored in Ontario and gained in Nova Scotia, pending some ongoing activism.

This exists specifically because it is classified as a medical issue, and is treated according to the recommendations of WPATH. There are some idiosyncracies, of course—a diagnosis of Intersex, for example, overrides a diagnosis of GID, and if someone is diagnosed as IS, the treatment is different (namely, GRS is not covered). Phalloplasty and metoidioplasty (FTM surgeries) are not covered in several areas because they are considered "experimental." Some provinces insist on treatment only in publically-funded hospitals, resulting in the rather unusual situation of Quebec sending patients to the U.S. or overseas, even though one of the top-rated (but privately-owned) GRS clinics in the world is located in Montreal. And many provinces direct transsexuals to the notoriously restrictive and obstacle-laden Clarke Institute (CAMH in Toronto) for treatment. Waiting lists can be long, and only a select few GID-certified psychiatrists are able to be a primary signature on letters authorizing surgery and funding. Still, the funding provides opportunity that many non-Canadian transsexuals would leap at within a moment, if they could.

Future Considerations

This possibility, remote as it may seem, is also out there for future American transsexuals. Both Democratic Presidential nominees have discussed developing a national health care program. The time is now for the trans, gay/lesbian/bisexual and allied communities to lobby insurance companies to develop policies that cover GRS. The time is now to lobby companies to seek out group policies for their employees with such coverage, and with more emphasis than the HRC's impossibly easy Corporate Equality Index (CEI), in which providing mastectomies for breast cancer patients qualifies as "transgender-related surgeries." The more prevalent health care coverage is for transgender persons when a national program is developed, the more effective the argument is that a national program should include it. Certainly, it will be much harder to lobby to have it specifically added later.

This possibility, remote as it may seem, exists because of the current classification. Even some existing coverage of and access to hormone treatment is called into question in a declassification scenario. And certainly, where coverage is not available, it is the impoverished, disenfranchised and marginalized of our community—who quite often have more to worry about than the stigma of mental illness—who lose the most.

So a total declassification is actually not what's best for the transgender community. Too, if anyone had been thinking that proclaiming that "transsexuality is not a mental disorder" would magically change the way that society thinks about transfolk, then they are spectacularly and embarrassingly wrong.

The Question of Reclassification

At some point in the future, I expect that we will find more biological bases for GID, and that transgender people will perhaps become a smaller part of the larger intersex community (rather than the other way around). Recent studies in genetics have demonstrated some difference in chromosomal structure in male brains versus female brains, and the UCLA scientists who conducted the study have also proposed that their findings demonstrate gender dysphoria as a biological characteristic. Other studies into endocrine disrupting chemicals (EDCs) could open new discoveries related to variance in gender correlation. A reassessment of GID is almost certainly something that will be on the medical community's table at some point in the future, but it definitely needs to be in the DSM somewhere. But for now, GID is not something that can be determined by a blood test or an ultrasound, and is not easy to verifiably place with biological conditions. The science is not there; the evidence and solutions are not yet at hand.

This is why reclassification is not yet feasible. It's difficult to convince scientific and medical professionals to move a diagnosis when the current model is workable in their eyes (even if not perfect), while the alternatives are not yet proven, cannot be demonstrated as more valid than the current listing, and no modified treatment system has been devised or proposed. Any move of the diagnosis is not likely to be very far from the current listing, and from the literature I've seen, I doubt that those in the community who advocate to changing or dropping the current classification would be happy with that. For some, even listing it as a "physical disability" could constitute an "unwanted stigma." I have heard one WPATH doctor suggest the term "Body Morphology Disorder"—for many, I suspect, this would still be too "negative."

"Unnecessary Mutilation"

That's not to say that complacency is an answer. In the face of conservative reluctance and new activism on the left by the likes of Julie Bindel, claiming that GRS is "unnecessary mutilation," we need to demonstrate the necessity of treatments, in order to ensure that any change would be an improvement on the existing model, rather than a scrapping of it. This is, of course, something that affects a small portion of the transgender community in the full umbrella stretch of the term, but the need for those at the extreme on the spectrum is profound—not simply a question of quality of life, but often one of living at all—or at least a question of being able to function. If and when a reclassification occurs, it will need to be this sense of necessity that will determine the shape of what will be written into any revision.

The solution isn't to destroy the existing medical model by changing or eliminating the current classification of "Gender Dysphoria." Collecting data, demonstrating needs, fighting for inclusion in existing health plans, examining verifiable and repeatable statistics on transgender suicide and success rates and other information relevant to the medical front is where medical-related activism should be focused, for the moment.

GID Reform Advocates

Issues of GID Diagnosis for Transsexual Women and Men

Gender Identity Disorder in Adolescents or Adults, 302.85

Section: Sexual and Gender Identity Disorders
Subsection: Gender Identity Disorders

"Gender Identity Disorder" (GID) is a diagnostic category in the *Diagnostic and Statistical Manual of Mental Disorders* (DSM), published by the American Psychiatric Association (APA, 1994). The DSM is regarded as the medical and social definition of mental disorder throughout North America and strongly influences the *International Statistical Classification of Diseases and Related Health Problems* (ICD) published by the World Health Organization. GID currently includes a broad array of gender variant adults and children who may or may not be transsexual and may or may not be distressed or impaired. GID literally implies a *"disordered"* gender identity.

Thirty-four years after the American Psychiatric Association (APA) voted to delete homosexuality as a mental disorder, the diagnostic categories of "gender identity disorder" and "transvestic fetishism" in the *Diagnostic and Statistical Manual of Mental Disorders* continue to raise questions of consistency, validity, and fairness. Recent revisions of the DSM have made these diagnostic categories increasingly ambiguous, conflicted and overinclusive. They reinforce false, negative stereotypes of gender variant people and at the same time fail to legitimize the medical necessity of sex reassignment surgeries (SRS) and procedures for transsexual women and men who urgently need them. The result is that a widening segment of gender non-conforming youth and adults are potentially subject to diagnosis of psychosexual disorder, stigma and loss of civil liberty.

A Question of Legitimacy

The very name, Gender Identity Disorder, suggests that cross-gender identity is itself disordered or deficient. It implies that gender identities held by diagnosable people are not legitimate, in the sense that more ordinary gender identities are, but represent perversion, delusion or immature development. This message is reinforced in the diagnostic criteria and supporting text that emphasize difference from cultural norms over distress for those born in incongruent bodies or forced to live in wrong gender roles.

Under the premise of "disordered" gender identity, self-identified transwomen and trans-men lose any rightful claim to acceptance as women and men, but are reduced to mentally ill men and women respectively.

DIAGNOSTIC CRITERIA

A. A strong and persistent cross-gender identification (not merely a desire for any perceived cultural advantages of being the other sex). In adolescents and adults, the disturbance is manifested by symptoms such as a stated desire to be the other sex, frequent passing as the other sex, desire to live or be treated as the other sex, or the conviction that he or she has the typical feelings and reactions of the other sex.

B. Persistent discomfort with his or her sex or sense of inappropriateness in the gender role of that sex. In adolescents and adults, the disturbance is manifested by symptoms such as preoccupation with getting rid of primary and secondary sex characteristics (e.g., request for hormones, surgery, or other procedures to physically alter sexual characteristics to simulate the other sex) or belief that he or she was born the wrong sex.

C. The disturbance is not concurrent with a physical intersex condition.

D. The disturbance causes clinically significant distress or impairment in social, occupational, or other important areas of functioning.

Specify if (for sexually mature individuals) Sexually Attracted to Males, . . . Females, . . . Both, . . . Neither.

Maligning Terminology

Of the disrespectful language faced by gender variant people in North America, none is more damaging or hurtful than that which disregards their experienced gender identities, denies the affirmed gender roles of those who have transitioned full time and relegates them to their assigned birth sex. Throughout the diagnostic criteria and supporting text, the affirmed gender identities and social role for transsexual individuals is termed "other sex." In the supporting text, subjects are offensively labeled by birth sex and not their experienced affirmed gender. Transsexual women are repeatedly termed "males," and "he." For example,

> For some <u>males</u> . . . , the individual's sexual activity with a woman is accompanied by the fantasy of being lesbian lovers or that <u>his</u> partner is a man and <u>he</u> is a woman.

Perhaps most disturbing, the term "autogynephilia" was introduced in the supporting text of the DSM-IV-TR to demean lesbian transsexual women:

> Adult <u>males</u> who are sexually attracted to females, . . . usually report a history of erotic arousal associated with the thought or image of oneself as a woman (termed *autogynephilia*).

The implication is that all lesbian transsexual women are incapable of genuine affection for other female partners but are instead obsessed with narcissistic paraphilia. The fact that most ordinary natal women possess images of themselves as women within their erotic relationships and fantasies is conspicuously overlooked in the supporting text.

Medically Necessary Treatment of Gender Dysphoria

Gender Dysphoria is defined in the DSM-IV-TR as:

> A persistent aversion toward some or all of those physical characteristics or social roles that connote one's own biological sex.

The focus of medical treatment described by the current World Professional Association for Transgender Health Standards of Care is on relieving the distress of gender dysphoria and not on attempting to change one's gender identity. Yet, the DSM-IV-TR emphasizes cross-gender identity and expression rather than the distress of gender dysphoria as the basis for mental disorder. While criterion B of Gender Identity Disorder may imply gender dysphoria, it is not limited to ego-dystonic subjects suffering distress with their born sex or its associated role. Ego-syntonic subjects who do not need medical treatment may also be ambiguously implicated. In failing to distinguish gender diversity from gender distress, the APA has undermined the medical necessity of sex reassignment procedures for transsexuals who need them. It is little wonder that the province of Ontario and virtually all insurers and HMOs in the U.S. and have denied or dropped coverage for sex reassignment surgery (SRS) procedures. Since gender dysphoria is not explicitly classified as a treatable medical condition, surgeries that relieve its distress are easily dismissed as "cosmetic" by insurers, governments and employers.

The transgender community and civil rights advocates have long been polarized by fear that access to SRS procedures would be lost if the GID classification were revised. In truth, however, transsexuals are poorly served by a diagnosis that stigmatizes them unconditionally as mentally deficient and at the same time fails to establish the medical necessity of procedures proven to relieve their distress.

Overinclusive Diagnosis

Distress and impairment became central to the definition of mental disorder in the DSM-IV (1994, p. xxi), where a generic clinical significance criterion was added to most diagnostic categories, including criterion D of Gender Identity Disorder. Ironically, while the scope of mental disorder was narrowed in the DSM-IV, Gender Identity Disorder was broadened from the classification of Transsexualism in prior DSM revisions and combined with Gender Identity Disorder of Adolescence or Adulthood, Nontranssexual Type (GIDAANT) from the DSM-III-R (1987, pp. 74–77).

Unfortunately, no specific definition of distress and impairment is given in the GID diagnosis. The supporting text in the DSM-IV-TR lists relationship difficulties and impaired function at work or school as examples of distress and disability (2000, p. 577) with no reference to the role of societal prejudice as the cause. Prostitution, HIV risk, suicide attempts and substance abuse are described as associated features of GID, when they are in truth consequences of discrimination and undeserved shame. The DSM does not acknowledge the existence of many healthy, well-adjusted transsexual or gender variant people or differentiate them from those who could benefit from medical treatment. These are left to the interpretation of the reader. Tolerant clinicians may infer that transgender identity or expression is not inherently impairing, but that societal intolerance and prejudice are to blame for the distress and internalized shame that transpeople often suffer. Intolerant clinicians are free to infer the opposite: that cross-gender identity or expression by definition constitutes impairment, regardless of the individual's happiness or well-being. Therefore, the GID diagnosis is not limited to ego-dystonic subjects; it makes no distinction between the distress of gender dysphoria and that caused by prejudice and discrimination. Moreover, the current DSM has no clear exit clause for transitioned or post-operative transsexuals, however well adjusted. It lists postsurgical complications as "associated physical examination findings" of GID (2000, p. 579).

Pathologization of Ordinary Behaviors

Conflicting and ambiguous language in the DSM serves to confuse cultural nonconformity with mental illness and pathologize ordinary behaviors as symptomatic. The Introduction to the DSM-IV-TR (2000, p. xxxi) states:

> Neither deviant behavior . . . nor conflicts that are primarily between the individual and society are mental disorders unless the deviance or conflict is a symptom of dysfunction. . . .

However, it is contradicted in the Gender Identity Disorder section (p. 580):

> Gender Identity Disorder can be distinguished from simple nonconformity to stereotypical sex role behavior by the extent and pervasiveness of the cross-gender wishes, interests, and activities.

The second statement implies that one may deviate from social expectation without a diagnostic label, but not too much. Conflicting language in the DSM serves the agendas of intolerant relatives and employers and their medical expert witnesses who seek to deny transgender individuals their civil liberties, children and jobs.

In the supporting text of the Gender Identity Disorder diagnosis, behaviors that would be ordinary or even exemplary for ordinary women and men are presented as symptomatic of mental disorder on a presumption of incongruence with born genitalia. These include passing, living and a desire to be treated as ordinary members of the preferred gender. For example, shaving legs for adolescent biological males is described as symptomatic, even though it is common among males involved in certain athletics. Adopting ordinary behaviors, dress and mannerisms of the preferred gender is described as a manifestation of preoccupation for adults. It is not clear how these behaviors can be pathological for one group of people and not for another.

EXPLORING THE ISSUE

Is "Gender Identity Disorder" an Appropriate Psychiatric Diagnosis?

Challenge Questions

1. Is gender identity a socially constructed notion or is there a true biological basis for one's sense of self as male or female, independent of genitalia?
2. If society did not have a binary view of the sexes, would questions of gender identity exist?
3. Is it necessary to have a diagnosis of GID in the DSM in order for transgender people to receive medical treatment?
4. Is it really necessary to have various labels for the variety of ways that people may manifest deviation away from traditional gender-relevant expectations? Who benefits from such categories?

Is There Common Ground?

It is important to realize that, while Allen and Winters take opposing sides to the question presented, both oppose the labeling of transgender or transsexual individuals as mentally ill. To a certain extent, the debate over the inclusion, reclassification, or exclusion of GID in the upcoming edition of the DSM exemplifies the phrase "You're damned if you do, you're damned if you don't." To remove GID from the DSM would in all likelihood help to reduce some of the stigma attached to transsexuality. However, many transsexual individuals need a diagnosable condition in order to receive adequate coverage for medical care. Could there possibly be a "correct" answer in this situation? Allen's essay, which acknowledges the stigma attached to the label of mental disorder and notes the possible benefits of re- or declassification of GID, focuses on the issue of access to medical care. The point is made that declassification would impact transgender and transsexual individuals in much different ways than the declassification of homosexuality affected gay men and lesbians. Unlike other sexual minorities, "transgender people—especially transsexuals—do have medical needs and issues related to their journey," Allen states. What would be the risks of removing GID from the upcoming DSM? Why would some transgender advocates argue for its continued inclusion? Allen also mentions the impact of nationalized health care on the GID debate. How would the discussion be different if the United States implemented health care coverage for all citizens? Winters focuses on deconstructing the current diagnosis of GID. Despite recent revisions, she states, the diagnostic criteria are "increasingly ambiguous, conflicted, and overinclusive." After reading the most recent DSM criteria for GID, included in the NO selection, would you agree? Fears that a revised classification would endanger medical care for the transgender community are essentially moot, states Winters, given the fact that the current diagnosis "fails to establish the medical necessity of procedures proven to relieve their distress." With the criteria put in place by the DSM, Winters argues, many insurers are already refusing to cover treatments, dismissing surgeries as "cosmetic" in nature, rather than necessary for treatment. Do you feel that total declassification is the correct step to take? Or would a revision of the current classification be more appropriate? What if these changes resulted in the denial of access to medical care for transgender or transsexual individuals? Is there a middle ground that reduces stigma while maintaining access to medical treatment?

ISSUE 21

Should Transgender Women Be Considered "Real" Women?

YES: **Lisa Mottet and Justin Tanis,** from *Opening the Door to the Inclusion of Transgender People: The Nine Keys to Making Lesbian, Gay, Bisexual and Transgender Organizations Fully Transgender-Inclusive* (The National Gay and Lesbian Task Force Policy Institute, 2008)

NO: **Jaimie F. Veale, Dave E. Clarke, and Terri C. Lomax,** from "Sexuality of Male-to-Female Transsexuals" *Archives of Sexual Behavior* (2008)

Learning Outcomes

As you read the issue, focus on the following points:

- What does it mean to say someone is womyn-born?
- What does it mean to say that women have shared experiences? Is being biologically born female enough to define shared experiences?
- What determines the basis of sexual attraction?
- Must transgender women show the same pattern of sexual attraction as biologically born women across multiple indicators in order to be considered "real" women?

ISSUE SUMMARY

YES: Lisa Mottet and Justin Tanis argue for recognizing diversity in all aspects of people's lives and reject efforts to categorize on the basis of rigid definitions.

NO: Jaimie Veale along with university faculty compared the sexuality of male-to-female transsexuals to biological females and found a number of differences that distinguish the groups in terms of patterns of sexual attraction to males.

In 1999, a controversy erupted between the organizers of the Michigan Womyn's Music Festival (MWMF) and Camp Trans over MWMF's policy toward permitting transgender women to attend the festival. To understand this conflict, some background is necessary. According to the MWMF founder Lisa Vogel, "Since 1976, the Michigan Womyn's Music Festival has been created by and for womyn-born womyn, that is, womyn who were born as and have lived their entire life experience as womyn." Camp Trans, an alternative music festival founded in 1994 to protest MWMF, is held on Forest Service land across from the MWMF. They believe that anyone who is a woman, regardless of the sex they were born as, should be permitted to attend. Vogel sent a letter to a member of Camp Trans that stated, "I deeply desire healing in our communities, and I can see and feel that you want that too. I would love for you and the other organizers of Camp Trans to find the place in your hearts and politics to support and honor space for womyn who have had the experience of being born and living their life as womyn. I ask that you respect that womyn-born womyn is a valid and honorable gender identity. I also ask that you respect that womyn-born womyn deeply need our space—as do all communities who create space to gather. . . . As feminists, we call upon the transwomen's community to help us maintain womyn only space, including spaces created by and for womyn-born womyn. As sisters in struggle, we call upon the transwomen's community to meditate upon, recognize and respect the differences in our shared experiences and our group identities even as we stand shoulder to shoulder as women, and as members of the greater queer community. . . . [T]he need for a separate womyn-born womyn space does not stand at odds with recognizing the larger and beautiful diversity of our shared community." This controversy raises the question of what is a "real" woman. It is clear that according to the MWMF credo, the lived experiences of womyn-born womyn is different from that of those women who were born biologically male and then chose to live their lives as female. This is the case in spite of the fact that the MWMF founders embrace all forms of gender variant women as long as they were born biologically female. This would include lesbians, bisexual, and polyamorous women who present their gender in a variety of ways (butch, bearded, androgynous, femme, etc.). One question to ponder as you read the YES and NO selections is how "common" do people's experiences have to be in order for them to have a common bond. Furthermore, what is the role of the patterns of sexual attraction in defining what it means to be a "woman"? The assumption is that heterosexual women have a clearly defined pattern of attraction to men. Gender variant women, on the other hand, may be lesbian or bisexual or polyamorous. Polyamorous women are women who have more than one intimate partner of the same or different sex at the same time. Thus, for the womyn-born womyn movement, it would appear that a variety of patterns of sexual attraction are acknowledged and accepted. Research has shown that among male-to-female transgender persons as well, a variety of sexual attraction patterns are possible, and some of these patterns would qualify as gender variant, that is, something other than females attracted to males.

It is interesting to ponder why for the womyn-born womyn movement, genitalia at birth have to hold the primary role in defining the foundation for share experiences. In many ways this presumption takes us back to the issue that opened this book—is anatomy destiny? What is it about anatomy at birth, independent of all the other ways in which women can differ, including sexual orientation, that is so important? As we noted earlier, biologically based theories of sex differentiation support the argument that genetic make-up and resultant hormonal influences determine fundamental differences between women and men. If so, what factors contribute to some men feeling an intra-psychic belief that they were meant to be women? And do these genetic and hormonal influences continue to make trans women fundamentally different than womyn-born womyn even after change of sex surgery and/or ongoing hormonal treatment? One fundamental belief of the womyn-born womyn movement is that prior to the transition to female, the biologically born men enjoyed the privilege of patriarchy for at least some part of their lives. Hence, they can never fully know and appreciate the discrimination and restrictions associated with being female and have the experience of privilege that womyn-born womyn can never know.

In the NO selection, Veale and colleagues take a close look at the variety of ways male-to-female transsexuals experience sexual attraction. They rely heavily on Ray Blanchard's theory that there are 15 aspects of sexuality that can be used to categorize people. Male-to-female transsexuals can be classi-fied as gynephilic (or lesbian, exclusively sexually attracted to adult females), bisexual (attracted to women and men), androphilic (or heterosexual, exclu-sively sexually attracted to adult males), asexual, and narcissistic or automono-sexual gender-variant persons (sexually aroused by the idea or impression of themselves as females). Veale's research indicates that male-to-female transsex-uals differed from biological females in a variety of ways, suggesting, at least when it comes to sexual attraction, this group really is different from women born as women. However, Mottet and Tanis argue against categorizing people based on gender identity or patterns of sexual attraction and then using those categories as a basis for discrimination. They suggest that some members of gender variant communities may in fact be transphobic. As you read the YES selections, consider this possibility. How exclusionary must an organization be before it is considered to be transphobic?

YES

**Lisa Mottet and
Justin Tanis**

Opening the Door to the Inclusion of Transgender People: The Nine Keys to Making Lesbian, Gay, Bisexual and Transgender Organizations Fully Transgender-Inclusive

Introduction

Thank you for picking up this guide and for your desire to discover new ways to help your lesbian, gay, bisexual and transgender (LGBT) organization become a more inclusive place for transgender people. It is exciting to see the ways in which our movement continues to grow and challenge ourselves to be more inclusive and more effective as we serve our communities.

In this guide, you will find practical ideas for how LGBT organizations can take concrete steps to provide a more welcoming environment for transgender people. We'll address directly the challenges and opportunities that present themselves in this process.

This resource is specifically written for LGBT groups and organizations that want to be more inclusive of transgender people. This will mean various things to different kinds of groups—from welcoming more transgender people on your soccer team to passing transgender-inclusive legislation to running transgender-specific programs at your community center. We encourage you to take the ideas in this guide and think of ways in which you can apply them to your unique organization and mission.

LGBT organizations are made up of a wide range of people, including family, friends, and allies. Our volunteers, staffs, and constituencies identify as lesbian, bisexual, straight, gay, transgender, non-transgender, queer, and more. When we refer to LGBT organizations in this guide, it is our intention to speak to this diverse group of people with the goal of helping our community become increasingly inclusive.

Other organizations that are not LGBT-specific in their focus may also find this guide helpful. Please feel free to translate the information from the LGBT experience to your own in ways that are useful to you.

Transgender Inclusion

Transgender people have been a part of the LGBT movement from its beginnings. As people began to see their sexual orientation as a healthy part of their identity and found the prejudice they faced oppressive, they found common cause with those who expressed their gender differently than the majority of society. Together, they began the work that we continue—striving to create a world where we are free to be ourselves and where our identities are never a justification for discrimination and violence.

Those who oppose our rights see LGBT people as a common community. We are targeted for stigmatization and violence together as a group because we break stereotypes. Our common vulnerabilities may have brought us together, but the LGBT community works together because we are working towards a common purpose, for the freedom to be who we are and the right to live with dignity and justice.

When we talk about transgender-inclusion in this guide, it is with the understanding that transgender people are inherently a part of the LGBT community and have been from the beginning. In some ways, the term "transgender-inclusion" is not perfect; it could be taken to mean that transgender people aren't inherently a part of something called the LGB(T) movement and that instead, transgender people have been added to the LGB movement. We use this term, despite this perceived limitation, because we believe it is the best term to describe the process of integration of transgender people throughout one's LGBT organization, and it is the term that our movement has been using for over a decade.

We also realize that the term "LGBT" sometimes glosses over the gap that exists between the realities of our community organizations (that they are not always inclusive) and the diverse and vast world of LGBT people. We know that our organizations want to accurately reflect and meaningfully serve LGBT people. Working together can be challenging, and we need to be intentional in order to create a truly diverse and vibrant community.

As Suzanne Pharr has noted in her ground-breaking book, *Homophobia: A Weapon of Sexism,* homophobia is driven by a rigid gender code. A long-time feminist, Pharr observed that women who break out of constricting gender roles and take leadership in their communities are often branded as "lesbian" to make them stop pushing for change—whether that change means better schools for their children, clean-up of a toxic waste dump, or marriage equality. Similarly, men who visibly challenge gender conformity—by confronting male violence, expressing emotion, or embracing their artistic or "feminine" sides— are punished both socially and in the world of work. Simply, gender bias and homophobia are inextricably entwined.

Gay, lesbian, and bisexual people have often constituted a significant share of our society's gender outlaws, standing side by side on the gender non-conforming continuum with our transgender peers and bearing the consequences of not matching the gender stereotypes of straight society. Accordingly, bias against gender non-conformity threatens access to employment and other key societal institutions for all of us and exposes us to violence and prejudice. While we may not all be in the exact same boat, we are certainly all in the same water.

The divisive and disappointing federal legislative battle around the removal of gender identity/expression protections from the Employment Non-Discrimination Act in 2007 should not confuse any of us. There is no secure equality for LGB people without protections for gender bias. On a parallel course, there is no true community and no authentic expression of queer life or culture without transgender people. Often the most stigmatized people in our ranks, gender non-conforming people have consistently led the charge for change in our movement and the society at large. We marginalize them/us at our own peril.

In different times and in different places, the LGBT community has varied between close-knit cohesion and an uneasy alliance between lesbian, gay, bisexual, and transgender activists. We have been divided along lines of gender, gender identity/expression, race, class, abilities, and more. But we believe that at the heart of the LGBT movement is a passion for inclusion and that at our best, and most effective, the LGBT community strives to open our doors to all who want to work together with people of all sexual orientations and gender identities and expressions.

We hope this book provides you with the concrete tools you need to fully realize your vision for a fully transgender-inclusive organization. There is so much work to do and so many challenges facing our movement. We must draw on the vast talents and strengths that our brilliant, diverse communities have to offer to achieve our goal of full equality.

Our Perspectives

The authors of this manual bring a variety of view points to our writing. One of us is transgender, and the other is a long-time ally. We have both had significant others who are transgender people. Both of us have spent our careers working within the LGBT movement, which significantly informs our perspective. We have also been active in a number of LGBT community organizations as participants, taking part in book clubs, political advocacy organizations, sports teams, and other groups.

We have been both leaders and members of the very kinds of organizations that we hope will benefit from this manual. In some cases, we've been very successful in bringing about the changes that we outline here. At other times, we've been met with resistance and have had the opportunity to learn how difficult this work can be.

Ultimately, we believe in LGBT communities—we believe in our drive for inclusiveness and in the strength of our vision. We have been proud to be a part of this movement and hope that this guide lends some ideas and experience that will help us move forward together into an even better future.

Opening the Door to a Transgender-Inclusive Movement

The question before us now is not whether transgender people are part of our movement, but rather how to build organizations in which the participation of transgender people is affirming for both them and for the groups to which they belong. The purpose of this guide is to consider how we can strengthen that partnership so that the political and social organizations that we have worked so hard to build can truly be as diverse, effective, and inclusive as we want them to be.

The Challenges We Face

One of the most significant challenges LGBT organizations face is that transgender (and bisexual) labels have often been added in name (the addition of the "B" and "T" to LGBT) without any authentic effort to integrate transgender and bisexual people and experiences into the organization. While often well-intentioned, changes in name only render the impact of adding those letters almost meaningless, as transgender people have learned the hard way. Because the addition of the "T" only sometimes translates into concrete programs or even a genuine welcome, trans people may view the "T" with suspicion or simply ignore it altogether.

Transgender people have also encountered overt hostility in some LGBT organizations. Some people—regardless of their sexual orientation—are uncomfortable with transgender people because of the transphobia that they have learned from the larger society. Sometimes lesbian and gay people recycle the homophobia they have heard and use it against transgender people, saying things like, "that's not natural," or "it's just a phase." Not intending to be hostile, some LGB people have pointed out the real differences between being LGB and T, and the different ways in which people experience discrimination, and have said that their organization should treat these issues differently. Whatever the reasoning, the result is that transgender people have learned, through painful experience, that lesbian, gay, and bisexual spaces are not always welcoming, safe environments for them. Using prejudice to exclude others based on their identity weakens our movement, and, as leaders, we must take whatever steps we can to counteract it.

Sometimes, gay, lesbian, and bisexual people genuinely want to welcome transgender people but don't know how. We may inadvertently include people in a way that demonstrates ignorance of the issues of gender identity/expression. For example, we might write a newsletter article on "LGBT marriage issues," failing to recognize that marriage rights for transgender people pose a different set of questions than same-sex marriage rights for non-transgender people. Or we might ask people if they are gay, lesbian, bisexual, *or* transgender, rather than seeing that a person can be lesbian, gay, or bisexual, *and* transgender. . . .

Looking at Our Missions

It is important that our organizations look carefully at our mission statements and make a decision about the inclusion of transgender people. While we would advocate that LGBT organizations are strongest when they are fully inclusive, you will have to make your own choices.

It is not acceptable, however, to just add the "T" to the mission or name of an organization out of perceived pressure to conform to a movement standard and then proceed to ignore transgender people. It is more honest to decide that transgender people are not part of your organization's mission and to say so than it is to try to *appear* inclusive but not *be* inclusive. If you feel your organization might fall into that category, you cannot change the past, but you certainly can change the future of your organization to fully live up to your name and desire for inclusion.

Mission statements of organizations that are fully inclusive of LGBT people should include gender identity/expression as well as sexual orientation. If transgender people are part of our mission, then we should do everything we can to fulfill the mission of our organization, including providing an equal place at the table for transgender people.

Transgender people can bring incredible gifts to our organizations to help us achieve the goals that we have as a community. Transgender people are often resilient, creative, and strong. They have survived the prejudices thrown at them by family, friends, and an all-too-often hostile world. They also seek what all of us seek in our LGBT organizations—safe and affirming places in which to be ourselves. By opening our programs—and our hearts and minds—to transgender people, we help to achieve the purpose that brought all of us together in the first place. . . .

Conclusion

By now you have a very good idea of what it is going to take to move your LGBT organization along in its journey to become fully transgender-inclusive. If you have a long way to go, you may feel overwhelmed. Rest assured, by slowly taking steps one by one, you will get where you need to go, and bring along the others in your organization with you. Many hands make light work. You will likely find the process enlightening and empowering. It certainly has been for us in our work in building transgender-inclusive LGBT organizations.

The work of trans-inclusion is critically important. Have no doubt that each of us doing our part will create a new world where it is safe and acceptable to identify as any gender and express our gender in any form we choose. As LGBT organizations demonstrate trans-inclusion, our example will be noted by other organizations and institutions we work with; indeed, we should be actively encouraging them to adopt these practices. Ultimately, our hope is that through each of us making our part of the world trans-inclusive, we will help spread trans-friendly attitudes and behaviors everywhere.

As Mahatma Gandhi said, "You must be the change you wish to see in the world." The power to change the world is yours and ours; we must recognize that power and use it to create a dynamic, inclusive LGBT movement. Hopefully, this guide will support that process. We look forward to working with you and your organization as we build an ever stronger, more powerful, and fully integrated movement for justice.

Transgender Inclusion: The Nine Keys for Success

#1 Work Toward Full Integration at Every Organizational Level

- Transgender people should be more than just clients; trans people should be in key leadership positions, serve on the board, act as volunteers, and be on the staff of an inclusive organization.
- Avoid the pitfall of tokenization or having one transgender person that the organization consults with on all trans issues.
- Unless trans people are fully integrated, transgender people will not be fully represented in and by your organization, which hurts not only the organization, but robs the movement of the chance to develop more experienced community members.

#2 Recruit a Broad Range of Trans People

- The work is never done; so one can never put this issue aside as complete.
- Not knowing trans people isn't an adequate excuse; there are transgender people interested and excited to work on LGBT issues. They can be found.
- The differences between transgender people must be recognized, both in gender identity and expression, but also in class, race, ability, age, and religious affiliation.

#3 Create a Welcoming Environment

- Physical space is important. Trans people need trans-friendly bathrooms. Some need a place to change into their gender presentation before a meeting or event.
- What you say really matters. Watch language on forms asking about gender and sexual orientation and think about whether the names of your organization and events are inclusive.

#4 Deal with Prejudice

- There is serious transphobia within LGB communities which must be addressed, not swept under the rug. Racism, classism, ableism, sexism, and other oppressions are also problems in nearly every environment and must also be addressed.

#5 Acknowledge Past Mistakes Regarding Trans Inclusion

- If your organization has previously done something that was not transgender-friendly, it is important to put aside defensiveness in the process of healing and repairing any rift that exists between LGB and T people in the organization.
- This is not always a fast process; typically, it will take time to rebuild trust.

#6 Have Trans-Inclusive Programming, Services, and Advocacy Positions

- There should be trans-specific programming/services; but they shouldn't be the only places trans people are expected to show up.
- Remember that not all trans people are gay/lesbian/bisexual, so include heterosexual transgender people and their families.
- For legislative- and policy-related organizations, the organization must take a non-negotiable stance on transgender-inclusion.

#7 Understand Transgender Experiences

- Be conscious of social and cultural differences that transgender people may have. Being trans is different than being gay.
- Do one's own education about trans issues; read a book, look on the internet, or do research so you better understand all of the different ways to be transgender and how that affects one's life.

#8 Understand One's Role as an Ally

- Being an ally means that one should help facilitate the trans community's goals and agenda, without undue influence on setting the agenda.
- However, you can (and should) still use your own critical thinking skills and contribute to agenda-setting and strategy when invited to do so by transgender leaders and colleagues.

#9 Have Fair Employment Practices

- Implement strong nondiscrimination policies, include nondiscrimination statements in job listings, establish transgender-friendly hiring practices, and provide trainings for employees on sensitivity.
- Provide transgender-related health care, integrate transgender-sensitivity into staff evaluations, ensure employees can update their name and gender in files, ensure that transgender status is confidential, and ensure that transgender employees are safe from harassment on the job.

Jaimie F. Veale, Dave E. Clarke, and Terri C. Lomax

NO

Sexuality of Male-to-Female Transsexuals

Since its beginnings in the early 20th century, research investigating the sexuality of male-to-female transsexuals has classified them into groups based on their sexual orientation. However, this approach has been disputed by a number of transsexuals. The present study attempted to shed some light on this issue by assessing aspects of male-to-female transsexuals' sexuality, including sexual orientation, autogynephilia, sexual attraction to transgender fiction, and factors relevant to evolutionary theory, among a non-clinical population. These variables were also compared to a group of biological females to ascertain similarities and differences in the sexuality of male-to-female transsexuals. Before outlining these aspects of sexuality, a brief review of some previous studies of male-to-female transsexual sexuality is given. In this article, the term transsexual refers to male-to-female transsexuals unless otherwise stated.

Research has shown that gynephilic (exclusively sexually attracted to adult females), bisexual, androphilic (exclusively sexually attracted to adult males), asexual, and narcissistic or automonosexual gender-variant persons can be distinguished. Automonosexuals are sexually aroused by the idea or impression of themselves as females.

Gynephilic transsexuals reported cross-gender fetishism that was not seen among androphilic transsexuals. Androphilic transsexuals also reported a greater level of childhood feminine gender identity than gynephilic transsexuals. . . . One relatively strong factor included erotic attraction to women and fetishism . . . , and low childhood feminine gender identity and less erotic attraction to males. . . . Thus, there were two distinct "types" of transsexuals: gynephilic and androphilic.

Using standardized self-report questionnaires, Blanchard provided evidence for the two-type model of transsexuality. . . .

He introduced the concept of *autogynephilia* . . . to refer to "a male's propensity to be sexually aroused by the thought of himself as a female." This concept formed the basis of Blanchard's hypothesis that there are two distinct manifestations of male-to-female transsexualism: "homosexual" and "autogynephilic." . . . Nonhomosexual gender dysphoria is the result of autogynephilia. Autogynephilic transsexuals are sexually aroused by stimuli

From *Archives of Sexual Behavior,* vol. 37, 2008, pp. 586–597. Copyright © 2008 by Springer Journals (Kluwer Academic). Reprinted with kind permission of Springer Science+Business Media via Rightslink.

that result in them to perceiving themselves in a more feminine way. Cross-dressing is the most striking example here—Blanchard believed that there was much commonality between autogynephilic transsexuals and transvestites. However, he believed autogynephilia can also encompass erotic ideas of feminine situations in which women's clothing plays little or no role at all, such as going to the hair salon or even doing knitting.

Blanchard believed that the sexual interest in males that arises in bisexual transsexuals was fundamentally different from the androphilic group. According to Blanchard, in bisexual transsexuals, autogynephilia produces a secondary interest in males to go along with the transsexuals' basic erotic interest in females. The interest was not in the male body or physique as it is for the androphilic group, but rather in the perception of themselves as a woman that males are attracted to. The inclusion of a male can add to the fantasy of being regarded as a woman for the bisexual group, and the attraction to a male would diminish if the bisexual transsexual was not being regarded as a woman. . . . Bisexual transsexuals were significantly more likely to report autogynephilic interpersonal fantasy—erotic fantasies of being admired by another person—than all of the other transsexual groups.

Autogynephilic sexual arousal may diminish or even disappear due to age, hormone treatment, and sex reassignment surgery (SRS), and yet the desire to live as a woman does not diminish, and often grows stronger, . . . like a heterosexual pair bonding: after years of marriage, sexual excitement with a partner tends to decrease; however, one continues to be just as attached to that person. Similarly, the desire to have a female body continues in a "permanent love-bond."

A number of subsequent findings have relevance to Blanchard's theory. Among transsexuals, gynephilia was significantly positively correlated with sexual arousal to cross-gender fantasy, and significantly negatively correlated with feminine gender identity in childhood. More recent studies have also reported the existence of cross-gender sexual arousal among transsexuals. Two further studies have found that transsexuals who were sexually attracted to males were significantly more feminine as a child and significantly less likely to report sexual arousal when cross-dressing.

Another interesting observation that has relevance to Blanchard's theory is the existence of erotic narratives that are found in transvestite publications and on the Internet that appear to be created for individuals with transvestic and autogynephilic fantasies. Nearly half of the stories ended with the indication that the main character will go on to live as a woman—an indication of transsexual fantasy among consumers of such fiction. The experiences in the transvestite fiction differed sharply from what the transvestite experienced in real life. These stories illustrate wish fulfillment of desires that are deprived of expression in reality. The themes of these stories merely provide insight into what transvestites find most pleasurable, but they are of little use in distinguishing individual's motives or reasons for cross-dressing. Many of these narratives can be interpreted as autogynephilic fantasies because the male is transformed into a female, not just through a change of clothes, but also through changes via a surgical, magical, or science fiction means.

One question this research is addressing is whether transsexuals are sexually attracted to this fiction.

Many transsexuals oppose Blanchard's theory of autogynephilia. It is clear that many transsexuals do not accept the underlying assumption of Blanchard's theory that persons with autogynephilia are males with a sexual fetish. Another phenomenon that added fuel to the argument was the release of Bailey's book [*The Man Who Would Be Queen: The Science of Gender Bending and Transsexualism*]. In this book, Bailey supported Blanchard's theory, and explained it in layperson terms in an attempt to popularize it among the general public. However, this has been very unpopular among transsexuals because among other things Bailey asserted that all transsexuals who do not believe in Blanchard's model are lying, either to themselves or to others.

Some further aspects of sexuality were of interest for the present study: sexual attraction to feminine males, sadomasochism, and aspects of sexuality relevant to evolutionary theory. . . .

Little previous research has examined attraction to femininity in males among gender-variant persons. Transvestites tend to avoid sexual encounters with males, with the exception of other transvestites; 26% of personal advertisements looking for transsexuals and transvestites were placed by self-described cross-dressers.

Several researchers have noted sadistic and masochistic tendencies in transsexuals and transvestites. If autogynephilia is a type of paraphilia as Blanchard contends, then we would expect to see a positive relationship between autogynephilia and sadomasochism and other fetishistic fantasies.

In accordance with sexual selection theory, males are more likely than females to report interest in uncommitted sex, interest in visual sexual stimuli, preference for younger partners, to value partner physical attractiveness, and experience of sexual jealousy more strongly than emotional jealousy. On the other hand, women were more likely than men to report concern with partner status, and to report experiencing emotional jealousy more strongly than sexual jealousy.

The aim of this research was to measure these aspects of sexuality among male-to-female transsexuals and compare them to those of a group of biological females, to ascertain similarities and differences in the sexuality of transsexuals.

Method

Participants

Transsexual participants were recruited from transgender social/support groups in New Zealand, and biological female participants were recruited through an undergraduate psychology class at Massey University in Auckland, New Zealand. These participants were given the option of either completing the questionnaire on the Internet or completing a paper version. Transsexual and biological female participants were also recruited via the Internet. The link to the survey was posted on a number of transgender, women's, and psychology online interest groups and email lists. Participants recruited via the Internet were given only the option of completing the survey over the Internet.

The questionnaire received a total of 361 completed responses; 327 of these were via the Internet questionnaire. Paper surveys were given to 71 people; 34 of these were returned completed, giving a response rate of 48%. Of the total, 127 responses came from biological females and 234 came from transsexuals.

Transsexuals ($M = 39.21$ years, $SD = 14.03$) were on average significantly older than biological females ($M = 30.63$ years, $SD = 11.90$), $t(359) = 5.83$, ($p < .001$). The majority (90%) of participants identified as European. Ethnic minorities were represented in 14% of participants. Participants in highly skilled occupations were well represented in this sample, with 46% of participants classified in the three most highly skilled categories on the New Zealand Standard Classification of Occupations. A large proportion (23%) of participants were students. The current sample appeared to be well-educated: 27% reported having a bachelor's degree, 16% reported having a master's or doctoral degree, and only 6% reported achieving 3 years of high school or less. Transsexual and biological female groups did not differ significantly in ethnicity, occupation classification, or level of education. Most of the transsexual participants (83%) had not undertaken SRS, and 61% of transsexuals reported that they were currently taking female hormones.

Differences between participants who completed and did not complete the entire survey were examined. Participants who did not complete the entire questionnaire were significantly less likely to be European, and significantly more likely to be Asian. . . . Completers and non-completers did not differ significantly in terms of gender identity, occupation classification, marital status, age, level of education, number of biological children, sexual orientation, or on any of the remaining variables.

Measures

Sex-Linked Behaviours Questionnaire

Sexual orientation was determined by responses to eight questionnaire items on sexual fantasy, sexual arousal, and sexual attraction, for example, "Rate the degree to which in your current sexual fantasies you are aroused by males." . . .

Attraction to Male Physique

This scale contains six items measuring sexual attraction to the male physique. . . .

Attraction to Feminine Males Scale

This scale contains six items measuring sexual attraction to femininity in males. . . .

Recalled Gender Identity/Gender Role Questionnaire

This scale measures recalled childhood gender identity and gender role; for example, "As a child, I put on or used cosmetics (make-up) and girls' or women's jewellery." This scale uses 5-point responses, with one or two extra response items to allow participants to indicate that they did not remember or that the behavior did not apply. . . .

Core Autogynephilia Scale

This 8-item scale was developed by Blanchard to measure sexual attraction to the fantasy of being a woman, for example, "Have you ever been sexually aroused at the thought of being a woman?" Changes were made to six of the questions so that participants were asked if they have ever been sexually aroused when picturing themselves with attractive or more attractive female physical features. The "attractive or more attractive" part was added to Blanchard's original version of the scale to make the questions more applicable to biological females. . . .

Autogynephilic Interpersonal Fantasy Scale

This 4-item scale measures the sexual arousal of being admired by another person as a female, for example, "Have you ever been sexually aroused while picturing yourself as a woman in the nude being admired by another person?" . . .

Fetishism Scale

This scale measures sexual attraction to inanimate objects, for example, "Were you ever more strongly sexually attracted by inanimate things than by females or males?" . . .

Masochism Scale

This scale measures masochistic tendencies, for example, "Has imagining that you were being humiliated or poorly treated by someone ever excited you sexually?" . . .

Sexual and Emotional Jealousy

This 4-item scale was designed to assess sexual and emotional jealousy, for example, "Rate how distressing imagining your partner falling in love with that other person would be." . . .

Preference for Younger Partners

This 11-item scale measures age preference for sexual partners, for example, "If someone showed definite signs of aging it would be difficult for me to be very sexually attracted to them." Nine of the items were scored on a 7-point Likert-scale format from *strongly agree* to *strongly disagree*. Two of the items ask participants to specify an age of desired partner. This was then subtracted from the participant's age to give a difference score. . . .

Interest in Uncommitted Sex

This scale is a 10-item measure of attraction to casual sexual relationships, for example, "Monogamy is not for me." . . .

Interest in Visual Sexual Stimuli

This scale is a 12-item measure of sexual interest in visual stimuli, for example, "Seeing my sexual partner undress is a real turn-on." . . .

Importance of Partner Status
This scale is a 12-item measure of concern with the amount of resources held by a partner or potential partner, for example, "I would like my partner to be from a higher social class background than I."...

Importance of Partner Physical Attractiveness
This scale is a 10-item measure of concern with the physical attractiveness of partners, for example, "I would be happy if my partner were more sexually attractive than I." ...

Attraction to Transgender Fiction Scale
This scale contains 12 items measuring sexual attraction to erotic narratives containing transgender themes. ...

Transgender Identity Scale
This 9-item scale measures cross-gender identification, and continuous commitment to cross-gender behavior through the desire to live entirely in the female role, for example, "If it were possible, I'd choose to live my life as a woman (or I now do so)." This scale was only completed by transsexual participants. ...

Additional information was collected from transsexual participants about the age they first desired to change their sex, how long they had been taking female hormones, and whether they had undertaken SRS.

Results

Comparisons Between Biological Females and Transsexuals

... After adjusting for age differences, transsexuals scored significantly higher on Attraction to Feminine Males, Recalled Feminine Gender Identity, Core Autogynephilia, Preference for Younger Partners, Importance of Partner Status, Importance of Partner Physical Attractiveness, and Attraction to Transgender Fiction. Biological females scored significantly higher on Emotional Jealousy.

Comparisons among Autogynephilic Transsexuals, Non-Autogynephilic Transsexuals, and Biological Females

Transsexual participants were categorized as autogynephilic or non-autogynephilic based on their scores on the Core Autogynephilia, Autogynephilic Interpersonal Fantasy, Attraction to Feminine Males, and Attraction to Transgender Fiction scales. These scales were selected because they were found most effective for classifying transsexuals into groups in a taxometric analysis using the same data as the present study. ...

All of the scales ... yielded a significant difference between the three groups except for the sexual orientation scales, and Attraction to Male Physique.

... Non-autogynephilic transsexuals scored significantly lower on Masochism and Interest in Visual Sexual Stimuli than autogynephilic transsexuals and biological females, who did not differ significantly from each other. Auto-gynephilic transsexuals scored significantly higher on Attraction to Feminine Males, Autogynephilic Interpersonal Fantasy, Preference for Younger Partners, and Attraction to Transgender Fiction, and lower on Sexual Jealousy than non-autogynephilic transsexuals and biological females, who did not differ significantly from each other. For Fetishism and Interest in Uncommitted Sex, autogynephilic transsexuals scored significantly higher than biological females, who scored significantly higher than non-autogynephilic transsexuals. Bio-logical females scored significantly lower on Recalled Feminine Gender Iden-tity than both transsexual subgroups, which did not differ significantly from each other. Autogynephilic transsexuals scored significantly lower than bio-logical females on Emotional Jealousy and significantly higher on Importance of Partner Status; non-autogynephilic transsexuals did not differ significantly from autogynephilic transsexuals or biological females for these variables. For Core Autogynephilia and Importance of Partner Physical Attractiveness, auto-gynephilic transsexuals scored significantly higher than non-autogynephilic transsexuals, who scored significantly higher than biological females.

Comparisons were made between autogynephilic and non-autogynephilic transsexuals on the measures that were only completed by transsexuals. Autogynephilic transsexuals had a significantly later age of first desire to change sex . . . , were less likely to be taking female hormones . . . , had fewer months taking hormones . . . , and less likely to have had SRS . . . than non-autogynephilic transsexuals. These groups did not differ significantly in age or scores on the Transgender Identity Scale.

Correlational Analyses

. . . Sexual Attraction to Males correlated positively with Core Autogynephilia among biological females and with Autogynephilic Interpersonal Fantasy among all participants. Sexual Attraction to Females correlated positively with Core Autogynephilia among all participants and with Autogynephilic Inter-personal Fantasy among transsexuals. Attraction to Male Physique correlated positively with Autogynephilic Interpersonal Fantasy among biological female participants. Attraction to Feminine Males correlated positively with Core Auto-gynephilia and Autogynephilic Interpersonal Fantasy among all participants. Attraction to Transgender Fiction was positively correlated with Core Auto-gynephilia among all participants and with Autogynephilic Interpersonal Fan-tasy among transsexuals. Recalled Feminine Gender Identity was not related to Autogynephilia variables for transsexual or biological female participants. However, Recalled Feminine Gender Identity was positively correlated with Sexual Attraction to Males among both transsexuals . . . and biological females . . . , and negatively correlated with Sexual Attraction to Females among both transsexuals . . . and biological females. . . .

Finally, in testing Blanchard's hypothesis that bisexual autogynephilic transsexuals are not attracted to the male physique, we found among trans-sexual participants classified as autogynephilic . . . , Attraction to Male Physique correlated significantly positively with Sexual Attraction to Males . . . , and this correlation was comparable to non-autogynephilic transsexuals . . . and biological females. . . .

Discussion

The results showed that male-to-female transsexual sexuality differed from biological females on a number of variables, and the largest differences were found when transsexuals were classified into two groups. Those classified as autogynephilic scored significantly higher on Attraction to Feminine Males, Core Autogynephilia, Autogynephilic Interpersonal Fantasy, Fetishism, Preference for Younger Partners, Interest in Uncommitted Sex, Importance of Partner Physical Attractiveness, and Attraction to Transgender Fiction than those transsexuals not classified as non-autogynephilic and biological females. Subject to further investigation, these erotic preferences—especially Attraction to Feminine Males and Attraction to Transgender Fiction—can be seen as notable components or correlates of autogynephilia.

Both groups of transsexual participants scored significantly higher than biological female participants on Recalled Feminine Gender Identity, and Importance of Partner Physical Attractiveness. It was unexpected that transsexuals would score on average higher on childhood feminine gender identity, because transsexuals would be given less opportunity to express their femininity and would be discouraged from doing so in their childhood. One possible explanation for this finding is that a large number biological females reporting sexual attraction to females were included in this study—such persons have been shown to recall less femininity in childhood. Transsexual participants, even those categorized as non-autogynephilic, reported placing greater importance of physical attractiveness of potential partners than biological females. The reason for this phenomenon is unclear—it is possible that transsexuals, being biological males, have been shaped by natural selection to view physical attractiveness as a marker of partner fertility; however, non-autogynephilic transsexuals did not score in a significantly more "masculine" direction than biological females on any of the other sexuality parameters relevant to evolution, but autogynephilic transsexuals scored in the more "masculine" direction than other participants on five out of seven of these variables. Overall, biological female and transsexual participants also did not differ on levels of Interest in Visual Sexual Stimuli. This is in spite of [the] claim that male-to-female transsexuals are more responsive to visual erotic stimuli, similar to other biological males.

The finding that transsexuals—even those classified as autogynephilic—did not differ significantly on Masochism from biological females was unexpected given previous reports of the prevalence of masochism in transsexuals, and reports of co-occurrence of fetishism.

Autogynephilic transsexual participants reported a significantly greater amount of sexual attraction to transgender fiction themes than biological females. Transsexuals most commonly endorsed themes of magical transformation into a female, having to be transformed into a female as part of a deal, bet or dare, and gender body swaps. However, some transsexuals endorsed all of the themes, and no clear pattern appeared among them. We conclude that sexual fantasy to certain transgender fiction themes does not appear to be predictive of transsexualism. This finding . . . [suggests] that these themes are of little use in distinguishing individual's motives.

Contrary to Blanchard's findings, when the transsexual participants were divided into autogynephilic and non-autogynephilic groups, they did not differ significantly on sexual orientation measures. Among transsexual participants, the Core Autogynephilia Scale positively correlated with Sexual Attraction to Females—in line with Blanchard's research. However, further analysis of the transsexual subgroups revealed notable diversity within the groups. The average score of Sexual Attraction to Males was higher for transsexuals classified as autogynephilic than for transsexuals classified as non-autogynephilic, although this difference was not significant, this is at variance with Blanchard's theory. Also, 68% of transsexuals classified as non-autogynephilic scored the highest possible score . . . on the Sexual Attraction to Females scale. Finally, among the transsexuals classified as autogynephilic, none scored low scores . . . on both the Sexual Attraction to Males and Females scales that would be expected if they were asexual—one of the sexuality subgroups of Blanchard's autogynephilic transsexuals. Possible explanations for this lack of asexuality include more liberal attitudes towards sexuality in today's culture, and participants in Blanchard's research reporting a greater asexuality if they believed this would increase their chances of receiving medical intervention. Attraction to Male Physique was positively correlated with Sexual Attraction to Males among autogynephilic transsexuals. If Blanchard's hypothesis that the sexual attraction to males experienced by bisexual transsexuals is to include them as props in the fantasy of being regarded as a woman, as opposed to sexual interest in the male body is true then we would not expect to see this positive correlation, or we would at least expect this correlation to be lower than the corresponding correlations for non-autogynephilic transsexuals and biological females. However, it is still possible that this attraction to the male physique could develop along with the secondary emergence of attraction to males that Blanchard describes. Also, contrary to expectation Recalled Childhood Feminine Gender Identity Scale did not correlate with autogynephilia measures.

We conclude that while Blanchard's two-group classification of male-to-female transsexuals appears to have merit for significant proportion of transsexuals, there is still diversity in the experiences of transsexuals, and a simple categorization may not completely represent this diversity.

Limitations

In the questionnaire, changes were made to the questions in the Core Autogynephilia scale so that participants were asked if they have ever been sexually aroused when picturing themselves with attractive or more attractive female physical features. The responses were also altered from a yes/no format, and the skip instructions were changed. All of these alterations to the scale made these research findings less comparable to Blanchard's research. Also, the Sex

Linked Behaviours Questionnaire, Core Autogynephilia, Autogynephilic Interpersonal Fantasy, Fetishism, and Masochism scales . . . were altered. . . .

A further limitation of this research was that it relied entirely on self-report. Blanchard reported that the group that he would later label autogynephilic may over report their femininity and under report the extent of their cross-gender sexual arousal. From clinical and research observations, previous researchers have claimed that non-androphilic transsexuals may consciously or unconsciously distort their responses to appear less autogynephilic. It is beyond the scope of this research to assess whether participants were distorting their answers. However, we believe participants would be less likely to consciously distort their responses in this study because their answers were anonymous and had no implications for whether they will receive treatment in a clinical setting.

Another limitation was the susceptibility of this research to manipulation. Although this is an issue with most Internet surveys, the contentiousness of the subject matter in this survey would make it more susceptible to dishonesty. Many transsexuals have strong feelings about autogynephilia and could have manipulated the survey by completing it many times with answers that they believe would either discredit or confirm the theory, depending on their beliefs. However, the length of the survey (162 questions) may have discouraged participants from answering it many times—our system showed us that most participants took longer than 25 min to complete it. In addition, we did not see any suspicious responding in the data, such as a lot of responses in a short period. Furthermore, distinct and often thoughtful comments were made by 71.4% of transsexual participants who completed the questionnaire on the Internet when given the opportunity to comment on Blanchard's theory of autogynephilia and on the survey in general. Although we did not see any signs of suspicious activity, we are aware that this may have been a possibility, and this is a considerable limitation to our findings.

The recruitment methods used in this research also contributed to a biased sample. The biological female participants were either recruited through first year psychology classes or through Internet mailing lists and message boards for persons with interests in psychology, sex research, or transsexualism (e.g., support groups for family and friends of transsexuals). The significant proportion of university students in the biological female sample resulted in a large number of participants in the 18–22 year age group. Among the transsexual sample, those who access online transsexual support groups and mailing lists were also likely to be overrepresented. Europeans were also overrepresented in the overall sample, and the participants appeared to be more educated than the general population. Also, a number of previous studies have shown that females volunteering for sexuality research are less sexually inhibited than the general population. It is likely that the present sample was biased in this way as well.

Finally, our findings bring up an area in need of further research. The concept of sexual attraction to oneself as a woman (autogynephilia) has never been assessed among biological female participants previously. Although a number of biological female participants endorsed items on the Core Autogynephilia and Autogynephilic Interpersonal Fantasy scales, no previous studies have reported biological females with such sexual attraction. Because of this, it is unlikely that these biological females actually experience sexual attraction to oneself as a woman in the way that Blanchard conceptualized it. However, the scales used in this research were not sufficient for examining this, so further research is needed to confirm it.

EXPLORING THE ISSUE

Should Transgender Women Be Considered "Real" Women?

Challenge Questions

1. What factors other than being born biologically female might create a foundation for shared experiences?
2. How do race, ethnicity, class, and sexual orientation, as well as other experiences such as having a physical disability or being a victim of sexual assault, define shared experiences?
3. Might womyn-born womyn find trans women threatening? In what ways and why?
4. How do discussions of patriarchy and male privilege inform discussions of what it means to be a "real" woman?

Is There Common Ground?

In July of 2008, it was announced that four Olympic athletes failed a gender test, the latest in a long series of challenges to the sex of female athletes. In 1968, the International Olympic Committee (IOC) began requiring certain female athletes, those for whom their masculine appearance and superior athletic ability raised questions about whether they were "real" women, to submit to genetic and blood tests. The goal was to determine their sex. The rule is that only women with two X chromosomes can compete as women (contrary to the opinion of most geneticists), with the exception of male-to-female transsexuals, but they must wait to compete for two years after the sex change surgery. In 1992, compulsory testing was abandoned but can be requested. Other questions arise for female athletes with other sex-related anomalies. The most recent case arose when the 2009 World Championship runner Mokgadi Caster Semenya was accused of being a hermaphrodite. The legitimacy of her gold medal has been called into question. Would this condition give her an advantage over other "normal" women? According to media reports in September of 2009, genetic testing revealed that Semenya is indeed intersexed; she has internal testes but no womb or ovaries and has testosterone levels three times higher than those typical of females. In October 2009 the International Association of Athletics Federations (IAAF) stated that these reports should be viewed with caution; however, in July 2010 she was cleared to compete. Nevertheless, this case raises intriguing questions regarding what determines one's sex. Because we now know that sexual development occurs on a continuum, from variation in number of chromosomes to various concentrations of estrogen and androgens (i.e., growth hormones) at different stages of prenatal development, the concept of sex as a simple dimorphic category is now questioned. For example, there are people who are intersexual, a group formerly termed hermaphrodite. These are individuals who are born with a blend of female and male sexual organs (approximately 1.7% of all live births). For many intersexuals, as well as infants with prenatal exposure to atypical levels of sexual hormones, genital size at birth becomes the primary basis for declaration of sex at birth. In these infants, it is the same tissue, but differences in size result in one of three natural configurations of external genitalia: female, male, or ambiguous. Gender identity for these persons is strongly influenced by whichever sex is declared at the time of birth. In contrast, transsexualism is seen as a medical condition in which a person is identified with the sex they were not born, that is, they are sexually dysmorphic (self-concept and biological sex do not match), and varies on a continuum in strength of the desire to become the other sex (ranging from cross-dressers to those seeking surgical alterations). Transgenderism refers to one's "gender identity," that is, identification as woman, man, mixed, or neither, that does not match one's assigned, or genetic sex. It is estimated that there are from 10,000 to 30,000 trans people worldwide, and that male-to-female outnumber female-to-male transgendered people. There are also people who consider themselves gender nonconformists. That is, they are neither transsexuals nor have a biological disorder. Rather, they oppose traditional standards.

What are the implications for what we now know about the varieties of gender identity and possibilities for being born intersexual or with ambiguous genitalia have for the concept of womyn-born womyn? Is womyn-born womyn a valid gender identity? What are the criteria for being considered a womyn-born womyn—XX chromosomal composition only? What about females with XO (Turner's syndrome) or XXX chromosomal make-ups? Must external genitalia be unambiguous? As long as women with any of these conditions are gender variant, do they qualify for the label womyn-born womyn? What are the implications of these variations for shared experiences and group identities? Consider other cultures in which more than two categories of sex are recognized and sometimes even celebrated (see Issues 3 and 20). How does an appreciation of such cultural variation help us discuss transsexuality, transgenderism, and gender variance? Does this knowledge strengthen or weaken the case that there are distinct and different gender identities that should be honored?

Contributors to This Volume

EDITOR

JACQUELYN W. WHITE is associate dean of research in the College of Arts & Sciences, a professor of psychology, and former director of Women's and Gender Studies at the University of North Carolina at Greensboro. She received her Ph.D. in social psychology, from Kent State University. Dr. White has conducted research in the area of aggression and violence for over 30 years, publishing numerous articles and chapters. She has conducted one of the few longitudinal studies of sexual assault and dating violence among adolescents and college students (funded by NIMH, NIJ, and CDC). Recent publications reflect an ecological developmental perspective to aggression and violence. She is a frequent speaker at national and international conferences. She is co editor with Dr. Cheryl Travis of the University of Tennessee on *Sexuality, Society, and Feminism: Psychological Perspectives on Women,* published by the American Psychological Association. She completed the "Gendered Aggression" chapter for the *Encyclopedia of Gender* (Academic Press) and "A Developmental Examination of Violence Against Girls and Women" for the *Handbook of the Psychology of Women and Gender* (Wiley).

In addition to her research activities, Dr. White served as the editor of the *Psychology of Women Quarterly* (2000–2004) and is a consulting editor for *Aggressive Behavior.* She has been president of the Southeastern Psychological Association, has been the treasurer of the International Society for Research in Aggression, and was the 2007–2008 president of the Society for the Psychology of Women Division 35 of the American Psychological Association. She has been a consultant on a project with the U.S. Navy examining the impact of pre-military experiences with physical and sexual abuse on military experiences. She has been the recipient of a number of awards, including the Women's History Committee Service Award given by the Commission on the Status of Women and the Greensboro YWCA and Kent State University's Honors Alumna of 2000. She was UNCG's 1996 Senior Research Excellence Award recipient, the highest research honor the university can bestow on a faculty member. She is also a fellow of the American Psychological Association.

Other awards include the 2008 recipient of the Carolyn Wood Sherif Award, given by the Society for the Psychology of Women, as well as both the Society's 2011 recipient of the Sue Rosenberg Zalk Award for Distinguished Leadership and the American Psychological Association's Committee on Women's 2010 Distinguished Leadership Award.

She currently co-chairs the National Partnership to End Interpersonal Violence and is co-editor of a two-volume series, *Violence Against Women and Children: Consensus, Critical Analysis, and Emergent Priorities.* She recently completed a NIDA-funded project on trauma and substance use.

AUTHORS

AGATSTON, PATRICIA W. is a Licensed Professional Counselor and Prevention Specialist with the Cobb County School District's Prevention/Intervention Center in Marietta, Georgia. She has written and spoken extensively on the subject of cyber bullying, and recently co-authored *Cyber Bullying: Bullying in the Digital Age* with Robin Kowalski and Susan Limber. Dr. Agatston is a trainer and consultant for the the Olweus Bullying Prevention Program, and is a member of the Board of Directors for the International Bullying Prevention Association and Connect Safely.

AHUJA, ANJANA is a former science journalist and columnist for the *Times*, with a degree in space physics from Imperial College London. She is a two-time nominee for the National Science Writing Awards and recipient of the EMMA award for Best Print Journalism. She recently collaborated with Mark van Vugt to write *Naturally Selected: The Evolutionary Science of Leadership*.

ALLEN, CHRISTOPHER T. is a senior research support specialist and couple CARE therapist with the Family Translational Research Group at the State University of New York at Stony Brook.

ALLEN, MERCEDES is a senior research support specialist and Couple CARE Therapist with the Family Translational Research Group at the State University of New York at Stony Brook.

AVERETT, PAIGE is a professor in the School of Social Work at East Carolina University, Greenville, NC. Her research interests are in sexuality, lesbian and gay studies, qualitative methodology, and social work pedagogy. Recent work includes a study of the influence of parent sexual orientation on emotional and behavioral problems of adopted children.

BAKER, SUSAN W. is a senior research support specialist and Couple CARE Therapist with the Family Translational Research Group at the State University of New York at Stony Brook.

BORKER, RUTH A. was the Coordinator of Women's Studies at Randolph-Macon Women's College, Ashland, Virginia. She also taught anthropology and women's studies at Cornell University, the University of California, Berkeley, and several other institutions. Her research focused on gender, language, and evangelical Christianity in Scotland and California.

BROOKS-GUNN, JEANNE is the Virginia and Leonard Marx Professor of Child Development at Teachers College and the College of Physicians and Surgeons at Columbia University. Her research focuses on designing and evaluating interventions and policies to enhance the well-being of children in poverty. Her scholarly interests include child and family policy, early childhood interventions and education, adolescent transitions and development, and neighborhoods and poverty.

BUITELAAR, JAN K. is a professor of psychiatry and child and adolescent psychiatry in the Department of Psychiatry at St. Radboud University Nijmegen Medical Center, Nijmegen, The Netherlands. His primary focus is on child psychiatry and he has published widely on ADHD, conduct disorder and autism spectrum disorder. He currently serves as head of Karakter Child and Adolescent Psychiatry University Centre and as editor-in-chief of *European Child and Adolescent Psychiatry*.

BUTTERWORTH, MOLLY is a graduate student in the clinical psychology program at the University of Utah.

CABRERA, NATASHA J. is an associate professor of human development at the University of Maryland. She directs the Family Involvement Laboratory at the University of Maryland, which explores ways that mothers and fathers are involved in their young children's lives and the influence that parents have on their children's development. Her research interests include parent–child relationships, children's social and emotional development in different types of families and cultural/ethnic groups, school readiness, fatherhood, predictors of adaptive and maladaptive parenting, and translation of research into practice and policy.

CAPECE, ELOKIN is the director of education at Planned Parenthood of Greater Memphis and a member of the MCS School Health Advisory Council. She also leads HIV education and screening efforts in collaboration with Queer as Youth, Many Men, Many Voices, and ¡Cuídate!

CARLI, LINDA is an associate professor in the psychology department at Wellesley College, where she has been since 1991. Her current research focuses on women's leadership, particularly the obstacles that women leaders face and ways to overcome those obstacles. Dr. Carli teaches a variety of courses, including organizational psychology, the psychology of law, and research in applied psychology.

CLARKE, DAVE E. is a senior lecturer in the School of Psychology, Massey University, Albany Campus, Auckland, New Zealand, and studies stress, personality, motivation, and gambling.

COHEN-KETTENIS, PEGGY T. is the head of the Department of Medical Psychology and director of the Center of Expertise on Gender Dysphoria at VU University Medical Center, Amsterdam, The Netherlands. Her primary research focus is on disorders of sex and gender development and sex hormone–behavior relationships. Current projects include studies of the effects of pubertal delay in adolescent transsexuals on psychological functioning, psychiatric comorbidity, and brain structure.

CORNYN, JOHN is a U.S. senator from Texas, who chairs the Senate Judiciary subcommittee on the Constitution, Civil Rights and Property Rights. He is a former state Supreme Court justice and state attorney general.

CRAIGIE, TERRY-ANN L. is a professor of economics at Connecticut College, New London, Connecticut. Her research covers the economics of the family, labor and urban economics, and applied microeconomics, and has recently focused on the causes and consequences of family formation on early child outcomes, as well as child support of complex family structures in large urban areas.

DEL GIUDICE, MARCO is a postdoctoral researcher at the Center for Cognitive Science in the Department of Psychology, University of Turin, Torino, Italy. His primary interests are in the evolutionary study of human development across the life span, with a special focus on the application of life history and sexual selection theory to individual and sex differences in attachment, mating, social competition, and personality.

DIAMOND, LISA M., psychology, University of Utah, focuses on two distinct but related areas—the nature and development of affectional bonds and the nature and development of same-sex sexuality. Her primary research questions are: (1) What are the basic psychological and biobehavioral processes underlying the formation and functioning of affectional bonds? (2) How are these processes related to sexual desire and sexual orientation. (3) What are the implications of affectional bonding for mental and physical well-being at different stages of life? In addressing these questions, she uses a diverse range of research methods, including in-depth qualitative interviews, controlled social–psychophysiological experiments, and assessment of naturalistic interpersonal behavior.

DOLEZAL, CURTIS is a research scientist at the HIV Center for Clinical and Behavioral Studies at New York State Psychiatric Institute and Columbia University. He is a co-investigator and data analyst for several projects at the HIV Center and has documented and manages several datasets covering the entire history of the Center. His research interests have included sensation seeking, drug and alcohol use, couple relationship quality, childhood sexual experiences, psychoendocrinology, and sexual risk behavior.

EAGLY, ALICE, a social psychologist, is the James Padilla Chair of Arts and Sciences, professor of psychology, faculty fellow of the Institute for Policy Research, department chair of psychology, all at Northwestern University. She has received numerous awards including the 2007 Interamerican Psychologist Award from Interamerican Society of Psychology for contributions to psychology as a science and profession in the Americas, as well as the 2005 Carolyn Wood Sherif Award from the Society for the Psychology of Women for contributions to the field of the psychology of women as a scholar, teacher, mentor, and leader.

FRITSMA, TERI is a senior project consultant for the Minnesota State Colleges and Universities System, curating several career exploration Web sites and developing Web-based tools for individuals exploring their career options. Her background is in employment research and labor market information, and her recent work has focused on skills assessments, green careers, and union membership among women.

FURNHAM, ADRIAN is a professor of psychology in the Research Department of Clinical, Educational and Health Psychology at the University College London. His research interests include complementary medicine; cross-cultural psychology, especially mental health and migration; organizational psychology; psychometrics, especially personality assessment; and economic socialization. He is the author of 46 books including *Culture*

Shock, The New Economic Mind, The Psychology of Money, The Incompetent Manager, and *The Dark Side of Behaviour at Work.*

GOLOMBOK, SUSAN is a psychology professor and director of the Family and Child Psychology Research Centre at the City University, London.

GUERRA, NANCY G. is the associate dean for Research, College of Arts and Sciences at the University of Delaware. She is also the director of Global Research Consortium and the editor of the *Journal of Research on Adolescence.*

HENLEY, NANCY M. is Professor Emeritus in the Department of Psychology at the University of California, Los Angeles. Her research focus is on power, gender, and communication skills, and has explored power and gender differences in nonverbal communication. Recently, Dr. Henley has studied how language is used to depict violence against women, lesbians, and gay men, and how differences in phrasing affect readers' understanding of the violence.

HESKETH, KYLIE is a senior research fellow at the Centre for Physical Activity and Nutrition Research in the School of Exercise and Nutrition Sciences at Deakin University, Melbourne, Australia. Her research has centered on the factors influencing children's weight status and preventing overweight through physical activity. Dr. Hesketh's recent research has investigated the factors contributing to physical activity in children, including the role of parents in preventing overweight and obesity.

HINES, MELISSA specializes in human gender development and is the director of the Hormones and Behaviour Research Lab at the University of Cambridge.

HYDE, JANET SHIBLEY is a professor of psychology and women's studies at the University of Wisconsin–Madison. Her research interests are in gender differences and gender-role development in children, with a recent focus on gender differences in the development of depression in adolescents. Dr. Hyde has received numerous awards for her teaching and research, including the APA's Award for Distinguished Service to Psychological Science.

JADVA, VASANTI is a research associate in the Center for Family Research, Faculty of Social and Political Sciences, University of Cambridge, Cambridge, UK. Her current focus is on families created using donor insemination, egg donation, and surrogacy, and she has also studied the experiences of individuals searching for, and finding, their donor relations, including donor offspring searching for their donors and donor siblings.

JONASON, PETER is a visiting assistant professor at the University of West Florida in experimental social psychology. He is interested in adaptive individual differences, conditional mating strategies, sex/dating research, personality research, animal models, dark triad personality traits, personality in nonhumans, religiousness, mate choice, mating strategies, short-term vs. long-term mating, intersexual conflict, and evolutionary psychology.

KAHNE, HILDA has a well-respected career teaching in academia with some research and administrative responsibilities. She has taught at Wellesley College (1948–1958), Radcliffe Institute for Advanced Study (1966–1977), Wheaton College (1977–1992). After retiring from Wheaton, she taught at the Heller School for Social Policy and Management (1992–2002) and has been at the Women's Studies Research Center since 2002.

KOWALSKI, ROBIN M. is a professor of psychology at Clemson University. Her research focuses on aversive interpersonal behaviors, including teasing, complaining, and bullying, and she has won several awards for her research and teaching. Her recent work, including a recently published book, has centered on cyber bullying.

KRAMARAE, CHERIS is a visiting professor at the Center for the Study of Women in Society at the University of Oregon, in Eugene. Dr. Kramarae's primary research interests have been in gender, language and communication, technology, and education. Her recent work has focused on gender and the experience of women in online distance learning environments.

LI, NORMAN P. is an associate professor of psychology at the Singapore Management University, School of Social Sciences, and adjunct assistant professor at the University of Texas at Austin Department of Psychology. He received his doctorate from Arizona State University and has numerous publications on evolutionary perspectives.

LIMBER, SUSAN P. is director of the Center on Youth Participation and Human Rights at the Institute on Family and Neighborhood Life and professor of psychology at Clemson University. Dr. Limber primarily studies the psychological and legal aspects of child protection, youth violence, and children's rights. Her work on the prevention of bullying has garnered several awards, including the APA's Award for Distinguished Contributions to Psychology in the Public Interest.

LINDBERG, SARA M. is a postdoctoral fellow at the University of Wisconsin's Center for Women's Health and Health Disparities Research. Her research interests are in the emergence of disparities in child health and well-being and the developmental origins of health and disease. Dr. Lindberg's recent work focuses on explaining how psychosocial and early life factors influence the emergence of disparities in pediatric obesity.

LINN, MARCIA C. is a professor of development and cognition in the Graduate School of Education at the University of California, Berkeley. She is a member of the National Academy of Education and a fellow of the American Association for the Advancement of Science, the American Psychological Association, and the Association for Psychological Science. Her research focus is on science teaching, gender and individual differences, and technology-enhanced instruction.

LIPS, HILARY M., a professor of psychology and the director of the Center for Gender Studies at Radford University, has published numerous books and articles related to the psychology of gender, including *Sex and Gender: An Introduction* (Mayfield, 2000).

LOMAX, TERRI C. is located at the School of Computer and Information Sciences, Auckland University of Technology, Auckland, New Zealand.

MALTZ, DANIEL N. is an anthropological bibliographer, whose work focuses on gender. Maltz proposes a two-cultures theory, which suggests that communication between men and women is complicated by their differing subcultures.

MANDEL, HADAS is a senior lecturer in the Department of Sociology and Anthropology at Tel Aviv University. Her research focuses on cross-country variations in gender inequality and their relationship to class inequality and the role of the welfare state. Her recent work has investigated the determinants of wage inequality across occupations.

MCKENNEY, SUSAN E. is a professor at the University of Twente and the Open Universiteit in the Netherlands, specializing in curriculum design and educational innovation. Her work has emphasized the supportive role of technology in curriculum and teacher development, with a recent focus on early childhood literacy. She has consulted broadly in the Netherlands, India, and southern Africa, offering research expertise in the design, evaluation, and revision of educational improvement initiatives.

MERHI, Z.O. is on the staff of Maimondes Medical Center, Brooklyn, New York, specializing in gynecology and obstetrics.

MEYER-BAHLBURG, HEINO F.L. is a professor of clinical psychology (in psychiatry) at the New York State Psychiatric Institute and Department of Psychiatry, Columbia University, and associate director of the HIV Center for Clinical and Behavioral Studies at New York State Psychiatric Institute, as well as director, Interdisciplinary Research Methods Core, HIV Center. He is also a full professional psychologist at New York Presbyterian Hospital. His primary research interests include developmental psychobiology of gender and sexuality, intersexuality/disorders of sex development, gender identity disorder, sexual risk behavior, and assessment of gender and sexuality.

MOTTET, LISA has staffed the Transgender Civil Rights Project at the National Gay and Lesbian Task Force since helping to establish it in 2001. In this role, she assists transgender activists and allies with all transgender-related legislation and policy. She co-authored *Transitioning Our Shelters: A Guide to Making Homeless Shelters Safe for Transgender People*, a joint publication with the National Coalition for the Homeless. Before joining the Task Force, Lisa was involved in leadership positions with various other LGBT organizations. Lisa currently serves on the Board of Advisors of the National Center for Transgender Equality and is on the board of the local LGBT soccer club in Washington, D.C.

NALAVANY, BLACE is a professor in the School of Social Work at East Carolina University, Greenville, NC. Her research interests are in childhood sexual abuse, learning disabilities, and adopted children with special needs.

Recent work includes a study of the influence of parent sexual orientation on emotional and behavioral problems of adopted children.

OLDS, TIM is a professor in the School of Health Sciences, Physical Education, Exercise and Sport Studies at the University of South Australia, Adelaide, Australia. His research has covered the mathematical modeling of cycling performance, anthropometry, and secular and geographic trends in fitness, fatness, physical activity, and food intake. Professor Olds developed the Multimedia Activity Recall for Children and Adolescents (MARCA), a computerized 24-hour use-of-time recall which permits the study of how people use their time, especially when undertaking behavioral change programs.

OLSZEWSKI-KUBILIUS, PAULA is the director of Northwestern University's Center for Talent Development (CTD) and a professor in the School of Education and Social Policy.

PATTON, GEORGE C. is Group Head of Population Health Studies of Adolescents at the Murdoch Children's Research Institute. Dr. Patton's research interests include overweight and obesity among adolescents, adolescent mental health, activity patterns, and global trends in mortality. His recent work has underscored the prevalence of mental disorders as a cause of disability among young people and the dangers of even low levels of alcohol consumption for adolescents.

PETERSEN, JENNIFER L. is an assistant professor in the Department of Communication at the University of Wisconsin–Milwaukee. Her research focus is on health communication, social support, and coping with illness, especially for individuals with stigmatized or rare illnesses. Recently, Dr. Petersen has been investigating the experiences of families in which the mother is living with HIV or AIDS.

RAMIREZ, IGNACIO L. is a professor in the department of sociology at Texas Tech University. His research interests include violence in intimate relations. His teaching includes social problems as well as law and policing.

REISMAN, JUDITH is the president of the Institute for Media Education, author of, among other publications, the U.S. Department of Justice, Juvenile Justice study, Images of Children, Crime and Violence in Playboy, Penthouse and Hustler (1989), Kinsey, Sex and Fraud (Reisman, et al., 1990), Soft Porn Plays Hardball (1991), and Kinsey, Crimes and Consequences (1998, 2000). She is also a news commentator for WorldNetDaily. com and has been a consultant to four U.S. Department of Justice administrations, the U.S. Department of Education, and the U.S. Department of Health and Human Services.

RYAN, SCOTT D. is associate dean and professor of child welfare at Florida State University, Tallahassee, Florida. He serves as director of the Institute for Social Work Research and as editor of *Adoption Quarterly*. His research interests are in adoption, especially adoption into families with gay and lesbian adoptive parents.

RIDLEY, KATE is a senior lecturer in physical education in the School of Education at Flinders University, Adelaide, Australia. Dr. Ridley completed her Ph.D. in 2005, where she co-developed and validated a Multimedia Activity Recall for Children and Adolescents (MARCA) to measure children's physical activity levels and use of time. Her research interest include the physical activity and sedentary behavior patterns of children, the relationship between behavior patterns, health, and academic outcomes, and the measurement of physical activity and energy expenditure.

SCHMITT, DAVID P. is a professor of psychology at Bradley University and founding director of the International Sexuality Description Project. His research interests include evolutionary and cross-cultural approaches to understanding personal relationships, sexual strategies, romantic attachment styles, and gender differences in human mating. He is also interested in the "Big Five" model of personality traits, risk factors for HIV/AIDS, and predictors of both sexual aggression and domestic violence across cultures.

SCHUMM, WALTER R. is a professor in the School of Family Studies and Human Services at Kansas State University, Manhattan, Kansas. His primary research interests include marital relationships, military families, and religion and families, as well as family research methodology and measurement. His recent research investigates the influence of parental sexual orientation on family outcomes.

SHACKLETON, JOHN is a professor of economics and dean of the Business School, University of East London. He was formerly dean of Westminster Business School and has taught at Queen Mary, University of London, and the University of Buckingham. Educated at King's College, Cambridge, and the School of Oriental and African Studies, he has also worked as an economist in the civil service, published widely in academic journals, and written for several leading think tanks. He has given evidence to parliamentary committees, has appeared frequently on radio and TV, and has lectured in many countries.

SHANNON, JACQUELINE D. is an assistant professor of early childhood education at Brooklyn College, CUNY. She is a member of the National Early Head Start Research Consortium. Prior to joining Brooklyn College, she was a research scientist at NYU and post-doctoral research fellow with NICHD. She also directed a home-based child development program in East Harlem serving families with children birth to three years. Her research interests include parenting (with a special focus on fathers) and young children's cognitive and social–emotional development within families living in poverty, using mixed methods.

STRAUS, MURRAY A. is currently a professor of sociology at the University of New Hampshire where he has taught since 1968. Dr. Straus is also the co-director for the Family Research Laboratory at the University of New Hampshire. He has been collaborating with researchers in 23 nations on a cross-national study of violence between partners in the dating relationships of university students.

SWAN, SUZANNE C. is an assistant professor in the department of psychology and the Women's Studies Program at the University of South Carolina. Before coming to the University of South Carolina, she was the director of Family Violence Programs at the Yale School of Medicine's Department of Psychiatry. She received her Ph.D. from the University of Illinois in 1997. Her recent work has focused on research with women who use violence in intimate relationships, with a particular emphasis on the contextual factors underlying women's violence. She teaches courses on the psychology of women, social psychology, and relationship violence.

TAMIS-LEMONDA, CATHERINE is a professor of applied psychology at New York University. Her research is focused on the cultural and social contexts of language and cognitive and social development in infants' first years of life. Through longitudinal inquiry she follows infants from birth through preschool, visiting babies and families in their homes, schools, and communities using naturalistic observations, interviews, and direct assessments of development. She is the principal investigator (for NYU as a local site) on the Father Involvement in the Lives of Low Income Children Project.

TANIS, JUSTIN joined the staff of the National Center for Transgender Equality as a program manager in August 2005. He works as a writer, Web manager, and designer for NCTE, creating publications, resources, and newsletters for the organization. Justin is the author of *Transgendered: Theology, Ministry and Communities of Faith* and contributed to the *Queer Bible Commentary* and *Take Back the Word: A Queer Reading of the Bible.*

VAN DE BEEK, CORNELIEKE is with the Department of Child and Adolescent Psychiatry, University Medical Centre Utrecht, and the Rudolf Magnus Institute for Neurosciences, Utrecht, Netherlands.

VAN GOOZEN, STEPHANIE H.M. is a biological psychologist interested in developmental psychopathology. Her research focuses on individual factors that explain or accentuate risk of developing antisocial behavior to those who live with early social adversity.

VAN VUGT, MARK is a professor of social and organizational psychology at the VU University Amsterdam and a research associate at Oxford University. His research is in evolutionary social and organizational psychology, with a special focus on the application of evolutionary psychology to leadership, cooperation, and other group processes. He is the author of numerous books, including *Naturally Selected: The Evolutionary Science of Leadership.*

VOOGT, JOKE M. is an associate professor in the Department of Curriculum Design and Educational Innovation at the University of Twente, in the Netherlands. The primary focus of her research is on innovative uses of information and communication technologies in the curriculum, with a special interest in the demands on teachers when integrating technology into the classroom. She also serves as editor-in-chief of the *International Handbook of Information Technology in Primary and Secondary Education.*

WAKE, MELISSA is a consultant pediatrician serving as director of research and associate director of the Centre for Community Child Health at the Royal Children's Hospital in Melbourne, Australia. Her research looks at the development and translation of community-based strategies that prevent or manage common childhood conditions—obesity, language and literacy delay, hearing, and developmental and behavioral concerns. Dr. Wake is also a senior research fellow with the Murdoch Children's Research Institute and Professorial Fellow with the Department of Paediatrics at the University of Melbourne.

WALDFOGEL, JANE is a professor of social work and public affairs at Columbia University School of Social Work and a visiting professor at the Centre for Analysis of Social Exclusion at the London School of Economics. Her research is centered around children, youth, and families, with a focus on the effect of children on women's pay and the influence of maternal employment on child outcomes. Current projects investigate the impact of public policy on child and family well-being, especially work–family related policies and child well-being in families at risk of breaking up or living in poverty.

WATERS, ELIZABETH is a Professorial Fellow of Public Health and Health Equity with the McCaughey Centre, School of Population Health, at the University of Melbourne, Australia. She is interested in adolescent health, measuring quality of life, and the prevention of childhood obesity. Dr. Waters is also coordinating editor of the Cochrane Collaboration Public-lic Health Group and a member of the WHO Expert Advisory Committees on childhood obesity prevention, childhood growth standards, mental health promotion and equity measurement.

WEBSTER, GREGORY D. is an assistant professor in the Department of Psychology at the University of Florida. He conducts research on prosocial and aggressive behavior from an evolutionary social psychological perspective. His research examines within-family resource allocation as a function of relatedness and emotional closeness. His aggression research examines relationships between different domains of self-esteem and aggression.

WILLIAMS, JOANNE is an epidemiologist in the Centre for Community Child Health at the Murdoch Children's Research Institute, Melbourne, Australia. Her research centers on children's health and activity patterns, with a recent focus on the risk factors for adolescent smoking and alcohol use.

WINTERS, KELLEY, formerly under pen-name Katherine Wilson, is a writer on issues of transgender medical policy, founder of GID Reform Advocates, and an advisory board member for the Matthew Shepard Foundation and TransYouth Family Advocates.